HIGH NOON IN SOUTHERN AFRICA

HIGH NOON IN SOUTHERN AFRICA

•

Making Peace in a Rough Neighborhood

Chester A. Crocker

W · W · NORTON & COMPANY

New York   London

First Edition

The text of this book is composed in Sabon
with the display set in Garamond Condensed.
Composition and manufacturing by The Maple-Vail Book Manufacturing Group
Book design by Jack Meserole

Library of Congress Cataloging-in-Publication Data
Crocker, Chester A.
High noon in southern Africa : making peace in a rough neighborhood
/ by Chester A. Crocker.
p. cm.
Includes index.
1. Africa, Southern—Foreign relations—United States.   2. South
Africa—Foreign relations—United States.   3. United States—Foreign
relations—South Africa.   4. United States—Foreign relations—
Africa, Southern.   5. Crocker, Chester A.   6. United States—
Foreign relations—1981–1989.   I. Title.
DT1105.U6C76   1993
327.68073—dc20   92–6387

ISBN 0-393-03432-1

W. W. Norton & Company, Inc., 500 Fifth Avenue, New York, N.Y. 10110
W. W. Norton & Company Ltd., 10 Coptic Street, London WC1A 1PU

1 2 3 4 5 6 7 8 9 0

To Saône, Sheba,
Rennie, and Becca

Contents

PART III

PART IV

PART V

Foreword

This book is simultaneously about an extraordinarily interesting and illuminating diplomatic process and about developments of major importance in Southern Africa. Here at Stanford University I am amazed how often students ask me about this American diplomacy. Somehow, the complex interweaving of the many strands of this undertaking—involving not only South Africa and the end of apartheid in an independent Namibia, but also Angola, Cuba, the Soviet Union, the "Front Line States" of Southern Africa, and the United Nations—has caught the attention of young people interested in diplomacy.

As Secretary of State, I worked for Namibian independence. Many others were involved, and their contributions, or the problems they created, are set out in this book. President Ronald Reagan's sheltering political umbrella made progress possible. But the man who mattered most was Chet Crocker. He unwaveringly upheld the American position while deftly and brilliantly weaving his way through a maze of international politics and conflict.

Namibia was the last vestige of Africa's colonial era. In 1978, United Nations Resolution 435 called for independence for Namibia and set out an elaborate transition process to achieve it. Why was this episode worth nearly a decade of agonizing effort? Why does it warrant book-length treatment? The implications ran far beyond the aspirations of the people of Namibia to sovereign control over their lives and territory. Independence would mean an end to South African-imposed apartheid in Namibia. What might that mean for South Africa itself? A precedent,

11

an experiment, a recognition that the white regime finally understood the inevitability of change? Who could know how the experience of being part of something that succeeds—achievement of Namibian independence and freedom from foreign forces—might affect all of Southern Africa?

In Namibia's neighbor Angola, the Soviet-supported regime was under pressure from anti-Communist guerrillas in the field. Their leader, Jonas Savimbi, was very much his own man and possessed immense charisma. Arrayed against Savimbi's UNITA were Fidel Castro's Cuban troops, sent to shore up Angola's crumbling Marxist-Leninist government. This was truly an international conflict of incredible complexity and meaning. We were not ready to see a new nation created only to become enrolled in the Soviet camp. Only if Cuban and South African forces departed Angolan soil could Namibian independence become a reality, and that country have a chance to achieve stability, internal reconciliation, and join in regional economic progress.

At the opening of the 1980s, it was clear that this task would not be accomplished unless the United States took a leading role. The improbable cast of nations and characters presented a unique challenge, requiring the classic diplomacy of juggling several balls in the air at once—but these were barbed balls, painful to catch and to toss accurately again. We had an adversarial relationship with Castro's Cuba. We had no diplomatic relations with Marxist Angola. Our support for Savimbi's UNITA was under constant domestic political attack. Our relations with South Africa were severely strained by its adherence to a racial policy wholly anathema to us. Confronting us at every turn was the Soviet Union, with the ideological contest of the Cold War at a stage of growing tension. And even our friends among European and African nation-states were skeptical, difficult, or hostile to our efforts at often-critical junctures.

This book is the story of Chet Crocker's near-decade-long struggle to devise a diplomatic strategy to deal with this conundrum and carry it through with skill, patience, courage, and dexterity.

On December 22, 1988, the international protocol bringing about Namibia's independence was signed at the United Nations in New York. When the moment came for the ceremony's official photograph, I made sure Chet Crocker was prominently placed at the center of the group. Every one of the assembled foreign ministers joined in paying tribute to Chet; they recognized that his personal commitment and creative diplomacy had been indispensable to this success.

GEORGE P. SHULTZ

Acknowledgments

The reader of this book will quickly recognize my many debts to others. Some of them appear in the story; others were invisible but indispensable partners. I cannot do them all justice. Frank Wisner, my senior deputy from 1982 to 1986, set an awesome standard of diplomatic creativity and effectiveness, which opened up the road for American policy across the African continent. I cannot say enough about my executive assistant Barbara Beckwith, whose unfailing grace and commitment to the cause from 1981 to 1989 made it possible to survive and, ultimately, prevail. Robert Cabelly brought his killer instinct and his nose for reality to the advancement of peacemaking, and, as he would say, "gave it his best shot" for over seven years. Assistant secretaries of state look to their legal advisers for fine judgment and fine print; Nancy Ely-Raphel took care of all that, and never permitted the rest of us to lose heart. The personal integrity and credibility of Larry Napper was one of our most potent secret weapons. No assistant secretary has ever learned as much from a desk officer as I learned from Bob Frasure, who helped to launch the ship in 1981–82 and worked to keep it afloat for years to come.

I owe big debts to many career diplomats, civil servants, and military officers. Some of them were: Nick Platt, Jim Bishop, Melissa Wells, Princeton Lyman, Chas Freeman, Paul Hare, Rich Sullivan, Roger McGuire, Robin Sanders, Sophia Porson, Dave Passage, Mark Bellamy, Frances Cook, Jennifer Ward, Alex Schiavo, David Dlouhy, Bill Pope, Marty Cheshes, Greg Bradford, Jeff Davidow, Dan Simpson, Gib Lanpher, Roy Stacy, Charlie Snyder, Ed Perkins, John Byerly, Ed Cummings, Tex Harris, George Moose, Nancy Morgan Serpa, Mike Ranneberger, Bob Oakley, Ray Smith, Jerry Gallucci, Mike McKinley, John Ordway, Bill Harrop, Lannon Walker, Bob Pringle, and Peter Eicher. Like other Americans, I owe a special debt to the family of Dennis Keogh, who lost his life in a bomb blast during a Namibian assignment for which he was the first volunteer.

A special word of appreciation is owed to David and Mollie Miller, the Batman and Robin ambassadorial duo who carried our flag high in Dar es Salaam, Harare, and Washington. Herman and Phyllis Nickel established our credibility with sane participants in the South Africa debate as our ambassadorial team in Pretoria, and prevented anyone else from capturing our flag for over four years. Like many others, I relied upon the quiet but strong leadership of Ed Perkins in Monrovia, Washington, and Pretoria. To my successor Hank Cohen, my deputy Chas Freeman, and my Pentagon counterpart Jim Woods, I owe a big debt for multiple contributions to all aspects of our diplomacy and for sustaining the interagency team that prevailed over all enemies, foreign and domestic, during the 1988 marathon. I worked under two immediate superiors, Larry Eagleburger and Mike Armacost, who offered wise counsel and inspired protection from Washington carnivores. Like their Pentagon counterpart, Richard Armitage, they knew that we had the right approach and, like him, they had the spine to say so.

Ronald Reagan gave me the opportunity to do the things described in this book. His confident instincts about America's world role and his stubborn sense of rectitude emboldened the activists in his ranks.

I would not have been able to sustain American policy in Africa without the leadership and unwavering support of George P. Shultz. It was Shultz who gave intellectual content to the Reagan era in foreign affairs, and it was he who set the standard for integrity in our public institutions. Long before the game broke wide open toward the end of the decade, Shultz created and sustained the running room that I and others required to do our jobs. He knew about motivation and downward loyalty; he knew how to lead, while delegating.

A number of people urged me to take the time after resigning from office to prepare this book. Chas Freeman literally insisted that I write about our joint exploits because history should be written by those who prevail. My friend Wolfgang Schürer understood that this was a book that had to be written, and did everything he could to encourage me. Any author-academic who does not have a friend like Peter Krogh, the dean of the Georgetown University School of Foreign Service, should immediately go out and look for one. The graceful wisdom and unstinting support of my publisher-editor Donald Lamm made this project a happy experience.

I owe a particular debt to the United States Institute of Peace—a publicly funded institution created by Congress in 1984 to support research, education, and information programs on international peace and conflict resolution. The award of a fellowship from its Jennings Randolph Program in 1989–90 enabled me to pursue this project. The book, of course, contains my views alone, and does not necessarily reflect the views of the Institute.

Through his impossibly high standards and his deeply held ideals, my father Arthur Crocker made it natural for me to battle for my beliefs and to imagine that government could be an arena in which to realize them.

Finally, I could not have carried out the assignment described in this book without the loving support and counsel of my wife Saône. She and our three daughters often paid the real price of my dream when the American diplomatic ship banged into rocks and shoals. They shared in my joy when we got to port, and understood that my odyssey would not end until this book was done.

Preface

This book tells the story of peacemaking in Africa in the 1980s. It is the record of an American diplomatic strategy which helped us to win the Cold War in the Third World. It tells the story of how Southern Africa's own thirty years' war was finally ended, setting the stage for the recent, dramatic turn away from apartheid and one-party dictatorship and toward democracy and political reconciliation in this vast region. The book is a case study of conflict resolution in a polarized region that cried out for third-party mediation. And, finally, it is a first-person account of policymaking in the Reagan era and what actually happened when a small group of people tried to make our foreign policy institutions work.

It is not every day that a thirty-nine-year-old academic gets a chance to apply his training and pursue his intellectual convictions in a government position tailored to his background. It is even less common for one to be given eight long years to see if he can realize his dream. Rarest of all is the story of an American public servant who was able to see a strategy through from conceptualization and implementation to the actual realization of the goal—in this case, a Southern African peace settlement.

I was fortunate in so many ways to have this opportunity to serve my country. With teammates from the Department of State and other agencies, I had the chance to put some good, logical ideas into action. But, if our ideas were so logical, why did it require an eight-year diplomatic marathon, a crescendo of domestic controversy, and recurrent waves of military escalation to arrive at peace in this part of Africa? That is the story of this book. Sensible concepts do not always appeal to wishful thinkers; further, we were dealing not with one but with several, interconnected wars. To achieve peace, the planets would have to come into perfect alignment.

I entered office several weeks before Ronald Reagan's January 20, 1981, inauguration, as a member of Secretary of State-designate Alexander Haig's "transition team" set up to help give the new administration a running start in foreign policy. After five months' service in my new job, Senate confirmation as Assistant Secretary of State for African Affairs came on June 9, after a protracted struggle waged by senators who considered themselves to be better judges than I of the President's thinking on Africa. I departed from my post on April 22, 1989, making me the longest-serving assistant secretary in the history of the Department of State.

It was not the smoothness of the ride that kept me motivated. We were dealing with a pretty rough neighborhood. And Washington itself is not always a warm, welcoming place, especially when seemingly arcane public policy issues become politicized. When a major domestic controversy over South Africa suddenly erupted in the mid-1980s, our efforts became ensnared in a nasty, partisan test of wills. Our concepts—so self-evidently consistent with responsible U.S. internationalism and activist diplomacy—became the target of bumper-sticker posturing. It was not pleasant to have one's record and values so grotesquely distorted. But we had asked for it. We had taken on a sweepingly ambitious brief in a part of the world few Americans knew. By doing so, we let ourselves become identified in the popular imagination with Southern Africa's violent brutality and political ugliness. As I wrote in *Foreign Affairs* in late 1989:

> Southern Africa is a beautiful region, magnificently endowed with human and natural resources, the potential economic engine of a continent, and a place whose web of racial and civil conflict tears at our hearts, urging us to engage ourselves. But at another level, Southern Africa can become, as former ambassador to Pretoria Ed Perkins put it, a sort of "political vending machine" into which we insert our coins to receive moral hygiene or instant ideological gratification. Featuring almost every form of odious human behavior—racism, brutal oppression, Marxism, authoritarianism, terrorist violence, organized butchery of unarmed villagers and gross official corruption—the region became a moralist's theme park.

But in the end, we got a lot done in eight-plus years. Our engagement in Southern African peacemaking had more profound consequences for the region than any of us in early 1981 would have predicted.

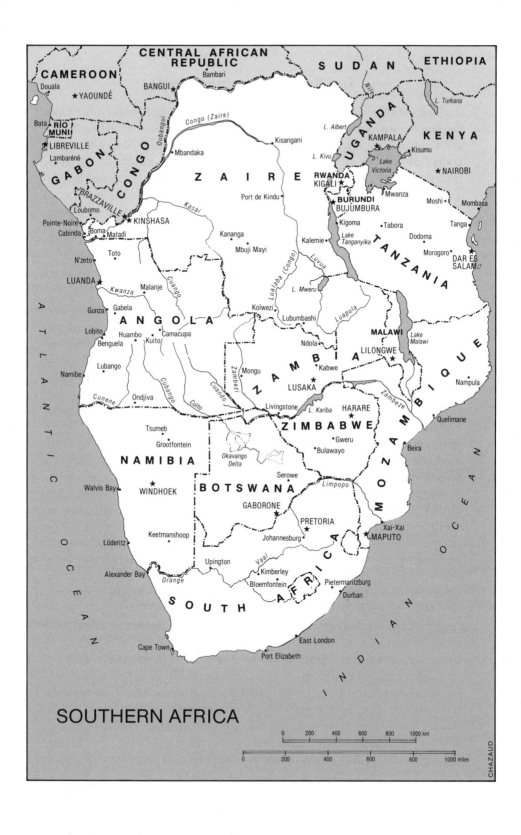

SOUTHERN AFRICA

The Roots of Regional Strife

The southern third of the African continent is not marked off from the rest by any natural or physical frontier. Central and Southern Africa shade into each other; the massive country of Zaire—larger than the United States east of the Mississippi—straddles the notional line. It is, nonetheless, helpful to think of a system of states stretching south from Zaire and Tanzania to the Cape of Good Hope. This is the portion of Africa colonized by Britain, Portugal, and Belgium—not France. Southern Africa is a huge zone, spanning twelve countries with a combined population of 150 million and a land area of about 3.6 million square miles (almost exactly the size of the United States). Economic and transport linkages, combined with imperial legacies and anti-colonial struggles, have helped to create a regional identity.

In modern times, the region has been shaped by these struggles against European control or local, white minority rule. Four nationalist insurgencies erupted between 1960 and 1967, and a generation of regional warfare ensued. Gradually, the South Africans projected themselves (or were drawn) into these conflicts to their north, whether indirectly as in Rhodesia (Zimbabwe) and the former Portuguese territories of Angola and Mozambique, or directly, as in Namibia and, at a later stage, Angola. The overwhelming economic and military power of the Republic of South Africa assured that it would become involved in events beyond its frontiers, especially after the last remaining European power—Portugal—pulled out in 1975, leaving behind a strategic vacuum which the Soviets promptly sought to exploit. By this point, South African leaders had already decided to help defend the shrinking "white redoubt" and to smash external enemies of their white-dominated domestic system. This greatly magnified the natural impulse of a regional hegemon toward intervention in the affairs of weaker neighbors. Those independent, black-ruled neighbors which imagined that they could support armed confrontation against South Africa soon began to pay the predictable price.

No conceivable combination of African conventional or guerrilla forces could take on the apartheid state in Pretoria. The weight and influence of South Africa could be felt throughout the region, parts of which functioned as dependent offshoots of the South African mining, transport, and communication systems. Banks, corporations, managers, and technicians were often South African-based. South African-style Roman-Dutch law and common commercial standards spread to a number of neighboring lands. South African import-export traffic, electricity demand, and tourism shaped the economy of southern Mozambique. The former U.K. colonies of Botswana, Lesotho, and Swaziland (along with South

African-controlled South West Africa) participated in a South Africa-dominated customs union. A high percentage of regional rail and air traffic traveled through South Africa, and hundreds of thousands of workers from as far north as Zambia and Malawi worked in South Africa's mines. This embryonic regionalism co-existed uneasily with Southern Africa's wars for nearly thirty years.

Few Americans knew anything of this pattern of events. In the 1960s and early 1970s, there were brief flurries of public awareness of strife in the former Belgian Congo (Zaire) and the war over Biafra's attempted secession from Nigeria. But the struggle against apartheid in South Africa itself was a cause confined to academic and Church activists. The famous Sharpeville massacre of March 1960—which catalyzed the British and Commonwealth anti-apartheid movement—and the subsequent trials and imprisonment of African National Congress leaders, including Nelson Mandela, made remarkably little impact on mainstream opinion in the United States. Even fewer Americans knew about the wars in Angola, Mozambique, Namibia, and Zimbabwe.

In May 1972, on the anniversary of African Liberation Day (a holiday established by the Organization of African Unity in support of the Southern African nationalist movements), several thousand anti-apartheid protesters and a few sound trucks showed up outside the State Department. After the Soweto crisis of 1976 and the death of Steve Biko in a South African prison the following year, there were more protesters in Washington. By 1980, a number of black American Church-affiliated and academic groups were working on South African issues and pressing for measures such as university divestment of the securities of firms invested in South Africa. But this activity, centered largely on the *internal* affairs of South Africa, had minimal impact on American society generally. The regional strife in Southern Africa had even less. These wars were the concern of some executive branch officials, a handful of congressional devotees, and small numbers of cognoscenti in universities and places like the Council on Foreign Relations, the Ford Foundation, the Center for Strategic and International Studies, and the Hoover Institution on War, Revolution and Peace. I was one of that small number, and here is where the story of this book begins.

PART I

1

A Mission to Accomplish

My earliest interests in school were in languages and literature. What should have been my junior and senior years of high school were spent tending bar on Lexington Avenue and working as a stock transfer clerk at a Wall Street bank. I arrived at Ohio State University without a high school degree in 1959, vaguely intending to major in classics. But several outstanding professors stirred a growing interest in modern European history. I became attracted to the study of imperialism and decolonization and the process by which a global political system had emerged after 1945.

Change on a global scale was an amazing idea, and especially the emergence to statehood of the formerly colonial and imperial domains of Africa, the Middle East, and Asia. These were the years of Africa's own emergence from European rule. My roommate, the late Henry Franklin Jackson, and I took every course and attended every lecture we could find on imperial history, comparative politics, African and Arab nationalism, and the struggle against apartheid in South Africa. A fascination with African decolonization brought Jackson and me together—the son of a poor, African-American farming family from Georgia and the son of a New York investment banker. It was a shared voyage of discovery. This was just before the days when most universities opted to make a statement by establishing formal ethnic heritage and regional studies programs—in a futile quest to combat Eurocentric parochialism with the divisive cocoons of multiculturalism. Our "African studies program" was a homemade blend of the best available courses and visiting lectures organized by a junior faculty member in his "free" time.

An undergraduate honors thesis on early British Labor Party foreign and colonial policies immersed me in such questions as the Anglo-Boer War and the creation of the Union of South Africa, the Agadir crisis, the founding of German South West Africa (Namibia), European settlement in Kenya and Rhodesia (Zimbabwe), the struggle over Indian colonial and military policy, and the policies of King Leopold of the Belgians in his Congo Free State (Zaire). Now, in the early 1960s, a nationalist wave had swept the empires away and an exotic array of "new nations" was taking their place.

Graduate school offered the chance to dig deeper into African affairs, and also to place these events in a context of contemporary global politics and American foreign policy. Johns Hopkins University's School of Advanced International Studies offered lots of both. The Cold War's spread to the Arab and African worlds in the 1950s and 1960s placed a special spotlight on the gradual British and French retrenchment from overseas security and defense roles, and on the choices that we and our NATO allies now faced in the developing nations. Vietnam was not the answer, but the protesters did not have one, either. Should containment become global, or should we simply avert our eyes from the likely consequences as Europe disengaged strategically from its former empires? What sorts of political and security roles should the United States foster with the "new nations"? Now that the drive for national independence was complete almost everywhere, people were beginning to ask if it had really been such a brilliant idea for Truman, Eisenhower, and Kennedy to hasten the Europeans' departure before any security mechanism could be devised to help maintain order in a world of new nations. A doctoral thesis comparing British and French approaches to decolonization exposed me to the awesome security challenges facing Africa's new rulers.

There was another reason why emerging Africa claimed my attention in the 1960s. I met my future wife in graduate school just as she completed her B.A. at the University of Cape Town, the English-speaking South African university whose faculty and students were so traumatized by the South African turmoil of the early 1960s. A native of Zimbabwe, Saône Baron left Africa to continue her education in the United States. Her family, remaining behind, soon found themselves caught up in the war sparked by Ian Smith's unilateral declaration of independence from the British in 1965. Portuguese-speaking Mozambique and Angola had already faced five years of anti-colonial war. SWAPO's insurgency began in 1966 in South African-controlled South West Africa (Namibia). Southern Africa had become the last frontier of the decolonization struggle.

One day in early 1966 my thesis adviser asked me what I wished to do with my life. Upon hearing of my continuing interest in Africa, he remarked, "Well, yes, but what would you want to do for a *living?*" In reality, Africa was never my exclusive focus; nor was my interest in it a career handicap. I landed a job as news editor with a monthly magazine called *Africa Report,* which offered its readers serious analysis and regular chronologies of events throughout the region. After several semesters of part-time teaching on African politics, I found myself torn between the narrow groove of African studies and the broader currents of global change and its implications for Western security. A phone call from a former professor opened the door to two years on Henry Kissinger's National Security Council. There, I served as a utility infielder, roaming far and wide, working on things like the Persian Gulf and Indochina, arms transfer policies and Indian Ocean naval balances. I tracked African developments, but did not work on them directly.

During the Nixon and Ford years, our government tried to restrain the Soviet thrust into Third World vacuums and troublespots, but it did so with a weak hand as a result of Vietnam. Sometimes, we lacked the finesse or the will to mount our own initiatives to counter our global adversary in a regional context. For much of this period, it seemed to me that we were imagining that Africa could be dealt with by leaving it to our allies or by quiet but cozy dealings with Lisbon and Pretoria. Belatedly, in 1975, we began to develop a serious African policy that went beyond the visceral instincts of busy people who spent 99 percent of their time tending other policy gardens.

By now I had left government for the School of Foreign Service at Georgetown University. It seemed to me to be clear that a test of wills had begun over the question of superpower conduct throughout the developing world. But a local test of wills had also broken out among rival nationalisms in some regions. It was unacceptable that the Western nations should watch from the sidelines, as the men with the guns on all sides took history into their own hands. Why should the fate of Southern Africa—the most westernized part of Africa—be determined in a shootout between those who were best armed? It would not be a pretty sight, especially given the considerable military staying power of an increasingly isolated, yet self-reliant Afrikaner state in Pretoria.

To me, the West was on trial in Southern Africa: our values and principles, our system and our global standing. It was time for the West to compete in shaping the destiny of this region. The Soviets and their proxies were moving forcefully to assert claims to regional leadership. The South Africans had responded to their loss of Western military support in the 1960s and 1970s by massive strategic investments in arms manufacture and nuclear and synfuels industries—and showed signs of preparing to go it alone as a regional superpower. The challenge was to identify strategies that were both credible and relevant to the region itself. Neither the globalists—who saw a Soviet hand behind every Third World problem area—nor the Africanists—who imagined that slogans like "African solutions for African problems" could ward off Soviet interventionism—had the answer.

Mine was a somewhat messianic message, but it was not without resonance in the policy arena. As a Georgetown professor and director of a small African program at its Center for Strategic and International Studies, I was well placed to speak on regional strife, Soviet-Cuban intervention, and Western diplomacy in Africa. I was delighted to be asked by George Bush to serve on his foreign policy advisory group during the 1980 primary campaign and, later, to head up an Africa working group for the Republican National Committee's foreign affairs advisory council during the Reagan campaign. When Al Haig asked me to join his "transition team," I realized that something more finite might be coming. Saône and I agreed that I should join the administration, although it would be tough: she had just enrolled in law school and we had three children in grade school.

Life as an Assistant Secretary

In December 1980 I had little idea what it would mean to head the Bureau of African Affairs. I knew or had met most of my predecessors and had a number of friends in the Foreign Service. But it was something else altogether to assume charge of the conduct of U.S. relations with the 46 nations of sub-Saharan Africa, where we had 44 embassies (all except colonial Namibia and unrecognized Angola), seven consulates, an American and foreign staff of 3,400 (supported by 135 people in the bureau in Washington), an operating budget of around $100 million—and lots of problems.

The awesome dilemma of Africa's economic crisis became a central topic as we sought to develop policy responses. We had to limit bilateral political damage while pressing African leaders to begin undoing twenty years of statist policies that had wrecked their economies and made them even more vulnerable to interest rate and commodity price fluctuations.

There was the continentwide pattern of Libyan subversion of vulnerable neighbors such as Chad and Sudan—an activity Colonel Qadhafi undertook (with ample Soviet and European hardware). Sometimes, Qadhafi acted in concert with the Ethiopian regime of Mengistu Haile Mariam—a thug and a leading Soviet client. We cared about African security. No Western or African objectives could be advanced without a degree of stability. Since we had neither the means nor the desire to carry this load alone, it was imperative that we consult closely with our key European allies, who had the ability to affect the situation in individual African capitals.

Then, too, we had a full caseload of "troubled friends" to deal with—countries historically close to us such as Liberia, Kenya, and Zaire, which had a reasonable expectation that we would be interested in their problems and prepared to be helpful. There was also a long list of important relationships to tend with friendly countries, where our bilateral interests and aid resources were less "exposed"—e.g., Côte d'Ivoire, Senegal, Nigeria, Zambia, Botswana, and Niger. In fact, we considered that all countries in the region (save Qadhafi's Libya and Mengistu's Ethiopia) were actual or potential friends. I did not view the search for enemies to be the primary business of our African bureau. We developed an agenda of working to turn our way the growing list of jaded Soviet clients and assorted quasi-Marxists—in places like the Congo, Benin, Guinea, Mali, Madagascar, Cape Verde, Guinea-Bissau, Sao Tome & Principe and, of course, Angola and Mozambique.

I spent the major proportion of my time on the events recounted in this book. But they represent only a portion of what we did in Africa in the 1980s. Early in my tenure, I realized that survival at the head of such a far-flung enterprise would depend upon recruiting top-class people to serve as deputies and regional or functional "office directors"—and then delegating as much authority as they could handle. To keep the pieces firmly in my mind and provide guidance, we ran coordination meetings five or six times a week. A superlative secretary–office manager and several staff assistants did the best they could to keep my four deputies and me organized, prepared, and in touch with life beyond the "front office." My senior deputy and I tried to be virtually interchangeable, backstopping each other whenever one of us was overseas. Portfolios passed back and forth with relative ease because of the long hours we spent briefing each other and developing our own institutional culture. It was the best way we could think of to run an ambitious and activist operation in a Washington setting that had long viewed Africa as the stepchild (if that) of American foreign policy.

AFRICA IN GLOBAL PERSPECTIVE

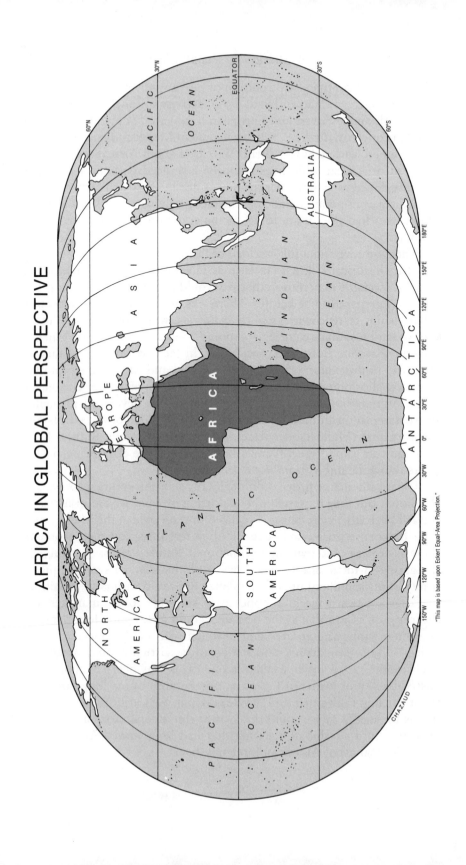

"This map is based upon Eckert Equal-Area Projection."

The Variety of Southern Africa

Facing a vast sea of distant, little-known countries and crazy-quilt boundaries, most Americans generalize about Africa. Speaking before American audiences, I am all too often asked questions about "famine in Africa" or "Africa's attitude" toward American policy. Yet variety is a primary characteristic of Africa's natural wonders, its climates, its ethnic and linguistic makeup, and its political cultures. Like its counterparts elsewhere, African diplomacy is shaped by culture, circumstance, and personality—the latter being especially important in non-democratic systems, the norm in most of Africa until the 1990s.

Africans have a deeply rooted cultural reflex of hospitality and politeness, which may mislead the novice visitor into thinking that the locals agree with him. Privately, the African message is usually couched in reasonable and friendly terms. But African states have also been among the world's great joiners of groups and interstate organizations in order to compensate for their general weakness and achieve some "strength in numbers." Sometimes, this leads to a sort of phony solidarity around a militant official "line" that appears in U.N. or Organization of African Unity resolutions (often driven by a radical minority). Observers who are confined to such manifestations of African diplomacy are severely handicapped in understanding the region's diversity and political behavior.

By the time I joined the Reagan team in 1981, only a limited number of African governments defined themselves as Marxist or pro-Western; most of them preferred a more "non-aligned" tag. And, in reality, ideology in the East-West or left-right sense was only a small part of the story. Often the colonial legacy of language, habits of thinking, and political culture was more significant. Africa's Portuguese and French speakers seemed to share a more natural rapport and a more comprehensible political idiom than either group did with the English speakers. At times, we heard the anglophones of, say, Zimbabwe or Tanzania, speak condescendingly of their northern and western neighbors as "French countries." This was an allusion to the pro-Western moderation and continued French influence in most of equatorial and Western Africa, in contrast to the anglophones' supposedly more nationalistic political style. We also heard the francophones respond with ill-disguised contempt for their critics' tendency toward strident posturing on Southern African issues even while they maintained intimate economic links with South Africa.

Partly for these reasons, staunchly pro-Western Zaire was not a member of the so-called "Front Line States" (a key political forum) or its economic equivalent, the Southern African Development Coordination Conference. This geographic and cultural chasm made little sense, and we ignored it. After all, Angola had more at stake in its relations with Zaire and the Congo Republic than it did with anglophone Zambia.

Angola and Mozambique, two Portuguese-speaking states, further confounded the stereotypes. Together with their lusophone brothers in Cape Verde, Guinea-Bissau, and Sao Tome & Principe, these states emerged at independence governed by avowedly Marxist parties. They appeared to be firmly linked to Moscow through a showy panoply of friendship treaties, party-to-party links, and military pacts. Their public rhetoric was vintage "non-aligned" and Marxist—a heady and hostile brew of anti-Western vituperation.

But behind the noisy facade, there were great differences and a more complex story. The lusophone states spent much of the 1980s seeking an escape from failure. They mounted a regional diplomacy which was at once more nuanced and more byzantine than that of their English-speaking co-members of Front Line States. Angola, Mozambique, and Cape Verde were capable of hunting with the hounds of Moscow and Havana while running with the hares of Washington and London. They left few stones unturned in exploring openings to the West and new channels to their regional nemesis, South Africa. Deals were discussed, and sometimes cut, that startled the strait-laced, moralizing anglophones.

These contrasts and generalizations also broke down upon closer inspection. The Angolans had lost so much more of their sovereign capacity for independent decision; their leaders lacked the internal mandate and the political will of their counterparts in Mozambique. There were similar sharp contrasts between English speakers such as the strident, newly independent Zimbabweans—the voice of believers in "armed struggle"—and the more statesmanlike message of the Zambians, champions of regional dialogue. Each government and its leadership was unique.

But some were more unique than others. South African diplomacy was a direct reflection of the National Party government's own needs, changes of mood, and internal preoccupations. The message from Pretoria to the neighbors swung like a pendulum between menacing toughness and an almost touching desire for acceptance by black Africa. The fact that many African regimes were prepared to meet and do business with the South Africans provided it was kept quiet only aggravated South African condescension toward black Africa. The South Africans were no more at home dealing with Western nations. Theirs was a true pariah politik.

At times, one wondered if virtually all the characters who populated the Southern Africa diplomatic landscape would not have preferred to live somewhere else, amongst other neighbors. But fate condemned them to live together in this rough neighborhood. They would make war unless they could be brought to make peace.

2

The Historical Setting

Southern Africa is a region at the periphery of modern world history, a place of peculiar parochialisms whose history has been shaped, in part, by the burdens of cultural and geographic isolation. At another level, the region is a microcosm that includes the full array of ideological conflicts, economic extremes, and antagonistic nationalisms found in the global system. The "end of history" is not in sight in Southern Africa. Western liberalism still contends with strong voices pushing Marxism, Leninism, state socialism, and many forms of ethnic nationalism.

Anti-colonial struggles first began to take violent form in Southern Africa in the early 1960s. The immediate issue in the region's four anti-colonial insurgencies (Angola, Mozambique, Namibia, and Zimbabwe) was self-determination of the indigenous, African majority population. These were nationalist rebellions in the tradition of the post-1945 decolonization process that produced scores of new nations in Asia and Africa. The Southern African wars of 1961–88 represent the final chapter in the global drama which ended the European maritime empires.

For the most part, Africa's decolonization was orderly and relatively peaceful: the anti-colonial struggles of Algeria and Kenya were exceptions proving the rule. In the case of Angola and Mozambique, however, the battle between nationalist guerrilla movements and the Portuguese armed forces dragged on into the mid-1970s. Portugal, the first European imperial power to colonize Africa, would be the last one to leave. The picture became even more complicated in the case of Namibia and Zimbabwe (Rhodesia), where insurgent guerrillas took up arms against local white authorities—not some distant colonial power. In Namibia, that authority was the government of South Africa, the *de facto* colonial power since World War I. In Zimbabwe, it was a rebel white regime that had seized "independence" from Britain in 1965.

This complexity was further aggravated when Portugal suddenly changed course in 1974, departing from Angola and Mozambique in indecent haste one year later, leaving behind a disastrous vacuum of power. A wholly new dimension was added when the Soviets and Cubans intervened militarily in 1975 to install a Marxist regime in Angola, and then developed close military ties with Mozambique, Zambia, and the anti-South African guerrilla movements SWAPO* and the African National Congress (ANC). These events cast a new light on the protracted but unsuccessful effort by African and "non-aligned" nations to assert effective U.N. authority over Namibia and bring the territory to independence from South African control. That effort included five different actions before the International Court of Justice and countless U.N. meetings, resolutions, and missions. Now, after 1975, SWAPO guerrillas acquired the sanctuary and backing of the Soviet-Cuban-dominated regime in Angola. But, at the same time, the Soviets' new strategic stake in Southern Africa was placed in question when post-independence rebellions broke out against the new Afro-Marxist regimes of Angola and Mozambique, a process fostered and exploited by the South Africans.

Western and U.S. policy toward Southern Africa during the last three decades has sought to navigate through this maze. The region became an increasingly polarized arena in which the outsider faced stark choices: engagement, disengagement, benign neglect, or distant sanctimony. If he engaged, he would have to tread at his peril through various political minefields laid by regional players eager to export their own causes and divisions.

For a variety of reasons, Americans have been willing importers of these partisan causes. The region's beauty, its drama, its larger-than-life "issues," and its vast geographic and psychic distance from our daily American experience, all combined to attract American attention. As a result, some of those minefields were laid right here at home. U.S. decisionmakers waited a long time—arguably, too long—before deciding that a global power requires a strategy for dealing with all parts of the

---

*SWAPO, the South West Africa People's Organization, is the Namibian nationalist movement based initially on the northern Ovambo people (about 50% of Namibia's population—Ovambos also inhabit an area of southern Angola). SWAPO began its military campaign against South African rule in 1966, finding sanctuary in Zambia and, later, Angola. SWAPO won a majority in the elections preceding Namibia's March 1990 independence.

globe. By the time they finally decided to do something, in 1975, strong negative dynamics were already firmly established. The Portuguese collapse created a regional vacuum, and the race to fill it had begun.

The Soviet decision to project military power into Africa—including the support of "proxies" in the form of thousands of Cuban combat troops sent to Angola and Ethiopia in the period 1975–78—placed the Western nations in a seemingly no-win situation. The actions of Moscow and Havana represented a geopolitical challenge with potentially global implications. Yet Western leaders had no interest in becoming hostage to the behavior of an increasingly isolated, bellicose, and militarily self-sufficient South African state. We could neither align ourselves with the land of apartheid, nor walk away and let nature take its course. The Soviets had developed the means for further expansionism into neighboring countries, while the South Africans had developed both the means and the rationale for military intervention beyond their borders.

The United States Enters the Diplomatic Game

The events of 1974–75 prompted a belated assertion of U.S. regional influence to stem further violence and polarization and to preempt further Soviet exploitation of regional strife. For the next six years, from 1975 to 1981, the Ford and Carter administrations sought to position the United States for leadership on the problems of Southern Africa by promoting negotiated solutions and peaceful change. For the first time, American policymakers began to articulate a regionwide vision, and Washington began to play a more active role in regional affairs. There were some differences in approach. Compared to its predecessors, the Carter team stepped up the rhetorical assault on apartheid and supported a mandatory U.N. arms embargo in response to the wave of unrest and repression in 1976–77. Compared to the Ford policy, it soft-pedaled and waffled about the inherently East-West dimensions of the troubling regional situation created by Leonid Brezhnev's interventionism in Africa.

But there were also important similarities between the Ford and Carter approaches. Both categorically rejected South Africa's apartheid policies. Both insisted on majority rule as the condition for Rhodesian independence and rejected the unilateral assertion of independence by the white minority. Both supported the principle that Namibia should move toward independence under the monitoring and supervision of the United Nations. (The U.N. had revoked South Africa's mandate over the territory deriving from the League of Nations, and in 1971, the International Court of Justice had declared Pretoria to be in "illegal occupation" of it, a judgment later reinforced by the U.N. Security Council.) Both carefully avoided dealing directly with the Angolan nettle left over from the fiasco of a failed covert intervention. Both attempted to pursue all of our regional objectives at once, then came to accept at least tacitly the need for some sequencing and priorities.

The British worked hard to persuade both U.S. administrations that the Rhodesian tangle was riper for a settlement than Namibia, and that it made no sense to pursue both with equal vigor. And they were correct: it would have been unthinkable that South Africa, having just experienced the collapse of the Portuguese imperial buffer, would rush to closure on Rhodesia and Namibia simultaneously even as it felt the local and external aftershocks of the Soweto crisis (1976) and the death in detention of black consciousness leader Steve Biko in 1977. In 1979, after repeated attempts had fallen short, the newly elected British government of Margaret Thatcher surprised the world and perhaps itself by negotiating a Rhodesian independence settlement. Zimbabwe emerged under militantly nationalist, anti-South African leadership in 1980.

By 1981, when the Reagan administration entered office, Southern Africa was no longer *terra incognita* for U.S. policy. Washington had established effective working relations with the British on Africa, an indispensable starting place since they had the greatest experience and the deepest policy linkages in the area. Washington played a key supporting role to the British in the negotiations leading to the independence of Zimbabwe in 1980. The United States had also developed close working ties with the African Front Line States—Angola, Botswana, Mozambique, Tanzania, Zambia, and Zimbabwe—so named because of their proximity to and role in the conflicts over Zimbabwe and, now, Namibia; and, to a lesser extent, with the wary South Africans, still deeply scarred by the Western collapse in Angola six years earlier.

At the same time, Washington had taken the lead on the question of Namibian independence with its British, French, German, and Canadian allies. In 1977, these were the five Western members of the U.N. Security Council; they converted themselves into the so-called "Contact Group" for the specific purpose of negotiating Namibia's independence with Pretoria and the Front Line States (FLS). The resulting "Western settlement proposal" of April 1978, endorsed as U.N. Security Council Resolution 435 in September 1978, was an impressive and ambitious piece of diplomatic work. It sought to convert the low-level bush war mounted by SWAPO in 1966 into a peaceful act of self-determination leading to statehood for Namibia.

A U.N. operation of unprecedented scope and complexity would be required in order to balance the interests of SWAPO, the internal parties operating within Namibia, the South Africans, and the neighboring African states during the delicate transition to independence. The settlement plan would basically govern the territory's transition. South African administrative control and responsibility for law and order would be offset by simultaneous U.N. monitoring and supervision, to be conducted by a U.N. Transition Assistance Group (UNTAG) consisting of up to ten thousand civilian and military personnel. The plan provided for the United Nations to:

- create acceptable conditions for an electoral campaign and organize and supervise "free and fair" elections;
- assure the repeal of discriminatory laws and the release of political prisoners (on either side);
- arrange the return of war refugees;
- monitor the Namibia-Angola border against infiltration;
- monitor the conduct of the local police, the confinement to base and scheduled departure of South African forces from Namibia, and the demobilization of local, South African-controlled territorial forces; and
- monitor and maintain a cessation of hostilities between the various forces.

The next two and a half years were taken up with efforts to obtain South African agreement to implement Resolution 435. By January 1981, when a new U.S. administration entered office, these efforts were continuing. At one level, the years 1975–81 represented an effective and fairly rapid assertion of U.S. leadership in a previously neglected region. The Soviets were unable to exploit racial and ideological tensions in Rhodesia for their own advantage or to block a U.S.-backed and British-orchestrated solution there. Similarly, they failed to derail or discredit the Contact Group's effort on Namibia, and were obliged to tolerate the adoption of Resolution 435 because it had firm Front Line State support. Western diplomacy appeared to have stemmed, at least for now, the tide of Soviet influence symbolized by Angola's alignment with Moscow and the strong Soviet influence within SWAPO and the African National Congress. The imaginative leadership of our U.N. ambassador, Donald F. McHenry, played a key role in these events.

But, at another level, the United States was trying to conduct regional diplomacy with a distinctly weak hand. The region was distant from American experience, a place where we had relatively few tangible assets and no basis for deploying or projecting American power. Our allies had greater links of history, trade, investment, and military acquaintance than we did. It was a place where we had to operate principally on the basis of our skill, our strategic vision, and our special diplomatic possibilities. Besides, U.S. engagement in regional problem solving contained risks and potential domestic downsides, but no guarantees of success. Previous administrations had already found out that African policies are seldom "popular" and often divisive. Kissinger's balanced activism in the waning months of the Ford administration did nothing for Ford's (or Kissinger's) position with those elements of the Republican Party where a strong strain of sympathy existed for the white Rhodesians and South Africans. Carter's hyperactive African diplomacy—with its visceral tilt toward the black African perspective and its schizophrenia toward Soviet-Cuban adventurism—was also divisive and controversial at home.

Moreover, Britain's successful handling of Rhodesia-Zimbabwe in 1979 did not necessarily augur well for breaking the Namibia deadlock. On the contrary, Pretoria had been stunned by the victory of Robert Mugabe's Zimbabwe African National Union (ZANU) in the April 1980 election. A militant African nationalist and a Marxist who was not fond of or beholden to Moscow, Mugabe represented a voice too strident and a message too complex for Pretoria. The South African government would hardly want to facilitate in Namibia the coming to power of yet another militant, Marxist-oriented guerrilla movement, SWAPO. Deeply critical of U.S. and Western conduct in Angola in 1975–76, the South Africans were unenchanted by the results of British and American diplomacy in Rhodesia. They began to see a pattern in these events that would undermine prospects for striking a deal on Namibia. Pretoria's circuits were becoming overloaded.

A long history of pro-SWAPO pronouncements and activities (including the General Assembly's 1977 endorsement of SWAPO as "sole and authentic representative of the Namibian people") had severely compromised the United Nation's standing as a decolonizing agent. Pretoria's stance on Namibia had become increasingly truculent and uncooperative during 1979–80. South African acceptance of the basic Western proposal embodied by reference in Resolution 435 became subject to a growing list of conditions, caveats, and ambiguities. At an abortive, U.N.-sponsored "pre-implementation" conference in January 1981—just days before the change of administration in Washington—South African delegates repeated numerous objections to Resolution 435, showed no real interest in discussing how to resolve them, and behaved in ways that seemed calculated to prompt a walkout by the Front Line States (FLS) and SWAPO.

But the FLS / SWAPO failed to oblige. On the contrary, they interpreted Pretoria's non-cooperation as either a sinister plot with the incoming Reagan administration or an interesting test of Western political will. Increasingly, as the new U.S. team settled into place, there were reports that the Africans, with support from the Soviets, Cubans, and elements of the Non-aligned movement, would soon take up the call for mandatory U.N. sanctions against South Africa for its failure to cooperate in implementing the Namibian plan.

To complete the picture, it is necessary to recognize that Western diplomacy from 1976 to 1981 had carefully avoided addressing the question of Angola. This was ironic. One might almost have thought that the United States had a case of strategic amnesia. After all, Angola, and the presence of Cuban forces there, was the principal negative factor that had prompted Western concern in the mid-1970s. That concern remained a subject of lively discussion and debate both within and beyond the Carter administration. At issue was not only Soviet-Cuban hegemony in Angola, but also the opportunity it offered to project Soviet power and influence to other states (such as Namibia) and to guerrilla groups such as SWAPO and the ANC (both, not coincidentally, based militarily in Angola).

But there were reasons why Angola had played almost no role in Western strategy apart from its role as a member of the Front Line States grouping. The 1975–76 Angola debacle left the West as losers in a proxy struggle. Whatever their real views about the Marxist MPLA regime, Angola's African neighbors were silenced by its propaganda and diplomacy stating that 25,000 Cuban troops were still necessary to ward off cross-border attacks by the South African Defence Force (SADF). Western attempts to raise the question of Cuban troops in Angola, it was argued, would have (a) undercut Angola's cooperation in the Namibia diplomacy, and (b) led to accusations that the West cared more about Communist presence in Angola than about colonialism and racism in South African-ruled Namibia. The Western Contact Group would be charged with siding against the "legitimate" government of Angola (recognized by everyone except Washington and Pretoria), and siding with South Africa and the South African-supported UNITA rebel movement in Angola.

To many observers in Africa, Europe, and the United States, such reasoning made good diplomatic sense. But it also made for an ineffective strategy. The issue of foreign intervention in Angola (both Cuban and South African) was uppermost in the thinking of decisionmakers in both Pretoria and Luanda. Long before the Reagan victory of 1980, Angolan leaders had recognized the connection between Namibian and Angolan events. They had made it clear in public and diplomatic channels that Cuban forces would depart only *after* a Namibia independence settlement under Resolution 435, thereby defining the South African presence in Namibia as the rationale for retaining Cubans.

In reality, there were a host of reasons why MPLA leaders preferred to postpone the issue of Cuban withdrawal until "later"—to avoid disrupting the delicate balances within their regime, to avoid annoying the Cubans (and Soviets), to cling onto their security blanket against UNITA and possible threats from Zaire, to avoid conceding the principle that the Cuban presence in Angola was anyone else's business. But South African control of Namibia and the SADF's looming presence on the border (or inside Angola) were the best possible arguments for delaying Cuban troop withdrawal until "later."

Meanwhile, a narrowly defined Namibia settlement (without reference to Angola) was unattractive to Pretoria for a host of reasons. It would entail the loss of a mineral-rich, strategic buffer zone larger than Texas without any compensating "quid"; the negative political imagery of a U.N.-led transition that would favor SWAPO; the risk of SWAPO exploiting its U.N., Soviet, Cuban, and MPLA support effectively to coerce its way into power, drawing encouragement from the nearby presence of a highly trained, mobile Cuban combat force; the desire to avoid abandoning Pretoria's black UNITA allies in Angola; the prospect of a chaotic exodus from Namibia of its white minority, leading to charges at home of a sellout; and the loss of Namibian bases for projecting military power into neighboring states. The SADF leadership and Prime Minister Pieter W. Botha himself (South Africa's defense minister during the events of 1975–76) would lose the means for continuing their "forward strategy" in Angola. There would be no compensation for the loss of their stake in the Angolan war. All these negatives played directly into the most neuralgic points of white South African and Namibian politics, summed up by the government's much-quoted opposition to a settlement that would mean "the red flag in Windhoek."

The South African leadership much preferred an "Angola-first" brand of linkage, just as the Angolans preferred the "Namibia-first" variety. The Angolan events of the mid-1970s were deeply etched in South African official memories as symbols of humiliation and Western weakness. A Namibian settlement that left intact the nexus of Soviet-aligned regimes, movements, and forces now in Angola would be both a strategic and political defeat. Angola epitomized Pretoria's preoccupation with a foe described in official rhetoric as "the total Marxist onslaught." On the other hand, Cuban troop withdrawal would remove the only conceivable conventional threat to the SADF's primacy for thousands of kilometers. South African negotiators raised the Cuban issue in their exchanges with U.S. and Contact Group representatives during 1977–80. They stopped short of formally insisting on linking the issues diplomatically; but the link already existed in the world of perceptions, and helped explain why South African diplomats came up with one caveat or condition after another for stalling on Resolution 435.

For its part, the Carter administration endlessly debated how to handle Soviet-Cuban adventurism in Africa, both as a matter of African policy and in the context of relations with the Soviets and Cuba. The events of 1975–76 in Angola had left a deep scar in the American political memory. As a result, Washington never established diplomatic relations with Luanda. During the Carter era (like the Ford era), we conditioned a future relationship on Cuban troop withdrawal—a position that effectively linked our Angola policy to a Namibia settlement: Luanda and Havana were most unlikely to approve Cuban withdrawal so long as the South African Defence Force remained free to continue operating into Angola from Namibian soil. Washington explored the chances for obtaining Angolan assurances that Cuban troops would, indeed, withdraw if Resolution 435 were implemented. But this went nowhere, and no specific formula for a link was established. As a result, some of the most basic security concerns of both Pretoria and Luanda were never explicitly addressed.

In January 1981, the incoming Reagan administration inherited a moribund diplomacy on Namibia and a worsening regional situation that mandated a review of U.S. options. We and our Contact Group partners were caught between increasingly polarized parties who showed every sign of hardening their positions. Even if Carter had been reelected in 1980, tough decisions on African policy would have been unavoidable. FLS wishful thinking, Soviet-Cuban obstructionism, and a growing South African determination to alter the U.N. Plan and delay a settlement would have posed a severe test of allied cohesion and leadership.

In the wake of the failed Geneva conference in January, the Front Line States and SWAPO hoped to enlist the Contact Group in support of expanded pressures on South Africa to implement Resolution 435 without further delay—pressures including, if necessary, the use of economic sanctions for which the Group had no enthusiasm. The Front Line African leaders hoped to "borrow" Western diplomatic influence to "deliver" Pretoria, thus averting a costly test of wills with their powerful neighbor and avoiding the need to rely on a protracted, Soviet-fueled armed confrontation whose outcome would be uncertain at best.

Pretoria, badly burned by the Zimbabwe outcome, was on a collision course with these trends. The fact that both Moscow and Pretoria had backed the wrong horses in Zimbabwe only added to the likelihood that they would compete for influence there—and in other neighboring countries. South African grand designs had been foreshadowed in public declarations back in 1979 calling for the creation of a "constellation of states" to include South Africa and its neighbors in a series of political, security, and economic agreements. Such proposals were backed by bellicose pronouncements warning its African neighbors to curb the guerrilla attacks being mounted from their territory against Namibia and South Africa. The clear message was that Pretoria was prepared to rely on its regionally dominant military power and to throw the sanctions threat back in the face of its authors. On the ground, South African military planners were stepping up clandestine activity in adjacent states, including Angola and Mozambique. Disaffected with the entire Contact Group exercise, the Pretoria leadership sought to promote a basic shift in the U.S. and Western approach: to place Namibia on the back burner and enlist the West as allies in support of an anti-Communist regional strategy.

The other four members of the Contact Group found themselves caught between the Front Line States, the South Africans, and a brandnew American team that was outspokenly critical of the Carter-era foreign policy record. Sensitive to U.N. pressures, these four governments sought Washington's early reendorsement of Resolution 435. Washington's Western allies, like the new and previous U.S. administrations, firmly opposed any discussion of mandatory U.N. economic sanctions. But there was equally little enthusiasm for a noisy debate and the use of the veto at the Security Council in New York. Our allies wished to avoid a rupture with the Africans over Namibia, one that could discredit fundamentally the 1978 initiative on Namibia. It was precisely to avoid a diplomatic vacuum in Southern Africa that the Western nations had developed the Namibia peace process back in 1977. A collapse in the process would hand Moscow a fresh opportunity to rekindle the fires of regional conflict in Africa. In sum, for domestic, African, and global reasons, our allies wanted to carry on with something like the Carter policy on Namibia.

The incoming Reagan team had other ideas. The dominant trend of thinking within the Reagan camp looked at Angola—not Namibia—as the Southern African issue that demanded urgent attention. A few of us considered them both to be important, and looked toward a regionwide framework for Western strategy. To understand fully the regional picture facing American policymakers, it is necessary to take a closer look at the Angolan legacy we inherited from the 1970s.

The Unlucky Angolans

Like nearly all African states, Angola is a geographic entity whose current borders were defined by European statesmen barely one hundred years ago. Its vastness is disguised on the map by the sheer enormity of Africa: 13.5 times the size of Portugal, its former colonial power, Angola is larger than the combined total area of France, the United Kingdom, Belgium, the Netherlands, Switzerland, and reunited Germany. With a population of perhaps 10 million, parts of Angola are empty of any form of human settlement, economic activity, or governmental presence. There is an abundance of rich, arable land ideal for staple food crops and tropical commodities; Angola's coastal fisheries were abundant before being pillaged by Soviet and other long-range fishing fleets. Angola possesses big league mineral, petroleum, and hydropower resources. With an end to thirty years of anti-colonial and civil war, and a competently managed reconstruction program, Angola could boom.

Unlike most African states, Angola's colonial history began nearly five hundred years before it gained independence from Portugal in 1975. That was time enough to build a few European-style cities and to implant a veneer of Portuguese language and culture among a small black and mestizo elite. Luanda, the capital, is older than Cape Town or Boston; Angolans from Luanda and its environs gained the most intense exposure to the Portuguese and profited most from the limited opportunities available to them. During these years, the vast hinterland generally remained isolated from Lisbon's direct influence. But the hinterland produced millions of Angolan slaves to be shipped across the Atlantic to Brazil and other lands in the New World.

More recently, in the post-1945 era, Portugal "exported" hundreds of thousands of settlers, officials, and soldiers to help farm, administer, and pacify Angola. The Portuguese found economic opportunity in Angola. Their jobs and businesses provided them a measure of status and wealth in a colonial social order. But fourteen years of anti-colonial warfare broke the morale of Lisbon's armed forces, which seized power in April 1974. Eighteen months later, in November 1975, Portuguese officials hastily lowered their flag and departed from Angola, leaving in their wake a chaotic three-sided civil war between rival liberation movements. Most of the 340,000 local Portuguese fled.

The exodus cost Angola the bulk of its trucks, tractors, and boats, and most of its commercial farmers, shopkeepers, maintenance technicians, building tradesmen, fishermen, engineers, accountants, mechanics, and merchants. Lisbon and the settler community had resisted until the end the notion of colonial stewardship in preparation for independence. The Portuguese had not planned to leave or to share their skills and jobs with Angolans. As a result, when the Portuguese did leave, Angola's economic and administrative heart stopped beating. No African country was born in more traumatic conditions. Angola's misery in the years since independence is like a mirror image of departed Portugal, Europe's most backward imperial power.

The manner of Portugal's departure goes a long way toward explaining how Angola came to be ruled by the MPLA regime. In the eighteen months between the April 1974 seizure of power by the Armed Forces movement in Lisbon and Angolan independence in November 1975, Portugal abdicated its governmental responsibilities. Angola and the other Portuguese colonies were cards to be played in the dramatic struggle between contending Portuguese factions at home. In January 1975, Lisbon and the three Angolan liberation groups (MPLA, FNLA, and UNITA)* agreed at the Portuguese town of Alvor to set up a transitional government of national unity to organize elections prior to independence on November 11. Within weeks, however, hundreds of Angolans had died in factional fighting. Portugal, having signed cease-fires with each group, did not have the political will, internal cohesion, or the physical means to impose itself. It could not lead Angola to an orderly, democratic independence. The Alvor agreement was, in reality, a figleaf to cover Portuguese disengagement.

The Angolan parties themselves concentrated on victory or survival. African leaders meeting under the aegis of the Organization of African Unity (OAU) had scant leverage on either the Angolan parties or their outside patrons. By August 1975, the MPLA held the upper hand in the region around Luanda, its ethnic power base. OAU leaders appealed in vain for the establishment of an effective cease-fire and elections. As the independence date approached, Portuguese forces withdrew from the countryside toward their departure point in Luanda, setting off another round of warfare that continued well beyond the agreed independence date.

---

* FNLA, the *Frente Nacional de Libertaçao de Angola*, was a Zaire-based nationalist movement whose ethnic (Bakongo) constituency lay in northern Angola; the FNLA lost the 1975–76 contest to the MPLA and then became the victim of Zaire's 1979 detente with the MPLA regime.

MPLA, the *Movimento Popular de Libertaçao de Angola*, was the Congo-based nationalist movement that drew support from the influential mestizos and Portuguese leftists, from the Mbundu ethnic group centered on Luanda, and from those most exposed to Portuguese colonial influences. Two years after seizing power in 1975, the MPLA became an explicitly Marxist-Leninist party, adding the term *Partido Trabalho* (Labor Party) to its name. It has held power in Angola since 1975.

UNITA, the *Uniao Nacional para a Independência Total de Angola*, was founded in 1966 by Jonas Savimbi after he broke with the FNLA's Holden Roberto. It operated out of Zambian sanctuaries, and was centered on the large (40%) Ovimbundu ethnic group in Angola's central highlands, drawing some support as well from other rural bases. UNITA survived the events of 1975 and developed into a nationwide insurgency against the MPLA regime.

There were no elections. Far from curbing the recourse to violence, Portuguese behavior encouraged it and literally invited foreign intervention in the fratricidal conflict. There was nothing particularly new about foreign intervention as such. The Soviets began financial and military aid to the MPLA before the anti-colonial struggle got under way in 1961; after a short hiatus in 1972–74, they resumed assistance in 1974. The United States had provided limited aid to the FNLA starting in the early 1960s, the Cubans began their MPLA alliance in 1965, the Chinese got involved with the FNLA in the early 1970s, and a number of African states supported one or another of the Angolan movements with arms, training, finance, political support, and sanctuary.

What was new were the context and the direct effect of foreign intervention. After Alvor, external aid ceased to be an anti-colonial gesture. It had become a bid to help one's favored faction take power and to block the competition. By November 11, 1975, the date of independence, Angola had been effectively thrown to the wolves and a feeding frenzy was under way. Cuban, South African, and Zairean combat troops had intervened directly. Mercenaries, advisers, and air force and armor crews were engaged from such countries as Algeria, Britain, China, Cuba, France, the Netherlands, Portugal, South Africa, West Germany, the Soviet Union, and the United States. Arms and financial support came principally from France, the United States, China, Czechoslovakia, Cuba, Belgium, Nigeria, South Africa, Saudi Arabia, and the USSR. The interventions came by land, sea, and air; Angola's notional "territorial integrity" was violated from the Atlantic and from facilities in Zaire, Congo, Guinea, Guinea-Bissau, Mali, Zambia, and South African-controlled Namibia.

There is something cruelly ironic in describing November 11, 1975, as the date of Angola's "independence." In reality, it became the date used by the MPLA to legitimize its armed seizure of power, backed by the Soviets and Cubans. It was also the date after which Angolans, not Portuguese, were formally responsible for trying to run an occupied country, overwhelmed by civil war and economic collapse. Angola would remain an occupied country for the next thirteen years, that is, until the 1988 settlement that provided for the removal of South African and Cuban forces (as well as SWAPO and ANC guerrillas). The last to leave were the Cubans, who completed their pull-out on May 24, 1991, five weeks ahead of the schedule established in the Southern African settlement of December 1988.

During the years after 1975, we rarely heard that the Angolan people had paid the price of their own leaders' fears and ambitions in 1974–75. Still less did we hear that the Angolans paid the price of Portugal's colonial collapse and its strange conduct in the months before it handed over to the MPLA the keys to Luanda. More often, we heard one form or another of conspiracy theory in which the West or South Africa was blamed for the Angolan tragedy. The Cubans intervened in Angola, according to common mythology, to defend it against the South Africans who had supposedly intervened first. In another variant, the Alvor agreement collapsed because Washington failed to support it and chose instead to pursue the "Cold War" option of covert assistance to the FNLA and UNITA, the MPLA's foes. Typically, the United States is blamed for not providing adequate support for "African solutions" and OAU leadership during the Angolan crisis. By backing horses (FNLA and UNITA) that also received backing from the South Africans, the United States is said to have offended Africans and assured the MPLA's "victory." By accepting South African aid, the losers were said to have earned their fate.

Until the archives are opened in a dozen capitals, there will be gaps in the chronology of decisions during round one of the Angolan civil war. But such myths do not stand up to scrutiny. The Soviets and Cubans, with the active connivance of pro-Communist elements of the Portuguese government, effectively installed the MPLA regime. Admiral Rosa Coutinho, Lisbon's man in Luanda at the time, has publicly declared that he did not consider elections to be a viable option and that he favored transferring power to the MPLA as "the only force capable of directing Angola." To that end, he actively facilitated the insertion of hundreds of Cuban advisers to set up training camps for the MPLA. His actions began as early as January 1975, when the Alvor agreement was being signed. By March, substantial amounts of additional Soviet hardware had begun to arrive, including armored cars, rocket launchers, and heavy artillery pieces. Portuguese officials who still controlled Angola's ports and airfields knew what was going on; if they opposed it, their opposition was remarkably passive. In June, Coutinho was in Cuba, coordinating the development of Cuban-MPLA military cooperation. By July, the MPLA had won the first battle for Luanda. Sometime in late July or early August, Castro made the fateful decision to send in combat troops, dramatically reinforcing the growing Cuban advisory presence. The first contingent of Cuban combat troops was spotted in Luanda in mid-September.

The ominous implications of this pattern were not lost on the leading Western powers, Angola's black African neighbors, or the South Africans. But they may have misread it as a tightly organized, Soviet-directed conspiracy. Looking back, it does indeed appear that Moscow pulled off a remarkably smooth and slick operation in Angola. After all, by March

1976, when the MPLA victory was evident, the Soviets were calmly asserting that East-West detente was never intended to apply to cases like Angola. By that time, Moscow had delivered $200 million in hardware to the MPLA, hundreds of Soviet advisers were in place, and Moscow had played a major role in ferrying some 14,000 Cuban troops to Angola.

But in the first half of 1975 the record suggests that the Soviets were carefully feeling their way forward. A case can be made that Moscow slid into its Angolan entanglement, acquiring a major new geopolitical position in the Third World almost by accident. The Soviets had long held misgivings about the MPLA, and had earlier cut back their support in reaction to its endemic factional squabbles. It was Portuguese Communists and their MPLA allies who took the lead in pressing for external support, and the Cubans—long committed to Third World "internationalism"—who quickly responded by putting their own people in place. The Soviets saw a real opportunity emerging in early 1975, and airlifted equipment from the USSR to Brazzaville at that early point. But they could not yet see how distracted U.S. decisionmakers would become as our collapse played out in Vietnam. They could not have imagined how reactive, slow, and ill-organized the Western powers would prove to be in Angola. Still less could they have predicted at that early stage the full extent of the American constitutional paralysis that would ensue when the Ford administration sought to orchestrate a complex, indirect, and largely covert response. As time passed, however, Soviet leaders came increasingly to realize that they would get a free ride to Angola.

In January 1975, Washington decided to channel several hundred thousand dollars in political action funds to the FNLA, the Zaire-based movement whose ethnic constituency lay in northern Angola. After months of delay, this decision was extended to include UNITA, a movement less known to Washington and the one with the largest ethnic constituency and the weakest army. Not until July was the decision taken in Washington to provide tangible military support; by this time the British and French had begun their own clandestine assistance programs. Only in August were U.S. officials in direct contact with UNITA on the ground.

These ill-coordinated steps produced a hodgepodge of cash, arms, advisers, and mercenaries channeled to the FNLA and UNITA through Zaire and Zambia, whose governments appealed for Western and South African help to check the MPLA's advances. The OAU's call for elections and a cease-fire would be meaningless if only the MPLA faction received effective support. Unhappily for Angola, this reactive Western / African response added up to less than the sum of its parts. Soon the FNLA's leadership had split, and its poor performance led belatedly to a decision to strengthen UNITA, the best-led of the anti-MPLA movements.

Meanwhile, an intense debate over Angolan developments had been under way within the South African government. Pretoria was in close contact with all the Western and African players, and was actively courted by FNLA and UNITA leaders as well as certain African governments to throw its weight into the balance. But the South African leadership hesitated, in part out of uncertainty as to how to read the confusing flow of events; in part to avoid the onus for intervening in what was still, in theory, Portuguese territory; and in part due to conflicting views over whether military or intelligence instruments should be utilized. By July, when the MPLA (with Soviet, Cuban, and Portuguese support) had gained control of Luanda, Pretoria began providing clandestine aid to the FNLA and UNITA. Zairean army units had started to deploy across the border into northern Angola in support of the FNLA. Washington, of course, was well aware of these moves: our winks and nods formed part of the calculus of Angola's neighbors.

In early August 1975, around the time that Castro made his decision to deploy thousands of combat troops to Angola, MPLA forces had moved south along the coast, pushing UNITA aside, and approaching the important hydroelectric and water-supply project operated by the South Africans at Calueque, near the Namibia-Angola border. Because of their importance to the Namibian economy, South African forces moved a short distance across the border to protect these facilities, thus beginning their own thirteen-year engagement in Angola. (Calueque would also be the site of the final Cuban–South African clash in June 1988.) Two months later, in October 1975, after large numbers of Cuban forces and equipment had begun to arrive in Angola, a substantial South African armored force crossed the border and rapidly advanced through the central highlands, reaching the coast north of the strategic Benguela Railway before "independence" day, November 11. The United States and other Western governments had done nothing to discourage Pretoria's mid-October intervention. For the first time, a rough balance of internal and external forces was within reach, precisely at the moment when Portugal formally withdrew. The music could not have stopped at a better time for the MPLA. Ensconced in Luanda, it declared itself to be the "Government of the People's Republic of Angola." It was at this point that the real test of wills began.

It soon became clear, however, that there was no contest. Havana and Moscow promptly raised the ante yet again, mounting "Operation Carlota" to surge additional forces and hardware. Havana and Moscow were determined to shore up the MPLA position and enable it to beat back the FNLA–UNITA–Zairean–South African coalition that might still have challenged the MPLA's hold on Luanda. The Cuban force was doubled in the next six weeks. In Washington, meanwhile, the Ford administration's position was rapidly unraveling. Reporting to six congressional committees on supposedly covert activities, the administration was soon deluged with leaks and "revelations" and found itself on the defensive for conducting a strategy of secret intervention in a distant, obscure Third World conflict. In the political climate of the time, it did not seem to matter that a coalition led by our global adversary had already become an active participant in Angola's undeclared war.

On December 19, the Senate voted to deny additional funding for Angola beyond the $32 million already committed (a sum that may have been 15–20 percent of Soviet assistance levels). The ban on U.S. aid to any Angolan faction was overwhelmingly confirmed in the House of Representatives on January 27, 1976, but the struggle was already over. The Cuban force doubled again that month, enabling the MPLA to neutralize the FNLA in the north and turn its attention toward UNITA. Soviet and Cuban officials openly declared that neither detente nor the views of African states in the OAU would cause them to cease support of the "legitimate" MPLA regime.

Africa's vulnerability to a Western collapse could not have been more apparent: on January 13, an Extraordinary OAU Summit deadlocked 22 to 22 (with 2 abstentions) on resolutions calling for the withdrawal of foreign forces and recognition of the MPLA regime; less than one month later, the MPLA regime was admitted to the organization as the government of Angola, its forty-seventh member. Zaire and Zambia folded shortly thereafter. The South Africans, who had become central players in a war they did not start, were left holding the can as Washington became reluctant even to acknowledge the obvious close links among all players in the Western-African coalition. Pretoria blasted what it saw to be Western flakiness, if not perfidy, and pulled out of Angola after cutting a side deal with the MPLA on the security of the Calueque water-power project.

The Angolan Legacy

Angola in 1981 remained the victim of these seemingly distant events. They represent the legacy which affected all protagonists in the Southern African drama. Portugal did not know how to redeem itself and set down a valid basis for productive postcolonial relations. Having left a power vacuum and helped the MPLA to fill it, Lisbon sought to co-exist with the unhappy results, seizing opportunities for its firms and nationals when they emerged.

But Portugal was itself as divided as Angola, and brought few strategic or economic assets to the process of ultimate rehabilitation and reconciliation. Portuguese who had fled Angola for South Africa or Portugal became a voice of bitterness and economic grievance. Those officials, technocrats, and intellectuals who had thrown in their lot with the MPLA—in some cases working within or for the government—became a standing lobby for normal relations with Luanda. The Portuguese government itself mirrored these and other tendencies long after the first round of Angola's civil war ended in early 1976.

As time passed and the Portuguese Communist Party passed gradually into political oblivion, the government in Lisbon was torn between exploiting its "family" ties to the MPLA and its disgust with Luanda's feckless subservience to Cuban and Soviet pressures. It was not until 1990, in fact, that Portugal was able to mount a coherent Angolan strategy aimed at ending the continuing civil war. As a result, Angola in the early 1980s was bereft of the kind of buffer and discreet leadership often provided by ex-metropoles in the affairs of their former colonies. This inevitably had an impact on the policies of other nations with interests or appetites, and it effectively eliminated the "middle road" in Angolan politics.

The second legacy from 1975–76 was the climate of sharply polarized East-West confrontation over Angola. Those events had lasting reverberations in the policymaking processes of both East and West. Angola signaled the demise of detente and the end of an era in which Africa had been buffered from the direct effects of superpower competition. Angola brought Africa into the mainstream of global politics. It also signaled a new Soviet assertiveness in distant troublespots, a confidence captured in Soviet military and party writings about the improving "correlation of forces." Cuban intervention forces, backed by growing Soviet logistic, air, and naval muscle, reinforced the "adventurist" Soviet image. Angola was the prototype for the application of the Brezhnev Doctrine in the Third World, a dangerous strategic precedent that was to preoccupy Western policymakers.

Whatever their initial perceptions of Southern Africa and Angola back in early 1975, the Soviets by 1981 had adjusted comfortably to their African gift. As the military and political patron of Marxist Angola, they provided it generous security support, and blanketed the place with Soviet and East European advisers. Angola became the flagship of Moscow's

Southern African policy, a staging point for supporting and influencing not only the MPLA regime but the SWAPO and ANC guerrilla movements as well.

Moscow had developed a "stake" in Angola. Its government could be relied upon to parrot the Soviet line internationally and to legitimize its support for the "liberation struggle" in Namibia and South Africa. The Angolan regime had ideal qualifications as Moscow's African client, being highly vulnerable and dependent; bereft of the most basic administrative, intelligence, and military skills; facing a range of tangible security threats—from UNITA, South Africa, and within the factionalized MPLA itself; and endowed with ample oil revenues to cover the hard-currency costs of Socialist solidarity.

The Soviet-Angolan military relationship was by no means a charitable venture on Moscow's part. Devastated Angola suddenly became a major buyer of arms: in a peak year such as 1984, Angola ranked seventh among worldwide arms importers, just behind Syria and Libya, and well ahead of India and Japan. Some $4.5 billion of arms were supplied to Angola in the first ten years of its independence, nearly 90 percent from the USSR. Arms imports soon dominated Angola's trade statistics and military spending absorbed up to 50 percent of the national budget.

Cuban interest in Angola had a sharper ideological focus and a distinct logic of its own. Angola (and Ethiopia in 1977–78) put Cuba on the geopolitical map after years of fitful and largely unsuccessful efforts to export "revolution" closer to home. Cuban military exploits in 1975–76 were translated into elaborate official myths of heroic resistance to imperialist intervention and South African aggression. Angola became a focal point of Cuban military planning and doctrine. By the 1980s, Cuban deployments in Angola were comparable on a relative scale to the U.S. presence in Vietnam at its peak. Cubans undertook to train thousands of Angolans in various fields, and Havana sent thousands of doctors, teachers, and civilian technicians to Angola, along with its military contingent of about 25,000 men in the early 1980s. Although there were many dimensions to Cuba's Third World policy, Angola represented Havana's largest foreign commitment and served as a showcase of Cuban "internationalism." Cuba received from the Angolans several forms of partial compensation (personnel allowances, fuel for transport), but Fidel Castro's primary interest in Angola was political: he gained a willing outlet for his grandiose, strategic mission.

In Washington, meanwhile, a parallel but contrary political imagery had built up since the drama of 1975–76. The phenomenon of Soviet-Cuban adventurism in Africa triggered debate among the Carter administration's factions about the merits of linking overall U.S.-Soviet relations to Soviet conduct in the Third World; linking U.S.-Cuban relations to Cuban troops in Africa; and linking U.S.-Angolan ties to a Cuban departure from Africa. Carter's malaise over Cubans in Africa was driven in part by a critical and anxious chorus in foreign policy journals, think tanks, congressional hearings, and media commentary. For many in the mainstream of strategic thinking, Angola came to symbolize Western disarray, excessive congressional restraint of the executive, and the Soviet challenge to the West in the Third World. In conservative quarters, Angola had become a call for revenge and a war cry in the resurgent campaign to restore covert action to its traditional place as a tool of strategy. Support for UNITA in its continuing struggle against the Communist-backed MPLA became an article of conservative faith, publicly espoused by candidate Ronald Reagan in his 1980 presidential campaign.

In sum, by 1981 the destiny of Angola was caught up in a powerful legacy of East-West conflict. It would have been difficult for Angolans of either the MPLA or UNITA persuasion (the FNLA had ceased to matter by the early 1980s) to escape this stark geopolitical context, even had they wished to. It served to shape their options, to define their hopes and fears (of support, abandonment, betrayal), and to limit the possibility of genuinely independent, non-aligned Angolan behavior. At the same time, it drove Angola's factions to seek sympathy and support at the extremes of the U.S. political spectrum where dogmatic thinking was most heavily entrenched. UNITA looked to the conservative right, while the MPLA sought support on the left; like their American "friends," both harbored deep suspicions of the State Department.

Isolation from American political reality characterized these Angolan movements. Each was overly dependent upon the self-serving, conspiratorial "information" provided by its primary backers (Soviet, Cuban, Zairean, South African). The continuing absence of U.S. diplomatic relations with Angola and, consequently, the absence of any U.S. official presence there compounded the Angolans' isolation and aggravated severely the obstacles to regularized, confidential communication.

Yet, non-recognition and the absence of diplomatic relations were an integral part of the 1975–76 legacy. They represented the principled American rejection of the MPLA's victory and the manner in which it took place. In the absence of basic change in Angola, such as an agreement on Cuban troop withdrawal, a reversal would be interpreted everywhere as a gift to Luanda and a blow to UNITA. For this reason, the Carter administration had shied away from recognizing and establishing relations with Luanda. To the dismay of the MPLA leadership, the

Carter team ultimately linked the bilateral relationship to Cuban troop withdrawal. It would have been politically unthinkable for the incoming Reagan team to go "soft" on Angola.

Yet another part of the East-West legacy was the congressionally imposed ban on U.S. military aid to any Angolan party. Originally adopted for one year in December 1975, the ban was extended in 1976 (the so-called "Clark Amendment," after its legislative sponsor, Senator Dick Clark of Iowa). The Angola ban remained painfully divisive: efforts to repeal it failed in 1977–78, but new bans on direct aid to the Angolan government were added in 1978–80. Under renewed pressure from UNITA sympathizers to review the ban, the House and Senate modified it during the 1980 campaign to permit U.S. military aid if authorized in advance by a congressional floor vote. But this was a purely symbolic shift since, presumably, executive branch advocates of aid to UNITA would wish it to be covert and not a topic of formal congressional action.

A third legacy from 1975–76 was the regional overspill from Angola's civil strife. Initially, it appeared that the MPLA would simply prevail nationwide, using its Communist alliance system and its symbols of governmental legitimacy to crush UNITA. Luanda would persuade or intimidate neighboring countries into accepting the outcome. This scenario was foreshadowed when the Zambians, isolated and exposed in their role as UNITA patron and South African partner, normalized relations with Luanda in 1976. UNITA personnel were expelled from their bases and UNITA supplies handed over to Luanda. Then, in March 1977, President Kenneth Kaunda hosted Soviet President Nicolai Podgorny on a state visit to Lusaka, describing the Soviets as "colleagues and comrades in the struggle"—a different formula from his earlier warning against the threat posed to Africa by the Soviet "tiger and its cubs." Zambia was protecting itself from a well-armed neighbor with clear superpower backing. He also hoped to regain the use of Angola's vital Benguela Railway to the Atlantic for his copper exports.

Angola's relations with Zaire, a neighbor similarly exposed and in need of egress to the sea for its copper exports, in 1977–78 appeared headed in the same direction. Emboldened by its late 1976 admission to the United Nations, the Luanda regime accused Zaire of continuing support for UNITA and the FNLA remnant. In March 1977, Angolan-based Zairean rebels known as Katangan gendarmes attacked Zaire's Shaba Province (Shaba is the modern name for Katanga, Zaire's copper-rich southern province). The attack was blunted with French and Moroccan assistance, but another more substantial attack followed in May 1978, resulting in major damage to the mines and combined French, Belgian, and U.S. military intervention to restore order. A few months later, the

United States helped to broker an understanding on the establishment of Zaire-Angola diplomatic relations and mutual pledges to deny facilities to rebels aimed at each other's territory. It began to appear that Angola's new Marxist leadership was getting its way.

But matters were not so simple. The MPLA leadership seriously underestimated UNITA. Driven into the extreme southeast of the country by advancing FAPLA*-Cuban motorized columns, UNITA's stragglers seemed to be finished. But as early as May 1976, UNITA challenged Luanda in a manifesto worded in Churchillian tones: "We will never accept a minority regime imposed by a racist European colonial power. We will fight in the jungles; we will fight in the mountains. We will infiltrate the cities. Let the Russians and their Cubans come by their tens of thousands, let them stay for years. In the end the people of Angola will win." The MPLA regime was trying to destroy a movement whose Ovimbundu ethnic base was Angola's largest, and whose rural-populist image contrasted sharply with the urban, privileged, mestizo-dominated and Portuguese-flavored leadership in Luanda. And it was taking on Jonas Savimbi, one of the most talented and charismatic leaders in modern African history, a man who would stop at nothing to advance his goals. By mid-1977, UNITA had recovered from the severe setbacks of the previous year. It had paralyzed the Benguela Railway with sabotage actions, and mounted sporadic guerrilla operations at sites across the expanse of south-central Angola. Savimbi's first offensive of the post-independence period kicked off a plan to establish a "Black African Socialist Republic of Angola."

Angola's independence and the MPLA's victory triggered a reversal of alliances among political movements. Previously, SWAPO and UNITA had cooperated closely, and both had drawn primary support from Zambian rear-base areas. SWAPO had used UNITA-controlled territory in Angola as a transit zone between Zambia and Namibia for refugees, supplies, and guerrilla fighters. The UNITA-Zambia rupture and the new availability of direct Angolan sanctuaries led SWAPO to shift its primary logistic lines west and north toward MPLA-controlled territory and the support of the Soviets and their allies.

At a stroke, the MPLA became SWAPO's primary African patron. The MPLA had allowed itself to become ensnared in SWAPO's war with Pretoria; Luanda's relations with the South Africans would now be a function of its readiness to support or restrain SWAPO. By offering SWAPO a new headquarters and extensive base facilities, the Luanda regime made itself an irresistible and obvious target for the South African Defence

---

* *Forças Armadas Populares de Libertação de Angola,* the MPLA's army.

Force, the region's most powerful military establishment. For its part, SWAPO became irreversibly entangled in Angola's civil war. SWAPO's destiny, like Namibia's, would be shaped by figures on a much larger canvas involving Angola and all who had interests there. SWAPO lost the support or even the neutrality of UNITA, which would now come under pressure from the SADF to help out in its anti-SWAPO campaigns. Sensing, belatedly, that Savimbi had been driven into a potentially dangerous South African embrace, the MPLA's first leader, Agostinho Neto, sought briefly in 1979 to open a channel to Savimbi. But Neto's sudden death in a Soviet military hospital stopped that initiative in its tracks. No MPLA leader for the next decade had the stature and self-confidence to pursue it. These developments virtually guaranteed that the Angolan civil war would continue to be internationalized.

The events of 1975–76 also had a traumatic effect in Pretoria, where Angola prompted a sentiment of revenge for past humiliation and an abiding suspicion of Western diplomacy. Against this backdrop, UNITA's determined leadership combined with its desperate physical predicament offered the South Africans a perfect opportunity. By helping UNITA rebuild and retrain as a classic guerrilla army, the SADF could keep the MPLA off guard. The South Africans would gain an ally against SWAPO, and hopefully ward off any further expansionist moves by the Soviets and Cubans. Meanwhile, the Angolan war could be manipulated well north of the Namibian border as a pressure point to restrain Luanda's support for SWAPO.

After former Defense Minister P. W. Botha took over as prime minister in September 1978, the way was open to a certain type of strategic and military thinking in the leadership in which Angola featured irresistibly as a theater of operations. Not only would there be a buffer for Namibia and a means of tying down the Communist intruders into this region of South African military primacy. There would also be the military basis for a "second track" of Namibian policy, to be pursued in tandem with the first track of Western-led negotiations, aimed at a settlement of some sort excluding U.N., Western, and perhaps SWAPO involvement. Beyond this, Angola offered a road to restored SADF prestige; perhaps, if enough effort were invested, it might even be possible for Pretoria's black UNITA allies to reverse the MPLA's victory. Certainly, a strong, pro-Savimbi stance by Pretoria was calculated to win the hearts of conservatives in places like the United States, the United Kingdom, Portugal, France, and Germany. Angola was perhaps the best place to force the feckless Western powers to choose between South Africa and the more militant black African states.

These events profoundly changed both the Angolan and Namibian conflicts. The Angolan civil war became part of a regional war in which the South Africans as well as the Cubans and Soviets were now central players. The SADF came to view Angola as the forward defense zone and strategic buffer for Namibia. The South Africans would help UNITA build a formidable guerrilla army in Angola's southeastern Cuando Cubango region. In the southwestern Cunene region, it would try to push SWAPO as far north as possible to deny it infiltration routes and sanctuaries near the heavily populated Ovambo districts of northern Namibia, SWAPO's ethnic heartland. Before long, Angola became the centerpiece of the SADF's anti-SWAPO strategy in the Namibian bush war that had started modestly back in 1966.

This trend toward regionalized warfare was already established in mid-1977 when the MPLA claimed to have evidence of South African intervention on UNITA's behalf. The following May, the SADF mounted an airborne attack on SWAPO facilities at Cassinga, some 150 miles north of the border. A few months later, UNITA claimed to be facing a "barbaric offensive" by some 20,000 Angolan, Cuban, and other Communist forces. By 1978, the basic military pattern of expanded regional conflict was set. Guerrilla campaigns and government offensives would ebb and flow across the Angolan countryside for years to come.

In sum, by 1981 the Angolans were deeply enmeshed in a destructive logic from which there were few escapes. Outsiders had acquired previously unimagined stakes in Angola's affairs. Regional conflict centered on Angola was expanding, and it was unclear exactly how to disentangle the Angolan civil war from the SWAPO-SADF conflict and the cross-border SADF-FAPLA clashes they spawned. Unless Angola had the vision and leadership to break the pattern, the country's future would be shaped by others—Cubans, Soviets, South Africans, and, possibly, Americans.

3

The U.S. Decision to Engage, 1981

Our policy review began under the State Department "transition team" before Reagan's inauguration. It continued for three more months, to the frustrated impatience of many African states and the gloomy fascination of our allies. Few outsiders realized how fundamental the review process was. At issue was the question of whether or not to take Southern Africa seriously as an arena for American policy. Should we pursue a Namibia settlement at all? Should we retain or scrap the broad thrust and specific policy parameters established during the 1975–80 period? How should we deal with the issue of Soviet-Cuban activity in Africa?

Reviewing the Options

The logic of the situation facing the incoming Reagan team suggested that we had basically three options. Although they were not articulated so precisely in formal policy papers, this was the range of options within which participants argued their case:

1. *to soldier on with the inherited Namibia-only approach*, recognizing its limited prospects but judging that an ongoing diplomatic process was the best way to buy time and avoid trouble with our allied and African partners;

2. *to downgrade Southern African diplomacy* in recognition that this was a polarized and unrewarding arena for U.S. leadership, and rely instead on public rhetoric and quiet signals to Pretoria to safeguard our interests; a more robust variant called for us openly to scuttle the Resolution 435 process, join South Africa in full support of UNITA's military efforts, and offer at least tacit support to Pretoria's "internal" option in Namibia; or

3. *to restructure fundamentally the negotiations to incorporate the Angolan factor and strengthen Resolution 435,* and thereby acquire new leverage while also accommodating diplomatic necessity.

The first option failed the tests of both feasibility and desirability: sooner or later, time would expire on it. The Contact Group had produced a plan, but it had failed to produce a settlement. The South Africans refused to cooperate, perceiving the plan to be weighted in favor of SWAPO. The West lacked credibility with the South Africans because it failed to take seriously their regional security interests. To continue the inherited policy would produce no fresh leverage to break the logjam. In addition, it would not address our concerns about Soviet-Cuban influence in both Angola and Namibia. Hence, option 1 became a strawman with no real support in the new administration.

The second option—a "no-policy policy"—might have been feasible. But it would have very high costs at the level of global alliance and African policy. In reality, it would slide over into a blank check for the least enlightened elements within the Pretoria establishment. If we intended to continue the long-standing U.S. opposition to mandatory U.N. economic sanctions, this "policy" would tacitly support whatever the South Africans came up with. There would be no Western-defined negotiating context. It would hand Moscow a huge gift, rupture our African and allied diplomacy, and weaken the pragmatists within P. W. Botha's inner circle in Pretoria.

The second option had no explicit adherents on Secretary Haig's review team. But it held strong attraction among right-wing Republicans and assorted hardliners and neoconservatives in and out of government who maintained contact with various parts of the South African lobbying structure in Washington. Six weeks of skirmishing and continuous redrafting were required to put option 2 to rest. This was less because of any acknowledged enthusiasm for it among the participants in Haig's review than because of their awareness that option 2 epitomized the stance of an orthodox right-winger. In the highly politicized hothouse of a new administration—the most conservative in modern U.S. history—senior policy officials tried to avoid statements that could be used against them. They sometimes posed as twentieth-century equivalents of Genghis Khan (now *he* had a coherent foreign policy), citing an imagined Reagan viewpoint that was much more extreme than the real thing. Members of Haig's review team generally understood the pitfalls of option 2. But they also recognized that it could become our policy unless we came up with something better.

To defeat option 2, we had to understand the mind-set of its open and closet proponents. To them, option 2 contained the seductive notion that we could somehow free-ride on the South Africans and avoid having to deal seriously with Southern Africa's messy polarization ourselves. The case *for* option 2 drew upon a range of attitudes and assumptions: (a) that South Africa was the West's only natural partner in the region and that the intelligence data and analysis brought to us by South Africans could be relied upon; (b) that African states were generally anti-Western and, hence, that U.S.-African diplomatic cooperation was not a credible means of countering the Soviets and Cubans; (c) that our Western allies' views on African issues could be ignored since other things were more important to them; and (d) that a sharp break with the past was desirable in order to give us the freedom of action and the leverage to block any further erosion of Western interests.

Unilateralists tended to view European and Canadian allies as spineless in their attitude toward Third World demands and Soviet obstructionism. The unctuous obfuscation that passed for diplomacy in too many European chancelleries was compared unfavorably with the straight-talking virility of Third World "allies" like South Africa. By the same token, the unilateralists' perception of African states and their leaders was seldom complicated by any firsthand acquaintance with Africa and Africans. SADF helicopter windows offered the lens through which the hard-core unilateralist viewed the politics of Mozambique, Angola, or—for that matter—Soweto. Their links to elements within both the Reagan camp and the South African security establishment were no secret to me.

There were no born-again unilateralists, the kind who speak in tongues, on the Haig review team. Instead, we comprised a delicately balanced mix of neoconservatives and "realists" from the Nixon-Kissinger mainstream of Republican strategic thinking. The argument between "realists" (dubbed "pragmatists" by their detractors) and "neocons" (dubbed "ideologues" by theirs) was not insurmountable. Sometimes we strengthened each other's cases. But important differences existed on handling questions of feasibility. We debated the trade-off between (a) achieving concrete results and (b) adopting "pure" positions of the sort we might wish to see attributed to us in print. Realists had less tolerance for the constraints imposed on U.S. policy by our own domestic structure; they had greater interest in the external behavior than the domestic affairs of foreigners. Neoconservatives saw themselves as intellectual populists; they were less interested in what we could accomplish in Southern Africa than what we should "stand for."

In this environment, a specialist on African affairs operated with both handicaps and advantages. Regional specialists—Arabists or Latin Americanists—labored under the presumption among their "generalist" colleagues of being incapable of hardheaded objectivity. Africanists probably carried the worst burden of perceived "clientitis" toward their region, a legacy in part of Kissinger's battles with the African bureau over Angola in the mid-1970s. In reality, most "generalists" happened to be Soviet experts, Europeanists, and specialists on strategic weapons. Though equally parochial in outlook, they fancied themselves as tougher-minded and more versatile than non-European regional experts. The latter, it was said, defined diplomacy as maintaining good relations with foreigners, while generalists understood that foreign policy was a contact sport whose goal was to score for the USA.

Fortunately, I had certain advantages as an alumnus of the Kissinger-Haig National Security Council in the early 1970s, where I had worked on Southeast Asia, Indian Ocean, Persian Gulf, civil defense, and security assistance issues—not African affairs. I had realist allies in the group and, like them, was somewhat suspect on account of my Kissingerian origins. As one of only two participants who actually knew Africa, I had some advantages. It helped to know the region, provided one avoided any trace of romantic attachment to it or any hint of belief that the United States should seek popularity there. As an academic and former denizen of a conservative think tank, I had aggressively criticized Carter's African policies. This gave me standing as one of the very few Africanists whose op-eds were read by Reaganites and neocons. Tactically, I had some running room to build alliances with most members of the Haig review team.

A number of arguments were proposed to keep the policy review more or less on track. First, option 2 was based on dangerous illusions: it would place us in a clandestine, pro-South Africa tilt that would soon blow up in our faces. American allies cared more deeply than some people recognized about certain Third World issues—problems that could be thought of as "defining issues" in their diplomacy. Southern Africa was a case in point, precisely because several allies (especially Britain, France, and Portugal) had such strong ties there. Their "exposure" on African questions derived from their involvement in U.N., European, French-speaking, Portuguese-speaking, or Commonwealth diplomacy. To be sure, cynical maneuvers among U.N. voting blocs accounted for the excessive Southern African emphasis in the United Nations. The "selective indignation" evident at international meetings—where was the majority's voice on Cambodia, Chad, Afghanistan, Lebanon, Nicaragua?—should not be permitted to "mau-mau" American policymakers. But, by the same token, it would be wrong simply to ignore or dismiss allied anxieties. The leader of the West should offer credible strategies through which members could cooperate to advance shared goals in the vast world beyond Europe. Failure to play this role could leave us isolated, encourage our allies to strike off on their own, and open splendid diplomatic opportunities for the USSR.

Second, realists argued that Africa was hardly a place of special American influence or leverage where a go-it-alone policy was likely to thrive. In fact, our allies—both within and beyond the Contact Group— offered us significant potential through their capacity worldwide to influence attitudes on African conflicts. Our decisions on Southern Africa had ramifications beyond that region. If we scrapped the inherited regional peace process set in place by the Ford and Carter administrations, or walked away from the whole exercise, we could endanger allied cohesion. Seen in this light, Southern Africa represented an inescapable burden, a thorn already placed in our flesh by history, a festering sore which literally invited Soviet mischief. Great powers do not have the option to duck the messy problems. Such issues need to be "managed" even if they cannot be immediately "solved."

The worst thing a realist can say about a policy proposal is that it is not "feasible." In the end, what matters is results, not good intentions or ideological postures. With George Kennan, realists take the Hippocratic Oath—above all else, do no harm—as their ultimate ethical guidance in matters of strategy. All of us in the Haig group could probably agree on a long list of things we felt strongly about: our uneasiness about a U.N.-led transition in Namibia; our questions about SWAPO's true intentions for an independent Namibia; our disgust at the hypocrisy of liberal opinion on African issues; and our ardent wish that the Cubans would leave Africa, that UNITA would reconcile with (if not replace) the MPLA, that African states would stand up to Moscow, and that South Africa would behave more reasonably on Namibia and move decisively away from apartheid and toward a negotiated and non-racial democratic system. But this was a wish list, not a strategy. Southern Africa was not a *tabula rasa* upon which we could etch a wholly fresh U.S. design. The historical context and the realities of regional politics had to be harnessed to our strategy.

The United States Chooses Linkage

In practice, Haig's senior team spent most of its time debating and refining one or another variant of option 3. But how should U.S. regional strategy be restructured? The people who participated in Haig's policy review were agreed on the need for a change away from the limp and indecisive stance of our predecessors. Tough-minded leadership was essential. If other governments wanted U.S. involvement and leadership, we would define its conditions. But few participants shared my deep feelings about the importance of shaping a coherent and credible African policy. In addition to Haig and myself, the participants included U.N. Ambassador Jeane Kirkpatrick, Counselor Bud McFarlane, Under Secretary for Political Affairs Walter Stoessel, Assistant Secretary-Designate for European Affairs Lawrence Eagleburger, Director of the Policy Planning Staff Paul Wolfowitz, Assistant Secretary for International Organization Elliott Abrams, Acting Assistant Secretary for African Affairs Lannon Walker (my deputy), and Haig's special assistant Harvey Sicherman and executive assistant Ray Seitz. Kirkpatrick's deputy, Ken Adelman (a former student of mine), was an occasional participant and an outspoken neocon.

As new players with lots of "external" alliances, we had ample temptation to brawl over policy and take our battles outside. We would succeed in defining a fresh strategy, however, only if we resisted that temptation. Our tasks were to identify what was missing in the inherited approach, control our weakness for ideological self-indulgence and wishful thinking, and operate within the parameters of regional reality—a lot of ifs. For the most part, this motley group remained on speaking terms while working to define a broad strategic approach that bridged the gaps between us.

There was considerable skepticism toward the U.N. Plan (UNSCR 435) as the only basis for a settlement. The very nature of U.N. bloc politics and Third World diplomatic authoritarianism (e.g., the prejudgment toward SWAPO) would skew any U.N.-supervised settlement to SWAPO's advantage. Some, but not all, of us assumed that SWAPO was and would inevitably remain a Soviet-oriented, Marxist movement. We agreed that a winner-take-all SWAPO victory posed risks for the West, especially if it continued to enjoy cross-border support from the Communist powers ensconced in Angola. Ronald Reagan had not been elected to make Africa safer for Marxism, still less to work for yet another Marxist takeover in the wake of the 1975–78 Soviet-Cuban gains in Angola, Mozambique, and Ethiopia, and the 1980 Mugabe victory in Zimbabwe. Some of us defined the primary goal in essentially negative terms: to prevent what Kirkpatrick termed a "less friendly" regime from taking power in Namibia, and to maintain opposition pressure on the Soviet-dominated MPLA regime in Angola. Others pointed out that the existing "regime" in Windhoek was a South African-run colonial authority; the issue was how to avoid exchanging one form of oppression and authoritarianism for another. To garner leverage and international support, we would need to aim higher, toward a strategy that could make *both* Namibia and Angola free.

Since it was not realistic to jettison Resolution 435 or to back a South African-rigged "internal" arrangement, we agreed that the Namibia settlement package should be strengthened. This could be accomplished, first, by altering the context in which it occurred—i.e., by broadening the agenda to incorporate issues of regional security like the Cuban presence in Angola. Second, it could be strengthened by entrenching basic constitutional checks and balances, minority rights and property rights. The neutrality and non-alignment of an independent Namibia might also be guaranteed as a means of preventing it from simply falling into Moscow's African orbit.

Most of the world assumed that Angola's fate had been settled five years ago. We disagreed; countering Soviet-Cuban adventurism was a primary concern. Before entering the government, I had written that our diplomacy should logically center on "the closely intertwined conflicts in Namibia and Angola"; connections between the two wars were so great that "we outsiders sometimes have a problem deciding which is the key to the other." I took issue with the advocates of the "Namibia-first" school of thought: the Angolan issues would not simply go away if Namibia were settled; in fact, a Namibian settlement in isolation could weaken UNITA, and undercut the chances for genuine political reconciliation. On the other hand, an "Angola-first" approach, downgrading Namibia and simply siding with UNITA, could also discourage reconciliation and reduce the chances for Cuban withdrawal. The proper course was to recognize publicly the legitimacy of UNITA's struggle and maintain pressure for Cuban withdrawal, while also pursuing an internationally acceptable settlement in Namibia, making adjustments to the U.N. Plan if necessary.*

My starting position before President Reagan's inauguration was to pursue parallel settlements in Namibia and Angola. I argued that U.S. credibility on the Namibia front—where an immediate diplomatic row

---

*The argument was published in "Southern Africa: A U.S. Policy for the 1980s," in *Freedom at Issue*, no. 58 (November–December 1980) with Mario Greszes and Robert Henderson; this article was reprinted in *Africa Report* (January–February 1981).

was brewing in early 1981—would give us the momentum and leverage to launch the separate Angola settlement process. One had to start somewhere, and Namibia was the place to start. By late January 1981, however, I began proposing that we seek a Cuban withdrawal commitment that would tacitly parallel South Africa's departure from Namibia under Resolution 435. Under this two-track approach, we would avoid explicit public linkage, but would signal to the parties privately that one settlement would not go forward to implementation without the other. This shift deflected unhelpful thinking about SWAPO and Resolution 435, undercut the arguments for something closer to option 2, and underscored my own personal commitment to obtaining both objectives. Serious reservations were expressed initially about the wisdom of making Namibia hostage to an ambitious Angolan agenda. It was argued that we should explore both tracks, keep our options open until we knew better the parties' bottom lines, and avoid an explicit link that could bring down the whole house of cards. These were powerful arguments.

But the shift to tacit linkage was the correct move. It strengthened my right flank in Washington. It would avoid rubbing everyone's nose publicly in a new Angolan condition. At the same time, if we were serious about revisiting the events of 1975–76, there was no reason not to commit ourselves categorically to achieving Cuban withdrawal as an integral part of the overall settlement. Why should we base our policy on vague Angolan assurances of eventual Cuban withdrawal with no safeguards?

The Cuban troop withdrawal link would bring pressure on Luanda to reconcile with UNITA. It would prevent a Namibia settlement from occurring at UNITA's expense. Cuban withdrawal from Southern Africa was inherently attractive in its own right and in terms of U.S.-Soviet relations. Finally, it would give us the leverage we would need to obtain South African cooperation on Namibian independence.

By mid-February 1981, there was substantial consensus between Wolfowitz, Abrams, Eagleburger, McFarlane, and myself on the tacit linkage approach. In early March, as pressure continued to mount for the new administration to declare itself on Southern Africa, we found ourselves still fighting off hare-brained vestiges of option 2. Soon my colleagues were drifting toward a rhetorically harder-edged option known as "explicit linkage." Under this model, we would proclaim boldly to the world our proud new strategy of liberating and democratizing two African countries for the price of one. If necessary, we would be prepared publicly to cast the Cubans as the obstacle to Namibian independence. The subtlety and flexibility I considered essential were rapidly going out the window.

Fortunately, it did not matter all that much. In the loose-knit procedural setting of the early Reagan period, many things were not spelled out—partly for tactical reasons and partly because there might be no consensus. Few distinctions were made between the strategic-military goal of Cuban withdrawal and the political goal of MPLA-UNITA reconciliation. Nor was the logical sequence between the two discussed or defined. Both goals could be embraced for now. It was better, in these dangerous early days, to leave awkward questions unasked so that they would remain unanswered. The pros and cons of tacit versus explicit linkage were discussed but not resolved. No one had offered an operational definition of the linkage. All this would have to be worked out later.

By the end of March 1981, President Reagan had approved a version of our much-discussed option 3, submitted to him by Secretary Haig. Neither the detailed terms of an acceptable outcome nor the exact tactics for achieving it were spelled out. Rather, the Haig proposal described a best-case outcome designed simply to overwhelm any conceivable resistance. It included: the drafting of a democratic constitution before elections in Namibia; internationally guaranteed neutrality for Namibia; Cuban troop withdrawal from Angola as well as political reconciliation between UNITA and the MPLA; the avoidance of noisy U.N. debates and strains in our allied relationships; improved relations with both South Africa and the other African states; and multiple setbacks to the Soviets and Cubans in the region. Among the proposed tactics were several items calculated to appeal: ready use of our U.N. veto power to defeat sanctions and public support for UNITA's leader Jonas Savimbi, as well as early efforts to assist him more tangibly.

Never mind that we had stacked the deck a little to obtain Reagan's approval, or that Reagan, as Haig would later put it, was "not too steeped" in the issues. At last we could begin to move out of our self-imposed diplomatic straitjacket. Finally, we had defined our own strategy, after over three months of ceaseless struggle to prevent others—allies, black Africans, conservatives and liberals at home, and especially the South Africans who had blanketed Washington—from defining it for us. The period of maximum danger was ending. We had changed course in our African policies. No one would mistake the Reagan approach for the Namibia-only, pro-Front Line States approach of Jimmy Carter and Andy Young. But we had fought off the pressures to swing the pendulum too far in the other direction. This was a centrist strategy, one with something in it for all Americans.

I was still three long months from being confirmed as Assistant Secretary of State for African Affairs, the post offered me by Reagan and

Haig. In fact, the Senate had not yet scheduled my confirmation hearings when I learned in late March that the President had agreed to our strategy. But at least I would now be able to operate with something closer to firm ground under my feet when I faced the Senate and began my first African mission as an unconfirmed assistant secretary.

The March 1981 decision provided my mandate for the next eight years. The basic concept was simple and clear: Namibian independence should be linked to the withdrawal of Cuban forces from Angola. Specifically, the implementation of Resolution 435 would be tied to implementation of a schedule for Cuban troop withdrawal from Angola. What we had done was to *expand the agenda* of the regional peace process begun in 1976. We planned to accept, confirm, and build upon the inherited formula, and thus to create a new one. The 1981 decision to link Namibia and Angola represented both continuity and change in U.S. policy. But the linkage strategy, by incorporating the Cuban issue, would fundamentally alter the political-diplomatic equation in the region. It is worth looking more closely at the goals and effects of our decision on linkage.

The Ambitious Logic of Linkage

By expanding the agenda and defining a new settlement formula, the Reagan team was seeking to acquire the leverage previously lacking. At the same time, we believed that we were promoting the outcome that best served U.S. interests. The new formula would give us a far better chance to nail Pretoria down to a categorical commitment to implement Resolution 435. There were reasons to believe that it would transform many of the negatives Pretoria perceived in Resolution 435. It would offer a major, visible, and strategic quid pro quo for agreeing to implement the Namibian decolonization plan: the reversal of South Africa's lonely humiliation in 1975; the removal of the SADF's only conventional equal; the likely reduction of Communist influence in the region; a serious constraint on SWAPO; and a likely boost for UNITA.

For these reasons, a settlement formula along such lines would put us in a far stronger position, first, to clear up once and for all the ever-shifting list of Pretoria's caveats and concerns about Resolution 435, and second, to obtain a firm commitment to settle. It would give us the potential to force decisions in Pretoria: to choose between cooperation or confrontation with the West, and between blind exploitation of its regional hegemony and the practical use of its power to support political solutions.

Linkage was also desirable in its own right. At the symbolic level, this would be the African version of the "America is back" message of the Reagan presidency. We would use the Kissingerian construct of linkage as a belated response to the Brezhnev Doctrine's application to Africa. The new strategy would challenge the legitimacy of the Cuban presence *and* the MPLA regime that depended on it. If Contact Group and African support could be developed for a linkage-based settlement, Moscow, Luanda, and Havana would have a hard time explaining their resistance to a package that would decolonize Namibia and terminate the South African threat to Angola. Properly orchestrated, the new approach would undermine the already hollow rationale behind Moscow's heavily militarized African diplomacy, and strain Soviet–Cuban–African relations.

The incoming administration did not view Southern African states as separate islands, each existing in its own cocoon. Rather, we recognized, and did not argue with, the inherent interdependence among them, despite their polarized politics. The prospects for reconciliation and negotiated political change *within* states (e.g., Angola, Namibia, or South Africa) were directly affected by the climate of security (or insecurity) *between* them. A broad regional agenda flowed from this logic. Cross-border violence by the SADF and by nationalist guerrillas throughout the region represented a two-way street leading nowhere. The wars of liberation had their mirror image in Pretoria's wars of destabilization; neither side could "win." These wars would stop together, reciprocally, or they would expand in a spiral of destructiveness. The case of Namibia and Angola was the principal and most dramatic example of this region-wide logic. There, we sought to resolve a set of problems and conflicts which were linked by history and geography. The wars involving SWAPO, the SADF, the Angolan forces of FAPLA, the Cubans and UNITA (and even the Angola-based ANC guerrillas) were all tangled up together.

To untangle these knots, the logic of linkage would need to start somewhere. What better way than to build upon the basis of the inherited Resolution 435 structure? This would offer us credibility at the crucial start-up phase and make us indispensable to our Contact Group and Front Line State partners. By resolving in some manner the "unresolved" issues from 1978–80, we would gain the leverage needed to launch the Angola "track" of the strategy. The goal would be a Cuban withdrawal timetable, defined in terms of phases and benchmarks in the U.N.'s Namibia plan. That plan included specific dates and numbers for SADF withdrawal from Namibia; once the Namibian election result was certified by the United Nations, seven months into the plan the SADF would be out of Namibia. Hence, the goal would be a timetable that both Washington and Pretoria could live with—on political and military grounds. At a minimum, that timetable should not hurt UNITA. Cuban troop withdrawal from Angola would logically create inexorable pressures for internal Angolan reconciliation between the MPLA regime and UNITA. (Of course, we would not be disappointed if it should happen in reverse: reconciliation would make decisions on Cuban withdrawal much easier for the Angolans. But we could not bank on this or insist on it.)

In sum, the logic of linkage blended nicely the broad political appeal of ending South African colonialism and racist practices in Namibia (a "motherhood" issue as well as wise diplomacy for global and regional reasons) with the "strategic" prize of uprooting the Cubans, freeing Angola, and undercutting Moscow in Africa. During the 1980 campaign, candidate Reagan had raised the issue of Cubans in Africa and asserted the importance of support for UNITA's efforts for reconciliation and against the Cuban-supported MPLA. The new administration, starting with the President, viewed the merits of a Namibia settlement as utterly dependent on the context in which it occurred. Failure to achieve a settlement was not necessarily the worst possible outcome.

On the other hand, the Reagan team had carefully chosen to stay with Resolution 435 and to avoid the trap of embracing South African "alternatives" that would scuttle the previous diplomacy. We would keep some distance from everybody—Africans, South Africans, even our allies—and maneuver to become the indispensable pivot amongst them. Our readiness to take South African interests into account, and to adopt a less hostile posture toward that country, can be seen, at one level, as shifting weight to correct what the South Africans perceived to be a stacked deck. A more finely tuned negotiating balance would give us a more fluid and malleable situation. Our new posture had a purpose: we wanted the South Africans to cooperate with our strategy by taking the right decisions. Thus, we had no intention of joining the Soviet bloc / Third World chorus whose vision of Namibian self-determination was reflected in their prejudgment that SWAPO was the "authentic" voice of Namibians.

Nor would we play along with the winner-take-all mentality that too often inspired both African and Western diplomats when discussing the "transfer of power" under Resolution 435. Namibia's ethnic balance could all too readily result in an unchecked SWAPO dictatorship, only adding to the chances that another misruled African state would emerge. Such an outcome would compound regional confrontation in Southern Africa, laying the basis for future conflicts and most likely opening up new fields of opportunity for Moscow and Havana.

This change of emphasis in U.S. policy would produce predictable complaints of a "tilt" toward Pretoria. But we would base our position on hard facts. The biggest "concession" of all in our settlement would be made by the South African government, which would be freeing Namibia. The United States would continue to support an internationally acceptable settlement; that was code language for a U.N.-supervised transition to independence in Namibia. In practice, the African Front Line States, SWAPO, our allies, and the South Africans would all have to approve it. No other kind of settlement would elicit U.S. support. Thus, there was plenty of balance in our strategy. If this was not good enough, then we would stand aside from the process and let others try their luck at prying the South Africans out of Namibia.

The Logic in Practice

The logic just described was based on cold realism and careful analysis of the region itself. It matched the hardball, geopolitical instincts and the conceptual style of the new administration. In linkage, we had a simple yet elegant strategic concept, backed by our always ample supply of strong convictions. But the art of peacemaking requires more than good ideas, realism, and strong convictions. It also requires the humility not to decide too much in advance and to leave plenty of room for the arts of diplomacy. We now faced the altogether different challenge of translating the linkage decision into a viable diplomatic strategy.

Indeed, a skeptic could have been forgiven for wondering, in 1981, why and how all of this would work. It may have been a logical scheme, but was it, in fact, so realistic? The United States would be asking over a dozen governments and two isolated guerrilla movements to cooperate with a fundamentally restructured negotiation. In a sharply polarized region, the United States was proposing to downplay or evade that polarity and move toward our vision of an overarching "common interest." In practical terms, the South Africans and the Front Line States were moving away from, not toward, common ground in early 1981.

Some observers and participants saw the new approach as overambitious or just plain naive. Privately, members of my Africa negotiating team conceded amongst themselves that the new strategy was a long shot. As the terminology of "linkage" and "constructive engagement" caught on, we joked about whether we would need expertise in animal husbandry as well as diplomacy to bring the parties together. We compared ourselves unfavorably with the vets at Washington's National Zoo, who were trying to breed panda bears in captivity. Al Haig looked at me after one strategy session in the spring of 1981 and asked, "Does this thing have a chance of working? We don't want to make all this effort for nothing." As a soon-to-be-anointed assistant secretary, I replied "Yes, if . . ." and cited a substantial number of necessary conditions. I wanted Haig to believe in the enterprise and to give me the freedom of action to do my job.

Linking one intractable problem to a wholly new issue was both ambitious and risky. As critics pointed out, the United States could, by overreaching, fail to solve either the Namibian or the Angolan problem. Washington would be falsely attacked internationally for abandoning its own child (Res. 435) or for blocking the plan's implementation with a new condition (Angola). Such charges were especially silly, but no less real, when made with table-thumping self-righteousness by the same gray Soviet diplomats who had done everything possible to block Resolution 435 themselves back in the late 1970s. Because of the change in strategy, we, ironically, would be accused of letting South Africa off the hook!

There was also the risk of losing our Contact Group and Front Line partners and becoming isolated with a new policy that went nowhere. The Carter and Ford administrations had declined to address directly the East-West issue introduced by the Soviets and Cubans in 1975. Having done so now, we would almost certainly be charged with caring only about the Cold War and not caring enough about freedom for Namibians. Never mind that our predecessors had tried it their way for four years; they had produced an impressive and skillfully designed plan— but no settlement.

The exercise of leadership always entails risks. We would bear the onus for the impasse if our linkage decision did not produce quick results. And that is what happened. For years to come the storyline would read that Namibia's independence had been blocked by the insistence of Washington on Cuban troop withdrawal. There was something perverse about the spread in the West and Africa of this mythology. It assumed that Pretoria *would have* agreed to implement Resolution 435 had it not been for our linkage decision—a silly notion. It further assumed that the originator of the linkage idea—rather than its opponents—was responsible for the delay.

Yet, in reality, we had used a fairly common tool in the arsenal of the mediator who faces an intractable logjam. Though none of us was self-consciously thinking in such terms at the time, the options are finite. You can try to engineer a "split-the-difference" compromise; you can seek a procedural solution (e.g., elections or arbitration); you can explore compensatory payments or side deals to alter the position of one or more parties; or, you can modify the agenda and redefine or restructure the issues in dispute. Only the last of these had any chance of working. There were two ways of doing it. The first was to break the problem down into pieces and go after them systematically—solving some, redefining others, handling the remainder by trade-offs between them.

In a sense, this is what the Carter administration had attempted to do. Once the Africans accepted Resolution 435, the Contact Group sought to resolve each of the problems South Africa raised as it began its protracted maneuvering in late 1978. Pretoria introduced a rolling series of concerns, caveats, and creatively worded conditions ("we accept on the assumption, *inter alia,* that our concerns about X, Y, and Z can be resolved"). In practice, there was probably no way to structure the issues of a strictly Namibian settlement so that Pretoria would approve it— without losing the approval of the other parties.

The other way to change the structure of the issues in a conflict is to increase their number and tie them together into a larger agenda. By linking one complex problem to another, we added massively to the size and complexity of our negotiating burden. But we also redefined and increased the number of relevant "parties," and increased the long-term odds of building a situation in which everyone wins.

The linkage formula that emerged in 1981 should thus be understood at several levels. It was, first, our attempt to mold a feasible and attractive settlement package. Linkage, at this first level, was an exercise in American strategy, motivated by the desire to advance American interests. But, at the second level, linkage was also an inherently logical formula, which addressed the underlying interests of the parties—defined narrowly as Angola and South Africa, but broadly also as the Front Line States, SWAPO, the other Namibians, other interested African states such as Congo and Zaire, our Western allies, the Cubans, and the Soviets. Had it not been a balanced and logical concept, ideologues and hardliners in various camps would not have been so quick to pour cold water on it.

But that did not make it any less ambitious. We would need to synchronize the "tracks" of two separate negotiations (on Resolution 435 and Cuban troop withdrawal) into one grand negotiation. If any major actor or variable was out of synch, the alignment of the planets would fail to occur. At a minimum, syzygy would require five separate conditions: (1) a reasonable degree of stability in the underlying regional balance of power, both in reality and in the perceptions of leaders; (2) a stalemate in the immediate military equations on the ground; (3) the strength, confidence, and coherence of leadership in key capitals, so that each could take big decisions in roughly the same timeframe; (4) the diplomatic skill to make the linkage formula come to life through a set of mirror-image, conditional ("yes . . . if") commitments; and (5) an acceptable forum or mechanism so that parties could communicate, maintain contact, and bargain.

The new initiative required U.S. diplomats to move continuously between these tracks of negotiation, shifting their weight and their message from one to the other with the flow of events. As Secretary of State George Shultz would later put it, we had to "carry water on both shoulders." The linkage formula determined which "side" we supported on a particular issue. We would be *with* the South Africans in pressing Luanda to offer proposals on a schedule for Cuban withdrawal, but *against* them if they overdid it, scaring off the Angolans and thus evading the need for decisions on Namibia. We were *with* the Angolans and the Front Line States in pressing Pretoria to resolve quickly all outstanding questions related to Resolution 435, but *against* them when they argued that it should be implemented unconditionally. Progress on one track, we believed, would create leverage for movement on the other; but the reverse was also true: the lack of progress on one track would reduce pressure on the other. We wished to achieve both objectives of our strategy, and would need to create momentum on both tracks to get there.

The decision to engage in Southern African peacemaking in 1981 was less a commentary on the "ripeness" of the region for peace than on the urgency of Western leadership there. If anything, the parties seemed to be moving away from common ground. The region was delicately balanced between its always bright potential and other forces hostile to compromise. One thing was certain: the future of this region would depend on whether we participated actively in shaping it. We engaged because we had a clear vision of our interests, a readiness to run the risks of taking a major initiative, and a desire to limit the damage of letting nature take its course.

But we also entertained the illusion, in 1981, that we might be able to pull the Namibia and Angola tracks together sometime over the next eighteen months (by the end of 1982). That seemed like an eternity in a professional environment where a six-week scenario represents long-term planning. As it turned out, we were off by a few years. The climate for decision was even less ripe than it had appeared to be. And the ambition of our task was greater than I had imagined. Perhaps it is just as well that no one told us in advance about the complexity of synchronous orbits.

But the perception of "ripeness" was not the main thing that attracted the administration to the linkage. It was not in the character of the early Reagan period to identify safe, predictable outcomes around the world and "go with the flow" of events and prevailing U.S. public opinion. There was an ornery quality to our approach, an eagerness to take on the odds. If our ideas were ahead of their time, we imagined that we could help to "ripen" the situation.

We were acting out of conviction. We knew what kind of settlement we wanted, and we decided to mobilize a complex diplomatic process to bring it about. But we were also building on a foundation laid in previous years; much of that foundation would be retained. Those few of us on the senior Reagan team who knew anything about the history of Southern African negotiations made an analogy to the decades-long Middle East peace process. Southern Africa, like the Middle East, was a region where the pursuit of negotiated solutions was in itself the essence of a regional strategy.

"Constructive Engagement" in Southern Africa

The Namibia-Angola initiative was the prime exhibit in a regionwide policy. It was by far the most salient African question reviewed by the incoming administration, and the only one, apart from policy toward Libya, that occasioned prolonged discussion. At first glance, it may seem strange that this arid land, whose population barely exceeded 1 million and whose GNP was a mere $1 billion, should so dominate our attention span. But we were by no means alone. Namibia was "hot" because a war was being waged over its ambiguous and contested status. After Zimbabwe's independence in April 1980, Namibia was "the next issue" and "the last colony" on the African political agenda.

However unlikely SWAPO was to dislodge the SADF, this low-level bush war against South Africa's "illegal" control of Namibia served as a lightning rod for outside interest. The presence of Communist military power next door in Angola alarmed conservatives and suggested lurid scenarios for future disorder. Namibia became the primary, residual focus of the political, diplomatic, Church, and Third World activist constituencies which had followed colonial questions since the 1940s. Religious linkages through missionary bodies put Namibia on the map in North America, Germany, Scandinavia, and Great Britain. The subject of Namibia took up man-years of debate and drafting at international gatherings (the Organization of African Unity, the Non-aligned movement, the United Nations, the Commonwealth). There was an obligatory stanza or two on Namibia in the countless joint communiqués signed whenever Third World potentates got together with each other or with others who had a weakness for public name-calling. Namibia served as the most active topic of diplomatic interaction between Africans and Americans, and was the only political topic on which Western and African countries maintained an ongoing negotiation.

In April 1981, during a twelve-nation tour of the Front Line States, South Africa, Kenya, Nigeria, Congo, Zaire, and Swaziland, the Namibia negotiations were the main subject of my exchanges with African leaders; nothing else even came close. It was a metaphor for South Africa's overall regional policy and the challenges facing Western diplomacy in the region. Black African leaders assumed that we had a posture or a position on the matter of apartheid. But few governments had an operational strategy toward developments *inside* South Africa in those days, and we were seldom asked to describe ours. None of my hosts even hinted at another set of priorities: Namibia was the number-one issue. We should concentrate our energies on getting Resolution 435 implemented, using whatever pressures were available (a few African leaders mentioned sanctions) to get the South Africans out of Namibia. Nothing should distract attention from this imperative. Later, there would be ample time to turn attention to completing the struggle against apartheid. It would be more likely to succeed when the rest of Africa was free and the South African government could not use neighboring lands— like Namibia—as a launching pad for strikes against African neighbors.

We fully shared this sense of the logical sequence, but our regional vision took the analysis several steps further. First, it was time to recognize explicitly in our policies that Southern Africa is an interdependent region: violence in one place triggers fears in another. External threats play directly into domestic anxieties; issues of political change within borders get tangled up with the question of physical insecurity across borders. This was as true for the Angolans as for the South Africans or the Zimbabweans. Governments were adept at transforming essentially domestic conflicts by referring to threats and scapegoats from across the border. The problem was compounded when external forces did, in fact, intervene with the instruments of violence. Once the issues became externalized (in fact or in perception) and the men with the guns began to shape the regional climate, politics degenerated into the art of making sure you ended up on the winning side. In such conditions, peaceful and democratic change must fail.

This was the most basic rationale for the regionwide pursuit of what I had labeled "constructive engagement" in an article entitled "South Africa: Strategy for Change," in *Foreign Affairs* (Winter 1980–81). Western engagement in Southern Africa was not for the purpose of imposing blueprints or timetables for change on the South Africans. We had neither the leverage nor the mandate for such a role. Rather, we had to engage in order to help foster a "regional climate conducive to compromise and accommodation" in both Southern and South Africa. The article painted a sober picture of a deeply troubled region.

In South Africa, the political trends within Afrikanerdom merited careful attention. There were some grounds for hope in the emerging coalition of "modernizers" and "reformers" assembled by Prime Minister P. W. Botha. But it was far from clear what they would do with the streamlined and centralized decisionmaking apparatus then emerging. There were some interesting changes under way or being debated in establishment circles. The basic purpose of "reform" remained ambiguous, but that was often the case. The article foresaw an aggressive external posture by the regionally dominant SADF, but cautioned against assuming that it was simply a voice for reactionary policy.

"A sustained and nimble diplomacy" would work to resolve regional conflicts and reduce violence. We could do this in several ways: by standing up for the very concept of negotiated, evolutionary change; by actively strengthening our relationships with leaders throughout the region without regard to race and ideology; by competing regionally for influence with the Soviets and Cubans and contesting the principle of external, Communist military intervention; and by working for a secure and prosperous region. We needed a policy of *"constructive engagement in the region as a whole."* This was the road to credibility and effectiveness; constructive engagement made no sense *except* as a regional strategy.

The implications of such a vision were numerous. As the Carter administration had itself discovered, U.S. signals to Pretoria on internal issues and regional diplomacy required some calibration. But rhetoric was a relatively minor issue. Another implication was the need for greater attention to the process of change. Too often, we talked only about the ultimate goal—a democratic, non-racial order—without addressing the steps and sequences that might lead to it. Such change would not be the result of one decision or one dramatic deal. There would be hundreds of decisions along the way; civil violence would accompany politics and negotiation; lesser forms of change would likely precede major change. Under certain conditions, the United States should be prepared to support evolutionary, "incremental" steps sometimes dismissed as merely ameliorative. To hold back, denying support to all partial, interim steps, was in effect a form of escapism. It would only encourage the South African government to believe that we sought its total capitulation and the black opposition to conclude that only a bloody upheaval could do the job.

On the other hand, it was not plausible to argue that "piecemeal reforms will lead inexorably to basic political change." Hence, our policy should rest on more modest claims: that white-led change had just begun, that blacks would assuredly gain greater organizational power from which to conduct their struggle, that incremental, ambiguous reform could have unintended consequences, and that much could be gained by pressing whites toward power sharing, while strengthening black empowerment efforts within South Africa.

I did not propose a dramatic departure from the last twenty years of American policy toward South Africa. Under constructive engagement, we would continue our adherence to the arms embargo, our refusal to make use of South African defense facilities, our categorical rejection of apartheid policies and institutions—as well as our rejection of trade and investment sanctions and all forms of economic warfare against South Africa, and our readiness to meet publicly with the top leadership as appropriate.

But there were important innovations in the approach spelled out in my writings before joining the new administration. The most significant was my insistence that the Western world take seriously its responsibility to create a regional climate conducive to negotiated solutions and political change. These things would not happen if Soviet-Cuban adventurism went unanswered and a cycle of reciprocal, cross-border violence was allowed to take root. The West needed to restore its credibility and compete throughout the region, supporting its interests in relevant ways—not wait to see which way the winds were blowing and go with the trends. We needed to understand the intimate link between regional security and internal change, and get the sequence right. As long as cross-border war continued, regional leaders would blame foreign enemies and seek foreign allies rather than reach out to their own people and create legitimate systems at home.

Inside South Africa, the Western world should also think about the sequencing and priorities of change. We should expand on the efforts of the private and non-profit sectors to promote U.S. and Western engagement in institution-building and black-empowerment programs. Politically and diplomatically, we would signal our support for a continuing process of change. In the crucial field of constitutional change, I argued that "piecemeal power-sharing steps deserve support if they are (a) consistent with the goal of expanded black political advancement, (b) demonstrably agreed to by the participants in them, and (c) not inconsistent with an open-ended process of change."

To judge by the standard of subsequent debate, one might have thought that this new approach represented a cozy alliance with apartheid. In fact, as I articulated the concept before entering public office, it represented an ambitious *regional* strategy linked to a purposeful and interventionist *bilateral* strategy toward the region's dominant state. Top officials of the government in Pretoria were quick to understand that this was not a formula for a love-in. They had read the words that best captured my message: "Clearly, the fundamental goal is the emergence in South Africa of a society with which the United States can pursue its varied interests in a full and friendly relationship. . . . As a multiracial democracy, the United States cannot endorse a system that is racist in purpose or effect."

I argued that the basic parameters of U.S. policy toward South Africa itself would be determined by events *within* South Africa. Our finite influence should be husbanded for occasions when it could make a difference and would be truly needed. The U.S. role in South Africa's affairs was likely to become more important as internal power relationships became more equitable. Moreover, "Pressure for change should be a central ingredient in American policy, and that pressure must be credibly maintained if we are not to send misleading signals to South Africans." But pressure alone was not enough. The West must show "a clear readiness to . . . engage credibly in addressing a complex agenda of change."

Within South Africa, the balance of coercive power remained overwhelmingly in favor of the whites, and a direct assault on white power was beyond the physical means of black South Africans. The government had the means to control internal opposition groups and to prevent the establishment of an internal guerrilla insurgency. It was also in a position to "punish severely any neighbors that support or tacitly tolerate anything more than a token guerrilla presence." This assessment, however, did not mean that I was forecasting peace: "There is every reason to anticipate continued and even gradually increasing political conflict and violence of several types ranging from sporadic terrorist acts to mass demonstrations, strikes, boycotts, urban disorder and sophisticated sabotage against South Africa's many soft targets."

It was clear that South Africa would not become free through revolutionary violence and direct assaults on the system. Black bargaining power would develop from non-military organizations created and based inside South Africa. The task of constructive engagement was to demolish the myths and fantasies of violence which for decades had transfixed black and white South Africans—the government's "total strategy" against the "total Marxist onslaught," otherwise known as the ANC's "armed struggle" campaign waged from neighboring lands vulnerable to the SADF's "destabilization wars." Our task would be to instill a new logic, under which all parties in Southern Africa would come to recognize that cross-border violence and armed confrontation are a two-way street. We would offer our diplomatic engagement to those governments in the region prepared to pursue negotiated solutions; this, we hoped, would strengthen regional stability and undercut the unilateral military game plans being considered by either Moscow or the hardliners in Pretoria.

Constructive engagement was an effort to short-circuit the military test of wills inevitably set in motion by the Portuguese revolution and the strategic changes of 1974–80 during which Angola, Mozambique, and Zimbabwe became independent. We offered an alternative road, directly challenging the Soviets and their Cuban and African allies as well as the South African government. We challenged those in the Front Line State capitals and the ANC who believed that the justice of the anti-apartheid cause would immunize them from the reality of South Africa's military supremacy. In sum, we proposed to eradicate a regional cycle of violence whose roots had already spread deep before we entered office.

The strategy of constructive engagement was not a gift to any "side," but a forceful assertion of leadership in support of American values and interests. We would seek strengthened and more constructive relationships with *all* countries in the region in order to bolster our credibility as a regional partner in peacemaking. I emphasized this point repeatedly in my first major speech as assistant secretary in August 1981:

> We cannot and will not permit our hand to be forced to align ourselves with one side or another in these disputes. Our task, together with our key allies, is to maintain communication with all parties—something we in the West are uniquely able to do—and to pursue our growing interests throughout the region. Only if we engage constructively in Southern Africa as a whole can we play our proper role in the search for negotiated solutions, peaceful change, and expanding economic progress. . . . The Reagan Administration has no intention of destabilizing South Africa in order to curry favor elsewhere. Neither will we align ourselves with apartheid policies that are abhorrent to our own multi-racial democracy.

When the debate over South African sanctions got going during the mid-1980s, it became accepted practice in the media to describe "constructive engagement" incorrectly as the Reagan administration's policy toward *the government of South Africa*. The policy would be characterized as one of "carrot but no stick" because of our firm stance against generalized economic sanctions. It would be said that we favored a strategy of "quiet diplomacy" or the use of "dialogue and persuasion" rather than pressure or sanctions. As the debate spiraled on, it overwhelmed rational discourse. Constructive engagement became distorted beyond recognition by critics who equated it, essentially, with opposition to sanctions which they further equated with support for apartheid. These caricatures of U.S. policy bore no resemblance to my self-evidently centrist and idealistic conception.

I have sometimes asked myself, though, if the debate of 1985–86 was really necessary. What could we have done to avoid this poisonous debate that did nothing to elevate its participants and still less to inform the public? In retrospect, it is probably not a good idea to assign descriptive labels to policies toward particular regions or countries. Many foreign policies—including some very good ones—are anonymous. We never made the conscious decision to apply the term "constructive engagement" to our Southern African policies. It had appeared in my *Foreign Affairs* article, and we just began to use it. There was no formal policy paper endorsing either the term or the specific content I had given it as a private citizen. Soon, the door was open for commentators and critics to cite every U.S. statement or decision as part of "constructive engagement." In some quarters, the label acquired mythic status as the American grand design that explained events in Southern Africa since January 1981. Once the labeling began, it descended into epithets whose very purpose was to distort a complex situation and win a partisan debate.

My article spoke of our support for evolutionary change as containing a "little-noted source of leverage," since we retained the option to pull back and cease our support; if we did so, no one else would take our place. In his first official press comment on South Africa in March 1981, Reagan said it better, noting that "many people, black and white, in South Africa are trying to remove apartheid," and adding: "As long as there's a sincere and honest effort being made, based on our own experience in our own land, it would seem to me that we should be trying to be helpful." We would elaborate on this "support the reformers" theme, carefully insisting that it applied to all races and to people in opposition as well as those in power.

Over the course of the next eight years, it became ever clearer to the practitioners—if not the critics—of constructive engagement that such conditionality is potent. By describing the region's possibilities, laying out our expectations, and ascribing constructive intentions to local parties, we laid the basis for future influence. When things turned sour, we had a far stronger hand to pressure the party that misbehaved. By 1985, for example, we were sharply distancing ourselves from both the South African and Angolan governments on account of their regional and domestic decisions. They came to pay a severe price for failing to live up to our stated expectations.

What threats could we wield to back up this intangible form of conditionality? Having previously gone the extra mile and given them the benefit of the doubt, we were in a strong position to blow their credibility out of the water. One tool was public statements and symbolic signals of displeasure or disgust—a joint press appearance by the U.S. and Botswana foreign ministers after an SADF raid on the latter's capital; public warnings to U.S. firms to think about the national interest before investing in Angola. In addition to distancing, there was the more drastic tool of policy reviews and threats of basic change in strategy. We could and did initiate such steps. We could also point darkly at others in our complex system, and warn that time was expiring—the old good cop, bad cop routine. (This classic tactic only works if the threat is under the effective control of the person wielding it.)

Perhaps the most credible threat of all is the threat to give up and go away. However perverse their conduct on occasion, and whatever they may have thought or said of our policies, none of the players in the Southern African drama of the 1980s wanted U.S. disengagement. They wanted American support for *their* side of the argument. Most important, at least some of the characters we were dealing with recognized that they, not we, would be the big losers.

But the message about conditionality got garbled for several reasons. Take, for example, the Reagan statement just quoted. It was followed by these lines: "Can we abandon a country [South Africa] that has stood beside us in every war we've ever fought, a country that strategically is essential to the free world in its production of minerals we all must have and so forth? . . . [I]f we're going to sit down at a table and negotiate with the Russians, surely we can keep the door open and continue to negotiate with a friendly nation like South Africa." It will be no surprise that various audiences in Southern Africa remembered the second quote longer than the first. At one level, the signal was wholly consistent with my vision: constructive engagement *was* the opposite of abandoning South Africa—it was aimed at saving that land and its neighbors from their own worst instincts. But at another level, the President's remark epitomized the insensitivity that would be the sad hallmark of his sporadic personal involvement on South Africa in the years to come.

One wondered what conclusions leaders of various races in Southern Africa were expected to draw from his strange terminology. Which "friendly nation" were we talking about? The one working ardently behind the scenes in Washington against my confirmation and for a very different policy? I wondered which side the President imagined the South Africans were on at the Battle of Gettysburg. Did he realize that he was repeating verbatim the theme song in press handouts of every South African embassy in the Western world? Did he know that hundreds of thousands of black Africans in Zambia, Kenya, Zimbabwe, Nigeria, Madagascar, Mali, Senegal, Chad, Togo, Ghana, Niger, and—yes—South Africa had fought with the Allies in both world wars? Or that the National Party of South Africa—the governing party from 1948 to today—agitated on the Nazi side and against South African entry into the war?

There were many reasons, beyond this episode, why the point about conditionality got garbled. My colleagues and I had no inclination to speak publicly of threats or deadlines for reaching agreements in the region. It seldom works, and it is hardly the way to engage others in one's diplomacy and ensnare them into decisions we wanted them to take. Confronted publicly, foreign governments are likely to give the wrong answers as a matter of principle.

Nor did I have authority to issue deadlines and threats. But I knew that there were people in Washington, in the executive branch as well as Congress, who would be eager to threaten or impose deadlines on the parties we were dealing with. They had a different agenda from mine. Both liberals and conservatives suffered from the illusion of American influence. They both enjoyed being seen to tell foreigners what to do— preferably in public—more than actually persuading them to do it. Neither was competent to judge the precise cause of the logjams and crises we ran into. Both would have been pleased if the process collapsed and their favorite "bad guys" took the rap. Both wanted to be the ones to set the terms of conditionality. If I could avoid it, control of the conditions of constructive engagement would never slip away from the hands of those committed to its success.

PART II

4

Engaging the Allies and the South Africans, 1981

The U.S. decision to mount a restructured peace initiative in 1981 carried with it some basic implications. Foremost among these was the need to reengage the South Africans in our diplomacy. Without Pretoria's participation, there would be no basis for proposing a fresh settlement strategy. Neither the African Front Line States nor our allies would participate unless we could demonstrate that we could get the South Africans on board.

Specifically, we needed an authoritative South African commitment in principle to implement a settlement based on Resolution 435. Pretoria, which accepted the original Western plan in April 1978, had never accepted a subsequent U.N. Secretary General's report on the details of the U.N. role or agreed to accept Resolution 435 which called for the immediate implementation of the plan in late September 1978. In reality, therefore, we needed not only a commitment to implement Resolution 435 but also some resolution of the issues that had stood in the way of such a commitment. We would have to get around or neutralize the rolling series of conditions South Africa had introduced during 1978–81 to fend off the day of decision on Namibia.

The Cuban linkage was the bait or "flypaper" we needed to launch our strategy. It would be the instrument of choice for influencing Pretoria to provide a categorical but conditioned commitment on Namibia.

The Botha government would be attracted to an approach which acknowledged that regional security was a "two-way street."

From April through September 1981 we worked to nail Pretoria down; by October, we had made sufficient progress to reengage our partners in the Western Contact Group and the Front Line States. It took another twelve months (to October 1982) to resolve all Namibia issues left over from the 1978–80 period. By mid-1982, we had launched the Angola "track" of our strategy, and were conducting something we termed "the Namibia-Angola negotiations," reflecting our linkage-based settlement concept.

It sounds almost smooth and straightforward. But the campaign to engage the South Africans in those early months of 1981 deserves a closer look. There was deep distrust in this highly complex relationship. The "understanding" we eventually reached with the Botha government in 1981 contained slippery ambiguities and unacknowledged differences. It meant different things to different people, and contained a little something for each of Botha's factions and most of ours. Eventually, we managed to nail Pretoria down. But this common interest would not remove the underlying suspicion that plagued our relations with South Africa during the 1980s.

Engaging a Pariah

Deep in the soul of Afrikaner politics resides the embattled spirit of an underdog ethnic nationalism which has only recently won its struggle. After their 1948 electoral victory, the National Party leadership erected a system that institutionalized white domination and advanced the political and economic interests of Afrikaners. Soon, however, it became clear that the great nationalist victory of Afrikaners (over everyone else, especially English-speaking whites) would lead to global ostracism and isolation. A Southern African Masada complex set in. When their ethnic dreams turned into nightmares for all South Africans, National Party leaders resorted to Orwellian double-talk to justify a growing mobilization of state resources to sustain the apartheid model. Externally, they waged a campaign of overt and covert actions to "sell" South Africa and elicit Western support, even while keeping the West at arm's length and investing massively in strategic self-sufficiency (e.g., in the arms, nuclear, and energy sectors).

By 1981, Afrikaner nationalists had begun to shed their illusions. It was becoming increasingly difficult to define what it meant to be a "Nat." Reform was no longer a dirty word after Prime Minister (later, President) P. W. Botha's "adapt or die" phraseology caught on in the late

1970s. Leading Afrikaans-speaking personalities were raising basic questions about the economic irrationality and political price tag of the status quo. South Africa's industrial relations were in the process of transformation as business leaders convinced the political establishment of the need to legalize the black trade union movement. This action alone drove a powerful stake into the heart of grand or territorial apartheid, demolishing the fantasy that whites only needed unskilled black workers as temporary participants in the urban, cash economy. No single change in the past twenty-five years did more to demolish apartheid and empower black South Africans in their own land.

These trends received scant attention beyond South Africa, which by now was firmly implanted in the liberal Western political imagination as a world-class pariah. Indeed, its leaders seemed to be increasingly accustomed to behaving like one. Their generalized commitment to reform was linked to a shrill rejection of Western "interference" and a tough external policy. A mailed fist at the frontier would buy time for domestic change.

We were the first people to attempt to engage the Afrikaners in a serious, reciprocal relationship since their 1948 victory. But it is not easy to engage a pariah, especially one so neuralgic about "foreign intervention" and at the same time so craving of Western acceptance. The South African establishment functioned as a secretive, ethnic cabal. Loyalty and solidarity were the supreme political virtues. The leadership seldom aired its very real inner differences, and it cut itself off from "external" advice and information. The result was a leadership that was at once tough and determined and, at the same time, unrealistic about its options. This helps explain how the Botha government could embrace the global message of Ronald Reagan—seeking to identify itself with Washington and acquire American "legitimacy"—while simultaneously viewing the Africa team in Reagan's State Department and its Southern African strategy as a dangerous threat.

From the earliest days of 1981, we and the South Africans lived in a shadowy world of multiple agendas and competing channels. One might have thought that dealing with Pretoria would be easier for us Reaganites than it had been for earlier administrations. We boasted solid conservative credentials and were known to hold less onesidedly hostile attitudes toward South African interests and the Afrikaners themselves. But matters were not so simple. Unaccustomed to "normal" diplomatic relationships with the external world, Pretoria's leaders treated it as an object of unending manipulation. No matter how forthcoming the position espoused by official Washington, the South Africans scrambled to get around our right flank. They used a host of lobbyists, consultants, and congressional "friends of South Africa" who had a natural interest in spreading the word that the State Department did not speak for the Reagan White House.

South African officials found our well-informed grasp of "their" region to be a little unsettling. They were not used to dealing with American conservatives who understood Afrikaner history and psychology. They were accustomed to American neanderthals who embraced them uncritically as the rulers of a vital Christian bastion against the spread of Soviet "control" and Marxist rule. Alternatively, they were used to being treated by liberals and the left as moral lepers worthy only of Western sanctimony. Over the years, they saw American visitors as belonging in one of two camps: there were the gold-chain Tarzans and peroxide Janes who raved about the climate, the golf, the wildlife, and the familiar frontier ethic; and there were the condescending poseurs of academe, the press, and the cloth, who rushed to judgment but never asked why South Africa is the only African country where things work.

By contrast, our conscious cultivation of leverage through a *conditional* offer of regional cooperation impressed Pretoria's leaders as serious and, perhaps, somewhat threatening. They detected a purposeful logic to it. We were not just another bunch of Americans looking for an overseas theme park. Later, our approach would be attacked by skeptics at home as "all carrot and no stick." But Botha and some of his colleagues sensed what we were trying to do. That was why they tried hard to undermine the State Department's Africa team.

Diplomacy on the Rack

We faced three closely related challenges. First, it would be necessary to retain overall control within our bureaucracy of the specific, operational content of our strategy. Second, we had to master the channels of communication between our new administration and the key players in Africa. Finally, we had to steer the pivotal South Africans toward a give-and-take pattern of cooperation with our strategy.

The first step was to establish coherence in American official ranks. Long after the basic strategy was endorsed by President Reagan in March 1981, there was a significant range of views on certain aspects. The differences did not disappear on June 9 when I was confirmed by the Senate in a vote of 84 to 7, after Jesse Helms's protracted "hold" on my nomination was finally broken. There was little consensus on such issues as: (a) what we meant by Cuban troop withdrawal; (b) what changes to consider in the inherited Namibia independence plan; (c) how to handle the public and diplomatic tactics of our "linkage" decisions (whom to tell what to and when); (d) how ambitious and concrete to be in proposing a democratic constitution for an independent Namibia; (e) whether to seek guarantees of Namibia's neutrality and non-alignment; (f) when to initiate direct discussions with the Angolan regime on the Cuban issue; and (g) how to obtain the support of Contact Group allies (Britain, Canada, France, and Germany) for our revised approach.

Each of these issues was a complex tangle, and it mattered how the answers came out. Over time, I learned that it seldom pays to force a decision on such matters in advance and in a vacuum. My role as the ranking Africa policy official of our government did not automatically give me a free hand or, even, an assurance of primacy and a veto on African issues. Rather, I would have to acquire such influence incrementally as the person directly responsible for implementing our strategy. To illustrate the point, it is worth looking more closely at how we managed allied relationships during the process of engaging the South Africans.

Ironically, the notion that our allied partners might offer useful counsel and essential political support and cover was more prevalent within the African bureau than beyond it. I found remarkably little awareness of the fact that the leader of the West must do more than take decisions unilaterally and inform our allies after the fact. Without allied participation, we could lose on every front—in Africa, in East-West relations, and in the arena of public opinion. To be sure, we would have to play hardball in the Contact Group: if the allies wanted U.S. leadership of the Namibia process, it would be on our terms or not at all. But, we would need to *listen, consult, and negotiate* in order to obtain allied cooperation and support. We did not wish to be left in splendid isolation at the lift-off stage.

My Africa teammates and I had two reasons to take the allied reaction seriously. First, we cared more than others about the fate of our initiative. After all, it was to be the centerpiece of our African policy and the basis by which we would be viewed throughout the region and beyond. Others, quite naturally, viewed African issues as of distinctly lower priority. In addition, it served our policy interests to take the allies seriously. They would give us a needed counterweight to the predictable South African drive for a thorough recasting of Resolution 435 and a Rambolike approach to Angola—a drive with sympathetic adherents within and beyond the administration. Allied input would give us leverage to steer the American policy process, and greater clout in our dealings with the parties. The allies realized that my Africa team represented a moderate version of the new Reagan era. We were the best they were going to get.

As early as February 1981, key allied officials had begun weighing in with the new Washington leadership, seeking to steer us away from formulas that would break all their diplomatic china in Africa. Their anxieties abated somewhat during my initial foray to Southern Africa, and they welcomed our candid briefing on that first mission in late April. As we will see, they offered vital support as we sought to ward off the moist advances of the South Africans and the shrill, all-or-nothing antics of the African–Non-aligned camp, egged on by Moscow's skillful diplomatic apparatus.

But the allies remained uneasy at the still vague formulas of our evolving approach. Their seasoned Africa experts were dubious of our grasp of the complex Africa brief. Some of them harbored doubts as to whether Reagan Republicans had the necessary genetic endowment to conduct an African policy. They fretted that we would give the store away to the South Africans. In part, they questioned whether the new U.S. Africa team could control the U.S. policy process. On this point, they had something real to worry about, and we found it useful, on occasion, to scare them.

Meanwhile, the South Africans had long ago mastered the art of placing a cat among the pigeons. Now, in the early months of the Reagan era, they purposefully fueled American divisions and allied nervousness. Like children running their fingernails down a blackboard, senior South African officials exploited the transition in Washington to press for maximalist U.S. positions that might cause the allies to bolt. Within days of Reagan's inauguration, South African diplomats in Washington began raising doubts about Resolution 435. In early March 1981, South Africa's state-controlled radio (SABC) editorialized that the onesided, anti-South African position of U.N. bodies had effectively killed Resolution 435. P. W. Botha told German parliamentarians that the U.N. Plan was "dead as a doornail."

That same month, senior South African military emissaries (not identified as such to U.S. consular officials who would have denied their visa applications) arrived in the United States to make their case "unofficially" to conservatives and ranking defense, intelligence, and policy officials such as U.N. Ambassador Kirkpatrick. They sought to undercut the evolving approach developed at State, and to discredit its Africa bureau in the eyes of conservatives. In mid-April, the South African government sought to trip me up on my first official visit to the region as a still-unconfirmed assistant secretary. P. W. Botha explained his decision not to receive me on the grounds that I had said unwelcome things publicly about the possible future role of SWAPO in an independent Namibian government, and also on account of my known opposition to the unauthorized U.S. visit of his military intelligence chiefs.

This gamesmanship was deadly serious. Some senior players in Pretoria had apparently concluded that I was not their candidate for the job. I would not last long in any event, especially if they succeeded in rejecting me as the channel for dealings with Washington. Botha's shirty treatment of Reagan's first emissary would create the impression that my mission had "failed." I could be portrayed as an "obstacle" to constructive relations, providing ammunition to right-wing conservatives in Washington who continued to string out the Senate confirmation process by "holding" my nomination from coming to a vote.

Other ammunition came from my previous writing on South Africa, the focus of much of the 100-plus written questions to which Jesse Helms of North Carolina demanded a reply even after my confirmation hearing in the Foreign Relations Committee in early April. Some of the questions appeared to have been inspired by people on the right fringe of the National Party who distrusted P. W. Botha's own reformist agenda! Additional ammunition came in May, when a series of classified papers drafted in my bureau mysteriously found their way to left-wing U.S. critics and activists, who promptly spread them to the media and around African capitals in an effort to discredit us as "colluding" with Pretoria.

The real motive and identity of the thieves was never established, but the theft temporarily weakened me; investigations were ordered, but the culprits were too good to get caught. Predictably, fingers pointed in my direction. Al Haig warned me to zip up my shop, implying that disaffected liberals there were to blame. I told him I thought it was another sort of inside job, and changed the combination on the safes in the front office. The air was understandably tense during a meeting with my key staff right after the document fiasco. People wondered if a witch-hunt was imminent. At a quiet moment, a mouse scurried behind my chair and down the hole carrying phone cables from floor to floor. "There's the mole!" exclaimed the quickest of us, breaking the tension.

Strenuous efforts were made by Helms to force me to fire my senior deputy and replace him with a Hill staffer who had very close ties to the intelligence apparatus in Pretoria. If I would agree, Secretary of State Haig informed me in May, the Senate "hold" on my nomination would be lifted. I refused to jettison Lannon Walker—an outstanding career officer whom I had known for years and whom I inherited from my predecessor. At the time, this stubbornness marked me as naive and impractical; I had declined to play the game. But keeping Lannon Walker at my side through April 1982 (beyond his normal tour of duty) was one of the best decisions I ever made. I learned a lot of tradecraft from this brilliant operator. He knew where all the African parties were coming from and offered an endless stream of inspired strategems for moving them down the track. Walker also understood the predatory games of Washington; he helped me to hone my skills in swimming with the sharks. By making Walker's tenure a condition of my confirmation, my opponents opened up the opportunity for me to make his tenure a condition of my staying: I told Haig that I would not want the job if some disaffected senator could dictate who my staff would be.

Eventually, senior people in the White House and State Department realized that they would have to choose between the Helms camp and their own nominees (there were several other "holds"). My "hold" was broken unconditionally in early June, sending a signal to the career ranks upon whom I would depend to conduct the President's policies for the next eight years. Despite Africa's lowly status as a controversial and second-order policy arena, Walker, his successors, and I recruited the finest people in the service to work with us. Years later, a top official of the incoming Bush administration asked me what was the secret for eliciting the loyal professionalism of the career service. Take a Foreign Service Officer to lunch, I replied.

Meanwhile, in response to our probes, South African diplomats offered up a thickening stew of desiderata. The U.N. Plan's security provisions relating to the U.N. military component (UNTAG) would have to go. Others stressed that U.N. civilian election monitoring was the most objectionable feature because of the United Nation's bias in favor of SWAPO. South African Foreign Minister Roelof ("Pik") Botha told Jeane Kirkpatrick in May that the entire military component of UNTAG ("blue helmets") was out. Some formula for weighted voting would be needed: otherwise, SWAPO would sweep the election in northern Namibia, provoking a Namibian civil war right next door to Soviet-controlled forces just over the border in Angola. My British counterparts, Derek Day and Len Allinson, looked at us knowingly and reminded us of their "many searing experiences" in trying to nail all this Jell-O to a tree.

Nothing would have pleased the hardliner faction in Pretoria more than a break-up of the Contact Group. They distrusted the Pierre Trudeau government in Ottawa and the new Socialist team of François Mitterrand in Paris. Hans-Dietrich Genscher, who dominated the foreign affairs machinery of the conservative-liberal coalition in Bonn, had made himself a *bête noire* in Pretoria by his dogged pursuit of the Namibian independence cause. After Zimbabwe's independence outcome became known in 1980, the South Africans also managed to contain their enthusiasm for Margaret Thatcher and her foreign minister, Peter Carrington.

These guys pinned their hopes on Ronald Reagan to scrap the U.N. Plan and join some cozy Pretoria-Washington axis directed against the many "enemies" who formed part of the "total Marxist onslaught."

My job was to press South Africa toward realistic negotiating terms without losing the confidence of superiors in Washington who often empathized with Pretoria's view of the United Nations, SWAPO, Angola, and even Hans-Dietrich Genscher! We had our work cut out for us. We would be trying to add Angola (and Cuban withdrawal) to the agenda and make needed improvements to Resolution 435 without losing the allies or the African Front Line States and SWAPO. We were on the foreign policy equivalent of the rack.

A further source of pressure came from the Africans. My April mission to the Front Line States went fairly well until we arrived in Mozambique. Its leaders appeared to have swallowed whole the Soviet and Cuban propaganda line that Washington had jumped into bed with Pretoria. Relations seemed close to a rupture on that front—a goal ardently sought by Pretoria as well as Moscow and Havana. More clouds gathered when the Front Line States met in a special summit in Luanda while my April mission was in full swing. A joint communiqué expressed "grave concern" at our stated intention to seek repeal of the 1976 Clark Amendment banning assistance to UNITA. It demanded the implementation of Resolution 435 without "any further delay, prevarication, qualification or modification." In calling for the defeat of "any maneuvers and schemes of imperialism and racism in the region," the communiqué reflected a dangerous polarization in the region and the virulent influence of our Communist adversaries. By late April, the Front Line States (backed by the full weight of the Soviet–East Bloc–Cuban diplomatic machinery in New York) organized a showdown in the Security Council over a series of four Namibia resolutions demanding that Resolution 435 be implemented forthwith.

The allies helped us to contain the pressure. They joined us on April 23 in a joint statement declaring that the Contact Group would be developing more specific proposals aimed at "strengthening the existing plan" and giving "greater confidence to all of the parties." One week later, the British and French joined us in a triple Security Council veto of African–Non-aligned–Soviet resolutions which would have imposed sanctions on South Africa if it failed to implement Resolution 435 unconditionally. The hardliners around Leonid Brezhnev and P. W. Botha must have been equally annoyed at their inability to split us from our allies. On May 3, allied foreign ministers meeting in Rome came together around a text declaring that Resolution 435 provided "a solid basis" for a settlement. Haig had what he needed for the May 14 arrival in Washington of his South African counterpart, Pik Botha, who had been pressing to visit since before Reagan's inauguration.

To Define a Relationship

All eyes were fixed on us. The African Front Line leaders formally opposed our approach of "strengthening" Resolution 435, and did not wish to discuss possible changes. Privately, they were saying that we would, first, have to get the South Africans to cooperate. The message, as conveyed by Tanzanian Foreign Minister Salim Salim, was, in effect, We think you are going about this in the wrong way, but show us it can work and we'll be with you. (This turned out to be a fairly accurate prediction of Front Line State conduct in the period to come.)

The allies were similarly focused on South African Foreign Minister Botha's first Reagan-era visit to Washington in mid-May. Allied experts coached us without mercy: Don't agree to negotiate a full-blown constitution in advance; protect the core of the UNTAG provisions without which the Africans will lose all confidence; explore carefully the idea of guarantees of Namibia's future status; watch out for the Angolan nettle and avoid Angolan conditions.

But the allies did not realize how little ground we had really covered with the South Africans prior to Botha's visit. The Haig-Botha discussion dealt with the big picture of our overall relationship and the question of where a settlement of the Namibia conflict fit into it. Botha had arrived with an eleven-point presentation purporting to define the basis for a new U.S.-South African relationship. Couched in terms of a *de facto* strategic alliance, it read as if drafted by first-term students at a South African military academy. All bases (especially naval) were covered: securing access to "critical minerals"; protecting the Cape sea route; strengthening the South African Navy's capacity to play a role in the Indian Ocean and South Atlantic; removal of Soviet and "Soviet surrogate" forces from Southern Africa; port facilities for U.S. warships in South Africa; and a settlement of the South West African (Namibian) problem in a manner that would produce a "moderate government, well disposed towards the U.S.A."

Haig sidestepped all this, focusing instead on the urgent need for a *political* strategy integrating the African, Cuban, allied, and Soviet dimensions into a coherent regional approach. This was Al Haig at his best: no one could outdo him in the virile language of geo-speak that entranced South African officialdom. He expressed understanding and support for Pretoria's concerns about the Soviets and Cubans (who must leave Africa). We supported Jonas Savimbi's battle for political reconciliation, but this would not be a part of the Namibia plan as such. Washington was dead serious about obtaining a Namibia settlement, and we wanted straight answers from Pretoria; *this would be a defining issue in our relations.* We needed to know whether South Africa was prepared to commit itself to a cooperative relationship on this regional agenda. We would shift our attention to other issues rather than be sucked into a drawn-out negotiating game.

After his meeting with Haig, Botha told the press that he could "see a very real possibility of moving ahead within the framework set out to me by the Secretary of State. . . ." The next day, I had extensive exchanges with Botha and his number two, Brand Fourie, Director General of the Department of Foreign Affairs. We danced imprecisely around the question of how the Angolan agenda would relate to all this: the United States, as Haig had said, would use its influence to achieve Cuban withdrawal and political reconciliation while the Namibia process moved forward. We agreed that Savimbi must not become a victim of a settlement. But we sparred on a number of specific issues: the role of the Namibian internal parties in the negotiation, the question of UNTAG, the question of how to guarantee the rights of non-SWAPO groups. I stressed that Washington needed a "conclusive list" of South African concerns and a commitment in principle to proceed toward a settlement.

But the South Africans, it seemed, could not help fantasizing about the true meaning of Reagan's election. The letter Botha sent Haig on May 19 began by positing that both governments agreed on a set of categorical strategic goals relating to the exclusion of all external Communist forces from the entire region. Instead of the UNTAG military component, Botha proposed U.N. civilian observers. A regional cease-fire would need to be negotiated with the neighboring states of Angola and Zambia to bring about a climate of stability *before* any settlement. And, a long list of guarantees was proposed, with South Africa itself to serve as one of the guarantors. Botha's wish list even dragged in the previously finessed question of Walvis Bay. (The legal status of Namibia's most important port, a territorial enclave on the Atlantic, remained in dispute. Its future was not defined in Resolution 435; Western and African negotiators intentionally left it to be resolved later, between the South Africans and an independent government of Namibia, a process that got under way in 1990.) Botha's letter stated that the "use" of Walvis Bay by a future Namibian government should be negotiated after Namibia's independence—a not-so-subtle move to preempt the outcome and obtain U.S. support for the view that its ultimate status was not a matter for negotiation.

Haig decided not to send a written, point-by-point rejoinder. Instead,

he referred back to the groundwork laid during Botha's visit, and declared
that the issues needed careful, in-depth review. To advance the bidding,
he proposed an early visit to South Africa and Namibia by his newly
arrived deputy, William P. Clark, a former judge and one of Reagan's
closest political allies from California politics. Meanwhile, I did not believe
it was wise or even possible to keep our Contact Group allies guessing
about the contents of Botha's letter. We needed them—both to help
maintain African confidence and to strengthen my hand internally and
with Pretoria.

The allies took fright upon seeing the letter: the grievous damage
Botha's positions would do to the entire U.N. framework was obvious.
German Foreign Ministry experts quivered with indignation at this bla-
tant example of "Boer cheekiness." Their Canadian counterparts added
that Canada's virginity on South African issues was what gave the Contact Group its African "credibility," and hinted darkly that Ottawa would
have to assess its continued participation. We knew that the Germans
were privately predicting the early collapse of the Group over the issue
of American tactics. The French had two positions: a Socialist one at
ministerial level mirroring the German malaise, and a far more practical
and creative line from my subministerial French counterpart, Jean Ausseil, who understood exactly what we were doing. London fretted sup-
portively; the Brits were anxious, above all, to get the process back on
the rails and keep the Group intact. Joint activity by our Group was
placed effectively on hold, while we prepared the Clark mission.

The anxious ministerial correspondence piling up on Haig's desk got
our attention on the eve of Bill Clark's June 10–13 trip to Cape Town
and Windhoek. (Harare, the Zimbabwean capital, was added for "balance," and to signal our backing for this one-year-old state whose policies were still in the formative stage.) Haig reassured his allied counterparts
that we were listening to them. Privately, he upbraided me for sharing
with them the contents of Botha's correspondence. We risked shaking
the allies' faith in us; they would badmouth us in Africa and raise doubts
in South African minds about our handling of privileged exchanges. He
had a point. But from my vantage point, the Group was proving itself
invaluable, bolstering our internal arguments on issue after issue. It did
not seem to me that dissembling or distorting the record with our NATO
allies was the best way to bolster their respect and support for American
leadership of the alliance. Swallowing his occasional doubts, Haig swore
me in as assistant secretary on June 9, just in time for my departure to
Africa with Bill Clark.

Haig's choice of Clark to head this mission was an interesting one.
Clark's grasp of world events beyond Sacramento and San Luis Obispo

was not renowned. Inside-the-Beltway sophisticates grumbled that he had slipped up during his own confirmation hearings when he could not correctly identify Robert Mugabe as prime minister of Zimbabwe. (Mugabe had no hang-ups about welcoming him to Harare, however, confessing that he had not initially known who Clark was, either!) Clark's diplomatic experience was nil. After the mission, tales of his naivete made the rounds back at State ("He thinks we can negotiate Cuban troop withdrawal with the South Africans!") His political instincts toward the Botha government were warm and often uncritical, just like Reagan's. In sending Clark to Cape Town, Haig risked compounding our problems and losing a measure of control over policy.

But Haig had his reasons for choosing Clark to head the mission and sending Elliott Abrams (Assistant Secretary of State for International Organizations) along as well as me and a trio of experts. Abrams, a former congressional staffer, had been a key colleague of mine in shaping the policy papers eventually approved by Haig and Reagan. We had a common interest in assuring the international viability of our strategy. Even at that early time, Abrams had begun to acquire a reputation among Republican politicos as a sort of neoconservative pit bull. He would offer the policy further political protection. If someone had to deflate the South African balloon in the name of Ronald Reagan, what better way to do it than by sending this cast of characters? The South Africans could not get around the right flank of Clark, Reagan's closest friend and ally in the entire administration, the man who had hired Ed Meese and Mike Deaver while Reagan was governor of California. If we hit rough road with P. W. Botha and company, better for that to happen on Clark's watch than Crocker's (or Haig's).

This, after all, was a time when Haig was anxiously trying to figure out where he stood with the Reagan inner circle. Whatever Clark's qualifications for the assignment, Haig had to think politically because he needed a way to communicate with Reagan and cut a channel through the phalanx of White House advisers (the "three mouseketeers," Haig called them) standing between him and the President. Clark, in sum, could help Haig with his broader problems, and he could help on Africa where Haig could be sabotaged if loony-fringe conservatives got too much White House attention.

Our planning for the Clark mission included a visit to Windhoek to discuss constitutional principles with the multiplicity of Namibian parties based there (including SWAPO's "internal" wing, which more or less spoke for the main leadership cadres in Angolan and Zambian exile). By now, Pretoria had backed away from insisting that a full-blown constitution be negotiated in advance of a settlement. Still, a set of agreed principles would be a confidence-building measure for Namibia's minority communities and the South Africans. Our tangible support for the idea would place us in a position to push Pretoria back on a number of its non-starters concerning security aspects of the Namibia transition and the question of guarantees. In addition, we had the Cuban card, and would look for ways to play it. From these discussions, we hoped to distill the understanding Haig had discussed with Pik Botha.

The Clark mission was a mixed bag. In a series of bizarre encounters, we turned the South African leadership around on the crucial role of UNTAG in the settlement; an UNTAG military component—whose size, deployment, and composition would be further negotiated—was accepted in the context of our explicit and categorical discussion of the Cuban link. In one exchange in Clark's Cape Town hotel suite, Pik Botha was regaling us with anti-U.N. horror stories when Abrams interjected, "Would it make a difference if the Cubans were to depart Angola in this context?" Botha and Haig had discussed the Cubans at length in Washington in May. But this sounded more specific, almost like a quid pro quo, which, in fact, it was. Botha conceded that this could change everything, and he undertook to consult with P. W. Botha, whom Clark would be seeing the next day.

In an evening surf-and-turf barbecue catered by SADF chefs at the Administrator-General's "castle" in Windhoek, Clark would embroider the point. Back in Washington, he had heard some fairly raw Haig commentary about how Reagan ought to smash the head of the Cuban serpent in its nest. Clark shared extracts of these wishful scenarios with his hosts over lobster tails and white wine. Pik Botha and Defense Minister Magnus Malan informed Clark that P. W. Botha had authorized them to concur with our request for flexibility on UNTAG. Years later, South African officials would try to deflect our pressures by asserting (incorrectly) that Washington had failed to live up to its commitment to force the Cubans out of Angola—which was not quite what Clark had agreed to.

Clark's hosts produced a slip of paper on June 12 that purported to reflect certain areas of broad consensus: opposition to a Marxist regime coming to power in Namibia; acceptance of the need for Cubans to leave the region and for Savimbi to receive appropriate help; the need for the rights of minority groups to be safeguarded; and flexibility on UNTAG, whose troops' arrival would be coordinated with Cuban departures from Angola. Clark seemed pleased with this fuzzy piece of paper. He commented on it favorably without reference to his traveling entourage, succumbing to his hosts' maneuvers to cut him off from his delegation. Clark, at one level, was an easy mark for Botha and Malan, and the paper will not be featured in the annals of U.S. diplomacy. One could drive a tank through its ambiguities and omissions. Vast amounts of work lay ahead of us to convert Clark's paper into something we could use.

But the paper was a start. It helped us gradually to reconfirm the central place of the United Nations as implementing agent in the settlement strategy. The South Africans backed off from the question of "paper guarantees": Cuban troop withdrawal, by transforming the regional balance, was the best means of guaranteeing the future conduct of Namibia and its government. As for the constitutional issues, these could be handled by a negotiated list of principles and voting procedures in Namibia's future constituent assembly.

If the specific accomplishments of the June 1981 Clark mission appeared modest, there was another side to the story. It would be hard to imagine a senior American official more favorably disposed to the Botha government than Clark on the eve of his visit. He had had some questions himself about whether the State Department was really working for Ronald Reagan; like too many politicos new to their bureaucratic assignments, he was not, at first, comfortable in the presence of inherited, career people. Imagining himself to be the guest of honorable people, he permitted his hosts to exclude or shunt aside members of his delegation and his local embassy team. Yet, by their offensively manipulative behavior, the South Africans managed to anger this naive but decent man. Nearly every schedule preference we had expressed for the visit was overturned by our hosts, starting with a heavy, formal dinner event on the evening of our arrival after a fourteen-hour flight. The venue—the SADF "castle" in Cape Town—could not have been more transparently chosen to create an imagery of U.S. identification with the South African military. The government sought, unsuccessfully, to press Clark to scrub meetings we had planned for him with non-governmental and opposition representatives.

On our arrival the first evening, Pik Botha and Magnus Malan whisked Clark to a VIP lounge where they handed him their proposed schedule for his visit, including an overnight visit to the "operational area" along Namibia's northern border. He (and we) would be outfitted in SADF khaki, transported to the edge of the war zone in SADF equipment, "briefed" by Malan's military intelligence people (the same ones who had entered the United States by the back door back in March), housed in officers' quarters, and escorted for a viewing of the anti-SWAPO combat zone before heading south to see a spectacular game park.

Abrams and I convinced him that the proposed schedule would discredit both Clark and his mission. It would enable the South Africans to paint us as having taken their side in the regional wars we had come to resolve. Clark, an avid outdoorsman, would have liked nothing better than to be able to accept this offer of geopolitical tourism on the fringe of Namibia's bush war. But he accepted our counsel and said no, prompting an angry P. W. Botha to go into a funk. There was a tense meeting: Botha apparently viewed the visit to the "operational area" as an initiation rite. Clark expressed quiet disappointment that his mission had failed, and spoke of flying home immediately (breaking off the travel to Namibia and Zimbabwe). At that point, Botha backed off, perhaps recognizing that he had gone too far. A few hours later, in my presence, he spoke warmly of Reagan and his emissary, but proceeded to openly warn Clark against listening to the counsel of "your advisers and your embassy here," wagging a knowing finger at me.

For months to come, Bill Clark would recount that never in "twenty years at the bar or in bar rooms have I encountered anything like the two Bothas." By stepping over the line, they forced him to draw one. While I might have drawn it somewhere else, they ran into the reality that even Reagan's closest friend would go only so far. The U.S.-South African relationship would be a reciprocal one, based on the regional equation we had defined. By abusing Clark's decency, they eroded their standing in his eyes. By trying to split the U.S. team, they drove it closer together. By trying to choose which U.S. officials they would deal with, the South Africans perversely strengthened my own standing. Soon, I became their principal American channel and interlocutor. No U.S. official higher ranking than me visited South Africa for the next eight years— none, that is, except Bill Casey, the Director of Central Intelligence.

Getting Control

Shortly after my return to Washington in mid-June, I remarked to a congressional committee that we had no intention of letting our credibility "be frittered away in a diplomatic charade." The South African government read this correctly as an encrypted signal that we had some lingering doubts about its seriousness, and it began to encourage us to launch the negotiating track. In other parts of Africa, my comments were misinterpreted as implying a desire to drop the Namibia issue altogether so that we could pursue a "normal" relationship with Pretoria. The British and other allies worried that we would unilaterally announce our conclusions from the Clark mission without consultations.

We were somewhat handicapped in explaining ourselves. Until Haig and Clark returned from extended overseas travel, we had no chance to put our heads together and figure out what to do next! Clark prevented any substantive briefing of the Contact Group or the African Front Line States pending his own report to Haig and Reagan. By late June, Canadian Prime minister Trudeau was complaining publicly in London about our stonewalling. On July 2, Haig wrote his allied counterparts to report that the South Africans had become somewhat more flexible on key aspects of the Resolution 435 framework. At the same time, the continuing "ambiguities" in Pretoria's position required him to write Pik Botha to nail down a clear and reasonable formula. He appealed for a bit more patience before holding a full-blown Contact Group consultation.

But privately, Haig was disappointed with Clark's report. There was still no firm basis on which to proceed. On July 5, Haig dispatched a courier to Pik Botha bearing a four-page letter summarizing the position and proposing a specific game plan for taking the negotiation forward. Our courier picked up Botha's reply on July 8. These two letters, as refined in September 1981, would constitute the core of the U.S.-South African "understanding" that enabled Western diplomacy in Southern Africa to proceed.

Haig opened by restating the case for a pro-active settlement strategy as the best way to maintain Western unity in the region and block further Communist exploitation of regional conflicts. It had become urgent, Haig argued, to have a credible, coherent plan to lay before the allies when the annual G-7 Economic Summit convened in Ottawa in a few weeks' time. Accordingly, he urged South African agreement to certain proposals which would become a "basis of understanding." Haig summarized where we stood: we would develop constitutional principles, drop formal guarantees, and leave Walvis Bay aside. He pocketed the South African concession on UNTAG—noting pointedly that we would assume that all transitional arrangements negotiated previously remained "intact," apart from the need to reach consensus on the size, composition, and deployment of the UNTAG military element. On Cuban troop withdrawal, Haig reiterated its central importance to both our countries. But he took issue with the wording given to Clark in Windhoek, which could be interpreted to mean that Cuban withdrawal must not only be negotiated but actually *carried out* before a Namibia settlement could be implemented. None of our allied or African partners could accept this, and we concurred with them.

Haig then outlined a three-phased approach to the negotiating process: in phase one, to last three to four months, the Contact Group would undertake to obtain agreement between South Africa and the Front Line States on constitutional principles (the myriad Namibian parties would be consulted but not asked to sign); phase two would commence once phase one had been completed and would serve to refine the complex

UNTAG arrangements; phase three should begin (after these Namibia issues were resolved, hopefully around March 1982) with Pretoria's providing a "date certain" for the start of implementation of Resolution 435 (sometime before the end of 1982). The United States would make use of this to obtain from the Angolans a specific commitment to a schedule for Cuban withdrawal "coordinated" with UNTAG's arrival and the SADF's departure from Namibia.

The Cubans would leave Angola, and Namibia would become independent, during phase three. To retain flexibility, we said nothing specific about the length of phase three or the exact nature of the timing link between Cuban withdrawals and the various components of the U.N. Plan in Namibia (including SADF withdrawals and elections). The three phases would be sequential, to protect everyone; the target dates would give the plan a tangible appeal for the other parties. The U.S. commitment to achieving all parts of the settlement was clear, and we needed a South African assurance that we could proceed in mutual confidence.

After consulting his prime minister, Botha accepted Haig's proposal as a basis of understanding, subject to a few, fairly concrete explanations and conditions. His reply underscored for the record that South African acceptance of a reduced and renegotiated UNTAG was the direct result of Clark's offer of a U.S. "commitment" to secure Cuban withdrawal. He seemed to recognize that this withdrawal would be part of, not a precondition to, phase three. In addition, Botha underscored once again Pretoria's insistence on the principle of U.N. "impartiality" as between the internal political parties and SWAPO, thereby telling us that this question would require further discussion. Once again, Botha raised a quibble about Walvis Bay. But it was an afterthought. So, too, was Botha's far-fetched suggestion that a truly free election in Namibia would not be possible unless UNITA had by that time achieved a "legitimate" role in Angolan politics.

At last, we could go back to our allies, and soon thereafter, we hoped, the African Front Line States. The South Africans had taken the juicy Cuban bait we offered, and appeared to accept our version of the Namibia portion of the deal. On July 19, Haig presented the gist of the understanding to our Contact Group allies in Ottawa, noting that there were important tactical issues to consider. Should we reveal the categorical Cuban link now, or wait until the completion of phases one and two? It would obviously be preferable to deal openly, but how would the Soviets react if we gave them the opportunity to shoot the package down before we could get our new process off the ground? Haig preferred to hold off on this decision until he had broached the matter with Andrei

Gromyko, his Soviet counterpart, in New York in September. The ministers would meet again that month: if things went well, we would launch our official Contact Group initiative in October with phase one proposals and, separately, approach the Angolan (MPLA) government in Luanda.

But the allies were extremely uneasy about the scenario they now faced. In mid-June, at the annual summit of the Organization of African Unity in Nairobi, a series of anti-Western resolutions accused us of a multitude of sins. The Africans' apparent loss of confidence in the process had been fueled by the prolonged delay, Soviet-Cuban propaganda, the distribution in Africa of sensitive documents that had been purloined from the African bureau, the evident anxieties of the allies themselves, and the bullish editorials emanating from the South African Broadcasting Corporation. Despite the best efforts of our diplomats in African capitals, conspiracy theory had become a growth industry, and our allies were feeling the heat.

This was the backdrop for our Ottawa meetings on July 19–21. There was a sharp intake of breath when Haig declared categorically that we could not obtain South African cooperation without a clear understanding on Angola. The South Africans would not leave Namibia without it; nor would we press them for a Namibia settlement in the absence of movement on Cuban withdrawal. A mournful Haus-Dietrich Genscher noted that this was a major change in the U.S. position; the allies had always supported a Cuban departure, but he feared that a linked condition would assure failure. French Foreign Minister Claude Cheysson wanted the Angolan track to be deniable, invisible, unmentionable in public, and certainly not an official agenda item of the Group. That said, he agreed that a good Namibia blueprint would create African pressures on Castro to pull out his troops. Mark MacGuigan, the Canadian, found our report and our position to be startling. Peter Carrington was equally taken aback, if less surprised, by Haig's vehemence. What could he tell Parliament about an Angolan precondition?

While they supported the goal, none of our partners could support an explicit, official Contact Group condition. Haig did not insist on direct, rigid conditionality; rather, there was an "empirical relationship" between Namibia and Angola. Washington could not go forward if the Group was going to split on this issue later, leaving the United States exposed. At a minimum, each ally should act, as appropriate, on the basis of a collective judgment that we should get the Cubans to leave Angola; and each should find ways to communicate that view to the Soviets, Cubans, and Angolans. Eventually, we reached a vague consensus that each would offer support on individual basis for the U.S. lead on Angola, and the Group would quietly discuss it.

Haig informed Pik Botha on July 20 that the Contact Group as such could not endorse the direct linkage of Namibia and Angola as integral elements of a single, phased plan. Our partners supported the goal of Cuban withdrawal from Angola, but viewed it as a separate endeavor, to be pursued in tandem with the phased approach on Namibia. The U.S. position supporting direct linkage would not change. Haig wanted to reassure the South African government while also warning it against actions or statements that would draw attention to allied differences on the principle of the linkage. It would also alert Botha that the Contact Group would not be a party to our understandings with South Africa relative to Angola.

Perhaps our message was too cryptic to be properly received. We may have underestimated the risks of upsetting the uncertain chemistry within the Botha government. Whatever the explanation, we received a reply from Botha on July 29 that further confused the issue. He interpreted Haig to be diluting the assurances previously offered, and then inaccurately described our understanding as calling for Cubans to have left, or be leaving, Angola by the time phase three *commenced*. Warming to the subject, Botha added that peace and fair elections were impossible as long as Cubans or "other hostile forces" remained in Angola.

Botha's letter was trouble, but we were unlikely to resolve the problem with a technical exegesis spelled out in further letters. The South Africans were not necessarily displeased to see us torn in multiple directions; some of them may still have hoped to split us definitively from the black Africans and our anxious allies. The latter had one especially well-founded concern. If we sought to formalize a Cuban condition for implementing an already approved U.N. settlement plan, we would be offering up a fat target in the United Nations. Efforts to amend or modify the existing U.N. Plan would be vetoed by Moscow unless the African states were strongly united in support of it. This was unlikely: the Angolans themselves could block consensus, and they were subject to massive Soviet and Cuban pressures. For these reasons, it made little sense to seek "official" linkage, at least at this early stage.

The next seven weeks were chaotic. At Ottawa, we had produced, at best, an ambiguous consensus. A joint Contact Group communiqué spoke hopefully of developing proposals to "complement and strengthen" Resolution 435 and provide the "confidence necessary" for all parties to settle. Contact Group "experts" (code for my counterparts and I) would meet in Paris on July 30–31, and ministers would meet again in New York in September. But Haig was angered by reports he received of an August 4 meeting between the British, French, German, and U.S. "political directors" (Lawrence Eagleburger, Under Secretary for Political

Affairs, led our side). The allies were distancing themselves from our Angolan agenda. Haig wrote his counterparts on August 7 to say that, until this was sorted out, the United States would not approve further Group meetings or the dispatch to Pretoria of a joint message seeking Pretoria's confirmation of the Namibia aspects of the package. To Haig, a continued stalemate on Namibia was less dangerous than allied disunity down the road. If we failed to reach agreement, we would all have a lot of explaining to do with our public opinion.

"Operation Protea"

Dozens of ministerial letters flew back and forth among the five capitals during August of 1981. Botha's unhelpful letter remained unanswered. As if to aggravate our difficulties, the South Africans mounted a major anti-SWAPO raid from Namibian bases into Angola on August 23. Code-named "Operation Protea" (after the national flower), the SADF action was aimed, like others before it, at destroying the bases and disrupting the infiltration routes used by SWAPO for its own periodic incursions into northern Namibia. But this action was on a larger scale (4,000 to 5,000 men) than before, and its timing did not help. From the outset, Haig ordered that we would respond to the SADF incursion "in context," calling for an immediate withdrawal, while also pointing to the fact of Angolan support for SWAPO's violence in Namibia.

In late August, Haig briefed his allied counterparts on a telephone exchange with Pik Botha urging a speedy pull-out. But there was no way to avoid an open split in New York: on August 31, we vetoed a Security Council measure condemning the raid, while the French voted in favor and the British abstained. Our public statements supported an immediate withdrawal, but not a onesided condemnation. Three days later, the General Assembly began a previously scheduled "special session" on Namibia, an event which rapidly descended into anti-American and pro-SWAPO feeding frenzy. Operation Protea ended on September 5.

These were not comfortable times for those of us trying to conduct an ambitious African strategy. It was a classic illustration of the tension between "globalists" and "regionalists." Haig wanted the Soviets and their surrogates to know that this was a new era. We did not intend that pro-Western states like South Africa would be written off as fair game for Moscow, Havana, Luanda, and their SWAPO guerrilla allies. The American veto would send a message. I had no problem with the point about Communist-backed violence. It was about time that Moscow's free ride in Africa came to an end. In fact, the need for a reciprocal framework of regional security was an essential plank in our whole campaign. But the dangers to U.S. standing in Africa and the threat to allied cohesion were also important. And, we had to be careful about the signals we were sending to Pretoria, as well as Moscow and Havana.

The reality of "Protea" and its aftermath is not easy to weigh. It is likely that the Soviets derived comfort from American isolation in New York, but they lost several men and their allies lost considerable equipment in these events. "Protea" was the start of a pattern that would gradually pressure Moscow and Havana to respond to South Africa's escalatory behavior in southern Angola. This response, in turn, would lead directly to the Soviet-Angolan military fiascos of 1985, 1987, and 1990.

Politically, "Protea" compounded the suspicion and paranoia we encountered in neighboring African countries whose governments would point to our U.N. veto as Exhibit A in their charge that the United States supported South Africa's regional policy—precisely the impression which short-sighted South African officials and Soviet diplomats both relished.

I thought a lot about South African motives at various points during the 1980s. This particular military operation had a tangible *military* rationale. Operation Protea severely disrupted SWAPO's position for a period of time, and pointed the way to a rolling series of such operations. They kept SWAPO off guard and enabled the South Africans to build a "salient" in Angola's Cunene Province which would become a free-fire zone for their anti-SWAPO units. During "Protea," the SADF captured large quantities of Soviet hardware and took out the Cuban-Angolan air defense facilities in such key towns as Cahama and Chibemba. There was heavy ground action at Xangongo and Ngiva as well; the SADF claimed to have inflicted severe casualties on SWAPO and Angolan forces (which were warned to get out of harm's way). But the SADF suffered ten killed and many wounded on their side—indicating that these were serious encounters with specific military objectives.

Agreement in Zurich

The Botha government also relished the *political* effect of taking strong action in August 1981 and experiencing a measure of U.S. understanding for that decision. Exploiting and testing the new signals from Washington was part and parcel of its pariah-politik. Perhaps, too, some South African decisionmakers hoped that their bloody strike into Cunene would force Washington to abandon its embryonic approach.

If so, they miscalculated. Haig relented on the "freeze" in a September 2 letter which produced an audible sigh of relief in allied capitals. Contact Group experts developed an extensive set of constitutional proposals during meetings held September 14–16. There was broad agreement on the Namibian agenda. As we approached the key ministerial meeting on the 24th, however, we realized that the gap in handling the Cuban linkage issue was not going to disappear. We could try to keep the Group formally in the center of all our efforts. But we Americans would have to play a non-stop dual role: as a Group member, and working solo on all aspects of the peace process.

A perfect example occurred as we sought to formalize the Group's reengagement in diplomacy by means of an exchange of letters between the Group itself and the South Africans. Its purpose was to elicit a South African confirmation of the phased approach on Namibia, identifying specifically the outstanding issues (and making certain that all issues had now been so identified). We worked hard to shape that letter so that it would elicit the "right" answer. But this was not enough. We would also have to coach the South Africans bilaterally on how to respond to the letter they were about to receive from the Group. Besides, we had to deal with the serious problems raised by Pik Botha's July 29 letter.

In a September 11 reply, Haig reiterated the bilateral, U.S.-South African understanding and explained why Angola would not be included in the Group's letter. Second, he pushed Botha back on the timing of Cuban withdrawal. We could not agree to Botha's "Cubans first" sequencing. Instead, we would be seeking from the Angolans a specific Cuban withdrawal timetable coordinated with the rest of phase three, including the benchmarks contained within the Resolution 435 plan. The United States would insist on maintaining the necessary tactical flexibility to obtain a settlement that would serve the interests of both countries. Americans sent a lot of messages to the South Africans in the 1980s; none was more important than this one. We simply refused to allow the South Africans to define the content of our linkage formula. That is what the negotiation would be all about.

Within hours of receiving these two letters, Botha was on the phone to Haig, inviting himself to Washington to sort out what he described as the growing misunderstandings between us before they leaked. I warned Haig that he would be seeing Pik Botha twice a month if he acceded to such requests whenever Botha became anxious. Haig persuaded the minister to lower the profile of the exchange: he would send me to a discreet European location and Botha should send his trusted deputy, Brand Fourie, to meet me. Reluctantly, Botha agreed, but on September 16, an exhausted and somber Botha spent ninety minutes with our chargé d'affaires, Howard Walker, cataloguing a litany of woe. He had been beaten up in his party caucus over the question of Namibia. Haig would not see him. He could not explain the letters to his government; Washington should remember that "I am not the South African government." He claimed that Haig was shifting the ground under his feet on Cuban withdrawal, and now the Contact Group was asking Pretoria to confirm that Resolution 435 remained "intact." Botha could not defend all this; if Pretoria had to answer the mail today, the answer would be no.

Fourie and his team arrived in Zurich on September 20. He brought his two best Namibia people from the Department of Foreign Affairs— Rian Eksteen and Derek Auret—as well as Army Chief of Staff General Johannes ("Jannie") Geldenhuys, who had played an important role in the process during 1978–80. For two days, we ranged over the negotiating history, the question of phasing, the issue of where UNITA fit into U.S. and South African policy, and the meaning of the Contact Group's letter about Resolution 435 remaining "intact." We planted the idea that our teams should constitute a reliable channel for assessing this intricate and difficult process.

But the centerpiece of discussion was phase three: how would Cuban withdrawal be linked to South Africa's commitments and UNTAG's arrival in Namibia? I began with a categorical confirmation of the U.S. pledge: we would simply not go along with a Namibia settlement that did not include Cuban withdrawal. The issue was how to mesh the Namibia and Angola tracks together. For our part, we rejected a "Namibia first" approach under which the South African Defence Force would be obliged to leave Namibia before Cubans departed Angola. We would not take their departure "on faith." But we also rejected as impractical an "Angola first" approach: no one else would buy it. Instead, we needed a coordinated, parallel approach. The exact scenario would have to be negotiated, and an agreement reached, before the U.N. presence was established in Namibia.

We did not envisage a lockstep, troop-for-troop pull-out schedule. But it must provide for rough, "functional equivalence" in the processes of withdrawal. We were grappling with a regional security problem, not an arithmetical one. The scenario must have an agreed starting point, an agreed ending, and a clear pattern of reciprocal steps during implementation. I explained in detail our notion of leverage: realistic progress on the Namibia issues would help us to overcome resistance to our Angolan agenda. An agreed package based on linkage would, in turn, build inexorable pressure on the separate question of Angolan political reconciliation. UNITA would be the beneficiary, not the victim, of our scenario.

The Zurich encounter of September 20–21 was the culminating point in our effort to engage the South Africans. Pik Botha's mood was transformed when he wrote Haig on September 23 to accept our approach to the linkage concept. South Africa could be flexible if the other side did the same. He now saw prospects for an "equitable" solution. A parallel message accepting the phased Namibia-only approach was sent to the Contact Group. This enabled Haig and his allied counterparts to launch the Contact Group initiative on Namibia. A joint communiqué after their September 24 meeting announced that the Group would now begin discussions with the parties, and table its constitutional proposals and a timetable for dealing with "the other remaining issues." The objective of these "further and final" negotiations would be the implementation of Resolution 435 sometime in 1982.

Controlling Our Channels

We had engaged the South Africans. We had engaged our Contact Group partners, and would begin in a few weeks the process of engaging the African Front Line States. At the time, of course, we still had little idea of what lay ahead. The idea of a settlement in 1982 was an abstraction. We hoped and believed it could become real; perhaps, if we said it often enough, others would come to share our belief and act accordingly. But we had given ourselves plenty to do.

We knew that it would be critically important to maintain productive channels of communication with Botha and his colleagues. And it would be vital to keep control of those channels. The Zurich meeting established an effective channel of communication at my level, strengthening my ability to serve as the voice and implementing agent of U.S. policy. But I remained concerned, on this score, at the protracted delay in getting a new U.S. ambassador in place in Pretoria. The post was now vacant. Howard Walker had been doing a super job as chargé d'affaires, but we needed an ambassador in place, and it mattered very much that Reagan name the right person. I had proposed Herman Nickel for the post back in April. A staunch proponent of the brand of hardheaded realism Haig and I favored, this veteran foreign correspondent was a natural for the job. He knew the country well—so well, in fact, that he had been chucked out of South Africa back in 1962. He knew the meaning of racism as the son of a Jewish mother living in Germany during World War II, before emigrating to the United States. He knew the ropes—especially the ropes with which American conservatives and South African hardliners too often hung themselves in this troubled relationship. An independent and broad-gauge fellow, Nickel had served as *Time*'s bureau chief in Tokyo, London, and Bonn. Earlier in his career, he had done volunteer legal research for former Justice Thurgood Marshall during his tenure as director of the NAACP's Legal Defense Fund.

But, despite his evident qualifications, it was now almost October.

There were other political candidates for the Pretoria post. One of these was a lawyer serving concurrently as an undercover police officer who had been named Outstanding Reserve Officer of the Year (1979) by Daryl Gates, chief of the Los Angeles Police Department. His credentials for the post included having guest-piloted most of the combat aircraft of the South African and the former Rhodesian air forces. I worried that the White House staff might not share my view of the downsides of selecting such a person. To the general relief of the Africa team, Herman Nickel finally received his presidential phone call on December 6, 1981. After another four months of paperwork, background checks, and confirmation hearings, he was able to present his credentials in Pretoria in April 1982. It was a strange and wondrous process, but at least the saga came out right. The ambassadorial channel would report to Haig and me.

The Characters and Their Motives

Who were these masked men from Pretoria? What were they like and what made them tick? After three intensive days traveling with Judge Clark in June 1981, his mild-mannered secretary was overheard to remark that she had "had enough of those jive turkeys." I might have used stronger language on that particular day, but I had been dealing with them and studying their actions for some years. Pik Botha and I, for example, had appeared together on an American television debate shortly before he left his post as ambassador to Washington to become minister of foreign affairs in April 1977 (a post he still held fifteen years later). Botha's legendary dramatic talents and his capacity to hold forth extemporaneously—leaving interlocutors numb or struggling to get a word in edgewise—were not news.

Dealing with the top leadership of Africa's autocracies is an acquired taste, and the Nationalist Afrikaner officialdom of South Africa is nothing if not African. They knew how to tell distant visitors what they wish to hear, hoping that there would never come a time to account for it all. Like their cousins in neighboring African lands, many of them believe that the external world thinks—or at least ought to think—about them as major factors in the global scheme of things. Our failure to do so is one of America's many shortcomings!

The top men from Pretoria sometimes behaved as if the government and the country belonged to them. It was a strange mixture. One found people of considerable talent and high integrity in the senior ranks of the political and security establishment. But we also experienced the arbitrary quality that comes when power is personalized and accountable mainly to itself. The ethnic insecurity of the Nationalist Afrikaner had become strangely wedded to an arrogance that excluded all outsiders. Too often in the past, South Africa's foreign relations were about finding foreigners who agreed with you (or could be paid to do so) and shared your long enemies' list. In such circumstances, it descended to an ideological rather than an analytical or strategic endeavor.

But no composite set of generalizations could capture a group of individuals which was anything but monolithic. Their decisionmaking was neither consensual nor collegial. Rivalries raged, typically just out of sight of the prurient foreign diplomat. While a common front was normally presented to us, the personalities we dealt with certainly had their differences. Bureaucratic struggles formed an essential part of foreign policy reality, and we made it our business to try to know who was doing what to whom. We found that the personal views and ambitions of individual officials could be as important as the agency they represented.

By placing our settlement scenario before them, we hoped to pressure P. W. Botha and his government to make a considered, strategic choice. They could have a settlement which respected many of their interests—and a more constructive relationship with us in the process; or, they could continue to play games and play for time on their own. We succeeded in part: the commitment they made to Washington over the course of July to September 1981 gave us the leverage previously lacking in Western diplomatic efforts on Southern Africa. We obtained the means to get the other parties to address the underlying problems of regional security, including the Angolan question. We also obtained a set of standards by which to measure—and sometimes influence—future South African actions. They would have to justify their behavior in terms of a commitment made to the most powerful "friend" they had.

But our initiative did not, and could not, *unite* the competing baronies and personalities in Pretoria in support of carrying out that commitment—wholeheartedly and coherently. Nor could it force the Angolans of Luanda and their Communist patrons quickly to seize the opening we had now created for a settlement without losers. At best, therefore, we had forced Pretoria to an understanding whose execution the South Africans by themselves could not guarantee. This would aggravate their well-known proclivity toward making tactical decisions and avoiding strategic ones.

Third, our initiative could not convert P. W. Botha, the hardened political organizer and former defense minister, into an instant champion of honorable disengagement from the bush wars which he knew South Africa would never lose. Having presided over the buildup of the

SADF and the burgeoning ARMSCOR military-industrial complex which supported it, Botha saw himself as the Charles de Gaulle of the Afrikaners. A proud nationalist, he had helped to make South Africa militarily independent of the distant but meddlesome British and Americans. He had salvaged residual defense ties with the French and Italians, diversified to other sources of technology such as the Israelis, gone to the arms market for selected items when necessary, and—above all—built up a major, indigenous capability in the manufacture of military equipment.

Botha would modernize and reform and strengthen South Africa, from the top and from within. The commitment to reform was as genuine as the commitment to become an autonomous regional superpower capable of assuring the defense of South Africa's interests in Africa. Now, in 1981, Botha committed himself to cooperate with Washington on our regional agenda.

Why did the South Africans say yes, enabling us to launch our plan? Some South African officials viewed our new approach in purely tactical terms: it would shift Western pressure to the Angolans and their Communist backers and dilute outside pressure for an early, Namibia-only settlement. Some may have made the judgment that we were hopelessly naive about Soviet, Cuban, and Angolan behavior. Our approach would run into a wall of Communist opposition, which would eventually persuade us to put negotiations on hold and join forces with South Africa and UNITA. Angola, under this logic, would become an irresistible honeypot for American conservatives.

Another argument for a positive reply to Washington was the very fact that we were advertising the centrality of the regional peace process in the U.S.-South African relationship. P. W. Botha and his colleagues were never really comfortable with this highly focused conception. They sought a far closer and more extensive relationship based on joint "understandings" on a whole series of regional political and military issues. But Haig and I had turned aside in May 1981 Pik Botha's grandiose notions of a new strategic partnership. We made it clear that we wanted results from a reciprocal relationship—not "better relations" as an end in itself or, still less, a strategic alliance. While disappointed with the parameters we placed on our bilateral dealings, South African leaders could still see the merit of cooperation with the United States—if only in hopes of deflecting problems on the internal front, while shifting the onus for achieving peace to other parties.

The more thoughtful players on the South African team could calculate that the U.S. plan might eventually work, but it would take time. The SADF and UNITA would have a key role to play in wearing down resistance on the other side. Saying yes meant agreeing to a settlement

... later. Our Namibia proposals also had some attraction for those South Africans (and Namibians) who cared about the perceived shortcomings of the inherited U.N. Plan and liked the changes we would introduce.

Those South African officials who worried about the open-ended political and financial costs of Namibia and Angola saw our initiative as a possible means to extricate South Africa from these conflicts honorably. Indeed, the Cuban link was the *only* credible argument they had to force the issue of Namibia within their government. After all, if it worked, the U.S.-led drive for Cuban troop withdrawal from Angola would be a marvelous result. It represented the best case against the proponents of a crude "forward strategy" aimed at postponing indefinitely a Namibia settlement and keeping the "enemy" as far away from the Republic as possible. More broadly, linkage offered an effective counter to a certain brand of military thinking and to the weight of the SADF itself in decisionmaking. Linkage could put a leash on the extravagant imagination of the prime minister and like-minded allies. It provided a context for asking hard questions about South Africa's foreign policy and regional strategy.

Some combination of these motives explains our success in obtaining the commitment in principle we needed. Later, when South Africa itself emerged as a controversial matter in U.S. domestic politics, it became fashionable to criticize the administration's actions during the early 1980s in various fields. The implication was that Washington had somehow "paid" Pretoria for cooperation on Namibia by offering up a collection of "carrots" and gestures. As evidence, critics cited the fact that we revised at the margins certain export controls (related to government end users and technology licensing). Training in the field of search and rescue (a regular activity in the rugged seas off South Africa) was extended to the South Africans. A few air ambulances were exported to Pretoria. We permitted the appointment of honorary consuls in additional U.S. cities and returned defense attaché staffing back up to the level prevailing prior to several incidents in the late 1970s. We relaxed somewhat our visa restrictions on visitors from official and quasi-official bodies, and suggested expanded cooperation in certain technical fields such as meteorology and agronomy. In international forums, we stated our convictions on the two-sided nature of regional violence and the foolishness of punitive economic sanctions as an instrument for ending apartheid or South African rule in Namibia—vetoing resolutions we did not like. We supported an IMF loan to South Africa in 1982 on the financial merits of the application.

It was relatively easy for the gullible and the conspiracy-minded to leap to the conclusion that such steps were the "carrots" for South Africa's cooperation in Namibia. But those critics misconstrue the nature of our influence as well as our own motivation. Some of these steps made sense on their own merits, whether Namibia existed or not. Some of them hinted consciously at the shape of a more normal, bilateral relationship that might become possible *if* there was regional progress and steady movement away from apartheid. However, none represented credible "quids" for Namibia. There was nothing tangible—no concrete goodies or sweeteners—which we *could* offer the South Africans that could begin to approach the size and importance of their perceived stake in Namibia (and Angola) in 1981. That was the reality, and they knew it. Those observers seeking some "smoking gun" to explain the Botha government's commitment need have looked no further than to our linkage-based strategic initiative itself: The American commitment to Cuban troop withdrawal from Angola far outweighed any tangible gesture we considered making.

We should look for a moment at the circumstances facing specific players on P. W. Botha's team in 1981. Pik Botha and his diplomatic colleagues found themselves in an interesting and ironic position. Botha himself had had a fast-track career, gaining the post of foreign minister at age forty-five in 1977. A champion high school debater, he entered the diplomatic service in 1953 after completing a law degree at the University of Pretoria. His assignments included tours as a member of the South African legal team in two South West Africa (Namibia) cases before the International Court of Justice (1963–66 and 1970–71). Botha's elevation to minister came in the immediate aftermath of the Angola fiasco of 1975–76; the SADF had pulled out of this entanglement with bruised public standing. By entering the prime ministerial sweepstakes in 1978, he took votes away from a front runner, Connie Mulder, thus giving the job to P. W. Botha. The change at the top had been occasioned by John Vorster's resignation over the so-called "Infogate" scandal in which the Department of Information and the Bureau of State Security (civilian intelligence) had covertly cooperated to purchase friends, newspapers, and influence abroad.

By 1981, Pik Botha was not quite fifty (about ten years older than I was). He had seen the rival Information and State Security bureaucracies discredited or neutralized (Information was added to his own portfolio in 1980). Mulder and the powerful State Security chief, General Hendrik van den Bergh, were no longer in the picture. State Security was renamed the National Intelligence Service, and it was headed by a thirty-year-old political scientist from the University of Potchefstroom, Lucas Daniel (Niel) Barnard, who was Botha's surprise nominee for the post in 1980. Barnard, in turn, was a protege of Orange Free State Party boss (and State Vice-President) Alwyn Schlebusch—one of the key men whose support had given P. W. Botha the premiership in 1978. In late 1980, two years after becoming prime minister, P. W. Botha handed his defense portfolio to his trusted associate, General Magnus Malan, a fifty-one-year-old career soldier then serving as SADF chief of staff.

All in all, one might have supposed that Pik Botha had a strong hand to play. Several rival agencies had new, untested leaders. No one in South African public life could rival his grasp of the international political scene, particularly the Namibia-Angola tangle and relations with Western nations. His extroverted manner and bombastic oratorical skills made him a striking and respected figure. Perhaps the most popular white politician in South Africa in the 1980s, Pik Botha was the man his party turned to when it faced a close by-election.

In addition, Botha had seasoned talent at his side in the Department of Foreign Affairs: his own former boss, Brand Fourie, a man of sixty-five who had held the top career position since 1966. Fourie had seen nearly twenty years' service in Europe and New York, and he had advised General Jan Smuts on the drafting of the U.N. Charter. An understated and gentle person, with a keen tactical mind and a calm personal manner, Fourie was the perfect foil for his mercurial minister. With their able, younger associates such as Neil van Heerden (serving in Bonn in the early 1980s), Sean Cleary (serving in Washington), Rian Eksteen and Derek Auret (the planning staff), Botha and Fourie could assemble a strong team.

Despite these advantages, their position was weaker than it looked. Pik Botha and his team saw the merit of our design, but they would need a lot of help persuading Prime Minister Botha and his inner entourage of advisers and staffers drawn from the security forces. They had international experience and analytical talent. But Pik Botha and his team lacked their own sources of intelligence and reporting from neighboring countries, and faced rival agencies which were in a position to cook the books seen by the cabinet. Pik Botha found it hard to counter something with nothing. It would be necessary for the foreign minister to coopt and engage the other players in his government. We often remembered his words to our chargé d'affaires: "I am not the South African government." After the key Zurich meeting in September 1981, we would meet Pik Botha (or Fourie) accompanied by an interagency team that typically included Malan and Barnard with several of their colleagues, as well as the Administrator-General of South West Africa (Namibia), Pretoria's ranking civilian official in Windhoek.

We came to know some of these so-called "securocrats" over the ensuing years. Despite the label, they, too, had little in common with each other. Malan said little, but appeared to enjoy the role of co-leader of delegation which Pik Botha gave him. The son of a professor of biochemistry, Malan valued credentials and was proud of his own formal military training, especially his attendance at the regular Command and General Staff Officers' Course in the United States in 1962–63. He rose steadily toward the top and then soared to the chief of defense staff position during his close association with P. W. Botha in the 1970s. A newcomer to politics, he first ran for a parliamentary seat in 1981. Malan was a reliable barometer of P. W. Botha's moods—including a strong attachment to the SADF's Angola role—though he was a more pleasant personality. We seldom learned much from him that had not been pre-rehearsed for his Mutt and Jeff act with Pik Botha.

Barnard, almost twenty years younger than Malan and Botha, did not presume to equate himself with them as the mere director-general (not minister or M.P.) of the National Intelligence Service. Barnard said little in plenary meetings. At the beginning, he was extremely reserved, even cold, toward my team. This may, in part, have been due to my role in discouraging his research in the United States in matters relating to nuclear technology acquisition while I was still at Georgetown University! We also worried that he might harbor a particular animus toward us, being a native-born Southwester (Namibian) from Otjiwarongo.

A young professor of international politics turned superspy, Barnard cultivated an image of inscrutability. Once he refused to identify the name of a local cheese being served at a state function—giving rise to hilarity in the U.S. delegation about the discovery of the National Intelligence Service's new "secret cheese." But we learned, over time, to respect Barnard, finding him to be a far more frank and forthright proponent of top-level hopes and fears than most of his colleagues. As the youngest top-level player on the South African team—heading an agency badly damaged by previous scandals—Barnard had a difficult assignment. Like other nationalist Afrikaners of his generation, he found the 1980s to be a crucible. We knew that he saw more merit in our agenda than he could openly acknowledge.

One of the least constructive characters we faced was Malan's chief of staff for military intelligence, Lieutenant General Pieter Willem van der Westhuizen. This was the fellow who had visited Washington without authorization in March 1981. An expert briefer, with a slick manner of stacking the deck, he traveled constantly to ply his trade across Africa, Europe, and the Americas. But he also made many of our negotiating rounds; eventually, we came to view those sessions he attended as unsafe for candid discourse. As the officer in charge of the SADF's undeclared wars and forays in neighboring countries, the forty-five-year-old van der Westhuizen doubled as the boss of the intelligence service nearest to P. W. Botha's heart. A prominent British businessman once compared Southern Africa to a vast warehouse with its share of rats seeking to steal the goods. Continuing the analogy, he noted that anyone in charge of warehouse needs a "ratcatcher." Van der Westhuizen was P. W. Botha's ratcatcher. The name caught on with the U.S. team.

It was in the Zurich airport that I first encountered another lieutenant general who became a core member of the South African negotiating team. Army Chief of Staff Johannes Jacobus Geldenhuys was waiting for his gear at the baggage carousel next to mine. He did not look much like a senior soldier; he looked like the sort of man who valued his privacy and disliked dressing up for formal events. It was not surprising to learn later that he had published poetry and children's stories. Geldenhuys said little in our plenary meetings; in private conversation, he was direct and unpretentious. At forty-six, he had risen through some of the toughest line commands in the SADF, including service in Namibia (and Angola as pre-independence defense attaché) for long periods. Geldenhuys knew Resolution 435 backwards and forwards, and had worked effectively with U.N. officials and the Angolans during the late 1970s. A soldier's soldier, Geldenhuys had been burned by politicians more than once, and he was wary. He also had the disconcerting habit of doing crossword puzzles or falling asleep during Pik Botha's windier monologues. But he supported the peace process. He knew from the start in 1981 that a good settlement might be possible if the politicians supported it. He would be proven correct.

5

The Contact Group Engages the Africans, 1981–82

During 1981–82, the Front Line States and our allies in the Contact Group became indispensable negotiating partners. Without them, we could never have completed the Namibia track of our linkage-based settlement. But the work was both intricate and cumbersome. It required what seemed like endless coordination with four NATO allies (Britain, Canada, France, and Germany) to mediate as a group between Pretoria and the six African Front Line nations (Angola, Botswana, Mozambique, Tanzania, Zambia, and Zimbabwe). To further complicate the scene, the Contact Group sought to maintain a balanced dialogue with both SWAPO and the forty-odd Namibian internal parties. The Front Line States served as the ally, patron, and adviser to SWAPO, while the South Africans enjoyed parallel links with some of the internal parties.

One almost needed a license to operate this unwieldy diplomatic contraption. It also helped to have a tolerance for the elaborate procedural minuets of multilateral diplomacy. If bilateral negotiation with the South Africans resembled a rugby scrum, this operation bore a closer likeness to diplomatic needlepoint. After sitting through a two-hour Canadian-chaired session drafting "oral talking points" for delivery by the Group's ambassadors in six African capitals, a colleague scribbled me a note saying, "If Haig knew what we are doing, you'd get fired."

Over the years since its formation in 1977, the Group had developed its own procedures, rituals, and an arcane theology. Often, it seemed that the medium of this Western-African diplomatic machinery was its only message. The emphasis was on process: parties spent long hours receiving, digesting, analyzing, drafting, coordinating, transmitting, and delivering rather formalistic messages. Everyone knew that the Group did not operate by majority voting. But the very nature of the context and the parties called for that conspicuous egalitarianism at which we Americans sometimes excel.

Yet, for all its seeming awkwardness, the Contact Group–Front Line State machinery could be made to work. Like mirror images, the African states were able to "deliver" SWAPO when the Contact Group demonstrated that it could "deliver" Pretoria. Generally speaking, it was understood that proposals came from the Group, e.g., the Western settlement proposal of April 1978, incorporated by reference in UNSC Resolution 435. The Front Line role was not only one of supporting, advising, and "delivering" SWAPO. They also buffered our diplomacy from the unhelpful interference of Soviet, Cuban, and radical non-aligned states whose motive was to poison the U.N. climate and discredit Western policy. The adoption of Resolution 435 in 1978 was itself due in part to the credibility and firmness of the Front Line States, which had prevailed over other voices in the United Nations. But their willingness to play such a role hinged on (a) their strong desire for a settlement, and (b) their perception of Western skill and determination in obtaining one.

Launching the New Strategy

It was not until October 1981 that we were in a position to table fresh proposals and launch our first official Contact Group mission of the restructured negotiation. The previous nine months had been consumed by internal policy reviews, followed by the protracted effort from May through September to reengage the South Africans. The resulting understandings saved Resolution 435 from permanent oblivion and laid the basis for completing the Namibia track on schedule the following year. This process had also engendered numerous, difficult debates within the Group, as our allies found themselves caught between their need for American leadership and their anxiety over the way we went about it.

No one opposed the goal of linkage-based settlement, but the Europeans and Canadians sought to avoid official, collective responsibility for introducing and defending the link. We argued that we could not proceed without allied support—i.e., no linkage, no U.S. leadership of the exercise. Allied reactions ranged from jaded realism ("Are you sure Pretoria is on board?") to resentment at our insistence on the revised basis for settlement ("We've never linked these things before"). We were accused of inadequately consulting our allies; we accused them of other diplomatic shortcomings.

By the end of September, this standoff was resolved. The Western Five, as the Group was sometimes known, agreed to proceed with the three-phased approach; all of them knew that there would be no phase three unless the Namibia and Angola tracks linked up at the end of phase two. We were back in business on the basis of U.S. concepts, but *de facto* Western unity would be accompanied by formal, official disunity on linkage. This messy outcome delighted East Bloc legal experts, and their cohorts in Africa and the West would debate the "legalities" of linkage long after it was an established fact of life. But it was a mutually acceptable outcome. We had our strategy and indispensable allied support on the Namibia track. The allies had their purity, some autonomy, and U.S. involvement in a restored peace process. It would now be much more difficult for anyone to block or escape from our new diplomacy.

Having crossed these hurdles, the Group was ready in October to mount a senior-level mission to all six Front Line capitals, South Africa, and Namibia in order to present the three-phased approach. The goal of phase one was to develop a set of democratic constitutional principles acceptable to all Namibian political parties. Achieving a broad consensus on constitutional principles would fill a key gap in the U.N. Plan, which had said little about constitutional matters or the workings of Namibia's proposed constituent assembly. They would serve as a confidence-building measure for Namibian parties fearful of eventual SWAPO rule, and could provide cover for Pretoria in its often-strained relations with them. We used the October mission to table a set of principles drafted by the Group's experts.

During the mission, everyone was on best behavior concerning the delicate linkage issue. Contact Group emissaries spoke circumloquaciously about how "progress toward regional peace could facilitate" South African decisions on Namibia. Front Line officials smiled politely and then turned to U.S. representatives for a translation. We predicted that progress on the "separate" Cuban issue would make a "decisive difference" in Pretoria. South African officials had the grace not to probe allied cohesion on the matter. In the privacy of bilateral conversation with African leaders, we described the link as both an essential South African requirement and the key to a settlement. They were equally blunt, warning us of South Africa's skill at devising excuses for not decolonizing Namibia, and sharing their concern that the Angolan regime was too weak and divided to part with the Cubans, especially in the face of recurrent SADF strikes into Angola. We stressed our commitment to both tracks of our strategy, making clear that it would remove the SADF threat to Angola. Such exchanges were to continue for years to come. A careful listener realized that we were hearing a message less of "principled" hostility than of pragmatic doubt that we could pull it off.

The October 1981 mission to Southern Africa was successful in its immediate objectives. All parties asked detailed questions about phasing. They acknowledged the merits of resolving one set of issues before moving onto the next, but settling nothing until everything was assembled in an agreed package. The parties promised us early reactions to the draft constitutional principles, and appeared to understand that the Cuban issue would be handled by the United States in separate, bilateral contacts.

By the conclusion of the mission, our eleven governmental partners may still have entertained doubts that we Americans knew what we were doing. But they were beginning to see firsthand that we could be both versatile and tough: in a matter of months, we had mastered this intricate Western-African mating dance; changed the regional negotiating structure without abandoning its key pillar; learned to work all sides of the street in a rough and polarized neighborhood; and maintained a difficult but essential balance in our posture toward cross-border violence.

Links, Leverage, and Phases

The Contact Group mechanism had begun to work. Virtually all "Namibia-track" issues were resolved between the October 1981 mission and the Group's joint communiqué to that effect on October 1, 1982. At the time, however, this progress was obscured by ambiguity and unavoidable confusion about the status of the linkage. The Angolans had publicly rejected the concept of linkage soon after they heard about it in 1981; the Front Line States, Soviets, Cubans, and others supported that position. Yet Angolan policy was itself based on linkage of the "Namibia first" variety. More important, the MPLA's rejection coincided with its own increasingly active engagement with Washington, starting in early 1982, focused on the U.S. settlement proposals. The Angolan two-track policy confused its African allies as well as the Western media, creating openings for detractors of U.S. diplomacy to stir up sterile debate.

At the same time, the reluctance of our partners to acknowledge publicly this reality greatly complicated our position. To avoid isolation on the matter, and also to facilitate what the Angolans were, in fact, doing, we avoided using terms like "precondition" (which has no place in diplomacy) to describe the linkage. Further, we believed that only by resolving all the items on the Namibia track would we acquire the credibility and leverage to press Luanda and its allies to take the big decisions on Angola. Until that moment came, the less stridently we discussed "linkage," the better. Another reason for publicly soft-pedaling the link back in 1982 was to camouflage its origins. No purpose could be served by our official confirmation that either Washington or Pretoria had come up with the linkage formula; instead, it "evolved" from our discussions with the South Africans on a settlement.

The result of all this was a lengthy string of official euphemisms to describe reality: a settlement would require *"de facto* parallelism" or "parallel movement"; "progress on one track will contribute to progress on the other"; the choicest was Secretary of State Haig's call for "empirical simultaneity." Such obfuscation was unavoidable. But it contributed to an atmosphere of innuendo in which our critics accused us of all kinds of sins: abandoning our principles, changing our minds, blocking a settlement, or buying time for South Africa.

To get beyond this turbulence, our best recourse was to clarify matters by resolving all the Namibia issues as quickly as possible. Here, too, there was a problem in that most of the items under discussion were on the agenda because Pretoria remained dissatisfied with aspects of the U.N. Plan (Resolution 435). A cloud of anxiety and hypersensitivity settled over us as we discussed how hard we should press and in how much detail for steps that would be seen as FLS / SWAPO concessions to the demands of Pretoria or the internal parties. Sometimes, this sort of thinking got out of hand: there was a ludicrous debate within our Group over whether it was "fair" to insist upon democratic checks and balances in Namibia's future constitution. We snapped ourselves out of such thoughts with the reminder that it was our obligation to do better in democratic institution building than had been done elsewhere in the region.

In December 1981, the Group received generally workable responses to its draft principles, and submitted a revised draft to the parties. The key constitutional issues were falling into place: an entrenched bill of rights, periodic elections under a secret ballot, an independent judiciary, a representative and balanced public service, and—of especial importance—a required two-thirds majority in the constituent assembly for adoption of the constitution. These items conformed to standard Western and international norms, and contrasted sharply with South Africa's existing arrangements in Namibia, such as racially and ethnically defined "second-tier" authorities.

Except for the Ovambo people, who constitute over 50 percent of Namibians and the main base of SWAPO support, Namibia is a land of black, mixed-race, and white minorities. The Contact Group attempted to assure these minorities some minimum degree of representation in the constituent assembly. We proposed that half its seats be filled by members from single-member districts and the other half by members chosen from party lists under a proportional representation system. Each voter would cast two votes. Derived from the West German constitution, this proposal was accepted by the South Africans. They believed that it could offer significant protection to minorities, or, at the least, that it could be so described to domestic and Namibian opponents of a settlement. South Africa's enthusiasm for the concept of "one man, two votes" was its kiss of death. The proposed electoral system prompted loud protests from SWAPO and other states and organizations no better acquainted than the South Africans with the fine points of democratic theory.

A protracted snarl ensued over the Namibian electoral system. It was alleged by SWAPO that "one man, two votes" was "an imperialist plot," a system too complicated for Namibian peasants (an odd charge coming from African freedom fighters). We offered another variant in April 1982: only one vote would be cast, but it would be counted twice, once for each set of seats. This model fared no better. Initially embarrassed by SWAPO's performance on the issue, the FLS found themselves unable to sell our constitutional Edsel to SWAPO. The Africans were dragged along by what had become an East-West test of wills, in which the Soviet diplomatic apparatus had become heavily engaged. By May, the FLS had endorsed not only SWAPO's rejection of "one vote counted twice" but also SWAPO's call for terminating the entire Contact Group approach and placing all issues on the agenda of a U.N. conference. This, of course, would have been the surest way to kill off the negotiations—Moscow's real aim. We ignored the suggestion.

Meanwhile, as early as November 1981, the Group had begun developing proposals for phase two issues: the South African demand for demonstrated U.N. "impartiality" as between Namibia's political parties during the transition to independence; and South African concerns relating to the size, composition, and deployment of the U.N. Transition Assistance Group (UNTAG), the U.N. civilian and military personnel who would supervise the transition process. These questions had a long and painful negotiating history; their resolution looked to be far more complex than the constitutional principles. Debates about UNTAG's size and role had thrown the peace process off the rails during the 1978–80 period. Solutions would have to walk a very fine line to gain the support of the parties who (correctly) saw UNTAG as defining the security environment during the Namibian transition period.

The South Africans were of two minds about UNTAG. On military grounds, they argued that it would have to perform extensive border surveillance to prevent SWAPO infiltration from Angola and Zambia. This role, taken literally, could require far more than the upper limit of 7,500 troops authorized in 1978 for UNTAG's military component. On political grounds, as we have seen, Pretoria argued for the smallest possible U.N. military component. Its negative attitude toward "blue helmets" was shaped by the U.N. General Assembly's endorsement of SWAPO as the "sole and authentic representative" of the Namibian people, and by the United Nation's ongoing provision of extensive diplomatic, financial, and propaganda support for SWAPO. By early 1982, South Africa's "no blue helmets" line had moderated only marginally: small numbers of U.N. troops could be deployed away from major towns where their imagery as the "ally" of SWAPO might sway Namibian voters.

By contrast, the Front Line States and SWAPO saw the equation in reverse. They wanted a large UNTAG military force, deployed not on the northern border but concentrated wherever the SADF or the Namibian police (SWAPOL) and territorial forces (SWATF) had the potential to misbehave. UNTAG, in the eyes of SWAPO and the Front Line States, was the primary guarantee that a climate would be established conducive to the holding of a "free and fair" election. UNTAG was also the main compensation in political and security terms for the hard fact that South Africa would remain the administering power in Namibia throughout the transition to independence.

There were other outstanding issues to deal with. In 1979, the Angolans had proposed that a demilitarized zone be established along both sides of the Namibia-Angola border. This proposal was designed in part to meet Pretoria's concern about border surveillance, and also in response to its demand that SWAPO bases in Angola and Zambia be monitored by the United Nations. Since UNTAG would monitor the SADF's confinement to two bases in Namibia during the transition, the South Africans wanted the same principle applied to SWAPO. These security questions had to be resolved one way or the other.

Finally, there was ambiguity about the question of the so-called "ethnic forces." These South African-controlled local battalions had grown steadily since 1978 and had recently been reorganized as the South West Africa Territorial Force (SWATF). This raised the question of whether the 1978 provisions for the "ethnic forces"—demobilization and disbandment of command structures—would apply to the Territorial Force. The U.N. Plan contained a delicate balance, effectively disarming both SWAPO's army (the People's Liberation Army of Namibia) and the former "ethnic forces." Any change would directly affect that balance. It could also force us to address the thorny question of how Namibia's future army would be composed. We were firmly committed to keeping this matter off the agenda.

Apart from the noisy debate about Namibia's electoral system, little of this complex agenda was publicly visible. But we had an ambitious target of concluding the settlement during 1982, and the Group worked intensively between December 1981 and May 1982 to review options and hammer out joint positions. In between such meetings, we consulted frequently with U.N. officials to explore our maneuvering room within the context of the U.N. Plan. Individual Group members talked informally with individual FLS members to lay groundwork and float ideas. At times like this, our partners offered indispensable support. They helped us mount man-to-man coverage across the entire political spectrum of the parties. We obtained independent assessments and reality checks that were not otherwise available. Our partners could say things on our behalf which we could not say ourselves.

But it fell essentially to us Americans to bring the South Africans along. We held extensive parallel exchanges with Brand Fourie and his diplomatic, intelligence, and military colleagues in London, South Africa, and several country estates in northern Virginia in late 1981 and the first half of 1982. Our goal was to probe in depth Pretoria's real priorities and prepare the South Africans to bite the bullet on phase two issues. They were beginning to realize that they would have to fall back substantially from their more extreme positions. Pik Botha revealed his mounting discomfort when he wrote to Haig about all the negatives of our settlement in a January 1982 letter. Botha wanted to know whether Haig had really thought all this through!

Fourie passed hints of ominous rumblings from P. W. Botha, who periodically vented his dissatisfaction with the narrow parameters of our dialogue. We discussed Namibia and Angola, Fourie noted; Botha wanted to discuss "strategic cooperation" and the U.S. attitude toward South African constitutional reform. Things might proceed more smoothly if Botha and Reagan could talk all this over, face to face. Meanwhile, there was some displeasure with Washington's determined drive to resolve issues and complete phases that would remain entirely hypothetical unless there was major movement on the Cuban withdrawal issue. At the time, there was no such movement, and the South Africans knew it.

This was a tricky situation. As our new ambassador, Herman Nickel, had reminded us, there were risks in concentrating too heavily on Namibia and Angola in our exchanges with the South Africans. They might perceive that we would be willing to subordinate our bilateral agenda in order to obtain their cooperation on regional issues. Accordingly, we regularly raised with top government officials the issues of reform and change that were of greatest interest to us. On the other hand, we had already made regional cooperation a defining issue in our relations back in May 1981. I judged it best to avoid the terrain onto which Fourie was inviting me. We did not want to get dragged into a South African trap of discussing "acceptable targets" or "understandings" for internal political change. Better to keep him focused on the matters at hand: the last thing I needed was an unstructured and uncontrollable Reagan-Botha summit.

The Story of a Breakthrough

Matters came to a head in May 1982, soon after the Front Line States and SWAPO had rejected yet again the latest Contact Group proposal on the Namibian electoral system. Having been handed this splendid tactical gift, South Africa suddenly lurched into a mode of impatient cooperation. In mid-May, Pik Botha led a large delegation to Geneva for another of our periodic bilateral consultations. We found new flexibility on some of the most sensitive UNTAG issues; Pretoria was also prepared to scale down its expectations on the question of U.N. "impartiality." It would consider sympathetically a new U.S. idea to finesse the electoral system issue entirely by simply deferring it for now. Moreover, to dramatize its new stance, Pretoria offered to set July 15 as the date for the SWAPO-SADF cease-fire envisaged in Resolution 435, and August 15 as the date for implementation to begin. Under this plan, Namibian elections and independence would occur during 1983. In vintage South African style, these proposals were accompanied by suggestions that Pretoria might have to review its options if the United States and our allies could not obtain rapid FLS / SWAPO agreement on a new Namibia package, as well as quick closure with the Angolan regime on an acceptable formula for Cuban troop withdrawal!

A few days later, after exhaustive review among senior officials, the allied foreign ministers held a special session in Luxembourg on the margins of a NATO ministerial session. In an upbeat communiqué on May 17, they sidestepped the phase one snarl and announced that phase two proposals would soon be presented to all parties. The decision had been made to pocket South Africa's newfound flexibility and convert it immediately into Contact Group proposals for FLS / SWAPO consideration. We would exploit Pretoria's sudden interest in rapid movement to test the other side. Meanwhile, we quietly but firmly reminded the South Africans that we had imposed no deadlines ourselves and would not look kindly on others' doing so.

The next few months were among the most productive of the entire negotiation. In June 1982, senior allied officials made a successful swing through Angola, Zambia, and Tanzania (chairman of the FLS) to elicit support for our phase two proposals. We invited senior officials from FLS capitals and SWAPO to join their Contact Group counterparts in New York to hammer out agreements on phases one and two; South African and U.N. officials would be available in the wings, thus enabling Group mediators to run an informal shuttle or proximity meetings.

The masterful performance of this small group of FLS ambassadors and senior officials during the summer of 1982 was a case study in coalition diplomacy. It was also a fascinating model of intergroup dynamics. Our agenda was to conclude and record a series of understandings on phases one and two. The most efficient way to muscle SWAPO and the South Africans toward agreement would be to mount a non-stop diplomatic process in one place. Experience had shown that periodic missions visiting multiple African capitals were an unwieldy procedure. They made effective coordination within and between the FLS and the Contact Group arduous, while offering both SWAPO and Pretoria many openings to impede or end-run our efforts. A continuous procedure from one place would also strengthen our hand in thwarting Soviet and radical non-aligned maneuvers.

New York was the agreed site because of the need for access to U.N. Secretariat personnel, and the presence of capable, literate officials in the U.N. missions of all the players. African and Contact Group teams were reinforced by top-level officials from capitals who camped out in the city for the better part of six weeks. New York had the added merit of being a place where senior diplomats could disappear from view to meet unobtrusively in its maze of hotels and restaurants. Most of the trial-ballooning and trading occurred over meals or drinks, not in official meetings where notetakers and listening devices would inhibit communication. Similarly, most of the real action took place in bilateral probes between two parties, not in plenary sessions of the fourteen interested players (six FLS governments, SWAPO, South Africa, the U.N. Secretariat, and the five Contact Group governments).

The state of relations among the various players necessitated the maximum caution over procedures. Experience had shown that SWAPO and South Africa were a combustible mix; Pretoria rejected the very notion of direct contact unless the internal Namibian parties were also present, a condition SWAPO would reject unless these parties were defined as part of the South African delegation. With an informal process we could deny these unruly characters any chance to anger and provoke each other directly.

The Front Line team faced a number of challenges. Knowledge of the negotiating history was uneven within African ranks, whereas both SWAPO and Pretoria had memorized their lines. FLS officials had to deal directly with us, while simultaneously "guiding" ill-informed or less constructive colleagues, preparing group positions before seeking SWAPO's acceptance, and warding off intrusions into the procedure by external parties hostile to it. In addition, they had to maintain some sort of loose contact with their own capitals without triggering the sort of top-level micromanagement that can bedevil an informal negotiating process.

Tanzania's Attorney General, Joe Warioba, and its U.N. ambassador, Paul Rupia, Botswana's U.N. ambassador, Joe Legwaila, and Mozambican presidential adviser Fernando Honwana, deserved particular credit for the successes achieved through this process from July to September 1982. Through a combination of tactical finesse and tough-minded pragmatism, they managed to discipline their group and control the agenda so that only the minimum number of choices and decisions was needed and old issues were not resurrected. Agreements took the form of letters, memoranda, and an informal checklist; in most cases, these documents remained "private." On some issues, agreement consisted of carefully defined "oral assurances" extracted from one side and passed to the other side on the condition that it henceforth drop the underlying issue.

To illustrate, on July 12, phase one was formally wrapped up by means of a letter from Contact Group governments to U.N. Secretary General Javier Perez de Cuellar. It transmitted the agreed constitutional principles, and officially finessed the previous snarl on electoral procedures. Our "mixed system" was dropped; the choice between one of the two systems would be made later by Pretoria, in consultation with U.N. Secretariat officials planning the UNTAG operation. (In late 1985, Pretoria informed U.N. officials of its preference for proportional representation, thus agreeing with both SWAPO and U.N. officials that a constituency-based system would be cumbersome in a territory without agreed districts or a recent census.)

On the constitutional principles themselves, the Contact Group letter simply recorded their acceptance by SWAPO and Namibia's internal parties, relying on private, oral FLS and South African assurances to this effect. Despite its informality, this agreement on constitutional principles stood up extraordinarily well for the next seven years. They resurfaced dramatically when SWAPO seized the high ground in November 1989 by proposing their adoption by the newly elected constituent assembly. The principles were unanimously confirmed as democratic guidelines for Namibia's constitution.

This procedural informality—natural, perhaps, in the American cultural context—was as much the result of Front Line innovation as our own. It avoided the need for more elaborate documents and approval procedures. It spared governments the need publicly to confirm where they had backed down from previous positions. It offered both SWAPO and the South African government a respectable form of due process. And it avoided subjecting the whole delicate exercise to the uncertain and often polarizing climate of bloc politics in the United Nations.

On the face of things, one might have expected real problems to develop within the FLS / SWAPO camp. Why would "moderate" Botswana, radically non-aligned Tanzania, and Marxist Mozambique find it possible to cooperate intimately with each other and with us, and to keep their FLS brothers and SWAPO in line? When former Tanzanian President Julius Nyerere first welcomed me to Dar es Salaam in early 1981 and heard me describe Washington's interest in the Angolan as well as Namibian aspects of a settlement, his eyes flashed with emotion. He accused us of reintroducing the Cold War and encouraging South African obstructionist tactics. How can you call yourself "non-aligned," I inquired, when you make such charges but turn a blind eye to Soviet / Cuban adventurism, which is where this sorry story began back in 1975? How can you expect the West to bring Pretoria to a settlement if you reject the only realistic and balanced basis for doing so? Nyerere was equally blunt: Of course, we Africans hold you in the West to a different and far higher standard since we expect nothing from the Soviets. But, he added, Africans trust Pretoria even less than Moscow.

My first reception in Mozambique in April 1981 could have been scripted in Moscow. The Soviets and Cubans had done their best to poison the well for U.S.-Mozambican relations, a task made easier by slick Communist intelligence operations and ham-fisted South African bullying. The Socratic dialogue of Dar es Salaam degenerated into polemics in Maputo. Compared with such scenarios, Botswana's leaders had accepted that we were innocent until proven guilty, and conducted themselves as worried friends—friends because they shared our desire to get *both* the Cubans and the South Africans out of places they had no business being in, but worried because they were not sure we were up to it.

A year later, in the summer of 1982, these differences of FLS culture and ideology seemed less apparent or pertinent. Warioba, Rupia, Legwaila, and Honwana, the leaders of the FLS team in New York, had much in common: they were all highly skilled people, who were used to operating on several fronts at once. They recognized the tactical advantages of using the new Western negotiating framework to test both the West and South Africa. Whatever their misgivings about the Reagan administration, they saw that the revised peace process on Namibia had built some momentum and had at least some chance of moving the South Africans. Not even the most skeptical of the FLS representatives wanted the West to disengage from its efforts as long as there was some hope to get Pretoria to settle on Namibia and, more generally, to curb its aggressive regional behavior. Whatever their differences on East-West issues, the FLS leaders had few illusions that Moscow could, or wished to, settle the region's conflicts.

This skillful pragmatism helped produce an impressive series of informal agreements on phase two issues. The toughest nut to crack were the security trade-offs between (a) UNTAG size and deployment; (b) the monitoring of SWAPO in Angola and Zambia; and (c) the DMZ proposal. We resolved it through a formula that had emerged from protracted consultations over the previous six months. The FLS / SWAPO agreed to accept that U.N. teams (under UNTAG control) would monitor SWAPO's bases in Angola and Zambia. This added a powerful element of balance to a package previously viewed as "onesided" by Pretoria. The Front Line States were now accepting responsibility for SWAPO behavior. In addition, though this was never officially recorded, SWAPO agreed not to raise its previous demand that it—like the SADF—was entitled to be monitored at "bases" inside Namibia. (The claim had always been a non-starter since SWAPO had no permanent military presence or "liberated areas" inside Namibia.)* To no one's real dismay, the DMZ proposal was scrapped. U.N. officials were clearly relieved, since they would have had to plan and operate a highly ambitious and costly surveillance scheme over a vast border region from the Atlantic to the tip of Namibia's Caprivi Strip.

In exchange for these moves, we and our allies prevailed upon South Africa essentially to drop its previous UNTAG positions. Pretoria agreed informally to accept the Secretariat's 1978 deployment plan; Pretoria sidestepped the clash on UNTAG numbers, tacitly accepting a 7,500-man "authorized upper limit" while expressing preference for lower numbers. (The Contact Group, FLS, and U.N. officials confirmed the upper limit while also recognizing that actual deployment numbers could be lower if prevailing conditions permitted.) The Contact Group, with

---

* SWAPO continued to pursue the goal of Namibian bases through military means. The last such attempt came on April 1, 1989, the starting point for implementation of the 1988 settlement. The decision of SWAPO's leaders to attempt a fait accompli by infiltrating two thousand men into northern Namibia cost SWAPO the lives of hundreds of its best fighters. But the settlement survived.

valuable help from U.N. officials, also managed to bury quietly the potential problem of UNTAG's national composition. We did this by assuring all parties that they would be appropriately "consulted" by U.N. headquarters, a long-standing practice in peacekeeping operations. In addition, we Americans quietly obtained the necessary oral assurance from General Geldenhuys that units of the South West Africa (Namibia) Territorial Force would be handled in accordance with Resolution 435's provisions affecting "ethnic forces"; this point was then conveyed orally to our Contact Group partners, the African parties, and U.N. officials, thus assuring that the matter would not be formally raised.

Similar compromises emerged on the politically charged issue of U.N. "impartiality." The Group persuaded the parties to accept a visually balanced package of measures under which both the U.N. system and the South African government would be obliged to behave impartially toward all Namibian parties during the transition. Pretoria's local administration in Windhoek would be expected to guarantee equal access to the media and freedom of association to all during the electoral campaign. Various U.N. bodies would cease their pro-SWAPO support activities once the implementation of Resolution 435 had begun; the U.N. Council for Namibia would also cease its political activities, and SWAPO itself would refrain "voluntarily" from exercising its U.N. observer role. The South Africans had made their point; but they would get relief only in the context of a settlement, and their own conduct would also be under scrutiny.

The "impartiality package" that emerged from the July–September 1982 diplomacy in New York was contained in an unsigned "checklist" and a memorandum recording a joint September 24, 1982, Contact Group / FLS conversation with the U.N. Secretary General. It would be difficult to imagine a less official record of a successful negotiation. Yet, for all practical purposes, South Africa had committed itself categorically to the specifics of an expanded and revised Resolution 435 package, which now had the full blessing of the FLS and SWAPO. On October 1, 1982, the Contact Group's foreign ministers saluted the "constructive and flexible attitude of the parties," and declared that "a valuable opportunity now existed to achieve a settlement within the time-frame envisaged. . . ." (i.e., one that could begin in 1983).

Victims of Our Own Success

Ironically, however, just when the benefits of harmonious collaboration between the Front Line States and the Contact Group were most apparent—at least to us—this working relationship came to an abrupt halt. Strains began to emerge within both groups. Publicly, a misleading impression had built up in the media coverage, which tended throughout late 1981 and 1982 to speak of a "deadlock" in the Namibia negotiations. The explanation for these misleading stories was that our very progress in New York sharpened an inevitable test of wills over the question of linkage. The result was a two-way diplomatic squeeze play. By resolving the Namibia issues, we had placed an increasingly bright spotlight on Cuban withdrawal from Angola as the *sole remaining obstacle* to a settlement. Feeling the heat, Angola and its FLS partners—backed by the Soviet bloc and radical non-aligned states—had mounted a vocal campaign attacking linkage and rejecting the "false sense of optimism" emanating from Western quarters. Much of the heat was directed at the Contact Group in hopes of breaking it up, leaving the United States isolated and under pressure to back down.

Already when I met with my allied counterparts in Paris in early August, we faced a mounting problem. It would have been preferable to register the "impartiality package" then emerging by means of public letter to Perez de Cuellar so that it could form part of the U.N. official record. But this would have sent the signal that all issues related to the Namibian independence plan had been solved. Logically, negotiation would then begin on the text of a Security Council resolution naming a date for the start of Resolution 435.

But that was impossible. Although we had successfully engaged the MPLA regime in Luanda in a discussion of the issue, we were not yet close to an agreement on Cuban troop withdrawal. Accordingly, the allied agenda in Paris was extremely complex: how to avoid a show-down with our African partners, how to "protect" them from the procedural gamesmanship of the Soviets, Cubans, and others, how to use our dramatic progress on Namibia as leverage to press for Angolan decisions on Cuban withdrawal (when the Group as such did not wish to speak to the issue), and how to explain officially to our various publics why the negotiation was not yet completed and identify the remaining obstacles.

Our Paris meeting coincided with preparations for the sixth round of U.S.-MPLA talks since January, and with continued SADF military operations against SWAPO in southern Angola. The allies were growing more anxious over the slow speed of the Angola negotiations and the sharp disparity between our quiet, unheralded progress in New York and the noisy debates over linkage. At our urging, the Group agreed to send separate but parallel messages to the FLS leaders, taking note of what had been achieved and pointing to the reality of Pretoria's insistence on a parallel commitment from Angola on the Cubans. Our strategy of pushing Namibia forward as quickly as possible paid off in the form of allied support, however anxious, for our campaign. The MPLA began to hear a loud and clear message on linkage from both African and allied quarters.

But the strains on Contact Group unity soon began to show, exactly as our opponents hoped it would. French representatives found it increasingly difficult to obtain ministerial approval for joint démarches like the one just described. In September, Paris dispatched its senior Africanist on an uncoordinated mission to Havana to discuss Angola. The visit occurred against a backdrop of inspired press reports hinting at France's departure from the Group. In October, French Foreign Minister Claude Cheysson—who had a weakness for African microphones and enjoyed burnishing his Third World credentials—told a Tanzanian audience that the Group's work was finished and that Cuban withdrawal was not its concern.

Strangely, this appears to have been the message that Tanzania's leaders wanted to hear. Setting aside the reality that a settlement was only possible with U.S. leadership, Nyerere and most others in the Front Line States nonetheless opted to reject officially our considered strategy for obtaining one. They would officially oppose linkage. Despite the evident success achieved by FLS diplomats in the New York talks, this was the last time that the Front Line States as a group played any substantive role in the diplomacy that produced the Southern African settlement of 1988. By the end of 1983, the Contact Group had also succumbed to African, non-aligned, and Communist pressure on its weakest links, France and Canada. But, by then, the FLS had forfeited their own collective role.

There was a real irony in this story. Moscow, Havana, and the Third World anti-linkage chorus made their points with Western public opinion and media. But Washington's drive toward a Southern African settlement made important and irreversible gains in 1982. South Africa had less room for maneuver on Namibia than ever before. The Namibia package was assembled and ready for implementation whenever we could ripen the Angolan side of the equation. But our timing goals would slip just at the moment when FLS cooperation and Contact Group unity also began to decline.

We would miss the concerted and tough-minded leadership of the African team in New York we enjoyed in the summer of 1982. Later, frustrated officials in Botswana and Mozambique would quietly point to a further irony: Angolan diplomats helped to stir up the strident, rejectionist FLS rhetoric of 1983–85 even while Angolan officials engaged ever more deeply in the U.S.-led diplomacy. Luanda's refusal to brief its FLS colleagues (except fellow Portuguese-speaking Mozambique) on the Cuban troop withdrawal negotiation reduced the Front Line States to an adjunct of Luanda's fitful public diplomacy. Whatever was said publicly, most of the FLS leaders welcomed periodic consultations with us, not least because it was the best means they had of discovering what the Angolans were really up to!

6

Engaging the Angolans, 1981–82

Cool analysis of the situation in 1981 would suggest that Washington should address itself to the Soviets or the Cubans (or both) rather than the Angolans. After all, there was a legitimate question as to whether the MPLA—the political movement which ran Angola's one-party Marxist state—could tell the Cubans to leave and whether they would do so if asked. Moreover, there was a deeper unknown: could the MPLA survive Cuban withdrawal in the absence of some understanding with UNITA? There were voices in Washington, in South Africa, and within UNITA which raised precisely these questions. From the outset, the American settlement effort was criticized as both pointless and naive; the only way it could get the MPLA to move was by offering things that should be withheld.

But we rejected that analysis. For one thing, the option to do business directly with the Soviets or Cubans did not exist in 1981. To approach either of them with the terms we had in mind would have required a readiness on our part to ask them for help and to give something in return, most likely on issues unrelated to Southern Africa. We knew that the Communist powers did not wish to drop their newly acquired African stake. Bargaining with them over the Cuban presence in Angola was intrinsically undesirable. It would also have the perverse consequence of legitimizing their regional roles—as expansionist and interventionist powers and as potential dealmakers. In the Washington political climate of the early 1980s, the idea of negotiating with them about Angola would have been rejected out of hand.

Nor, in my judgment, could it have worked. Both the times and the logic of the situation argued for a regional, African approach. We would inform the Soviets and Cubans of our intention to negotiate the Namibia-Angola settlement directly with the parties concerned; point out that such a settlement was balanced and in everyone's interest; and warn them not to block an initiative which could attract African support and which was, in any case, the only alternative to expanded war.

These bold phrases directed toward the Soviets and Cubans (who, of course, interpreted them against a wider backdrop of issues in their relations with the United States) were easily uttered. But obtaining MPLA support for the U.S. initiative was another matter altogether. In light of earlier history, MPLA leaders looked upon us with the deepest suspicion. What they heard from their friends and from South African enthusiasts of the linkage approach only deepened it. The Angolans lacked the most rudimentary grasp of U.S. political reality. The complexities of U.S.-South African relations did not fit the Marxist stereotype, either. Angolan officials seemed, at times, overwhelmed by the weight of legacies they knew little about.

Our refusal since 1975–76 to establish diplomatic ties sent a powerful message which undercut the MPLA's legitimacy and made the regime nervous. It offered us potential leverage and gave us a card to play. But, at the same time, it profoundly complicated the task of bringing the MPLA to a deal. The lack of official U.S. presence in Luanda prevented us from gaining firsthand mastery of the MPLA's byzantine modus operandi. Access to the key players was sporadic and difficult. We seldom had a precise sense of who was doing what to whom within the MPLA. Direct communication was fitful and interrupted, and we relied heavily on third-party channels.

Despite the vital help of a long list of intermediaries, there remained an "empty chair" with our name on it in Luanda, which we could not fill for reasons of policy and politics. Some states had established formal relations with Luanda while maintaining warm political ties and even tangible assistance to UNITA. Some of our African and European partners advised us to do the same thing (without changing our policy). But the legacy of 1975–76 made it impossible for us to adopt this Old World realism: how could we fill the empty chair without giving the MPLA a major, unearned gift and without weakening UNITA? At a minimum, we would want to balance our communications and data gathering by establishing a State Department liaison link with UNITA in Angola or a neighboring country. In the event, however, my team and I enjoyed direct and authoritative channels with *neither* Angolan party. In the case of UNITA, we relied either on other governments or the U.S. intelligence

community for communications. These handicaps are all the more striking in light of Angola's central place in our ambitious strategy of peacemaking.

But this was only the beginning of our difficulties. We came into
office eager to send the message that the constitutional paralysis and
partisan strife over America's world role was over—and that the executive's prerogatives on such matters as covert action were being restored.
Accordingly, Secretary of State Haig testified before the Senate in March
1981 in favor of repealing the 1976 Clark Amendment. Angola was the
only country in the world subject to such a legislative ban on U.S. covert
involvement. Our campaign to repeal Clark was designed to show that
we had the option to back our diplomacy with physical power; no decision had been made actually to intervene. We made a substantial effort
to obtain repeal, succeeding in the Senate in October, but running into
resistance in the House. To my dismay, the issue was traded away by
Republican conferees in a December 1981 House-Senate conference on
the foreign aid bill: it was deemed too "expensive" in the context of
other high-priority items in this complex legislative package.

This skirmish demonstrated that Angola remained a divisive topic,
symbolizing an underlying argument over goals and tools of American
policy in the Third World. By trying to repeal Clark and then falling
short, we had the worst of both worlds. Other nations would draw their
own conclusions about American credibility. U.S. negotiators would have
to engage Luanda without having either the potential "carrot" of establishing relations or the potential "stick" of aiding UNITA.

Getting to Know the MPLA

We soon discovered that we were dealing with a weak and fragmented regime, unaccustomed to negotiating on its own behalf. Led by
a strikingly handsome and highly articulate young president named Jose
Eduardo dos Santos, the MPLA nonetheless never recovered from the
death in 1979 of Agostinho Neto. Even he—poet, physician, founding
father, and "Immortal Guide of the Angolan Revolution"—had barely
mastered the movement's many personal, ideological, and racial antag-
onisms. Portraits of Neto and dos Santos would jointly adorn Luanda's
public buildings for years to come, subtly suggesting the source of the
latter's legitimacy and the hope that he, too, would unify the party.

Dos Santos joined the MPLA as a teenager and was a leading youth
activist at the age of nineteen in 1961, the year the anti-colonial war
began. Eighteen years later, he was the consensus choice to succeed Neto
as president. In between, he acquired a Soviet wife, a Soviet petroleum

engineering degree, and a string of rapid promotions. His success in countering the effects of damaging splinter movements was recognized by elevation to the Central Committee and the politburo in 1975 on the eve of independence. He held three ministerial portfolios, smoothly surviving a bloody coup attempt in 1977 that was put down with Cuban help. When dos Santos took over as president upon Néto's death in 1979, he was intimately aware of how close that coup came to success, how carefully the Soviets and Cubans had played their cards during the hours of uncertainty, and how many top people were killed or placed in detention. He knew how easy it was to antagonize one or another of the MPLA's power bases—government bureaucrats, military officers, party potentates, white and mestizo ideologues of the left (the "internationalists"), and the black moderates and nationalists who resented their prominence. Above all, dos Santos had a healthy awareness that his presidency rested on the premise that he would respect the baronies around him and work for compromise among them.

We had, of course, been dealing with Luanda on the Namibia issues in 1981, but it was a very different matter for the MPLA to discuss our overall relationship, including the U.S. view of linkage. It was, therefore, something of a surprise in December 1981 when dos Santos signaled his desire to meet with us bilaterally to discuss "all problems of common interest that fall into a bilateral framework and which could lead to the normalization of relations between the two countries." The proposal came just as Jonas Savimbi was undertaking a well-publicized visit to Washington. It signaled that the Angolans were not playing hard to get. They had their own agenda.

We scheduled a meeting with Foreign Minister Paulo Jorge in Paris in January 1982. I had first gotten to know Jorge during a swing through the Front Line States in April 1981. He revealed some of his nature on that occasion by opening our exchange with a pointed query: "In what capacity are we meeting, Mr. Secretary . . . are you speaking to me as the Foreign Minister of the Government of the People's Republic of Angola?" Jorge enjoyed semantic combat and the chance to wrong-foot his American interlocutor. I replied that he was surely well aware of the long-standing U.S. policy of non-recognition as well as the reasons for it. My presence in Luanda reflected the reality that his government existed, that Angola was a member of the FLS group working on the Namibia issue, and that we believed Angola was in a position to play a decisive role in the peace process. We were, in sum, pragmatists who dealt with reality as we found it.

This reply gave Jorge the sort of opening he relished: Angola was weak and vulnerable, but it had a "responsible and principled stance" and a "legitimate" government, which enjoyed universal recognition except from Washington and Pretoria (sneer). Angolans operated on the basis of internationally accepted "principles," including the U.N. Charter's Article 51 concerning the right of states to self-defense (i.e., Cuban troops) and U.N. resolutions regarding SWAPO ("sole representative" of the Namibian people) and Namibian independence (under UNSC Res. 435). If the United States wished to play an acceptable role, it, too, should respect such principles. It should not ask Angolans to support changes in the "established legal basis" for a settlement, but should use its "friendship" with South Africa to get it to implement U.N. resolutions. Nonetheless, the Angolans, "as a gesture of good faith," were prepared to meet with the U.S. delegation, despite the absence of official relations between the two states!

And so it went. Jorge was always doing us favors like that one. He enjoyed debate, and made good use of his Cartesian-Marxist intellectual formation to engulf his adversary in a miasma of juridical formalism. In this respect, he was by no means alone among MPLA officials, but he was especially good at it. He had honed his skills as an "external representative" of the MPLA from 1961 to 1975 and as Angola's foreign minister since 1976. One struggled in vain to find in him a trace of interest in communication or in identifying possible common ground. U.N. or OAU resolutions, doctrines, and abstract principles were his preferred weapons in laying claim to what he described as the "correct legal and ethical" position. Anyone who ever dealt with Brezhnev-era Soviet diplomats will be familiar with the pattern, except that Jorge's style and delivery were clearly Portuguese. The tone of prosecutorial superiority was complemented by the air of quasi-erudite discourse one might find among café intellectuals in any large European city.

Married to a Cuban and holding dual Portuguese and Angolan nationality, Paulo Jorge had studied at the University of Lisbon before joining the MPLA and building close links to its powerful mestizo faction. He symbolized the MPLA's continued reliance on external power bases. An "internationalist," his position depended on the factional status quo within the party, as well as the political status quo within Angola. Jorge made us forget that we were negotiating with an African country. Nor were we alone in this sentiment: a leading African diplomat once quipped to me that he knew an upcoming FLS ministerial summit would be counterproductive if Angola were represented by "that white Portuguese Communist."

But it is rare that you can choose your interlocutors in diplomacy. Jorge was the official "front door" to the MPLA, so we did our best to work with him. When Jorge and I met in Paris in January 1982, it was my first occasion to present a complete picture of the new American strategy for Southern Africa, including our sensitivity to the security concerns of both Angola and South Africa. Our approach, we argued, would offer a definitive test of Pretoria's acceptance in principle of Resolution 435; Angola could test our good faith and enable us to test South Africa's. The way to do this was to develop with us a formula for Cuban withdrawal, related in some credible fashion to the timetable already built into the Namibia transition plan.

It was a complex brief, requiring that we touch upon all the relevant tenets of inherited Namibia theology. To get the Angolan's attention we needed to offer him a reasonably candid picture of decisionmaking within the South African government and of what would be required to force a basic decision in Pretoria. We described in matter-of-fact terms our analysis of the "practical necessity" of obtaining a specific schedule for Cuban withdrawal from Angola. We also outlined the advantages for Angola of our settlement package, which—by resolving the interrelated regional security issues—could open the way to national reconciliation and economic progress for Angola and normalization of U.S.-Angolan relations.

Jorge listened politely, smiling indulgently as I fumbled my way through the tabs in my eight-pound Department of State briefing book, covering the lengthy "talking points" so carefully crafted by my staff. I knew that he would be unlikely to respond constructively to either threats or false warmth, but hoped that my "big picture" would tempt him to explore our logic and gain a feel for our realistic, objective analysis of the various regional problems.

But Jorge had neither the mandate nor the inclination to do so. This round of meetings included over twelve hours of verbal sparring, relieved only by several fine French meals which conclusively demonstrated that the Angolan entertainment budget substantially exceeded our own. Jorge expressed interest in the U.S. plan for "phasing" the strictly Namibian agenda items. Angola had a clear track record from the 1978–80 period of supporting the Namibia settlement process, he correctly argued, and would continue to play this role. But he flatly rejected any link or "parallel commitment" on Cuban troop withdrawal. The U.S. team was cross-examined as to why Cuban troops in Angola were any different from U.S. troops in South Korea or French troops in Djibouti. He pointedly observed that U.N. resolutions already applied to Namibia, while there was "no juridical basis" for raising the Cuban issue; to do so would be to equate the aggressor (South Africa) with the victim (Angola).

I noted then, as I would in countless meetings to follow, that the United States considered South Africa's occupation of Namibia and its periodic incursions into Angola to be illegal. But the conflict was not, in reality, a legal one, and it would not be resolved by legal argument. There was a basic security problem and we were seeking a practical solution to it. If we failed, the Angolan regime would face a genuine security threat in the south for the foreseeable future. The only way that SADF military action could be restrained was in the context of a credible regional peace process. Neither SWAPO, nor the MPLA and the Cubans, nor U.N. resolutions would get the SADF out of Namibia in the absence of a regional settlement.

Jorge's response was revealing. In the past, during the struggle, the MPLA had controlled only limited assets: its supporters and fighters, its spirit, and its external representatives in various African and world capitals. Now, the MPLA controlled the Government of the People's Republic of Angola, the army of Angola (FAPLA), the flag, the capital city and most major towns, and a seat in the United Nations. Jorge professed to be less impressed by the obvious absence of governmental authority or sovereignty in major parts of the country. It was the viewpoint of a liberation movement which was pleased to have won control of at least some of its supposed territory. But it was also a strikingly clear echo of Portugal's own experience in Angola: only in the last fifty years before independence did Lisbon gain control of the vast, raw hinterland.

Angolan Tactics and American Themes

The January 1982 meeting in Paris represented the real beginning of a sustained U.S. drive with the Angolans. (An earlier meeting between Secretary of State Haig and Jorge at the United Nations the previous October had been a brief courtesy call, confined to generalities.) It signaled that the Angolans, for their own reasons, had agreed to engage in the U.S.-led diplomacy. Jorge and I each professed to find the meetings useful.

Significantly, Jorge never suggested that the question of apartheid within South Africa should take precedence over the regional agenda of reducing violent conflict. Namibia came first. While he differed with us on the structure of a Namibian settlement, Jorge expressed interest in hearing specific proposals, and told us that he would seek a mandate from his leadership to enter into more detailed discussion.

We soon learned how the MPLA would play its cards. Details of our discussions were promptly leaked to a leftist French news magazine by the high-living hardliner Jorge had assigned as MPLA ambassador to Paris. Then, on February 4 in Luanda, Jorge and his Cuban counterpart Isidoro Malmierca published a joint declaration. These two doctrinaire ideologues must have had fun penning this verbose polemical rationale for Cuba's Angolan adventure, intended as a response to "an infamous and malintentioned propaganda campaign of the imperialists."

The declaration proceeded to rehearse their version of history since 1975. It claimed that the presence and departure of Cuban forces was a "bilateral matter between two sovereign states." It argued that plans for gradual withdrawal had several times been thwarted by renewed SADF attacks on Angola, most recently in August 1981 during South Africa's "Operation Protea." Citing the U.S. veto of the U.N. Security Council condemning that operation, the two ministers declared that the Cuban presence in Angola was justified by "the external aggression from the racist and fascist South African troops, in close alliance with the USA. . . ." For a punch line, Malmierca and Jorge embraced their own version of linkage: the two governments would "analyze reinitiating the gradual reduction of Cuban forces" *after Namibian independence* in accordance with Resolution 435, provided that this produced a "truly independent government" and complete South African withdrawal. Almost as an afterthought, they added that when and if this happened, "Cuba reiterates that it will abide, without hesitation, by any decision that the sovereign government of the People's Republic of Angola makes about the withdrawal of said forces."

These were not new positions. But the declaration represented the first authoritative Angolan reply to the U.S. initiative. It became the MPLA's opening bid. Optimists in the United States and the Contact Group capitals took heart from the postscript, viewing it as a revealing assertion of Angolan independence. Others saw the declaration as a victory for Castro and the Soviets, who had a witting ally in Jorge. The MPLA was now locked into a negotiating stance that was a clear non-starter in both Washington and Pretoria. To complete the picture, Jorge was quoted on the very day of the declaration urging the other four members of the Contact Group to pressure the United States to drop the Cuban issue and return to an unadulterated Resolution 435.

Angola's public adoption of "Namibia first" showed that we had gotten their attention. It also validated the intimate connection between events in Namibia and Angola, though the precise nature of that link remained in dispute. But by going public with such a position, the Angolans provided ample ammunition for skeptics in Washington and Pretoria who wondered about the point of continuing direct talks at all.

In reality, however, there was little choice. Failure to pursue the Angola track aggressively would leave us in the dark. The only alternative— favored by some of Secretary Haig's advisers and sometimes by Haig himself—was to stop the entire process dead in its tracks, declaring publicly, in effect, "No Angola, no Namibia." In my judgment, we had not yet built either the credibility or the leverage to force decisions in Luanda, Havana, and Moscow by threatening, as Haig put it, to "go cold turkey." Such a move would have placed the entire strategy at risk.

The MPLA had reasons for keeping the direct channel open to Washington: to hold the high ground and be seen to be working for peace. Later, in February, the MPLA came back to propose another round of talks with Jorge, again in Paris. We accepted the proposal. By doing so, we, too, would gain the high ground for cultivating the U.S.-Angolan dialogue. More important, we would have the opening needed to test the MPLA's internal consensus and its margin of maneuver vis-à-vis the Cubans and Soviets.

To do this effectively, we would have to make artful use of the rather modest arrows in our quiver. We would need to signal our readiness to discuss the MPLA's fears. To demonstrate our optimism, we would continue to refer to normalization as the logical result of a regional settlement. In the meantime, we planned to continue extending Export-Import Bank credits for development of Angola's offshore oil resources, in which U.S. firms already played a key role. We also decided at this time to co-host with a Washington-based think tank a conference on Angolan economic development. These moves would help portray our own hopes for a brighter Angolan future.

But we would remind the Angolans of the pressures they faced. The situation on the ground in Southern Africa contained the strongest, practical pressures for a settlement. It was a simple fact that the SADF's support for UNITA and its periodic anti-SWAPO operations in southern Angola would only end if a settlement were achieved. While we would condemn Pretoria's intervention, we would also note that there was an obvious two-way link between SADF and SWAPO violence—a link that would only disappear when the Namibia conflict was resolved. That, in turn, now hinged on reaching agreement on Cuban withdrawal.

In our March 1982 meeting with Jorge, we decided to change tactics. Rather than focus primarily on the principle of a linked Namibia-Angola settlement, we would float the idea of an interim security mechanism that would reduce the violence, create a climate of confidence, and help us to tie the Namibia and Angola issues together. We called our concept a "pre-implementation cease-fire." The cease-fire would take effect immediately after Pretoria announced a "date certain" for the start of implementation of Resolution 435—the point at which Namibia's transition to independence would begin. Hostilities would end; the SADF would return to its bases in Namibia; Cuban, MPLA, and SWAPO forces would pull north to agreed distances from the Namibia-Angola border; and a verification mechanism would be established to monitor performance and assure that no party took advantage of the new situation.

Jorge took careful notes on all this while asking lots of questions about how the cease-fire would work. We were baiting the hook: our proposal had been crafted to offer Luanda interesting openings to explore U.S. thinking.

This proposal for disengaging the various armies clearly foreshadowed subsequent stages of the negotiation. But in early 1982 neither the South Africans nor the Angolans and Cubans yet recognized the incipient military stalemate they faced, and each of them exaggerated their bargaining power. We too exaggerated our own leverage as mediators, imagining that we could simultaneously cool off the war, channel the South Africans toward cooperative behavior, twist Angolan arms on Cuban withdrawal, and create space for UNITA.

Nonetheless, the cease-fire concept served a useful purpose as the lead item for six months of bilateral diplomacy and as the pivot for whatever other leverage we could muster. Jorge and I concentrated on it during an inconclusive March meeting in Paris and returned to it again briefly in early April on the occasion of a separate Contact Group mission to Luanda. Jorge, however, remained true to form, sharpening his well-honed dialectical skills but doing nothing to advance Angolan interests. We found ourselves hankering for a more constructive Angolan interlocutor.

But first we would need some basis for leapfrogging above or around him. Jorge was a devotee of protocolary gamesmanship. A perceived slight could lead him to downgrade the dialogue on the grounds that, as a full minister, he outranked me. We had no desire to end up in the hands of his deputy, Olga Lima. This stunning black Angolan on Jorge's team played her role as assistant prosecutor as intensely as Jorge himself, though the effect was muted somewhat by French couture, rhinestone-studded horn-rim glasses, and layers of blue-green eyeshadow. Unlike Jorge, Lima had a sense of humor and was capable of enjoying a point of agreement. However, we doubted that she was a secret fan who would strive to help us obtain an Angolan proposal on Cuban withdrawal.

Reaching Out to dos Santos

Happily, our slow start with the MPLA was immediately followed by significant breakthroughs on Namibia between May and August 1982. Our need for the Front Line States' help on the matter of U.N. monitoring of SWAPO bases in Angola and Zambia served as the occasion for a

Contact Group mission to Southern Africa in June. We decided to send two of the finest diplomats I knew to get directly to President dos Santos.

Ambassador-at-large (and General) Vernon ("Dick") Walters led the mission, making expansive use of his broadly defined job description as roving presidential emissary. A former deputy CIA director and confidant-interpreter for U.S. presidents since FDR, Dick Walters was ideally suited to the task. A jovial extrovert, Walters works his magic through a purposeful, multilingual charm, which often takes the shape of a perfectly chosen anecdote. An ardent cold warrior and avid Savimbi fan, Walters might have seemed an odd choice to help us woo the MPLA leadership. But his warmth, directness, and superb language skills made him an instrument of choice for cultivating dos Santos, perhaps Africa's most frightened Marxist.

Frank Wisner perfectly complemented Walters. The dean of Southern African specialists in the career service, Wisner had recently accepted my proposal that he return from his post as ambassador to Zambia to become my senior deputy and alter ego. No aspect of Angola's sad history or of Southern Africa's multiple conflicts escaped him. He had played a central role in the Ford-Kissinger Africa team, living through the trauma of 1975–76 in Angola. At home in the intellectual and foreign policy universe of Europe, Asia, Africa, and the Middle East, Wisner possessed a breadth of foreign affairs background unmatched in our government. His polished, low-key manner and personal warmth made him the perfect candidate to help Walters.

The June 1982 Walters-Wisner mission lived up to expectations. They had done their homework, and wowed dos Santos with their detailed grasp of both Angola's concerns and the intricate Namibia brief. Our basic message was that rapid progress had been made on most issues. Monitoring SWAPO camps was the last serious hurdle. To deal with practical security issues, we had tabled the cease-fire proposal,* and were still awaiting Angola's reply. We had been informed in May that Pretoria was ready in the immediate future to announce a date for the state of Resolution 435 implementation.

Before proceeding, however, Pretoria would want to have a concrete Angolan commitment on Cuban withdrawal. The South Africans would expect a withdrawal schedule to be completed by the time of their own

---

* To the great amusement of the MPLA team, we informed them that "PIC," the acronym we had selected for our pre-implementation cease-fire proposal, had to be replaced because Foreign Minister Roelof "Pik" Botha was uneasy at its similarity to his nickname. Instead, we now called it the "CBI" (cease-fire before implementation). Pik Botha's nickname is a diminutive of the Afrikaans word *pikkewyn*, or penguin, a creature he was said to resemble as a youngster when dressed in his Sunday suit.

final departure from Namibia (i.e., at independence, which could be seven to twelve months after the start of implementation, depending on how long it took the Namibians to write their constitution); but there was wide flexibility within that time period.

Walters added for good measure that we had informed the Soviets and Cubans of our strategy and urged them not to pose obstacles to a settlement which was pro-African, not directed against them. We had no plans to aid UNITA, and expected it not to exploit the cease-fire. Finally, Walters shared our decision to provide some $7.5 million in humanitarian aid to Angolans via the International Committee of the Red Cross.

Dos Santos's response was the strongest we had heard to date. The Angolans would support U.N. monitoring of SWAPO camps as part of the Namibia package. On the cease-fire, they had no problem with keeping the Cubans and SWAPO away from the southern border; the former were not in the south in significant numbers and the latter would remain north if the cease-fire was linked to an early date for Resolution 435. It would not be fair, however, to expect the Angolan forces not to exercise sovereignty over their own territory: FAPLA should return to its "traditional garrisons." We viewed this, at the time, as a qualified acceptance of the cease-fire, and we subsequently pressed the South Africans to accept a FAPLA presence at the border.

Dos Santos declared that he was prepared to cooperate in the search for a "just solution." He appreciated our efforts but urged us not to "equate victim and aggressor." If the South Africans left Namibia, the Cubans would leave—why not take Angola's word for it? Walters and Wisner observed that even if Washington were prepared to take it on faith, there was no way to sell that to Pretoria. The South Africans were bound, under Resolution 435, to a rigorous and detailed schedule of political and military obligations (see Appendix 1). A credible commitment, perhaps in the form of a letter, would be needed. The Angolan president did not close the door; rather, he undertook to think further and added that "maybe some new ideas will emerge in a few days or weeks."

Vague as it was, this exchange offered grounds for believing that we were finally speaking to the right person. We decided to mount a full court press. Walters and Wisner returned to Luanda in late July, but found dos Santos distracted by the need to reshuffle his top people. There were signs of factional divisions in his regime, due in part, we learned, to debate over the negotiations with Washington. He apparently did not have a consensus behind him. This situation was aggravated by military flare-ups in the southern Cunene Province, where the SADF had mounted another round of anti-SWAPO operations. By publicly embracing linkage, proposing early dates for a cease-fire and Resolution 435, and simultaneously declaring its intent to continue such operations until a cease-fire was signed, Pretoria had abandoned any trace of subtlety. Its actions temporarily blew the few decisionmaking circuits that were operational in Luanda. The situation crowded our space as mediators, causing the MPLA to wonder whether we were choosing not to lean on South Africa.

Walters and Wisner distanced the United States from South Africa's impatient diplomatic demands and its military incursion into Angola. Angola could help us by restraining SWAPO and working with us to create the political context for an early agreement. As an example, the two U.S. diplomats saluted Luanda's help in solving the issue of U.N. monitoring of SWAPO bases in Angola.

Out of respect for Angola's reluctance to equate Cuban withdrawal with South Africa's obligations under Resolution 435, we agreed to explore an Angolan concept put forward earlier in July: Angola would provide its specific commitment to a "third party," which would serve as its "guarantor." Walters informed dos Santos that this idea had promise; we had already discussed it with the French, the Contact Group member closest to the MPLA. To help stimulate a concrete Cuban proposal, the U.S. team suggested that Luanda consider proposing a schedule that would, nonetheless, remove all Cuban troops during the first seven months of the Namibian independence process.

The Angolan leader listened politely to the U.S. presentation, and promised to study our ideas before authorizing a "formal" reply. The MPLA's formal response, however, was not what Walters and Wisner had hoped for. Luanda accepted the cease-fire framework and proposed a series of specifics on FAPLA garrisons and border posts, a joint SADF / FAPLA liaison mechanism, and the 16th parallel as a line of Cuban restraint. These terms would not be easy to sell in Pretoria. But their specificity confirmed the MPLA's interest in an early cease-fire, a reduction in SADF pressure, and a direct channel to the South African leadership. We had a live negotiation under way on the ceasefire. But on Cuban withdrawal, the MPLA retreated to the extreme formula that Cuban troops could depart only "after Namibia's independence." The U.S. team made clear that this was a complete non-starter.

Luanda's performance on the crucial Cuban issue could be explained in several ways. Perhaps the MPLA leadership was simply too divided in July 1982 to move under the combination of international pressures. Alternatively, it was holding out for further U.S. concessions before offering a specific proposal. Some of us wondered if positive movement on the cease-fire issues would be used as a decoy for basic intransigence on Cuban troop withdrawal. Others wondered if the MPLA did not feel more comfortable continuing to fight with familiar friends and foes rather than take chances for peace with uncertain partners.

Driving in Angolan Snow

Lacking hard answers, we had to operate by instinct. We had created a regional peace process and established ourselves as the pivotal actor. The process was on track—barely. To protect it, we had to keep moving forward or we would simply stop, rather like driving a car in deep snow.

By this time, we had begun the practice of communicating with Luanda through the British, who had placed their people and secure telex facilities at our disposal. This solved the immediate dilemma of how to avoid going through unhelpful MPLA channels in order to reach the specific individual we wanted to talk to in Luanda. In this business, channels of privileged communication are as vital as identifying solid interlocutors. The intimate working relationship we developed with the British in Southern Africa would soon become essential.

Early in August 1982 we used this system to sound out dos Santos's foreign affairs adviser, Carlos Fernandes, on the idea of a quiet meeting in a third country to review the bidding. This initiative to extricate him from his surroundings failed. Instead, we used the British channel to set up another Wisner mission to Luanda and to pass to the MPLA a South African message concerning the military situation in Cunene Province. We were faced with substantial preparatory work for this meetings. Our new Secretary of State, George P. Shultz, had just taken over from Al Haig; I would need his support for our basic approach and his approval of any new moves for the Wisner mission.

One such move was a conversation on Angola with Shultz's Portuguese counterpart, Futcha Pereira, in which we urged him to propose to the leadership of Cape Verde that they host direct South African–Angolan talks with possible U.S. participation. The parties would require direct talks to hammer out cease-fire details too intricate and delicate to handle by mail. We knew that they were oddly fascinated to hear directly from each other at the table, without having to depend solely upon American accounts of each other's positions. But meeting officially with the South Africans was a sensitive matter for the Angolans; a discreet signal from their closest Portuguese-speaking cousins in Cape Verde was the best approach.

To encourage MPLA leaders to drop their rigid attitude toward Cuban withdrawal, Wisner was authorized to inform them that we were pre-

pared to establish a "liaison office" in Luanda once a settlement including Cuban withdrawal was in progress. This interim step would enable
the United States to play a role in monitoring implementation. But it
was also a step toward establishing diplomatic relations; we would state
our intention to normalize relations during the implementation phase.

In another gesture toward Angola's stated concerns, Wisner would
take with him a document entitled "Procedural Framework." Responding to the MPLA's "principled" rejection of direct, explicit linkage between
Resolution 435 and Cuban withdrawal, this paper described an artful
finesse. There need be no bilateral Angolan–South African treaty. Instead,
the MPLA would supply the United States with a confidential, written
commitment concerning a schedule for Cuban withdrawal and reiterate
its support for Resolution 435. (The schedule would, of course, have
been negotiated in detail through us and agreed to by Pretoria.) The
South Africans would simultaneously provide to the United States a parallel assurance of their intention to implement and abide by Resolution
435, to refrain from the threat or use of force against Angola, and to
respect its territorial integrity and sovereignty. These assurances would
enable the United States and our allied partners to seek U.N. Security
Council action authorizing the implementation of Resolution 435. The
"Procedural Framework" would not only sidestep MPLA hang-ups about
any formal agreement "equating" the two pieces of the package; it would
also save face for Havana while avoiding the possibility of a Soviet veto
in the United Nations Security Council. We decided that Wisner would
table the idea in Luanda at roughly the same time as we showed it to
Pretoria, giving each of them the impression that the other was seriously
interested.

Thus equipped, Wisner spent four days with the Angolans in August.
He presented our latest ideas together with a blunt warning that the
United States could not sustain an endless series of meetings without
results. We were convinced that there were ways to respond to all the
Angolan concerns. Rather than debate history or the legalities of linkage, we needed to deal with reality: there would be no settlement unless
both South Africa and Angola approved it. South Africa's potential flexibility was impossible to for us to test in a vacuum. Peace could not be
defined as the precondition of a settlement; peace would have to be built
by both sides.

Wisner was armed with detailed answers to the security concerns
raised by dos Santos back in July. The Angolan had claimed that UNTAG
would not protect Angola from continued SADF attacks—via UNITA and
directly. Cuban withdrawal, he had argued, would further weaken Angola,
making it more vulnerable to attack *even after Namibia's independence*

from South Africa. Wisner focused on the underlying strategic logic of our ideas. Implementation of Resolution 435 would instantly alter the security environment of the region. The SADF would have to withdraw fully from Angola *prior* to implementation. Then, under the rigorous and detailed provisions of the U.N. Plan, SADF forces would be confined to two bases under U.N. monitoring and rapidly withdrawn from Namibia to South Africa. Within twelve weeks, 90 percent of SADF forces would leave Namibia; the residual element of fifteen hundred men would depart after the Namibian election was certified some sixteen weeks later. Thereafter, all SADF forces would be south of the Orange River, nearly 1,000 kilometers from Angola's border. This process would, by definition, fundamentally change the nature and extent of the South African relationship with UNITA. Once the U.N. forces had arrived and the U.N. timetable had started, the process would gather momentum. Thus, it was far-fetched in the extreme to imagine that the SADF would return to Namibia, attack UNTAG, incur global wrath for doing so, and then proceed to resume attacking Angola.

In addition, we stressed, there was a fundamental difference between the situations of the parties. The schedule for South African troop withdrawal from Namibia had already been negotiated and was clearly defined in a four-year-old U.N. Plan. Neither we nor the South Africans were proposing to reopen it. By contrast, there was an almost infinite variety of hypothetical Cuban withdrawal timetables that could be proposed within the period between the start of Resolution 435 and Namibia's independence. It simply made no logical sense to argue that *no* schedule within that period could protect Angola's security. For good measure, we also stressed that the relevant time period for the schedule was not seven months (the elapsed time prior to Namibia's election) but something more, perhaps twelve months (the elapsed time prior to Namibia's independence). Pretoria was already committed to a heavily front-loaded schedule for pulling its forces from Namibia. Surely, a proposal could be shaped that would result in the removal of significant SADF forces well before major Cuban departures would occur.

This was the logic of our case. It was a logic we would use for the next six years, not only with the Angolans but with the allies, the Soviets, the Cubans, the Front Line States, and others. For obvious reasons, it was not a logic we could employ explicitly in discussions with the South Africans (who would find out what we were saying anyway), with UNITA (which would leap to the conclusion that the State Department sought its destruction), or with conservative U.S. critics (who presumed in any event that we were engaged in selling the family jewels to the Communists).

The U.S. mediation strategy in 1982, as later, could only be grasped by people prepared to study the negotiation and come to grips with its military and political logic. This was the only way to master such central points as the fact that Resolution 435 and Cuban troop withdrawal were both processes, not events. A settlement might become possible if one process (Cuban withdrawal) of unknown duration could now be defined in terms of the other process (Resolution 435), which was already fixed in detail. We were not demanding troop-for-troop linkage or symmetrical parallelism between Namibia and Angola, and we would reject South African efforts to do so.

We would frequently find that our interlocutors in other African countries were privately surprised at the "reasonable" and "balanced" meaning of linkage in practice. But Wisner encountered fears and skepticism in Luanda. The MPLA pressed for further assurances, such as an explicit South African commitment, guaranteed by others, to end all support to UNITA. We stated flatly that this would not fly: Pretoria would reject any proposal that it publicly abandon an ally, and would likely respond by demanding that the MPLA publicly abandon SWAPO and the ANC. Besides, our "Procedural Framework" already covered the point implicitly. We also stressed that the SADF's *capacity* to provide logistical support to UNITA would dramatically decline under our settlement scenario.

But the Angolans fretted. It was as if they viewed South Africans as possessing some miraculous white magic that enabled their SADF to defy the laws of logic and geography. This may explain another fear which began to be vented by Jorge to Wisner: what was to stop Pretoria from simply concentrating its military might in Walvis Bay? Here, too, the answer was a matter of political and military logic. We and our Contact Group partners were on record firmly opposing any significant buildup in Walvis Bay in the context of a settlement. Walvis Bay was a training base with the capacity to house perhaps one brigade of ground troops. When and if the South Africans decided to decolonize Namibia, that would alter the strategic equation in Southwestern Africa. It contradicted political logic to believe that they would use a distant and potentially vulnerable enclave in order to launch operations across Namibian land and airspace into Angola.

The MPLA did not give Wisner a Cuban proposal with specifics on numbers and dates. But they agreed in principle to consider Cuban withdrawal *during* the implementation period, a shift from the previous stance (only *after* Namibian independence). By mid-September, we found ourselves at an increasingly interesting juncture. We had obtained South African approval of the "Procedural Framework" concept (though not all the wording) and the Angolans appeared interested in it. The concept of a pre-implementation cease-fire and direct talks to define its terms was in play. Military activity in southern Angola had begun to phase down as SADF units pulled back. We awaited word from Luanda to schedule another round of talks at which we hoped to receive a serious proposal. We, ourselves, had specifically cited our goal of reaching a settlement during 1982. While not discussed as a deadline, this was a valid target, both within and beyond the Contact Group. Having a target date had played a useful purpose in breaking quickly through the Namibian agenda items of phases one and two in New York. Now, we hoped that it would help us to obtain a concrete Angolan proposal.

But two sides could play this game. At an early September African summit in Lusaka, MPLA diplomats fueled the virulent anti-linkage sentiment. By not informing their FLS colleagues of our latest exchanges, Luanda was, in effect, acting in concert with the Soviets, who chose this moment to start campaigning in New York for a U.N. debate on linkage.

From their side, the South Africans had become irritated at the growing list of U.S. proposals, all of which seemed to be aimed merely at getting the MPLA to make an opening proposal. Impatient and shirty, they continued to hint that time was running out before they might have to explore unspecified "other approaches" on Namibia. These pressures had begun to take their toll on allied unity. My French counterpart, Jean Ausseil, was losing the struggle for his minister's support and badly needed early ammunition from the next U.S.-Angolan meeting.

Our September 1982 meeting in Luanda did not provide it. Confined largely to tedious exchanges with Jorge, we found ourselves bogged down in protracted discussion about cease-fire details. As though to demonstrate his seriousness, Jorge showed an interest in meeting the South Africans at Cape Verde to discuss a cease-fire. But we knew that the political context did not yet exist for productive discussion. Wisner returned from Luanda convinced that dos Santos lacked a mandate to take a major move.

Neither Wisner nor I were to return to Luanda for nearly two years. This was also, happily, our last encounter with Jorge. Well, almost the last. A few weeks later he delivered a vituperatively anti-American speech before the U.N. General Assembly. Jorge paid a pro forma courtesy call at the New York hotel suite of George Shultz in October. Shultz, who had seen the speech, made a few brief remarks before tossing it in disgust across the table toward Jorge. So ended the first phase of our Angolan engagement.

7

The Angolans Get Serious . . .
and Scared, 1983

By the end of 1982, our Namibia strategy was virtually complete. On the parallel "Angola track," the gradual shifts in the MPLA's position were accompanied by a maze of reservations and conditions. Most important, we had failed to obtain anything approaching a realistic Angolan proposal on Cuban troop withdrawal. We had transformed the regional agenda by redefining the "deal" needed for a settlement. But we had nothing tangible to show for our efforts on Cuban withdrawal and, consequently, precious little ammunition to use with Pretoria. If this state of affairs continued, our negotiating partners would seek cover, and the South Africans would assert that they should be relieved of the obligation to stick with our initiative. The Soviet–Cuban–Angolan nexus would be strengthened. Cross-border military clashes could escalate. In Washington, both the left and the right would start rattling their cages.

In practice, the negotiating situation was extremely difficult to read. Was the glass half full or half empty? During a November swing through seven African countries, Vice President George Bush had forcefully articulated the U.S. vision for achieving a peaceful region, arguing that Cuban withdrawal was "the key to the settlement." Bush's African hosts remained silent or were publicly critical of U.S. policy on Namibia and Angola, creating a public impression of impasse. Also in November, the South Africans (who were not on the Bush itinerary) sent Foreign Minister Pik Botha to Washington for meetings with his new U.S. counterpart, George

P. Shultz. Botha, taking note of the progress on Namibia, publicly declared that there was "a real chance" for the U.S.-led settlement process; but he described Pretoria's requirements in terms that sounded like an "Angola first" form of linkage.

In early December 1982, events introduced new layers of complexity. First, the SADF mounted a bloody raid against ANC personnel in Lesotho, the small but independent state completely surrounded by South Africa. The raid led to unanimous U.N. Security Council condemnation, and seemed to be an omen of what British U.N. Ambassador Sir John Thomson termed "further twists to the menacing spiral of violence in Southern Africa." Yet, at the same moment, top-level South African officials held surprise bilateral meetings with the Angolans (at Cape Verde) and the Mozambicans (at the border town of Komatipoort). American officials did not take part, but described the meetings as a "hopeful sign."

A few days before the Cape Verde meeting, my deputy, Frank Wisner, was in Maputo laying the groundwork with the Machel government for our ambitious Mozambique strategy in talks described publicly as "frank and productive." Within hours of the Angolan–South African meeting at Cape Verde on December 7–8, the MPLA Central Committee announced the grant of "special powers" to President dos Santos in view of "the grave situation facing the country." According to the Angolan media, the leadership "rejected" once again U.S. efforts to create a link or relationship between Namibia and Cuban troop withdrawal. During the same week of December 1982, I was meeting in Moscow with Leonid F. Il'ichev, one of Soviet Foreign Minister Andrei Gromyko's deputies, for an exchange on African problems. It was the second such meeting in recent months, the first since Brezhnev's death, and the only example of continuing U.S.-Soviet regional exchanges at the time.

The attentive newspaper reader—to say nothing of the well-informed Western journalist—could hardly be blamed for asking what was going on here. Who was in charge? What was the agenda? Was there a deadlock or not? At moments like December 1982, we often asked ourselves the same questions. We knew that "stalemate" was not an accurate description of the situation. Rejections of linkage had become a somewhat tedious ritual often used to disguise a far more fluid reality. Our real uncertainty was over the direction of the flow, and whether it supported or hindered our agenda. We attempted to convey a sense of calm omniscience amidst all this confusing activity.

We knew after my Moscow mission that exchanges with Il'ichev were unlikely to offer any basis for forward movement. This old warhorse excelled at waging verbal combat and reading line-by-line from his single-spaced talking papers. Moscow was using these exchanges to fish for information and to make a "principled" record of staunch opposition to our strategy. Il'ichev offered no hint as to Soviet priorities or possible terms, and used the most rejectionist official quotes from Angolan, SWAPO, and other African sources to prove that we were wasting our time.

The ardor of these sentiments convinced us that Moscow was not totally certain of its control over the MPLA. But the tone signaled that the Soviets would wait for further events or move invisibly behind Angolan decisions. By talking to them, we had stripped away the claim (heard in both Western and Soviet bloc circles) that we were unwilling to do so. But their dogged refusal to engage in serious discussion only confirmed that they viewed our settlement as a threat to be blocked. Sowing doubts in Luanda, offering expanded military aid, and working for paralysis within the MPLA all served this goal.

What about the South African raid on Lesotho? Did this action, taken in the midst of openings to Maputo and Luanda, signify that the right hand did not know what the left hand was doing? A leading Afrikaans-language newspaper editor commented that there must be "a screw loose somewhere." He was correct, at one level: such actions inevitably sowed fear and suspicion about South African motives. But, at another level, the garbled message was intended. Many officials within the security and foreign affairs establishment saw merit in a "thump and talk" approach to their neighborhood. They saw it as underscoring Pretoria's regional dominance and demonstrating South African independence of any external power.

We had been informed in advance of the South African encounter with the Angolans at Cape Verde. But it strained our imagination to suppose that these characters would communicate effectively, lacking a common language, agenda, or political idiom. A mediator can hardly make full use of his skills when warring parties choose to meet bilaterally without him. We doubted that they would stick to the tough political decisions each of them faced, and we were correct to be concerned. As we later learned, the South Africans bluntly told the MPLA that if the local parties worked something out, the United Nations and outside powers would go along with it, even if that meant deviations from Resolution 435. The Angolans were warned that they faced disaster if they continued to harbor SWAPO and ANC fighters. The South Africans also urged the MPLA to reconcile with UNITA, while the MPLA in turn proposed that the South Africans hold direct cease-fire talks with SWAPO. Both suggestions were ignored. Angolans probed South African interest in Cuban troop withdrawal, but were stonewalled, leaving the intended impression that this was an American issue which might be sidestepped if the MPLA would strike a direct deal.

That deal, as presented to the Angolans at Cape Verde, was a heavily modified version of our cease-fire concept: an immediate military standstill by FAPLA and SADF forces within Angola, followed by SADF withdrawal back to Namibia, in return for the removal of SWAPO and Cuban forces beyond restraint lines several hundred miles north of the border. A verification mechanism would be set up as of February 1, 1983. According to the South Africans, the MPLA team "welcomed" these diversionary proposals, but expressed reservations about the exact location of the proposed SWAPO and Cuban restraint lines (250 and 175 miles north of the border, respectively). When our ambassador to Zambia, Nicholas Platt, visited Luanda in late January to get the MPLA's version of what was going on, he heard a very different story from Paulo Jorge's deputy, Vice-Minister Venancio da Moura. The Cape Verde talks had produced nothing except an agreement on terms for an exchange of prisoners. The South Africans were showing no restraint. The Angolans had agreed to meet with them in response to U.S. and Contact Group efforts, but had heard only "insincere, dishonest" proposals. Da Moura shed little light on Angolan priorities: he appealed for another U.S. mission to Luanda, but gave Platt no reason to recommend one. Da Moura also managed to convey the false impression that the MPLA would not pursue its separate discussions with Pretoria.

In reality, the Angolans and South Africans remained in contact through the Cape Verdeans about a further meeting, which occurred in late February 1983. By this time, the South Africans had dropped their public optimism of just a few weeks earlier. Reacting angrily to a fresh round of SWAPO guerrilla incursions, top government leaders spoke menacingly of their readiness to assist rebels in neighboring states whose governments harbored Marxist guerrilla movements. The South Africans appeared to have convinced themselves that the MPLA was engaged in treachery. Specifically, they accused Luanda of building up its forces for action against UNITA while also helping SWAPO to stockpile weapons and mount infiltration across the border. The South Africans sent lower-level representatives to this meeting and used it to assert their manhood, subjecting the Angolans to threats and verbal abuse. The meeting broke up after opening exchanges.

These Angolan–South African meetings were widely interpreted at the time as evidence that the United States had been sidetracked by parties eager to escape our agenda. A bilateral cease-fire arrangement, it was argued, could relieve the pressures on Luanda and Pretoria, stabilize the immediate security picture, and leave the Cubans in Angola and the South Africans in Namibia. But, in fact, something more complex was occurring. The pressures mounted by our regional initiative had altered the equation.

Initially, our pressures drove Luanda and Pretoria toward each other: each sought to explore a limited, partial peace that had little to do with a regional settlement. But they quickly discovered the problems in making such a deal. A vast communications and ideological gulf made it hard to collude at the expense of third parties. Profound suspicions existed on both sides. The South Africans' cultural arrogance toward black Africans and the SADF's assumption that it held the high cards militarily all added up to a crude diplomatic performance. The Angolans might bite their tongue (thus contributing to South African self-delusion), but they retaliated by engaging in their own form of Afro-Marxist duplicity— leading Pretoria on with come-hither looks while savaging South African credibility with third parties as soon as the meeting was over. In addition, both parties soon found that there was no real basis for the separate, limited deal they had explored. This lesson would be learned, more than once during the 1980s, and each time it would end up by strengthening our hand.

The MPLA Starts to Move

Another key development was the gradual strengthening of dos Santos, Angola's cautious leader. This, too, was a direct consequence of the changed situation in the region. Since his elevation to the presidency in 1979, dos Santos had based his position on the constant search for consensus among the MPLA's deeply entrenched regional, ideological, and ethnic factions. Until late 1982, however, we had seen little evidence that he had made headway in forcing the tough issues onto the agenda of his party, or in acquiring the personal standing and clout to take major personnel decisions. Dos Santos seemed to require everyone's blessing and to have almost no room for maneuver.

Admittedly, the MPLA was notoriously difficult to read. Insider gossip among Luanda-based diplomats and journalists often proved wide of the mark. Senior government figures were difficult enough to reach, and the top party ranks were even more elusive. Relations between the party, the security services, the presidency, and the armed forces remained obscure. Half-baked theories flourished in the dark recesses of Angolan politics, nourished by a steady diet of rumors about impending party purges, cabinet shuffles, and ministerial scandals. Yet the more dramatic scenarios that might clarify things never seemed to happen. Instead, we witnessed an apparently endless game of maneuver, captured by a colleague's description of the regime as "shoats tussling under the blanket in Luanda." These factional tussles seldom had simple ideological or ethnic explanations. Mestizo intellectuals valued job security as highly as their Marxism, and some were known to prefer their Marxism over any presumed warmth toward the USSR.

Yet something of real importance must have happened between the abortive Wisner-Jorge exchange of September 1982 and Wisner's first encounter with our next Angolan interlocutor in March 1983. The best explanation is that Dos Santos cut down to size the primary factions within the *apparat*—the so-called "internationalist" clique, representing the party's mestizo and Marxist intellectual wing, and the black nationalist faction (sometimes termed "Catete group," after the hometown of key figures), whose "Africanist" leanings had to do with jobs, race, and rivalries going back to the liberation struggle. Dos Santos shuffled, removed, or discredited some key representatives, while avoiding the risk of party purges that could provoke a *coup d'état*. He used the December 1982 meeting of his recently enlarged Central Committee to create a carefully balanced politburo. These moves cleared the way for what he hoped would be a team of loyal, competent technocrats and proven security and military officers drawn from various camps within the party. These were the moves of a leader still improvising to consolidate his tenuous grip on authority, not of one who could dominate his party by force of personality.

Dos Santos took advantage of "external" developments to obtain a strengthened mandate from his party. These developments included a steadily expanding UNITA threat beyond its core stronghold in the southeast, and the sporadic but expanding SADF cross-border operations in Cunene Province. Military pressures and crude, diplomatic signals from Pretoria obliged Luanda to react in some fashion. But the MPLA also faced Soviet and Cuban pressure not to cooperate with Western diplomatic initiatives; the Communist powers backed their arguments with major increases in military credits.

On the other side, our regional strategy forced the MPLA leadership into a continuous need to make choices and define positions. By the end of 1982, the Angolans found themselves running into the consequences of our initiative on all fronts. Our opening to the Machel government in Mozambique, for example, was no secret to the Angolans who, in a sense, constituted its primary foreign audience. Faced with these multiple challenges, dos Santos persuaded the December 1982 party meeting to grant him "special powers" to act within the context of an "overall emergency plan." Special committees on economics and defense and security were established under presidential appointees. Some key personnel moves strengthened his authority, enabling him to deploy his most talented people internally and on the diplomatic front. When it became clear in February 1983 that the Cape Verde channel to the South Africans would produce nothing, dos Santos listened to Mozambican advice and contacted us through special channels that would not leak within the Angolan system.

The Angolan signal ended six months of treading water and two years of dealing with the wrong sort of MPLA negotiators. We had long realized that Manuel Alexandre Rodrigues was the man we should be working with in Luanda. Known by his *nom de guerre* of "Kito," he was one of only four lieutenant colonels in FAPLA and he had previously held a range of top security positions—supervising the police and FAPLA political commissars and heading FAPLA's finance offices and inspectorate general. A politburo member, Kito now served as interior minister, and he headed the party's pivotal control commission. He often served as acting president when dos Santos traveled abroad.

This was a man who knew where to find the levers in the bureaucratic and military machinery of Luanda. With the backing of the late president, Agostinho Neto, Kito had played a central role in 1977–79 when he led the Angolan team dealing with the South Africans and the Contact Group on Namibia. Kito had also arranged a modus vivendi on security issues with the Zaireans during this period. Dos Santos's decision to name him to lead the talks with the South Africans in December 1982 was nothing new; he had been dealing with them for six years. But it suggested that he was again becoming the *de facto* foreign minister.

We were delighted to have this confirmed by the message that Kito wished to meet us discreetly in Paris in mid-March 1983. The approach had been carefully scripted. The groundwork was laid in our opening to the Mozambicans and, especially, in Frank Wisner's skillful approach to Mozambican Security Minister Jacinto Veloso, a close confidant of Kito's. By this stage, the two Southern African governments were proceeding in a sort of loose tandem, held together by culture, shared history, and close personal relationships, now further cemented by the intervention of a wealthy Nigerian jet setter, Chief Anthony Oladeinde Fernandez, who mixed business and politics in the classic African manner. Chief Fernandez liked to wash down Big Macs with Château-Margaux while brainstorming with Kito and Veloso on the best approach to Ronald Reagan's Washington. He helped bring us together with Kito by offering support and facilities. The plan was that Wisner should meet Kito for an in-depth, one-on-one exchange, without notetakers, after which other members of the U.S. and MPLA teams would have a more formal encounter "for the record." Assuming the talks held promise, there would be an early follow-up in the United States.

When he drove up to the entrance of Bois Feuillette—Chief Fernandez's unfurnished château at Pontpoint, near Senlis, outside Paris—Wisner was greeted by the owner and by Veloso, who introduced him to Kito. The chaperons then faded tactfully away while Kito and Wisner disappeared into an empty bedroom featuring a card table and two straight-back chairs. The American and Angolan would have to furnish their own heat to ward off the March chill and their own language skills. Wisner's fluent French was better than Kito's, but Kito—the number-two or -three person in the MPLA hierarchy—had the advantage of status over Wisner, who ranked somewhat lower in our echelons.

These differences did not hamper them in the arts of precise and candid communication. When they emerged from this bizarre venue two and a half hours later, a fresh start had been made. Kito had been blunt in characterizing the South Africans' performance at Cape Verde and equally direct in citing the MPLA's fears—fears of Arab, African, South African, and private U.S. help for UNITA; fears of SADF destabilization of the region; and fears of U.S.-South African diplomatic engagement. History had placed us on opposing sides, and the MPLA would need many reassurances before it could reach a settlement including Cuban troop withdrawal. But Luanda recognized that the Soviets were a troublesome, sometimes unresponsive ally, which could not solve Angola's problems. Neither would the South Africans. That was why the leadership had decided to explore working with the United States for a solution.

Wisner took Kito back through that history to place the relationship in a global perspective. The United States sought to break the cycle of East-West divisions and regional violence, and to achieve stability and security in Southern Africa, so that Angolans and Namibians could build their own societies. How the MPLA and UNITA sorted out their differences was an Angolan matter, to be addressed once South African and Cuban forces were removed from the conflict zone. To get from here to there required the creation of a new political context. Washington had to deal with the divided ranks of the government in Pretoria. Without powerful ammunition, we could try to persuade, restrain, and educate the South Africans; but they would remain on Angola's borders and would not have to choose.

Kito took careful note of all these arguments, planning his approach back in Luanda. Wisner's forceful logic and his respectful presentation were hard to resist. Before leaving Paris, Kito told us that he was convinced of the need for Angola to provide a Cuban departure schedule: "The ball is in my court"—magic words in the ears of a mediator. After consulting Dos Santos, Kito would come back to us.

Kito Comes to Town

The Kito Rodrigues phase of our Angola negotiations lasted from March 1983 to April 1987. It was hard not to respect this extraordinarily versatile man. Born in 1943, he had managed by the age of thirty-nine to master a range of key posts in his chaotically ill-organized system. Quiet but warm in manner, he used a universal language of gestures and anecdotes to convey the essence of sensitive points without revealing too much. Educated in part by U.S. Protestant missionaries, Kito seemed to have a special taste for American college and professional basketball. But he had a soft spot as well for the melancholy *morne,* the enchanting folk songs of Cape Verde's seafaring culture.

For a negotiator, the most intriguing thing about Kito was an artful ambiguity about his own mandate. This must have been a survival skill learned on the job. Kito, we were soon to discover, had as many enemies at home as we did. Did his grasp of the centrality of the Cuban issue mean that the MPLA regime itself was ready for serious business? We were not the only ones with questions. If Kito were to engage his own position and the word of his president, it was essential that he develop a confident sense of the people he was dealing with on the American side; did Wisner speak for Crocker (about whom Kito had heard much but knew little)? Did we speak for Shultz and Reagan? If Dos Santos and Kito were to build a consensus for bold departures in Angolan policy, they would want solid answers to a host of questions about their U.S. interlocutors. They would want to know our attitude on the question of eventual diplomatic relations and investment and trade links. It would also be important for them to understand better the character of our relationship with the South Africans: How much influence did we have? Were we prepared to use it? Did we speak for ourselves or for them in putting forward negotiating concepts? How much did we know about SADF operations, and did we "approve" of them?

The MPLA leadership remained profoundly ignorant of the American system and political realities. Their information about American policymaking was unhappily based on sporadic reports from domestic academics and activists ardently opposed to our policies, supplemented by Soviet and Cuban input, the BBC, and Radio South Africa. In the absence of a permanent U.S. presence on the ground in Luanda, we found that paranoia and well-managed disinformation efforts regularly poisoned the well.

With the aid of Chief Fernandez and Jacinto Veloso, the Mozambican, the MPLA leadership organized a ten-day fishing expedition in April 1983 to find answers to their many questions. First to arrive in Washington was Energy and Petroleum Minister Pedro de Castro Van Dunem ("Loy"), accompanied by Herminio Escorcio, director of the state oil company, Sonangol. An ambitious and articulate representative of one of the MPLA's leading dynasties, Loy was openly bullish about a greater U.S. role in Angola's economy, especially the petroleum sector, which accounted for over 80 percent of Angola's exports. American firms (headed by Gulf Oil, but also at the time including Texaco, Mobil, Cities Service, Getty, and Marathon) were well represented in Angola, and already produced the lion's share of this output. Loy wished us to know that Angola believed in maximizing production, regardless of price. Was the Export-Import Bank prepared to support Gulf in a major expansion of the most promising fields in the north, offshore of the Cabinda enclave?

We told Loy that the Gulf / Sonangol application for some $400 million in Export-Import financing would be acted upon according to its economic merits. But we also used the occasion of Loy's visit to remind him of a basic fact of life: diplomatic ties could only develop in the political context of a settlement entailing Cuban withdrawal. Large-scale U.S. participation in Angolan economic development, beyond the enclave oil sector, would depend on conditions of peace and security. Loy left Washington satisfied that he had been well received and that the U.S. government was not opposing the growing role of American oil companies on political grounds. (The Ex-Im loan was approved in 1984.)

The main event was an extraordinary one-week visit to the United States by Kito and Veloso from April 9 to 15. It was not every day that the interior minister of a Third World Soviet client state (two of them, in fact) visited Washington. We pulled out all the stops to host the security chiefs of Angola and Mozambique, the principal victims of Pretoria's military pressure. Deputy Secretary of State Kenneth Dam hosted a working dinner for them at the Metropolitan Club, where they heard deputy NSC adviser Bud McFarlane and AID Administrator Peter McPherson eulogize Reagan's commitment to peacemaking. During a formal office call at the State Department, George Shultz reinforced the message, while Kito pitched for U.S. recognition and told Shultz that Southern Africa could assure his name in history. Over at the White House, Kito was open-mouthed as Vice President George Bush identified the United States with the MPLA's regional goals, including respect for the sanctity of Angola's internal affairs. Bush advised Kito for good measure that Shultz and his State Department team were the people to work with. Kito and his escorts left Washington moved by the seriousness and coherence of the U.S. team.

But Kito also left the United States with something tangible: two draft Cuban troop withdrawal schedules, to be presented to the MPLA leadership in Luanda. Wisner and Kito, with deft input from Veloso, had begun the discussions at Chief Fernandez's U.S. headquarters, a lavish estate in Greenwich, Connecticut. After several days' work in Greenwich, Kito and his escorts traveled to Washington to refine the timetables, prepare them as typed documents, and review the steps ahead. The genesis of these documents sheds an interesting light on the question of mandates, illustrating our dilemma as mediators.

Until April 1983, the MPLA had ruled out as a matter of principle giving us a specific Cuban timetable. When Kito arrived in Greenwich, the MPLA position had changed: a Cuban timetable defined in reference to the Resolution 435 schedule would now be possible. But that did not mean that Kito had brought proposals from Luanda. Rather, the discussion began with Kito asking us to tell him what sort of schedule we needed as ammunition with the South Africans. We were being asked to make the opening bid in our own mediation!

Wisner and I had talked over the tactics in detail. For two years we had been resisting South African efforts to nail us down to a specific definition of the Cuban linkage. The last thing we needed was to become prematurely committed to any such specifics. It was essential to avoid U.S. fingerprints on any early proposals: there was nothing remotely resembling a policy consensus or an authorized position in Washington. We had neither a specific mandate on this question nor any incentive to seek one. Our approach should be to probe Kito's authority and the parameters of his instructions, and then to work with him in shaping an MPLA proposal.

The Angolan's response was a diplomatic classic. He wished to get on with it, to avoid the need for protracted back and forth. He could speak for his government and even give an indication of what sort of timetable it might be able to live with. But he could not commit Luanda to a timetable without first submitting it to the leadership at home *and* to the Cuban government (since Cuban troop withdrawal obviously involved Cuban interests). Kito urged that specific ideas be developed and put on paper for him to take home.

Since the Angolan did not have an opening proposal, it would be necessary to create a "non-proposal" and to help him sell it back home! Rehearsing ground covered in 1982, we told Kito of the infinite variety of possible proposals and the ways in which they could protect the MPLA's security interests. For example, by the end of the third month of the transition period, when 95 percent of the South African forces had withdrawn from Namibia, would it not be possible for Cuban withdrawal to be 40 percent completed? Kito jumped on this to say that Cuban departures could not begin before the third month. Aha! We had our first MPLA proposal; but we warned that it would be an extremely hard sell in Pretoria. To this, Kito replied gloomily that the South Africans wanted strict linkage in order to force a change of regime in Angola—a statement confirming the MPLA's fear of UNITA (even after the South African force had moved 1,000 kilometers away from the Angolan border).

In the midst of this exchange, Wisner placed before Kito some illustrative timelines laying out the SADF's withdrawal commitments under Resolution 435 and, in the next column, two hypothetical Cuban timetables. Reflecting closely held brainstorming within our team as well as the input of Veloso, these "non-proposals" represented our best effort to focus MPLA thinking and get the bidding started. Both schedules brought Cuban forces down from 25,000 to 22,500 at four months; 17,500 at six months; 12,500 at seven months, when the Namibian election would be held; and some 6,000 at nine months. One model removed the remaining Cuban forces by the time of Namibian independence (i.e., approximately the twelve-month point), on the explicit condition that South African respected Angola's territorial integrity. The other called for the residual to be withdrawn in equal monthly increments of five hundred men during the twelve months *after* Namibian independence.

Kito was not surprised. The two sides agreed that the timetables had no author—they had "evolved" from discussion in a process that could be likened to immaculate conception. Kito found the two-year plan more attractive, even though it was categorical and contained no explicit "condition." The problem was the regime's security, he acknowledged, not the principle of Cuban withdrawal. In fact, he volunteered, the Cubans were more anxious to leave than the MPLA were to see them go. He worried about any areas where a proposal was silent or ambiguous. Drawing on analogy from Angolan lore, Kito noted that houses are built in the valley while wolves howl from the hilltops. If the howling stops, does that mean that the wolves have come down to attack or that they have disappeared over to the next valley? Until every hypothetical question was answered, the MPLA wanted Cubans to help guard their house. After twelve months, the wolves of South Africa would be gone, leaving the "semi-wolves" of UNITA. Ideally, the Angolans would want assurances at every stage, and an undertaking that logistic and other support for UNITA would cease.

Kito pressed the theme that Washington should exert greater effort to "control" the SADF's operations, and complained that FAPLA forces were being bombed at the 16th parallel in preparation for a move against FAPLA's southernmost air defense and infantry garrisons. We told him that the South Africans were on notice of our strong concern about the need for mutual restraint. We did not believe as of mid-April that fresh offensive operations were imminent. But we also knew that SADF planners were busy in the wake of recent incidents of SWAPO violence. In the current climate our leverage was finite; a breakthrough on the settlement process was the best way to strengthen our hand and terminate the SADF's capacity to intervene in Angola.

As for Kito's fear of UNITA, the Angolans should focus on the SADF link, which would be transformed by a settlement, and not waste their time fretting about the bogeyman of private U.S. links, rumored Israeli plans, or alleged Saudi and Moroccan aid. These were either marginal or nonexistent factors in the military balance. Rather than demanding that Pretoria commit itself to abandon UNITA—a demand that would prompt counterdemands for the MPLA to abandon SWAPO and the ANC—Luanda should get serious about a political opening to UNITA. This was the fastest way to end foreign intervention. It would be downright dangerous for the MPLA to isolate Savimbi or to leave him dependent on the not-so-tender embrace of the SADF military intelligence leaders.

Having talked to Luanda by phone, Kito described the figures in the two-year Cuban timetable as close to what Luanda might accept. We agreed on a press line noting simply that there had been "progress toward defining a basis for accelerating the present negotiations for Namibia's independence." This low-key posture would protect Kito at home and enable us to hold close the exact state of play pending further word from Luanda. But Kito's non-polemical approach, his realistic grasp of regional dynamics, and his surehanded optimism all gave us reason to think that we were on the verge of obtaining a credible and authoritative proposal.

"A Wolf on Every Hill"

With the benefit of hindsight, it is easy to conclude that we were wildly unrealistic to believe that Kito could deliver what he virtually promised in April 1983 (assuming that he was leveling with us). But the problem was not with our analysis of the inherent long-term balance between the parties. Nor was it with our analysis of where the logical middle ground of a linkage-based settlement would turn out to be. Indeed, the negotiating parameters contained in the April 1983 two-year timetable bore a striking resemblance to the terms of the December 1988 New York accords.

Our main problem lay rather in substantially misconstruing our negotiating partners. We knew that we were not dealing with an African strongman, but we also knew that dos Santos's position in mid-1983 was stronger than it had been two years earlier. What we failed adequately to recognize was the depth of fear and indecisiveness from which he had started and the distance still to go before Angolan leaders could serve as valid negotiating partners on gut issues of war, peace, and survival. We failed, in other words, to grasp the extent of the MPLA's disunity, the essential weakness of dos Santos's position vis-à-vis his senior party colleagues, and the regime's degree of dependence on and vulnerability to its external allies. Above all, we underestimated how frightened dos Santos and his team were by the world they lived in. Kito's telling metaphor about wolves on the mountain rings in my ears to this day. He returned to it again during a private conversation in late 1984 when he confided that "in Angola, there are many kinds of wolves, and there is a wolf on every hill."

We also exaggerated the Angolan leadership's understanding of the process of international negotiation. As the months dragged on, it became clearer that the MPLA feared that making a proposal—any proposal—would commit them, trap them, and signal weakness.

In mid-May of 1983, Chief Fernandez reported that our splendid reception of Kito in Washington, combined with Angola's obvious need for peace, had enabled the dos Santos / Kito team to carry the day after a bitter debate within the leadership. He cautioned, however, that the Cubans and especially the Soviets would need very careful handling. Dos Santos would have to visit Fidel Castro and the Soviets, whose military support remained vital, to persuade them that our settlement would not represent a defeat or humiliation. Wisner should be prepared to fly to Luanda to receive the MPLA's approved proposal toward the end of May.

In early June, the Contact Group foreign ministers held a special meeting at the Quai d'Orsay, the historic headquarters of the French Foreign Ministry—a scenario to gratify our hosts and tranquilize the antsy Germans and Canadians. Shultz stressed the need for strong nerves and collective effort to keep the restive South Africans in line, bolster Angolan confidence, and turn aside the slings and arrows aimed at us from predictable quarters. Turning to me, he asked when we could expect to receive the Angolan proposal. "By next weekend," I responded without hesitation, as my mind jumped to Kito's latest messages and his travel schedule.

During the course of the next five years, I often thought back to that

Paris meeting and to one of the worst forecasts I ever made. Shultz never once alluded to it, but it was prominently embedded in my memory until the moment arrived, in October 1984, when I could at last bring to his desk an MPLA bid. In retrospect, there had been mounting evidence of a concerted campaign against our diplomacy since the day Kito left Washington. In late May, we faced a noisy and unhelpful session of the U.N. Security Council whose stated target was South Africa's continued control of Namibia. The real target of the nearly eighty speakers—mostly Soviet bloc and non-aligned members—was the Cuban linkage and its American authors. Events like this do not just happen: they are carefully and professionally scripted.

The interesting question for us was to track who were the leaders of the pack and who were mere camp followers. Were the MPLA leaders, in Leninist terms, "useful idiots," who could be counted on by Moscow to block our ambitious diplomacy? Was the MPLA regime itself behind the U.N. games, or was it an unwitting victim of its own official rhetoric and ideology? The answer is that elements of the regime were hard at work to discredit Kito's opening to Washington. Our old friend Paulo Jorge pushed the line that it would represent a loss of face for Angola to make a proposal that included Cuban troop withdrawal. Angola, the Front Line States, the Organization of African Unity, the Non-aligned movement, and various U.N. bodies were on record against linkage, he argued. Why should Angola now embrace it? The hardliners running the Angolan media echoed Jorge's themes.

They were not alone. Shortly after Kito had left Washington, SWAPO held a rare Central Committee meeting inside Angola. Its final declaration blasted our efforts as "a mere rescue operation for the white racists in Namibia," and demanded that we "desist from all attempts to highjack the Namibian revolution." SWAPO urged that the Security Council "resume and exercise its full responsibility for the speedy implementation of Resolution 435"—a theme the Soviets had been pushing since the fall of 1982. It is difficult to believe that Kito enjoyed reading this SWAPO outburst.

Dos Santos returned from a much-publicized visit to Moscow in late May, just as the U.N. Security Council debate was cranking up in New York. We viewed his visit as a critical test of his leadership and of the MPLA's freedom of maneuver. But we were disappointed in our hopes for early clarification. The public line from Moscow reiterated the rejection of linkage, reaffirmed Soviet military support for Angola and SWAPO, expressed Soviet support for dos Santos's efforts for peace in Southern Africa, and demanded South Africa's withdrawal from southern Angola. Against this backdrop, the silence from Kito was troubling. Had dos

Santos not told the Soviets of his "decision" to move ahead in the negotiations?

Dos Santos had reasons for avoiding a direct challenge to Moscow. He faced mounting military pressures from Pretoria and UNITA. There were people in his own ranks whose allegiances were ambiguous. The Russians, Cubans, Portuguese Communists, and East Germans were omnipresent in Luanda, and they had clout. There was a widespread belief that the Soviets had initially backed the failed Nito Alves coup attempt against dos Santos's predecessor back in 1977 because they wanted someone more "reliable" than Neto. Moreover, it was known even to us that the Soviets were not pleased with recent personnel moves clipping the wings of Lucio Lara, the hardline, mestizo ideology secretary, and others in the "internationalist" camp. We had also seen signs of Soviet discomfort at the renewal of active U.S.-MPLA discussions in March and April. The position of dos Santos was dicey.

But members of the Angolan elite could be heard talking with increased openness of their disgust with the fruits of Soviet assistance. American diplomacy was stimulating an inevitable historical process of Angolan self-assertion to which the Soviets had no sure response. It would not work for Moscow simply to cozy up more closely to the mestizos, a mere 1 to 2 percent of the population. Crude Soviet bullying could backfire, driving the MPLA either toward us or still further into the embrace of the Cubans (who had supported the regime during the failed 1977 coup). The Soviets could not afford to ignore their tangled history with Castro and the possibility that Soviet and Cuban interests might diverge again at some point. Soviet officials must have realized that their plodding but systematic efforts to obstruct us had not stopped Luanda from edging toward our settlement terms. To counter the trend, they would rely upon a three-pronged strategy: playing upon MPLA fears; aggravating its divisions; and offering assurances of continued, robust military support.

By July 1983, it was clear that the always fragile MPLA "consensus" behind dos Santos had become threadbare. The Soviets and Cubans may have aggravated these divisions, but they did not invent them. The recent ascendancy of Loy and Kito in Angola's foreign economic and political relations—as well as their growing status in the party pecking order—aroused predictable jealousies on the part of those who had been sidelined.

In the poisonous Luanda climate, anyone who took initiatives opened himself up to opposing maneuvers. An ambitious personality like Kito became a target partly because of his foreign associations. Veloso, Kito's white Portuguese friend who served as Mozambican security minister, aroused hostility and suspicion as a neocolonial alien. It was no secret in Luanda that Kito enjoyed Chief Fernandez's purposeful hospitality and found his tastes congenial. As for Wisner and me, it need hardly be added that Kito could get into trouble for being dependent on the voo-doo dolls of left-wing African politics!

By July, we saw growing signs of impending paralysis in Luanda; party meetings had produced little except rumors of a scandal in Ango-la's diamond-trading operations, a topic enthusiastically pursued by fac-tions known to be unhappy at Kito's rise. A major ruckus had been stirred up in Luanda over testimony I had given in the U.S. Congress five months earlier. At that time, I had restated our long-standing position that UNITA was a "legitimate" nationalist movement, whose interests would have to be taken into account if there were ever to be peace inside Angola. There was nothing new in this; it had been said in public repeat-edly, and Wisner had told Kito a blunter version of the same thing. I had also declined to speculate in public testimony as to which other coun-tries helped UNITA. (This is standard practice in response to invitations to disclose sensitive intelligence data in public.) A loaded version of these proceedings ended up in the hands of Kito's opponents, and we now faced urgent appeals from Luanda for explanations. The official estrangement between our two capitals made it easy to exploit local gullibility and factional paranoia. In addition, the opponents of Wash-ington possessed superior debating skills—powerful tools inside a divided leadership. Neither dos Santos nor Kito was a person to dominate a tough discussion.

A Shifting Military Balance

There is a fine line in statecraft between pressures that trigger new thinking and pressures that drive the target into a Masada mentality, or deeper into the arms of one's adversary. Our experience in 1983 dem-onstrated the point. But it also underscored the unusual complexity of a tangle of several overlapping conflicts: the anti-colonial struggle in Namibia, the Angolan civil war, and the regional war triggered by SADF support for UNITA and MPLA support for SWAPO. Our strategy had mul-tiple objectives and obliged us to play multiple roles.

For example, we understood that South Africa's expanded anti-SWAPO operations in southern Angola in the early 1980s were discrediting the myth that guerrilla violence could "liberate" Namibia. This was not altogether a bad thing if one wished to obtain a political solution. Simi-larly, Pretoria's steadily growing support for UNITA could serve to remind Luanda of how much better life would be with a settlement that would send the SADF home, at last, to South Africa. Did this logic mean that we were on the side of South Africa and UNITA, and against SWAPO and the MPLA? At one level, it was important for Luanda, SWAPO, and their Soviet and Cuban backers to know that it was a new situation after 1981. If they obstructed our settlement terms, the price and the pain would grow. South African power was one of the anvils of our diplomacy.

But the new situation was not as simple as it looked. We knew that it would not help us in Luanda to be perceived as riding on a South African tank to the negotiating table. If *that* were the game—"settle or else"—there was no need for a mediator or, indeed, for a diplomatic process. In reality, South African military power was an anvil, not the hammer. We had different interests and different policies. And we had other anvils. The United States was not conducting an Angolan strategy, but a Namibia-Angola strategy. Paradoxically, our squeeze play represented SWAPO's best chance of obtaining an election and Namibian independence. It would also produce what the MPLA said it most wanted: an end to the possibility of continued SADF logistic support to UNITA and of SADF intervention inside Angola. This explains why our relationships with South Africa and UNITA became so ambivalent and strained. As the wars heated up in 1983, Washington was the object of growing distrust on all sides, and the sentiment was mutual.

Had our strategy been simply to wink at SADF cross-border operations (or actively encourage them), the military record of 1983 would have turned out rather differently. The SADF would have retaliated promptly against a large, provocative SWAPO infiltration campaign in February through April 1983 by mounting punitive actions into Angola. (SWAPO had used the FAPLA and Cuban forces as a shield and a launching pad for their incursions into Namibia.) Instead, the SADF hit SWAPO hard and flexed its muscles with a major force buildup, but the big punch never came.

One reason why it never came is that we insisted on South African restraint. In mid-March, we held a three-day review of regional trends at a retreat in rural Virginia with the top South African national security team; our principal message was a warning that Moscow and Havana would raise the stakes, pouring in more men and modern hardware, rather than be humiliated or driven out of Angola by force. South African officials grumbled, but their intelligence chiefs did not debate our analysis. SADF operations were scrubbed or cut back to avoid further acrimony with us and to minimize contacts with the Angolans and Cubans. From March through July, we warned senior South African officials that we were not prepared to have them use the cover of our relationship to pursue an aggressive policy of air strikes and raids that could derail our hard work with the MPLA. The South Africans clearly wished to avoid the charge that they had undercut our talks with Luanda.

The Soviets, meanwhile, had been moving more or less as we had predicted. They helped FAPLA and the Cubans complete an impressive series of parallel defense lines around modern firebases and air defense facilities in Cunene Province. Begun in late 1981 after the SADF's major operations of that year, this program was stepped up in the immediate aftermath of dos Santos's return from Moscow. By mid-1983, the Soviets, Cubans, and Angolans had altered the balance in Cunene, making it far less vulnerable to SADF air action than it had been two years earlier.

Nonetheless, the Angolans sought to hold us responsible for each military incident, and then to condition their own moves on U.S. gestures and South African good behavior. The harder we tried to meet Kito's requirements, the clearer it became that Luanda was just not up to producing the proposal he had promised. Ironically, the MPLA's lack of response over the months of May through September strengthened the hand of those (both in South Africa and in the United States) who argued that we were wasting our time talking to these feckless Marxists when we should be supporting Angola's real winner, Jonas Savimbi of UNITA. Pressures began to mount within the administration for a basic review of our policy and for me to threaten Luanda with a deadline.

Part of the explanation could be found in the fact that the *other* Angolan conflict, the civil war, was going badly for the MPLA. Since the previous October, UNITA had begun to move beyond its core zone of operations. By mid-1983, UNITA forces were nearly double their 1981 strength, reflecting the infusion of expanded South African support. Savimbi had taken the offensive on many fronts, stepping up classic guerrilla operations in the central highlands—UNITA's ethnic home base. This made life increasingly difficult for FAPLA / Cuban garrisons at the central city of Huambo and other towns along the strategic Benguela Railway. From the southeast, UNITA's forces expanded to the north and west, bypassing major enemy garrisons along the way. Soon they had effective control of much of eastern Moxico Province. Relying largely on foot soldiers and human porterage over vast distances, UNITA guerrillas had also begun to hit at transport routes in northern Malange Province (Kito's home) and the diamond-producing regions of nearby Lunda Sul and Lunda Norte.

UNITA's gains in 1983 were among its most dramatic in the long civil war. Bombs started to go off across the huge Angolan countryside in places where this was not supposed to happen. Journalists, invited to visit and travel with UNITA, began writing stories that pointed to an almost certain continuation of the trend. UNITA captured a number of expatriate technicians from Western and Eastern countries, and skill-fully exploited their public relations potential. Western businessmen became increasingly nervous as UNITA actions moved north and west.

This pattern of events made a mockery of the official line that UNITA could be dismissed as "armed bandits" or "puppets" of Pretoria. Dos Santos had no really attractive options. In the end, he could not ignore the advice of his own military and decline the support on offer from his Communist allies. The Angolan regime would have to respond militar-ily, expanding the size of its low-quality defense establishment of some 35,000 men and equipping them to contest UNITA gains. Angolans, not Cubans, would have to do the brunt of the fighting: neither ally liked the image of Cuban forces fighting the Angolan people. In these circum-stances, the MPLA and its allies decided to beef up Angola's forces and equipment in preparation for future counteroffensives.

Thus, the changing military balance between the MPLA and UNITA in 1983 distracted dos Santos's attention from diplomacy and undercut his ability to pursue it. This became clear when Chief Fernandez returned to Washington in mid-July with a long list of requests for assurances related to UNITA. We sent him back to Luanda armed with a strong letter to dos Santos from Under Secretary of State Lawrence Eagleburger, my immediate superior in the chain of command. The United States had no plans to assist UNITA, and did not encourage others to do so. We hoped to see the civil conflict resolved among Angolans with no outside inter-ference, and looked forward to the time when Angola would be free of South African military pressure or occupation. The administration would use its full weight to obtain a favorable South African response if the Luanda government would give us a credible proposal.

The Washington Timetables Collapse

In early August, we still had no direct reply. Instead, we had word that Kito and his associates were "fighting like hell" to salvage the famous two-year proposal for Cuban withdrawal. There was one decision which Luanda wanted more than all others: the establishment of diplomatic relations with the United States. We will never know if this move would have enabled dos Santos and Kito to impose their will and move forward in the negotiations. They wished us to believe it would transform the situation; officials in a number of Western and African governments agreed. Such a bold stroke, it was argued, would have stunned Angolan fence-sitters and broken the logjam. It could have placed the Soviets and Cubans on the defensive and given us the capacity to apply our influence directly to the Brownian motion of Angolan politics.

In mid-August, I asked Shultz to consider the idea of offering Luanda diplomatic recognition in return for a credible Cuban withdrawal commitment. There was no guarantee that it would work, and the downsides were obvious, especially in Washington. On balance, however, I believed that it would send a signal to all parties that we were deadly serious and determined to compete with our global adversary. Shultz and I knew that American political realities were moving in precisely the opposite direction. MPLA dithering made this idea an even harder sell than it would have been six months earlier. We would be accused of handing Luanda an unearned gift at the moment when there was considerable "hype" in Washington around the "UNITA is winning" theme.

So much hype, in fact, that it had begun to permeate our foreign policy apparatus and parts of the intelligence community. The story paved the way for conservative friends of UNITA to persuade NSC Adviser Bill Clark that he and I should meet Savimbi in Europe. Such a meeting would be purposely leaked in order to rattle the MPLA's cage and tilt the administration visibly toward UNITA. Thus, there were two directly cross-cutting proposals in play within our government. I had no illusions that Shultz would be tempted by the prospect of a bloody ideological row to take up my ill-timed suggestion during the summer of 1983. The idea got buried in his vacation reading.

Our analysis for Shultz was based on African reality rather than wishful thinking (to put the best face on it). It was true that UNITA was on a roll. But to extrapolate that a UNITA victory lay around the corner ignored all battlefield logic. Savimbi's strategy was to maximize pressure for a political deal with Luanda. This, however, did not imply that he could mount frontal assaults on MPLA strongpoints. UNITA forces would quickly become vulnerable targets for better-equipped FAPLA and Cuban conventional troops if they tried to seize and hold major towns. Yet MPLA rule would not be threatened so long as it held the capital and major provincial centers. Even if rural insecurity spread and the country's economy fell still further, it was likely that the MPLA would survive. A UNITA "victory" in the military sense would become possible only if the SADF intervened massively and the Soviets and Cubans walked away— an unlikely scenario. We continued to place our emphasis on political solutions. Indeed, as we told anyone who would listen, our settlement package was the best thing that could happen to UNITA.

We deflected Clark's suggestion of a high-profile meeting with Savimbi, and his urgings that we give Luanda a deadline to produce a serious proposal. Such crude tactics were not going to bring this fish into our net. Instead, in August 1983 two of my aides paid Savimbi a discreet visit in Jamba, his bush capital in the isolated southeast corner of Angola.

This was our first direct contact with the UNITA leader in some eighteen months. Upbeat about his recent gains, Savimbi was far more sober than the growing chorus of South African-influenced UNITA supporters in Washington and other Western capitals. He recognized that the Soviets could, and probably would, raise the ante in support of their Angolan clients, and he knew that there were limits to South Africa's readiness to support his cause.

Jonas Savimbi had a world-class strategic mind, and was quicker than most to understand his own position. He grasped our emphasis on Namibia and Cuban withdrawal from Angola, and saw that the Clark Amendment limited our options. But that did not mean that he trusted us or sought to be helpful. Savimbi would have preferred a more direct and public U.S. alignment with him and a less "balanced" U.S. stance on the civil war—a stance more akin to the one he heard from American and South African conservatives and intelligence officials. Dubious about the MPLA's capacity for independent decision—and fearful of our budding diplomatic engagement with Luanda—he told my colleagues that Washington should make a more direct effort with the Soviets, focusing on both Cuban withdrawal and Angolan reconciliation; the latter, of course, was his number-one priority. At times, he seemed less convinced than we were that Cuban withdrawal would almost by definition lead to Angolan political reconciliation.

It was difficult not to be impressed by this Angolan, who combined the qualities of warlord, paramount chief, demagogue, and statesman. His toughness and courage were as legendary as his ferocity toward those who crossed him. Since breaking with the MPLA in the mid-1960s, he had built up a remarkable grass-roots movement in the towns and rural areas of Angola's hinterland. UNITA clearly was the most potent organization in Angola (leaving aside the Cuban Army). The periodic waves of distrust that got between us were especially frustrating because I respected Savimbi as a serious and capable person. Fluent in three African and four European languages, and well schooled in modern history and world politics, Savimbi was more sophisticated in his grasp and judgments than his Western champions and most fellow African leaders. And yet, he lived in God-forsaken isolation—caught between Angola's corrupt and ineffectual Marxists and their cynical Communist patrons on one side, the staunchly supportive but kleptocratic Zairean regime of Mobutu Sese Seko, and the endlessly manipulative and condescending Afrikaners to the south. Later, when Savimbi and I became caught up in an adversarial game, I knew that it was bad for both of us. But apart from sporadic direct meetings like this one in mid-1983, there was little we could do to prevent third parties from impeding our communication and poisoning our relationship.

Seeing the centrifugal tendencies all around us, Shultz had asked me in late July if we could find a way to freeze the diplomacy in place and hunker down for a while. We would need to fend off pressures for a basic policy change from the White House and other elements of the bureaucracy. But the problem was how to keep some heat on all the parties. As he left for his August vacation, I recalled for Shultz our earlier agreement to consider developing a more substantive exchange with the Soviets. Back in June, we had received a Soviet "non-paper" taking us to task for "hardening" our position by "equating" the security concerns of Angola and South Africa. By way of reply, we might propose that African questions be placed on the agenda when Shultz next saw his counterpart. A follow-up session at the expert level could follow. We would never know if the Soviets had defined their terms for a settlement in Southern Africa unless we probed more deeply. Shultz had put this idea to the President, but as yet there was no decision. (Back in July, I had also noted that there had been no contact with the Cubans since Dick Walters's tête-à-tête with Castro eighteen months earlier. The absence of such contact meant that we were flying partially blind and could not explore and compare the positions of the three Marxist allies.)

On August 14, while we were sorting out these thoughts, meeting with Savimbi, and awaiting the MPLA's reply to the Eagleburger letter, UNITA overran Cangamba—a major center in Moxico Province. This victory, aided at the end by South African air strikes, followed a two-week siege that cost FAPLA hundreds of killed and captured troops (UNITA acknowledged 60 dead and 250 wounded). The Cubans also took casualties, and evacuated a major contingent from the town before it fell. Two days later, we learned from Chief Fernandez that his efforts to help the MPLA leaders compose a "letter of commitment" were running into heavy weather. But the campaign was still alive; the embattled Kito had been joined by planning minister and economic "czar" Lopo do Nascimento.

The Chief arrived in Washington on August 25 bearing a reply to Eagleburger's letter signed by Deputy Foreign Minister da Moura (who pointedly noted that he was replying to a letter addressed to his president). There was some good news: Angola accepted "in principle" the withdrawal of Cuban troops as a contribution to peace in the region, and it was prepared to negotiate the necessary agreements. But da Moura got tangled up in procedural and substantive preconditions, including the immediate end of South African support to UNITA and SADF operations in Angola. A few days after this letter was signed, dos Santos made a public statement, in the presence of U.N. Secretary General Perez de Cuellar (who was visiting him at the time), agreeing to provide a Cuban withdrawal "timetable" (a term previously shunned) if four conditions were met: early implementation of Resolution 435 (i.e., a commitment by Pretoria to an early date); immediate and unconditional SADF withdrawal from Angola; an end to South African "aggression" against Angola; and an end to its military support to UNITA.

It is not a simple matter to make peace when one party demands the fruits of a settlement before placing his opening bid on the table. On the other hand, if we assumed that dos Santos was merely stringing the process along, we might never know whether he could produce. We chose to interpret da Moura's message in the best light as a formal political commitment to our settlement formula, the precursor to actual delivery of a Cuban withdrawal proposal. Vice President Bush agreed to write dos Santos an encouraging reply that accepted the MPLA letter as a solemn commitment, underscored the urgent need for a specific Cuban withdrawal proposal, noted that a proposal would commit Luanda to do nothing until the entire settlement was agreed, and offered to meet with dos Santos when we received a proposal.

This was powerful ammunition. Fernandez, Kito, and da Moura did their best during protracted conversations with dos Santos at the presidential compound in Luanda, September 1–3. They drafted for the president's review a carefully worded reply to Bush that was to have covered the two-year Cuban schedule developed in Washington. But it was too late. Several weeks earlier, shortly after the fall of Cangamba, the politburo had reached the decision to proceed no further—at least for now. Dos Santos had chickened out, going along with a skeptical majority. Kito had lost control of the negotiations. Bitterly disappointed, he sent us a terse message of regret.

It is interesting to ponder what really happened to defeat the 1983 draft Cuban withdrawal proposal. The Soviets do not appear to have "vetoed" it, though they sought to scare the MPLA by pointing out all the problems it posed. The Cubans wished to participate in preparing Angola's positions, but they counseled the MPLA not to reject the proposal. The events of July and August appear to have blown the circuits in Luanda. Had the MPLA said yes, it is possible that some circuits would have blown in Pretoria as it confronted decisions it did not expect to have to face.

In the event, dos Santos sent Fernandez back to us on September 6 carrying a frightened and useless reply. The MPLA, he said to Bush, would not undertake commitments it could not honor or which would mean "suicide." Before Angola and Cuba could make specific proposals, it would be necessary to create a climate of trust. Dos Santos repeated his four conditions and declined to continue the dialogue unless outside aid to UNITA ceased. Wisner told Fernandez that Washington would react angrily to the letter and disengage to let events take their course.

Getting the point, the Chief (with input from Angola's U.N. ambassador) said the letter should not be officially "delivered"; instead, they would try again for fresh instructions. During September, various gambits for prying a proposal out of Luanda were launched—only to be derailed, reportedly because of anxiety over continuing UNITA attacks in the central highlands. The MPLA did not want a rupture with Washington. But, as Kito put it, "the coffee is too hot; the United States must cool it or we'll have to wait for it to cool."

By October 1983, it was difficult to escape the conclusion that dos Santos had failed our test. What we still did not know was the reason: was he too weak to move, or was he maneuvering for better terms and a stronger negotiating position? In early October, he told reporters that if he moved forward on the Cuban issue, he would then be hit with demands to reconcile with UNITA. The comment, like his four conditions, revealed the growing salience of UNITA as a huge question mark hovering over the entire peace process.

Crossing a Swamp at Dusk

The final three months of 1983 were like crossing a swamp at dusk, not knowing the depth of the water or the shortest way to firm ground. Our Contact Group partners, dismayed by both the military and the diplomatic news from Southern Africa, began groping to define their mission. London and Bonn were committed partners, and sought to do what they could to help keep the Group together. The French exploited this dynamic artfully, while maneuvering to distance themselves from Washington and awaiting the time and place for a dramatic exit. The Canadians watched the French in wide-eyed admiration.

Picking up on an idea circulating with Perez de Cuellar and his Secretariat team in the wake of their August mission, the British wondered if the Group might not induce the South Africans to pull out of Angola. The purpose would be to create a better climate for our talks with the MPLA. This idea had merit as a source of possible leverage. But it would not be easy to maintain the necessary balance using the Group as an instrument. In the end, we decided to pursue the British idea through other channels (with London's full knowledge and support). In an exquisite illustration of bad timing, Foreign Minister Claude Cheysson announced on December 7, 1983, that France was "suspending" its participation in the Group, which should remain inactive "in the absence of any ability to exercise honestly the mandate confided to it."

In retrospect, the French departure gratified the Soviets, Cubans, SWAPO, and the Paulo Jorges of the world—in Africa and the West. But the real damage was modest. Once Canada followed suit, this left a compatible rump of three like-minded allies who held ad hoc encounters whenever there was a need. The Group's work as a negotiating entity for Namibia was completed. However, its impending dissolution was a psychological and public relations blow—useful ammunition in the hands of critics and adversaries of our efforts. Inside the administration, we fretted about it as another sign that things were not going well.

One exception seemed to be de Cuellar's late August 1983 report to the Security Council on his mission to Southern Africa. To his surprise, the South Africans organized a warm and courteous reception. He, in turn, appears to have surprised them by the reasoned openness, balance, and non-ideological fairness which were the hallmarks of his stewardship as U.N. Secretary General.

As a result of this visit and his stops in Luanda and other Front Line capitals, de Cuellar could report that virtually all obstacles to the implementation of Resolution 435 had been removed. He categorically confirmed Pretoria's readiness to proceed on the sole condition that agreement could be reached on Cuban withdrawal. De Cuellar of necessity distanced himself from the Cuban linkage (having no authority to endorse it). But his authoritative description of the state of play sent a powerful signal of Pretoria's continued commitment to the linkage deal and of the progress we had made since 1981 in removing many other obstacles.

The de Cuellar report was a two-edged sword. Its detailed treatment of the Cuban issue provoked an intense, emotional reaction from some African U.N. delegates in New York. One exchange between a key FLS ambassador and de Cuellar degenerated into a shouting match. The reason was that his report could be interpreted to validate our version of the situation: Namibia could become free if only the MPLA regime would bite the bullet. This was intolerable. The ideologically "correct" conclusion to be drawn was that the United States and South Africa were using the Cuban issue to block Resolution 435.

When I paid a courtesy call on Paulo Jorge in October, he demanded a specific answer to the question, "Has the United States finally dropped the doctrine of linkage?" I responded that we were trying to solve a practical problem, not to sell doctrines. But Jorge had exactly the opposite interest, and he got busy stirring up the troops. A few weeks later, Security Council debate began on the implications of the de Cuellar report.

We knew exactly what the Soviet-Angolan game was: to force a lonely American veto on a resolution condemning linkage.

After protracted internal discussion, we decided not to play. Instead, we would let the anti-American claque in New York slay the dragon of linkage. U.N. resolutions could not kill it, because we had no intention of changing our policy. We would negotiate the removal of offensive language directed at us, and then abstain when the vote came. The result was U.N. Security Council Resolution 538 of October 28, a ten-paragraph measure asserting that Resolution 435 was the sole and exclusive basis for Namibia's independence and condemning South Africa's insistence on linking it to "irrelevant and extraneous issues" described as "contrary" and "alien" to Resolution 435. It tasked de Cuellar to report back to the Council by December 31, and alluded vaguely to "appropriate measures" being taken in the event of continued obstruction by South Africa.

Decades of East-West political warfare and Third World diplomatic hypocrisy led to such U.N. silliness. Our finesse saved the world organization from looking even worse. However, our handling of Resolution 538 did not amuse the South Africans. Nor was it generally interpreted in Washington as a victory of statesmanship. We could explain our vote to doubters. But some within the administration found it demoralizing to have let the resolution pass, resulting in U.N. condemnation of the doctrine that formed the essence of the President's African strategy. (The Angolans were not the only ones with a Paulo Jorge problem.)

On October 31, three days after Resolution 538 passed, I received a piece of paper saying that Shultz had asked the Department's Policy Planning Staff to coordinate a policy review and report conclusions to Eagleburger. It was hard to argue with the facts. From Shultz's viewpoint, an in-house review was the best way to protect a policy for which he had to provide cover all over Washington. The terms of reference prejudged nothing. Instead, they asked where our current approach stood, whether there were other ways of achieving our current goals (including dealing directly with the Soviets and Cubans), and whether any of those goals should be changed. This was a relatively benign charter. Nonetheless, it was hardly comforting that such a review was considered necessary.

Moscow Plays a Card

On November 11—the eighth anniversary of Angola's independence—dos Santos summed up his hardline message in a final exhortation: "Let us, therefore, strengthen our unity as we struggle. Let us organize the armed defense of the people to defend the revolution." The Angolan leader, jubilant over Resolution 538, declared that the "great imperialist dream of changing political power in Angola" would never come about. Nor had "imperialism" been successful in its campaign to bring about Cuban withdrawal.

One week later, on November 18, officials at the South African U.N. Mission were startled to receive an approach from two Soviet counterparts bearing a message for Pretoria. Moscow was concerned over the situation in Southern Africa. South Africa's military actions, including its support for UNITA, were unreasonable and counterproductive. After the recent U.N. vote, South Africa was now completedly isolated on the linkage issue. It should face the reality that the United States could not bring about Cuban withdrawal and that "the Chester Crocker cycle has now been terminated." The Soviets urged a speedy pull-out of the SADF from Angola. Without threatening Pretoria, the Soviets recalled their Friendship Treaty with Angola and said they would supply "all support necessary" for Angola's defense. Up to now, they added, the USSR had had "only nominal" involvement in the region.

If the real purpose of the message was to open a channel with us on Africa without having to ask, the Soviets must have been disappointed by our failure to request an explanation. But it is unlikely that this was their motive. The final quarter of 1983 was hardly a time of promise in U.S.-Soviet relations. Soviet positions on regional problems appeared to be ossified under the domination of the military and the Party. We were in the long season of no decisions and no compromises in Moscow. To make matters worse, the entire gamut of issues on the agenda was soured by the September incident when the Soviets shot down a Korean civil airliner. By mid-October, Shultz had decided that we would not initiate further contacts in the sporadic U.S.-Soviet dialogue on Africa.

Is it possible that the Soviets were uneasy about the flow of events and seeking to bluff Pretoria out of Angola? Did they wish to avoid sliding deeper into their own Angolan swamp? It would have been in character for them in late 1983 to expand arms supplies reflexively. We also know from subsequent events that decisions were taken around this time to embark on a substantial program to expand and modernize FAPLA. The Soviets were playing a long game; it was not inconsistent to inform the South Africans of that reality and, perhaps, limit its costs.

In addition, the Soviets must have been aware by mid-November 1983 of the discussions in Luanda, Cape Verde, London, New York, and Washington about ways to achieve an SADF pull-out from Cunene Province. It was no secret that we and others were making plans to create a new window for diplomacy. If there was to be some form of South African gesture in Angola, Moscow would want credit for having "demanded" it. Besides, the Soviets and Angolans were not yet prepared for a major counteroffensive.

Soviet predictions of our impending demise were premature. Toward the end of November, I reviewed the bidding with Perez de Cuellar at his U.N. offices. Already anticipating his next report back to the Security Council, the Secretary General wondered if we had anything up our sleeves? He was a quiet believer in our quest for peace in Southern Africa, who wished to be able to report something positive by the December 31 deadline set in Resolution 538.

I decided to take him into my confidence and told him that I would be leaving in a few days to meet with Pik Botha in Rome to discuss ways of breaking the impasse. I promised de Cuellar I would seek something for his report. One possibility was to seek a formal South African decision on the Namibian electoral system—the last "loose end" left from 1982 and an item specifically called for in Resolution 538. But we favored a larger play, one that could transform the broader climate for peacemaking. De Cuellar and I agreed that it would be ideal if a formula could be devised to get the SADF out of Angola.

For nearly two months we had been working on this concept. Good ideas have many parents. Our version took shape in discussions with Chief Fernandez, the British, the Portuguese, Martti Ahtisaari (de Cuellar's special representative for Namibia), and Aristides Pereira, the president of Cape Verde. As we proposed it to the Cape Verdeans, they would host a quiet U.S.-MPLA meeting to help restore bilateral confidence and review our respective agendas. At that meeting, we would undertake to seek from Pretoria a thirty-day "cooling-off" period of maximum SADF restraint. In return, we would expect Luanda to give us its Cuban withdrawal proposal. We would seek to convert the temporary military standdown into a reciprocal disengagement of military forces. Pereira agreed to put these ideas into play with his Angolan cousins, suggesting a December–January timeframe.

On this basis, Wisner and I secured Shultz's approval in mid-October to sound out UNITA and the South Africans on the concept of a cooling-off period as a means of restoring pressure on Luanda. The MPLA did not bite at first, citing vague politburo guidance to place our talks on hold. We approached Savimbi to explain our thinking and obtain his tacit agreement not to disrupt the intricate security equation we were trying to create in the Cunene region (immediately to the west of UNITA's southeastern strongholds). Savimbi was polite but skeptical—probably unsure of Washington's commitment to the concept and uncertain as to South Africa's reaction. But Luanda's reticence and UNITA's uncertainty were short-lived. Soon, the agonizing disappointments of 1983 would become a thing of the past. We did not yet realize it, but when the morning light returned we saw that we had finally reached the edge of the swamp.

8

Breakthroughs and Opportunities, 1984

Within a matter of weeks in late 1983 and early 1984 we created a window for our diplomacy, reversing the previous cycle of escalation. We exploited this new opportunity with all the energy at our command, and came closer to our objectives than would have seemed possible while we were "crossing the swamp" in late 1983. In orbit between the United States, Europe, and Africa, my teammates and I averaged nearly one senior level meeting a month with both the Angolans and the South Africans, in addition to frequent exchanges with Contact Group members, the Cape Verdeans, key FLS leaders (Mozambique, Tanzania, Zambia), UNITA and SWAPO leaders, and other "regulars" like the Zaireans and Portuguese. Much of this diplomatic activity was directed at planting ideas, providing ammunition to troubled negotiating partners, brokering understandings, goading the parties to deliver on past promises, and exposing their double games. But all of it sought to refocus attention on our vision of a different Southern Africa—one where neighbors could negotiate their differences and have the self-confidence to address their internal traumas.

American diplomacy came close to breaking the regional cycle of violence in 1984. The cross-border war finally came to a halt under the cease-fire / disengagement accord negotiated with U.S. help in February 1984 at Lusaka, Zambia. A parallel peace process was launched by Mozambique and South Africa with U.S. support one month later on the other side of the subcontinent. By November 1984, we had opening bids on the crucial Cuban withdrawal timetable from both sides. We had also slowed the cycle of military escalation. For a brief moment, it seemed that the parties' separate orbits could be synchronized. Our task was to freeze this moment and hold the orbits together. When the ground started to shake under our feet in late 1984, that task became impossible. It would take years to recapture the lost moment.

Peacemaking with Kaunda of Zambia

The story of 1984 starts with Kenneth Kaunda. Whatever our problems might be with the Front Line States as a group, we made an effort to stay in close touch with Kaunda. The Zambian leader was a veteran of regional politics since the late 1960s and a key player during various phases of the conflicts over Rhodesia (Zimbabwe), Angola, South Africa, Mozambique, and Namibia. He would soon take over the role of FLS Chairman upon Julius Nyerere's resignation as Tanzanian president. The Zambians had serious interests at stake. They lived next door to the war in Namibia, and they shared a long border with parts of Angola controlled by both the MPLA and UNITA. They also hosted the exiled political headquarters of the African National Congress of South Africa, certain SWAPO offices, and the United Nation's educational arm, known as the U.N. Institute for Namibia.

Landlocked Zambia lived at the epicenter of a bad neighborhood where transport routes and clandestine operations shaped foreign policy. Kaunda had burned his fingers backing political factions that lost out at the time of independence in both Angola and Zimbabwe. Painful experience explained a certain flakiness in his diplomacy, a tendency to seek short-cuts and go with the flow. At times, his moves were inconsistent with the main lines of our regional strategy—and arguably with his own interests. The United States and Zambia were neither allies nor foes; rather, we were sometime associates, depending on the circumstances.

Kaunda was inspired by the desire to cool down the regional conflict. He would mount risk-free forays of statesmanship, but the governing principle of Zambian policy was to discern the prevailing wind. Part romantic and part African mystic, he possessed neither academic attainments nor the intellectual pretensions that can accompany them. Known for the trademark white handkerchief he carried in one hand and the tears he often shed while describing Southern Africa's racial strife, Kaunda ran a somewhat eccentric operation out of his State House mansion.

An eager statesman and globetrotter, Kaunda always struck me as a somewhat lonely man, who suffered under the self-imposed isolation common to the presidents of African one-party regimes. His conversation was laced with references to distant places and far-away problems—Korean unification, the ABM Treaty—suggesting a statesman's pride and the ever present fear of African marginalization in global affairs. A charming visitor, he traveled to Washington equipped with his guitar in readiness to perform African hymns for American VIPs. But Kaunda was also a consummate host and facilitator. He put Zambia on the map as a catalyst for peace by welcoming itinerant visitors and warring neighbors to his presidential mansion. Golfers could try their luck on his combination game park / nine-hole course where "State House rules" included unique penalties (for hitting peacocks) and rewards (the use of impala droppings to improve one's lie). A committed teetotaler and vegetarian, Kaunda offered his guests the best of Anglo-African cooking as well as a choice between South African Reisling and a non-alcoholic "State House" wine.

Despite the man's accessibility and charm, it was no easy matter to read Kaunda's thinking. He listened to many voices, ranging from British businessman Tiny Rowland, the buccaneer chief executive of the Lonrho Group, to a resident Indian swami. On one occasion, descending from the modest State House office of his top foreign policy adviser, I literally bumped into the head of South African military intelligence. The Zambians looked the other way as I greeted General Pieter van der Westhuizen, the darker face of Pretoria's Januslike foreign policy. To get U.S. views across as effectively as possible in this diplomatic bouillabaisse, Washington maintained a strong presence in Lusaka, assigning a string of the finest officers in the Foreign Service as ambassadors.

Access to Kaunda and the one or two other men who mattered in Zambian foreign policy was not a problem. Kaunda received visitors at his mansion with a prompt and civil courtesy. Usually, the first step was an exchange of official statements before the local media in Kaunda's cabinet room. This was the perfect device for structuring a meal of diplomatic sound bites to distract Zambian television viewers. On camera, we would cite shared goals, profess mutual respect, and refer vaguely to the current diplomatic situation. If he felt it to be necessary, Kaunda would allude politely to some differences with us over means. After dismissing his media, Kaunda would ask us to outline our thinking and present our analyses before inviting his officials to pose questions or offer comments.

With this ritual out of the way, Kaunda dismissed most of his team and asked if our ambassador and I would like to join him in his library where the real meeting would take place. He expected us, at this point, to reveal the most sensitive "news," and put forward ideas on how to advance the regional peace process. We did so in the knowledge that others with different interests had preceded and would follow us in those same chairs. Kaunda would protect our confidence, just as he generally protected the confidence of others. He would offer suggestions and counsel when asked, but would seldom volunteer his own innermost thinking.

We knew that he shared to a degree our exasperation at the opaque indecisiveness of the Angolan leaders in Luanda, who seldom produced the kind of solid ammunition we needed to move the South Africans. But Kaunda did not think he was in a position to do much about it. Zambia, like the great majority of African states, does not possess the kinds of power that could be brought to bear on decisionmaking in a neighboring capital. Besides, the nature of his position constrained him from pressuring—or being seen to pressure—a fellow African president facing South African military operations, American diplomatic initiatives, Soviet and Cuban intrusion into his every policy move, and a factionalized politburo. At best, we could hope that Kaunda would support our tactical ideas and help persuade his FLS counterparts—especially dos Santos—that American negotiators were sufficiently skillful and dedicated to have some chance of belling the South African cat.

We knew (and Kaunda knew that we knew) that he maintained a discreet means of communication with his former Angolan favorite, Jonas Savimbi of UNITA. Savimbi was now publicly ostracized for the convenient reason that he had accepted South African help, an item in the secret file of many key actors in the region. Kaunda fully understood that the Angolan civil war would continue to rage—at one level of technology and cost or another—until Angola's factions cut a deal. In that sense, he had long been a champion of Angolan reconciliation. But he felt unable to force the issue or explore the basis for dialogue unless dos Santos asked him to play this role. Relations with Savimbi became increasingly restricted by secrecy and taboo, while Kaunda developed his role as careful, correct, and benign mentor to the person he described as "the young man in Luanda."

Publicly, Kaunda seldom departed from the FLS liturgy on Southern African issues. But he was not content with a regional policy comprising nothing more than overheated rhetoric and anti-South African solidarity rallies. He knew that the Front Line States would gain little from armed confrontation with South Africa. Accordingly, he sought in his fashion to strengthen the alternatives. This explained his decision to reach out in 1982 to arrange a meeting in Botswana with P. W. Botha, his South African counterpart—an action taken on the strength of his own vision. For the same reasons, Kaunda would agree to play host to South Africans, Americans, and Angolans in the meetings that produced the February 1984 Lusaka Accord.

A great believer in dialogue and personal diplomacy, Kaunda based his policy on personal feel, spiritual conviction, and bits and pieces of other peoples' policies. When U.S. diplomats appeared to be on a roll, Kaunda went out of his way to associate with us. His policy and ours became tactically synchronized into a joint operation requiring frequent and fast communication. Nor was "KK," as he is known, unique among the FLS leaders in enjoying reflected light. During the brightest days of 1984, Julius Nyerere of Tanzania offered his strong encouragement and full support.

Emboldened by success, Kaunda later tried his hand with his own formulas. Lacking all but the most rudimentary diplomatic and intelligence capabilities, KK was highly dependent on his partners. He ran into trouble later in 1984 when his diplomacy got badly tangled up with Pretoria's regionwide peace offensive, SWAPO's drive to claim a place at the table, and Luanda's confused search for painless options. We tried to steer him away from such miscues, and Kaunda gave us sporadically useful advice and help in return.

Making Peace by Stopping War: The 1984 Lusaka Accord

The basic concept behind the February 1984 Lusaka Accord was to create a climate of reduced violence and greater confidence so that Angola would table a proposal on Cuban troop withdrawal. But it was no simple thing to achieve a "cooling-off" period and break the cycle of cross-border warfare begun in the mid-1960s. No Angolan–South African security framework had ever existed since round one of the Angolan civil war in 1975–76. Our concept envisioned that political decisions would flow from military ones. Both sides would contribute.

The outlines of the Lusaka Accord took shape during the intensive diplomacy of the previous nine weeks in Rome, South Africa, Zambia, and Cape Verde. In Rome, on December 5, 1983, I met with Pik Botha for the first top-level U.S.-South African exchange in a year. Relations had frayed during the course of our long drive to obtain an MPLA proposal. I told Botha that Washington wanted a significant South African military gesture for a finite period as a means of levering reciprocal moves from Luanda. The United States was not prepared to have its diplomacy stalled while South Africans stoked regional wars and the "military track" became an end in itself. This applied in Mozambique, just as it did in Angola-Namibia.

Protracted conflict was not what we had in mind when we started our efforts in 1981, I reminded him. It was not serving either South African or American interests: it would erode what had been accomplished so far, undercut MPLA moderates, and further entrench the Cubans and Soviets. Our objective was to get the Cubans out and reduce Soviet influence in the region—not to bleed the Cubans or try to force the Soviets out by vain efforts to destroy their MPLA client. Letting military events take their natural course would lead us nowhere since no party could win. The recent Soviet message to Pretoria could be interpreted in various ways, but it would be unwise to ignore Moscow's escalating military assistance or to assume that the Soviets could be bluffed out of Angola.

Ever the consummate performer, Botha slipped into his Godzilla suit to rebut my pitch, using the standard lines of South African geo-speak. The Soviets, he began, would eventually be forced out by the intractable reality of black Africa. Already the balance had moved against them. UNITA was now far stronger than in 1981 (true), and by riding out the conflict, the West and South Africa could wear down the Marxist coalition (far less likely; such pressures work only when linked to a credible diplomatic track). We argued over whether it would make more sense to negotiate Angolan internal reconciliation first, since the MPLA was obviously troubled by fear of losing the Cubans. We argued about the net effects of a prolonged, bloody stalemate, with Botha taking the bullish view. We pointed out that this was the game the Soviet military would be comfortable to keep right on playing, especially during a succession of dying Soviet leaders.

In a rhetorical crescendo, Botha suggested that perhaps we should just call off our fragile new relationship. Referring to the friction over SADF military action during 1983, he said, "I cannot keep saying yes to your requests." Washington should stop asking Pretoria for things to help fend off the pressures we faced to deliver "results" in Southern Africa. Go ahead and impose sanctions, he bellowed. Yes, South Africa might have to face ten years of isolation, but it would reemerge stronger as blacks throughout the region, their backs against the wall, reversed ground and appealed for an end to external sanctions. Waxing eloquent, he asked what more he could do after three years of effort to "help" Washington force the Cuban issue. We told him to turn the tables on his (and our) growing list of detractors. It was time for a strong and credible peace initiative.

This was an important exchange. It captured the essence of Pik Botha's diplomatic art. By playing devil's advocate to my more nuanced reading of the Angolan situation, he was making a hawkish record to take home.

But he was also rehearsing the lines he knew he would hear back in the locker room of South African policymaking. He was carefully absorbing the argument and analytic input we provided. Botha partially agreed with us, but he could not carry the debate at home unless he had powerful ammunition. Often, we were his only "independent" source of analysis on regional military developments and Soviet affairs. It could make a difference if he returned to his locker room with the word that senior American officials did not believe the Soviets could be forced out of Angola.

The exchange accurately reflected the foreign minister's (and Pretoria's) sense of timing. Washington was prepared, if necessary, to play a long game, grinding down resistance to the settlement concepts we had designed. For us, there were few acceptable alternatives; we certainly had no interest in the unilateral options Pretoria had hinted at periodically since the late 1970s. I was not prepared to entertain even the possibility of a Southern African policy based on letting nature take its course. The South African sense of timing was different. Botha had interpreted the U.S. initiative of 1981 as an interesting and attractive idea which, unhappily, was not working. This delay in ripening a settlement exposed him to continuous challenge at home. He faced pressure from the security establishment to redefine South African strategy in the direction of unrestrained and open-ended regional interventionism. Prime Minister (later State President) P. W. Botha sympathized with his military advisers; and, in addition, as the top political leader he naturally viewed regional scenarios in an ever-changing domestic political context.

From Pik Botha's perspective, my colleagues and I were constantly asking him to restrain his military, pacify his irascible state president, block alternative South African strategems, and basically to freeze the Namibia situation for the indefinite future—regardless of the budgetary and political implications. It was as if we wished him to keep the Namibia engine running year after year, fuel topped up and a full crew in place, in the hope that there would someday be an Angolan train it could hitch up to for the final leg of the voyage.

Despite his familiar bluster, however, it was obvious that Botha saw an opportunity in our Rome message. When I reiterated the merit of acting now, before the next rainy season when SWAPO's forces would begin their southward infiltration campaign, Botha interrupted the discussion and excused himself from the room. He said he wished immediately to phone Defense Minister Magnus Malan to mention a South African initiative that could be placed on the agenda of the State Security Council in Pretoria one week later. Botha returned to the room looking like he had just landed a nice fish.

It was not exactly the fish we were hoping for. On December 6, the SADF mounted "Operation Askari"—a five-week operation that included air sorties as far as 200 miles north of the Namibian border and ground action 125 miles into Angolan territory. It was the largest SADF operation in Angola since 1981, and appeared to be aimed both at preempting SWAPO incursions and at distracting the MPLA and Cubans from their anti-UNITA counteroffensives. "Askari" was also the South African government's reply to the Soviet warning message of November, and its answer to the progressive hardening of the FAPLA / Cuban defense lines (next to which SWAPO liked to locate).

It was not uncommon for the South Africans to try to associate us with actions such as this long-planned military operation. But Pik Botha had a serious purpose. He wished to use our Rome meeting and "Askari" to launch a new regional initiative. On December 15, Botha wrote his new friend, the U.N. Secretary General, to announce that Pretoria was prepared to begin on January 31, 1984, a "disengagement of forces which from time to time conduct military operations against SWAPO in Angola," provided that "this gesture would be reciprocated by the Angolan government." Specifically, the Angolans should ensure that their forces, the Cubans, and SWAPO did not "exploit the resulting situation." In this initial version, the South Africans were not proposing to negotiate a permanent arrangement. Rather, they would pull out unilaterally for thirty days; if the other side responded appropriately, the period of disengagement and restraint could be extended.

A confusing spectacle ensued. First the MPLA (December 31) and then SWAPO (January 5, 1984) accepted the South African proposal, subject to conditions of their own which were complete non-starters—e.g., a pledge by Pretoria to begin implementing Resolution 435 fifteen days after the end of the thirty-day period. The MPLA sought to pass the buck for controlling SWAPO to the U.N. Secretary General by requesting him to undertake consultations with SWAPO and the South Africans about a cease-fire. SWAPO grabbed this opportunity to assert itself as "the other party" in the Namibia conflict; a cease-fire was fine if it were linked to an irreversible commitment to begin the transition to independence. Pretoria, of course, had no intention of gratifying SWAPO in this manner, or of committing itself to proceed with Resolution 435 in the absence of a deal on the Cubans. Soon, Pik Botha and SWAPO President Sam Nujoma were trading public insults.

At this delicate juncture, we faced yet another test in the U.N. Security Council: a draft Soviet–Non=aligned–African resolution condemning South African military action in Namibia and Angola, demanding that Pretoria provide war reparations to Angola, and calling on member states to render "all necessary aid" to the MPLA regime. It would be difficult to imagine a less helpful form of U.N. activity at a time when serious diplomacy had just begun to take hold. The British joined us in abstaining on Resolution 546. Botha dismissed the resolution with contempt. Meanwhile, Malan claimed victory in the SADF's current "preemptive operations" against SWAPO, and spoke favorably of negotiations to resolve regional differences. (By now, Pik Botha's initiative was looking more attractive to the SADF, which had run into some newly delivered air defense missile systems; it was the right moment to scale back Operation Askari.)

On January 10, the Mozambican security minister, Jacinto Veloso, summoned our ambassador in Maputo and introduced him to Kito Rodrigues, our elusive Angolan interlocutor. Having held us up for the past four months, the Angolan breathlessly proposed a meeting at Cape Verde in ten days' time! He handed over a complex draft agenda, including all the MPLA's desiderata from the previous two years, plus the immediately relevant items (a thirty-day "truce," restrictions on SWAPO operations) and the basic linkage formula (Resolution 435 and Cuban withdrawal). But the encouraging thing was Luanda's uncommon sense of urgency. On their side, the South Africans were uneasy about the ambiguity of their own proposal and the responses to it. They began to explore with us the best way of obtaining "agreement" on it. They had no intention of pulling completely out of Angola without getting something specific in return.

The trick at this point was to avoid procedural snags and focus attention on obtaining a military standdown. Three-way talks between the U.N. Secretary General, SWAPO, and the South Africans had to be avoided. There was nothing for these parties to negotiate about: all necessary arrangements for putting Resolution 435 into operation had already been agreed. We decided to place a positive interpretation on the South African proposal *and* on the MPLA and SWAPO responses to it. The conditions and caveats would be quietly set aside and, if possible, ignored. South Africa's initiative would remain "unilateral," and we would now work with the MPLA to obtain its "unilateral" response.

On January 20–21, 1984, Frank Wisner met with Angolan Vice-Minister Venancio da Moura at Mindelo on the Cape Verde island of Sao Vicente. These wide-ranging talks turned the page with Luanda. In a joint minute rather grandiosely entitled the "Act of Sao Vicente," the Angolans undertook to control SWAPO once the SADF had withdrawn and FAPLA units could reestablish effective control of the vacated area. The United States undertook to use its influence with South Africa to support the disengagement. Both of us agreed on the need to exploit this opportunity to resolve the larger issues (including Resolution 435 and Cuban withdrawal). Each side stated its position as to how the process should unfold.

On the strength of the Cape Verde meeting, I traveled to Cape Town to nail down the outlines of the deal with the South Africans and brief our UNITA and FLS partners on developments. But on arrival at the Fleur du Cap meeting site outside Cape Town on January 27, I found Pik Botha and the entire security establishment preoccupied by a tangle of diversions. Botha asked us to support a scheme he attributed partly to Kaunda for a grand summit in Lusaka that would include the United States, South Africa, Zambia, SWAPO, the internal parties and the Namibian Administrator-General as well as the MPLA and UNITA! The summit would "converge with" and broaden the January 31 disengagement, giving Kaunda something to offer to SWAPO, Botha lamely argued. My teammates and I glanced at each other: this would be another one of those meetings that open with outlandish South African gambits. (Later we learned that the Lusaka "open house" proposal was intended to deflect P. W. Botha from still less promising ideas, such as a speech abandoning Resolution 435 altogether and handing responsibility for Namibia to the local, white-led power structure.)

To get past this new hurdle, we conveyed the solid news from Cape Verde of the MPLA's commitment to reciprocate the SADF's pull-out. The real issue was how to proceed after the first thirty days. There was also the problem of how to assure smooth communication, especially in the early days when military incidents would be almost inevitable. And there was the matter of verification and how to handle possible violations. Would it not make sense to plan for a trilateral U.S.–Angolan–South African meeting soon to hammer out a package of reciprocal commitments? The South Africans grumbled as if they were still wondering about the wisdom of their own proposal ("We made the offer only because the United States asked us to"). But they were impressed with our firm assurances from Cape Verde. If Luanda was prepared to police SWAPO and keep the Cubans well north of the previously SADF-occupied salient— and if the United States would provide cover in the United Nations in the event of MPLA / SWAPO bad faith—they would go ahead as planned. The South Africans were also prepared to join a three-way meeting with the MPLA in mid-February. We had our basis to proceed, and notified the Angolans immediately of the outcome at Fleur du Cap. Pik Botha succeeded in shifting his president's January 31 speech in a more statesmanlike direction, stressing the urgency of an internationally acceptable Namibian solution.

It was a good thing that we had a head start in planning an early trilateral meeting. By February 4, the air was thick with reciprocal accusations and confused reports from southern Angola. The South Africans were still in the salient they occupied athwart SWAPO's primary infiltration corridors. The loosely worded December 15 proposal did not mean that the SADF would be out of Angola by January 31, but that it would begin a thirty-day withdrawal process and start observing a cease-fire on that date. Meanwhile, the South Africans reported intercepting a group of some one hundred SWAPO fighters who had crossed into Namibia. This appeared to be an effort by SWAPO to demonstrate that it had forces within Namibia when the shooting stopped.

Despite the extreme fragility of the situation, the parties stayed with us. When I visited with him on January 29, I found Kenneth Kaunda effusively supportive of what we had accomplished at Cape Verde and Fleur du Cap. President Nyerere of Tanzania echoed Kaunda's line, closing our meeting with the words, "Let me know if I can help"—not his original reaction when we met in 1981. SWAPO president Sam Nujoma, in remarks from Lusaka that coincided with my visit, publicly committed SWAPO to respect the disengagement. MPLA officials told us that SWAPO would pull its forces north of the Namibe-Lubango line, 200 miles north of the border.

This seemed an excellent time to reach out to the SWAPO leadership. We had picked up evidence of SWAPO's deep suspicion about the disengagement, combined with a fear of being sidelined and losing its freedom of maneuver. I asked my special assistant Robert Cabelly to track Nujoma down and deliver a personal message from me, appealing for restraint and assuring him that our goal was to achieve a Namibian settlement. Cabelly was especially well suited for this mission. As my special assistant and senior intelligence staffer, Cabelly spoke with blunt authority. No American knew more about South African decisionmaking; his unvarnished account of the facts of life could, ironically, impress Nujoma that he was being taken seriously. We did not want to elevate SWAPO to the status of a party (a move that would have caused us untold headaches with other non-state parties, as well as with Pretoria and the FLS). But we saw every reason to treat it with respect. The gesture of sending Cabelly to brief Nujoma in person would reinforce my regular channel of communication with his highly effective U.N. representative (and *de facto* foreign minister), Theo Ben Gurirab.

Years of effort by U.S. diplomats to gain a measure of Kaunda's confidence paid off in February 1984. We had kept him closely informed of our settlement drive since the beginning. This made it possible for us to approach KK on very short notice to seek a venue for direct, three-way talks with the MPLA and the South Africans. Kaunda's instinctive reading of the flow of events persuaded him that our request was a golden opportunity. After comparing notes with dos Santos in Lusaka on February 5, he quickly agreed. The stage was set. This would be the high point of Kaunda's involvement in the Namibia-Angola peace process.

At this juncture, Lusaka was the ideal venue. For the South Africans, Lusaka symbolized public respectability and confirmed political status. For the skittish Angolans, the Zambian capital offered ideal protective coloration for their dealings with South Africa (and the United States). As for us Americans, a Zambian venue would legitimize our strategy and anchor it amongst the Front Line States right on the heels of their campaign to exorcise the demon linkage by organizing a U.N. resolution to "reject" it. And not least, the choice of Lusaka would give Kaunda himself some stake in the continued health of the peace process.

Lusaka is a sprawling city of teeming residential areas, verdant suburbs for expatriates and diplomats, and extensive government facilities. Its modest commercial shopping district and "international" hotels are not the place for discreet diplomacy. Kaunda offered us his vast conference center at Mulungushi Hall, a facility indistinguishable from scores of look-alikes scattered around the globe. His people organized a series of interlocking rooms where smaller or larger exchanges could be held over tea and room-temperature soft drinks.

We had worked out a scenario in which delegation heads would arrive after two days of "preparatory" work among political and military experts. Kaunda held preliminary bilateral sessions with each delegation upon arrival to hear its assessment, gauge the mood, and offer his support. This enabled him to remain informed without committing him to any substantive role. It was both logical and helpful that he would defer to us as broker and mediator between Luanda and Pretoria, rather than trying to insert himself directly into the substance. The broad outline of a deal had been prepared before anyone arrived in Lusaka, but a lot more hard work was required during the "preparatory" talks.

Our "working-level" team, led by Bob Frasure (then serving as the Africa man in our London embassy), Ambassador Nick Platt, and Jim Woods, my Defense Department counterpart, quickly discovered that three-way meetings were a bad idea. Angolan and South African representatives would not say anything useful to each other in our presence, and they refused to meet without us. But by engaging these wallflowers in separate rooms, the American team discovered that they were eager to come up with something concrete. The problem was that they had no mandate to propose anything! It fell to us to define the formula, sell it to each side, and then help them hammer out the plan for putting it into action.

Once I and the other delegation heads (Kito and Pik Botha) arrived, Kaunda opened the only plenary meeting of full delegations with a prayer reminding all parties of the urgency of peace—and promptly left us to make our remarks, ratify the accord prepared by the experts, isolate any remaining issues, and arrange our joint press guidance. At the conclusion of the meetings on February 16, Kaunda offered more prayers and a fine banquet. Throughout the meetings, he maintained an open door at State House for delegations to seek his counsel or lobby their cause.

The Lusaka meetings ranged over a large agenda. Our tasks were (a) to strengthen the fragile "peace" on the ground; (b) to define and establish a new military regime in the salient of Angolan territory being vacated by the SADF; and (c) to explore ways to extend the parties' commitments beyond the first thirty days. Each of these items had multiple parts. The new military regime had to be defined geographically. An understanding was required on the return of FAPLA forces to this area; a monitoring mechanism and channel of communication would be needed; so, possibly, would joint patrols and jointly manned border posts. Beyond these immediate tasks, we wanted Lusaka to serve as a psychological watershed pointing toward accelerated progress in the political discussions.

The Lusaka Accord of February 16 created the new security regime. By defining a no-go zone for SWAPO and Cuban forces in a large area of Cunene Province, the accord created a balanced context for South African withdrawal and Angolan reassertion of sovereignty. Pretoria and Luanda approved detailed arrangements for phased withdrawal of the remaining South African forces and phased introduction of a FAPLA presence in the territorial salient described by the signatories as "the area in question." Geographic lines, timeframes, and reciprocal obligations were spelled out with military precision. SWAPO infiltration routes would be jointly monitored during the thirty-day disengagement period.

To handle the functions of verification and communication, the parties created a bilateral Angolan–South African Joint Monitoring Commission, to which U.S. observers would be welcomed. The commission held an inaugural ministerial meeting in Lusaka. Its first on-site meeting would take place on February 25 at the Cunene town of Cuvelai—an important garrison town in the north-central part of the salient. The thirty-day clock would start at Cuvelai, and meetings of the Joint Monitoring Commission would be held as required at towns under FAPLA or SADF control as the South Africans moved south to the Namibia border.

•

Lusaka was a sweet success, which quickly bolstered our fortunes in Africa, Europe, and Washington. Kaunda was tickled with the high visibility pay-off for his gamble in hosting talks that had stopped the war between his neighbors. Pik Botha, Magnus Malan, and their team were delighted to be on the high ground and quick to pledge their close cooperation in achieving a Namibia-Angola settlement. They were predictably unrealistic about their own bargaining position; but it was refreshing to be dealing with a government committed to a regionwide peace offensive rather than having to do all the pushing ourselves. Botha would be off to Maputo in a few days time carrying a draft non-aggression pact for discussion with the Mozambicans. The South African penchant for self-destructive tactical maneuvers remained much in evidence, and their overconfidence was troubling. But it was at least plausible to believe that Pretoria was on a more constructive path.

Our side discussions with Kito confirmed the distinctly more constructive Angolan outlook which Wisner had detected at Mindelo a few weeks earlier. He was relieved to hear that Savimbi had just assured me he would not disrupt the new arrangement. Kito appeared to grasp the utility of the American dialogue with UNITA and to see the clear distinction between the U.S. and South African roles. Yet, when we discussed the timing of our next bilateral meeting to review the broader negotiation, he underscored that the MPLA would closely watch the disengagement process before taking further steps. The United States, he argued, should persuade Pretoria to stop pumping up UNITA. Otherwise, it would be "difficult" to resist the pressures to accept more Cuban troops and more Soviet hardware. What Kito did not tell me was that trilateral Angolan–Cuban–Soviet discussions had already endorsed a major further expansion of Soviet arms deliveries over the next twelve to fifteen months.

The Slow-motion Disengagement

Within days of the Lusaka Accord, South African and Angolan officials were enmeshed in operating their new mechanism, the Joint Monitoring Commission. Kick-off sessions of the commission at Cuvelai produced agreement to move the formal start of the thirty-day disengagement process back to March 1. But a month later, the commission was still deep inside Angolan territory. Joint patrols had actually clashed with SWAPO units (to Pretoria's delight and Luanda's deep embarrassment), and modest SADF units remained within the salient. They would remain deployed in Cunene Province for many more months: the "final" pull-out of South African forces under the Lusaka Accord did not occur until April *1985*, one year behind the original schedule.

What happened? Basically, neither side had a powerful incentive to move the commission swiftly to the border. SADF representatives on the commission sought to maximize the use of joint patrols aimed at SWAPO, and resisted moving south until previous SWAPO incidents were investigated. They pressed for credible FAPLA efforts to prevent SWAPO infiltration. In addition, the South Africans argued that a follow-on mechanism (including provision for joint patrol) would be essential as soon as the Joint Monitoring Commission reached the border. They warned against moving to the border until its charter had been agreed. In other words, the South Africans wanted to retain the functional equivalent of their Angolan salient under a new rubric.

On the Angolan side, all sorts of motives came into play. The very fact of delay in implementing the Lusaka Accord served as a strangely useful tool of MPLA diplomacy: it enabled Luanda to deflect U.S. pressure to get on with the principal negotiation, and it permitted Luanda to berate Pretoria publicly for not meeting the agreed deadline (April 1, 1984) for completion of the disengagement. But the public posture bore little relation to reality. In our discussions with MPLA officials over the fourteen months following Lusaka, we never detected a trace of Angolan impatience to have the Joint Monitoring Commission reach the border. They quickly recognized that the South Africans liked the symbolism of the commission. Keeping it in play kept the SADF on a leash. We sometimes wondered, too, if FAPLA units did not prefer being co-located with SADF units: they certainly lived better this way, and probably lived longer, too. The result was a bizarre spectacle in which the two governments officially attacked each other's failure to move forward, while their military personnel attached to the Joint Monitoring Commission were shacked up together in Angolan camps like common-law partners.

Neither side made it easy for us to devise a formula. South Africa wanted a continuing right to participate in joint patrols inside Angola after the disengagement was complete, a notion the Angolans quickly rejected as an unacceptable infringement of sovereignty. By May, MPLA officials were saying that they could not extend the disengagement unless we could arrange a SWAPO-SADF cease-fire accord that would give them political "cover" by linking the disengagement to Resolution 435. In other words, the Angolans were not prepared physically to restrain SWAPO once the SADF had completed its withdrawal. They wanted SWAPO to suspend its violence in the context of a cease-fire accord with Pretoria. SWAPO, of course, was eager for such an accord but would try to link it to a date for Resolution 435. The problem with this Angolan position was that it gave SWAPO and the South Africans a veto over the next step. The poisonous chemistry of distrust, fear, and hatred existing between them virtually assured the collapse of any plan dependent on their joint endorsement.

From April to November 1984, we tried to meet all these concerns and devise a formula for extending the Lusaka Accord. In an effort to meet the Angolans' requirements, we convened a meeting in July 1984 at Cape Verde between SWAPO leaders and a South African team headed by the Namibian Administrator-General to approve a "cessation of hostilities." The Cape Verdeans and Angolans joined us as chaperons for the event. Despite weeks of careful, detailed work on a draft agreement, the July meeting broke down in a few hours. Arrogance and ineptitude on the South African side and self-destructive intransigence on SWAPO's caused the breakdown.

We resolved at that point never again to put the South Africans and SWAPO in the same room until everything had been agreed and implementation was within sight! We made a final stab at getting agreement by suggesting that they send parallel letters to the Secretary General. But SWAPO refused to cooperate on any formula unless Pretoria provided a "date certain" for Resolution 435—an impossible demand until we had obtained agreement on a Cuban withdrawal schedule.

Thus, the Lusaka Accord had a range of consequences. It eventually cleared the way for unprecedented progress in the main negotiation by creating conditions in which Luanda finally came forward with its first Cuban withdrawal proposal. At the military level, it led to a fairly effective cessation of cross-border violence for over a year. Yet there were also perverse consequences: the Angolans and South Africans were unduly "comfortable" with a limited deal that made the status quo less costly. Pretoria could defang SWAPO, reduce its military and diplomatic exposure, and concentrate on helping UNITA. Luanda gained a breathing space to build up strength for possible future contests. And it achieved the gradual return of Cunene territory, while continuing to attack Pretoria for "delays" in fulfilling the Accord.

During 1984, some ninety South African and five Angolan complaints of violations were raised on the Joint Monitoring Commission. But the overwhelming majority of such complaints were filed away and ignored. The top-ranking SADF officers responsible for the disengagement became convinced that the Angolans and SWAPO were conducting a deceitful charade to cover up continuous SWAPO violations. But they received little support from higher-ups in Pretoria's civilian leadership, which was more interested in exloiting the Lusaka Accord as a political win. We heard parallel complaints from Angolan officials involved with the commission. Just as SADF officers were certain that FAPLA passed intelligence to SWAPO and "protected" it from commission monitoring, FAPLA officers were certain that the SADF used the commission to help out UNITA with intelligence and advice that undermined FAPLA's war effort. Both sides treated the Lusaka Accord as an alternative context for prosecuting the underlying conflict.

The Games Regimes Play

Pretoria's regionwide peace offensive in the first half of 1984 became one of the great bum's rushes in modern diplomatic history. After signing the February 1984 Lusaka Accord, the South Africans mounted four months of non-stop diplomatic activity. Non-aggression pacts were signed with Mozambique and Swaziland in March. Paralleling the Joint Monitoring Commission meetings inside Angola, the South Africans used Kaunda's hospitality and the Lusaka framework to schedule monthly encounters in Zambia with Angolan and Zambian leaders. In mid-June, all this regional diplomacy was rewarded when P. W. Botha was welcomed on a seven-nation tour of Western European capitals, a first for any South African leader.

In all his years of public life, P. W. Botha had never ventured out of his South African cave for an overt, acknowledged visit to a Western country. His lack of acquaintance with the Western world was, in fact, one of our underlying problems. We were delighted that Europeans were prepared to throw a coming-out party for the Bothas. It was a form of Western recognition for statesmanlike behavior; yet we could remain in the background, not a bad outcome for both domestic political and foreign policy reasons. Nor did we necessarily oppose the pace of Pretoria's post-Lusaka peacemaking efforts. It made good sense, in fact, to keep the Soviets and Cubans off balance by creating a steady stream of "new facts." It was also wise to diversify the diplomacy in several directions: none of South Africa's neighbors wanted to monopolize the stage as Pretoria's steady date.

But Pretoria needed to act wisely, on the basis of reciprocity, and in a manner that could inspire African trust and confidence. I soon found myself warning Pik Botha of the need to present his neighbors with bite-size decisions and, especially, to coordinate his moves with us and them *before* taking action. But the South Africans remained true to their traditions of crude unilateralism. Sensing an opportune moment to burst through the bonds of isolation, they seized it in a graceless dash to establish a regionwide *Pax Pretoriana*.

Pik Botha's breathless diplomacy was accompanied by glowing SABC radio broadcasts about the burgeoning prospects for peace among African brothers if the principles of regional cooperation, non-interference, and respect for territorial integrity were respected. But, in the next line, came the warning: unless neighboring states agreed to stop supporting guerrilla violence by hosting anti-Pretoria rebel movements, there would be a regional conflagration. Neither the United Nations nor any outside power would come to the rescue. By swaggering, the South Africans overplayed their hand, undercutting the very neighbors who could have been their most effective partners. As Kaunda put it to me in May of 1984, the Front Line States wanted peace and were prepared to deal pragmatically with Pretoria. But the terms would be *negotiated*. They could not build a durable new relationship with a South Africa whose regional policy consisted of "sign or else."

This was not the only problem. To bolster their cause with the Front Line States, the South Africans were not above muddying the waters by hinting that Cuban troop withdrawal was an American preoccupation. In a late April pronouncement, P. W. Botha stated that if there was no progress on Resolution 435 and Cuban withdrawal, Pretoria would not block Namibians from "planning their own future"—terms that encouraged the listener to believe that linkage might be negotiable. Kaunda, disappointed at delays in implementing the Lusaka Accord, was groping for short-cuts to get things back on track. And the Angolans, SWAPO, and the Front Line States, were ready to listen to South African hints about finding a way around the Cuban issue.

We were not happy when Kaunda chose to support these diversionary gambits in mid-May by hosting meetings between SWAPO and the internal Namibian parties of the so-called "Multi-Party Conference." Kaunda's goal was an all-party Namibian consensus on a settlement formula that would lead straight to Resolution 435 without the geopolitical complications of linkage. He later claimed to me that he had agreed to chair the meeting on the basis of a "misunderstanding" of the South Africans. Masters of ambiguity, they professed to be open-minded about formulas for achieving peace. No one should deny the Namibians the right to work out their own future, they declared; anything the Namibians could agree upon was certain to receive the endorsement of the outside world!

What the South Africans never told Kaunda and the others in so many words was that they had no intention of implementing Resolution 435 in the absence of Cuban withdrawal. They had their own agenda: (a) to test SWAPO's attachment to the U.N. Plan and its openness to invitations to return home to discuss possible alternative roads to "independence" (i.e., without U.N. involvement and under South African control); (b) to give the isolated Multi-Party Conference some external exposure and stature as SWAPO's equivalent; (c) to avoid the appearance of a U.S.-led process and assert themselves as an African regional power; and (d) to signal the Angolans that they might escape the rigors of linkage if they could persuade their SWAPO guests to leave Angola and return home peacefully to Namibia.

This second Lusaka meeting in May 1984 predictably collapsed in confusion and recrimination as soon as SWAPO asked direct questions about how Resolution 435 fit into the picture. It fell to us to conduct an extensive mission of "clarification," then pick up the pieces and continue. We told Pik Botha what we thought of his effort. Botha categorically reaffirmed Pretoria's adherence to the Cuban link, and stated that he had told Kito the same thing in Lusaka a few days before our meeting. But just to make sure, we told everyone in the region exactly where Pretoria stood. We did not oppose contacts between SWAPO and the Multi-Party Conference. But they made sense only as part of a broader effort to sustain the negotiation over Cuban withdrawal and Resolution 435.

In late May, I found Kaunda to be genuinely disappointed when I confirmed once again that there was no way round the Cuban link unless SWAPO and the Front Line States were prepared to abandon Resolution 435—a move we would strenuously oppose. He seemed to be depressed at the realization that others were prepared to play these games at his expense, but also at the stark implications of our message. He had little confidence that the Angolans could move on the Cuban issue, and feared that our renewed pressure would only drive the MPLA closer to Moscow. We saw it somewhat differently. The confusion and double games had wasted nearly four valuable months. But Pretoria's maneuvers weakened its capacity for independent mischief at our expense. These events would help us reassert our centrality in the diplomacy.

Immediately after speaking with Kaunda, I went over this same ground with Kito. As we had feared, the recent follies had distracted MPLA attention from the main negotiation: Kito had nothing new for us on the Cuban issue, and he explained this by pointing to delays in the Lusaka disengagement process. The MPLA's continued dithering was depressingly familiar. I warned that, from the American perspective, our dialogue risked being viewed as a onesided charade.

At one point, Kito and I retired with a few aides to the study in Nick Platt's Lusaka residence. Bob Frasure got their attention by comparing Angola to seventeenth-century Germany halfway through the Thirty Years' War. The United States was trying to find a short-cut around the next fifteen years. The South Africans, we added, were in a position to take decisions and create their own facts; they were not in a mood simply to sit still. I told the Angolans that Washington saw no prospect that either the MPLA or UNITA could prevail militarily. Kito did not disagree, but instead asked morosely what Luanda should do. We gave him a choice to take back home: Angola could regain the initiative by moving promptly to give us a serious Cuban offer which we could use with Pretoria; or, Angola could work out its problems with the SADF by itself and Washington would simply disengage from the process.

This stark choice had probably occurred to the MPLA leadership before, but they preferred to keep both options open and to play for time with both Washington and Pretoria. Now, we were in a strong position to paint in dramatic colors the fundamental differences between American and South African policies. We supported the earliest possible completion of the disengagement. We saw no alternative to Resolution 435 and were not prepared to lend our support to other scenarios. Unlike South African officials in their bilateral meetings, we did not insult the MPLA as too weak and too fearful of UNITA to be capable of agreeing to Cuban withdrawal; nor did we wag our fingers in their faces and say that they would be destroyed unless they settled with Savimbi first.

It may be that the MPLA was under Soviet and Cuban pressure to play along with Kaunda and the South Africans—while keeping its distance from the United States. Ironically, from an ideological perspective, dealing with the South Africans could be explained as a practical necessity; dealing with the United States was something else. There may also have been Soviet-Cuban differences on the matter. Moscow, after all, had pronounced our efforts dead in late 1983. In March 1984, Cuban Vice-President Carlos Rafael Rodriguez told an interviewer that Cuba was "prepared for the moment when it is necessary and appropriate to begin the process of withdrawal." A few days later, Castro welcomed dos Santos to Havana and fully endorsed the Angolan negotiating position, including the MPLA's four conditions for Cuban withdrawal.

Whatever the explanation for the Angolan tactics, the MPLA leadership could credibly argue by June that having the Americans involved as mediators offered the best way to proceed. Dealing bilaterally in a dark closet with the South Africans might bring hints of relief from the Cuban demand, but it also brought ambiguity, arrogance, insults, and games. In early June, after comparing notes with Kaunda in Luanda, dos Santos saluted Kaunda's efforts and politely urged him to continue "his diplomatic initiative."

At Last, the Real Bidding Starts

When the Angolans joined us at Cape Verde in late July 1984, on the occasion of the abortive SWAPO encounter with the South Africans, Kito pressed Wisner for a bilateral meeting. This was the first time in memory that they had taken the initiative. According to Kito, dos Santos was now ready to bite the bullet on Cuban withdrawal, assuming only that something could be done about the MPLA's SWAPO problem. Luanda would soon hand us a proposal along the lines of the famous April 1983 draft timetable worked out in Washington. It would provide for 75 percent of the Cubans to depart by the time of Namibia's independence, though total withdrawal would depend on fulfillment of some vaguely phrased conditions relating to UNITA. The Angolan bid would come to us through a Portuguese-speaking intermediary, such as Cape Verde or Mozambique, which would act as "guarantor" and provide cover for dos Santos's move.

This was splendid news. We also learned that, at dos Santos's request, the Cape Verdeans had held a series of meetings in early July 1984 with Castro. The Cuban leader said that he was ready to disentangle himself from Angola under the right conditions. These talks paved the way for a successful visit to Havana by Kito, who discussed "the proposal" with the Cubans. Kito declared that Angola was now in a position to make a "sovereign decision."

Wisner responded to the news by informing Kito that we had now approved the major Export-Import Bank credit sought by Gulf Oil and Sonangol for expanded Angolan offshore exploration and production. In addition, he was able to share with the Angolan the broad thrust of an internal review of the politically sensitive matter of U.S.-Angolan relations. The MPLA had signaled back in January the high priority it attached to establishing diplomatic relations and conducting a top-level dos Santos–George Bush meeting as part of a settlement scenario. In March, Shultz and NSC adviser Bud McFarlane had presented to Reagan a carefully formulated scenario in which:

1. We would inform the MPLA of our readiness to recognize the Angolan government once agreement had been reached on a Cuban withdrawal schedule and a date for implementation of Resolution 435;
2. Bush and dos Santos would meet as soon as the settlement package was agreed on all sides;
3. Savimbi would be invited to Washington, and we would make clear our readiness to work for negotiated political reconciliation within Angola; and

4. the United States would establish diplomatic relations with Luanda, open an embassy, assign an ambassador, and conduct normal bilateral business *as Cuban troop withdrawal actually progressed.*

Reagan approved this carefully hedged formula, though not without voicing some misgivings about being asked to announce a move that conservatives would denounce as the "sell-out" of Savimbi. We held the news of the President's decision very closely; we did not want the Angolans to know of it until they had shown evidence of renewed seriousness in the talks. And it would be dynamite within the Beltway unless we had in hand a credible Angolan proposal, pointing toward an early settlement. In any event, Kito was most pleased with the broad picture Wisner painted. This would strengthen dos Santos's position with those who were still opposed the talks.

The meeting in Cape Verde coincided almost exactly with a rare, direct feeler we received from the Cubans. Initiated by an official known to have Castro's confidence on sensitive matters, the Cuban probe focused on our settlement formula, in particular, our view of Resolution 435. We confirmed our long-standing support of the U.N. Plan as the centerpiece of the settlement. The Cubans matter-of-factly noted their assumption that Cuban forces would withdraw in the context of an overall settlement. They also saw merit in direct U.S.-Cuban discussions to support the peace process.

There was no enthusiasm in Washington for gratifying this Cuban request. We assumed that the Angolans and Cubans would coordinate closely, and told Havana that the settlement would humiliate no one. While not endorsing a separate bilateral negotiation with Havana, we saw merit in a periodic exchange of ideas.

After July, things moved forward fairly steadily. Dos Santos made positive public remarks about the prospects for peace in early August. Despite our inability to resolve the problem of SWAPO's role in the disengagement, we soon had word that Kito would meet us again in Cape Verde later that month. The Angolans had moved beyond their earlier paralysis over the stalled disengagement and were apparently ready to table a bid. When I arrived in Praia on August 28, however, President Pereira informed me in some embarrassment that Kito had just left the island capital for Cuba; there was some mix-up in schedules, and Kito needed to run the latest Angolan position by the Cubans before he could see us. Aristides Periera is the sort of man you could imagine as your favorite uncle. The gray-haired dean of lusophone African leaders, Pereira exuded a soft-spoken, homespun wisdom. He spoke when he had something to say and his advice was given sparingly. When Pereira told me that Kito and the Cubans were "establishing a timetable," I took him at his word.

The situation made for an annoying yet amusing diplomatic and logistical tangle. I had other travel commitments in Southern Africa and had planned to brief certain regional leaders, including the top South African negotiating team, on the results of the Cape Verde meetings. It would be rather odd for a U.S. assistant secretary of state to camp out in Praia for days on the chance that Kito might pitch up, pushing the rest of the schedule back accordingly. But it would also be problematical to meet the South Africans as planned, since they knew that we were to have seen Kito first. They might take turns laughing at the MPLA and the Americans, a prospect I did not relish. We decided instead to proceed with our original schedule. We would carry out our consultations with the South Africans as if we had just completed a constructive round of discussion with Kito, who had gone on to consult Castro before coming back to us with a joint position. Meanwhile, we would put out an all-points bulletin for Kito and try to get him to meet me one week later.

Kaunda and the Cape Verdeans tracked Kito down and arranged for a rendezvous on September 6–7 in Lusaka. Our August 31 meeting in Pretoria went better than expected. Pik Botha was delighted when I informed him (based on Pereira's rendition of Kito's position) that the Angolans were ready to put the Joint Monitoring Commission problems to one side. He was even more interested in my analysis that Kito and the Cubans were clearly working on a withdrawal proposal and that Pretoria should be ready for serious bargaining in the near future.

The South African performance was a fascinating blend of skeptical bluster at the negotiating table and enthusiastic but nervous interest in informal side conversations. Privately, Pik Botha confirmed that I was right: something important was happening. He had met Kito in Maputo a few weeks earlier, and heard from him that the MPLA was prepared to reach a deal. Pledging Botha to keep this "secret" from the Americans (we never learned how many layers of invention lay in the tale), Kito had asked Botha what Pretoria required in terms of Cuban with-drawal—in effect, seeking a direct version of South Africa's opening bid. Botha replied (we were told) that (a) Cuban withdrawal did not have to start before the beginning of Resolution 435 or to match SADF with-drawal from Namibia on a troop-for-troop basis, but (b) that Cuban withdrawal should be complete by the time of the Namibian election (seven months into the transition).

Botha and I solemnly swore to keep each other fully informed in the period ahead. At his request, the details of our exchanges on Angolan decisionmaking were not shared in plenary discussion. He was obviously not unhappy that the ice might be breaking in the negotiation. Equally interesting, Botha (in the presence of Malan and Brand Fourie) raised the sorts of questions likely to be raised by doubters in their own ranks in the event that solid prospects for a settlement materialized. Why should the Soviet Union "permit" the MPLA to do a deal on the Cubans, and let itself be outmaneuvered in Angola as was occurring in Mozambique? As for the MPLA, how on earth could they be seriously considering Cuban withdrawal when they continue to reject talks with UNITA and even carry on with public bravado about mounting a military offensive against the rebel movement? "Who the hell are they kidding?" thundered Botha.

In one-on-one exchanges, he returned again and again to the question of our shared interest in UNITA's welfare. Why would Ronald Reagan want to sacrifice UNITA and help dos Santos? Botha knew that we had serious answers to his polemical questions. Unless Savimbi's forces were only half as good as we both knew them to be and the MPLA's were three times better, there was no way that a reasonable Cuban timetable could do anything but advance UNITA's goal of Angolan reconciliation. Without the Cubans, Luanda would *have to* open up political discussions with UNITA. Botha accepted that we knew what we were talking about. Our intelligence was continuously updated and cross-checked from multiple sources. Whatever he thought of our answers, Botha knew that he had no better source of analytical input, and no better means of demolishing the specious nonsense that often passed for "information" in Pretoria.

We left Pretoria after the August 31 meeting knowing that the government continued to operate under illusions fed by a dangerously warped policy and intelligence process. But the private chat with Botha meant that he and his allies saw a real opportunity for an early settlement. We spoke of an accelerated negotiating timetable immediately after the American elections in November (all bets would be off without a second Reagan term). We discussed the idea of a visit by P. W. Botha to the United States in April or May 1985 to meet with President Reagan and conclude the settlement. Under this scenario, the Namibian elections could be held before the end of 1985, with independence to follow in the first half of 1986.

A radiant Kito flew into Lusaka on September 6 in his newly acquired Gulfstream executive jet. While waiting for him to show, I had spent the past five days bouncing around the skies of Central and East Africa in a USAF Beechcraft Commander, a modest mode of transport appropriate for Air Force attaché missions to places like Malawi and Uganda where

I had just paid courtesy visits. Kito seemed almost to swagger as he greeted me at Kaunda's Mulungushi Hall and motioned me to the meeting room.

He then handed me a document entitled "Proposal for a Possible Withdrawal of the Cuban Internationalist Troops from the People's Republic of Angola." We huddled with our interpreter to digest its main points. The document was a draft outline of principles and specific proposals for inclusion in a final agreement to be signed by Angola, South Africa, and SWAPO, and "guaranteed" by the U.N. Security Council. The MPLA's famous four "conditions" reappeared in slightly revised fashion (South African agreement to implement Resolution 435; an SADF-SWAPO cease-fire; completion of SADF withdrawal from Angola; and the end of all South African support for UNITA). The specifics on Cuban withdrawal were minimal: 5,000 troops of Cuba's "southern troop group" would depart "as a goodwill gesture" when the SADF presence in Namibia had been reduced to 1,500 men—that is, at month seven of the transition, the precise moment when Pik Botha had told Kito that *all* Cubans should have withdrawn from Angola. The remaining (unspecified) Cubans in the southern group would depart in not more than three years. No Cuban forces would deploy south of the 16th parallel (few had ever been sent that far south, in practice). The 10,000 troops of Cuba's "northern troop group" would be withdrawn according to a separate schedule to be determined by Angola and Cuba (i.e., not subject to negotiation with the United States or South Africa).

Here, at last, was an Angolan bid. I noticed the elated expression of my legal adviser, Nancy Ely, a core member of our negotiating team since the Judge Clark mission in June 1981. She—like Wisner, Frasure, Cabelly, and a few others—had logged hundreds of thousands of miles on three continents in our drive for a settlement. Ely, who had worked closely with our predecessors during the Carter era, had become a champion of our settlement who kept us believing in ourselves. She made an unmatched contribution to U.S. credibility in the eyes of skeptical allied and African officials. For all of us around that table, this was a wonderful moment.

And yet, we were also dismayed. The Angolan bid was so vague and awful! What were the Angolans doing carving up the Cuban troop contingent into pieces and telling us that one of them was non-negotiable? How many Cubans troops was the proposal based upon? Was the three-year plan for the so-called "southern group" serious? What happened to the timetables we had been discussing for the past eighteen months? What were the specifics of the schedule—all we had was one benchmark, one line of geographic restraint, and an endpoint for *partial* Cuban withdrawal. Compared to the detailed provisions related to the SADF in Namibia under Resolution 435, this was a joke.

The next morning, we appeared with long faces. Treating the proposal with appropriate respect as a "significant political step" by a "sovereign government," we made all the obvious points about how hard this would be to sell. Much greater specificity would be necessary. We had grave reservations about taking this to the South Africans in its current form, and urged the Angolans to avoid a situation in which the other party could make light of Angolan sincerity about a settlement. While we understood that Luanda might not start by tabling its final offer, this proposal represented backsliding from previous U.S.-Angolan discussions, and would not be easy to explain in Washington either.

The Angolan team manfully defended the document, placing special importance on the distinction between northern and southern forces. Kito explained that as Resolution 435 cut SADF support for UNITA, this would relieve pressure on FAPLA, enabling it to take up the Cuban burden in central and southern areas of the country. But the Cuban "northern troop group" would remain vital "to defend us" in Luanda, several other key northern centers, and the oil-producing Cabinda enclave in the far north between Congo and Zaire. In other words, the regime did not wish to negotiate away this all-risk security blanket in its own ethnic and economic heartland. The Angolans confirmed that there were now 30,000 Cuban troops in the country, an increase from the 20,000–25,000 figure generally used in the early 1980s. Applied to the MPLA proposal, this meant that Luanda's opening bid offered a withdrawal of 66 percent of the Cubans over three years (compared to 75 percent in the first year, as discussed in Washington in April 1983 and mentioned by Kito to Wisner in July 1984).

My final private exchange with Kito on September 7 was bizarre. I pressed Kito again on what had happened to the earlier Cuban schedules. Opening his folder, he pointed to the provisions in the 1983 schedules A (twenty-four months) and B (twelve months). "Huh?" I said. Kito nodded and said that either schedule could be accommodated under paragraph 4 of his proposal (the one stating that the southern group would leave in three years). "It could?" I asked. Kito expressed complete confidence that he could persuade dos Santos (and presumably the Cubans) to reduce the time period substantially, although a three-year schedule for southern troop group withdrawal would be "easier." I reminded him that it would be a lot harder in South Africa, whose forces were expected to depart Namibia completely in seven months. Kito suggested that we obtain South Africa's reaction to schedules A and B to test the water, though we could not indicate that either of them had the MPLA's approval.

After several more exchanges and another new wrinkle involving third-party "guarantors," I realized that things were getting out of hand. We could not present to the South Africans this hodgepodge of possibilities, suggestions, and Kito's personal forecasts as the considered position of the government of Angola. Nor did we have the slightest interest in floating schedules A and B in front of the South Africans without identifying whose ideas they were. At my urging, Kito agreed to return to Luanda with a U.S.-drafted, two-year withdrawal plan modeled on schedule A of 1983. We adapted for the figure of 30,000 troops and began Cuban withdrawal at the four-month point; we also defined Kito's 10,000-man northern contingent as the residual to be withdrawn during the second year, provided that South Africa respected Angola's territorial integrity. (This timetable would remove 66 percent of the Cubans in the first year, instead of the first three years.) In a jointly signed cover sheet, Kito and I described this new variant as a "U.S. understanding of possible details in the context of the proposal put forth by the Government of Angola."

I left Lusaka knowing that we had crossed a major watershed in the negotiations. The very fact of a Cuban withdrawal proposal defined in terms of Resolution 435 was a big victory. Its content was another matter. There were many possible explanations for the MPLA's backsliding, but it was difficult to be reassured by Kito's nonchalant suggestion that Luanda could be flexible on specifics. We could only hope that our new two-year amalgam would fly when Kito returned to Luanda.

Refining the Angolan Proposal

When our discussions with the MPLA resumed on September 28–29, 1984, the venue was Luanda, our first visit there since the fall of 1982. Frank Wisner and his delegation were received at dos Santos's presidential compound, Futungo do Belas—a former beach resort complex on the Atlantic coast south of Luanda. Fittingly, the road to Futungo passed through the city's abandoned shopping areas, teeming tenements, shanty towns, and roadside squatter camps, before reaching vistas of the beautiful shoreline, a huge poster of Castro exchanging fraternal smiles with the late leader Agostinho Neto, and finally, near the entrance, a former country club housing dug-in tanks and Cuban infantry. The road to Futungo was an Afro-Marxist theme park.

Wisner was greeted by Kito, da Moura, and a new face, FAPLA Chief of Staff Colonel Antonio dos Santos (no relation) Franca "Ndalu." Like Kito, Ndalu was a politburo member and beneficiary of a 1982 personnel shuffle. He exuded a low-key, authoritative competence of the kind not in surplus in the MPLA. A mestizo born in Mupa in Cunene Province,

Ndalu had touched a lot of bases in his forty-six years: a teenage soccer star in Angola and Portugal, he served in the Portuguese Army before joining the MPLA, pursuing coursework and military training for eight years in Cuba, and undergoing staff officer training in the USSR. We would come to know this gracious and politically astute Angolan well in the years ahead.

Kito welcomed Wisner with a cheery reference to our earlier chat about the Thirty Years' War; the Angolans had now decided to be pragmatic so as to avoid the second half of the conflict! But it quickly became evident that he had run into heavy weather on his return from Lusaka several weeks earlier. His list of complaints included alleged Zairean support for expanded UNITA operations in the north. Publicity surrounding Savimbi's recent visit to Cape Town—including a Botha-Savimbi photo in the influential weekly *Jeune Afrique*—seemed particularly to rattle Luanda. As Kito put it, this sort of thing could "destroy the whole process." Not mentioned, but part of the regional background, was the triumphal conclusion (coordinated with music from the film *Chariots of Fire*) of "Operation Thunder Chariot," the largest SADF military exercise held inside South Africa since 1945. This two-week SADF display was not aimed specifically at the Angolans, and it occurred thousands of kilometers from Angolan territory. Nevertheless, it served as a reminder of their friendly neighborhood hegemon.

The two-year Cuban withdrawal proposal Kito had calmly discussed with me in Lusaka now seemed to scare him. There were more wolves in the Angolan hills. Kito ardently defended his draft three-year proposal, especially its political principles ("you only care about the Cubans"), and the distinction between southern and northern troops. Ndalu spoke expansively about why FAPLA would need three years to generate the additional forces, train the necessary pilots, and purchase and digest the modern hardware required to fill in behind the Cubans. Wisner stressed the necessity of specifics so that the timing, rhythm, and numbers in the timetable would be apparent. If we were to force Pretoria's factions to make up their minds and respond seriously, it was important to put forward a plan that incorporated *all* Cuban forces.

A philosophic debate ensued. We sought their "best" offer (with any conditions they required); they were giving us their "safest" offer, with the footnote that Cubans withdrawal could go faster if things went well. Kito insisted that the northern contingent of Cubans was not negotiable, arguing that it concerned Zaire (not South Africa) and the potential threat of Cabindan secession. We pointed out the centrality of South Africa—not Zaire—in the Angolan strategic equation. (While the Zaireans maintained a political relationship with UNITA and offered it sanctuary and diplomatic-intelligence support, UNITA did not receive appreciable tangible help through Zaire at this time.)

In addition to these problems, Kito offered nothing by way of greater specificity on the southern troop timetable within the three-year period; by implication, 5,000 Cubans would leave as a "gesture" at month seven (month four in our variant), but the remaining 15,000 southern group Cubans would not leave until the very end. It made no sense. Wisner told Kito that he could not recommend that Washington present such lopsided proposals to the South Africans. As Wisner prepared to leave for the airport, the MPLA team stepped next door for final instructions from dos Santos. But a forlorn Kito returned to propose a two-week adjournment in the talks. Despite the risks of further drift, Wisner stuck to his position. We knew that Luanda was getting very close to making its bid formal and official. But we still hoped to improve the Angolan opener. Our credibility depended on obtaining from the MPLA a viable, concrete proposal.

The Soviets, at this stage, were showing little interest in serious exchanges on Southern-Africa, apart from the occasional low-level fishing expedition by officers from their Washington embassy. Meanwhile, we were receiving quite different vibes from Havana. The Cubans had no shortage of information, having clearly been involved in shaping MPLA positions. In discussions with our "interest section" in Havana, they described the exercise and the U.S. role in positive terms, volunteering their intention to cooperate with the process and all but asking us to accept some form of explicit Cuban participation. As on previous occasions during 1984, it appeared that Castro saw the train moving and wished to be aboard: it would be a stain on Cuban honor if a linkage-based settlement occurred without Cubans playing an acknowledged role. Moreover, we had hinted to the Cubans earlier in the year that our settlement could find ways to recognize the contributions and interests of all. But we stopped short of spelling out what this might mean in practice, and did not offer Cuba a place at the negotiating table.

When Wisner returned to Luanda in mid-October, the MPLA had its act together. There were fresh documents, including a "chronogram" (a graphically displayed timetable), a restated "plataforma" (statement of principles), and a new Angolan-Cuban joint text (dated October 9), spelling out in further detail the proposal and eloquently arguing for its terms as proof of Angolan goodwill and seriousness. These documents consciously blended together a set of basic principles, the notion of a specific Cuban timetable, and the concept of a geographic redeployment northward of Cuban forces. All elements were defined in terms of Resolution 435 and argued so as to highlight the point that Cuba and Angola could pose no conceivable threat to Namibia or South Africa. This package enshrined linkage in all but name. Interestingly, the September "plataforma" was retroactively edited to add Cuba to the list of signatories of a proposed four-way international agreement (Angola–Cuba–South Africa–SWAPO) to be endorsed and "guaranteed" through the U.N. Security Council.

The Cuban timetable itself was a marginal improvement:

- the 20,000 Cuban troops in the Southern group would be withdrawn over a period of three years, starting with the beginning of implementation of Resolution 435;
- of these, 15,000 would depart Angola in two years (5,000 between months 4 and 8; 5,000 between months 12 and 16; and 5,000 between months 20 and 24). During this period, they would not go south of the 16th parallel (150 kilometers north of the Namibia border). In effect, these provisions would remove the Cubans from Angola's southernmost defense lines (including the primary Namibe–Lubango–Matala–Menongue line about 300 kilometers north of the border). The remaining 5,000 southern troops would spend their third and final year north of the 13th parallel that lies alongside Angola's central Benguela Railway. They would depart between months 32 and 36;
- the remaining 10,000 troops of the northern group would be withdrawn according to a timetable to be negotiated between Cuba and Angola; they would remain north of the 13th parallel.

Secretary Shultz approved our recommendation that this proposal be transmitted to the South African government. We were not going to get a better opener; this version had Cuban fingerprints all over it, and was therefore both more authoritative and less likely to be easily modified than its predecessor. (Interestingly, Kito urged Wisner to keep U.S. exchanges with both the Cubans and the Soviets to a bare minimum, presumably to avoid complicating his agenda and to limit our involvement in volatile alliance affairs. Yet he made it obvious that the MPLA had shared less information with Moscow than with their Cuban co-authors.)

After all that had taken place, we could not refuse to forward the mail on the grounds that it did not meet up to our earlier expectations or that the South Africans would treat it disdainfully. Our very best case scenario was a settlement which achieved total Cuban withdrawal by the time of Namibian independence—roughly twelve months after the start of Resolution 435. But we had long recognized, within our own negotiating team, the likelihood that we might have to live with some form of Cuban troop residual for some period of time after independence.

Besides, it was not a question of trying to sell the October 9 proposal to Pretoria. We looked at it quite simply as a viable place to start the bidding process and move toward direct negotiations. In the circumstances, our best course was to hold the news tightly in diplomatic channels and elicit a counterproposal from the South Africans. We also viewed the proposal as evidence of an Angolan and Cuban decision in principle to negotiate a regional settlement on the basis of the American formula of 1981. Both the Angolans and the South Africans had now *endorsed our formula*. Never mind the continuing public rhetoric about a "categorical rejection" of linkage—the phrase used when dos Santos, to our dismay, forwarded his proposal to Perez de Cuellar in mid-November. This was merely a word game to cover his tracks. The Angolans were "rejecting" it only if "linkage" were defined as requiring Cuban withdrawal *prior to or exactly in parallel with* SADF withdrawals from Namibia—something we had never done.

9

The Gathering Storm, 1984–85

The bidding had finally started. The cross-border war was on hold, the regional balance heading back toward stalemate. Yet eight months later, in June 1985, the political basis of the Southern African negotiation was rapidly falling apart. We were barely on speaking terms with the parties; diplomats had trouble being heard above the din of soldiers and politicians. It seemed that the key power centers were spinning away from each other in non-synchronous orbits. Our moment had passed, perhaps permanently, and a sense of gloom descended.

I believe that we were closer than is generally realized to a regional settlement in 1984–85. Moreover, I am certain that there are well-placed people in South Africa, Angola, and Cuba who quietly have entertained the same thought. A skeptic, of course, could argue that the Angolan bid of October 1984 was merely a cynical pose, a tactical move to shift the pressure to Pretoria and buy time by pretending to negotiate. This was a game both sides could, and often did, play. We would never know the answer: it is hard to prove a negative.

The October 1984 proposal nonetheless changed things. Once the MPLA (and the Cubans) took the crucial step of offering a proposal within the parameters of our strategy, the way was clear for *the possibility* of an open-ended sequence of bargaining moves. Had the voices of realism (both civilian and military) within the South African government been stronger and better organized, Pretoria could have seized and exploited the opening that now—for the first time—existed. Unhappily for everyone in Southern Africa, the South African leadership had already begun to abandon its previous, tentative pursuit of constructive regional and internal policies. The machinery of rational decisionmaking had begun to collapse.

Bad Behavior at the Ilha do Sal

These problems became evident when I flew to Cape Verde at the end of October to share the MPLA bid with the senior South African negotiating team. The South Africans informed us that they would prepare a counteroffer for cabinet approval within about two weeks. Their reaction to the MPLA bid was predictably scathing: it was "a war plan." Luanda aimed to use Resolution 435 "as a means to destroy UNITA," which would lose its SADF support upfront while the Cubans remained on to help the MPLA for the indefinite future. But, at the same time, the South Africans quickly recognized that the very fact of the Angolan proposal fundamentally changed the situation. The bidding over terms and principles had started. For the first time in years, the ball was now in South Africa's court.

The new situation changed the character of our bilateral discourse with South Africa. Before, we were with the South Africans in pressing Luanda to make a bid. Now, we would distance ourselves from the negotiating positions of both sides, align ourselves with the process itself, and ardently defend the integrity of our formula. Quickly sensing the changed situation, the South Africans immediately began to insinuate that my colleagues and I were deviating from previous positions by merely presenting this lopsided Angolan bid.

But the chilling thing about the Cape Verde meeting was the chemistry within, and the behavior of, the South African delegation. American officials found their motives openly questioned in side conversations. Why didn't we want Savimbi to become the president of Angola (as if this objective were within the grasp of American, or South African, decisionmakers)? Revealing his agenda in an unguarded moment, Defense Minister Malan asked me, "Why don't you get involved in Angola and Mozambique?" My special assistant Robert Cabelly probed SADF military intelligence boss Pieter van der Westhuizen about the signals being sent by his covert operations far north of the border. "It tells the MPLA you want to kill them, not do a deal," Cabelly noted. "I agree," replied the man we had nicknamed "the ratcatcher of Southern Africa."

There were many such unguarded moments during those two long days and nights on Sal Island, the windswept moonscape where South Africa had constructed the Cape Verdeans' international airfield. We met at the Morabeza hotel and sports complex on the northeastern shore of Sal, a meeting site frequented by a motley array of airline crews, sport fishermen, and windsurfers. The Morabeza did its best to maintain a business-as-usual atmosphere for its regular clientele. But this was not easy. Twenty or so of the top ranks of Pretoria's national security establishment set a tone somewhere between Club Med and an adult-style *Lord of the Flies*. There was rampant strife in their ranks. Pik Botha, the official delegation leader and spokesman, confided to me that he had brought this horde along in order "to implicate" them. (Four departments and agencies plus the Administrator-General's office in Windhoek were represented on Botha's team.)

Like paint remover, the non-stop alcohol intake stripped away any veneer of Afrikaner solidarity. They disagreed about everything: Savimbi's prospects in the Angola, the relative importance of the Angolan war for South Africa, the role being played by the United States, the hopes for Namibia's internal parties, how to handle growing black unrest at home, and the right course in Mozambique. So deeply did they disagree about Mozambique that Botha excluded Van der Westhuizen from our restricted discussion of that topic. Later, when Cabelly approached the fuming "Wessy" to compare notes, he growled: "You're wasting your time talking to them [Botha, Malan, Fourie, Barnard, Geldenhuys]—*I run Mozambique.*"

After our presentation of the MPLA proposal, another debate broke out among the South Africans over the Angolan military balance. This "lively conversation," as one participant delicately described it, focused on the standard SADF military intelligence line that the MPLA was on the verge of collapse. Savimbi would soon seize power. Why listen to Luanda and the Americans? Just play along and wait until after the U.S. election. We know how to organize our "friends" and "UNITA's friends" in the West for a change in U.S. policy. Pretoria's veteran statesman Brand Fourie offered a caustic comment on the rosy nonsense about Savimbi's impending victory: "Sure, sure, maybe six months, maybe six years." There was nothing remotely approaching a consensus on Angolan policy within the government.

Namibia fared no better. The official Department of Foreign Affairs line remained one of solid adherence to South Africa's responsibilities under Resolution 435. But the Administrator-General and his staff in Namibia, who reported directly to State President P. W. Botha, habitually sought some room to maneuver between Pretoria's baronies and the local Namibian political forces. Under the incumbent Administrator-General, Dr. Willie van Niekerk—a hardline gynecologist-politician whose dream was to abort Namibia—this became a menace. He and his people gleefully informed us that the Multi-Party Conference had written P. W.

Botha proposing that Resolution 435 be altered to require a constitutional conference *before* elections. There was also talk of a "deadline," after which unspecified events would occur and Resolution 435 would lapse. The saner heads from Pretoria knew that these rumblings were idle. In the real world, South Africa could not unilaterally settle the Namibian problem. But there was a risk of myopic miscalculation. Such mischiefmaking only served to place us on the defensive and discredit the settlement exercise in the eyes of others.

We used the Cape Verde meeting to send some messages of our own. In particular, we warned the South Africans that the growing township unrest and their response to it were becoming a more serious political issue in the United States. We came down hard on the importance for South African, as well as American interests, of avoiding official brutality at home and of making the regional peace process work with Mozambique and Angola. The Pretoria-organized talks between the Maputo government and RENAMO* had just collapsed in mysterious circumstances. Botha reported to us the story of RENAMO's Evo Fernandez being called away from the table for an unidentified overseas phone call, after which he broke off the talks. These were painful exchanges. A clearly frustrated Botha put up a good story, but he was probably beginning to accept that we knew far more than we could share with him about the contradictory, self-destructive policies of his own government.

The Cape Verde encounter served as a warning of things to come. One wondered about the "policy process" among grown men who took such evident delight in making spectacles of themselves in the presence of foreigners, strangers, and their own young countrymen (and women) from South African Airways. We watched in amazement as a member of the South African cabinet willfully delayed a SAA jumbo jet and then tried to intimidate its outraged commander into silence. It reminded me of another time when Gabon's president, Omar Bongo, held a UTA jumbo on the ground in Libreville for two hours during a refueling stop in order to conduct a conversation with me. These African leaders, white and black, represented a laboratory for Lord Acton's dictum about absolute power. Some members of the Pretoria gang, when free of the scrutiny that normally accompanies high office, behaved as if South Africa and everything in it were their personal possessions. At a deeper level, this

---

* The South African-backed rebel movement established in the late 1970s by the Rhodesian special forces to pressure the new Mozambican regime to cease support of guerrilla operations by the Zimbabwe African National Union. Initially, the movement was called the MNR (Mozambique National Resistance), reflecting its anglophone Rhodesian roots, but it was retroactively given lusophone legitimacy with the name RENAMO (*Resistencia Nacional Mocambicana*).

mixture of self-indulgence and bullying was adolescent. Could these guys get their act together when times got tough and fundamental choices were needed?

Before we left Cape Verde, Pik Botha authorized me to report to Shultz that South Africa was prepared to free Namibia, provided it could depart honorably. He saw "possibilities" in the new situation, and expressed interest in the idea of a trilateral meeting with the Angolans at Cape Verde once Pretoria had made its counterproposal. I reminded Botha of his earlier trial balloon suggesting a spring 1985 scenario for settlement. Botha looked at me with an expression indicating either silent disbelief or a sudden digestive problem. What he actually said was that a visit to the United States by his president might make sense provided we had "something to announce." Botha still knew what we wanted to hear, but his performance was anything but reassuring.

On November 15 I traveled to Pretoria for two days to receive a South African opening bid approved by the cabinet on the eve of our arrival. The counterproposal, interestingly, was modeled on the Angolans' composite document—a statement of political principles, followed by a timetable. On the plus side, Pretoria committed itself categorically to implement Resolution 435 as soon as agreement was reached on Cubans. It also pledged best efforts to achieve an early completion of the disengagement, and stated a continued readiness to work out an end to violence with SWAPO. South Africa supported the concept of Security Council endorsement of the final package as a form of recognition of the "commitments and contributions of all interested parties."

But Pretoria demanded a Cuban timetable providing for precise parallelism with the SADF's own withdrawal schedule under Resolution 435— the Cubans should draw down to 12,000 by six weeks, 8,000 by nine weeks, and zero by 12 weeks! To top this off, the South Africans wanted the Angolans to provide a full list by name of all Cubans in Angola (sic) and a list of the assignments and locations of all Communist bloc advisers (sic). Now we had Pretoria's own anti-MPLA "war plan."

The South Africans had, as promised, quickly delivered their "considered" response. It was a maximalist position, mirroring in a way the MPLA's opener. We saw little to be gained by using our capital at this point to push for a more serious South African position. Our goal was to launch the process of exchanging positions and then move toward three-way talks. I told Botha matter-of-factly that Washington would not endorse Pretoria's opener any more than we had signed on to Luanda's. The South African side erupted for a moment, but things calmed down when we reiterated our basic commitment to a settlement including total Cuban withdrawal and our fundamental opposition to any deal that could help the MPLA destroy UNITA. At a joint press conference at the end of this meeting, Botha did us a favor—surprising his own delegation—by stating publicly that South Africa could not accept a "permanent presence of large numbers" of foreign troops in the region, a phrase he proceded to define as "more than three to four thousand." The obvious implication to well-informed observers, of whom there were mercifully few in the Pretoria press corps, was that the concept of a Cuban residual after Namibian independence was not totally excluded. It was an interesting way to "make policy."

There was something slightly odd in the South African performance. More revealing than Botha's oratory was the generally disengaged and uncommunicative attitude of his entire team on the subject of our negotiation. General Geldenhuys, one of the key men capable of making either peace or war on Botha's side of the table, abandoned his customary sports pages and slept through the entire proceedings. In addition to their discord over regional policy and their anxiety to slam the ball back into Angola's court, these officials appeared increasingly distracted by the wave of black unrest rolling across South Africa. It was a combustible mixture, especially when one recalled the attitudes of P. W. Botha.

Back in February, when we were developing the Lusaka Accord, Botha had written Reagan to express his misgivings about the drawn-out regional peace process and the burdens he carried as a "supporter of the West." After praising the President's tough stand against Moscow and politely complimenting America's "agile" diplomats, Botha had predicted that the Soviets would never tolerate a Western victory in the region. Moscow had Cuban infantry brigades, thousands of Soviet advisers, tanks and helicopter gunships at its disposal to back up Soviet strategic interests. Botha wanted to know whether he would be left standing alone, still the victim of a Western arms embargo, when the U.S.-led drive for negotiated settlements predictably collapsed under the weight of Soviet obstructionism and massive military support to its clients.

Botha had never been much of a fan of constructive engagement. He was deeply suspicious of our agenda and our past refusal to define with him the limits of internal change. Now that things were heating up internally, he was aware that he might be "alone" on the home front as well. He craved another definition of US policy.

Another deeply suspicious leader who might have preferred an alternative American script was UNITA's Jonas Savimbi. When I met him in Pretoria in mid-November, it was another in a series of attempts to build (or restore) mutual confidence. Typically, I would find that Savimbi's mind had been poisoned by misinformation, lies, and distortions deliberately planted with him by opponents of our strategy. I challenged the conduct of his Washington representative, Jeremias Chitunda (UNITA's highly able vice-president), who seemed to spend much of his time cultivating suspicion among conservatives that the State Department was selling out UNITA. After an exhaustive briefing on the state of play in the negotiations, Savimbi said he was reassured.

Savimbi and I exchanged notes on African attitudes toward reconciliation between UNITA and the MPLA. We had helped open up a channel between dos Santos and Zaire's leader, Mobutu Sese Seko, UNITA's staunch supporter, in order to press the reconciliation agenda. We discussed the emergence of a more balanced French policy toward Angola, and the best ways for UNITA to get its message across in the West and Africa. The UNITA leader craved such firsthand contact with the point man of U.S. African policy. Yet we could never satisfy him or deter him from going around us at home. Instinctively suspicious of diplomats, he fretted that we would cut a deal in Luanda at his expense. He, like the SWAPO leadership, wanted to be treated on the same footing as a government. Before we parted, he casually sought my reaction to a possible trip to the United States—his first since late 1981. It was a not-so-subtle-test: "We know you don't want to be seen talking to us." I showed polite interest. This ploy could be part of some larger game plan. We did not yet know how ambitious his SADF and U.S. support network would be in their efforts to overturn U.S. policy.

One man who could have enlightened me was Defense Minister Magnus Malan. But instead of discussing Angola, I found him unusually communicative about the domestic situation in South Africa. In the privacy of his living room, he spoke heatedly about the mounting township crisis and the urgent need for black-white negotiation. Scathingly critical of the South African police, Malan argued that the security forces should have waded in with full power at the outset of the unrest in September— "not with bullets but with manpower to break the cycle of intimidation, arson, and violence."

I warned Malan about reactions in the United States if the spiral of violence and repression continued. I stressed the urgency of a credible signal of the government's intent: movement on the issue of equal citizenship and a bill of rights for all South Africans might be such a signal. Malan listened courteously and referred me to other ministers. But his mind was elsewhere. Like his boss, he was a wishful thinker who preferred the advice of people who agreed with him, whether in the South Africa lobby in the United States or within his intelligence establishment at home.

In November 1984, we had only the dimmest notion of how deep South Africa would sink into the abyss in the coming few years. In the circumstances, we thought it was best to drag the South Africans gradually into a give-and-take negotiation on Namibia-Angola. By proceeding in this manner, we made some implicit assumptions. Was time working with us or against us in terms of the capacity of the sides to take decisions? At what stage should we bring them together to hear, blame, provoke, threaten, and test each other? When should we put our own views on the table as mediators? The risk of a damaging explosion from premature direct talks seemed greater than the risk of delay. At the time, we were awed by the enormity of the gap to be bridged between the Angolan and South African positions on the Cuban timetable. After all, Luanda had offered 67 percent withdrawal over three years, with the 33 percent residual to remain in Angola "until the end of never"; Pretoria wanted total Cuban withdrawal in twelve weeks!

We were also accustomed to the rhythm of a long-distance, indirect mediation. Subconsciously, we may have projected into the future this familiar but inefficient rhythm. The novelty of *substantive* bidding may have obscured the possibilities for *transforming the process* so as to jolt the parties and bring about rapid, continuing movement. We later learned that the Angolans were suspicious that the United States was cooking the messages carried back and forth in our indirect shuttle. Since it was impossible to station U.S. diplomats in Luanda, the time may have arrived to institute a more or less continuous shuttle—so that issues could be aired before they festered—until we got tripartite talks under way. With hindsight, time was rapidly running out on us. Soon, the South African crisis and the American domestic reaction to it would engulf our regional strategy in controversy, threatening its very existence. We continued the deliberate pace of our mediation when we should have been pulling out all the stops.

Games and Maneuvers

On November 17, Angolan President dos Santos sent Perez de Cuellar a letter containing the full text of the MPLA proposals plus his own further commentary, and requested that they be circulated as an official U.N. document. The South Africans followed suit as soon as they learned of the Angolan maneuver; the documents were published on November 26. After the event, we heard various explanations for this gross breach of diplomatic norms. Angered and offended by "onesided" or "selective" leaks in the media, the Angolans said they had to clear up the record. The negotiation involved much more than Cuban troop withdrawal, and people had to know that the Angolans had not compromised their basic principles.

Perhaps going public was merely a leap for the high ground, and a device to wrong-foot the United States or South Africa. Luanda may have calculated that its opening bid, if publicized and fully ornamented with bells and whistles, would be seen as a "major gesture." This would gain them credit in Africa, and internationally, and protect them from pressures to move further. Given the diplomatic isolation of their opponent and the generally credulous Western press coverage of Southern Africa, there was no doubt who would win this game.

In any event, the publication of both proposals advertised the huge gap and severely hampered flexibility. This complicated our options for advancing the process. If the time was not ripe for trilateral talks, we had two choices: to put forward our own ideas or to press for a second MPLA bid. It was premature, we judged, to table American proposals, so we would have to coach the MPLA on the shape of a rebid that would be conditioned on major South African moves.

This was the awkward tactical scene when Wisner visited Luanda early in December 1984. The Angolans appeared fairly comfortable with their new position and under no particular pressure to take another step. Wisner warned Kito that the South Africans were in a similar frame of mind. The sides could be setting the stage for a test of strength: the South Africans had provided their own "war plan" in response to the MPLA's. There was a delicious irony in the way the MPLA's position had evolved from one of dogmatic refusal to discuss anything but Namibia and Resolution 435 into gradual acceptance of the idea that Cuban troop withdrawal might be a powerful instrument to remove the SADF threat, and finally, to attempts at using Resolution 435 to achieve an Angolan outcome (the destruction of UNITA) which was beyond Luanda's military reach. Kito nodded gravely as Wisner described how the South Africans would lick their chops at this shift of focus away from Namibia. Wisner outlined all the key areas for possible revision of the MPLA offer, and Kito agreed to get back to us. He pressed hard for Wisner to spell out the U.S. position on terms for settlement, claiming that the Angolans wished to stay close to that position.

For months, the MPLA had been dodging South African proposals for a ministerial-level meeting to decide on completing the disengagement. Luanda and Pretoria disagreed about the structure and role of a follow-on mechanism to the Joint Monitoring Commission. Rather than risk a blow-up, the Angolans preferred to continue cohabiting with the SADF in the commission facility at the town of Ngiva, while claiming publicly that Pretoria was violating the Lusaka Accord. Wisner told Kito that we were tired of providing cover for this dance. The liaison office we had opened in Namibia was starting to take flak at home and in Africa from critics who charged that it implied acceptance of the South African-controlled status quo there. (It was closed in early 1985, several months before the last SADF forces left Angola in April.)

On December 28, 1984, I received a lengthy written message from Kito responding to Wisner's earlier points. Buried in a swamp of pseudo-juridical verbiage was the notion that the MPLA could not negotiate with us over the northern troop group without compromising its position "rejecting" linkage (sic). As for the southern troop withdrawal schedule, thirty-six months was close to the "absolute minimum"; any adjustment could only occur within "very narrow and restricted" limits. The message contained one new formula: the MPLA would not oppose U.N. verification of Cuban troop withdrawal, provided that it received guarantees of the end of South African assistance to UNITA and attacks on Angola. Kito concluded with a series of questions which shed light on their current concerns: they wanted us and the South Africans to take their "plataforma" seriously (an issue of face); there was a suspicion that we were engaged in "salami slicing" tactics in league with Pretoria; and, they wanted to see some South African cards before playing any more Angolan ones.

The Storm Clouds Gather

By mid-January 1985, neither side wanted to move, and the Angolans had begun badmouthing our negotiating procedures. At home, the violence in South Africa and controversy over the U.S. policy response mushroomed into a major political story. We decided to give the talks a jolt. When Wisner made his next visit to Luanda in late January 1985, he told the Angolans we would be prepared to convene a trilateral meeting and table our ideas once we had explored possible common ground with both sides. Each side, we hoped, would help us define a basis for negotiations. We needed to know what the MPLA could consider in exchange for South African moves.

After some initial confusion about this approach, Wisner told dos Santos bluntly that we were hearing less and less about the entire peace process from the South Africans. We were not seeking specific MPLA concessions, but rather a broad "hunting license" in order to get the attention of the distracted Bothas. Dos Santos said he now understood our game plan. When Wisner and Kito returned to the meeting room, they put aside a polemical Angolan position paper and focused briefly on the content of such a hunting license. Kito passed Wisner a yellowing copy of the two-year Cuban troop withdrawal schedule the two men had worked on at Chief Fernandez's estate in April 1983. We could hunt with this. The Angolans would be interested in South African reaction to it, but did not want their name attached. This was all the guidance we were going to get.

At the time, we sensed a more assertive and macho tone on the Angolan side of the table. It could have been simply an effort to force us to shift our pressure onto Pretoria. It could also have reflected a mix of support and "advice" from Luanda's allies. Or, the MPLA may have perceived that the South Africans were in trouble at home and facing mounting Western pressure. As for the conflict between the MPLA and UNITA, it continued to spread across Angola; but UNITA's momentum was ebbing and the MPLA was building up for major countermoves. Soon the diplomatic test of strength would be paralleled on the ground. The parties still had a lot to learn.

One cue we probably paid insufficient attention to was Kito's pitch to Wisner back in early December for direct Cuban participation in the talks. Previously, Kito had expressed the preference that we not discuss the details with either Moscow or Havana. Now, he seemed to be under instructions to raise the matter. Separately, FAPLA chief of staff Antonio dos Santos Franca "Ndalu"—a man always in close contact with the Cubans—told us that both the Soviets and Cubans had become distrustful of the Angolans. And we knew from our own contacts that Castro sought to become a visible player in the process. We ignored Kito's signal.

It is impossible to know whether an American decision to grant Castro admission to the diplomacy would have breathed new life into it at this crucial moment. Possibly, the Cubans had come to believe by early 1985 that the settlement train was slowing and there was no reason to be on it. But a case can be made that we missed an important opportunity to test the Cubans. At the time, we reasoned that it was preferable to confine the talks to the directly affected regional parties and prevent any U.S.-Cuban complications from being introduced into an already complex agenda. It was difficult enough sustaining our African policies in Washington, without the added burden of having to meet some Cuban demand or to explain why we had "legitimized" Castro's African policies.

Ironically, the South Africans appeared open to Cuban participation when I met them in February, believing that it might stiffen MPLA spines against Soviet pressure. Jonas Savimbi, in a reflective moment, volunteered that Castro probably wanted to leave Angola but had trouble figuring out how to do it. But I told them that we were adamantly opposed for both regional and global reasons. I believed that the Cubans would obstruct us at the table. And, in any case, I was certain that my political superiors would reject the idea.

On the surface, the January–April 1985 period saw continued forward movement. I took our Angolan hunting license to Pretoria and Cape Town in mid-February and precisely inverted Wisner's earlier pitch to the MPLA. The Angolans were confused, I argued. The regime was divided, scared, under heavy Soviet pressures, and hoping to survive by avoiding big decisions. The United States and South Africa had a choice: We could let nature take its course, or we could try to force another major decision in Luanda.

I told the South Africans that we risked becoming sitting ducks for domestic and foreign critics in both our countries. Vociferous opponents of U.S. policy were exploiting the uncertainties of our regional diplomacy, as well as the internal South African scenario of unrest and repression. Another Soviet succession loomed, and the era of plodding, reactive gerontocracy in Moscow would soon be over: we should act now, before a more formidable Soviet leadership had the chance to consolidate. Our regional accomplishments to date—on both the Mozambique and Angola-Namibia fronts—remained fragile and reversible. Accordingly, we wanted a green light to return to the Angolans and say that Pretoria was prepared to take a major step if the MPLA would do likewise. We would not commit the South Africans, but would suggest the possibility of their considering a two-year withdrawal schedule with a modest Cuban residual in second year *if* the MPLA would accept that the bulk of Cuban forces would depart in nine to twelve months.

There were predictable eruptions on the South African side of the table. It might be better if the United States just dropped constructive engagement: the Front Line States got much more out of it than South Africa, Pik Botha declared. The more South Africa changed, the more hell it took from the West. "The price of constructive engagement is too high," Pik Botha shouted at me. He realized that South Africa had become a burden to Washington, but the United States had become a bigger burden to his government. His president had been enraged by the conditionality theme—"as long as we do this, you will do that"—in a recent speech by U.S. Ambassador Herman Nickel. By asserting the notion that good relations depended on a continuing coincidence of interests (on both internal change and regional security), Nickel had merely described the facts. But it appeared that P. W. Botha was in no mood for facts. According to his foreign minister, he believed it would be better if we just came out and said that we basically agreed with our domestic critics!

As for my proposals, Pik Botha fumed that his government could not survive Resolution 435, a SWAPO victory, and "partial Cuban withdrawal." Reminded that we were proposing total Cuban withdrawal over two years and that he had himself publicly accepted the concept of a residual of 3,000 to 4,000 Cubans, Botha said he had been talking of Cuban "nurses and doctors." His government—for good or ill—was on record for "total bloody withdrawal" by the end of Resolution 435, which he equated with the Namibia election date (month seven). It could not change now without paying a huge domestic political price. It would be far preferable to drop both Resolution 435 and Cuban withdrawal, stop trying to "freeze" Namibian politics, hand over greater autonomy to the Multi-Party Conference, and encourage its members to do a deal with SWAPO.

Getting things like this off their chests was a form of occupational therapy for the increasingly defensive South African leadership. We managed to turn Botha and Malan around by using two arguments. First, our proposed "hunting license" was the best and only way to seize the initiative. It should be linked to a firm and unilateral decision by Pretoria to complete the disengagement, even if it remained impossible to get the MPLA to negotiate a successor security mechanism to the Joint Monitoring Commission. Malan agreed that this could be done so long as SWAPO infiltration did not blow up in the government's face; he promised a decision in a few weeks.

Second, a properly front-loaded two-year Cuban timetable would actually serve UNITA's interest, since it would accelerate pressure on the MPLA to make peace with it. If we waited around until the end of Reagan's second term in hopes of getting an ideal Cuban timetable, while the Communist powers sustained their defense buildup, we were letting them define our fate. This was hardly doing UNITA a favor. It was hard for Malan and Botha to argue with this logic. If we got 80–90 percent of the Cubans to withdraw in the first year, that had to help Savimbi. Malan groused that we were really asking for Pretoria's bottom line before getting Luanda's. "We're not at the point of bottom lines . . . yet," I replied. Mixing his metaphors creatively, Botha observed that "all our bottom lines are broken."

When I saw Savimbi in Cape Town a few days later, it was clear that he had been sympathetically briefed (perhaps by Botha and Malan jointly). The Angolan guerrilla chief agreed that if we could get 20,000–25,000 Cubans out of Angola by the time of Namibian independence, this would be major progress. He held out little hope that the United States could persuade Luanda to do it, but there was "no harm in trying." It was important to force the pace and seize the initiative. Savimbi put down a marker questioning the total figure of 30,000 Cubans (suggesting that the real figure might be as high as 45,000), and urging that the residual numbers and timeframe be as low as possible. It would be important to have safeguards against MPLA / Cuban reneging once the implementation phase had begun, since it would be hard for an isolated South Africa to stop the U.N. transition process dead in its tracks. (Clearly, Savimbi and his hosts had been engaged in intense consultations.)

UNITA remained frustrated with a negotiating mechanism that excluded them formally and with an agenda that might "force" national reconciliation later, but did not explicitly provide for it now. His main lament was that we had not publicly declared which side we were on in the Angolan civil war; our active and visible diplomacy with the Marxist MPLA demoralized UNITA. Savimbi did not press for military support; UNITA was "overextended" from past gains but not hurting for hardware supplies. He requested—and I agreed—that we step up our public references and private messages to African leaders signaling our support for the legitimacy of his cause. We parted with Savimbi telling me that he was pleased with our meeting and supported our attempt to increase the heat on Luanda in tandem with his own military efforts. I did not ask his approval of a specific schedule. But my comments and his answers shaped the ideas we would be placing on the table. He knew what to expect and did not oppose it.

Before I left South Africa, Botha and Malan reaffirmed that having Savimbi's support would be a "powerful inducement" for their government to support our approach. They were making no commitments as to bottom lines, but agreed that our target of over 20,000 Cubans withdrawn in the first year and a one-year residual of 5,000–6,000 men would change the scenario "dramatically" for the better. They also embraced our 30,000 figure on the number of Cubans deployed in Angola: Botha said that it coincided with his own "inflated estimate used for propaganda purposes."

We now had several, comparably vague "hunting licenses," and the parties knew what we were up to. Our internal deliberations in February and March focused on whether to table a U.S. negotiating document. The parties were stuck, and there was no reason to believe that our patience would produce movement. In fact, the process could unravel in the absence of some intervention to end the gridlock. The time factor was working against us in terms of both domestic opinion and events in the region. Acting now was a possible method of holding the process together and pushing the parties to confront choices they might wish to avoid.

But it was also possible that an attempt to "hot-wire" the negotiation would backfire. Taking a position on where the "point of compromise" should be would identify us irrevocably with a particular outcome.

One or both parties could respond by staking out positions as far away as possible from the common ground we sought to define, thus getting each other off the hook. Shultz, the former professor of industrial relations and Secretary of Labor, was uneasy. You cannot settle a dispute if the parties are not ready to settle. We were pressing. But he accepted that that it was our best option in the circumstances.

With his blessing, we melded the parties' positions into a single text for presentation to the parties as a "basis for negotiation." The document was also described internally and to the parties as a "synthesis" of the two proposals on the table and, more importantly, of what we had heard from them in our shuttles. We carefully stated that this was *not* a U.S. proposal, but, rather, a single documentary basis for further negotiation. In fact, the one-page "basis for negotiation" was a classic mediator's attempt to leapfrog over a procedural logjam and step up the pressure for compromise on both sides.

The "basis for negotiation" included a restatement of the commitment to Resolution 435 and reciprocal assurances that South Africa would respect Angola's territorial integrity and Angola would respect Namibia's. Angola "in that context" would commit to the withdrawal of 24,000 Cubans (80 percent of the total) during the first twelve months from the date of implementation of Resolution 435; a minimum of 12,000 (40 percent) would depart by the end of the eighth month. The residual of 6,000 (20 percent) could remain north of the 13th parallel for up to one additional year. During this schedule, Cuban forces were not to participate in offensive operations. The United Nations would verify withdrawals, and the U.N. Security Council would adopt a resolution to "guarantee" respect for all the commitments made by South Africa, swapo, Angola and Cuba, and the United Nations itself, related to both Resolution 435 and Cuban withdrawal, which would thus constitute a "single binding accord." The "basis for negotiation" sought to address all key points of principle (to avoid the charge that we only focused on the Cubans). The timetable itself was a simple two-year plan.

In presenting the document to Kito in Cape Verde on March 18, I told him exactly what the United States was trying to do: accelerate the talks and bring about a settlement now. We are asking Angola to help us to force decisions in South Africa, I told him. If Angola was constructive, the South Africans would find it hard to stonewall us. I asked Kito to take our document home to review it with his leadership, and then to answer two questions: Is it acceptable as a basis for further negotiation? And what problems or concerns does it raise for the Angolan government?

Kito was both upbeat and evasive. His government had been waiting for Washington to declare *its* view on the issues. Had we done so earlier, much time could have been saved. He believed our document could serve as a basis for negotiation and would so recommend to his government. But Kito also insisted on misinterpreting it as a "U.S. response" to the Angolan "plataforma" of October 1984, and was very slow to grasp what we meant when we said that this document would serve as basis for discussion. To the Angolans, it meant agreeing to "receive" it for purposes of discussion—one of those grand gestures for which MPLA diplomacy was renowned. Kito waffled when we underscored that we had in mind setting other proposals aside to focus on this one, but he described our document as a good basis for discussion.

Things Fall Apart

The South Africans were less flattering. When I described the document as a tool to force MPLA decisions (as we had discussed five weeks earlier), Pik Botha said it was a tool to force decisions in South Africa. He did not like the lack of detail on withdrawal benchmarks during year one of the schedule. More important, he insisted on labeling the move as a "deviation" from our understandings of 1981. I rejected the charge categorically. Botha said ominously that he could recommend nothing to his government without first getting the reaction of Savimbi. This was a precise echo of Brand Fourie's warning to me in Washington in early March. It was deliciously ironic to hear South Africa's white leadership nail its fate to the mast of a black Angolan freedom fighter. Somehow this was starting to sound more like an escape hatch than a consultative process.

Nothing was going well in South Africa or U.S.-South African relations on that day, March 21, 1985. Botha hinted that his government was becoming more open to the schemes emanating from the Administrator-General's office in Windhoek to devolve greater authority on the Multi-Party Conference. No one—not the United States and not the United Nations—could tell South Africa that it had to remain in charge as the administering power of Namibia until a settlement was reached. Our discussions of Mozambique were equally gloomy.

But the worst news came last. As we prepared to leave the meeting room, Botha informed us that there had been a bloody clash between black funeral mourners and police at Uitenhage, near Port Elizabeth, in South Africa's Eastern Cape region. Police had killed nineteen blacks in one of the worst incidents of political violence since the Sharpeville tragedy—exactly twenty-five years ago to the day—when some sixty-nine black protesters were mowed down by security forces. Uitenhage brought the death toll in 1984–85 political violence to some 250 people. A week later, Pretoria banned meetings of the United Democratic Front (UDF), the internal, umbrella opposition group allied with the African National Congress. South Africa's internal political crisis got into high gear at the precise moment when we tabled our "basis for negotiation."

The next day, March 22, three of my closest colleagues flew into Jamba, Savimbi's southeastern Angolan headquarters, to brief him on the "basis." But someone else had gotten there first. UNITA's top team recited scores of rehearsed questions indicating that the well had been systematically poisoned in advance. Our document was "unacceptable." It would "destroy UNITA," and the government in South Africa would be told of UNITA's firm position. U.S. diplomatic strategy had produced "not one inch" of progress in four years. UNITA's specific comments tracked the South Africans' own comments the day before. But there were also some new themes and political terminology that were clearly made in Washington: why did the State Department "refuse to recognize UNITA"? UNITA's secretary general, Nzau Puna, demanded to know whose proposal this was—was it a "U.S. government proposal or something else"? Savimbi raged at the fact that I had sent my colleagues to see him—a courtesy saving him the trip to Cape Town, a tiring journey— when I had personally met with MPLA leaders a few days earlier. The UNITA performance on March 22 was an offensive act of political theater that would not have occurred without the backing of influential people in both Pretoria and Washington.

On April 17, a marching band playing "My Darling Clementine" led several hundred SADF troops back across the border into Namibia, thus concluding the 1984 disengagement process some fourteen months behind schedule. A few weeks later, in a meeting in Maputo, the Angolans once again refused to extend the border security mechanism once its final thirty days ran out. This essentially doomed the limited disengagement pact. Meanwhile, on April 18, one day after the last troops withdrew from Angola (though not for long), President Botha announced in Parliament that his government had approved proposals setting up an "interim government" in Namibia, based on the Multi-Party Conference, to take over a range of functions from the Administrator-General and prepare proposals for the constitution of an independent Namibia. Botha added that the people of Namibia "cannot wait indefinitely for a breakthrough on the withdrawal of the Cubans from Angola."

South African leaders seemed by now to be calculating how best to discredit the American-led diplomacy of the past four years. And they succeeded. On May 6, we received a message from Luanda in which Kito largely ignored the U.S. "basis," claiming that the South Africans had created major obstacles to moving ahead. Kito said that the settlement process could not proceed until these obstacles had been removed. Pretoria seemed to be determined to grant Angola the high ground at just the time when Angolan planning for a major anti-UNITA offensive was becoming evident.

On May 22, an SADF commando unit was intercepted by Angolan forces as it sought to sabotage Gulf Oil's installations at Malongo, in the northern enclave of Cabinda. We had entered the dark ages. On June 2, Savimbi publicly announced his rejection of the "basis" document. A short while thereafter, Pik Botha handed us an almost contemptuous reply to the "basis"—a reply that accused us of a sell-out and counter-proposed that 90 percent of the Cuban forces in Angola should withdraw in the first twelve weeks of the transition, while the remainder departed over the course of the next twenty-one months! On June 14, the SADF killed fourteen people in a raid against alleged ANC targets in Gaborone, the capital of Botswana.

We recalled Ambassador Herman Nickel in protest. South Africa's veteran professional, Ambassador Brand Fourie, had left his Washington post a few weeks earlier and retired from the diplomatic service. By June 1985, our relations with South Africa had sunk to their lowest level in the modern era. Pundits pronounced constructive engagement dead. On the left and right, American ideologues rubbed their hands in delight.

10

The Exceptional Mozambicans

We turn now to the strange case of Mozambique. Few countries have gained independence carrying such a burden of irresponsible colonial rule and reckless decolonization. Fewer have so quickly aggravated their own problems through policies that produced a string of man-made disasters and invited the hostility of powerful neighbors. No African government in the 1980s shifted course as drastically or creatively in an effort to cope with the results.

Mozambique entered the 1980s led by a ramshackle, Marxist regime more committed to the Soviets than the ruling party, FRELIMO, had been during the anti-colonial struggle. When Portugal suddenly pulled out in 1975, the leaders of FRELIMO made just about every wrong policy choice it is possible to make. Elaborate statist agricultural schemes were imposed, despite the lack of the most basic administrative talents to back them up. Abstract slogans became a substitute for policy. Local ethnic and religious sentiments were ignored, creating a reservoir of rural animosity toward the regime and compounding the dangerous vacuum created in the countryside when Portugal and several hundred thousand Portuguese settlers pulled out (the latter crossing into South Africa). Maputo adopted a self-destructive "confrontation" stance toward white-ruled Rhodesia, and then South Africa; a substantial number of Zimbabwean and South African guerrillas found sanctuary in Mozambique, creating a state of undeclared war along thousands of kilometers of indefensible borders.

The rulers of this tragic land have experienced Africa's steepest learning curve. Extreme adversity has triggered drastic reappraisals of policy and an eclectic and pragmatic open-mindedness, commodities that until quite recently were in remarkably short supply in Africa. The pay-off for these decisive moves has been a long time coming. Famine, insurgency, and massive refugee flows still torment its people, and the state-party apparatus of the governing FRELIMO movement controls less of the countryside than it did ten years ago. Millions of Mozambicans have died or been uprooted by a vicious war. But as Mozambique struggles to get back on its feet and its people gain the chance to heal their wounds, outsiders in and beyond the region would do well to study one of the first laboratories of African "new thinking."

Shedding the "Enemy" Image

My early official experience with the country did not always kindle these warm sentiments. It was April 1981, and I was about to sit down in the un-air-conditioned VIP lounge of Maputo Airport to begin my first Mozambican press conference. A colleague asked, "Why are you doing this to yourself? Just look at these slugs." Glancing at the collection of reporters from Soviet, Chinese, Yugoslav, East German, and European Communist news organs, I knew he was right. None of the assembled worthies, including a handful of Mozambicans from the government press agency, wished American diplomacy well in early 1981; several posed the sorts of questions one might expect in a criminal proceeding.

My first official visit to Mozambique had not gone well. The government had recently expelled several U.S. diplomats on trumped-up charges, and claimed to see an American hand in a recent South African commando strike on ANC offices in the capital city. Local officials argued that Washington had initiated the deterioration in relations, and demanded that we provide assistance to show our "goodwill." Not a born diplomat, I informed Foreign Minister (now President) Joachim Chissano that American taxpayers did not have an obligation to write checks to prove anything to his government. Standing up, Chissano terminated the exchange.

Diplomats accredited to capitals like Maputo tend to evaluate the visits of foreign dignitaries by the access they gain at the very top. My tentatively scheduled chat with President Samora Machel was scrubbed, and so the mission would be deemed a flop. I wondered at the time if Chissano and Machel were free agents who had planned this foolish scenario. Did they not realize that an abortive visit was calculated to delight South African hardliners and American fringe conservatives? It

seemed incredible that the top people in Maputo could believe in antag-
onizing the top Africa official of a popular new U.S. President as the way
to win hearts and minds in Washington. Did they really believe that we
Reaganites were a monolithic army of one-dimensional cold warriors
who had already written them off? If so, why had we bothered to come?

Next door in South Africa, the senior government ranks had answers
to these questions. Though they were divided on many things, they sus-
pected that my colleagues and I were trying to develop a balanced regional
policy that advanced American interests. That would mean straddling—
not fueling—the region's divisions and seeking to resolve conflicts which
the Soviets would otherwise exploit. They worried that we would reject
their attempts to define who our friends and enemies should be. Mozambique, according to the script being developed in South African official circles and among their right-wing American contacts, was supposed
to become an enemy for the new Reagan administration. It was already
on Pretoria's enemies' list, and was fast becoming the site of Southern
Africa's most brutal proxy war.

First impressions are dangerous things. I often thought back to my
first encounter with Chissano. A slim man of average height, with dart-
ing eyes and an intense countenance that seemed to mask a strong and
possibly ominous force, he reminded me of a cat ready to pounce. Fluent
in a number of Western languages (including English) as well as several
African ones, it was possible to imagine this fellow mastering by sheer
force of intellect the dangerous power politics of a violent liberation
struggle to become perhaps the second most powerful man in the country. (African foreign ministers rarely rank so high.)

It was also interesting to speculate on his private relationship with
Machel, a former hospital orderly catapulted from the humblest origins
to become the boss. The contrasts could not have been stronger. Chissano exuded the air of a generic senior official, with his cool aplomb in
Western business suit and his command of international codes. Machel
had the swagger and visibly pumped-up presence of a former laborer
who had just seized the master's estate. "Welcome to the Gang of Five,"
he bellowed at my four Contact Group colleagues and me as we entered
his modernistic presidential compound for consultations in late 1981.
Sporting combat fatigues and holstered sidearm, Machel seated himself
amidst a sea of Brazilian designer leather and chrome, looking as if he
were trying out for a movie role as Third World dictator. Chissano spoke
in paragraphs. Machel regaled us with the sort of cadenced rhetoric
familiar to readers of interviews in government-owned media organs.
Powerful in its own way, Machel's speech contained exquisite timing,

and one could get carried away by the rhythms of his Portuguese diplomatic rap—a challenge for the finest interpreter.

The relationship gradually became more interesting in late 1981 and 1982 as mutual stereotyping waned and each side did some homework on the other. Our British partners, who knew the place well, shared their own experience from the 1979 Lancaster House talks that ended the Rhodesian war and led to Zimbabwe's independence in 1980. The Mozambicans had been quick learners in the late 1970s, too. Having made the commitment after independence in 1975 to provide sanctuary for the Zimbabwean liberation war against Ian Smith's white minority government in Rhodesia, the FRELIMO government paid a heavy price in terms of Rhodesian counteraction. By 1979, the Mozambicans wanted the war to end, and they deployed some of their ablest people to London to assist the British in obtaining the requisite concessions from all sides, including the Mozambique-based ZANU wing of the Patriotic Front. Sadly, this diplomatic victory came too late to forestall Rhodesia's anti-FRELIMO counterinsurgency war from taking root in the central areas of rural Mozambique amongst disaffected FRELIMO people and ethnic groups underrepresented in the Machel regime. These were the origins of what had become by 1982 the MNR (renamed RENAMO) insurgency, a proxy war inherited from the Smith regime by the South African Defence Force.

Maputo had sent Fernando Honwana, a special adviser to Machel, to work on the fringes of Lancaster House in 1979, and he was an immediate star performer. Thus, we were delighted to learn in June 1982 that he would represent Mozambique at the New York proximity talks on Namibia; it signaled hope for constructive help from the Front Line States. Mission-educated in English-speaking Swaziland, Honwana came from a prominent Mozambican family whose members have made their mark on its political life. Before his tragic death in a 1986 plane crash that also killed Machel, Honwana made countless contributions to Mozambique's "new thinking" and to the steady improvement in the U.S. bilateral relationship.

I was to work as well with his brother Bernard, who became minister of culture and who possesses many of his brother's qualities. But Fernando was a diplomat's diplomat. He had the rare ability to grasp and articulate perfectly the internal political logic of warring protagonists and to suggest practical solutions that respected the core values of all parties. This enabled him to analyze correctly the mirror-image anger and fear of SWAPO and the South Africans as we grappled with defining the United Nation's role in the Namibian transition to independence. It is interesting, given the regime he represented, that Honwana could be courteous and gracious toward anyone except blind ideologues, whether American or African. Such individuals offended him and contradicted his instinct to empathize and understand.

If anything, these qualities were strangely reinforced by an officer training course in North Korea, an assignment he felt obliged to accept in the knowledge that his country's armed forces were a disorganized shambles that desperately needed competent leadership. By the mid-1980s, when the Maputo government was working to construct a new relationship with South Africa, Honwana would seek us out to gain understanding of what made his neighbors tick. He realized that no one understood them better than we did, least of all the suffocating blanket of Communist advisers still present in most of his government's ministries. Facing the ambidextrous actions of Pretoria after the 1984 Nkomati Accord that was to have ushered in a new era, Honwana unerringly asked us the same questions we asked ourselves. He asked about people, the authority relations between them, and the ammunition they might need in order to turn things around and make the agreement work. These were the practical questions of a problem solver. Honwana died before he could see the new Southern Africa that has emerged in recent years. But he was one of its founding fathers.

Our relations with Mozambique began to improve somewhat as the U.S.-led Namibia diplomacy got into gear in October 1981. Chissano paid a visit to Washington that same month. His top-level interlocutor was Deputy Secretary William P. Clark (later Reagan's National Security Adviser). Judge Clark, as he is known, was not renowned for his affinity with African Marxists. But this time, Chissano opened with a proposal that the United States and Mozambique discuss their differences and try to define a more positive relationship.

Oddly, he and the homespun Clark hit it off quite well, comparing notes on the region's ills and the Namibia-Angola diplomacy. Chissano had reason to seek some basis for dialogue with us. Things were going from bad to worse inside his country, our emergent regional diplomacy was becoming the focal point of activity by this point, and our credibility in Pretoria made Washington a logical place to visit. Clark's receptivity to Chissano surprised people who knew him only as a rather innocent hardliner. His feel for the region's complexities had grown fast during his visit to South Africa in June, when he was subjected to elaborate diplomatic highjinks and the sort of wet embrace reserved for a long-awaited suitor.

The Clark-Chissano meeting was the first, tentative step in a process that would gradually lead to dramatically improved bilateral relations. By mid-1982, when Chissano paid another quiet visit to the United States, he contacted us again for a no-holds-barred exchange on where his country was headed. Mozambique provided first-class leadership in the FLS– Contact Group talks in New York that summer. Secretary George Shultz held constructive talks with Chissano in October. But it was a series of visits to Maputo by my senior deputy, Frank Wisner, starting in December that opened a wholly new chapter in relations. No one was better equipped than Wisner for this pioneering diplomacy in a place so caught up in the Marxist-apartheid nightmare that Southern Africa risked becoming. He knew how to navigate the shoals of culture, ideology, and fear that had blocked communication with the leadership of this traumatized land.

Soon we were in touch with additional members of the top political leadership. The Mozambicans sought U.S. understanding and diplomatic support in checking tough South African military and economic pressures. They wanted to upgrade the bilateral relationship to ambassadorial level, and requested official encouragement of private investment as well as official humanitarian and development aid from the Americans. Most interesting from our point of view, they thought in broad, regional terms, grasping instinctively the link between events in Angola and Mozambique, in South Africa and Zimbabwe.

Our priorities in these early encounters were to shift Mozambique away from its self-destructive confrontation with Pretoria, to foster rethinking about its ruinous domestic policies, and to explore its readiness to abandon its close Soviet and Cuban alignment and behave like an independent, non-aligned country. We also sought its help in our dealings with the MPLA regime in Angola. Wisner argued that one could not expect to restrain the military behavior of South Africa, the dominant power in the region, unless that restraint was reciprocated by neighbors who provided sanctuary and support for the ANC and SWAPO.

By early 1983, this dialogue was paying off. In the months to come, U.S. food aid began to flow, and talks were held on an aid program to support the market sector and agricultural policy liberalization. Agreement was reached on exchanging ambassadors. Mozambique decided to freeze or curtail security ties to Communist states, to seek "associate" status with the European Community under the formula in place for other African states, and to apply to join the World Bank and International Monetary Fund. As a signal to the Western private sector, an oil-exploration contract was signed with Exxon, and Lehman Brothers was signed on to provide advisory services on debt restructuring.

On the regional front, we placed Mozambique at the center of an increasingly intense regional agenda. It was no longer difficult to persuade Machel, Chissano, Honwana, and their colleagues that the primary victim of a Front Line State strategy of confrontation with South Africa would be the Front Line States themselves, and especially Mozambique. Whatever the sentimental and political value of the "armed struggle" to its ANC and SWAPO partisans (and their Western fan clubs), it was nothing but a boomerang as a strategy. Whether singly or in combination, the Front Line States could not possibly take on the South Africans. That would remain the case as far ahead as one could see. Pretoria's practitioners of "forward strategy" found Mozambique to be an especially attractive target for obvious reasons: its evident vulnerability to a murderously efficient proxy war; its proximity to the core of South African military and economic power; its close links to the East; and, above all, its key role as a sanctuary and transit base for ANC personnel and supplies.

The challenge was to define the alternative to armed confrontation. Working closely with the Mozambicans, we would need to neutralize the forces of polarization and legitimize the notion of a regional security framework with benefits for all. We started by mounting a two-pronged initiative in early 1983 that soon opened the door to fundamental regional change. First, we discussed ways to break out of the sterile mold that had characterized the U.S.-Angolan discussions so far. In essence, this meant obtaining access to the core of the MPLA politburo and sidetracking Luanda's officious and hostile foreign minister, Paulo Jorge. The Mozambique leadership, working closely with Chief Fernandez, the Nigerian businessman, delivered exactly what we needed: by March 1983, we had opened a direct channel to Angolan Interior Minister Manuel Alexandre Rodrigues "Kito," at the time perhaps the number-two or-three man in Luanda.

We came to view the Mozambicans as partners who wanted us to be successful in resolving the Namibia-Angola wars. They understood that we were serious about getting a regional settlement, and needed help in building the necessary access in Luanda. At the same time, we understood that they were allies of the Angolans, sharing a common language and colonial history, a common experience of close Soviet ties and of South African destabilization pressures.

We also understood their motives in helping us on Angola-Namibia. They hoped that we would assist them in coping with their South African problem. This would form the second half of our 1983 initiative. We had prepared the ground with Pretoria's top officials, arguing that cooperation with us on regional diplomacy could pay major dividends. It could open the way to direct dialogue with two key Marxist neighbors on issues of war and peace, trade and cooperation. It could offer South Africa a conditional exit from the diplomatic doghouse. Many African states, including these two, refused to meet its officials, or did so only in the closet. It would offer Pretoria an ideal opening to bargain for FLS restraint on ANC guerrilla or terrorist actions. And it could provide the context for cooperation in undercutting the Soviet position and eliminating Soviet military influence and presence.

The South Africans seemed to get the point. In December 1982, after we had prepared the way in all three capitals, the Angolans and Mozambicans each held the first in a series of bilateral meetings with the South Africans. Machel's readiness to take the plunge on both fronts emboldened the skittish Angolans, creating a window for intensive regional diplomacy during the first half of 1983.

Viewed from Mozambique, American progress in getting Angola and South Africa to the table would (1) strengthen rational minds in Pretoria; (2) enhance the chances for an effective U.S. restraining influence there; (3) legitimize Mozambique's own quest for a modus vivendi with Pretoria; and (4) give us an incentive to invest our energy and prestige in a Mozambique–South Africa peace process. At the very least, such an approach could enable Maputo to test American intentions and our ability to deliver.

Machel understood that the triangular relationship between Angola, Mozambique, and South Africa could become a source of leverage for his regime, which was essentially powerless. Only Washington could make this triangle work; it would certainly not work by itself, given the depth of hostility and suspicion then existing, and no other external power had our potential to move the truculent South Africans. A similar logic operated for the Angolans, who were pleased to have company and a form of "cover" from their Mozambican country cousins as they explored their U.S. and South African diplomatic options.

Unhappily, military incidents intervened to place a severe strain on the new exchanges, triggering recriminations and sometimes retaliation. The triangle could produce negative as well as positive feedback. Maputo and Luanda maintained very close contact on regional issues; their moves and moods often seemed synchronized. An upbeat or negative assessment of South African intentions would quickly pass from one lusophone capital to the other, where it became input for policy decisions. We sometimes wondered if the men with the guns were in tacit collusion to sabotage the fragile chances for regional peacemaking.

The Angolan–South African meetings became the victim of such violence and a lack of clear leadership, as we have seen. Similar reversals occurred in Mozambique–South African relations. Some progress seemed to have been made at the second ministerial-level exchange between them in early May 1983 to discuss questions of border security, mechanisms for investigating incidents, and the issue of Maputo's support for the ANC and South African assistance to RENAMO. Then, on May 20, 1983, ANC operatives exploded a car bomb in front of an office building used by the South African Air Force in Pretoria, killing eighteen people and wounding nearly two hundred.

As the most important proximate sanctuary for the ANC, Mozambique was automatically the top suspect in South African eyes. Three days later, the South Africans mounted an air raid on Maputo, claiming to have knocked out a SAM site and killed forty-one terrorists. (Mozambican officials claimed the toll was six civilian dead, several abandoned houses, and a destroyed jam factory.) A few months later, the SADF mounted a daylight commando raid on ANC facilities in the heart of Maputo.

The Road to Nkomati and Beyond

The Mozambican leadership in the 1980s contained a rich variety of personalities, credentials, and ethnic backgrounds. It included Indians (mainly Goans), mestizos, whites, and Africans. It included technocrats, apparatchiks, and veterans of the anti-Portuguese struggle. But during his lifetime, there was never any doubt that Samora Machel was the boss of this diverse lot. Physically a diminutive man, Machel had the courage to take risks and lots of flak. He had the strength to modify his views and admit his bewilderment when things went wrong. Despite his best efforts, things often went wrong for Mozambique.

We may never know whether in early 1983 Machel had already written off Moscow as irrelevant to, or even the cause of, Mozambique's mounting problems. He may, on the contrary, have hoped that his early initiatives with us and with the South Africans would trigger Soviet competitive reflexes and more staunch Soviet support. Whatever his assumptions, Machel knew that he was venturing onto a vast, unmapped minefield that contained multiple dangers: the threat of a brutal Soviet retaliatory squeeze; the risk that Pretoria would exploit his moment of maximum vulnerability; the concern that any shift would subject him to ostracism by ideological "progressives" and fellow travelers at home and abroad; and the risk that the United States and other Western powers would fail to support his bold moves.

Before his death in 1986, Machel experienced all of these dangers to one degree or another. Success seemed to elude him. And yet, he had made the right choices. As he would do again and again, this unsophisticated but street-smart ruler demonstrated his grasp of the arts of political maneuver. His game was to acquire help for his collapsing country and leverage on his vastly more powerful neighbor. It was a case study of the diplomacy of weakness.

One of Machel's (and later Chissano's) key lieutenants for the most delicate missions was Jacinto Soares Veloso. A white Mozambican of Portuguese descent, Veloso rose to membership in FRELIMO's politburo over the years since he joined the movement in 1963. He had defected from the Portuguese Air Force by flying his plane across the border to Tanzania, site of FRELIMO's headquarters during the anti-colonial struggle. Educated in both Mozambique and Portugal, Veloso was the sort of person who enjoyed the challenge of dealing across cultural chasms. He seemed to be almost magnetically attracted to the most delicate political assignments.

Machel chose Veloso to lead his country's side in most ministerial-level talks with the South Africans, both before and after the Nkomati Accord of March 1984. Veloso, who spoke excellent French and passable English, did much of the market testing and advance work for Machel's diplomatic debut in Western Europe in late 1983 and his U.S. debut in the fall of 1985. When Machel decided in early 1983 to help us reach out to the key Angolan players, it was Veloso who showed up as a combination coach, escort officer, and chaperone for the MPLA's Kito Rodrigues. A frequent visitor to Luanda, Veloso read the MPLA's pulse regularly and did what he could to strengthen the arguments for making peace.

Jacinto Veloso was the first senior Mozambican to receive a guided tour—in Kito's company—of political Washington in 1983. He helped us to conceptualize and then articulate the earliest versions of possible schedules for Cuban troop withdrawal from Angola. In the process, he became identified with an enterprise that appeared to be booming in April–May but which had run aground by August amidst factional recriminations and mounting paranoia in Luanda. The shifting currents were even more ominous for highly exposed people like Veloso in his own home capital. When the high hopes created by signature of the Nkomati Accord in March 1984 were followed by mounting disappointment at Pretoria's double-dealing over the next several years, he must have faced times of real danger.

I used to marvel at the way he worked. Veloso never appeared to be relying upon briefing papers or written instructions. He had no supporting staff to keep notes or prepare messages. He gave no sign of ever receiving or sending diplomatic cables. As far as one could tell, Veloso's mandates and assignments were sweepingly broad—generic instructions of some sort from Machel to "go chase those cows." The record of his far-ranging personal diplomacy was largely in his head, supplemented by occasional handwritten scribbles in a small notebook he carried along. Filing systems, Xerox machines, cable clearances, trip reports, decision memoranda, and other ephemera of the modern bureaucratic state were utterly alien to his experience.

One would know that the conversation had taken an important turn when Veloso unobtrusively reached for his little book. On the other hand, like many top-level diplomats accustomed to working in delicate matters, he would cross his legs and look mildly perturbed if a U.S. staffer began taking actual meeting notes; the clarity and directness of his contributions began suddenly to suffer. Veloso, in other words, operated on the not unreasonable premise that no record should be kept of important and sensitive conversations until the point was reached when the parties wished to create one.

At the start of a meeting, he would mumble the minimal diplomatic "grace notes" in one language or another, and quickly shift to the listening mode. If you said something original or candid, the odds were high that the conversation would open new horizons and be mutually worthwhile. Idealistic platitudes led to stony silence and slightly impatient fidgeting. You knew you had reached him when a wry smile began to curl across his thin-lipped, slightly chubby face. A one-time director of his country's security police, he behaved like a man with as many enemies as friends. Behind the masks of official role and ideology that it was necessary to wear, Veloso was a man who liked to do crossword puzzles and go fishing.

The final months of 1983 were an especially busy time for Machel's lieutenants. He had made the basic decision to go beyond his earlier feelers and strike a deal with Pretoria. The economic and military pressures generated by the SADF / RENAMO proxy war had begun to affect nine out of Mozambique's ten provinces and to disrupt the lives of perhaps half its people. The rural economy and foreign trade were collapsing; schools, clinics, and most other forms of central government presence in the countryside were being systematically destroyed. It was becoming clear to the authorities in Maputo that they faced a brutally effective adversary, whose strategy was to destroy the social and economic fabric of village life; the uprooted rural villagers fled to safety (if they were lucky) or else were "recruited" into service as laborers, porters, or fighters. The Machel government, whose early actions had done so much to create conditions for rural insurgency, was on the ropes.

Second, it had become clear that the Soviets—with whom Mozambique had signed a Friendship Treaty—and their allies were simply not prepared to get more deeply stuck into the African quagmire. They did

Savimbi briefs the press from his Jamba headquarters in late 1987.

Sharing a light moment with former Tanzanian President Julius K. Nyerere during the April 1981 round of consultations with Front Line State leaders.

Left to right: U.S. delegation members Doug McElhaney, Nancy Ely, Elliott Abrams, South African Foreign Minister Roelof "Pik" Botha, U.S. Deputy Secretary William P. Clark, South African head of Namibia planning Rian "Kudu" Eksteen, U.S. Ambassador Bill Edmondson, and Chester Crocker. Botha points out convergence of oceans on Cape Sea Route off Cape Point, South Africa.

U.S. and South African sides square off at Fleur du Cap immediately prior to Lusaka tripartite meetings that produced the Lusaka Accord. Crocker flanked by U.S. Ambassador to South Africa Herman Nickel and Southern African Affairs Director Daniel Simpson. South African delegation led by Pik Botha, flanked to his right by Defense Minister Malan (obscured), Namibia Administrator General Willie van Niekerk, National Intelligence Service Director General Niel Barnard, State Security Council secretary General J. van Deventer, and to his left by Foreign Affairs Director General Hans van Dalsen and presidential advisor General Jannie Roux. *(Credit: South Africa Digest)*

At the conclusion of the Lusaka Accord, February 1984 *(left to right):* South African Defense Magnus Malan, CAC, Namibia Administrator-General Willie van Niekerk, Angolan Interior Minister Alexander "Kito" Rodriques, U.S. Ambassador to Zambia Nicholas Platt, Angolan Defense Minister Pedro Maria Tonha "Pedale," Angolan Vice Foreign Minister Venancio da Moura, and South African Foreign Minister Pik Botha.

Crocker greets SWAPO president (now president of Namibia) Sam Nujoma upon his arrival for discussions after the Lusaka Accord is signed.

Oval Office, November 1984: discussing the violence in South Africa and Round One of the U.S. debate on sanctions.

UNITA president Jonas Savimbi in conversation with Vice President George Bush during the January 1986 Savimbi visit to Washington. The administration moves forward to provide assistance to UNITA.

With George Shultz, appearing before the Senate Foreign Relations Committee, July 1986, on the day after the Reagan South Africa speech. *(Credit: Jose Lopez NYT Pictures)*

On Secretary Shultz's plane during January 1987 African trip. *Left to right:* AID administrator Peter McPherson, CAC, press spokesman Chuck Redman, DOD deputy assistant secretary Jim Woods, Africa bureau military adviser Col. Greg Bradford, George Shultz.

South African gunners during the 1987 Angolan offensive.

UNITA forces return from the front with Soviet armored equipment captured from retreating MPLA units.

Angolan, American, and Cuban military experts chew over the complexities of keeping the forces apart during the late July 1988 talks on the Namibia-Angola border. *From left:* Maj. "Ita" (Angolan intelligence), Col. Antonio Jose Maria (security adviser to Angolan President dos Santos), Lt. Col. Charles Snyder (military adviser to Crocker), the late Col. Jesus Morejon (Cuban military intelligence).

Crocker exchanges congratulations with Congo President Denis Sassou N'Guesso after signature of the Brazzaville protocol in mid-December 1988.

December 22, 1988, signing ceremony at U.N. Headquarters. *Left to right:* South African Defense Minister Magnus Malan; South African Foreign Minister Roelof "Pik" Botha; U.N. Secretary General Xavier Perez de Cuellar; Chester A. Crocker; Secretary of State George P. Shultz; Angolan Foreign Minister Alfonso "Mbinda" Van Dunem; Angolan armed forces chief of staff Antonio Franca "Ndalu" dos Santos; Cuban Foreign Minister Isidoro Malmierca; and Cuban Defense Minister General Abelardo Colome Ibarra. *(Credit: U.N. Photo)*

First organizing session of the Joint Commission, New York, January 1989. *From left to right:* Soviet ambassador at large Vyacheslav Ustinov, Angolan Delegation head General Ndalu, Cuban delegation head Carlos Aldana Escalante, South African delegation head Neil van Heerden, and Crocker. *(Credit: Brian F. Alpert)*

Crocker flanked by Cuban Vice Foreign Minister Ricardo Alarcon *(left)*, special assistant Robert Cabelly, and Jay Taylor *(in rear:* head of U.S. Interests Section in Havana); upon arrival in Havana, March 1989.

Fidel Castro greets delegations for Joint Commission meeting on the eve of the settlement implementation; March 1989.

Alex Schiavo *(left)* interprets between the Cuban head of delegation, Carlos Aldana, and Crocker; March 1989.

Deputy Assistant Secretary of State Frank G. Wisner with Mozambican President Samora Machel.

Crocker and Soviet Deputy Foreign Minister Anatoliy Adamishin confer at Windhoek airport en route to emergency meeting of Joint Commission at Mt. Etjo, Namibia; April 1989.

not want Mozambique to join COMECON.* Unlike oil-producing Angola, Mozambique did not have the necessary foreign exchange earnings to pay for large-scale, sustained imports of Soviet hardware. Moscow was not prepared to extend a blank check of military credit. Nor were vast military supplies the answer: the FRELIMO regime, founded on a guerrilla base during the colonial period, had abandoned its authentic military roots and lost its way in an inappropriate morass of procedures, tactics, and doctrines aped from Soviet and East Bloc military manuals. Moscow transferred few skills. Thousands of Communist military advisers retained control of logistics, maintenance, and training—for reasons of policy, and out of disdain for Mozambican capabilities.

The result was increasingly obvious to the regime itself: its armed forces were ill-trained, ill-led, lacking the most rudimentary equipment (including boots), and unable to rely on essential supplies (food and ammunition) in operational conditions. The Soviets were not the answer. And, unlike Angola, there were no Cuban troops in Mozambique to man key logistics and specialist services, air force, air defense and armor units, to hold key strategic positions or conduct joint operations. Furthermore, Machel—looking carefully at his options and at Angola's sad experience in the Cuban embrace—did not relish that scenario.

Third, Machel became persuaded that the only way to bring RENAMO under control was through South Africa, and that the best way to influence Pretoria was through the West. For all the military backwardness of Mozambique, it possessed the capability to gather and assess the evidence of systematic South African help to RENAMO. The Soviets and their allies must also have been in a position to know what was going on. That support included cross-border logistic, transport, communications, and intelligence help, as well as the provision of sanctuaries and training facilities on South African territory. South African ground, air, and naval forces violated Mozambican sovereignty with impunity on a regular basis, spreading captured arms and equipment (from Angola) across the countryside. Given these stark realities, Mozambique's leaders decided to see whether they could alter South African behavior.

Machel's October 1983 tour of Western Europe set the stage for six months of heightened diplomacy that culminated in the signature of the Mozambique–South Africa non-aggression treaty known as the Nkomati Accord. Many hands had been at work in the lead-up to the signing ceremony at the steamy little border town of Komatipoort on March 16,

---

* The Council for Mutual Economic Assistance, the Moscow-dominated regional economic grouping which linked the USSR, Eastern Europe, Mongolia, Cuba, and Vietnam.

1984. The Portuguese government had become far more sanguine about Machel and his prospects during 1983, in sharp contrast to the deep gloom in Portuguese assessments of Angola. Lisbon urged its European allies and the United States to bolster Machel as he approached the toughest decisions. Lisbon shared our sweeping goals, but it was also motivated by more tangible hopes that peace would bring opportunity for its citizens and firms. Portugal was particularly interested in seeing the massive Cabora Bassa hydroelectric project return to operation so that South African electricity purchases would help defray the project's large debt-service burden. In December, Portugal took the initiative to host a renewal of direct Mozambique–South African talks.

But Machel's and Botha's officials played the primary roles in negotiating the Nkomati Accord. Subtitled an "agreement on non-aggression and good neighborliness," this was a remarkable document. It literally and explicitly prohibited the parties from engaging in, or permitting the launch of, any form of armed attack on each other—by regular or irregular forces, directly or indirectly—or from providing any kind of military aid whatsoever to each other's armed enemies (i.e., the ANC and RENAMO), including such activities as organizing, recruiting, arming, hosting, or training such forces, and offering them shelter, weapons storage, transit, bases, communication, or broadcasting facilities. Nkomati was supposed to be the ultimate all-risk, no-loopholes insurance policy; it was the product of deeply suspicious, traumatized minds on one side and small-town lawyers on the other. Nothing would be left unspoken so that the other guy could come back and say, "Oh, we never said we'd cut *that* out."

In order to obtain iron-clad written commitments from Pretoria, Machel had signed the most comprehensive security agreement with South Africa in the region's history. By any measure, it was a great accomplishment for South Africa's diplomats and security bureaucrats, so eager for external recognition of its legitimate security interest against guerrilla infiltration and terrorist violence. But Nkomati was hardly an isolated or unique agreement. Comparable arrangements, typically informal and secret, already existed to thwart ANC operations from or through Zimbabwe, Botswana, Lesotho, and Swaziland (the last accord was published after Nkomati). Machel knew all this very well. If anything, the Nkomati Accord was less onesided than these other arrangements, because Machel wanted it—and its intended results—as much as Botha did.

Machel staged with South Africa a high-profile diplomatic scenario for signing Nkomati. This would give him credit internationally for realism ("One does not choose one's neighbors," he declared shortly before the signing); and it would surely give Pretoria a bigger stake in the success of their common enterprise of regional peacemaking. Perhaps he also had had enough of the slimy hypocrisy that sometimes passed for statesmanship—the fiery, anti-apartheid speeches from places far less vulnerable or needy than Mozambique, speeches often accompanied by secret visits to Pretoria to plead for railway wagons, foodstuffs, vital spare parts, or other goods. Perhaps he considered it more dignified and honorable to stand publicly before the cameras with Botha under a scorching African sun, as a co-equal partner, jointly creating a new regional order.

On March 16, Machel spoke eloquently of escaping the "process of confrontation," and described the accord as "laying the foundation for a definitive break in the cycle of violence that had been established in this region of the continent. A violence that was above all the result of the burdensome legacies we carry with us." Referring to Africa as "a continent of survivors" of slavery, foreign conquest, and repression, Machel spoke of Nkomati as "the only rational alternative for our future to be free of the spectre of violence and destruction."

The Mozambican leader was more or less alone that day at Komatipoort, his FLS partners having declined invitations to attend the signing. Though he received a lukewarm endorsement at the next FLS summit and from individual FLS leaders, the general reaction in African and Third World circles was one of sullen shock. Mozambique had had enough. The ANC's military wing had obviously suffered a body blow; its entire Mozambique logistic network would become the casualty of Nkomati over the coming months. The bitterness of ANC official spokesmen toward Machel was carefully muffled, directed instead at Pretoria for seeking to impose such accords and at the West for supporting Machel's course.

Machel's people attended proximity talks under South African auspices with RENAMO's "external" representatives in October 1984 to work out terms for an internal cease-fire. And when RENAMO representatives mysteriously broke up those talks, walking out at the very moment when a deal was within sight, Machel held the South Africans partly responsible. He was correct to do so because elements of the Pretoria government, working with like-minded Portuguese interests within and behind RENAMO, had helped to orchestrate the walk-out.

Within months of the signature of Nkomati, it was obvious to officials in Maputo that something was fishy about the chemistry within the bilateral Security Commission set up to monitor and supervise implementation. Evidence of a continued flow of material support to the rebels from South African territory gradually mounted. Efforts by official spokesmen to explain why Pretoria, the regional hegemon, could not fully control what was happening on its territory were received with knowing but nervous laughter in Maputo.

Machel, sensing confusion in South African ranks, consulted us intensively in 1985–86. At one moment, he received contrite noises and pledges of tangible aid from top levels in Pretoria who were visibly scrambling to "save Nkomati"; at the next, he was given fresh evidence of unauthorized flights and intensive unidentified radio transmissions emanating from across his eastern borders, from Malawi south to South Africa's Transvaal Province. Anyone who knew the region knew that such activity could only have one source.

But it was hard for Machel to believe that this was all a coherently organized act, authorized at the top. It looked more like one bunch of guys dashing around to cover for another. Machel may never have believed or understood the inner complexity behind South African ineptitude and deceit in its Mozambique policy. Indeed, it is hard to explain. How could the government in Pretoria have permitted one of its most striking diplomatic accomplishments to be so promptly discredited? What purpose could be served, short term or long term, by acting to destroy what confidence existed in one's solemn word? Perhaps it was an exaggeration to speak of a "South African foreign policy" in the mid-1980s.

Machel appeared to understand the complexity of RENAMO's origins and makeup, though he preferred to simplify the story. He realized that its leadership responded to disaffected African ethnic constituencies in central Mozambique, to diverse South African official interests, and to revanchist Portuguese constituencies resident in South Africa, Portugal, and even Brazil. He had an inkling, also, that a RENAMO support infrastructure, spawned under Pretoria's aegis, ranged from anti-Communist Islamic potentates in the Persian Gulf and Comores Islands to European conservatives and a motley assortment of right-fringe U.S. activists.

Machel's response to this complexity was to use Nkomati as a sword, holding Pretoria responsible for the mayhem inside Mozambique without actually blaming Botha himself or abrogating the agreement. This gave Machel and his government the keys not only to Pretoria's international standing but also to the minds, hearts, and wallets of the Western world. Mozambique was probably better off with Nkomati than it would have been without it, even though the agreement did not bring peace. What it did do was to turn the tables, giving Maputo an instrument with which to pressure and discredit South Africa and to gain external support.

The American Battle over Mozambique

The story of Mozambique after Nkomati is full of twists and contradictions. The government and people came to benefit from unprecedented flows of humanitarian assistance and development aid from Western nations and the international financial agencies. But rural security got worse and RENAMO became more aggressive. By the end of the 1980s, the Maputo government had achieved universal recognition and had thoroughly isolated RENAMO internationally. Yet it had also concluded that a military solution to the rebellion was beyond reach.

By the time Machel made a long-anticipated visit to Washington in September 1985, Mozambique was becoming the largest recipient of U.S. aid in sub-Saharan Africa. To the dismay of the "once a commie, always a commie" conservatives, the administration had proposed to Congress a modest military assistance program. Its goal was to support Machel as he carefully reduced his dependence on Communist military aid, looking to Zimbabwe for combat support in central Mozambique and to Britain for army training. Washington sought to follow up and consolidate its own success in changing the political map of the region. But our very clarity of purpose threatened vested ideological interests, and triggered a protracted debate over Mozambique. The military aid was blocked, and economic aid subjected to a series of harassing conditions.

Machel arrived to meet the most conservative President in modern American history, and witness the spectacle of seeing him attacked from the right *and* from the left for his African policies. If Machel put his ear to the ground upon arrival in Washington, he would have heard loud rumblings of debate on policy toward Mozambique, Angola, and South Africa. Congress had just repealed the Clark Amendment banning aid to UNITA, and the question of how and when to respond to the ongoing Soviet / MPLA offensive in Angola was a lively topic of discussion. The administration had announced its own South African sanctions initiative a few days before Machel's arrival in order to send needed signals to P. W. Botha and his neighbors while also preempting congressional sanctions measures.

Machel understood our reasoning, and no doubt enjoyed the domestic debate over how we should "punish" the bully next door. But he must also have wondered whether Washington could remain engaged as a serious and steady African player in the face of these strident and contradictory domestic voices fighting over policy. Fortunately for Machel, the British, who by this point appeared to support U.S. policy more strongly than we did, helped to smooth the way. They did so by quietly passing the word to Reagan that Margaret Thatcher had become an ardent Machel fan. There could be no stronger endorsement.

Machel used every tool at his command. Walking into the Oval Office where Reagan's somewhat ill-at-ease National Security team awaited this controversial African visitor, Machel grinned at Reagan, moved in for a two-armed Afro-Marxist embrace, and declared in dramatic Portuguese: "My friend Ronald! I've so long waited for this moment!" Reagan beamed back, charmed by the warm spontaneity of this most undiplomatic character. There ensued a friendly exchange in which Reagan heard Machel describe the latest revelations of South African bad faith on Nkomati, and replied by praising Machel's decision not to cancel the accord.

Machel's visit to Washington provided prompt but temporary relief for both him and us. Reagan, like Thatcher, understood that support for Machel and his traumatized people represented enlightened statesmanship. His support for the cause was reinforced by glowing reports he received from his daughter, Maureen. She was impressed with this vivacious and direct African potentate, having met him while serving as the leader of several U.S. delegations and goodwill missions in the region. (Maureen Reagan and Samora Machel, I later reflected, were truly a magical combine: two irrepressible extroverts with backbones of steel, they would have made a winning tag team.)

From our perspective, the Maputo government was either doing, or attempting to do, the right things on regional policy, on relations with South Africa, on domestic economic issues, and in its shift toward closer Western ties. We, therefore, wished to be in a position to offer timely assistance and to lead the Western effort to convert this golden opportunity into a success story.

It was not to be. It seemed that the stars were never in perfect alignment over Mozambique. By 1986, the battles over Mozambique policy within the South African government were over. The SADF covert operations guys had prevailed; links with, and support to, RENAMO's war effort were sustained, along with help for its increasingly aggressive external relations campaign. Washington and other key Western capitals pressed Pretoria repeatedly, in public and private channels, to make Nkomati work. But until late 1987 when South African diplomats began their comeback, it was a sterile exchange.

Inside the country, the war became a prolonged and bloody seesaw affair whose primary victims were civilians. FRELIMO's soldiers, for the most part, saw no incentive or purpose to stand and fight, a fact that caused resentment among the 6,000–10,000 Zimbabwean troops who helped hold the country together. On the other hand, RENAMO never posed a threat to seize power or even to hold major centers. That was not the intended purpose of this movement or its backers, who sought instead to keep Mozambique on its knees and free of ANC presence; to maintain pressure for some eventual negotiation over issues of policy, power sharing, and property rights of former Portuguese owners; and to prevent or reduce FLS use of Mozambique's transport corridors and keep trade flows dependent on South African facilities.

So the war ground on. Economic policy reforms produced quick results around some urban centers. But rural insecurity and governmental disorganization sharply limited their impact. It was impossible to attract much outside investment. When Machel's Soviet-piloted aircraft crashed near the Mozambique–South Africa border in October 1986, it seemed a sad metaphor for the fifty-three-year-old leader's career. His 14 million people were still suffering their worst years. These were years when 3–4 million of them would depend for survival on emergency food aid, 1.5 million became displaced persons or refugees, and the RENAMO campaign of destruction reached new levels of brutality.

In Washington, partisan strife over Mozambique became one of our biggest headaches during most of the second Reagan term. In my eight and a half years at the helm of the Africa bureau, no policy battle was more bitter. Few presidentially approved policies were more shamelessly undercut by people in the President's own party, his own administration and, even, his own White House staff.

By the time Chissano visited Washington in early October 1987, he had already come to grips with the reality that the civil war could not be resolved militarily. He described to Reagan and Shultz a range of reforms, including the restoration of religious freedoms and church properties and moves to open up the political system. It was a good thing that he was able to state his readiness to work with us and other countries to find "a political solution": Reagan was still taking heat from conservatives over Mozambique. We had just gone through a bruising, ten-month struggle over a routine rotation of ambassadors in Maputo. The nominee—a distinguished career officer named Melissa Wells—had become snared by conservative maneuvers in the Senate.

Amazing as it may seem, the challenge we faced from within and beyond the administration was the demand that we abandon and cut off aid to the struggling Maputo regime and help RENAMO as "freedom fighters" under the Reagan Doctrine. In their quest for American backing and "recognition," the movement's external representatives churned out manifestos on democracy, Christianity, and capitalism. Elements of the RENAMO lobby developed data and arguments to suggest that REN-AMO was winning. It was time to scrap the "State Department policy"; at a minimum, we should open channels to RENAMO and avoid "taking sides." Cable television viewers could tune in presidential hopeful Pat Robertson on his Christian Broadcast Network promoting a version of RENAMO crafted by evangelical Church sources with connections in South Africa, Zimbabwe, and Malawi.

All of this made it almost impossible at times to conduct our policies and maintain our programs. But we had support at the top. Thanks to his esteemed fellow conservative Margaret Thatcher, as well as Shultz, National Security Adviser Frank Carlucci, and especially his daughter Maureen, Reagan stuck with the policy. Another reason why we prevailed was the outstanding humanitarian research undertaken by a refugee specialist named Robert Gersony. He had previously undertaken impeccable research on refugee disasters in other parts of Africa, Asia, and Latin America. In light of the mounting refugee numbers crossing from Mozambique into South Africa, Zimbabwe, and especially Malawi, it made sense for Gersony to probe the root causes of the exodus.

Gersony spent weeks in the refugee camps ringing Mozambique, systematically interviewing their inhabitants in order to compile a profile of the conditions from which they had fled. When his horrifying results became available to top levels within the administration in April 1988, we quickly decided to brief the Congress and publish the report before it leaked and we faced accusations of "suppressing" it. The report painted a picture of rural catastrophe, forced labor, degradation of women and youth, and the deaths of perhaps 100,000 civilians; it was worse than anything we had imagined. RENAMO's open and closet admirers in Washington made a fierce but futile effort to discredit the work. These events, and the defection to FRELIMO in March 1988 of its Lisbon spokesman, Paulo Filipe de Oliveira, were major blows to RENAMO. The South Africans would soon be finding ways to distance themselves from the movement and promote a genuine settlement.

PART III

11

Sanctions and Sanctimony:
The South Africa Debate of 1985

Africian affairs has long been the stepchild of U.S. foreign policy. Largely ignored by Congress and the media during Reagan's first term, the State Department Africa team concentrated its "outreach" efforts on traditionally moderate constituencies that were readily accessible—business and labor organizations, Church groups, public affairs councils, educators, think tanks, and foundations. We had only intermittent success in keeping lines of communication open to the twin poles of "movement": conservatism, and liberal and black activism. Gradually, we had learned not to fool ourselves; these power blocs had very different agendas and goals from ours. They had no incentive to work with the State Department on anything. Their role was to protest, raise funds, gain national attention, and thereby expand their political base for future battles. To the extent that they were interested in U.S. foreign policy, it was to replace our strategy with something else. Meanwhile, the less ideological majorities in both parties, like public opinion generally, simply did not show much interest in African policy issues during Ronald Reagan's first term.

Within the executive branch, we operated in relative obscurity. We enjoyed solid, if sometimes distracted and incredulous, support from our political masters. Internal sabotage occurred from time to time, but it was not generally of a type or at a level that could threaten policy coherence. By the time of Reagan's overwhelming reelection in 1984, the

Southern African peace process still rested, and was seen to rest, on a broad mandate from the most popular American President in modern times to his Secretary of State and, through him, to me. We had the luxury of conducting foreign policy on its merits; we were accustomed to a relatively low profile in the United States. By the standards of other U.S. policies in other regions, we had a long leash and a high degree of autonomy.

Had we been able to capitalize on the splendid opportunity that emerged in 1984, our defenses would have been stronger when a multi-front assault on our African policies opened up at home. But those chances slipped by. It quickly became apparent that the "centrist consensus" of which I had written in 1980 still did not exist. And, now, we would really miss it: Africa was about to come of age as an object of mainstream American domestic politics. It would do so at a historical moment when we had assumed the lead role in a regionwide peace process whose nearest conceptual parallels were in the Middle East, a region about which Americans were better informed and less likely to lose their bearings.

By the end of 1985, the free hand we had previously enjoyed became an object of nostalgia. Suddenly, we found ourselves ensnared in the polarization, hypocrisy, and purely political logic that flourished just outside our doors in Washington. Africa would now become the ultimate "freebie" in American foreign policy. Remote from the American experience, Africa was the stuff of legends and stereotypes: it was the last remaining land of white hats and black hats, a Manichean playground for underemployed Western activists on the right and the left. Where else was there such a pure play on racism or anti-communism? Where else was there so little need for knowledge, experience, or self-discipline? Since our tangible strategic and economic interests in Africa were so modest, there was literally no penalty when politicians were caught playing with matches. There was no one to hold participants accountable if they made matters worse in the name of "doing something" about the region's many evils.

Since it did not really matter what one did or said, there was every incentive to view African policy as a bidding war in which you staked out "foreign policy" positions in order to "prove yourself" at home. Conservative Republicans viewed Africa as elephant country—a place to hunt for anti-Communist trophies to hang on the wall and to demonstrate doctrinal manhood in support of freedom fighters. Having just been trounced by an incumbent President who took forty-nine of fifty states, Democrats badly needed issues and causes to rally around. If the mounting violence in South African townships could be pinned on Reagan and his policies, this would open up a new "civil rights" front. The regional turmoil across Southern Africa was a gold mine, containing a bonanza of raw material for lobbyists, politicians, and fundraisers. But nothing could rival the special agony of South Africa itself in the mid-1980s. The land of apartheid was the mother lode of icons and symbols.

The Domestic Roots of Debate

Looking back, it is easy to see why the center did not hold during the South African sanctions debate of the mid-1980s. The United States had never in its history had a serious national discussion about any aspect of African policy. Debate and dialogue about African issues had previously occurred at the margins of our foreign policy process, among experts (Africanists) and a familiar band of corporate, religious, foundation, and media enthusiasts, plus activists on the fringes of their respective parties.

This was ironic. After all, 12 percent of the American people trace their ancestry to African shores. The story of racism, segregation, the civil rights struggle and equal opportunity are among the most neuralgic in American politics. South Africa's 340-year history of European settlement, colonial conquest, imperial warfare, minority domination, and (after 1948) legally entrenched racism is not without a certain resonance for Americans of all races—however vastly different the circumstances and political histories of the two lands. With hindsight, it is astonishing that apartheid had never before burst upon the American public consciousness as a topic of mainstream media interest and public debate. Other Western nations such as Britain and the Netherlands (South Africa's former colonial powers) had experienced their own apartheid debates over twenty years earlier in the aftermath of the 1960 Sharpeville massacre. The lines of European public opinion had become clearly established and remained relatively stable thereafter.

Strangely, this process of creating a stable framework of opinion never occurred in America—the land where Martin Luther King, Jr., and his allies built a national movement on the principles of peaceful protest against racial injustice. South Africa, after all, was the place where the techniques of non-violent resistance used by King in the United States were first developed by the South African-born Gandhi.

Even in quiet times, South Africa is a land that fuels strong emotions and big thoughts. Yet it had never touched the American public at large. The country and our policy toward it remained the preserve of a tiny black and white elite in a few American cities. It stayed that way from the time of apartheid's creation, starting with the National Party victory of 1948, through the heyday of classical apartheid in the 1950s and

1960s, to the beginnings of apartheid's dismantling in the late 1970s and early 1980s.

When the issue finally burst upon us in 1984–86, the air instantly became charged with the electric currents of racial politics. Almost overnight, American politicians, officials, pundits, businessmen, journalists, Church leaders, and trade unionists found themselves dealing with something white hot. They also found themselves face to face with what I once unguardedly described to a Senate committee as "the moral equivalent of a free lunch." A regatta of a thousand ships set off on a race for the moral high ground. But they did so without benefit of a chart, a clock, or a compass. Suddenly, all past standards of measurement were overtaken by events. Economic sanctions proposals which had been rejected by a liberal, Democratic administration in 1979–80 quickly became the opening position for moderate Republicans seeking political cover during the spring of 1985. Government reform moves previously considered beyond reach were now dismissed as "cosmetic" by Americans who had no concept of their significance (and who preferred, in any event, to take their cue from government opponents). These were truly inflationary times.

As for U.S. policy, it became a silly caricature of reality in the hands of critics ("gentle persuasion," "quiet diplomacy," "all carrot, no stick," "rapprochement with Pretoria"); it would almost have been amusing if the mainstream print and electronic media had not permitted our critics to get away with it. Unhappily, they generally did. An exception was Ted Koppel. After "Nightline" spent a week in South Africa, he wrote a *Newsweek* column in April 1985 recounting why South Africans of violently opposed views had taken the time to appear on the show. They appeared, Koppel wrote, because they all wanted American participation in the process of change, and they saw "Nightline" as an opportunity to advance their cause "by addressing the curious amalgam which is the American political structure." Koppel then addressed himself to American viewers, including me:

> And they were talking to you, Chester Crocker. Your theory of constructive engagement, set against the backdrop of an increasingly aroused public, is the right one. It permits the calibration of pressure, rather than the stark alternatives of abandonment (which would be self-destructive) or superpower bullying (which is almost always counterproductive). The news from South Africa is tragic, but our capacity to affect change there is greater than it has ever been.

Almost overnight, the Reagan administration found itself in the midst of a debate over whether "constructive engagement" or an alternative "policy" of sanctions was the right way to end apartheid. As if South Africa were an island in the South Atlantic, this debate totally ignored our regional strategy. It completely overlooked the logical necessity for regional peacemaking to *precede* basic internal political change in South Africa. That sequence was accepted by other governments ranging from the Soviets to the Front Line States and our European allies. In late 1985, a Marxist African head of state even complained to me that the combination of township violence and the American sanctions campaign would delay into the indefinite future the hope for a Namibia settlement!

But Koppel had a good point about the potential growth of U.S. influence on domestic change: for a short while, it *was* on the rise. Constructive engagement could have been strengthened by the heightened public concern behind the sanctions campaign. But that would depend on many factors, including the quality of our own management of the issue, the degree of partisan poison injected into the debate, and the ability of two very different political systems to remain in rough synch with each other as South Africa's ordeal unfolded. In the event, none of these equations came out right.

Republicans controlled the executive branch and the Senate. Under the perverse logic of Washington, officeholders are identified with the events—however distant and beyond U.S. control—that occur on their watch. This is especially true for the chief executive, the person centrally responsible for the conduct of foreign policy. Messy and tragic events abroad are deemed to require an American "response," regardless of what tools of policy may potentially be available or their relevance to the situation at hand.

As South Africa's black townships descended into a swamp of mass protest, police repression, and black-on-black coercion, we soon found that there was muck on our shoes. Put there by the media and our political opponents, the muck was even harder to remove because the administration *did* have a policy toward Southern Africa and we had blessed it with a name. By the summer of 1985, Reagan and other top officials regularly faced press questions along the lines of: "Mr. President, another thirty-nine blacks died in continuing urban violence in South Africa during the last two weeks. Hasn't the time come to move beyond your policy of constructive engagement and silent diplomacy?" The sanctions campaign had two targets, not one.

The Free South Africa Movement which emerged in late 1984 was a coalition of anti-apartheid and pro-sanctions groups spearheaded by TransAfrica and its founder-director, Randall Robinson. For some years, grass-roots activists had been pushing the idea of "divestment" of the securities of American firms with a direct investment stake in South Africa.

An embryonic network of state and local activists already existed. TransAfrica, founded in 1977 as a national and Washington-based black lobbying group on African and Caribbean issues, advocated a policy of comprehensive economic sanctions against South Africa.

The nationwide South African unrest and official repression of 1984 lit a match ideally suited to the needs of Robinson and other figures who drew together the various strands of the American anti-apartheid movement. An articulate advocate, who knew how to frame the issues and use the media, Robinson emerged as the lead witness for a cause defined in stark tones as one of solidarity with a rebellion against apartheid. He had first come to my attention when his group distributed (and later published) classified U.S. policy documents to African leaders attending the 1981 Organization of African Unity summit meeting. It struck me as interesting that Robinson consistently rebuffed our overtures for dialogue during Reagan's first term. He cherished the imagery of confrontation. Both before and after the protests began, he made a point of canceling, boycotting, or walking out of meetings scheduled between concerned black Americans and administration officials. He wanted attention and confrontation, not communication.

The prime goal of the Free South Africa Movement which came to life on Thanksgiving Day, 1984, was to generate media coverage, using a campaign of carefully scheduled demonstrations and rallies in major media markets. A key device was to stage the arrest of politicians and other celebrity "picketers" outside the South African Embassy in Washington. Arrests were scheduled by appointment and coordinated with camera crews and TV newsrooms. In the name of freeing South Africa, the movement created an American media happening. It drew strength from a network of friendly media organizations, civil rights, academic, labor, and religious groups, and state and local political activists.

The movement also drew strength from the presence in the United States of Bishop Desmond Tutu, who had received the Nobel Peace Prize in October 1984 for his work on behalf of racial justice in South Africa. Tutu's eloquence about injustice and his strident rhetoric attacking constructive engagement as a form of collusion set up a picture-perfect confrontation between him and Reagan—an imagery Tutu fostered skillfully with the press at the conclusion of December 7, 1984, meetings with Reagan and Bush.

Desmond Tutu and Randall Robinson complemented each other well: the courageous South African prelate with a sharp tongue and a well-developed taste for liberation theology, and the American activist who knew how to simplify South Africa's trauma into a series of emotive, civil rights sound bites. The two men had the perfect allies in their campaign to change American policy: Pretoria's ministers of brutality, perversity, stupidity, and bad timing—a collection of characters who behaved like walk-ons in a Hollywood script. Incredibly, these guys actively facilitated foreign media coverage of township unrest, imagining that the TV footage would help their cause by focusing on "terrorists and hoodlums" causing the violence, and not on the police and defense forces conducting their heavy-handed township sweeps. (Media coverage of political violence was curtailed in late 1985, over one year after the authorities had first encouraged it.)

If one stopped to think about it, the situation was bizarre. Where else in the Third World would scores of foreign journalists be welcomed in to cover a story of nationwide urban unrest? For South Africa's dominant urban black protest movement, the United Democratic Front (UDF), the political tinder being ignited in the United States by the Free South Africa Movement, Bishop Tutu, and the TV footage was a gift from the gods. A tactical alliance mushroomed before our eyes. Each partner made the other into a larger-than-life threat to the local status quo.

Another clue to the political roots of the controversy was the almost instanteous reflexes of a group of some thirty-five Republican members of the House of Representatives. On December 4, 1984—one month after Reagan's smashing victory, two weeks after the arrests began outside the South African Embassy, and one day after I had briefed Reagan on the gathering storm—these Republican worthies released the text of a threatening letter to the picketee, South African Ambassador Brand Fourie. Its thrust was to attach explicit, bilateral conditions to their continued support for constructive engagement: an "immediate end to the violence in South Africa accompanied by a demonstrated sense of urgency about ending apartheid." If these things did not happen, they would "recommend" a curtailment of new U.S. investment in South Africa and diplomatic and economic sanctions. Led by Vin Weber (Minnesota), Bob Walker (Pennsylvania), Newt Gingrich (Georgia), and other figures in the Conservative Opportunity Society (dubbed "conservative opportunists" by many fellow Republicans), the group knew exactly what they were doing: a locomotive was headed down the track toward their President, and they had no intention of standing in its way. They also had no intention of letting the "race issue" within the burgeoning South Africa debate go by default to the Democrats. The letter was early proof that American domestic politics would interpret sanctions as the equivalent of "doing something" about apartheid.

Another clue to the domestic politics of the drama came when I was summoned one week later to Senator Ted Kennedy's northern Virginia estate. I had been asked to brief the Massachusetts legislator for his suddenly arranged visit to South Africa. He was the essence of civility. But Kennedy's well-scripted civil rights photo opportunity became an embarrassing fiasco: contending black organizations differed over how he should be received, and he was not given the telegenic platforms he had expected.

I next saw Kennedy in his Senate office for a trip read-out in late January 1985. After opening pleasantries, the senator suddenly began berating me, Reagan, our embassy in South Africa, and U.S. policy. He would see to it that changes in our policy happened fast, he growled. Voice rising, face reddening, he rendered the ultimate judgment that nothing had changed in South Africa since the visit there by his late brother Robert in the 1960s—by implication, a benchmark event in South African history. As I left his office, I glanced back to see if I could locate the switch that must have been flipped on for my benefit. Kennedy was by no means the only white American politician who saw it as his civic duty to hector, bully, and preach to fellow countrymen in need of moral instruction about racism. He was just the first out of the blocks.

The battles over U.S. African policy that began in November–December 1984 continued in one form or another for some thirty-four months, ending symbolically with the Senate's approval of Melissa Wells in the fall of 1987 as U.S. ambassador to Mozambique after an ten-month confirmation struggle. Along the way, we won some engagements and lost some. And our regional strategy of peacemaking came perilously close to destruction.

Starting in December 1984, a rising share of our time was taken up with the poisonous debate over South Africa. Each crescendo and turning point meant another round of high-level strategizing within the administration; another round of appearances on "Face the Nation," MacNeil/Lehrer, and the Brinkley show; another series of hand-holding sessions with corporate, labor, minority, and religious leaders; and a fresh series of calls on individual legislators and their staffs. By mid-1985, the Africa team at State was conscious of the quiet circling of predators. Our approach to Angola, Namibia, Mozambique, and the other Front Line States came under conservative attack just as the attacks from the left began to draw blood. A Hill staffer was overheard gloating to an administration soulmate that "Crocker is about to run out of silver bullets."

What Went Wrong?

Ted Koppel had written in April 1985 that constructive engagement, conducted against the backdrop of an aroused public, could enable us to "calibrate" pressures and enhance our influence on P. W. Botha's government in Pretoria. Theoretically, this might make sense. But the good cop, bad cop analogy—arming a reasonable and balanced policy-maker with the "threat" of a meaner alternative—does not always work well in American foreign policy.

Koppel's model might have worked if the good cop and the bad cop were working for the same police chief. In this case, the bad cop was not trying to help Reagan, Shultz, and me; he was trying to discredit, undermine, or replace us; and he sought to compel us to redefine U.S. policy. Not surprisingly, we refused to oblige: our role in life was not to serve as agents of the opposition party or to defer to a 535-member committee known as the Congress. The fundamental issue underlying the debate was a struggle over *control of U.S. policy toward South Africa.* You can hardly "calibrate" policy when it is the object of a test of wills between rival forces.

As a result, by mid-1985 the message we were sending to the South Africans became louder. But the signal heard by the Botha government and its black opponents had become a high-decibel garble. In Washington, we had the task of responding to a rapidly deteriorating situation in South Africa while fighting off a challenge from domestic opponents. These twin factors required us to toughen our own message. But it did not strengthen our hand with the government, which perceived us as changing our strategy to compete with our critics. U.S. influence, if anything, declined, and our garbled messages virtually invited the South African parties to escalate their own test of wills. The violence and oppression in South African sparked the American debate, and that debate helped fuel South Africa's fires.

The second problem with the good cop, bad cop analogy was precisely the definition of policy and the standards of measurement used in calibrating it. Our policy contained a *dual* conditionality: regional cooperation and internal reform. It is not uncommon in statecraft to advance a multiple agenda in its relations with another state. In the case of major states (China, Brazil, Mexico, Saudi Arabia, Iran, India, or Thailand), we seldom have the luxury of having only one goal toward which all of our leverage and creativity are applied. As the dominant power of the subregion from Zaire south to the Cape, South Africa clearly qualified as a major state. Historically, administrations prior to Reagan's pursued a multiple agenda toward South Africa, recognizing that it was essential to engage Pretoria regionally. Like us, they pursued each of their agendas, keeping them on completely separate tracks and handling them in very different ways. Like us, they had no desire to hand the South Africans any excuses for refusing to cooperate in U.S. regional diplomacy, thus letting them off the hook. Like us, they carefully avoided defining precise targets and explicit conditions related to internal political change.

American administrations defined our goal within South Africa as peaceful change away from apartheid and toward a democratic, non-racial order. They articulated general political formulas consistent with that goal—e.g., full political participation (Carter-Mondale), government based on the consent of the governed (Reagan-Bush). In the 1980s, we also signaled our readiness to support—and give recognition to—incremental steps along the road of reform, *provided that they were not inconsistent with the concept of an open-ended process of change.* But the exact steps, timing, and eventual constitutional formulas were for South Africans, not outsiders, to define.

The reason for this caution was self-evident. First, South Africa's white leadership would have been only too willing to engage us in discussing some sort of "understanding" on issues of political change. They found our broad formulations to be too open-ended. I regularly fended off suggestions from Pretoria that we define our own bottom line for South Africa; as Pik Botha put it to me in February 1985, "Let's get down to brass tacks. What do you want of us, and in what timeframe?" It would have been downright dangerous to our long-term interests in democratic change for us to engage the Nationalist Afrikaner government in a negotiation on these matters. Moreover, it would have been suicidal for me to seek from the Washington "policy process" an authoritative position on them. Second, it was not the United States (or Britain or Europe) with which Pretoria should negotiate a future political system, but its own unenfranchised people. Our role was to facilitate negotiation, not to become one of the parties ourselves. As I had argued in my 1980 *Foreign Affairs* article during the final months of the Carter administration:

> U.S. officials correctly insist that the timetable and the blueprint for change in South Africa are not for outsiders to impose. Yet, without Western engagement in the region as a whole, it will not be possible to assure that South Africans are permitted to build their own future. The American stance must be firmly supportive of a regional climate conducive to compromise and accommodation in the face of concerted attempts to discredit evolutionary change and to exploit the inevitable ambiguity and periodic "incidents" that will accompany political liberalization.

There was nothing particularly dramatic or controversial about these sentiments when they appeared in print on the eve of the Reagan era. In fact, they represented basic continuity of policy. By early 1985, however, a highly partisan debate had broken out which purported to measure U.S. policy exclusively in terms of South African internal reform. Gone was the dual conditionality (regional and internal) that had earlier defined our relationship with Pretoria. U.S. audiences tuned out our effort to describe our regional strategy and its regional context; we were charged with ducking the "real" issue.

As a result, we gradually lost the ability to tell South African officials with a straight face that their cooperation on Namibia, Angola, or Mozambique would make any difference to the domestic debate over sanctions. We withdrew Herman Nickel, our ambassador in South Africa, in June 1985 explicitly to protest SADF raids into Angola (the Cabinda raid on U.S.-owned oil facilities) and Botswana. This move was also designed as a rejoinder to Pretoria's cavalier and even arrogant response to U.S. negotiating proposals tabled in March. Yet by July and August 1985 it had become obvious to Pretoria that American banks, American congressmen, American media, and (for that reason) American officials were focused mainly on the issues of violence and reform within South Africa. From a South African perspective, the test of wills over control of U.S. policy was having the effect of changing the focus of that policy.

Consequently, the administration spent the years 1985–86 engaged in battle on terrain selected by our domestic political opponents and accepted uncritically by virtually all other participants. U.S. policy would now have to stand or fall solely on the basis of how Americans judged its results in ending apartheid itself. It was a stacked deck. We had never claimed that constructive engagement could end apartheid—any more than our predecessors had made such lofty claims for their strategies. Nor had we ever set deadlines for the achievement of specific reform targets.

Where, I wondered, was the sense of history and perspective in this sudden spasm of American self-righteousness? After all, the era of racism and white domination in South Africa began in 1652; three hundred years later, the National Party had mounted a horrendous plan to convert this legacy into the statutory-constitutional dogmas of apartheid. Where was the American body politic during the 1950s, the era during which apartheid was built and an ANC–South African Communist Party coalition mounted the so-called "Defiance Campaign" against the hated pass laws? Where were the protests during the early 1960s, when the Rivonia trials resulted in Nelson Mandela's imprisonment and the banning of the ANC? These were the formative events for people of my generation who knew South Africa, the events that triggered the ANC's decision to go underground and resort to violence. These were the events which had caused an exodus of thousands of white and black South Africans, molding a generation of political leaders, journalists, and authors. Ironically, Americans discovered the existence of apartheid only in the mid-1980s, the very moment when its own inventors were beginning to cast it off and when the black opposition had finally found the organizational means to mobilize an effective movement of resistance.

The American sanctions debate of 1985 interacted precariously with South African decisionmaking; it was unclear which society was having the more harmful consequence on the other. Not only did we face a reversion to mindless, self-destructive regional behavior by Pretoria. By July 1985, South Africa's internal crisis had deepened. Some five hundred blacks had died in the previous nine months of violence. In response to the continuing unrest, the South Africans on July 21 declared a partial state of emergency, widening police powers to crack down on the activities of black organizations. A few days later open-air funerals were banned, and in early August we learned that sixteen top UDF leaders would face treason trials. Prominent prelates like Reverend Allan Boesak, the ranking churchman in the mixed-race branch of the Dutch Reformed Church, defied the new protest restrictions, while Desmond Tutu boycotted a meeting with P. W. Botha. The test of strength was fully joined.

Meanwhile, by late May Senate Foreign Relations Committee chairman Dick Lugar had begun publicly to modify his stance on sanctions legislation. Previously leaning toward legislation that would threaten future sanctions, he now moved toward a two-phased approach: immediate application of certain measures, and adoption of others within eighteen to twenty-four months unless "significant progress" occurred in ending apartheid. Lugar moved quickly, giving ground to his left whenever necessary in an effort to preempt a partisan bidding war on sanctions. His committee generated a bi-partisan bill in early June. Meanwhile, on June 5, the House had voted 295 (including 56 Republicans) to 127 in favor of a measure imposing an immediate ban on new investment and gold-coin imports. In a procedural fluke, a total boycott bill proposed by Representative Ron Dellums (Democrat of California) passed the House on a voice vote, an event pointing to the confused rush for cover among legislators of both parties.

On July 11, the Republican-controlled Senate voted 80 to 12 in favor of a sanctions measure carrying the endorsement of the Republican and Democratic leadership. The bill would ban new bank lending to the South African government and its state-controlled agencies, create a total ban on nuclear-related trade, codify existing curbs on computer exports, and mandate corporate adherence to the previously voluntary fair employment policies known as the Sullivan Principles. A ban on new investment and the import of South African gold coins (Krugerrands) was threatened for later.

Conservative Republicans opposed to South African sanctions meanwhile had taken the lead in organizing the repeal of the 1976 Clark Amendment prohibiting U.S. military aid to any Angolan faction (read UNITA). This effort succeeded easily in the Senate in June. The key vote in the Democrat-controlled House came on July 10 (one day before the Senate sanctions vote), when a bi-partisan coalition (including sixty Democrats) approved repeal with a 51-vote majority. We had long favored repeal as sending a signal that would strengthen our hand with Luanda.

Other players had another agenda. In recounting his maneuvers with certain Republican senators and CIA director Bill Casey, former NSC staffer Constantine Menges wrote that the senators saw the repeal as offering President Reagan "the opportunity to jettison this failed State Department policy." He encouraged their aides to send Reagan "a factual criticism of the current policy, then present *an alternative pro-Western policy*" (emphasis added), which Menges proceeded to draft for them.

A few days after the House vote, the MPLA regime announced an apparent suspension of negotiations with Washington. To complete the picture, conservative Republicans had managed to kill our request for a modest military assistance grant to the government of Mozambique. A worldwide foreign assistance authorization containing the ban was signed into law by Reagan on August 8. Behind the scenes, NSC staffer Menges (and his soulmates) coached Hill staffers on the need for a "shift to a U.S. policy of full support for the pro-Western armed resistance, RENAMO. . . ."*

On July 15 *The Washington Post* published a lead editorial entitled "Africa Policy in the Shredder." Not an advocate of sanctions, the *Post* explained that congressional voices were reacting to the perception of "administration tiptoeing on apartheid" while Pretoria seemed to be "thumbing its nose at Ronald Reagan and at America." Not only was there a test of wills at home and within South Africa; now, we were being urged to engage in a test of strength with the South Africans and other evil foreigners. Our ardent defense of current policy somehow suggested that we were defending apartheid (or Marxism). Less balanced observers went further. Anthony Lewis on the Op-Ed page of *The New York Times* on June 2 interpreted Pretoria's conduct as "deliberate insult to the United States" and a "contemptuous violation" of its commit-

---

* Constantine C. Menges, *Inside the National Security Council* (New York: Simon and Schuster, 1988), pp. 236, 238.

ments to us. The May 1985 Angola raid was a "calculated embarrassment to U.S. policy" and a "deliberate slap in Mr. Crocker's face." I should give Pretoria a deadline to shape up or else I should ship out.

Progressive and conservative critics alike wanted graphic displays of America's manhood. By jingo, this was no time for U.S. officials to pussyfoot around with nuanced explanations of the "regional context" or to expound upon our "finite influence" in advancing some nebulous peace process. The way to deal with a sick society and a rattled and divided regime was to strike a virile pose and increase their economic and political isolation. The way to deal with the Angolan and Mozambican regimes was to equate them (despite their massive differences), to stop talking to them, and to side openly with their enemies.

Under instructions from Shultz, we had carefully avoided boxing ourselves in by threatening a presidential veto of sanctions. Our reaction to the Lugar Bill was that it contained some positive aspects, but we remained opposed to punitive economic sanctions (i.e., those directed not at the government but at the South African economy as a whole). In fact, much of the Senate package consisted of a codification of current executive regulations and policy. The endorsement of the Sullivan Principles—named after the Reverend Leon H. Sullivan, a black Baptist minister from Philadelphia who had devised this code of conduct in 1977 as a condition for U.S. corporate presence in South Africa—was most welcome. The Sullivan effort made a practical difference. Its fair employment practices set the standard in South Africa and hastened key labor law reforms. Hundreds of millions of dollars in social spending by the Sullivan signatories supported the vital opening of opportunity and the transfer of skills to the black community. We also welcomed expanded Senate funding for our government assistance programs for South Africans in the fields of human rights, community self-help, black education, and business development. The thing to be avoided was current or prospective damage to South Africa's economy—as well as the imposition of a legislative straitjacket that would sharply reduce our flexibility and control of policy.

Shultz was disgusted by, but resigned to, the partisan times we were facing as people looked toward the mid-term elections of 1986: "It's just that sort of period." If we lost on the Hill, so be it; but we would not change our policy. "Trade and financial sanctions will just hurt the wrong people and give us less to work with." We were not against pressures, including sanctions; we were against the wrong kinds of measures in the wrong hands. Shultz counseled me to insulate our strategy, steel ourselves against hostile verdicts, and await openings to bring our influence to bear. We had the right policy, but it could accomplish little while the South Africans were battling each other in an existential test of wills. He did not rule out tactical adjustments to distance ourselves from the mess and bridge toward better times.

In late July, we and the British abstained in the U.N. Security Council, permitting passage of a French-sponsored resolution calling for repeal of the recently imposed state of emergency and urging a suspension of new foreign investment in South Africa. The last item was a splendid Gallic gesture: investors were already leaving South Africa in droves. A few days later, a major U.S. bank refused to roll over its South African debt. South African leaders did not yet realize it, but they were sitting on a financial volcano. Two thirds of the country's foreign obligations were concentrated in short-term loans due within one year; nearly 40 percent were due in six months. Bad political decisions could easily trigger a chain reaction amongst foreign creditors.

By mid-August, the House and Senate conferees had put the finishing touches on a compromise sanctions package. To clinch the deal, Lugar and Majority Leader Bob Dole accepted an immediate ban on Krugerrand imports; the list of threatened measures to be considered by the President after twelve months now included a ban on the import of coal and uranium and denial of most-favored-nation trade status. We knew that the votes were there in both houses to pass a sanctions bill immediately after the August recess.

Matters came to a head in the worst of circumstances in August and early September. Far from being able to "calibrate" pressures on P. W. Botha's government in the good cop, bad cop fashion Ted Koppel had suggested, we could no longer control either the pressures or the incentives in the bilateral relationship. More than ever before, we needed the parties in Southern Africa (especially the South Africans) to cooperate and be responsive. But their incentive to cooperate with us declined as the test of wills heated up between the administration and Congress. We needed "results" from Southern Africa at precisely the moment when we were least likely to get them.

Regional leaders began to understand that they could influence the factional strife breaking out among Americans. Leaders of the UDF, the South African government, UNITA, the MPLA, or the Front Line States would now think twice before deciding whether or not to "help" American diplomats battling to maintain policy control. They had options across the spectrum of American politics. Our divisions magnified theirs, and vice versa. Splits within the Botha camp helped accentuate splits within the Reagan camp. There were powerful voices in both camps which viewed the State Department as the enemy and which worked assiduously to poison the well for our strategy.

Worse, the test of wills tended to encourage polarization at both ends of the U.S.–South African relationship, empowering the extremes and undercutting the center. In a belated riposte to our having yanked Ambassador Nickel back in June, Pretoria withdrew Herbert Beukes, its new ambassador-designate, from Washington before he could present his credentials! Our diplomats faced steadily more chilly treatment from South African officials who began to echo their president's revealing dictum to visiting Americans: "Sanctions are your problem, not ours." In a parallel gesture, black activists began boycotting meetings with us (and denying the fact of ongoing meetings) as a statement of protest at the administration's opposition to economic sanctions. Both developments undercut State Department influence and temporarily isolated us. Meanwhile, on the conservative and left-wing fringes of our system, relationships flourished: the Robinson-Tutu alliance was paralleled by the links between Botha's narrowing circle of security advisers and a network of conservatives on the Hill, in the lobbies and parts of the evangelical movement, and within the intelligence community and the White House staffs.

Even in normal times, most people resist doing things under overt pressure from foreigners. That is more true of nationalistic people like the Afrikaners, whose identity has been defined by a rejection of foreign domination. Back in February, Pik Botha had told me that his president could no longer accept being told "as long as you do this, we will do that." The price of constructive engagement was becoming too high for P. W. Botha. Americans, on the other hand, make a habit of "intervening" in the affairs of other people, and we are not reticent about taking public credit when something "good" happens. Afrikaner hypersensitivity and American insensitivity made for a combustible mix. Earlier in the year, Botha went so far as to reverse a positive decision immediately after Reagan had taken personal credit for achieving it!

Sanctions, Signals—and Rubicons

As we headed toward the first climax of debate, a mythical dichotomy took hold: would we stay with constructive engagement and veto the sanctions legislation looming ahead of us (running the risk of a veto override), or would we "acknowledge" that our policy had "failed" and that it was time for sanctions? In reality, it was a phony choice. Sanctions had been incorporated in U.S. policy since the voluntary arms embargo of 1962. There were a number of sanctions (bans on trade of arms and military or nuclear-related technology, restrictions on computer licenses for certain buyers) already built into long-standing U.S. policy. Moreover, the dichotomy was false because sanctions are not a policy; they are one possible instrument of policy. Their use needs to be properly understood.

The threat of sanctions can sometimes bring influence, if carefully targeted and skillfully deployed. But, as with other types of threat, credibility is greatest when you never actually have to carry out the threat. Once implemented, the influence derived from the threat is gone and you end up with less than you had before.

Now, you are dependent on the raw coercive potential of the sanction itself—a very different matter. Measuring coercion is an intricate art. How is success to be measured? The arms embargo successfully raised the price and complicated the acquisition by the SADF of a wide range of items. A more or less permanent constraint was placed on certain defense options by the prohibitive cost of strictly domestic procurement. On the other hand, the embargo led South Africa to create one of the largest and most diversified arms industries in the southern hemisphere. Sanctions created pressures for self-sufficiency, and South Africa became a significant player on the world arms-export markets. South Africa's aggressive regional policies of the 1970s and 1980s would have been impossible to sustain had Pretoria remained dependent on Western nations for imported arms.

If U.S. (or Western) economic sanctions were to reduce South Africa's GNP by 2 percent and increase unemployment by 20 percent, would that be "success"? Clearly not: the goal was not to impoverish the country. The problem is to identify how—if at all—tangible pain can produce a predictable political consequence such as reform or negotiation. Punishment, presumably, is not an end in itself; the likelihood of unintended consequences is simply too vast.

The third approach to sanctions is to view them primarily as a device for "sending a message." Sanctions could represent a gesture of annoyance, disapproval, censure, disgust, or principled opposition. They could underscore our disgust at the legally entrenched racism of apartheid and our disapproval of the means being used to repress the black resistance movement sweeping across the South African landscape. Congressional sanctions advocates, in their more candid moments, conceded that sanctions were unlikely to affect events on the ground in South Africa very much. The purpose was "to make clear where we stand" and to distance ourselves from something ugly and unpleasant. But the problem is that multiple audiences receive the message, and it may translate differently in different places. The real audience most U.S. politicians cared about was their own constituency, not the embattled foreigners 8,000 miles away.

By the summer of 1985, there was a strong case on domestic policy grounds for the adoption of some additional sanctions. By defusing a domestic debate, sanctions might enable the executive to return to the business of conducting foreign policy. But what about the signals being sent to South Africans? What, exactly, was the intended message of proposed U.S. sanctions? There were fine lines to be walked here. It was good foreign policy to underscore American solidarity with the quest for freedom by South Africa's black majority. This message was wholly consistent with the message we had been trying to send all along.

But was it good foreign policy to imply that we supported the opposition no matter how it behaved and no matter what the government did? Obviously, we were against the brutalities of police violence against unarmed protesters. Were we also against the gruesome actions of militant township "comrades" who were using the vacuum of authority to build a revolutionary power base? Was the "necklace" (the victim is placed inside a gasoline-soaked tire and ignited) permissible since blacks did it to blacks? South Africans would view U.S. sanctions as an act of alignment with the black opposition and against P. W. Botha's government. Which terms and conditions would be set for this act of taking sides and who would set them? It was important to ask whether we might not unwittingly maximize racial polarization if we conveyed the signal that any "side" had a veto on our policy or that we were, in practice, calling for nothing less than a revolutionary transformation. Some sanctions proponents may have favored this goal. We did not. The end of apartheid was not the only objective: it mattered equally how it was ended and what replaced it.

Finally, what about our Southern African regional equities? We saw no reason at all to reassess the logical sequence of peacemaking and change: apartheid would be dismantled and democracy built in South Africa only after the region had made peace with itself. Unless carefully controlled, the sanctions signal could backfire, setting back both our regional and internal South African goals, and placing them in competition with each other.

These vital distinctions about sanctions got lost because the debate centered on American—not South African—political reality. It would take serious diplomacy to promote an end to township violence or the beginning of negotiations. It would require a carefully calibrated use of U.S. influence to encourage Botha's early return to the agenda of reform and regional cooperation. Sanctions, on the other hand, were a blunt and onesided instrument. They would represent a jolt to Botha's authority, and a boost for the militant opposition. At one level, this could be useful; but only if we remained in a position to reverse ground and go the other way if circumstances warranted it. We had no desire to fuel the vicious and bloody test of strength that had already begun. It was not a test that black resistance organizations could possibly win.

By mid-1985, it was clear that circumstances had changed, both in Africa and at home. One close colleague sent me a handwritten memo urging that we trim our sails to the swirling political winds by moving sharply to the right on regional issues like Angola and Mozambique and sharply to the left on South Africa. It would disarm critics, stem the bloodletting at home, and prevent us from becoming sitting ducks. The idea was not without merit. After all, constructive engagement offered a conceptual framework for regional peacemaking at a particular historical juncture, not a static prescription engraved on stone tablets.

But such maneuvers would not be so simple to orchestrate once the domestic battle had been joined. For one thing, media and political opponents were desperate for any evidence of a shift. They would describe it as a defeat and a "concession" under duress, no matter how we described it. It would not be easy to sell this imagery to a top leadership structure supporting the most popular American President in decades. In fact, the administration was anything but united on how to handle the increasingly painful South Africa debate. Shultz, McFarlane, Bush, and Jim Baker knew that the time was approaching to put the issue behind us somehow—making the necessary healing gestures domestically and adopting modest additional sanctions. But this was not the message Reagan heard from CIA Director Casey, Chief of Staff Don Regan, Senate conservatives, former NSC adviser and confidant Bill Clark, the Orange County (California) kitchen cabinet, the guys at the Heritage Foundation, and their soulmate, White House Communications Director Pat Buchanan. The advice from this quarter was to sharpen the issues and win the debate.

While Shultz, McFarlane, and I exchanged ideas in August 1985 for defusing the congressional sanctions drive, Buchanan was helping to organize conservative and evangelical activist groups who might rally around the pro-South African views espoused by the Reverend Jerry Falwell. While we were moving toward a scenario for embracing elements of the congressional package, the polarizers wanted to confront the sanctions movement. This varied input was perfectly reflected in the bobbing and weaving of Reagan's own press comments during August and September of 1985. One day, he categorized the Botha government as "reformist"; shortly afterward he retracted this judgment as "misleading."

Our domestic and foreign policy interests pulled us in very different directions. At home, our prime goal had now become to get out of the corner into which we had been painted. The telegenic racial brutality of apartheid and our resistance to economic sanctions had now become a choice issue for the Democrats and a primary source of division among Republicans. The party of Lincoln risked being viewed as the party of Helms and Falwell. Across the land—in boardrooms, city councils, and college campuses—the apartheid-sanctions issue was getting uglier. Sit-ins, shanty towns, and demonstrations were breaking down university resistance to divestment demands. I believed strongly that we needed to lance this boil on our body politic before old divisions were rekindled, putting an end to the generally civil climate of the post-Vietnam era.

But the foreign policy arguments generally cut the other way. By standing tall, Reagan would come across worldwide as a tough and principled leader who did not abandon his convictions to curry political favor at home. At some future point, a firm stand would serve us well with Pretoria. If we were suddenly to become more flexible on sanctions, Botha and his associates would dismiss the move as pure politics. They would assume (correctly) that we had caved in to domestic pressures and were running scared of the Free South Africa Movement and the Congress. With some exceptions, black South African leaders might be pleased to see us impose new pressures "against apartheid," but they, too, would perceive that we had acted under duress. This would not strengthen our hand either at home or abroad.

A firm administration stance could temporarily inflame opinion in other parts of Africa, and hand a propaganda weapon to the Soviets. But no real damage would be done. If we caved in to the pressures, it would actually undercut the position of our most important allies in places like London, Bonn, and Tokyo where governments agreed with us completely on the need to remain engaged. They faced no serious domestic pressures, but if we shifted ground it would create diplomatic momentum which they could not ignore—in the European Community, the United Nations, and the Commonwealth.

Falling into the Rubicon

It was against this backdrop that we received faint signals in late July and early August 1985 from Pik Botha, the reformist-survivor and the most internationally minded of the senior players in Pretoria. There had been no senior-level contacts since March. We had made clear since recalling Herman Nickel from Pretoria in June that we were prepared to work to define the steps necessary to restore a working relationship. But we were not interested in meetings and discussions for their own sake.

Thus, before proceeding to schedule any high-level contact, we needed a clear, authoritative signal of South African intentions regarding the region and domestic reform. In the period since March, we had seen a basic change in Pretoria's regional policy. With the state of emergency and increasingly tough actions against black opposition groups in July, we had seen a shift away from the politics of reform to the politics of repression. It almost seemed as if Botha's truculent defiance was aimed at eroding the position of those Western leaders most committed to preventing the destabilization of Southern Africa.

On August 2, Pik Botha suggested that we meet urgently to discuss the road ahead, including plans for a major address by P. W. Botha on August 15 at his annual party conference. Such a meeting would afford us an ideal occasion to weigh in and to help the good guys. We realized that Botha was running with the hares and hunting with the hounds. He probably sold this gambit to his president by suggesting that meetings with senior U.S. (as well as U.K. and German) leaders just before the speech would imply Western association with its contents. We had long become accustomed to such maneuvers by Pretoria. At the same time, we knew that the foreign minister was a lonely player in the policy scrum, a key figure whose voice the president needed to hear. If we did not provide him with reliable information and solid ammunition for use at home, who would?

Moreover, we wished to coach Pretoria on what was needed to break the downward spiral of internal violence, to promote dialogue, and to reverse the erosion of Western confidence that was plaguing South Africa. Botha needed to hear once again that continued regional misbehavior would have a bilateral price. Finally, we needed an authoritative rendition (however self-serving) of Pretoria's latest thinking on such internal issues as the state of emergency and the prospects for the release of ANC leader Nelson Mandela—a key to engaging the black opposition in dialogue.

This would not be the first such encounter. Back in January 1985, Frank Wisner and I had spent hours closeted with Defence Minister Magnus Malan and National Intelligence Service chief Niel Barnard—two of P. W. Botha's closest security advisers—during the course of their unannounced visits to Washington. We had shared our view of the broad areas where bold leadership would make a difference: opening negotiations with the full range of black leadership; ending "forced removals"; scrapping the Mixed Marriages and Immorality Acts, the pass laws and the entire system of influx control, and the Group Areas Act; extending freehold urban land tenure to blacks and opening central (white) business districts to black entrepreneurs; extending full citizenship rights to all South Africans (including blacks in and from the homelands); and the establishment of a justiciable bill of rights for all citizens.

Malan and especially Barnard had welcomed our suggestions. It was not a question of cutting a deal; rather, we were trying to communicate. Elaborate provision had been made to avoid any disclosure of these January 1985 exchanges. The South Africans talked to us openly of their sputtering dialogue in secret channels with the exiled ANC leadership (a dialogue we were also tracking through our own ANC contacts). We encouraged them to challenge their interlocutors with serious ideas. And we were scathing about Pretoria's failure to engage in the work of the multi-racial negotiating forum sponsored by KwaZulu Chief Minister Gatsha Buthelezi which had produced a democratic constitutional model for the province of Natal. Malan and Barnard berated us for the lukewarm Western reaction to their government's 1984 constitutional reform; we responded that change which excluded the black African majority could hardly resolve the country's dilemma, as the UDF-led protest campaign made clear.

Barnard acknowledged the extreme constipation of Afrikaner politics, where change was equated with weakness and leaders could only move when visibly dealing from positions of strength. These men were acutely conscious of the need to overcome their people's isolation and combat the illusion that they could ignore the external world. They desperately needed coaching on how to interpret the American political system. I concluded at the time that such exchanges were the only way to avoid an irreparable breach. If we could continue them invisibly and quietly—as these top officials clearly wanted—it might stimulate creative action by Pretoria.

But that was not to be. As the months passed, it became less and less feasible to orchestrate the kind of secret, high-level exchanges that would be necessary really to move Pretoria. In our eyes, Pretoria's actions became ever less responsive, while our voice seemed to them ever more shrill. During the nearly five-month hiatus since I had tabled our "basis for negotiations" paper in Cape Town, the climate had perceptibly chilled. The Botha government made some substantial reform moves (e.g., scrapping the Mixed Marriages and Immorality Acts) and committed itself to suspending forced removals, reviewing freehold land tenure, addressing the citizenship issue, and extending political rights to blacks.

But it combined these moves and promises with severely repressive steps. Worse, it failed utterly to seize the initiative and create a climate for negotiation. Instead, Botha remained mired in concepts and terminology that could not be sold beyond his party. His private correspondence with Western leaders and his parliamentary statements were larded with such phrasing as: "Structures must therefore be developed for Black communities outside the national states [i.e., homelands] through which they can decide for themselves on their own affairs up to the highest level." No reactionaries were going to accuse P. W. Botha of "selling out the interests of the white man"!

Given this background, it took some persuading to convince Shultz and McFarlane that it made sense to respond positively to Pik Botha's feeler. (I also argued that McFarlane should lead our side in order to associate the White House more closely with our message. Bud McFarlane was familiar with the regional brief, and he had at least a passing acquaintance with the burgeoning South African issue.) A meeting would be a high-wire act on both sides. In reality, the Pik Botha–Bud McFarlane encounter in Vienna on August 8, 1985, was a diplomatic act of last resort. Highly visible, the very fact of the meeting immediately raised expectations. Both men needed to return home with something. Our congressional calendar created an impending deadline for action on sanctions legislation. P. W. Botha's mid-August speech erected an early test of exactly what U.S. diplomacy could achieve. This scenario might be attractive to a doctoral candidate in political science, but it was a diplomat's nightmare.

Pik Botha was at his thespian best in Vienna, walking out on limbs far beyond the zone of safety to persuade us that his president was on the verge of momentous announcements. We learned of plans for bold reform steps, new formulas on constitutional moves, and further thinking relative to the release of Mandela. For his part, McFarlane was at his orotund best, carefully avoiding any hint of Yankee preachiness and solemnly conveying the President's determination to play a constructive role. Each man heard some of what he wished to hear. We tried to help Pik Botha carry the day upon his return. He offered a guidebook to help interpret the upcoming speech.

But when August 15 came, P. W. Botha fell into the Rubicon he had promised to cross. He put aside the speech drafted for him and substituted his own visceral xenophobia. There were general statements placing influx control and citizenship on the agenda, accepting the notion of black participation in national politics, and calling again for negotiations. But the Rubicon speech at Durban fell massively short of what was required. It was an angry man who appeared on television sets around the world, reacting against the demands of his critics and distant foreigners. Instead of sending a healing message as the leader of all South Africans, he used the code language of an embattled minority in a polarized conflict. Far from restoring foreign confidence and enticing blacks to the negotiating table, Botha's speech provoked black leaders to defy government authority. It triggered a stampede to the exits by foreign bankers and investors. Somehow, the government had failed to distinguish between seizing the initiative and reasserting control.

The day of the "Rubicon" speech, Shultz, McFarlane, and I compared notes gloomily. McFarlane was irate at Botha's performance, which he privately compared to film clips of Alabama police chief Bull Connor. Publicly, McFarlane remarked that the government in Pretoria "has labored and produced a kind of a cloud." Much less charitable commentary soon flowed from the White House and State Department. I had the unpleasant assignment of making a previously scheduled address to the Commonwealth Club in San Francisco on the day after Botha's Rubicon. I damned it with faint praise—we would look for "clarifications and implementation" of his program, but in the meantime I used terms Shultz had given me that morning as we edited my draft: "What we define as a Rubicon is when negotiation is no longer about whether apartheid is to be dismantled but is about how and when." At the same time, I appealed for both the government and the black opposition to look beyond the abundant procedural and substantive obstacles and get on with the essential task of negotiation. And I appealed to Americans to "remain builders and not destroyers . . . using the influence that derives from being present, having programs and people there, and from having contact and communication with all parties."

But the die was cast. Within days of Botha's Rubicon, Pik Botha was on the phone to me warning of unilateral action by his Reserve Bank if American and other foreign banks refused to roll over their short-term loans. On August 27, Pretoria closed the exchange markets, and it declared a unilateral moratorium on debt repayment a few days later. One of South Africa's most cherished possessions—its repute in the financial world—went out the window. The president of South Africa had led his country into the era of economic sanctions—financial sanctions, imposed not by the Free South Africa movement or the U.S. Congress but by the Western marketplace, which had lost confidence in his government. P. W. Botha had created a panic, and Western governments would soon scurry to adopt sanctions of their own.

Reagan Opts for Sanctions

On September 9, 1985, President Reagan signed Executive Order 12532 establishing by his personal authority a program of sanctions against South Africa. Inspired by the House-Senate conference committee bill, it effectively preempted a Senate floor vote on that measure and, hence, forestalled for the time being any further congressional action on sanctions. We had orchestrated the finesse with Senators Lugar and Dole after protracted discussion within the administration over the pros and cons of three options: signing the bill after the Senate approved it; vetoing the bill and accepting the risk of an override; and preempting it by executive order.

Of these options, the third was by far the most attractive—provided it was feasible. Preemption would maintain both the principle and the practice of executive branch control of foreign policy. While we would be moving under the threat of imminent congressional action, we would still be the ones defining, interpreting, implementing, fine-tuning, and adapting policy to a highly fluid situation. And we could strengthen our own hand by visibly agreeing that "something had to be done" about events in South Africa. Second, there would be no "reversal" or "defeat" imagery to deal with, and the President's political and constitutional authority would be fully protected. As a practical matter, no one wanted the distasteful job of trying to sell Reagan the idea of simply signing the congressional bill. And no credible player believed that it was wise simply to veto the measure, bearing in mind the 80–12 vote in the Senate back in July. Third, the preemption route enabled us to select out those elements of the bill we liked (or could tolerate) and scrap the less acceptable parts.

Reagan's executive order dropped all reference to the threat of future economic sanctions, and argued that our measure targeted apartheid itself—not the very people we were trying to help. Reagan's order banned: bank loans to the government (and government-owned or -controlled entities); computer exports to specified governmental agencies; nuclear trade; and Krugerrand imports. Export assistance facilities would be denied to firms that did not adhere to the Sullivan Principles. Funding was increased for "positive measures" programs for black South Africans. And a blue-ribbon advisory committee was established to advise Shultz on means to support the U.S. goal of peaceful change in South Africa.

The third option worked because Shultz and McFarlane had the credibility and the leverage to control its implementation and to persuade the Senate Republican leadership to work together with us (under the quite overt threat of a presidential veto). The senators would get the credit for steering a responsible middle course that upheld the authority of their President. They would have to grab the bill off the table and declare that the President's action provided the previously lacking leadership on the issue.

The signing was accompanied by a forceful presidential statement—the kind of statement that healed and made clear where we stood. After declaring that he respected and shared "the goals that have motivated many in Congress to send a message of U.S. concern about apartheid," Reagan said that his package was "aimed against the machinery of apartheid, without indiscriminately punishing the people who are victims of that system." He also announced that U.S. Ambassador Herman Nickel would return to his post:

> I am now sending him back, with a message to State President Botha underlining our grave view of the current crisis, and our assessment of what is needed to restore confidence abroad and move from confrontation to negotiation at home. The problems of South Africa were not created overnight and will not be solved overnight, but there is no time to waste. To withdraw from this drama—or to fan its flames—will serve neither our interests nor those of the South African people.

The Reagan executive order of September 1985 was the appropriate response to a rapidly deterioriating situation. Our policy machinery got us through this first crisis. To be sure, we had now joined the "signal-sending" school of South African policymaking. And we were now enmeshed in the perverse logic of sanctions: if they appeared to work, there would be demands down the road to increase them (or at least maintain them in force, rather than lift them to reward good behavior); if they appeared *not* to work, there would be demands to maintain them until they did or to increase them (as the original legislation had provided). We were stuck with this one-way, ratchet effect.

But we had reasserted our leadership. And we had bought ourselves a period of time—perhaps six to nine months—in which to get a handle on events, reverse the dramatically negative cycle, and pick up the pieces of the stalled Namibia-Angola peace process.

12

The Right Strikes Back, 1985–86

William J. Casey wanted to be Reagan's Secretary of State. He worked tirelessly as Director of Central Intelligence until his death to get a comparable "policy role," even if he could not have the job itself. The nomenclature of titles can be deceiving. The intelligence boss wears several hats: as chief collector, analyst, and purveyor of intelligence reports and assessments; as the bureaucratic manager of clandestine services; as the coordinator of intelligence (and counterintelligence) targeting and prioritizing; and, as the CEO for covert action programs. If the incumbent wishes and the political leadership encourages or tolerates it, the CIA director has the resources to make a serious run at becoming a rival foreign minister. He has the networks, the budget and personnel resources, the private and dedicated communications capabilities, and the access to senior levels in Washington and abroad. He is in a position to play the role of prosecutor, judge, and jury in the highly judgmental business of analyzing the world.

The United States is not the only country where such things can happen. There are a number of African countries where intelligence chiefs have become *de facto* foreign ministers. In a few cases, such as Zaire and South Africa, the government seemed to take a page from Reagan's book by tolerating chaos and ambiguity in the relationships among senior people.

Statesmen depend massively on reliable information. I never had enough, and I made it one of my cardinal principles to acquire as much of it from as many credible sources as possible. My assistant Robert

Cabelly spent 75 percent of his time digesting, analyzing, acquiring, comparing, and exchanging information within and outside our government. To help compensate for other liabilities, we wanted the best data and analysis available. My colleagues and I developed enormous respect for the intelligence professionals—both analysts and operators—with whom we interacted in Washington, Europe, and Africa. Their standards were second to none. The diplomats of great nations must be able to count on clandestine capabilities. I remain an ardent advocate of the United States maintaining the capacity for effective covert activity in support of foreign policy objectives.

The problem arises when the varied intelligence functions are so organized and managed as to encourage policy conflicts and the abuse of power. If only one government had these problems, the risks would be severe but nonetheless manageable because other governments could put an end to the games and maneuvers emanating from that source. Sooner or later, the offending government would be obliged to make up its mind about which foreign policy was its real foreign policy. But when several governments share this structural problem, there are grave dangers. Ultimately, foreign policy becomes an unprincipled battleground where one power center uses its information from and access to foreigners in order to sabotage a domestic rival. Control over channels of communication with foreigners becomes the object of heated argument, often leading to bureaucratic treaties that split the difference—leaving everyone frustrated and inclined to play games. Established policies, lines of authority, and essential ethical standards are all placed at risk. In this case the result, as we will see, was to encourage a pattern of collusion between forces opposed to our settlement strategy.

Powerful voices within the South African government were opposed to constructive engagement and the Namibia-Angola peace process from the outset in 1981. They wished to believe—and led P. W. Botha to believe—that Reagan's 1980 victory was the prelude to a love-in with Washington. In practical terms, this would take the form of a *de facto* strategic alliance against the "total Marxist onslaught"—defined for Western audiences as the Communist conspiracy to seize control of Southern Africa. The bad guys in the scenario included Moscow, the East Bloc, Havana, the Front Line States, swapo, the anc and its internal offshoots, and almost any other institution (e.g., the BBC, *The New York Times,* the State Department, or the West German Foreign Ministry) that stood in the way of a maximal definition of Pretoria's security.

We soon became identified in the minds of these South Africans as a threat. For one thing, we knew too much about them and their region. Knowledge is power—including the power to undermine one-dimensional thinking. For another, we represented a painful memory: names like Haig and Eagleburger symbolized continuity with the Kissinger era and the Angolan disaster of the 1970s. We also had a well-advertised agenda of advancing Western interests, checking Soviet-Cuban gains and opportunities, and steering South Africa and its neighbors toward political settlements and peaceful change. Some South Africans correctly saw that these concepts represented a golden opportunity for their country— and for them—to get a handle on the hawks in their midst. But the hawks saw it differently. We were trouble.

Pretoria's hawks tried every device they could think of to undercut us: feeding information to hostile senators who sought to block my confirmation; sending secret emissaries to Washington to try the "back door" to the President and other senior players like Casey and U.N. Ambassador Kirkpatrick; seeking to discredit and exclude me from top-level meetings with their senior officials; hiring lobbyists of their own to promote their policy preferences with favored American interlocutors; and passing self-serving "information" to our government through intelligence liaison channels. In practice, the hawks had their own diplomatic service, with their own message, code language, channels, delivery system, and network of friends scattered amongst conservative circles in predictable places around Washington and other Western capitals.

This underground alternative diplomacy was a direct threat to South African diplomats and to us as well. Its messages and démarches could cause conservative activists in Washington to vibrate purposefully within hours. Pretoria's diplomats were only dimly aware, at times, of what their fellow countrymen were up to as they visited the United States on false passports and bogus visa applications to conduct "unofficial" diplomacy. But the inquisitive ones had a general sense that there was massive indiscipline in their own ranks. They also realized that the range of views within the Republican Party and the Reagan administration was vast. Washington offered fertile soil for subversion. As Pik Botha remarked to me in May 1981, after an afternoon of meetings on the Hill, "Jesus, Chet, I thought *we* had a conservative problem!" In reality, we both did.

We labored hard to control end runs and other maneuvers aimed at exploiting our divisions. But we probably became aware of only a fraction of them. Factional collusion thrives on common interests. We knew, for instance, that elements of the South African security establishment looked on their Angolan war as a prize possession—an end in itself, a source of prestige and status, the basis for retaining control of Namibia, and a means of assuring plentiful military and covert action budgets. They also realized that Angola, properly handled, could be used to

strengthen ties with Western conservatives, providing an insurance policy for the future.

This much was obvious. It was equally obvious that some U.S. conservatives lapped up South African criticisms of our strategy for achieving a Namibia-Angola settlement. In the fantasy world of the American
right, victory can only be achieved by physical muscle and sinew—that
is, by the direct actions of the Defense Department and the CIA and
their foreign clients. This was precisely the scenario promised by SADF
"intelligence" officers (often working with UNITA representatives and
lobbyists dependent on Pretoria). Never mind that such a settlement was
beyond anyone's reach. If Pretoria's hardliners and their American
counterparts realized this, they made it their purpose not to say so.

A variety of American networks were accessible to the hardliners
from Pretoria. For true believers—credulous individuals who contributed funds to help disguised SADF fronts deliver radios and Bibles to
RENAMO in Mozambique—the motive was support of a politico-reli-
gious cause. For wealthy conservatives—the sort who loaned the UNITA
leadership VIP aircraft and subsidized expensive overseas offices and
lobbyists—the motive was the thrill of bankrolling an invisible, priva-
tized foreign policy apparatus. For institutionally based activists, the
motives could range from empire building and fundraising to the simple
ambition to participate on the right side in Washington's wars. Careers,
lifestyles, organizational budgets, and even electoral campaigns can be
based on causes like "the struggle for freedom in Southern Africa,"
whether that struggle is anti-Communist or anti-apartheid. Finally, for
actual or would-be policy players, the motives ranged from personal
ambition or jealousy to deep ideological conviction.

Sympathy for the hardline South African viewpoint and ardent distrust of the State Department were two sides of the same coin. Belief in
the chimera of a UNITA military victory and support for policies based
essentially on coercive instruments—military intervention, arms trans-
fers, covert action—were also sides of the same coin. In Southern Africa,
the "overt" route of intervention or large-scale military aid was simply
out of the question: it would not sell politically, in the Congress or with
the media and public opinion. But covert action was another story. In
the imagination of conservative activists, covert action was the "strategy" of choice. It represented a welcome return to the good old days of
unfettered clandestine interventionism. It would serve to avenge the
Angolan defeat of 1975–76.

A strategy based on covert action, by definition, represented a challenge to State Department management of the policy process. It would
become a political tool and a bureaucratic method of empowering the

CIA. And why not? After all, the U.S. link to UNITA originated in the 1970s as an intelligence relationship, conducted principally in intelligence channels. Naturally enough, UNITA leaders looked at the CIA as their past supporters—and, hopefully, their future ones. As guerrilla strategists, their view of the State Department was shaped by automatic distrust of our diplomatic dialogue with Luanda and by whatever input they gleaned from the intelligence services of Zaire, South Africa, and the United States.

We faced nothing less than a continuing challenge to our control of Southern African policy. Generally, we could tell what we were dealing with by reading the attack journalism in publications like the Aida Parker *Newsletter* (renamed *The Naked Truth*) or *The Citizen* (South African publications), as echoed in places like *Human Events* or the *Conservative Digest*. Letter-writing campaigns generated by U.S. activist groups bore an uncanny relationship to occasional congressional initiatives and themes we would pick up at meetings with certain officials from Pretoria.

Boys Will Be Boys

In early 1983—just as a promising chapter opened in our talks with the Angolan regime—we became aware of a shadowy activity called "the UNITA project." Its apparent goal was to undercut the U.S.-led negotiations on Namibian independence and Cuban withdrawal from Angola. Instead, the United States should support an interim, South African-controlled arrangement in Namibia and a UNITA victory in Angola. The "project" was inconsistent not only with presidentially approved U.S. policy but also with official South African policy.

This move coincided with UNITA's stepped-up military campaign on the ground, starting in the second half of 1982. By mid-1983, UNITA had gained the military initiative, and the time was ripe for a new political assertiveness. Whereas in 1982 UNITA had a minimal, low-budget external presence, new UNITA offices were popping up across Europe a year later. Its entrée in Paris and Lisbon had suddenly improved, and UNITA's presence was strengthened in Switzerland, Germany, Denmark, and Britain. UNITA was getting big league help in raising its political profile as a "winner" in Europe and North America. Its U.S. representatives were being escorted by well-connected right-wing organizations (e.g., the American Security Council) to "brief" officials in the Defense Intelligence Agency and the Congress.

We learned that this lobbying campaign was directed by Americans working for the military intelligence directorate of the SADF. The South

Africans (civil and military, official and corporate) never had a problem finding capable lobbyists. One of the top South African lobbyists (earning a reported six-figure fee) was Stuart Spencer, one of Ronald Reagan's 1980 campaign managers! Bill Casey, another campaign manager, had replaced John Sears, another South African lobbyist. (Spencer eventually stepped aside after the potential for major embarrassment, to say nothing of mixed policy signals, was brought to the attention of people in the White House.)

When NSC Adviser Bill Clark asked me, in the summer of 1983, to give the MPLA "a deadline" before breaking off the talks, he added that he was taking heat from well-placed "UNITA supporters" in town. Oh really? Where had they come from? Who mobilized them at this particular time? When he told me that he was willing to help me arrange a European rendezvous with Savimbi, who "did not wish to meet with the State Department," I twitched, having heard that line somewhere else. We declined the offer and arranged our own meeting at a location in Africa.

In May 1983, as a gesture to our allied and African partners, Shultz held a courtesy meeting with SWAPO president Sam Nujoma in New York. A few weeks later, Eagleburger delivered a comprehensive speech on U.S. Southern African policy. Neither event represented any change in policy whatsoever. But you would have guessed otherwise from the hysterical right-wing reaction. Howard Phillips of the Conservative Caucus wrote that Shultz had given "de facto recognition to a communist gangster who, in a civilized society, would be brought to trial for the terrorist murder of hundreds of innocent civilians. . . ." As for a policy he termed "the Eagleburger Doctrine," it represented the "abandonment of Jonas Savimbi whose UNITA forces now control roughly two-thirds [sic] of Angola. . . . Savimbi and South Africa have defeated the Soviet proxies in Angola and Namibia. Now, Eagleburger proposes to give the Communist International through diplomacy that which it has been effectively denied on the battlefield."

By 1984–85, we became accustomed to a common theme in various intelligence reports suggesting that RENAMO was inexorably winning in Mozambique. Yet, despite our requests, it somehow was never possible for U.S. intelligence to document RENAMO's barbaric modus operandi or the pattern of continuing South African support. We had to track the story down ourselves. In 1984, not long after the Nkomati Accord was signed, General Pieter van der Westhuizen (head of Pretoria's military intelligence) had assured me with a grin that the FRELIMO government's collapse was imminent. RENAMO, he said, was "the fastest-growing liberation movement in the Third World." Yet only we asked how he knew and why he smiled when he said it.

Only we were bothered by the fact that U.S. intelligence reports and summaries prepared for senior officials tilted consistently toward a bearish view of FRELIMO and a bullish view of RENAMO. RENAMO's military prospects never quite lived up to the high hopes of elements in the Washington intelligence community. But the inspired analyses were enough to kill off our initiatives to beef up regional economic assistance to Mozambique and its neighbors in 1985–87. They created an intimidating climate of opinion.

By the early months of 1985, South African diplomats quietly pleaded with us to help their minister by sharing with him our information concerning continuing SADF support for RENAMO. Reluctantly, the seniormost people in their ministry had become convinced that certain defense colleagues were systematically lying to them and misleading their state president. Pik Botha would need "ammunition" to lay out the case before P. W. Botha (assuming he did not know). When I arrived in Pretoria in early February, Pik Botha himself made a veiled plea that I present to his president a request in Reagan's name for SADF support of Machel, the FRELIMO leader. This would help consolidate the position of the Maputo regime and avert a scenario that could play into Moscow's hands. I had to sidestep these dangerous requests, which could have been a trap or a counterintelligence game. We could not serve as the eyes and ears of a beleaguered foreign ministry seeking to survive its own interagency struggles.

Even more glaring was the game playing on Angola. Magnus Malan must have had a reason for asking me—at Cape Verde in October 1984— "What side are you on? Why don't you get *involved* in Angola? We have a really basic difference on this." He wanted there to be a basic difference—one that his people could exploit by spreading it to UNITA and all over the right-wing diaspora with which he maintained personal and interservice contact in Europe and the United States. This would enable them to target Shultz and me for blocking a shift in policy.

The plot thickened in 1985 as the apartheid debate escalated. During a February mission, Botha initially told me that Savimbi wished never to meet with State Department officials again. A few days later, Savimbi and I had a constructive exchange in Cape Town. I had my "hunting license" to obtain a new opening from Luanda. Now, Botha and Malan told us that if we could keep Savimbi "on board," their government would cooperate fully with our campaign for a settlement. The message was meant to convey P. W. Botha's strong, emotional commitment to the UNITA chief. But it was also a dare: no one was in a better position than Malan's own people to destroy Savimbi's confidence in us and to manipulate him into attacking "State Department policy." Malan added, tellingly, that Savimbi thought we were discouraging UNITA's African and European friends from being supportive. It was a cock-and-bull story: we were, in fact, doing the opposite. A few weeks later, a report reached State Department principals from Casey himself claiming that we were discouraging support for UNITA in Europe. Who created such reports, whose only purpose could have been to undercut Shultz's Africa team?

Interesting coincidences abounded. When we presented our "basis for negotiations" paper to the parties in March 1985, someone had clearly gotten to Savimbi before my colleagues Tim Carney, Robert Cabelly, and Bob Frasure arrived at his bush headquarters in Jamba to brief him. The guerrilla leader who five weeks earlier had given an emphatic green light to our proposal to force the pace of decisions in Luanda had now become persuaded that we aimed to destroy him. Within days of this encounter, we learned in Washington of a new intelligence community study of the impact of Cuban troop withdrawal on the Angolan military balance. Savimbi himself would be "interviewed" to provide input for this "intelligence assessment"—a clear challenge to State Department control of the negotiations.

Conservative activists also played a role in this tale of indiscipline. They, too, had become convinced that Reagan's African policies were not sufficiently Reaganite. The mounting attacks we faced from the left on South Africa created vulnerabilities they were quite prepared to exploit. As a Senate staffer pointedly remarked, "You cannot expect conservatives to do battle for you on South Africa if you stonewall us on Angola, Chet." Never mind that they agreed with our South African position: Africa was a "freebie" and politics came first. In reality, we were not stonewalling Hill and movement conservatives on Angola. We scheduled meetings galore with senators, congressmen, and conservative editors. We took our case to public meetings of activist organizations like the National Conservative Political Action Committee. We explained, we briefed, we reiterated once again our support for the UNITA cause and for repeal of the Clark Amendment. We demonstrated how and why our strategy was gradually grinding down resistance to Cuban troop withdrawal—the best thing that could happen to Savimbi. The only thing we did *not* do was promise to scrap the President's Southern African strategy.

•

The second Reagan term ushered in a wave of personnel changes that, over time, undercut what little systemic discipline had previously existed among foreign affairs agencies. There was a sharp decline in the competence and coherence of White House policy management after the 1984 election. The NSC function was hamstrung by these changes, gradually opening the way for still greater interagency warfare. They also opened the way for aggressive freelancing by new players like Communications Director Patrick Buchanan, a voice of "movement" conservatism and an eager articulator-communicator of "the President's message" on whatever subject he happened upon. Buchanan knew before he arrived in the job that the State Department was enemy country. A skilled infighter, he quickly inserted himself into the pipeline of ideologues, activists, and officials working to force a change in U.S. policy.

Taking a suggestion from fellow political appointee and close friend David Miller—our ambassador to Tanzania and now Zimbabwe—we arranged to meet Buchanan to chew things over in late May 1985. Heritage Foundation president Ed Feulner joined Buchanan, Miller, and me. We brainstormed tactics for shoring up the administration position on South Africa. But when we turned to the Southern African *regional* strategy, our success in subverting Moscow's African clients was dismissed as evidence of our own heresy. Once a Marxist, always a Marxist. Our tactic should be to polarize the region by aligning ourselves with anti-Communist freedom fighters (and their invisible backer, South Africa). This would supposedly rally the troops at home, bolster the friendlies overseas, and force fence-sitters to chose.

One day later, on May 22, Luanda announced the capture of SADF commandos attempting to sabotage Gulf Oil's Cabinda facilities in the name of UNITA. Tough U.S. protests over this stupid blunder and the SADF strike into Botswana in June quickly chilled our relations with South Africa. But they also chilled relations between realists and polarizers in Washington. We began receiving mail on Republican Party stationery informing us that we were on the wrong side: Gulf Oil was propping up the Marxist MPLA and deserved whatever it got from the freedom fighters (that is, SADF commandos masquerading as UNITA). By this time, the MPLA was worming its way off the hook we had tried to set with our "basis for negotiations." But it was impossible to reset the hook when the South Africans had effectively cut our line.

I flew to Africa for a quick meeting with Savimbi to try to restore the relationship. He had already allowed himself to be maneuvered by conservative activists into splitting publicly with us. It was becoming difficult to maintain a civil discourse with his Washington representative. Savimbi began by venting well-rehearsed opposition to the Cuban withdrawal terms contained in our proposals and demanding a change in our basic approach so that "national reconcilition" would come first. He had had "no choice but to attack the State Department because we think we are to be sacrificed."

We parted more amicably several hours later, with Savimbi agreeing that we should pursue our diplomacy. But his spokesmen and lobbyists continued their attacks on "the State Department policy." At about this same time (early June), New York gubernatorial candidate Lew Lehrman showed up at Jamba for the inaugural meeting of something entitled the "Democratic International," a gathering of the leaders of U.S.-funded, anti-Communist guerrilla groups from around the globe. The main purpose of the rally was to obtain media coverage associating UNITA with the other groups. Lehrman read a letter written over Reagan's signature proclaiming that "your struggle is our struggle."

By now, Senate Conservatives were pawing the ground to bring the repeal of the Clark Amendment to the floor. Repeal was a long-standing administration goal, one I had worked hard to achieve back in 1981. It would obviously strengthen our hand in the protracted campaign to get the MPLA to deal. By mid-1985, it would send mixed signals to everyone, but it still made sense and we decided that it was better to let Congress take the lead while we offered quiet, behind-the-scenes support. The proponents of Senate repeal won handily on June 11.

Two days later, the SADF mounted a commando strike on purported ANC houses in Gaborone, the capital of Botswana. We yanked our ambassador in protest. A few days later, Pik Botha delivered to the American chargé in Cape Town a contemptuous reply to our March "basis of negotiations" paper, a reply that would enable Pretoria to say that it had answered our mail. Reacting to the recall of our ambassador and the sharp signals we were trying to send, P. W. Botha fumed: "If there are elements in Washington who think South Africa is going to be run by the United States, then it must be made quite clear that these elements are heading for a confrontation with the South African government and people." A few weeks later, in July 1985, the Senate passed a South African sanctions bill and the House repealed the Clark Amendment. The MPLA cited these developments as their excuse to "suspend" talks with the United States, and the Soviets and Angolans kicked off the biggest anti-UNITA offensive ever launched!

American "policy" toward Southern Africa in the middle of 1985 was an amazing sight to behold. Some Americans were busily preparing sanctions packages against South Africa. Another group of Americans were telling Pretoria, in effect, "not to worry, we want to help you clean out the commies in your neighborhood." A third group of Americans (the administration) were signaling P. W. Botha both to provide a statement of intent on reform and to get back on track with our regional strategy. He knew which message he wanted to hear. America's fragmented political system and undisciplined executive strengthened the phalanx of wishful thinkers surrounding South Africa's isolated leader. We probably contributed to Botha's self-destructive behavior.

Looking back, it is hard not to search for connections between all these events. For example, how exactly did Lehrman dream up the idea of carrying the Buchanan-Casey battle cry to the remotest reaches of Angola's Cuando Cubango Province? Who do you suppose drafted the letter and lobbied tirelessly until it was approved and signed by Reagan or his signature machine? Who coordinated the logistics, communications, press coverage, and security of travelers from around the world into a military camp appearing on no published map in a war zone accessible only to South African military pilots and friendly air service contractors?

We knew that Bill Casey paid "goodwill" visits to a number of African capitals and held his own private exchanges with senior intelligence and political leaders. We facilitated those visits and provided background material for him at the request of his staff. Such travel is a standard activity for a director of central intelligence, especially a forward-leaning one who wished to get firsthand orientation, show his flag, cultivate local relationships, and catch up with his ambassadors ("station chiefs"). We did *not* know about the cooperation he promoted with the leaders of South African military intelligence in connection with our Central American strategy. Casey was after sources of Soviet hardware; the booty captured by the SADF in Angola was a perfect source. Pretoria was eager to please, delighted to be "wanted." As the ranking official responsible for U.S. foreign policy toward Africa, I might have dreamed up other ways to diversify the sources of arms supply to the Contras. Casey's senior colleagues were uneasy about it. But General van der Westhuizen must have thought it was a fine idea. The Angolan honeypot was working like a charm.

The repeal of the Clark Amendment became effective in October 1985, the start of the new fiscal year. This gave Washington players several months to fight over the future of U.S. policy. The Angolan war heated up, providing a dramatic backdrop: by late summer, word of a major MPLA offensive against UNITA strongholds had begun to leak out beyond the experts. The stage was set for one of the least comprehensible and most misread policy reviews of the 1980s.

Doctrines I Have Known

Hovering over the participants was the question of how the Reagan Doctrine ought to be applied to Africa. The issue was fraught with theological significance. The answer would determine not only the immediate question of how and when we should help UNITA but which other African "freedom fighters" should benefit from this newly visible but well-established tenet of U.S. policy. Equally important, the answer would probably reflect the balance of forces between the battling Reaganites. After the first climax of policy debate on South Africa in August and September, we plunged into a probing search of our ideological manhood.

The practice of helping anti-Communist guerrillas was first applied in Afghanistan toward the end of the Carter administration. But it was the Reagan team which elevated the aiding of "freedom fighters" into a full-blown, global campaign. It developed early on as a primary focus of U.S. policy toward South Asia and Central America. In June 1983, Shultz had testified before the Senate about the importance of ensuring that "those who have a positive alternative to the Soviet model receive our support." By 1985, the basic concepts became the focus of addresses by the President and his top people. Soon, observers began explicitly to discuss something called the "Reagan Doctrine."

Its logic was impeccable: Soviet imperial expansion had created imperial vulnerabilities that could be exploited at low cost. It was much more expensive and challenging to sustain an incumbent government than to back a rebel movement. By providing tangible as well as moral support for anti-Communist insurgents, the United States could raise the price of the Soviets' Third World empire. Properly applied, the strategy made eminent sense. We would help the Soviets learn that it was one thing to seize power using instruments of coercion; it was something altogether different to prop up year after year a collection of feckless and bankrupt regimes that lacked a popular mandate and depended overwhelmingly on Soviet guns to survive.

The concept served to underscore our seriousness about global order and reciprocal restraint beyond the zones of armed confrontation in Europe and Northeast Asia. The Reagan Doctrine gave us the leverage to insist that Soviet policy in "regional conflicts" would be on the bilateral agenda. It also made sense as *one element* of a strategy for advancing U.S. goals in specific areas of the Third World. As Shultz wrote in *Foreign Affairs* early in 1985: "Americans have sometimes tended to think that power and diplomacy are two distinct alternatives. The truth is, power and diplomacy must always go together, or we will accomplish very little in this world." Shultz cited Nicaragua, Afghanistan, Cambodia, and a place identified simply as "Africa" as "dramatic and heartening examples of popular insurgencies *against* [emphasis in original] communist regimes." Americans, he added, had a noble tradition of "supporting the struggle of other peoples for freedom, democracy and independence." We could not permit the Soviets to proclaim that their empire was irreversible while everything else was up for grabs. The official launch of the "doctrine" by Reagan came in his 1985 State of the Union address, when he declared that the United States must not "break faith with those who are risking their lives on every continent, from Afghanistan to Nicaragua, to defy Soviet-supported aggression and secure rights which have been ours from birth."

So, if the basic idea was sound, what was the problem? In fact, there were plenty of problems. In the right hands, good ideas can strengthen the statesman. In the wrong hands, doctrines can become a substitute for thought—or the basis for an ideological *auto-da-fé*. Set loose amidst the intra-Republican turf battles of 1985–86, a powerful idea became a further incentive for conflict. Who would supervise its implementation? Activists who could not find Beira or Eritrea on a map would soon be asking why we were "blocking the President's policy" in Mozambique and the Horn of Africa as we fended off the bad idea of providing U.S. support to rebels in these places.

Another problem was that the specific structure of the Namibia-Angola tangle did not fit the model as neatly as some other cases did. We were dealing with Pretoria, SWAPO, the internal Namibian parties, Cubans, the MPLA, the Front Line States, and UNITA. It was not a simple two-part equation. This made it difficult to follow Shultz's counsel in a major address to the Commonwealth Club in San Francisco that February: ". . . it must always be clear whose side we are on."

U.S. sympathy for UNITA and for its avowed objective of reconciliation was no secret. Yet even here there was a problem. If we shifted our focus to the internal Angolan struggle, we would be diverting attention away from the regional conflict. By coming out and flatly "taking sides" in an internationalized civil war, we risked losing most African and allied partners and letting Pretoria off the hook. As with the South Africa debate, we were being pressed to focus increasingly on the *internal* affairs of the parties. Yet this was not where we had relevant leverage. There was simply no action-forcing event or coercive pressure that could possibly produce "reconciliation first"—in either Angola or South Africa. We could not just "demand" it; had we tried, our partners would have run for the exits. Cuban troop withdrawal *had* to be the engine to drive the train of Angolan reconciliation.

Luanda was under no illusions: we had repeatedly pointed out to MPLA officials that strong pro-UNITA sentiment made it impossible for us to take their side in the internal conflict. They accepted our mediating role on the regional issues in order to test and perhaps benefit from our potential leverage with the South Africans. Nonetheless, if we now advertised that we planned to ally ourselves with their internal enemy—in association, however arms-length, with their regional enemy—we would be literally inviting Luanda to call it off. Perversely, that would let *them* off the hook in our negotiation.

Above all, the unveiling of a new policy doctrine required that we identify criteria that could help us decide where and when the direct application of American power could advance our goals. The antidote to reflexive policymaking was to think carefully about each case of regional conflict and *to decide each case on the merits*. It would be necessary continuously to remind ourselves that aiding anti-Communist rebels was not by itself a strategy. The mere application of power in the absence of a considered political-diplomatic strategy can achieve nothing: it is like pushing on a string. As with sanctions, aiding rebels was one of many policy tools that might be used to support our strategy. The ultimate criterion, as in the application of sanctions, should be the likely results of U.S. action.

This was best stated in testimony in early May 1985 before the Senate by Richard L. Armitage, Assistant Secretary of Defense for International Security Affairs. A devotee of the Reagan Doctrine in Afghanistan, Armitage was well placed to caution his audience about the need for criteria. These should include: the direction the target country was moving in; the dynamics surrounding the conflict, including the availability of regional partners prepared to work with us; likely Soviet reactions—i.e., the risk of an expansion of the conflict; our capacity to provide suitable assistance and to do so consistently and reliably; the values and worthiness of our local ally ("not every group that professes anti-communism deserves our support"); and the question of overt versus covert support.

Armitage's 1985 testimony remains one of the wisest iterations of the Reagan Doctrine. As with our sanctions hassles, we badly needed standards, and we needed some ground rules on the perennial problem of who would control the action. If the idea of aiding African "freedom fighters" caught on, Congress would want some of the action. Meanwhile, Africa was the one region where there were no "freedom fighter" programs (as of mid-1985), and it was obvious that political pressures were mounting to go after Soviet clients there as well. As one intelligence officer remarked to me at the time, "Casey wants to have at least one covert war in each region." It all clicked together.

Africa was a place where self-described Marxist and Socialist regimes remained plentiful in the mid-1980s; but it seldom meant much. Generally, these labels were the diplomatic equivalent of early designer sunglasses—they made a fashion statement revealing that the bearer was behind the times. Very few African Marxists were worth going after, even if you had extra time on your hands. Most spent the 1980s flirting with us in ill-disguised contempt for Moscow. The mind boggled at the prospect of heavy-breathing conservative activists pouring over U.N. voting records and other "data" in search of African enemies. Nor would it have been difficult to find ample supplies of "pro-Western freedom fighters"—if they knew you were in the market on a given day. But UNITA was the only movement I knew that merited consideration for U.S. support. UNITA was a legitimate, nationalist movement—an indigenous phenomenon born of the grim realities of the Portuguese and Soviet-Cuban empires. RENAMO, the hottest guerrilla property in General van der Westhuizen's inventory, was an African Khmer Rouge.

Thus, we needed criteria. In the early months of the second Reagan term, the President and Shultz generally skirted references to specific African countries where the United States should support anti-Soviet rebels. But by the time of his October 1985 address to the United Nations, Reagan was ready to name names, citing the cases of Ethiopia and Angola along with cases in other regions. These wars were the consequence of an "ideology imposed from without, dividing nations and creating regimes that are, almost from the day they take power, at war with their own people," a problem that leads to "war with their neighbors." Reagan solved the internal versus regional dilemma by lumping them together when he called on the "warring parties" to negotiate cease-fires, political reconciliation, and foreign troop withdrawals as a "first step," prior to U.S.-Soviet negotiations to guarantee these outcomes. But until reconciliation had occurred, U.S. support for the "struggling democratic resistance forces must not and shall not cease."

The Aid-to-UNITA Saga

By mid-October 1985 a variety of bills had been introduced in Congress calling for overt (publicly acknowledged) U.S. military and humanitarian assistance to UNITA. Enthusiasm was running high among UNITA's backers in both parties. The multi-brigade MPLA offensive against UNITA positions at Mavinga and Jamba, backed by over $1.5 billion worth of

Soviet hardware and hundreds of advisers, had been blocked by UNITA with a decisive assist from regular SADF air force and ground units. The political trend was clear.

Yet, just days before Reagan's U.N. address, Shultz had written House Minority Leader Bob Michel urging him to discourage support for the first of these bills, a measure that would provide $27 million in overt, non-lethal aid. The legislation, Shultz wrote, was "ill-timed and will not contribute to the settlement we seek. I feel strongly about Savimbi's courageous stand against Soviet aggression, but there are better ways to help. A determined effort on our part to pursue the negotiation is a good approach." Shultz had signed that classified letter on my recommendation. When it was promptly leaked, there was blood all over the floor in Republican Washington. For years to come, the Shultz-Michel letter would be quoted as evidence of original sin at the State Department.

What was going on here? Back in February in his Commonwealth Club speech, Shultz had described UNITA in glowing terms, and spoken of the need to "be clear whose side we are on." While stopping short of calling for direct U.S. assistance (still prohibited by law), he had certainly pointed his audience in that direction. Had he changed his mind since February? Had he succumbed to the subversive logic of Crocker and Department "careerists"—the voodoo dolls of movement conservatism? You would have thought so to read the scorching columns of *The Washington Times*. The real story is more interesting.

Starting back in July, we began an interagency policy review. It was triggered by the many negative regional developments of recent months—as well as the repeal of the Clark Amendment and the desire in some quarters to force a change in strategy. The review sputtered along in desultory fashion, becoming by October a frustrating stand-off. We, of course, wished to integrate the new "flexibility" given us with Clark repeal into our existing negotiating strategy, and retain control of the process. Participants from the Defense Department and CIA challenged the basic viability of the current strategy. Ranking CIA representatives scathingly attacked the fruits of our diplomacy to date, and argued for a prompt decision to implement a program of military aid to UNITA. Debate dragged on about the real significance of the fighting in southeastern Angola. Some claimed to see Angola as the flagship of a new Soviet military assertiveness in regional conflicts, while we underscored the ebbs and flows of this inconclusive struggle and the long lead times preceding any specific military event.

But there was one subject on which everyone agreed: aid to UNITA, when and if we approved it, must be covert, not overt. There was a strong common interest here. Any move toward publicly acknowledged assistance would severely jeopardize the prospects in Congress for separate, clandestine activity. (There would be no rationale to go for both.) Since overt programs cannot be conducted by a clandestine service, this would threaten Casey's ambition to become the lead policymaker on Angola and the benefactor of UNITA. Moreover, an overt assistance program would eliminate even a trace of "deniability," removing the veil of ambiguity that we wished to maintain. An acknowledged activity of this sort would draw prurient press interest and hand our adversaries a propaganda bonanza. It would undercut the advocates of compromise in Luanda, forcing them to "react." It would also subject our entire policy process to a level of congressional intrusion that no one wanted.

Finally, there was the problem of *how* to deliver U.S. assistance. We were determined that any U.S. help should not go through South African hands in Namibia. But Angola's other neighbors—Zaire and Zambia—would be exceedingly unlikely to approve any overt activity from their territory: whatever their views might be on the merits, no African country would wish to be seen officially cooperating in the delivery of U.S. aid to a rebel movement in Angola. These governments had backed UNITA's cause in 1975–76, and their scar tissue was still visible.

It sounds straightforward, but that did not mean that it was a simple argument to sustain with the Hill. Africa, remember, was a freebie, and this was politics. For many, the goal was simply to engineer a recorded vote in favor of "freedom fighters" and against a pro-Soviet regime; this was a way to strengthen one's right flank or to offset a perceived electoral liability on some other issue. Others may have had a more ideological motive: they simply wished to place perceived opponents of helping UNITA on the defensive.

Gossip about the ongoing review within the administration caused conservative antennae to twitch. Shultz's letter to Michel could be cited as "evidence" that the State Department did oppose helping Savimbi. In fact, Shultz supported aiding UNITA, and he gave me categorical instructions: we were to develop options for assistance which best supported our settlement strategy, and to implement them in a phased manner that supported U.S. diplomacy. This was precisely what the legislative language repealing the Clark Amendment had provided. Power would be used to support diplomacy; it was not an alternative to diplomacy.

A careful reading of Shultz's letter—"there are better ways to help"—was code language for stating his preference for covert assistance. But that did not stop some from claiming that Shultz was subverting Reagan. A few weeks later, returning from his first Soviet summit in late November, Reagan cleared Shultz of the charge in press remarks that also pierced our precious veil of ambiguity: "We all believe that a covert operation would be more useful to us and have more chance of success right now than the overt proposal that has been made in the Congress." Whoops! Reagan rewrote in a sentence the lexicon of clandestine diplomacy. We would get immediate "credit" for intervening no matter what the final shape, timing, or content of our decisions.

Did I favor aiding UNITA? Pressed to give a short answer, I would have replied, "Later, if necessary." I had worked hard for Clark repeal in 1981, and believe to this day that our hand would have been substantially strengthened had we achieved it then. (It was my superiors in the administration who pulled the plug on our repeal drive in December 1981 in order to trade it for some "higher" priorities in that year's U.S. foreign assistance bill.) In July 1985, I cheered the results on C-SPAN in my office as sixty Democrats joined in the House's vote for repeal. One could even imagine, for a naive moment or two, that this represented a refreshing bi-partisanship behind Ronald Reagan's crusade for freedom from Communist tyranny around the world. The repeal of the Clark Amendment signaled the end of an era of American schizophrenia about our global role. I also thought back to the many times I had bemoaned the absence of the policy tools enjoyed by my counterparts dealing with Latin America or the Middle East. Until now, we had had to rely almost exclusively on our wits, our logic, and the inherent leverage built into the regional power balance.

Repeal changed the equation we faced. It would send a signal—a useful one—to Moscow, Havana, and Luanda that we had options if they continued to use our diplomacy as a cover for the pursuit of unilateral, military objectives. Now we could threaten to raise the price. Now we had the basis to acquire a stake of our own. Looking down the road, our "free hand" in Angola could help reduce Savimbi's excessive dependence on the South Africans, freeing him to play his cards as an Angolan nationalist and curbing Pretoria's tendency to manipulate the Angolan leader for its own purposes. Now, we could play the assistance card so as to guarantee that UNITA could never become the victim of a Cuban withdrawal settlement; it could also give us leverage as the question of Angolan reconciliation ripened.

But I was not happy about the decision we were taking. It was being driven by the wrong people in Washington, for the wrong reasons. It was distressing to hear the advocates of immediate aid brush aside all consideration of diplomatic consequences and leap to the false conclusion that the Angolans were the ones blocking a settlement. The reality was far more complex.

It was even more distressing to hear so little discussion of what the military consequences of doing so would be. Despite Clark repeal, we knew that there was no stomach for substantial U.S. military involvement in Southern Africa. The long-term durability of bi-partisan, congressional support was unknown. No one was proposing a significant assistance program. The Soviets were in the Angolan business at a level 50 to 100 times higher.

Therefore, it was important that we not delude ourselves. We could help in specific areas and make a contribution to UNITA morale and, at the margins, its capabilities. But there was no question of creating conditions for a UNITA victory. The underlying Angolan military balance was beyond the reach of anything under consideration in Washington. If we were lucky, U.S. military help might reinforce the stalemate at higher levels. On the plus side, this could bolster UNITA defenses against future offensives and underscore the futility of Soviet-Angolan attempts to destroy Savimbi. But it could be downright dangerous for both UNITA and the South Africans if our support led them to miscalculate and overplay their hand. Unless we controlled every aspect of U.S. strategy, we could end up with a mortally wounded diplomacy and nothing to replace it. Covert action—like sanctions—is not a foreign policy.

For all these reasons, it was important that we do everything possible to avoid disclosures concerning covert action. Reagan himself blew our cover. We also argued that we should first use the threat of U.S. intervention to press the MPLA to move forward. We should stage a variety of covert pressures over a period of time, starting with modest measures and moving toward more coercive ones. This "incremental" approach would string out the decision process, giving us maximum openings to work on the Angolans. It might also keep Pretoria in line. On this basis, I told Shultz in late October that I could recommend giving a green light.

Shultz favored adding some muscle to our diplomacy: we had been conducting an ambitious strategy of regional peacemaking with our hands tied. He also knew that there was no way to stop the train heading down the tracks toward us; the firestorm after his letter to Republican Michel made that much clear. Third, he knew that the anxiety level on his Africa team was rising. Shultz no doubt wondered if we were capable of shifting gears. I wondered if he understood how the shift looked to a cadre of officers who had seen the United States self-destruct in Angola just ten years earlier.

Nonetheless, Shultz agreed in early October to hold off a decision while we made one more run at the MPLA leadership. Citing a string of excuses, they had not met with us since March, thus undercutting the minority in Washington who still believed in the negotiation. Meanwhile, in late September, a low-key, civilian-military team of South Africans had arrived in Washington at their own initiative for talks on

Namibia and Angola. The timing was interesting. The signal came just as the fighting in southeastern Angola was cresting and the South Africans were under pressure to decide on how and when to intervene on Savimbi's behalf. It was also just two weeks since Reagan had issued the executive order imposing limited sanctions on Pretoria, and six weeks since our Vienna rendezvous with Pik Botha prior to P. W. Botha's Rubicon speech.

We explored in detail with the South Africans our "basis for negotiation" proposal of March, answering a long list of questions and offering preliminary interpretations on key features of the proposal. The visitors seemed to be gathering information that could serve as input for a "revised" reply—their snotty June reply having become a real bone of contention between us. They also wished to test the vibes emanating from our Angola policy review, and to gauge where they really stood in American eyes on the Namibia-Angola issue. When they left, the South Africans can have been in no doubt about the trend of thinking in Washington and the enormous tactical opportunity opening up before them. We eventually received Pretoria's revised reply on November 22. It was a constructive document that accepted our core proposals subject to various conditions that would need to be negotiated or buried later.

Whatever their motives, the South Africans had quickly shifted to the high ground by this action. They committed themselves officially to a series of positions that would arm us to lean on Luanda: acceptance of our proposed Cuban troop withdrawal schedule providing for 80 percent to leave during the first year, and the remaining 20 percent during the second year—provided that (a) agreement could be reached on a satisfactory verification plan; (b) the tempo and rhythm of first-year withdrawals would assure that the withdrawals were "irreversible" by the time of the Namibian election; and (c) agreement could be reached on the role, composition, and deployment of Cuban forces during the withdrawal process. Pretoria also wanted assurances from Washington about our position on U.N. sanctions and our relationship with the MPLA regime and with UNITA.

Against the backdrop of our internal review of Angolan policy, Frank Wisner met twice with Ismael Gaspard-Martins, one of the MPLA's most impressive senior officials and minister of commerce at the time. Martins was in town to demonstrate Luanda's interest in U.S. commercial ties and to probe the implications of the Clark Amendment repeal. Though not in the inner policy loop, Martins would pass messages reliably. Wisner spoke of the rapidly mounting sentiment to help UNITA; by resisting the Soviet-Cuban military presence, Savimbi had won the respect of the last three American presidents and a growing body of congressional opinion. Angolan diplomatic inaction and military offensives were playing directly into the hands of those who wished to see a basic change in U.S. policy.

Martins spoke of the need to create a better climate of trust, suggesting that Luanda could not negotiate while Pretoria's air force was bombing FAPLA positions near Mavinga at the Lomba River. In phrases we were to use again and again, Wisner observed that peace could not become a precondition of talks to achieve peace. It was important for Luanda not to misinterpret the U.S. sanctions debate or the unrest within South Africa. The anti-apartheid sentiment here was not a pro-Angolan sentiment; if anything, sanctions fervor on the American left had kindled the pro-UNITA drive among moderates and conservatives. As for Pretoria, it was plain to see that the South Africans were not on the verge of collapse.

A few days later, Under Secretary of State Michael Armacost and I met with President dos Santos at his suite in the U.N. Plaza Hotel in New York on October 22. We painted a classic good cop, bad cop scenario for the Angolan leader: pressures were mounting quickly in Washington, and people were saying that Luanda had decided to wage war against UNITA. Six months had been wasted. The current MPLA offensive showed that military solutions would not work. Soon, the U.S.-Soviet summit would be held, and the question of regional conflicts was certain to arise. It was urgent for the MPLA to demonstrate its true intentions.

Dos Santos professed incomprehension at the apparent change in the American posture. Angola was "the victim" of one act of South African bad faith after another, and now the United States was discussing aiding Angolan "armed bandits." Angola would need "assurances" that Washington would not aid UNITA; it could not negotiate under threats. In the end dos Santos thought again, and proposed an in-depth round of talks to occur immediately after the summit. Our March "basis for negotiation" would be the focus of discussion. Two days later, on October 24, Reagan delivered his U.N. address aligning us clearly on the side of "freedom fighters" and placing regional conflicts high on the summit agenda.

The Angolans Blow Another Chance

The first U.S.-Soviet summit of the Reagan-Gorbachev era was not exactly the ideal venue for substantive discussion of Southern Africa. There was an overall superpower relationship to discuss and an arms control agenda to define; within the framework of regional conflicts, Afghanistan ranked first on both sides. In the event, Angola was barely mentioned at Geneva. It was probably just as well. We left the door open, and avoided playing any high cards before we had developed and demonstrated our UNITA aid option.

I flew from the summit to Dakar and Lusaka to brief key leaders and meet with Kito Rodrigues on November 27–28 in the Zambian capital. With a straight face, Kito declared that this meeting had come at Luanda's initiative and was "exploratory" in nature. He had brought nothing new, and proposed that we start where we had left off on March 18, 1985, and then review the intervening events which had deadlocked the process. In the MPLA's view, those events—highlighted by the SADF's Cabinda raid back in May—fully validated Luanda's insistence on refusing to include the northern contingent of Cuban troops in the timetable. On top of this, the U.S. position had hardened and Luanda did not know where we were headed.

I erupted: there were perhaps ten people left in the United States who believed in these negotiations, and five of them were sitting across the table from him in Lusaka. The lack of Angolan seriousness and the dramatic escalation of the war against UNITA had severely undercut us. Luanda's whining chorus of requests for assurances, gestures, and clarifications had placed U.S. officials in an impossible position. The Angolans seemed to believe they were negotiating with us, instead of working with us to bargain with the South Africans. Thus, all the talk about the right "climate" or "necessary preconditions" only confirmed our suspicions that Luanda was playing for time.

Finally, I informed Kito of the latest news from South Africa. Not only had Pretoria provided a conditional acceptance of our "basis" proposal; it had also replied to the United Nations concerning the leftover issue of selecting an electoral system to be used in the Namibian election. This effectively concluded every substantive agenda item related to the Namibian settlement plan. Kito was beginning to see our point. But he had no mandate to play any cards. Instead, he asked me to sign an upbeat press communiqué, which I refused to do, and invited me to return to Luanda in two to three weeks. The MPLA would demonstrate its seriousness by offering better proposals on the Cuban timetable; it might even be possible to consider some evolution on the northern troop issue. Before leaving Africa, I visited Johannesburg to brief the South Africans, and met with Savimbi in Zaire to invite him formally to visit Washington at the end of January. (The UNITA leader's CIA liaison and U.S. lobbyists had already begun planning the trip, but this made it official.)

This was the last meeting we held with the MPLA before we notified Congress in mid-December of the President's decision to mount a covert program of assistance to UNITA. Implementation would begin in early

1986. The phased, multi-track scenario we had proposed back in September was premised on using the threat of intervention to lever the Angolans forward. Recent South African moves made the scenario more credible. But the MPLA's performance in late 1985 guaranteed that we would soon shift to a fast track.

Still, we refused to give up on the Angolans. I made a final visit to Luanda from January 8 through 10, 1986, at Kito's invitation. Dos Santos set the stage by whisking my Pentagon counterpart Jim Woods and me out to his palace at Futungo do Belas for a media-drenched act of political theater. Reciting the MPLA's many "gestures of goodwill" and its interest in a comprehensive regional settlement, dos Santos asked me if "the [upcoming] visit by Savimbi [to Washington] and the military and other aid that the U.S. government plans to give should be considered a form of pressure or a declaration of war"; whichever, Luanda would get more help from its socialist friends.

We learned from several European and Arab diplomats that Soviet and Bulgarian diplomats had papered the walls of Luanda with their version of our March 1985 "basis for negotiations" within two weeks of my handing it to Kito. Now, ten months later, Kito had just concluded another round of arms supply talks in Moscow. The MPLA had just concluded a successful party congress, interpreted as further strengthening the personal position of dos Santos. Though the offensive against UNITA had been defeated, the Angolans were more confident that they had stemmed the rising UNITA tide of 1983–85. To do so, they had become, if anything, more dependent on Soviet help, a situation that probably reduced the freedom of action of Kito and the "peace party."

Despite his invitation, Kito had nothing to tell me—no new position, no agenda for talks, nothing much to say about the substantial evolution in South Africa's positions. The Angolan handed us a formal paper, which asserted that our "basis" was not acceptable, and stated that the withdrawal of the northern contingent of Cuban troops remained nonnegotiable. Kito impressed Woods and me as almost relaxed and confident. I looked at my watch in disgust. As we headed for the exit, Kito shifted ground, stating that a South African commitment to a "date certain" (sometime in mid-1986) would energize the talks and might even make it possible to negotiate the northern troop issue. Here we were once again, bouncing between alternative Angolan positions, one formal and rigid, the other oral and flexible.

In late January 1986, Wisner met with Kito at Claridge's Hotel in London. (Savimbi had already arrived in the United States for a high-profile Washington reception that would be the envy of a European head of state. Neither dos Santos nor P. W. Botha ever made it to Washington during the Reagan era; neither of them ever forgave us.) Kito told Wisner that the "date certain" proposal would make a powerful difference in Luanda; Wisner replied that Pretoria would require something concrete in return like an MPLA confirmation that the negotiation covered *total* Cuban withdrawal. Kito winced. The Soviets, he explained, were exploiting Angola's dependence. Before leaving, Kito promised Wisner we would hear within one week about obtaining a commitment to negotiate total withdrawal in return for a July or August 1986 "date certain."

In mid-February 1986, I confirmed to the Senate the widely known fact that the provision of "appropriate and effective" support to UNITA had begun. On March 4, the South Africans announced their readiness to begin implementation of Resolution 435 on August 1 if agreement could be reached by that time on the Cuban issue. On March 6, I met in Geneva with Vladillen Vasev, a senior Soviet counterpart. We hoped to use Pretoria's proposal as a fulcrum for assessing the real Soviet attitude and, if possible, for wedging the MPLA into a serious response to the South African offer. Instead, we found the Soviets beside themselves in their anxiety to discredit the "date certain" offer. On March 18, dos Santos wrote to U.N. Secretary General de Cuellar to announce that Angola was "deeply outraged" by American decisions, which "jeopardized its credibility as a mediator." He called on the U.N. Secretary General to assume the lead role in obtaining the implementation of Resolution 435. The Angolans never seemed to miss an opportunity to miss an opportunity. The Soviets were delighted.

By the end of March 1986, it was generally assumed that our regional diplomacy was dead. Bill Casey and his South African counterparts had what they thought they wanted. In fact, the basic U.S. strategy did not change. We had become an indirect party to the Angolan civil war. But we also had a thoroughly logical two-track strategy of diplomacy backed by aid to UNITA. Shultz's dictum would turn out to be correct, however difficult it might be to shift our gears. And we would soon start to think about developing a third track focused on the diplomacy of Angolan national reconciliation.

If only we could master the wars within our own constellation! On March 14, *Washington Post* correspondent David B. Ottaway wrote an article wondering "how long Crocker can last"—pegged to recent demands by Jesse Helms and other conservative senators that Shultz fire me. I was said to be "a man with enemies on all sides" because of my efforts to sustain a rational American policy amidst the South Africa and UNITA aid controversies. Most controversial of all were the words:

Yet to the chagrin of his detractors, he has proven an extraordinarily good bureaucratic infighter. And he is a master of the linguistic ambiguity that is the trademark of his temporary profession. His double-edged or round-about replies to questions have been known to drive congressmen and reporters to despair, leaving nagging doubts about whether he really said "yes" or "no" to a delicate question.

Actually, it was all very clear. I had a goal. And we had a Secretary of State with integrity.

13

The Great Foreign Policy Robbery of 1986: South Africa, Round Two

In June 1986 the phone rang in my State Department office late on the afternoon of Friday the 13th. Nancy L. Kassebaum, the Republican chairperson of the Africa subcommittee of the Senate Foreign Relations Committee, was on the line. We respected each other. I knew a lot less about Kansas politics than she knew about U.S. relations with Africa; but we could learn from each other. The problem was that our roles and interests differed, especially when African issues became really hot. I needed a tough-minded ally to help sustain our cause in Congress. She needed a politically attuned ally who could ensure that the administration provided political "cover," the crucial garment in Washington's couture.

The senator's message was stark, her tone anxious. She did not know what more she could do to warn us that the President had to "get out front" on the South African issue fast or the Republican-controlled Senate would march off in its own direction. Kassebaum and other restless Republicans were seeking a meeting with Reagan to plead that he give a radio address professing his disgust and dismay over recent South African events. He should send out a presidential envoy to talk plainly to P. W. Botha, and to take "a visible lead" and "do something" about South Africa. The senator was good at predicting the political weather in Washington. Her Africa committee assignment made her a lightning rod for the electric discharges going off over the issue of South Africa around the nation.

I urged Shultz to compare notes with Kassebaum and Senator Richard Lugar, chairman of the Foreign Relations Committee. An orgy of self-destructive decisions in South Africa had set off big waves in the United States. Within days of Kassebaum's call, the Hill and the media were in an uproar, and I found myself on television defending and explaining U.S. policy five times in ten days. There were not a lot of other volunteers.

What had happened? The Reagan executive order of September 1985 had provided an opportunity for the South Africans to return to the path of constructive change and regional cooperation. Reagan's action had enabled us to send *our* signals: by imposing some additional restrictions on our bilateral relationship, we just barely retained control of the U.S. end of the economic relationship. The window was opened wider by a diplomatic initiative taken by the Commonwealth nations in October 1985. The "Eminent Persons Group" (EPG), consisting of senior figures from Commonwealth member countries, had a mandate to develop a "negotiating concept" that could foster talks between the government and black opposition leaders.

Initially, it looked as if the leadership in Pretoria intended to make creative use of that opportunity to defuse the crisis of confidence that had erupted back in July and August 1985. But things lurched badly off the track in late April and May 1986. Suddenly P. W. Botha abandoned any semblance of constructive interaction with Western capitals. Like a caged animal, he lashed out in all directions in angry frustration. On May 19, while the Commonwealth EPG was in the middle of a key mission to the region, the SADF crashed across the borders of Zambia, Zimbabwe, and Botswana against ANC targets. Shortly thereafter, an SADF hit team struck ANC targets in Swaziland, and commandos attacked Soviet and Cuban shipping in the southern Angolan port of Namibe. The Commonwealth EPG promptly succumbed to these provocations and called off its mediation exercise—blasting Pretoria as the obstacle to negotiations and letting the Lusaka-based ANC and the imprisoned Nelson Mandela completely off the hook.

It was almost as if elements of the Pretoria government had consciously dreamed up the best possible way to get credit for scuttling the Commonwealth exercise. On their side, some elements within the group seemed to be just as happy to disengage in a manner that would place the full onus for a breakdown on Pretoria. The British—the Commonwealth country with the most clout and the most to lose—were horrified at this turn of events. On June 12, the EPG announced the collapse of its mission, and called for the imposition of comprehensive and mandatory (i.e., U.N.) economic sanctions. On the same day, Botha reversed his earlier moves to loosen up internal security measures and imposed a nationwide state of emergency. Another one thousand oppositionists were detained, and fresh curbs placed on the press. On June 18, the U.S. House of Representatives passed a bill that would impose total trade and investment sanctions on South Africa.

A series of external clocks were ticking: in the Congress, in the diplomatic networks of the Commonwealth and the European Community, and in the boardrooms of U.S. corporations caught up in pressures from shareholders, state and local governments, universities, institutional investors, and from the Reverend Leon Sullivan, who had set a two-year deadline of his own in 1985. These clocks paid no attention to Southern African time; they were set to foreign time and political imperatives. As peacemakers, we were caught between the raw forces operating on the ground and these ever-changing foreign clocks.

As this second phase of the crisis over South Africa came to a head, we would need a coherent strategy. A showdown was approaching. By early August, the Commonwealth would be holding a mini-summit and Prime Minister Thatcher would be totally isolated in her firm, anti-sanctions stance. She faced mounting pressures from Fleet Street and the City as well as the anti-South African chorus of the other Commonwealth members and the organization's secretariat. In late June, Thatcher and German Chancellor Helmut Kohl managed to block sanctions proposals in the European Community, but not before Thatcher offered up Sir Geoffrey Howe, her Foreign Secretary, to take on a European Community–mandated diplomatic mission to the Front Line States, the ANC, and South Africa. His assignment—to pick up the pieces of the prematurely aborted EPG exercise—had all the hallmarks of a kamikaze mission. Unless Howe could pull out of a suicide dive, this mission would only feed the pro-sanctions sentiment within both the European Community and the Commonwealth. By mid-August, our Senate would have had plenty of time to catch up with the House. The tides of opinion in these forums would reinforce each other, leaving us face to face with a repeat of the 1985 scenario.

Botha's Dilemma

Pretoria's angry defiance represented a sharp change of signals from before April 1986. Had P. W. Botha, as Bishop Tutu quipped, "lost the convictions of his courage"? Had he become the prisoner of a dangerously narrowing circle of advisers who preferred simply to block Western "meddling" and pay whatever sanctions price followed? Did the perceived imperative of breaking the back of black resistance gradually come to outweigh all other considerations? Were P. W. Botha and his inner circle led to believe that Reagan and Thatcher would protect them forever against the sanctioneers or that they did not really want Pretoria to negotiate with the ANC and its internal allies? It was a tangled tale.

P. W. Botha's record is full of ironies. His government introduced a significant collection of piecemeal reforms, improving the lives of black South Africans in many fields and removing or modifying a variety of classical apartheid practices. For the first part of his stewardship, he was unquestionably the most reformist and "moderate" leader South Africa had known since the National Party took power in 1948. Yet Botha's government will be known as the one that introduced a draconian state of emergency in which thousands died, some 30,000 were detained, black groups were put out of action, and the press severely restricted. The leader whose "adapt or die" slogan in the late 1970s signaled a less ideological and extremist vision, ended up by destroying foreign confidence, undercutting his own diplomatic achievements in Africa, and sabotaging those Western leaders most inclined to give him the benefit of the doubt.

Botha had an extraordinary opportunity for constructive leadership in the 1980s. During the first half of the decade he faced benign external circumstances. He built up an impressive party, military, and bureaucratic machinery as his base of power. A man of courage, he did the unthinkable for an Afrikaner leader by splitting the National Party in 1982–83 over the introduction of a tricameral constitution which enfranchised so-called "Coloreds" and Asians to elect their own chambers of Parliament. Suddenly, the National Party had become a potentially centrist, reformist party by proclaiming its readiness to do without the 20–25 percent of hard-core conservative voters.

Botha's constitution also brought autocratic personal power to unprecedented heights, occasioning talk of an imperial presidency. (There is a story that during their triumphal European tour in June 1984, his wife Elise ignored the injunction that only royal visitors wear white to a papal audience, remarking, "*Ons is mos royal*—But we are like royalty"). Authoritarian and hypersensitive to criticism, Botha became a perfect foil for the many foes he acquired. A bully, he was capable of reducing his cabinet colleagues to tears. This was the image that came across on television during his disastrous Rubicon address of August 15, 1985.

But, at his peak, Botha had an unassailable power base for pursuit of a sustained program of autocratic political reform. Sadly, he never figured out how to link this power base to a coherent reform strategy. Compared to the more sweeping reformist visions found amongst leading Afrikaner political thinkers in the early 1980s, Botha's notions were incomplete, vague, and lacking in realism about timing. He tried to remedy the historic wrong done by his predecessors who had disenfranchised the Coloreds and Asians thirty years earlier. But he stopped short of engaging blacks in negotiation about power sharing: his 1984 constitution excluded the African majority.

By 1985–86, when he sought to open such a dialogue, it was late in the day. His own actions, in the eyes of blacks, represented the ultimate insult to their aspirations. Ironically, he catalyzed a tide of black anger that sparked three years of urban unrest and fueled the most successful organizational drive in the history of black South African politics. By 1986, the United Democratic Front had managed to place the Botha government on the defensive and increasingly to isolate it through alliances with the Western anti-apartheid movement.

This was the backdrop for understanding Botha's zigzag performance in 1985–86. In early 1985, Pretoria hinted at movement on the question of citizenship for all South Africans. It recognized that the homeland policy was not an adequate answer to the issue of black political representation. Forced removals of settled black communities were suspended for a time while the policy of urbanization was placed under review. Some central business districts were opened to all races, and the Pretoria authorities raised the black education budget. Laws banning interracial sex and marriage were repealed. After a hiatus and the Rubicon fiasco, Botha's reform initiatives resumed in September and October 1985: he renewed the pledge to move on restoring citizenship to homeland blacks. And he appeared to accept the principle of extending the vote to blacks in an "undivided" South Africa (i.e., reversing apartheid's fragmentation of the country) by talking about some form of black political representation "up to the highest level" in a new constitution. An official panel recommended that the pass laws (*de facto* internal passports for blacks) be abolished. On a separate track, Pretoria took a series of steps toward renewing its participation in our regional diplomacy.

Meanwhile, to Botha's exasperation, white business leaders and opposition parliamentarians broke new ground by meeting with ANC representatives in Lusaka in September and October, and calling publicly for negotiation with "acknowledged" black leaders. This ran directly counter to Botha's preferred strategy of isolating militant black leaders and groups, and promoting negotiation among "moderates" of all races.

His aim was to draw the sharpest possible line between them, to gain allies, and to undercut the dangerous momentum achieved by township radicals. But his effort to control the selection of interlocutors had the effect of legitimizing more radical voices.

The issue of ANC violence came to the fore in November and December 1985 when a series of bomb and landmine attacks killed white civilians in rural and urban areas. By late 1985, the ANC had begun taking public credit for incidents involving "soft" as well as government targets. This syndrome triggered a surge in white sentiment to crack down further, and aggravated Botha's tendency toward the "iron fist." Security force actions escalated against ANC targets in the Front Line States and radical groups within South Africa. A spiral of terror and counter-terror had set in. The question of violence began to figure prominently in the bargaining positions of the various sides, especially in the context of the Commonwealth group initiative launched in October. Botha began to specify the renunciation of violence as a condition to dialogue with opposition movements. In turn, the black opposition began enunciating rigorous preconditions of its own: an end to the state of emergency, removal of security forces from the townships, and the release of Nelson Mandela and others from their long imprisonment.

This cycle would not have been easy to break for a more imaginative and less angry leader than Botha. Within South Africa, he could find little solid support to his left or his right, and the center was shrinking. Externally, his financial and political relationships were eroding. He and his colleagues could not unilaterally stop the violence or start a process of negotiation—even if they genuinely wished to do so. But they could—and they did—work to shift the onus to others.

Here was a real irony. ANC terrorist incidents were, in part, an effort to show the world (including South African blacks) that *Umkhonto we Sizwe* ("The Spear of the Nation")—the ANC's underground and largely exiled armed wing—actually existed. ANC pronouncements were laced with talk of the "armed struggle." It was a claim to manhood and revolutionary status at a time when new forms of militant but non-military leadership and organizational power were springing up like spring flowers across the blighted urban landscape of South Africa.

The "armed struggle" never amounted to much more than a costly inconvenience to the security forces—an inconvenience that was gradually eliminated during the course of the 1980s. But it served Pretoria's interest to focus attention on the ANC's violence: in the first place, the imagery of battling Soviet-backed terrorists organized in underground cells or cross-border guerrilla camps was a straight shot at the emotions of Western conservatives; second, this was a good way to smear the

UDF, the township "street committees," and the "comrades" with one broad brush; and third, if talks ever became a reality, the ANC's inability to control internal violence and its internal differences over the issue of violence would be useful to Botha and his men.

It was no easier to "reform" South Africa than it was to end its hideous violence. Botha could offer up gestures to foster a climate for reconciliation, but there was little mileage in it when each unilateral move by Pretoria was ignored, rejected, or discounted as having been extracted under pressure. The Botha government was bound by the basic logic of white South African politics: there were only so many cards in the deck, and it was essential to get something for them. Otherwise, it was preferable—in fact, imperative—to play for time, reassert control, and establish a stronger position from which to negotiate.

The American Response

This was the backdrop to my arrival in P. W. Botha's Cape Town office on January 13, 1986, bearing a letter from Ronald Reagan. By the norms of correspondence between heads of state, it was a detailed and lengthy message. Reagan asked Botha to exchange views with me about ways in which 1986 could become a year of decisive accomplishment. He urged Botha to seize the initiative and take bold steps on reform and negotiation, pledging to offer support and credit along the way. I was primed to elaborate: if there was a "context" which we could support, we were prepared to suggest the possibility of a meeting between the two leaders.

But Botha seemed as expert as the MPLA leadership at missing opportunities. Events of the past year—including our own actions and signals—had wounded him severely, exacerbating his already emotive brand of leadership. Whereas Pik Botha, the foreign minister, welcomed me warmly ("You've been away too long"), his president stood stiffly on his side of the room and asked, "Why are you here?" as I entered his office. Before I could reply, he wanted to know if I had met secretly with ANC leaders in Lusaka before coming. P. W. Botha never trusted me, being convinced that my personal agenda was to impose SWAPO rule in Namibia and ANC rule in South Africa. He saw me as a wolf in sheep's clothing. But, now, he generalized his complaint. He had been let down by two Republican administrations (Ford in 1975–76, and Reagan now), and he wanted me to know that he preferred dealing with the Carter administration—at least he knew where he stood. We Republicans could not even retain control of our own political system.

He told me bluntly that he intended to stay on in his job. I should inform Reagan that South Africa was going forward "with confidence"; Botha then proceeded to hand me a boilerplate document prepared by his Foreign Ministry and distributed to a wide range of know-nothing Western visitors. The West had become defeatist and soft, using the language and concepts of our enemies (and his). We applied double standards, blasting Libyan terrorism and backing Israeli counterterrorist actions but ignoring the evils of ANC violence. Western actions were destabilizing South Africa and causing his opposition to escalate its demands. Botha was too proud to open up to me. He was too angry at history to concede his need for help from a country he perceived as a principal source of his problems. It was a chilling encounter. It would also be our last.

But P. W. Botha's nasty performance was by no means his final word, or even the real response to U.S. cajoling and hints of our readiness to help. Botha had ridiculed our decisions on Angola, describing our plans to help UNITA (someone had briefed him quite accurately) as "chicken-feed." Did the South African leader resent the end of his monopoly relationship with Savimbi, or was he irate because the black guerrilla chieftain had an invitation to Washington and he did not? But separately, Botha's diplomats seemed much less hostile. They appeared interested in the notion of announcing a "date certain" for implementing a Namibia settlement if a Cuban withdrawal deal could be worked out. One well-placed Afrikaner insider told me that Namibia and Angola would be far easier to accept than major domestic change. In another side conversation, Pik Botha suggested that we might be able to get important things accomplished if we would reengage aggressively and at the highest levels. Clearly, our aloofness since the events of August–September 1985 had gotten the attention of P. W. Botha's team. It was possible that the Reagan message would not be dismissed, after all.

Pik Botha had spoken of the possibility of paying us a return visit. But General Pieter van der Westhuizen arrived in Washington first, showing up as I returned. Just as I had touched lots of bases in South Africa, the new secretary of Botha's State Security Council camped out in our midst for days. He was shopping for support for his boss, arguing that U.S. help would encourage Botha to move forward. His meetings with his friend Bill Casey, with NSC Adviser John Poindexter, with former NSC Adviser Bill Clark (now a private citizen), and with me must have enabled the general to prepare an interesting report back to his boss. I never found out what it said.

I told Van der Westhuizen that a presidential meeting might be possible if we could agree on the necessary political context. This would require major moves by Pretoria to create a climate for talks with black leaders. P. W. Botha's "ratcatcher" was less than pleased when I proposed quiet talks between Pik Botha and me in Europe to talk it over—a proposal which, incidentally, removed him from the loop. In any case, Van der Westhuizen wanted a P. W. Botha visit without strings.

Around the time of Van der Westhuizen's return, P. W. Botha replied to Reagan's letter (and, indirectly, to my version of the "context" required for a visit). It was a plaintive message. All the pressure was being placed on one side—he could not *force* black leaders to negotiate. The West was building up expectations that went beyond his political limits. Botha appealed for less one-sidedness from Washington, for a moratorium on punitive actions and threats. In the same breath, he endorsed the basic line of the Commonwealth EPG initiative calling for matching commitments to end violence on all sides. Botha was prepared to release Mandela in return for a pledge that he would not "personally" be involved in violence. Unlike his tone with me, Botha's message was respectful and appreciative. He really wanted that visit.

And he must really have believed it was within reach. After all, he knew that the idea for such a visit had well-placed support in Washington. It was not my idea. I first learned of it when approached back in December by Bill Clark for my reaction. Since Botha's Rubicon speech, the United States had been aloof; this was unhealthy. Reagan, Clark added, had the idea of "talking sense" to Botha in a quiet meeting, which could be held outside the Washington spotlight. I found it implausible that Reagan had just come up with this concept in an idle moment. Poindexter said that the idea had come from Van der Westhuizen, Bill Casey's former intelligence counterpart. This, then, was the background to my January visit to South Africa. It explains the general's puzzlement upon hearing of the rigorous conditions I had worked out with Shultz and Poindexter after my return.

Botha's January 31, 1986, speech to Parliament contained some interesting elements. There was a firm commitment to terminate the hated pass laws. (They were rescinded in April, and a white paper issued to describe a series of fresh departures in urbanization policy.) The president announced his intention to "negotiate" the creation of a "national statutory council" to serve as a multi-racial advisory forum (including blacks) pending further constitutional changes. His prose included sweeping commitments (this time, in a more comprehensible code) to such democratic norms as an undivided South Africa with a common citizenship, equality before the law, and the rule of law. Finally, Botha offered a new wrinkle on the release of Mandela: he could be freed as a humanitarian gesture if the Angolans would free a captured SADF special forces officer and if the Soviets would free Andrei Sakharov and Anatoly

Shcharansky. Botha had changed his mind: Mandela's release would now become dependent on the decisions of two Communist dictatorships.

This speech offered a welcome contrast to the Rubicon precedent. But it was no basis for an invitation to Washington. How should we proceed? There was no reason to suppose that Botha and his factionalized establishment, left to their own devices, would come up with a winning formula to break the country's downward spiral. On the other hand, it would be a real high-wire act to bring Botha to the United States. A firestorm of protest would occur unless such a visit resulted in major accomplishments. Anything less than a capitulation by the National Party would be portrayed by the Free South Africa movement and a supporting media chorus as a total sell-out. Leaving aside the domestic politics, we viewed a possible Reagan-Botha meeting as a key component in a strategy that would unfold between Washington and Pretoria over an extended period of time.

On the other hand, the South African government viewed such a visit as an end in itself, a symbolic act of U.S. recognition of Southern Africa's most important leader, and a supportive signal that the leader of the West accepted the need to deal with and through him. Pretoria, we judged, was prepared to pay for such a visit. But it had initially been misinformed by other American voices on this point, and it would clearly not pay any price. We would have to conduct a controlled, in-depth test of precisely how we could benefit from the situation. No one in our government but the State Department Africa team had the literacy to conduct that test. We must be the ones to do it if we wished to prevail in the barely visible tussle over South African policy.

I met Pik Botha in Geneva on February 12–13, 1986, armed with an elaborate series of steps we wished Pretoria to take, sequenced with supporting moves we would be prepared to make. The scenario carried all the way up to the beginning of black-white negotiations and the scrapping of all apartheid laws. Supporting moves ranged from Botha's possible visit to providing help with banks and third-party governments, and the eventual removal of existing U.S. pressures. This was a sweepingly ambitious scenario.

Pik Botha made a valiant attempt to dress up his brief. He had worked very hard on the January 31 speech by his boss, and he had thought that it would set the context for a meeting of between the two presidents. But after hours of formal discussion which must have seemed to him like cross- and re-cross-examination, an exasperated Botha said he could not seem to give me the "clarity" I needed to facilitate a meeting. In fact, our questions had forced him to free-lance beyond his normal expansive limits. Pretoria, we learned, continued to think principally in terms of what external pay-off it could get for taking the step of releasing Mandela rather than of how the release itself could create a new political context inside South Africa.

At a private dinner outside Geneva, Pik Botha told me, "We can't possibly meet your price." He had never believed in this idea: he realized that our "domestic political requirements" obliged us to set the price too high for his government—at least at the present time. Maybe later. In the meantime, he hoped that we would continue to press for reform and to give credit where it was due.

Back in Washington, I found that the air was full of talk about a possible presidential emissary to "reaffirm" on behalf of the White House the terms for a possible visit. South African Ambassador Herbert Beukes appeared to be under instructions to ascertain the prospects for such an emissary, who might merely indicate to P. W. Botha that a meeting was not excluded at a later time. Beukes informed me that "other voices" were already asking why Pik Botha and I had failed to organize a presidential visit! In mid-March, it came to my attention that Casey had told P. W. Botha that I was supposed to have invited him to Washington during my January visit to South Africa. Botha, according to the story, replied that I had not done so, but had discussed the idea inconclusively in Geneva. We thought we had killed the idea of another emissary. But, apparently, there was a self-appointed one in our midst. P. W. Botha was continuing his efforts to exploit alternative channels to Washington—channels made available to him by our official indiscipline.

In March, Pretoria lifted the partial state of emergency and released most of the remaining detainees (some 8,000 had been detained since the emergency began in June 1985). The Commonwealth EPG tabled a "matching commitments" formula with Pretoria, Mandela, and the exiled ANC, which aimed at establishing agreed conditions for the start of negotiations. Detentions would be suspended, troops removed from the townships, Mandela and others released, and the ANC and Pan-Africanist Congress unbanned; and the ANC would agree to suspend violence and enter into negotiations. The Commonwealth initiative had Mandela's support and the support of some within the Pretoria government (including several senior ministers in periodic contact with Mandela). P. W. Botha had lots of reservations but had not rejected it. In early April, in response to Thatcher's request, Reagan wrote Botha endorsing the initiative and urging that he explore fully this opportunity to bring the violence under control and begin the process of dialogue.

When I met Pik Botha in Geneva again on April 21, I found him far more upbeat about reform prospects. President Botha had just announced the abolition of the pass law system of black "influx control." The foreign minister now agreed with me that 1986 had become the crucial year. The Commonwealth group idea had many positive features—not least as a means of getting the Mandela issue resolved and bringing other black leaders to the negotiating table, whether the ANC chose to participate or not. But Botha still was searching for an external safety net: Pretoria wanted to obtain American and British guarantees that South Africa would not be hammered by further sanctions in the event that all hell broke loose upon Mandela's release and the government was obliged to crack down again. He must have known that no foreign government could offer his security establishment such a blank check; but the question told us what he was facing at home. Mercifully, the subject of a Reagan-Botha meeting did not arise.

When details of the pass law reform were published on my return to Washington, we hailed the move as "a major milestone on the road away from apartheid . . . perhaps the most conspicuous discarding of discriminatory laws in recent South African history." But this was to be the high water mark of 1986. Within weeks of lifting the state of emergency, urban unrest began to escalate once again. Activist-led boycotts of white businesses in several areas of the country and continued labor troubles were driving white attitudes in the wrong direction. The existential test of strength within the black community—and between it and the government—was the dominant fact of political life.

Beneath the surface, the government remained profoundly split. Some saw the Commonwealth EPG as an ideal vehicle for forcing the ANC and its allies to make hard choices. Others wanted to prevent negotiations until the government had first smashed the black resistance movement. Security force planners were straining at the leash to mount strikes against neighbors, and broke off the leash in two separate incidents on the very day that I had met Botha in Geneva.

In late April, we began hearing ominous South African comparisons of our mid-April strike on Libya and their "anti-terrorist" strategy in Southern Africa. We and other major Western nations also began to receive urgent South African appeals that the Western powers address the issue of violence in South Africa at their upcoming Group of Seven economic summit in Tokyo. African policy officials in several Western governments, including ours, worked hard to get some appropriate language on South Africa into the draft communiqué. But we lost this battle: on May 5, the Tokyo summit issued a statement condemning terrorism and the Libyans, but making no reference whatsoever to developments in South or Southern Africa.

It was a major blunder to utterly ignore Botha's appeal for a signal that we were at least paying attention to the delicate process under way in his country. Western governments, after all, were his most demanding critics and the only source of constructive influence on him. Did we simply not give a damn? Something snapped in the man; xenophobic anger overtook his common sense. Within two weeks, the EPG initiative and the tentative hopes for reform and negotiation lay in ruins. As we have seen, Botha unleashed his security establishment, and turned decisively toward the road of repression. The partisans of polarization—in Western capitals, in black Africa, in the Commonwealth, among black South African opposition leaders, and within Botha's government—would soon have the upper hand.

How We Lost the Second Sanctions Battle

These were not great moments in South African decisionmaking. Botha was repeatedly led astray by listening to the sycophants and wishful thinkers in his inner circle. His sense of strategy was flawed by his very African penchant for believing that distant foreigners were the source of his problems and could become his *deus ex machina*. Although he was the supreme leader of a regional superpower, P. W. Botha, ironically, had the mind of an embittered Third World dictator seeking foreign help against local enemies.

But these were not great moments in American diplomacy, either. It was not a question of whether to "help Botha," but of how best to help ourselves. The place to start was by continuing to place hard choices before him—not easy ones. We needed to make him think. Our inability to get Western leaders to take South Africa seriously at the Tokyo summit helped to guarantee that they would have to do so later. Similarly, our own multiple channels and indiscipline hurt the realists and helped the wishful thinkers around Botha. Our changing signals on terms for a Reagan-Botha meeting led to cynicism: did we have *any* bottom line, or would we just keep asking for more than he could deliver?

In an ideal world, we would have defined clearly and sharply what it was that we needed from Pretoria, pushed the message consistently from the top, bridged our position to that of the key Western allies, and stuck to it rigorously. But by the end of June 1986 we had few good options left. We still had a sound regional strategy; but we could not conduct it under current circumstances. We had at best two to three weeks before the Republican Senate leadership would begin to chart its own course—just as Nancy Kassebaum had warned. The administration was increasingly isolated on South Africa, which had once again become an angry, festering sore.

Meanwhile, the game was nearly over for a growing number of major U.S. corporations with investments in South Africa. It was becoming ever more arduous to ward off domestic pressures for disinvestment from South Africa. Some of the roughly 350 American firms involved were starting to pull out. Yet this, in our view (and theirs), made no sense whatsoever in South African terms: it would remove a positive, though limited influence, as equal opportunity and black advancement programs under the Sullivan Principles would be eroded. What would replace them? Disinvestment would predictably hand U.S. corporate assets over to others with fewer principles at bargain prices. But in the United States, the protests, shareholder proposals, public and employee relations problems, and restrictive local and state ordinances related to South Africa were all having an effect—though not, perhaps, precisely the effect intended. They were wasting the time, money, and energy of top leadership in boardrooms across the country.

In an ultimate affront to the rage and fear engendered by the South African drama, apartheid was becoming a first-class nuisance. Corporate leaders had little doubt that staying in South Africa was the right thing to do. But, in cost-benefit terms, they could not justify spending 25 percent of their time on debates over their activity in a country that accounted for perhaps one half to 1 percent of their business. They had better things to do. In a rebuff to Marxist devil theory, our government was urging U.S. firms to hang on well after many of them had decided to leave. As Shultz and I heard in a meeting with the CEOs of IBM, General Motors, Johnson & Johnson, and others on July 1, 1986, the "flak factor" was completely out of hand. An immediate and forceful expression of presidential leadership on the issue was imperative.

We were hearing the same message informally from members of Shultz's advisory committee, established by Reagan's 1985 executive order. This was not altogether surprising: selected largely for its bi-partisan respectability and representativeness, the group echoed America's high-prestige boardrooms. An exception was former Under Secretary of State Larry Eagleburger. A rock-solid champion of our regional strategy, he knew that we faced a politically driven stampede. But the best defense would be a forceful assertion of presidential vision to clarify U.S. goals, supported by the adoption by the President of a range of political and mild economic sanctions. Eagleburger understood that a way must be found for both the administration and Congress to get credit for any policy adjustments made.

A policy review under such circumstances would have risked everything, serving up our strategy as an entrée to the carnivores of Washington. That did not stop Poindexter from informing the press in late June that a review was under way—a claim the White House spokesman described as exaggerated and the State Department called premature. Some congressional voices wanted us to undertake a truly dramatic initiative, such as inviting Botha and Mandela to Camp David where Reagan would "take them to the woodshed." The mind boggled.

By early July, internal State Department planning focused on a package of new moves. First, we prepared a list of largely non-economic sanctions aimed at getting the attention of Pretoria and white South Africans generally. Such measures might be announced immediately, in hopes of maximizing their current impact in Pretoria and with restive Republicans in Congress. Or, we might make a "down payment" of such measures now, but signal that further measures would be the subject of consultations with Commonwealth and European Community leaders in light of the results of Sir Geoffrey Howe's mission to the region. Strengthened allied coordination would be a central element of either approach: the South Africans would have greater reason to respond if the principal Western nations were clearly united.

We developed a parallel package of initiatives to expand funding for our assistance programs for black South Africans and for the regional Front Line State economies, focusing particularly on the key transport sector. This was partly a way of making a gesture of support for the victims of Pretoria's bursts of brutality; and partly a way of underscoring the message that we wished to strengthen the region's economy, not weaken it by punitive economic sanctions whose main victims (apart from black South Africans) would be South Africa's neighbors.

We also developed ideas for raising the profile of our dialogue with the ANC leadership, and using it specifically to test the organization's seriousness about negotiation. We would use our contacts to focus on the shape of a post-apartheid future, underscoring our conviction that Marxist-Leninist principles were the last thing South Africa needed. Raising the visibility of our ANC contacts would directly confront Pretoria's absurd attempt to dictate who should be on the other side of any future table. It would remove the risk—which I had managed so far to prevent—that we might be maneuvered by Pretoria and its U.S. sympathizers into rejecting contact with the ANC unless it "changed its spots" as a precondition. The PLO parallel was to be avoided at all costs.

However unattractive some aspects of ANC policy were, the government itself was anything but a rose. Meeting visibly with the ANC would set an example to Pretoria: talking to someone does not mean that you approve of them or agree with them. Placing our weight solidly behind negotiation would be the best way to signal to all parties the alternatives they faced. We would contrast South Africa's bright potential with the grisly alternative if whites continued down the road of defiant repression and black militants continued to believe that they could overwhelm the state.

We also grappled with how best to deliver the new messages and implement a supporting diplomacy. Should we strive for dramatic effect by mounting a high-profile diplomatic initiative? This course would offer the best immediate impact, especially in the congressional context. But the impact was likely to be short-lived; there were no grounds for believing that anything much could be accomplished in the awful climate of mid-1986. Why advertise the limits on our influence by trying to sail into the wind? A mission by Shultz to the region would be postponed; it made more sense for the regional parties to know that we strongly supported Sir Geoffrey Howe's mission.

From every quarter, we heard the message that Reagan needed to lead if he wished his party and his country to follow. While the State Department message on apartheid and sanctions was somewhat effective, that did not cut ice politically when the President was "invisible" or sending garbled messages on the worsening situation. As a friend in the House put it, the President needed to do something unequivocal, to "light a symbolic candle for apartheid's victims." In early July, I laid out for Shultz a scenario including consultations with Howe after his first round of meetings in Africa, a quick vetting in the interagency process of our "new wrinkles," the drafting of a major speech for delivery by Reagan, and parallel testimony by Shultz, who was scheduled to appear in the Senate Foreign Relations Committee on July 23. The Reagan speech would, of course, be the centerpiece.

Shultz was uneasy about hanging our South Africa policy from a presidential speech. Speechwriting could be difficult to control. It could become a substitute for a policy review. There was also the question of the President's own instincts on the issue. Sadly, Reagan failed to convey a sense of outrage on racial issues. His comments regretting the violence and killings were linked to the argument that much of it was blacks killing blacks, a point which implied that the problem was "tribal." Reagan, like Botha, drew sharp distinctions between "responsible" black leaders (a phrase familiar to South Africa watchers) and the militants of the UDF and the ANC. When pressed on whether he would ever "go beyond friendly persuasion," Reagan fell into the trap of saying that Botha himself was trying to eliminate apartheid. While there was a kernel of reality in his arguments, the President tended to discredit his case by sounding so much like the government from which he was so reluctant to distance himself.

But we had little choice, so we began work on Reagan's speech. Our first drafts would have had Reagan address the debate as the leader of Abraham Lincoln's party. He would have reached out to all Americans and tried to unify them behind a shared statement of our values and interests, defining "constructive engagement" correctly as U.S. involvement in the struggle for peace and justice throughout the region. He would also have reached out to Botha and to white South Africans generally, making clear that the United States did not want one evil system replaced by another, and signaling an understanding of white anxieties and fears. But he would have added that Americans were united in outrage at the recent turn of events, the government's failure to grasp openings, and the destructive cycle of bad decisions including Pretoria's latest crackdown and its bullying of neighboring countries in May–June 1986. And he would have reached out to black leaders across the spectrum, making clear that we shared their aspirations for liberty, equal opportunity, a rightful share of power, an end to racism.

These early drafts would have announced a sweeping series of fresh initiatives—a sizable U.S. commitment ($200 million) to enhanced assistance programs for black South Africans and the neighboring states; a renewal of Reagan's 1985 executive order plus additional, targeted sanctions against South African Airways and tough new visa restrictions on official visitors to the United States; a prohibition on new investment by U.S. firms which did not adhere to the Sullivan Principles; and allied consultations on strengthening the U.N. arms embargo and banning computer sales to government agencies. These moves were linked to a renewed effort to launch negotiations where the Commonwealth initiative had just left off.

Shultz found the tone of our early drafts to be messianic, taking on responsibilities beyond our leverage. Some of the proposed moves would be a hard sell in the White House. And it was tactically wrong, Shultz believed, to shoot all our bolts at one time in a presidential speech now scheduled for July 22. Our best shot would inevitably be labeled inadequate by some at home. Besides, we would get more mileage from a series of actions and gestures, a phased approach, one that left people here and in South Africa guessing as to what we might do next. In addition, we should avoid unilateralism; instead, Shultz believed we should tie our own diplomacy to the European Community–mandated Howe mission and explicitly bridge our funding initiatives to broader Western ones. Our ultimate sanctions decisions should also reflect these allied consultations.

Reagan, we agreed, should still state his reservations about punitive economic sanctions, but also note that the United States did not oppose sanctions on principle: they were a last resort when all else fails. He would note that the United States was already applying more sanctions to South Africa than our allies did. He would not rule out further measures, but would stress instead the central importance of having the industrial democracies speak together as a force for moderation and reconstruction. Thus, Reagan would create a two- to three-month "window" for rethinking in South Africa, consultation with our allies, and preparing a future report to the Congress and the American people.

A draft speech along these lines finally went to the National Security Council on July 8. But by July 13, I had to report to Shultz that we were in deep trouble. Our draft had basically been ignored. What came back to us was identified as a "Buchanan/NSC" draft. This label confirmed the appalling news I was hearing from my NSC counterpart. Poindexter could not (or would not) control the process at his end; the only way he could get White House Chief of Staff Don Regan's chop was by letting Pat Buchanan do what he wished with the speech. Permitting Communications Director Buchanan to mess with the basics of American foreign policy was to me almost obscene. How could the National Security Council have sunk to such depths of irrelevance?

Whatever the answers, the only thing standing between the State Department and the hard right was the common sense and good judgment of Don Regan. The value of that protection was revealed—a few days later—when Regan spoke to journalists about the importance of South African mineral exports, wondering if American women were "prepared to give up all their jewelry." * Shultz's caution about speeches suddenly flooded back to me. The interagency "process" was in the hands of people who knew dangerously little about everything from American foreign policy and Southern African affairs to the structure of the diamond market.

The Buchanan draft was a stridently polarizing message. It would give no U.S. senator apart from Jesse Helms and a few associates any ground to stand on. A presidential veto of economic sanctions was threatened up front. There were two or three lines about Pretoria's official violence and nearly a page about ANC terrorism and the "necklacing" of blacks by township comrades. South Africa was compared favorably to the rest of Africa, and our interests in the region reduced essentially to an anti-Communist manifesto. The *real* bottom line was to keep South Africa's minerals and ports out of Soviet hands! There was no diplomatic game plan, no effort to reposition ourselves in the

---

* *The New York Times,* July 20, 1986.

debate, no call for contact and negotiation with the ANC, no regional assistance program in the Front Line States, and no real call to action or threat of action. This draft was not even equivocal; it was pro-Pretoria.

But the speech itself was not our only problem. In a meeting with South African Ambassador Herbert Beukes, he revealed specific knowledge of virtually every new angle we had been considering, as well as the efforts of Defense Department and CIA officials to water them down or reverse them. Beukes spoke of "assurances" he had received from the White House that Pretoria need not worry. The subversion occurring in our own ranks took multiple forms. We learned that the CIA had distributed a draft "special estimate" on the ANC around town, despite opposition to its contents by most of the intelligence community. The purpose of the draft was obvious: to discredit the concept of higher-level American contacts with the ANC and to undermine the argument for pressing Pretoria to unban and negotiate with it. The movement was described in familiar, Buchananesque terms.

The battle of the speech drafts lasted from July 13 to the day of the speech, July 22. We managed to correct many of the glaring problems. But inevitably a paler and more ambiguous message resulted. It no longer sang. It contained too many opaque phrasings aimed at retaining ideas without giving offense. Inevitably, the key elements of our original action plan were whittled down and a number of major issues sidestepped.

On July 19, we received a draft that was frustratingly close but still not enough to help the administration seize the initiative. Alongside our vibrant language on apartheid, we found formulations that looked as if they came from the editors of the South African Broadcasting Corporation: instead of eliminating all apartheid laws, the Buchanan-NSC draft sought the elimination of "the vestiges of apartheid." Instead of seeking a democratic system in which the rights of majorities, minorities, and individuals would be protected, the Buchanan-NSC draft sought a government (no reference to "democratic") which would protect the rights of "all peoples." This was vintage Afrikaner-speak, and would instantly be recognized as such by anyone half-literate on the subject. So, too, would the heavily caveated references to U.S. communication with all parties "committed to peaceful change"—wording inserted to provide a base from which to fight against our plans for meeting with the ANC at higher policy levels.

On the way over to brief the press and hear Reagan deliver the speech, Shultz and I passed by Poindexter's office just as the door opened. Out they came, the President's own South Africa lobby: Bill Casey, Pat Buchanan, and several aides. Shultz growled that they would be well advised to keep their hands off the latest draft we had seen. But the crime had already been committed. Now, we supported the elimination of "apartheid laws" (not "all apartheid laws"); we favored the unbanning of "black political movements" (not "all black political movements"). The words "democratic" or "democracy" did not figure in the President's vision for a future system. Now, we said little specifically about black fears and anger but spoke eloquently about "the social, economic, and physical security of the white people in this land they love and have sacrificed so much [sic] to build."

With this speech, the "great communicator" became the great polarizer. Botha must have been delighted to read one sentence: "Then, there is the calculated terror by elements of the African National Congress: the mining of roads, the bombings of public places, designed to bring about further repression, the imposition of martial law, eventually creating the conditions for racial war." The abuse of logic reminded one of other times and places; South Africa's state of emergency was now the fault of the ANC. But Botha must have particularly enjoyed hearing that he could choose which blacks to talk to: "the South African Government is under no obligation to negotiate the future of the country with any organization that proclaims a goal of creating a Communist State—and uses terrorist tactics to achieve it."

Had anyone stopped to consider that Sir Geoffrey Howe would be seeing Botha in a few days in order to take up the EPG's concept of "matching commitments" on violence between the government and the ANC? Had anyone thought about the inconsistency of those sentiments with another part of the speech, which expressed support for the mission of Thatcher's foreign secretary? Botha must have been intrigued to receive a letter from Reagan, dated July 22, repeating this theme, and talking earnestly about the urgency of creating a negotiating framework.

We lost the sanctions debate on July 22, 1986. The day after he had met with Republican senators on the issue, Reagan lost most of them. He gave them no ground on which to stand against the pro-sanctions crusade. His strident pro-Pretoria tilt disarmed those in Congress who preferred to let the executive branch conduct policy toward this complex region. The speech triggered a bi-partisan storm. It literally forced a split in his party in the Senate—a mere three months before a mid-term election—and obliged legislators to make the best of a bad situation. Soon, they would be trying to do from the outside what we had been trying to do from within: to reposition ourselves by sending some more signals, to heal our own needless wounds, and to acquire some fresh leverage for the next act in the drama. But, no matter how skillful, legislators cannot conduct diplomacy, and most of them realize it. Only we could have done these things in mid-1986. But the daylight robbery masquerading as the "U.S. foreign policy process" had not permitted us to do our job.

Seizing Defeat from the Jaws of Defeat

These dramatic conclusions did not all become clear in one day. We did not give up trying to find a way to assert leadership. Testifying in the Senate the next day, July 23, Shultz offered testimony based on the speech that Reagan should have given. He stressed the importance of negotiation in South Africa, and spoke of his firm plan to advance that process by meeting with the ANC's leader in exile, Oliver Tambo. Shultz spoke enthusiastically of our interest in bolstering the regional economy through assistance to transport systems among the Front Line States.

On sanctions, Shultz declared: "We are prepared to take action, with our allies, to change the mix of our pressures—positive and negative— to meet the rapidly changing course of events in South Africa and to play an essential supporting role in advancing South Africans toward the objective of a decent, democratic, prosperous and civilized society for all who live there." His bottom line was that the administration sought to work closely with our allies. To do so, we required maximum flexibility and discretion: "This is not a situation in which we can afford to be locked in the straitjacket of rigid legislation, no matter how well intentioned, or carefully drafted, to anticipate events that may or may not occur."

By July 24, the White House line was changing hourly. Reagan responded to shouted press questions at a South Carolina photo opportunity by shouting back: "We haven't closed any doors." His press spokesman said that the Reagan speech had only ruled out punitive or "broad" economic sanctions; this did not mean that he was against other measures. Pressed for examples of the sort of measures Reagan might consider adopting, the spokesman blurted out such things as a ban on South African Airways landing rights in the United States, visa restrictions, the freezing of certain bank assets, and perhaps some of the measures under consideration by the European Community and the Commonwealth. We were coming back full circle to where the early drafts of Reagan's speech had started. But this was foreign policymaking on the run—running down a slippery slope.

By now, Nancy Kassebaum had introduced a bill to ban new investment. Senate Majority Leader Bob Dole called on the floor of the Senate for the appointment of a presidential emissary to swing into action. Dick Lugar circulated the outline of proposed legislation, including items like air links and visa restrictions, plus trade bans on certain products from

South Africa's parastatal companies (e.g., the iron and steel company ISCOR).

NSC and White House officials began casting about for fixes that would hold things together at least through the August congressional recess. Elaborate scenarios were rushed in our direction: a presidential envoy to be announced immediately, renewed confirmation of U.S. support for the U.K. mission (in Pretoria for another round on July 29), a meeting of key Western foreign ministers to be called by the British immediately after the Commonwealth Summit, due to open in London on August 3, and travel by the U.S. envoy to Southern Africa in time to meet Botha before his mid-August party meetings and our mid-August congressional recess.

But such frantic maneuvers would only set us up for ridicule. Our hopes now were dependent on Howe's African mission. By July 29, Howe had been insulted by both Front Line State Chairman Kenneth Kaunda and P. W. Botha. The ambitious ideas coming from Poindexter's office were chilling in their naivete. If we sent out a presidential envoy, which U.S. policy would the envoy represent and to whom would the envoy report?

I became Washington's envoy, and my brief was simply to consult the Europeans in an effort to shore up *their* moderation, since this might help keep Congress from going too far off the reservation. Mark-up of the Lugar legislation began on July 29, and it was soon amended on the Senate floor (by narrow majorities) to include a broad range of high-sounding but patently protectionist import bans borrowed from the Commonwealth list of measures Thatcher was resisting in London. Our best hope would have been for the Senate to buy time—using reports to Congress and links to allied decisionmaking—during which the European, Commonwealth, and American decisions could be sorted out.

But Thatcher now had no choice but to give some ground at the Commonwealth mini-summit. On August 5, a majority at the mini-summit endorsed a sweeping list of non-binding (voluntary) economic and other sanctions measures, ranging from visa, tourism, and air links to bans on new investment and loans and imports of South African agricultural goods, coal, uranium, and iron and steel. This meeting only fueled the bidding war on the floor of the Senate, making it more difficult for Lugar to hold the line. Britain took the modest step of accepting the voluntary ban on new investment and on tourism promotion, pending consultations with the European Community in early September.

On August 15, the Senate voted 84 to 14 for a sanctions bill; the President had carried about 25 percent of his own party. The bill would end landing rights; ban new investment and new public and private sector loans; entrench in law the President's September 1985 executive order; prohibit petroleum exports; and ban imports of agricultural and fisheries products, coal, uranium, textile products, and imports of iron and steel. An awesome range of executive branch reports were tasked on everything from Western dependence on strategic mineral imports to the role of the South African Communist Party in the ANC. A series of specific "conditions" were identified—most of them borrowed directly from the EPG exercise—which South Africa would have to meet before sanctions could be lifted. The President was instructed to report back in one year as to which additional measures he favored imposing if there had been no progress. In a sweepingly unconstitutional seizure of prerogatives, the bill purported to instruct the President on how to vote in international gatherings and how to conduct his diplomacy.

It was a stampede. By now, over sixty U.S. firms had pulled out of South Africa (GM and IBM would follow suit in October). On August 25, the California Senate approved a bill requiring the divestiture by state pension funds of some $11 billion of equity in companies doing business in South Africa; Republican Governor George Deukmejian would sign the bill this time around, having vetoed it in 1985. Such measures had already passed in nineteen states and sixty-five cities. What was happening? It was not that the wisdom of going down this road had suddenly become apparent. On the contrary, a chorus of caveats were voiced. But there was an urgent, burning need to send messages, take stands, express disgust, respond to the black South African–American campaign, reject Botha's own defiance, and to show some distance from Ronald Reagan's apparent refusal to lead on an issue perceived overwhelmingly as a civil rights matter. For politicians this was, after all, an election season.

Meanwhile, in South Africa political polarization and violence grew apace. Pretoria threatened sanctions against its neighbors to retaliate for their own calls for sanctions. Botha told his governing National Party at a special convention that the outside world should not "underestimate" his people: "I'm not a jellyfish, we're not a nation of jellyfish." In Parliament a few days later, opposition deputy Helen Suzman—the distinguished anti-apartheid campaigner and champion of black rights—said that Pretoria's emergency regulations had been written by "men drunk with power, men on a high who have paid scant attention to clarity of language and none whatever to the law of natural justice." The government's response was to accelerate the stampede to full-blown martial law. The test of strength had entered a new phase.

The EC members were not so readily stampeded. On September 16, they adopted bans on new investment and the import of iron, steel, and gold coins. As we had hoped (and quietly advocated), a proposed ban on coal imports valued at $1.3 billion was dropped from an EC list approved earlier (thus saving thousands of black miners' jobs). We hoped that Europe's moderation would give us ammunition and enable the Washington "policy process" to redeem itself.

When the Congress returned from its summer recess, Reagan renewed the 1985 executive order for another year. But no new sanctions cards were played, and the general administration line remained opposed to the Senate bill. Authorized leaks began to seep out that we were about to appoint Edward Perkins, a black Foreign Service Officer, as our next ambassador to Pretoria. It became known that Shultz was planning a two-week Africa trip that would include stops in Southern Africa and be aimed in part at energizing negotiations.

The struggle between the executive and Congress suddenly clarified on September 12, when the House passed the Senate sanctions bill by a vote of 308 to 77. Rather than run the risk of a time-consuming process and a possible "pocket veto" by the President, the House Democratic leadership had decided to drop a more draconian House bill. A ten-day clock started ticking for the administration to decide whether to sign the legislation, veto it, or let it become law without taking any action. Reagan's sentiment was strongly in favor of vetoing the bill. But there would be no hope of sustaining a veto unless it were accompanied by a credible alternative—that is, by fresh evidence of administration initiatives, backed by another set of sanctions promulgated by executive order, as in 1985. The time had come to deal.

Strangely, however, there seemed to be little inclination to play this hand. Shultz had developed an excellent working relationship with Lugar, and had the credibility to negotiate on the administration's behalf. But Lugar, who had pulled last year's bill off the table at administration behest, was not interested in last-minute maneuvers this time around. He told the administration that it had forfeited the opportunity to lead on South Africa. The Senate (led by Lugar) had produced legislation which he strongly believed to be responsible and moderate. Reagan should sign it to unify and strengthen America's voice and place the country on "the right side." Regan and Poindexter undertook their own probes of Senate Republicans and found (surprise!) that there was a range of views. Dole encouraged them to believe in the veto option and undertook to poll his fellow Republicans on what would be needed to sustain a veto.

Lots of trial balloons went up. Anything remotely resembling an "initiative" was seized upon by one or another faction and leaked by "sources" to test or stimulate a congressional reaction. Everything we did—or considered doing—was interpreted by others as mere tactics. This was the case with the bruited Shultz trip to Africa and the imminent announcement of a new ambassador. It was the case when I met with Oliver Tambo in London on September 20 to lay groundwork for an October visit by Shultz to Africa that would include a stop at ANC exile headquarters in Zambia.

At around the same point, the State Department and the Agency for International Development (AID) put the finishing touches on a $500 million supplemental assistance proposal that arose out of an August mission to Southern Africa led by AID administrator Peter McPherson. It would include such beneficiaries as Mozambique and Zimbabwe—places that were not exactly top choice in Helms's country. These moves made foreign policy sense; properly construed and orchestrated, they could have helped us tactically as well. But that was expecting too much: Senate conservatives, activists, and the Casey–Buchanan–Regan axis worked to thwart us.

With twelve hours to the deadline for decision, there was still no coherent position. Some White House elements spent their time reassuring noisy but politically irrelevant right-wing activists. It baffled us at first: did Buchanan think we could make a deal on sanctions with the far right? But then we realized that his goal was to prevent any deal, and afterwards—if Congress overrode the President's veto—find a way to blame others. Poindexter and Regan appeared unwilling to tell Reagan the hard fact that he was headed for a political and foreign policy disaster. Hence, they denied their subordinates the authority to propose serious and substantive new ideas in their Hill soundings. Officials in the NSC staff and the White House legislative office sought to mobilize Dole and others to line up a firm bloc who could sustain a veto. But they fell short because they were unsure of the ground under their own feet. Congressional staffers informed us that they had no confidence in what they were hearing from White House aides, and were uneasy that Shultz was not participating in these encounters. No one had a mandate to talk turkey in these circumstances.

A week before the deadline, the State Department recommended that Reagan veto the sanctions bill and issue a strong and principled veto message. It would applaud significant portions of the bill with which we had no problem, giving particular credit to its original Senate drafters who had tried to act with restraint before the bill became mired on the Senate floor. The message would announce the Shultz mission, our assistance initiative for Southern Africa and black South Africans, and the ambassadorial appointment of Edward Perkins. Then it would describe in non-polarizing terms our constitutional and foreign policy differences with some portions of this highly complex legislation. And it would outline a new executive order, including the bill's general statement of policy goals (which, in fact, had been drawn largely from administration pronouncements) and a number of the sanctions drawn from the legislation or the EC measures (e.g., air-landing rights, the ban on iron and steel imports).

Had our advice been followed, there is reason to believe that Reagan's veto could have been sustained. This was the way—the only way by late September—to prevent a highly destructive shift of policy control away from the executive. It was the way to reach out and do some healing without a philosophic flipflop on the sanctions issue. It was the way to regain needed leverage for the next phase of our diplomacy. We would have stuck to our principles, while giving a little ground in practice. It was still possible to avoid making the South African situation worse. An overridden veto, by contrast, was the worst outcome imaginable. Reagan's previous vetoes had been overridden only four times—none on highly visible issues. The hemorrhaging of the President's constitutional authority in foreign affairs would only get worse if he lost this battle. (The last overridden veto on a foreign policy matter had occurred over the highly contested War Powers Resolution in 1973.)

But that is what happened. The White House prevailed upon Shultz to attempt to interest Nancy Kassebaum in a deal on September 26 with a midnight deadline just hours away. (The senator was as amazed at the administration's ineptitude as Shultz was embarrassed at being in this position.) It was a polite but short meeting. Reagan's uninspired veto message was signed a few hours later. A warmed-over version of July 22, the ANC was attacked by name. No new initiatives of any sort were announced. The message expressed a desire to "work with Congress" in developing an alternative program of "executive actions" consistent with the recent EC decisions.

We made a final, final effort with Senate Republicans on September 29. (The House overrode the veto that day by a vote of 313 to 83.) Shultz and I reviewed the reasons for sustaining the President's authority in foreign affairs. An override would make it impossible for the administration to proceed with its planned diplomacy and force Shultz to cancel his mission. In Africa, an override would encourage leaders to think they could pick and choose which Americans to deal with. A divided policy could not work. We had been hoping for a helpful Reagan letter to Dole, putting some meat on the bones of his veto message. But that, too, was gutted by the domestic White House people. On October 2, the Senate overrode Reagan's veto, 78–21. We were just 12 votes short—

and we might have had them if permitted to do our job. Shultz promptly canceled his African mission.

Iran-Contra in Microcosm

By the end of 1986, the Iran-Contra mess threatened the Reagan presidency. But the passage over Reagan's veto of the Comprehensive Anti-Apartheid Act was Iran-Contra in microcosm. The protracted struggle over sanctions risked hobbling our diplomacy in an entire region, just as Iran-Contra made fools of us in the Middle East. Like Iran-Contra, the South Africa policy fiasco was scandalous. There was no discipline, no system, and apparently no means of keeping unauthorized personnel away from the vital machinery of decisionmaking. Every major element of our Southern African policies—policies Shultz had obtained presidential approval for—was the object of one form of sabotage or another in the NSC, the domestic White House, the CIA, or the Defense Department. Foreign officials informed us of the treacherous conduct of our "colleagues" in other agencies. But foreign officials were also beginning to wonder if anyone in the administration was in charge.

The funereal gloom in my office became especially heavy on the morning, a few weeks after the veto override, when we learned of the death of Samora Machel. The mounting surge of right-wing sabotage against our Mozambique policy would only increase with the death of this man who had impressed both Reagan and Thatcher. RENAMO personnel were using their connections to obtain access to offices in the White House and the Defense Department—a scenario almost designed to advance Soviet interests in Africa.

In 1986, RENAMO had set up shop with an office in the Heritage Foundation, a conservative think tank conveniently located on Capital Hill. Soon it became even more difficult to move any foreign assistance requests for Mozambique through the labyrinthine executive and legislative procedures. Sympathetic friends of a serious African policy, never many to start with, began to disappear on Mozambique. My superiors in State let out an audible groan when I approached, knowing that they would be asked to carry water to fratricidal Republicans and bemused Democrats on Mozambique. Other agencies, egged on by the RENAMO lobby, pressed for a Mozambique policy review, an idea that gathered force when Machel died and was succeeded by the less familiar and charismatic Chissano.

When he heard the news of the crash, Charles (Chas) W. Freeman, the senior deputy I had recruited to succeed Frank Wisner only six months earlier, looked at me quizzically. He had joined my team from his post in Thailand with high spirits to apply his renaissance intellect to a wholly new region. Freeman had a consuming appetite for serious foreign policy, and he had heard that we were in that business in the African bureau. But he quickly adapted, developing new layers of steel plate to cover an already tough hide. Between the body blows and self-inflicted wounds of 1986 he never winced. He just looked at me and said with an icy grin, "You never told me how much fun this would be."

Our relief that the sanctions debate had finally ended was outweighed by the outcome. And it was overshadowed by the knowledge that we had entered the period of maximum danger, the period of angry recrimination and the search for scapegoats. On the Hill and within the administration, there were whispers about the role of Shultz and myself in creating the mess. Deep down, most members of Congress knew very well that they could not conduct our diplomacy. Some of them were relieved that the battling might end now. But that would only happen if we could get our act together.

One of my closest partners urged me to resign swiftly. My resignation could be seen as an act of protest at the sheer incoherence within the administration as well as the terminal sanctimoniousness sweeping the land. It would be a chance to blow the whistle against the hijacking of U.S. policy in broad daylight, splitting our party, damaging the President, and handing the sanctioneers a needless victory. It would also afford me the freedom to state that constructive engagement was the only wise course, even if P. W. Botha and Ronald Reagan were not, perhaps, the ideal leaders to make it work. I dreamt of jackals tearing at a carcass left by lions on the African veldt.

But my resignation would have gratified too many of the wrong people. We still had the right strategy. I had no idea when we might be able to reactivate it or how much damage the battle in Washington would do to our basic framework. But I was hopeful that the parties would someday return to the regional peace process, provided *we* did not abandon it. I remained a believer in what we had set out to do, and particularly in the logic behind it: Southern Africa would achieve peace on a regional basis *before* fundamental political change would come to its troubled societies. As a practical matter, however, South Africa would probably not return to the peace process until after the government had effectively reasserted its control at home. This was tragic for all those who would pay the price in the test of strength that lay ahead.

But I could wait. I would not resign while George Shultz remained as solid as a rock in his support of my stewardship. Shultz knew better than I why we had lost the sanctions battle. He faced structural disarray on multiple fronts. To me, the African policy drama of 1985–86 was outrageous. But it required Iran-Contra—a few months later—and the basic personnel shake-up that ensued for the administration to restore itself. Only then would we regain the coherence to exploit the splendid global opportunities opening up before us. If Shultz was prepared to stay on and lead through all of this—saving the President from himself in the process—it seemed trivial for me to think of resigning.

PART IV

14

Angola and the Art of Indecision, 1986–87

By June 1986, Pretoria's renewed lurch toward repression and its attacks on its neighbors had triggered the collapse of the Commonwealth initiative and the final phase of our debate on sanctions. But the South Africans were not the only ones misbehaving. Back in February, Castro made a speech linking Cuban troop withdrawal from Angola to the end of apartheid, and declaring that Cubans would remain for another thirty years if necessary. In early March, the MPLA rebuffed the South Africans' conditional offer of a "date certain" one day after it was announced. Citing our new relationship with UNITA, dos Santos wrote a polemical letter to U.N. Secretary General Perez de Cuellar attacking our "credibility as a mediator" and calling on de Cuellar to take over the job.

Soon, we began hearing a refrain from multiple sources that "the Crocker initiative" was dead. According to this African, non-aligned, and European diplomatic "buzz," the regional balance had shifted against Pretoria. Now, the United States was itself isolated and it might soon be possible to force us to abandon linkage. This must have been music to the ears of my Soviet interlocutor, Vladillen Vasev, whom I met in Geneva on March 6, 1986 (just before the dos Santos letter to de Cuellar). Vasev mouthed the lingo of "new political thinking" he had just picked up from Mikhail Gorbachev's report to the 27th Congress of the Communist Party of the Soviet Union. The time had come, Vasev intoned, "to activize collective means to unblock regional conflict situations." But this crafty old veteran still wallowed in old thinking. He blasted the South African offer of a "date certain" as simply "the same old demand" for linkage, and noted with a grin that the peace process was dead-locked. It would only move if we abandoned our strategy and met Moscow "halfway" in the search for "an honest solution." Soviet obstructionism got another boost on April 8 when the Front Line States issued a communiqué fully supporting the MPLA's moves and echoing the call for the United Nations to replace Washington.

The U.N. Secretariat Tries Its Hand

In response to these maneuvers, we made it clear throughout our diplomatic network that we were prepared to receive Angola's positions via U.N. Secretariat officials, if Luanda preferred to avoid dealing directly with Washington. Turning the other cheek in this fashion placed the onus squarely on the Angolans to explain themselves. By appealing to the U.N. Secretary General to step in, the MPLA set itself up for another, unintended test. De Cuellar's special representative for Namibia, Martti Ahtisaari (concurrently a senior official in the Finnish Foreign Ministry), paid several visits to Luanda in response to dos Santos's March appeal. The Soviets may have hoped that U.N. officials would simply issue a report blaming Pretoria and Washington for the blockage. But they should have known better.

Ahtisaari was the perfect stand-in for us during these difficult months. He and Brian Urquhart—the United Nation's distinguished under-sec-retary general for political and peacekeeping matters—had been extremely helpful in 1981–82 in sensitizing me to the negotiating history and the requirements of U.N. peacekeeping. Urquhart epitomized the ideal of the practical peacemaker. No official in the U.N. system (and few diplomats anywhere) knew the issues or the players better than Ahtisaari. Few men cared more or worked harder so that Namibia would become free. Formerly accredited as ambassador to Tanzania, Zambia, Somalia, and Mozambique, Ahtisaari had acquired rich experience in African affairs. He had played an important role on the Namibian issue as the Secretary General's "special representative" for Namibia from 1978.

We kept Ahtisaari closely informed of the details of our negotiations throughout the 1980s. Accordingly, he was in an excellent position to take up where we had left off. This was an extraordinarily tricky under-taking for an international civil servant. The U.N. Security Council itself was on record "rejecting" linkage, despite the Angolans' *de facto* accep-tance of it in the 1984 proposal. Ahtisaari knew very well that Moscow and its clients were seeking not only to kill our diplomacy but also to destroy the link once and for all. His formal U.N. mandate was to obtain independence for Namibia, not to "sell" Cuban troop withdrawal, so he had to play his cards carefully.

But Ahtisaari's high credibility and diplomatic skill enabled him to speak with candor. He asked dos Santos all the right questions during his missions to Luanda starting in March 1986: Exactly what role did the Angolans wish the United Nations to play? Did the Angolans have new ideas for advancing the goal of Namibian independence? Did Luanda have anything new to say (to the U.N.) on its bottom-line terms for Cuban withdrawal? A substantial reduction in the timetable for withdrawal of the southern contingent of Cuban forces would be warmly welcomed by de Cuellar and could strengthen the United Nation's hand in responding to the Angolan request. The Secretary General was only prepared to work on the South Africans if there was some prospect of results.

The Ahtisaari missions of March and May 1986 paid off. Dos Santos not only confirmed the 1984 MPLA bid (thus confirming the continuing validity of our package deal). He quietly added, when reminded of what Kito had told Wisner and me, that Luanda could even consider reducing the time period for withdrawal of the southern Cuban contingent from three years to twelve months. Properly packaged as a "proposal," this could have provided the basis for some movement in the process. But dos Santos simply described it as an illustration of Angola's hypothetical flexibility; the 1984 "plataforma" remained valid. He offered nothing on the northern Cuban contingent, which remained off limits for discussion.

On the matter of how the United Nations should proceed, dos Santos simply urged Ahtisaari to go see the South Africans. In an ironic way, these exchanges actually confirmed that the basic structure of the process remained intact. Yet, by breaking off contact with us and kicking the can with the United Nations, dos Santos gave the impression of wandering about without any coherent strategy. Or perhaps he was just avoiding basic diplomatic decisions while he concentrated on the war against UNITA and waited for developments in South Africa (and Washington). Whatever the explanation, the gist of Ahtisaari's thinking would soon circulate amongst Western and African officials in New York: that is how the United Nations works. It would be hard to paint a glowing portrait of a government which appealed for U.N. involvement and then ignored the chance seriously to test its adversary.

Secretariat officials could do little more than communicate in an even-handed manner with both sides, and factually report on the logjam as the August 1 "date certain" approached. In fact, August 1 passed with barely a ripple. De Cuellar received a civil message from Pik Botha affirming that Pretoria remained prepared "to enter discussions at any time" to resolve the Cuban troop issue. We took the line that August 1 was a lost opportunity, not a deadline. The ball remained in Angola's court to demonstrate its seriousness about a negotiated settlement: the last move had been South Africa's November 1985 message accepting key parts of our 1985 "basis" proposal.

The Dust Settles and Pressures Mount

Later in August, dos Santos received visits from Andrew Young and Jesse Jackson. He may have believed that severing contact with us and schmoozing publicly with leading domestic critics of our efforts would pressure us in the midst of our sanctions fracas at home. But Young and Jackson gave him good advice: this was not the way to play his cards with the Americans. Reversing his ground, dos Santos then invited Reagan to visit Angola and other Front Line States to see the situation for himself. As an alternative, he invited himself to Washington. He called for the immediate establishment of diplomatic relations and an end to the U.S.-Angolan estrangement, and pledged to redouble his efforts for Namibian independence.

A Reagan visit to Luanda! I could just imagine the reaction of White House officials responsible for planning presidential travel. Fortunately, matters never got this far. No reply was needed since we never officially received the invitation, which appeared in a joint communiqué signed with Jackson. Later, when Kaunda of Zambia renewed it formally on behalf of the Front Line States, we replied by proposing the Shultz trip (canceled in early October after the sanctions veto was overridden). The real significance of dos Santos's hints and announcements in August 1986 was that he was already seeking a way out of the corner into which he had painted himself.

The U.S.-Angolan freeze triggered by our UNITA decisions had lasted six months. At the Non-aligned Summit meeting in Zimbabwe in September 1986, dos Santos took a markedly more moderate line, reiterating earlier Angolan-Cuban positions on the negotiations. Castro, by contrast, stressed his new linkage of Cuban withdrawal to the end of apartheid—a line not mentioned by his Angolan counterpart. The Cuban leader rubbed African participants the wrong way with rhetoric that portrayed him as the arbiter of Southern African events.

On September 24, Under Secretary of State Michael Armacost exchanged views with Angolan Foreign Minister Afonso Van Dunem

"Mbinda," Paulo Jorge's successor, in New York. Mbinda was upset that his president's invitation had not been received, and asked if we preferred to receive a written one or a personal envoy. Armacost politely noted that this was all rather premature: such summitry requires a political context. Did Angola have anything new to say on the negotiations? Mbinda defended his government's past actions, but steadily avoided substance, offering merely to pass along our "renewed desire" to advance the peace process.

That same September dos Santos informed de Cuellar that he was withholding his hypothetical offer of better terms for the timing of Cuban troop withdrawal (the hints given to Ahtisaari in March and May). He pointed to continued SADF attacks and Pretoria's continued insistence on discussing total Cuban withdrawal. In a November speech, dos Santos suggested that the resumption of direct negotiations with us depended on a positive U.S. response to his quest to establish diplomatic ties, a complete non-starter. He also claimed to be awaiting a meeting between Shultz and the Front Line leaders as a group, suggesting that he still felt the need for cover. By the end of the year, we still did not know whether Luanda had reached any basic decisions about war and peace. The Angolan leader was doing what the MPLA did best—avoiding major decisions.

His balancing act reflected the pressures and trends surrounding dos Santos. Of these, the war always came first. During the 1986 dry season, FAPLA forces avoided any major offensives. But after receiving substantial infusions of Soviet hardware, they kept UNITA under sustained pressure across a large southern arc extending around the edges of its southeastern stronghold. UNITA had proven that it could not be wiped out, but it often found itself on the defensive against more heavily armed FAPLA units. Its best response—as always in guerrilla operations—was to spread the government forces, avoid creating concentrated targets, and strike government positions at times and places of its own choosing. Temporarily, however, UNITA's attempts to take the battle to the enemy seemed unimpressive. From Luanda's perspective, the trends could have been worse. Rather than take major risks, the MPLA leadership coalesced around simply playing for time. The military situation did not oblige dos Santos to decide on major moves.

On the other hand, it made little sense for Luanda to continue isolating itself. By late 1986, we had orchestrated a range of indirect pressures on the Angolans to do something. Luanda's officials took heat from our European allies and their African friends for their continued lack of participation in any visible diplomatic process. Edging back toward the table would keep dos Santos's options open and deflect these pressures. As part of this process, dos Santos now authorized Manuel Pacavira, his ambassador in Havana, to pay a series of visits to Washington, where he quietly established a channel to my deputy, Chas Freeman. Pacavira's bottom line seemed to be that the MPLA was "prepared to be flexible" if conditions could be arranged that would permit a resumption of acknowledged negotiations.

There were other pressures for dos Santos to contend with in the final months of 1986 and early 1987. Jonas Savimbi had published a UNITA "peace platform" and he pushed his vision of Angolan reconciliation during a swing through Western European capitals in late October. The UNITA leader realized the need to make continued political headway with Western and African opinion. This was the way to pressure Luanda for talks and sabotage its campaign for strengthened political and economic ties in Europe. Eager to break out of a no-win defensive situation in the southeast, Savimbi was caught between his dependence on SADF help and the MPLA's conventional superiority on the margins of his areas of control. Dos Santos predictably snubbed any notions of negotiating with Savimbi, but he felt the need to counter UNITA initiatives by upgrading his own program of "pardon and clemency" and suggesting a broadened participation in the rubber-stamp People's Assembly. Behind the scenes, several MPLA officials were authorized to make "unacknowledged" contact with UNITA officials in European capitals. Nothing much came of this, and the door slammed again when the contacts leaked.

By January 1987, when Shultz made his often-postponed African trip, his itinerary carefully avoided Southern Africa. But stops in Nigeria and Côte d'Ivoire offered the opportunity to advance the "national reconciliation track" of our diplomacy and to coordinate closely with Savimbi as well. Our goal was to encourage key African leaders to consider what they might do to legitimize the objective of Angolan political reconciliation. One gambit we discussed was the reopening of the Benguela Railway bisecting Angola's central highlands and linking the Zambian and Zairean copperbelt to the Atlantic coast. The beauty of the concept was that the railway would have appeal as a means of reducing the hinterland's dependence on South African-controlled transport routes for moving their foreign trade. Yet, since the railway passed through UNITA-controlled areas, Savimbi's approval would be required. It might be a start to dialogue. U.S. political support for UNITA in key countries like Nigeria, Kenya, and Côte d'Ivoire created yet another problem for the MPLA leadership to contend with as it sought to continue avoiding decisions.

By early 1987 chaos in the Angolan economy was spreading. Oil output was growing rapidly as Western firms backed the development of this enclave sector surrounded on all sides by economic collapse. But total Angolan export revenues plunged by 40 percent in 1986 as a result of a collapse in world oil prices (oil now represented 90 percent of exports and nearly 70 percent of government revenues). The MPLA faced mounting economic pressures that obliged the regime to seek an eventual Western exit from the Marxist quagmire. Angola suffered from five separate curses: the Portuguese colonial legacy; the broader African economic crisis of the 1980s in which Angola shared; the specifically Angolan brand of Marxist economic policies; the scourge of war (absorbing 50–60 percent of foreign exchange and 40 percent of government spending); and the special curse of oil riches, which postponed the day of reckoning.

By the end of 1986, the effects of massive bureaucratic controls, official corruption and ineptitude, and heavy deficit financing had finally caught up with the MPLA. It was beginning to pile up arrears in its foreign debt, including military-related debt to the Soviets and Cubans, who were not amused at the loss of hard-currency payments. Four hundred state enterprises and a bloated overhang of security and regulatory officials had destroyed both agriculture and industry. The only areas of growth (apart from the oil enclave) were in foreign debt, official corruption, and ensuing political scandals.

The pressure for major economic reform which had swept the rest of sub-Saharan Africa had washed up on Angolan shores as well. Advocates of economic reform began to find their voice, and the MPLA leadership decided to announce a plan for economic and financial adjustment. Dos Santos began placing higher priority on cultivating ties with Western governments and bankers, especially European ones, and on meeting the criteria for admission to the World Bank and the International Monetary Fund.

As Angola's largest creditor, the Soviets bowed to the inevitable and rescheduled the huge debts piling up from arms sales that averaged over $1 billion a year, roughly comparable to total civilian imports in 1986. They, too, now supported Angola's turn to the West for improved economic ties: it was their only hope of getting paid. Arrears had also begun to build up on Angolan hard-currency obligations to the Cubans (averaging perhaps $300–400 million annually for support of Cuban troops, advisers, and civilian technicians). The economic crisis had finally begun to spill over into the sacrosanct military sphere, causing periodic strains on the Soviet–Cuban–Angolan triangle.

From Brazzaville to Luanda: Reengaging the MPLA

We resumed bilateral negotiations with the Angolans in Brazzaville, the Congo capital and former federal capital of French Equatorial Africa, on April 5, 1987. The black Mercedes sedans of Congolese protocol came to a stop outside a modest villa located in a residential complex originally built to house African summit meetings. We entered, turned up the air conditioning, and fended off requests for a scene-setter interview by Congolese television. We had traveled twenty-four hours on the explicit pledge by President Denis Sassou-Nguesso that Kito Rodrigues would head the Angolan side. Kito had confirmed the arrangement via the British. Vice Foreign Minister Venancio da Moura met with us the first day; by leaning hard on Luanda, Sassou managed to produce Kito the next day. A major diplomatic embarrassment was narrowly averted. After all, it was but a one-hour flight for the Angolans.

Washington was not particularly close to the Congolese, but we had quickly accepted Sassou's invitation to resume direct negotiations in his capital and had parried the initial MPLA suggestion of meeting in Paris. Everything discussed in a Paris encounter would miraculously leak to unhelpful journalists. We owed nothing to the French, who had spent much of the past three years making hay in the Third World at the expense of our policies. Fellow Marxists in rhetoric, and sporting a familiar African one-party system, the Congolese were the MPLA's only friendly neighbor. During the Angolan liberation struggle, they provided the MPLA with sanctuary and support. Cuban troops bound for Angola still utilized the Congolese port of Pointe Noire. The MPLA leadership should be comfortable meeting in Brazzaville.

We also saw an interesting chance to build upon Sassou's own motives. Central Africa needed peace. The confrontation in Angola risked exacerbating his already strained relations with Zairean President Mobutu Sese Seko across the great Congo River that separates Brazzaville from Kinshasa. A trained eye could spot the plainclothes Soviet intelligence operatives sprinkled at key points around town. But Sassou was far from being a Soviet client. A visit to the presidency quickly suggested that his Marxist tendencies were of the Louis XIV–Yves St. Laurent variety. He sought out the advice of his friend David Rockefeller to reinforce his American option. In addition, Sassou was the 1987 chairman of the Organization of African Unity. By hosting the resumption of our bilateral talks, he would be legitimizing them. In doing so, he would acquire a stake in our success. OAU chairmen are measured in part by their contributions to the resolution of disputes. We could build on these foundations.

Our instinct was correct. The Brazzaville meeting signaled the end of the formal, fourteen-month hiatus in negotiations. The endorsement of the acting OAU chairman offered a symbolic blessing. U.S. leadership of the regional peace process regained its luster, enabling us once again to mobilize and sustain pressure for a settlement. The Soviets understood this very well, reacting angrily to Sassou's initiative on which they had apparently not been consulted.

The April 1987 Brazzaville meeting also coincided with the passing of our political nadir in Washington. The bureaucratic and personnel shake-up flowing from Iran-Contra and the departure of Bill Casey (for health reasons) created a new foundation for the conduct of U.S. foreign policy. The arrival of Frank C. Carlucci as NSC Adviser, followed by Howard Baker in place of Donald Regan as White House chief of staff, restored the basic coherence of White House operations, and strengthened the administration's overall decisionmaking capabilities. Having served three tours in Africa during his Foreign Service career, Carlucci brought an unprecedented level of literacy to the administration's top ranks. His selection of Hank Cohen—one of the ranking Africanists in the service and my eventual successor as assistant secretary in 1989—as NSC Africa director reinforced the change and brought us an ally where we had often faced treachery in the past. To restore coherence, a sweeping series of NSC policy reviews was ordered. A revitalized National Security Council fended off Defense Department efforts to put our Front Line State and Mozambique policies up for grabs until the more critical South African and Angolan reviews were complete.

All this came none too soon. By the spring of 1987, we already faced murmurs of liberal congressional sentiment for another round of anti-South African sanctions if progress had not occurred by the first anniversary of the October 1986 legislation. Meanwhile, Senate conservatives introduced bills to cut off all U.S. assistance to Front Line States which supported any black South African movement that practiced "necklacing." This was a back-door attack on the ANC and our dialogue with it. South Africa's neighbors were being targeted in apparent retaliation for the passage of anti-South African sanctions. In both the House and Senate, legislation was introduced calling for full economic sanctions against Angola, including mandatory disinvestment by U.S. oil companies operating there. (Angola, at the time, was our second-largest trading partner in black Africa, despite the absence of diplomatic relations.) Our test of strength over Mozambique policy with the right wing was in full swing.

The shake-up in Washington gave us a fighting chance to win some of these battles and conduct our strategy. We moved quickly to implement the earlier, contested decision on contacts with the ANC. Shultz met with its exile leader Oliver Tambo in Washington on January 28—sending the important signals to multiple audiences which we had tried in vain to convey during the saga of 1986. It was an unprecedented U.S. action, causing significant right-wing indigestion, but charting the way toward the essential and inevitable task of negotiation among South Africans themselves. Shultz made clear that the meeting was not a gift to anyone, but a chance to probe and communicate. He told Tambo that we all knew what we are against in South Africa, but what kind of a future system are we for? What about the role of Communists in the organization? The last thing Africa needed was more Marxists. What contribution was the ANC prepared to make toward getting negotiations started? Was it prepared to set aside violence? He told Tambo that his waffling replies were "disappointing." This was the way to use U.S. influence: neither P. W. Botha nor the ANC's exile leadership were especially thrilled by the meeting. But that was not its purpose.

We faced a delicate task in deciding the proper stance toward bilateral Angolan economic relations. On the one hand, it made no sense at all to apply sanctions that would simply hand U.S. investment assets and opportunities to the Europeans. The MPLA would lose no foreign currency earnings from "sanctions" against the Angolan oil industry: it would find alternative markets, and alternative foreign oil companies to explore, develop new fields, and exploit the resource. Already a 1986 ban on new Export-Import Bank credits had handed lucrative opportunities to French and British exporters enjoying the support of their export credit agencies.

But, on the other hand, we needed all the leverage we could find with Luanda. The threat of further economic restrictions would carry some political weight in Luanda, where MPLA officials were hypersensitive to the slightest variations in our tune. In a few fields, we could deny technologies the MPLA wanted (e.g., dual-use civilian aircraft and radars). Our review came out right eventually: Reagan approved a policy of continued economic pressures, but stopped short of shooting American corporations in the foot, an increasingly common Washington pastime. A total economic embargo was proposed in the Senate by Robert Dole and Dennis DeConcini. But it fell short (61–38) in July 1987, enabling us to control the signals sent to Luanda.

We learned of the MPLA's imminent return to the table through nine distinct channels in early 1987, ranging from Western businessmen to the Mozambicans and Martti Ahtisaari. There was a momentary gnashing of teeth in some quarters of the administration and Congress over the prospect of renewing official contacts with Luanda. Had not the MPLA become our adversary with the decision to aid UNITA? Would not a meeting reduce pressure on Luanda and demoralize Savimbi? We believed otherwise. Shultz had made it clear to Savimbi in January that we would continue our multi-track strategy. Carlucci was comfortable; to keep him that way, I asked Hank Cohen to join me in the trip to Brazzaville, just as I had asked my Pentagon counterpart, Jim Woods, to accompany me to Luanda on my last trip there in January 1986. These would become good habits for the period ahead.

So, our Brazzaville meeting was something of a turning point. Substantively, however, it turned out to be a dry hole. For starters, da Moura and Kito described this as a "preparatory" meeting. Kito made much of having flown over to Brazzaville despite being acting president of Angola while dos Santos traveled overseas. This showed Angolan "goodwill" and enabled him to confirm the MPLA's "flexibility" on the southern troop contingent schedule. But there was no new official position. Asked why Luanda and SWAPO had done nothing to exploit Pretoria's "date certain" offer back in 1986, Kito replied that people sometimes distrust "those with big hands and startling proposals." I bit my tongue as I asked our Angolan friend what the next step should be. He invited me to Luanda for an official meeting in the near future (no date). He referred to the Angolan dialogue with Ahtisaari, and hinted that the northern Cuban contingent could also be discussed.

Experience had taught us to deflate expectations whenever we dealt with the Angolans of Luanda. Soon afterward, we learned that Kito had visited Brazzaville without having received the necessary "endorsements" at home. In other words, he had been sabotaged by domestic (or foreign) enemies for responding to our entreaties through Sassou that he personally attend. As Sassou would later describe it to me, "Kito burnt his wings." I often wondered exactly who had lit the match and why. It was the last time we would ever encounter this talented Angolan in the negotiations, and it would take another fifteen months (to July 1988) for the MPLA to field anyone comparable to head up the Angolan negotiating team.

Why *did* Luanda return to the table in April 1987? The probable answers range from the desire to gain the high ground, to deflect pressures from all quarters to reengage, to killing time while preparing for another bash at UNITA, and probing our intentions and our latest thinking. Just two weeks earlier, Ahtisaari's deputy, Hisham Omayad, had probed dos Santos again about reducing the southern contingent timetable, as had been discussed during 1986. Dos Santos informed Omayad that South Africa was now much weaker than before because of regional and internal developments, and claimed that his government had the upper hand regarding UNITA. While Angola faced problems, it was now in a stronger position and could not be expected to make the sorts of concessions that might have been considered earlier.

Whatever the precise mix of motives, Kito's and da Moura's performance in Brazzaville ended any illusions about the chances for immediate movement. The MPLA leadership was indulging in some dangerously wishful thinking about the regional situation. Dos Santos's apparent decision to return to a U.S.-led process and deactivate the U.N. track was followed by an unpublicized exchange with the South Africans later in April, presumably to compare their signals with ours. If nothing else, he would learn that Pretoria and Washington were barely on speaking terms, and that South Africa was less responsive to the United States— not more—in the wake of the sanctions fracas.

Six weeks after the Brazzaville encounter, Shultz received a letter from Mbinda, his Angolan counterpart. We were invited to Luanda in late June. (This would slip further to mid-July.) The bad news was that Mbinda had capitalized on Kito's woes to flex his ministerial muscles: he and his ministry had assumed charge of the talks. We groaned. Mbinda also noted that he preferred to communicate directly with U.S. officials (in third countries or via emissaries) rather than using British channels. We groaned again; British communications were one of the very few things that worked in Angola. Mbinda, contradicting Kito, stated that the northern contingent was *not* on the agenda. Finally, he complained about the "interlocutor chosen by your country": I had been discourteous in refusing to accept his deputy, da Moura, as my interlocutor and in twisting arms to get Kito to post in Brazzaville.

The decision to replace Kito with Mbinda seemed almost to confirm dos Santos's preference for treading water. Major diplomatic initiatives would hardly be entrusted to a cipher like Mbinda, who appeared not to grasp how the world was organized. A reserved and insecure member of the MPLA's well-placed Van Dunem clan (other Van Dunems held key justice and economic portfolios), Mbinda had worked previously in the presidency and a series of party jobs (youth, propaganda, information services, and foreign relations). Appointing him foreign minister had been an insult to foreigners; assigning him the task of dealing with us was an unfriendly act.

Nor were we especially encouraged by the signals we received from Minister of State for Production Pedro Van Dunem "Loy," who visited the United States for three weeks in June as the guest of non-governmental groups and personalities such as David Rockefeller. Loy was, at this time, a sort of economic czar and considered to rank with Kito near the very top of the regime. A rising star, the forty-seven-year-old Loy came across to Westerners as a soft-spoken, cherubic presence. His brief in the United States was to "educate" Americans and promote closer relations. He declined to engage in discussion of the negotiation, confining himself to general claims: for example, the MPLA hungered for peace, but it could not be asked to commit suicide. Loy described South Africa as a regional superpower which continued to occupy parts of Angolan territory. Angola was being asked to do without its Cuban "deterrent" and yet nothing was being offered in its place.

One fruit of Loy's diplomacy was the visit to Luanda in late June of a congressional delegation led by Congressman Howard Wolpe (D-Mich.), chairman of the Africa subcommittee of the House Committee on Foreign Affairs. Though no friend of the administration's policies, Wolpe performed a useful service by urging the MPLA leadership to make a major move. It could be linked to whatever conditions the Angolans required, but should cover *all* Cuban troops over a specific timeframe. Nothing else would move the administration in Washington, and only Washington could move Pretoria.

The developments of early July were mixed. We became aware that dos Santos had decided to mount a long-planned military offensive against UNITA. Another round of MPLA-initiated fighting would cast a pall over our efforts and probably provoke South African countermoves on UNITA's behalf. As for the South Africans, official repression in the wake of sanctions had taken a severe toll on black resistance movements and their leaders. Acts of violence had declined but a mood of angry confrontation prevailed in the townships, and the Botha government seemed to recognize that it could not restore the pre-1984 status quo. Reformers within the system were trying to mount an initiative aimed at the release of Mandela and the start of black-white talks, but these were fragile initiatives which would be quickly blown out of the water through any association with the United States. In early May 1987, parliamentary elections had given Botha a clear-cut law-and-order mandate, while the right-wing Conservative Party replaced the liberal Progressive Federal Party as the official opposition in the white chamber.

We carefully tested the water from time to time, but it was premature to try to reengage the South Africans. Our official dialogue was severely strained, even artificial. Pretoria was isolated and inward-looking. Its strategists were preoccupied with restoring internal order and coping with the changing military picture in Angola. They had no consensus or game plan for either. We worked hard in 1986–87 to engage our major allies in crafting a joint statement of democratic principles for a future after apartheid. The statement would have presented a tough challenge to South Africans of all races to look beyond the test of strength and clarify their vision of the country's future. But our allies had been burned by the previous year's events, including the fratricidal strife in Washington. We would have to go it alone: Shultz presented a powerful vision of hope for a democratic, post-apartheid South Africa in a New York speech in October 1987.

Recent events also raised basic questions about Soviet policy. Their basic message to Luanda was that the MPLA should solve its problems unilaterally—through military action, and by mounting its own internal political offensive to counter UNITA's call for reconciliation. Soon it would be apparent that Soviet arms and advisers were playing a central role in support of the MPLA's biggest effort yet to achieve a military victory. "New political thinking" had not yet made it to Southern Africa.

July 1987 in Luanda: "Basically a Waste of Time"

Following Mike Armacost's recent Moscow visit for talks on "regional issues," we decided that I should hold another meeting with the Soviets. The dialogue had tactical utility even if we had little reason to anticipate a constructive turn in Soviet conduct. To get maximum benefit from the exchange, I would see them just prior to my mission to Luanda. Anatoliy Adamishin, a deputy foreign minister, had recently taken on the African account in a reshuffle carried out by Eduard Shevardnadze. On July 2 we met with Adamishin and the veteran Vasev in London.

Adamishin's primary expertise lay in West European affairs. When he criticized U.S. policy, he sounded like a trendy European intellectual: we had become "more ideological" than the USSR, our fixation with "leaning on the USSR" would distract us from "more important issues" like Islamic fundamentalism and Third World debt. Adamishin could be gracious—"It's a pleasure to work with an old African wolf like you"— and his quick intellect meshed well with a good sense of humor. Sometimes, however, that humor reverted into familiar Soviet sarcasm: "You have more influence than we do, if you would only use it." He was capable of the kind of slick sincerity that made a new acquaintance instinctively check his wallet. But this youthful and charming official was one of the most attractive personalities on Shevardnadze's marketing team.

We had a prolonged session. Adamishin had come to probe our flexibility on the Southern African peace process. His basic pitch was that the talks were hopelessly deadlocked. But, at the same time, the prospects for U.S.-Soviet cooperation were better in Southern Africa than in any of the other regional conflicts (i.e., Nicaragua, Afghanistan, Kampuchea). This was the bait. If we were to work together, however, it would require that we establish a "new mechanism" for negotiation, perhaps upgrading the United Nation's role, and specifically the role of the Security Council, which would provide a context in which "to unite" the efforts of the United States and the Soviet Union. At present, the United States tried to serve as the pivot of all contacts, and played too many roles at once.

I examined the bait while avoiding the hook. I pointed out that if we emphasized purely procedural questions and ignored the substance, we would only be inventing new means of registering our substantive differences. Moreover, I questioned whether the talks were, in fact, deadlocked. The basic concept of linkage was clearly enshrined within the negotiating positions of both sides. But a substantial gap remained to be bridged on the Cuban withdrawal timetable. In this regard, the role of the Soviet Union and Cuba could be far more constructive. Instead of fueling the war, Moscow could encourage its friends to make peace. Instead of linking Cuban withdrawal to the end of apartheid, the Cubans could arrange to depart in the context of our settlement framework, which contained something for everyone.

Adamishin rejoined that Moscow had "no solution." But one way out of the deadlock was to break the link between Namibia and Angola and make the deal "less onesided." Namibia, he declared, was "ripe"— why not start there? The Soviet bottom line, it seemed, was to support its Angolan ally, defined as the victim of aggression, while seeking some solution that did not "harm the interests of the Soviet Union." As for the Cubans, Adamishin described them as "hostages" rather than fighters in Angola—a phrase Castro would have found interesting.

We left London wondering how much Adamishin really knew about the sweepingly ambitious Soviet-Angolan military plan about to be launched against UNITA. We wondered, too, how confident he was about the "deadlock" he had described with such apparent certainty. For our part, we had received reports from multiple sources, including MPLA officials, that Luanda intended to table fresh proposals at our next meeting. They had selected the timing after several postponements; presumably, they had something to tell us.

This was the logic behind our hopes as we returned to Luanda for talks on July 14–15, 1987, after an absence of some eighteen months. But Mbinda opened the meeting by announcing that he had no agenda and no proposals. Worse, he delivered a scathing diatribe about the U.S. role and argued that Washington needed to "rehabilitate itself" as an interlocutor by making a "gesture" (code for promising to abandon UNITA). It could have been an Angolan U.N. speech. Who on earth were the Angolans taking advice from? He was so badly briefed that he apparently did not realize that the administration had just helped to defeat sanctions legislation against his government in the Senate. Bristling, I told Mbinda that we had come to test the accuracy of the Soviet predictions we had just received in London. The Angolans were living up to Soviet expectations.

At this point, to save the mission from complete collapse, a coffee break was suggested. One of my colleagues whispered to me that da Moura, Mbinda's deputy, was thoroughly discomforted. Mbinda was at sea in discussing the negotiating history, and spoke with no apparent knowledge of previous exchanges with Kito and da Moura. Being ill-prepared for the exchange, he went on the offensive. Mbinda's ministry almost certainly had few files or memoranda of previous exchanges. Officials who know that they are surrounded by potential enemies do not put anything interesting on paper. The big question was whether or not there was anything interesting to put on paper. The only way to find out with these characters was to give them every opportunity to come up with something.

Carefully we recounted past U.S. and U.N. exchanges on reducing from three years to one year the timetable for withdrawal of Cuban troops in the southern zone. What "guarantee" or condition was Angola hinting at in return for such a move? Dos Santos, Kito, and Loy were well acquainted with the concept. The U.S. government could not be expected to guess at Angolan terms. Guarantees could take many forms: the *physical* guarantee of getting the SADF out of both Angola and Namibia under our settlement; the *juridical* guarantee of Security Council endorsement of the final settlement package; possible "side assurances" to each party by the mediator; the option of making Namibia formally a buffer state through a neutrality agreement; or the possible emplacement of a U.N. or inter-African military presence on the Namibia-Angola border after Namibia's independence. We asked Mbinda and his colleagues to think it over.

On the second day, the tone improved. Mbinda thanked us for our "interesting new ideas," then proceeded to reject some and ignore the others, leaving us as before with his opening position. The question of the Cubans in the north was not part of this negotiation. Angola and Cuba would address it when there was a fundamental change in regional conditions, including "the end of apartheid." What if we said one year for the southern contingent, three years for the northern contingent, consideration of an African force to fill in behind the Cubans, and a "process" of U.S.-Angolan normalization starting at the beginning of a settlement, I asked. Mbinda asked about the South African position. When I reiterated Pretoria's acceptance of the twenty-four-month, 80–20 percent withdrawal scheme, he looked surprised.

Mbinda and chief of staff Ndalu raised again the question of aid to UNITA. I advised them to drop it. The South Africans would respond by demanding that Luanda cut off all support to the African National Congress of South Africa. Did we really wish to expand the already complex agenda? As for U.S. aid, I warned that this demand would oblige me to raise the question of Soviet aid to Luanda.

We told the Angolans that we had no choice but to report to Washington that Luanda remained exactly where it was in October 1984—with the famous "plataforma." The United States could not negotiate with itself. Both Da Moura and Mbinda looked mournful. We would get a new position at "the next meeting"; perhaps the southern timetable could be reduced to thirty months. Our ideas merited "further study."

There were two ways to interpret our experience in Luanda in mid-July. Possibly, the MPLA leadership had not yet jelled around a new position but was, indeed, working on one. The meeting should have been postponed, but our hosts wished to avoid coming under further heat for the umpteenth postponement. Under this theory, the meeting failed due to characteristic Angolan disorganization and diplomatic ineptitude. But when a statesman is beset with hopes and pressures for results, it is sometimes hard to accept that failure flows from such random, non-rational sources.

I returned to Washington convinced that there were more sensible explanations. The Angolans were facing external pressure to rebuff us. Moreover, they were focusing on their dry season military offensive and on aggressively wooing European officials and lenders to help shore up their collapsed economy. The French and Portuguese were falling all over themselves to explore Angolan commercial opportunities. Against this backdrop, I concluded that Luanda wanted the appearance but not the substance of negotiation.

We acted in accordance with the "rational" theory of Angolan behavior. On July 22, I participated in a press conference on the U.S. Information Agency's Worldnet television system. The program had a wide African and European media audience. Asked about the Luanda talks, I replied: "Despite Luanda's earlier promises, no new proposals were made . . . and the talks were basically a waste of time." I referred to "clear disunity within the Angolan leadership" and "no clear instructions from the top." The MPLA was "still focused on military solutions."

Later, we backgrounded the press with the line that Moscow and Havana were blocking dos Santos from moving forward.

These remarks immediately ricocheted around Portuguese-speaking Africa. Da Moura quickly told his media that the MPLA did not consider the talks a waste of time, while Mbinda claimed to have heard new ideas from Washington in line with Angola's own thinking. At a regional summit meeting in Lusaka, dos Santos went further, making a public, presidential commitment: Angola would soon propose to the parties the framework for an overall settlement, to be signed by Angola, Cuba, South Africa, and SWAPO under the aegis of the U.N. Security Council. It was marvelous: we seemed to have found an MPLA hot button.

The Luanda government was scrambling for the high ground and committing itself to constructive action. Was this for show? Or would dos Santos now assert himself to demonstrate not only his interest in peace but also his capacity for independent decision? Even if he did, it looked to us as if Moscow and Havana had other intentions. I told Shultz as late as July 25 that we should lower our sights and muster whatever pressures we could to blast the process out of deadlock before our time expired. This would include expanded help for UNITA to reinforce the stalemate. But we should reconcile ourselves to the prospect that Luanda and its allies were playing a long game. In these circumstances, there would be little to discuss with the South Africans for the foreseeable future. The season for soldiers—not diplomats—seemed to be returning.

15

The Final Shoving Match, 1987–88

In July 1987, the end of Southern Africa's wars seemed like a distant dream. But the final eighteen months of the Reagan era proved to be the most eventful in the modern history of the region. We could not yet hear the rapids, but we were about to enter the fast water. The climax of the pre-negotiation period lay just ahead. By January 1988, the Cubans had joined our peace process as acknowledged participants, and we had achieved agreement on the basic linkage principle—Namibian independence and *total* Cuban troop withdrawal. By May, we had reengaged Pretoria and enticed the Angolans, Cubans, and South Africans to the table for direct talks under U.S. mediation in London. This nine-month period leading up to London was a time of decisive flux in the thinking and behavior of the parties. Regional experts and geopolitical pundits outdid themselves to explain things. Inside our government, officials argued their favored theories. But, ultimately, we had to rely on our instincts. We would need quick reactions to exploit the historic opportunity opening up before us. We seldom had a full deck of information, and could only see a fraction of what was happening around us.

Castro's Bids to Join the Settlement

The first major development in this new phase was a five-day visit to Cuba by dos Santos starting July 30, 1987. At its conclusion on August

3, Castro and dos Santos signed a communiqué confirming their readiness to modify their 1984 proposal and their willingness "jointly to pursue the negotiations resumed in Luanda in mid-July." On August 4, Mbinda sent us an Angolan-Cuban "response" to our "proposals" of two weeks earlier. In essence, the new proposal offered a reduction from three years to two years in the timetable for the withdrawal of the 20,000-plus Cubans in the southern sector (i.e., south of the 13th parallel which roughly bisects Angola). A phasing plan defined in 5,000-man increments was included. The proposed package agreement would, as dos Santos had said at Lusaka, be signed by Angola, Cuba, South Africa, *and* SWAPO, under the aegis of the Security Council's five Permanent Members acting as "guarantors." The new bid (like the old one) explicitly excluded the roughly 15,000 Cubans in northern Angola until an "appropriate time," when Angola and Cuba would review the possibility of their withdrawal. (We believed there to be about 37,500 Cubans in Angola at this time.) It was also linked to familiar conditions pertaining to a date for implementation of Resolution 435 and an end to all support for UNITA and all interference in Angolan affairs. Mbinda proposed U.S.-mediated talks among military experts and proximity talks to bring SWAPO into the loop.

The August 4 proposal itself was a modest step forward. By splitting the difference with us on the southern contingent and linking this move to a series of patently unacceptable conditions, dos Santos ran no risk that Pretoria or Washington might agree. By asserting Angola's capacity for decision, he was seizing the high ground at the very moment when his forces were gathering for their largest-ever bash at UNITA. Luanda promptly leaked its new proposal to advertise the move as a sign of Angolan "good faith."

Nonetheless, we finally had Angola's second bid in the drawn-out negotiation. Despite its obvious shortcomings, we welcomed the fact of a new bid as a significant step. So did Neil Van Heerden, the newly appointed director-general of South Africa's Foreign Ministry, who commented (before seeing the terms) that his country favored talking to neighbors and solving regional problems rather than leaving it to "big brothers far away whose interests are not always supportive of the region." He added, however, that it was highly unlikely that the MPLA "would be allowed to do anything which does not fit in with the Soviet plan." As soon as the terms were leaked, Pik Botha predictably rejected the new proposal.

The terms of the August 4 proposal were far less interesting than its genesis. What had happened during dos Santos's long visit to Havana? The "buzz" among Luanda-based diplomats was that dos Santos carried the plan with him and, after tough exchanges, persuaded Castro to go along. In return, the MPLA leader agreed that Cuba should join the negotiating process effective immediately. This would save Cuban face.

But reality was far more subtle and interesting. On July 27, we had received an unofficial go-between bearing a message from Castro to the top level of the administration. The message distilled hours of conversation with the Cuban leader. Castro had chosen his emissary carefully, and he knew precisely which senior administration figures would receive his message. He proposed that Cuba should join the U.S.-MPLA talks. Cuba was prepared to work with the United States and the Angolans to get a solution. If a negotiated settlement did not occur, Cuba was fully prepared to stay and fight another ten years if necessary. On the other hand, if Cuba participated in the negotiating process—which clearly and directly affected Cuban interests—this could help bring about a solution. Having Cubans at the table would naturally facilitate progress. Castro wanted an urgent reply: he had to know the U.S. answer before dos Santos's arrival in Havana in forty-eight hours.

It was obviously important to Castro to nail down the procedural issue immediately. What was the rush? Would the MPLA leadership resist? We did not know. Was a visible Cuban role the quid pro quo for Castro to go along with our peace process? Yes, in the sense that it would be very hard to save face without it. But there was much more to it than that. A visible role at the table would bring status as a legitimate participant in the African peace process. U.S. acceptance of that reality would be a major plus for Castro.

There was also the inference that the substantive provisions of a deal entailing Cuban troop withdrawal were of vital importance to Castro. This was not something that could be left to others less knowledgeable about Cuban priorities and less reliable in support of Cuban interests. As Castro put it to me face to face in March 1989, "We respected your diplomacy and we were prepared to contribute to a settlement, but not just any settlement: it must be an honorable one and it must provide security for our people as they departed and for Angola as well." Although Castro's message was guarded, one could infer that Cuba was interested in winding down its Angolan entanglement. Of course, Cuba would complete its mission with pride and dignity, however long it took. Castro remained a believer in his "internationalist" cause in Africa. But he seemed to be saying that it would be good if the twelve-year engagement of Cuban forces in Angola—a commitment more onerous in percentage terms than the U.S. engagement in Vietnam at its peak—could be concluded on honorable terms. We also knew, though not from Castro's message, that this massive burden was not popular in Cuba. There was serious concern in the regime that returning troops would bring an AIDS menace to Cuba. And Angola was no longer keeping up with its hard-currency payments to Cuba.

There were two further factors impelling Castro to bid for a role at that moment in the summer of 1987. In the first place, he and his military were utterly disdainful of Soviet strategic planning. For twelve years, the civil war had ebbed and flowed across the vastness of the Angolan landscape. As dos Santos would state publicly in a highly conservative estimate in mid-August, 60,000 lives had been lost (the true figure may have been four to five times greater) and one tenth of the population had become homeless in the war. Yet the government and its superpower ally, in the Cuban view, had no strategy. Every hill and each village of forty huts was treated by Angolan military planners as a significant "target." Soviet planners favored tactically complex and ponderous ground advances that took FAPLA units hundreds of kilometers away from their rear support bases.

This was a low-intensity bush war spread across a vast country where high-value targets were scarce. The key military resources were reliable people and the capability for sustained and rapid maneuver. Soviet-led FAPLA offensives bore little relation to Angolan conditions. The arts of surprise and mobility were as alien to Soviet planning as the concept of logistics was to the Angolans. The Cuban military did not share Soviet assumptions about likely enemy countermoves; a debate had broken out over probable SADF ground and air responses to yet another FAPLA thrust toward Mavinga and Jamba. The Cubans argued against the 1987 Soviet-Angolan battle plan, and played only a minimal role in it.

It was the Soviets who pushed this offensive; they had the influence to prevail in allied decisionmaking since they paid the bills and provided the hardware. More precisely, it was the Soviet military and Communist Party hardliners who wanted the offensive—Shevardnadze and Adamishin did not yet run Soviet African policy. Castro felt that he was a "hostage," to use Adamishin's term, to a poorly led strategic alliance and an inept local regime. By joining the diplomacy, he might gain options and greater influence on decisions that affected Cuba.

A second factor was Castro's long memory and his deep commitment to Cuba's distinct role in the world. The whole edifice of Cuban policy was based on the fierce pride of a small state whose leader has a grandiose sense of destiny. His African ventures, as he liked to point out, predated the rise of Soviet strategic interest in the region in the 1970s. Cuban policy contained a blend of old-fashioned military adventurism and a sort of Robin Hood Marxism based on solidarity among the underdogs. Castro had helped to shape the events of 1975–76 in

Southern Africa. As time passed, he hungered to shape the next phase of regional development. He had made a serious bid for a place at the African peace table back in 1984, the last occasion when there was real fluidity in the process. For Castro, the new global fluidity represented both an opportunity and a potential threat. He never forgot how the superpowers settled the 1962 Cuban missile crisis over his head without reference to his interests. That must never be allowed to happen in Angola, the flagship of Castro's "internationalist" policy. Cuba needed a major, visible role.

In July 1987, of course, we did not see all these things—or could only dimly perceive them. The idea of dealing directly with the Cubans over Angola was a highly sensitive topic, fraught with domestic political overtones. It was much easier to dwell on the downsides of accepting a Cuban role than to imagine the advantages. Castro would crow about his recognition as a legitimate player; he might inject extraneous bilateral issues onto the agenda and then use Angola as a precedent for asserting a "right" to be at other tables such as in Central America. We had little reason at this point for *assuming* that he wanted out of Angola and none at all for believing that we (or the South Africans) would want to pay his price for leaving. I had no basis in July 1987 for believing that Castro's thinking might be significantly more advanced than that of either the Soviets or the Angolans.

We quickly decided on a "diplomatically correct" reply to Castro's feeler, stating that it was up to the MPLA to decide how it wished to proceed on the matter of having Cubans at their side in the negotiations. We also noted that we could not predict whether Pretoria, in response, would seek any change in the definition of the parties involved. We sent our reply to Luanda as well as Havana, embellishing somewhat for the MPLA's benefit Castro's implication that Cuban participation would make a major difference.

We sought to create an interesting dynamic between Luanda and Havana. The Angolans might not be thrilled about a format for talks which advertised their continuing dependence on the Cuban armed forces twelve years after their "independence" in 1975. The imagery of Cubans sitting at the table would only reinforce the logic of the entire U.S. strategy. At a minimum, our message would pose an awkward choice for dos Santos. By leaving the door open to possible Cuban participation, our reply appeared to accede to Castro's request; we would avoid making ourselves a target by objecting. There would be ample opportunity later to shape the precise terms, including those for the Cubans.

Dos Santos, we learned, was indeed upset when he first received word of Castro's signal to Washington. Clearly, it was news to the Angolans.

While they fully accepted the need for Cuban participation at the right moment, they considered the Cuban move premature and did not appreciate being blind-sided like this by the Americans on the eve of an Angolan-Cuban summit meeting. By the time of his visit to Havana, however, dos Santos had agreed to Cuban participation and the two leaders appeared to have patched things up. We soon learned that the MPLA leaders had chosen to interpret our position as an invitation to include the Cubans. But it was nothing of the kind. No decision had been taken within the administration on Cuban participation. We had basically ducked.

A Changing Climate for Negotiation

Between August 1987 and late January 1988, there was almost too much going on at once. Issues of procedure and questions of substance were tied up in an ever-expanding gridlock. The MPLA now refused to meet with us "formally" without the Cubans! Seeing the importance that Luanda and Havana attached to this Cuban link, we began to treat it as a major card: if they wanted it so badly, we should get something for it.

Within weeks of their August 4 bid, we informed the Angolans that further improvement in their proposal would be necessary *before* we would take it to Pretoria and seek to reengage the South Africans in the process. This was partly a matter of our own best judgment. The scar tissue from the 1986 sanctions fiasco was only a year old, and we did not wish to approach the South Africans until we had something powerful and credible from the Angolans in our hands. Besides, we had little choice once the Angolans published their August 4 proposal: the South African foreign minister had rejected it out of hand. That was not surprising. We had long told the MPLA that Pretoria would continue to reject categorically any formula for partial Cuban withdrawal. We certainly hoped that they would!

It had become a classic mediating dilemma. The South Africans had accepted the basic timing in our two-year, 80–20 percent withdrawal proposal of 1985. What to do when one side accepts the essentials of the mediator's own compromise, while the other side digs in at a considerable distance away? We pressed the MPLA to bring the southern troop schedule down further, to one year (from two), and to acknowledge the necessity of dealing with the northern contingent as well. But Luanda was irked that we declined even to go through the motions of "presenting" their already published proposal to Pretoria.

These issues provided the raw material for two "informal" meetings with the Angolans in September—first in Luanda, and later in Brussels, where I caught up with Mbinda during his president's European travel schedule. Hank Cohen and I met with dos Santos in Luanda to share a White House message urging the Angolan to follow up on his August 4 proposal with further decisive action. We told him that the issue of Cuban participation was very difficult for us at this stage. Cuba was no friend of the United States, and it was a political matter for us to include them. We had not expected the Angolans to agree.

Producing the original of one of our messages of late July, dos Santos said he had assumed that we had no problem. "I went to Havana and agreed. Now we are in a very sensitive situation for which we are not to blame." He pleaded with us not to create "the impression of a rift between Angola and Cuba" because the Cubans were "friends who had made many sacrifices for Angola." Further, dos Santos pledged that the Cubans would not inject any extraneous matters into the already complex agenda or seek to pursue bilateral issues. We were not surprised to learn a few days later that Jorge Risquet Valdes, one of Castro's closest advisers and political allies, had shadowed our travel to Angola, perhaps in hopes that a place would be set for him at the table.

When Mbinda and I resumed talks in Brussels on September 24, we had another stand-off on the Cuban role. I sought to coach him on what a big issue Cuba was in U.S. politics. Mbinda was testy: where were the American replies to Angola's questions about the Cuban role and aid to UNITA? Angola had done its homework, but we apparently had not. We were refusing to "negotiate" with him, to open the process to his ally, or to reengage with his adversary.

As we spoke, officials in Washington were debating formulas under which the administration might permit Cuban participation. No one wanted to create problems with the president's staunch Cuban-American supporters. Perhaps we could live with a joint Angolan-Cuban delegation or Cuban "advisers" to the Angolan team. But I could not yet offer this to Mbinda.

Instead, I leaned forward and outlined a "personal" suggestion for Mbinda to take to his leader: the Cubans of the southern contingent would depart in one year (by which time Namibia would be independent); six months later the northern forces would begin their withdrawal, and would all depart within the next eighteen months. (In effect, I was coaching the MPLA to table a three-year schedule for *total* Cuban troop withdrawal. If Angola would propose this formula, the Cubans could come to the table. For our part, I would recommend to Washington that we take it to Pretoria as a major forward step by Angola. I reminded Mbinda of our long-standing position on the incremental establishment of diplomatic relations, starting when the settlement was agreed. I would also recommend that the United States drop political objections to Angola's application to join the IMF.

Had Mbinda and his government been quicker, they would have jumped at it. Fortunately, they did not, and I never had to try to sell this package back to Washington. It would be four months before we saw the Angolans again, and from then on we steered our conversations in other directions. But it would take hard work to wean the MPLA away from the flawed conception—for which we were partially responsible—that they were negotiating with us.

The South Africans showed interest in our September MPLA meetings, and complained that they were not being kept fully briefed. We had kept Pretoria generally informed, but we had no intention of sharing the details of Angola's opacity or our own tactics for trying to build on it. Still, it was good that the South Africans were beginning to show a flicker of interest in the diplomatic process. We learned from an early November probe that Pretoria's top career diplomats were trying to generate support for opening an authoritative channel to U.S. negotiators. But they ran into a brick wall at the political level: our ties remained so severely strained from the events of 1985–86 that it was politically impossible for Pik Botha to meet with me.

In early October the Soviet-FAPLA offensive was smashed at the Lomba River near Mavinga. It turned into a headlong retreat over the 120 miles back to the primary launching point at Cuito Cuanavale. In some of the bloodiest battles of the entire civil war, a combined force of some 8,000 UNITA fighters and 4,000 SADF troops destroyed one FAPLA brigade and mauled several others out of a total FAPLA force of some 18,000 engaged in the three-pronged offensive. Estimates of FAPLA losses ranged upward of 4,000 killed and wounded. This offensive had been a Soviet conception from start to finish. Senior Soviet officers played a central role in its execution. Over a thousand Soviet advisers were assigned to Angola in 1987 to help with Moscow's largest logistical effort to date in Angola: roughly $1.5 billion in military hardware was delivered that year. Huge quantities of Soviet equipment were destroyed or fell into UNITA and SADF hands when FAPLA broke into a disorganized retreat.

In a splendid paradox, the Soviet Union had become the largest external source of arms to UNITA and South Africa. The 1987 military campaign represented a stunning humiliation for the Soviet Union, its arms, and its strategy. It would take FAPLA a year, or maybe two, to recover and regroup. Moreover, the Angolan military disaster threatened to go from bad to worse. As of mid-November, the UNITA/SADF force had destroyed the Cuito Cuanavale airfield and pinned down thousands of FAPLA's best remaining units clinging onto the town's defensive perimeters. There was a risk of a complete FAPLA collapse in the south of Angola.

As the extent of the disaster became known, U.S. officials began to pick up hints of mounting disgust with the Angolan fighting from Soviet diplomats and academics. Nonetheless, the Soviets reminded us that they and the Cubans were central players in the drama and could not be excluded from efforts to resolve it. One well-placed Soviet sought to educate us on the need to factor in Cuba's "inferiority complex" in dealings with us. This could be remedied by showing some respect for Cuban pride. Another senior official informed us that the Cubans now realized that they would have to withdraw their troops from Angola. Shevardnadze confirmed to Shultz the need for Cubans to join the talks. These were delightfully self-serving conclusions at a time when Soviet strategy lay in ruins.

In the lead-up to the December 1987 Washington summit between Reagan and Gorbachev, there was a regular rhythm to meetings between Shultz and Shevardnadze and their senior aides. Ministerial sessions shaped overall priorities and provided guidance for the work of subordinates on arms control, human rights, regional conflicts, and bilateral concerns. The ministerial agenda on both sides was crowded. Its content was shaped by perceptions of movement on one issue or another. It would be a struggle to get Africa on the top-level agenda, but it would be difficult to generate pressure for Soviet decisions *unless* our principals showed interest in Southern Africa. We would need a strong case. Citing battlefield and diplomatic reports, I told Shultz in late October that we were facing the best opportunity in six years for a real breakthrough. This turned out to be one of my better predictions.

But it took a while to come true. When Mike Armacost and NSC staffer Peter Rodman met with Deputy Foreign Minister Yuli Vorontsov and Vladillen Vasev in Geneva on November 15, Vasev did most of the talking for the Soviet side. The Soviets seemed edgy and defensive. Solutions must be based on "the lawful rights of governments." U.S. support of UNITA was "unhelpful," suggesting that we wished to revisit the events of 1975. When Vasev pressed the idea of including the Cubans in the talks, Armacost quietly agreed that we could consider this if the MPLA put forward interesting new ideas. Asked if the Cubans were ready to leave, Vasev replied affirmatively, but added that the Soviet Union was not prepared to "throw Angola to the wolves." The Soviets were humiliated, trapped, and at odds with themselves. They were in no mood to reverse course in Southern Africa or to hand us a diplomatic victory. But they were groping, and their strategy was in tatters.

In an exchange with Cuban Vice Foreign Minister Ricardo Alarcon on November 4, he complained to a U.S. official that the United States had "changed its mind" about Cuban participation since August. Washington must not be serious; valuable time had been wasted. Were we trying to split the Communist allies? A veteran and loquacious diplomat, Alarcon knew us well. He enjoyed conducting dialectical combat with aggressive facial expressions, while waving a long Cohiba cigar for emphasis. But on this occasion he was mild. Cuba and South Africa had no quarrel, he noted. The Angolans might be worried about the prospect of Cuban troop withdrawal; but no one stood to benefit from it more than the Cubans themselves. Alarcon expanded on this theme a few days later at a lunch with an American diplomat in Havana: a settlement would enable Cuba honorably to terminate a very heavy commitment.

However, in a November 20 exchange in Mexico City, Alarcon said he no longer felt "the same optimism" as before. An early U.S. meeting with the MPLA—even with Cubans present—would not necessarily be fruitful. He advised us against pressing for an early rendezvous with the MPLA. What had changed? The Cuban cited the mid-November visit to Savimbi's Angolan headquarters by President P. W. Botha and members of his cabinet. This cast a pall over any talk of peace. He quoted from hardline statements by Botha, Defense Minister Malan, and Chief of Defense Staff Geldenhuys which laid out a bold rationale for SADF intervention: facing a choice between seeing UNITA defeated or halting "Russian aggression," South Africa had chosen the latter. The survival of UNITA served essential South African national interests, Geldenhuys had added, by blocking SWAPO and ANC ability to use much of southern Angola as a launching point for infiltration. Somehow, it did not seem credible that these remarks had transformed Cuban thinking. Something else must be happening.

The Washington summit of early December 1987 was dominated by the successful conclusion of the INF Treaty and by discussion of Afghanistan and the Persian Gulf. At one point, Gorbachev noted to Reagan that he saw good opportunities to move ahead with the search for political solutions in Central America, Cambodia, and Southern Africa. These issues had caused tension in superpower relations; thought should be given as to how the superpowers could cooperate in their own interest and in the interests of the regional parties. Gorbachev offered no specifics, and appeared to be thinking generically. Reagan did not address the Angola-Namibia case, and Gorbachev did not return to it.

By mid-December, Mbinda had taken a page from the gloomy Cuban book and backed away from an earlier proposal for a December meeting. He wanted a further, one-month delay. The "present climate" did not favor talks. Since Brussels, we had failed to give him "satisfactory" answers to his demands concerning U.S. aid to UNITA (described as "agenda item #1" on the MPLA list) and Cuban participation. Luanda was displeased with Reagan's public references to UNITA's "heroes" at the Battle of Lomba River and with Savimbi's statements citing the effectiveness of U.S. military support. The Angolans did not believe negotiations should take place while there were still thousands of SADF troops in Angola in contravention of U.N. Security Council Resolution 602.

That resolution, adopted unanimously on November 25, condemned the intervention and called for SADF withdrawal by December 10. Pik Botha rejected the resolution; South Africans would remain in Angola as long as the Cubans and Soviets did, and as long as Pretoria's security required it. On December 5, Chief of Staff Geldenhuys announced that his forces had completed their task and had begun a tactical disengagement under "operational" conditions—i.e., a slow pullback that might be interrupted by combat.

The Turning Point

The second half of 1987 was the great turning point in the long history of the Namibia and Angola conflicts. This was the moment when the situation "ripened." The Soviets and Angolans had labored strenuously to smash UNITA, and had instead been thoroughly defeated. Meanwhile, the heavy concentration of FAPLA conventional power for the failed offensive opened up a rich field of opportunity for UNITA guerrilla action in other parts of the country. By November, neither Luanda nor Moscow appeared to know which way to go. These developments, by themselves, might have sobered up the Marxist allies. Yet, by themselves, they were unlikely to give American statesmen a real opening. South Africa and UNITA could hardly be expected to draw the same conclusions from what turned out to be their greatest victory in the war. As for the Soviets and Angolans, a time of humiliation is not necessarily the ideal moment for peacemaking—unless it is a dictated peace, something which was never in the cards.

What made the second half of 1987 decisive was the impact of these developments on the Cubans and the Cuban response to them. In July, Castro had made a bid to join the diplomatic process, and failed. By Cuban choice and well-established practice, his forces had played a distinctly secondary role in the August to November fighting. Cubans manned the Lubango-Menongue defense lines well to the northwest of Cuito Cuanavale, supported the FAPLA logistic effort, flew air sorties, and provided the garrison strength that freed up FAPLA units for battle. But the

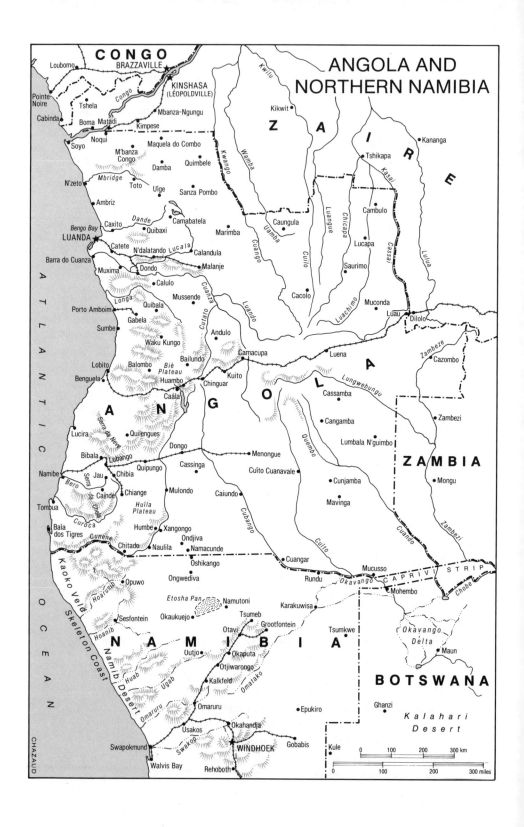

ANGOLA AND
NORTHERN NAMIBIA

government in Havana disagreed with the Soviet plan and had done little to advance it. By November, it was fair to say that the Cubans had a lead role in neither the diplomacy nor the war.

The situation offered Castro a unique moment to shape his own destiny in Africa. He was free to seize the opening for leadership among the Communist allies. He was not tainted by association with failed stratagems. But, at the same time, the situation presented a unique challenge to Castro. Were his troops in Angola for a serious purpose? Were they prepared to join the fray at a moment of extreme peril for the bloodied FAPLA forces in the southeast? Just as the South Africans had perceived a dramatic choice before them back in July and August, this was a time of testing for the Cubans. The extent of the UNITA / SADF victory created a crisis at Cuito Cuanavale.

Castro would later argue that Angola's independence and its "revolution" (the MPLA victory of 1975) were at risk. After it was all over and peace had been achieved, Castro remarked to me that UNITA and the South Africans—by aggressively exploiting their big win—made a strategic mistake: "They created a crisis and forced me to act." According to this logic, the SADF should have pulled back after smashing the FAPLA offensive at the Lomba River, instead of creating an Angolan "Dunkirk" at Cuito Cuanavale. Discounting for Castro's retroactive hyperbole, it seems clear that events forced someone to do something.

In early November the three Communist allies met during the seventieth anniversary of the Bolshevik Revolution. Castro faced Angolan bitterness over Cuba's lack of role in the offensive. Dos Santos found himself facing Soviet pressure for hard-currency payment before fresh arms commitments were agreed, and he was worried that he might be pressured to cut a deal with UNITA. Castro found the Soviets flaky. They talked of "political solutions" as well as of the need to bolster Angolan defenses, but they had no effective strategy for dealing with the Angolan mess.

This was Castro's magic moment—now, he could be the decisive strategist who shaped events. Castro later told me that he worked out his plan with dos Santos on November 7 and then "informed" the Soviets. Soviet officials confirm that Castro made the big decision at around that time, and that his military game plan was greeted with initial Soviet skepticism. It is unclear whether the Angolans realized at the time why Castro was now prepared to assume the strategic lead.

Cuba would dispatch up to 15,000 additional troops to Angola, replace some conscript units, and deploy major elements of the vaunted 50th Division and other front-line combat units and top-rated air force pilots. The Soviets eventually agreed to equip some Cuban units directly from the USSR, but most brought their modern hardware from Cuba. Castro directed four of his most decorated and experienced commanders from earlier African wars (Angola, 1975–76, and Ethiopia, 1977–78) to assume charge of operations.

Effective immediately, Cuban ground forces would be authorized to move south of the 15th parallel (at Menongue and Lubango), their traditional southern perimeter and primary defense lines some 200 miles north of the Namibian border. Additional Cuban forces began arriving in Angola on November 15, one week after dos Santos endorsed Castro's plan in Moscow. The first priority would be to deploy ground and air forces to help FAPLA hold Cuito Cuanavale. By taking up positions around the periphery of this besieged town and pinning down its ragged FAPLA defenders, the SADF and UNITA apparently aimed to seize it. The Cubans would help FAPLA block their path. The first three hundred Cuban reinforcements began arriving in Cuito Cuanavale in early December. A Cuban infantry regiment and a tank company arrived somewhat later from Menongue to stiffen the beleaguered Angolans. The much-decorated General Cintra Frias was placed in command of the position, bypassing the FAPLA chain of command. By March 1988 the Angolan position had finally stabilized after a series of inconclusive encounters between SADF, UNITA, FAPLA, and Cuban forces.

Castro's plan was to block the SADF in the southeast, and then to move a major combat force into the southwest, Cunene Province. This was the zone covered by the 1984 Lusaka Accord until mid-1985, the place of soft sand and scrub through which SWAPO infiltrated to reach Namibia. It was also the place where an intermittent SADF / SWATF presence moved in and out to break up and preempt SWAPO actions. Token FAPLA units stayed as far out of sight as possible, hunkered down in bush camps and a few towns populated largely by wild dogs and helia monsters.

Much of the southwest could be considered a no-man's-land. The South Africans looked upon it as a free-fire zone for their lightly armed special forces (seldom more than 1,000 men), and they traditionally controlled its airspace. Castro aimed to fill this zone with a major deployment of modern, conventional combat power. With the support of FAPLA and SWAPO units, the Cubans would reoccupy Cunene Province right up to the Namibian border. This would be a bold reassertion of Angolan sovereignty. It would permit SWAPO to regain access to its best sanctuaries and infiltration routes into Namibia's Ovamboland (SWAPO's ethnic heartland). And, perhaps most important, it would be the grand strategist's classic "flanking maneuver": a dramatic *drang nach sudwesten* to pry the SADF out of *southeastern* Angola. This was Castro's plan—

though there is evidence that General Arnaldo Ochoa Sánchez, Cuba's distinguished African war hero who was shot by firing squad for corruption and treason in 1989, had a hand in designing it.

By February 1988, an advance force of 3,500 Cubans had moved south into Cunene Province. Cuban arrivals surged in from March to May; by late May they had established a new southern front running some 250 miles in rough parallel with the Namibian border and coming to within 12 miles of it in some places. The front was manned by 11,000–12,000 of Cuba's best units, organized in three task forces along the rudimentary lines of communication in Cunene Province. FAPLA elements and several large SWAPO detachments accompanied the Cuban shield. The front was protected by late-model MiG-23s and helicopter gunships located at newly upgraded airbases at Cahama and Xangongo (40 miles from the border). The Cubans had some two hundred tanks and ample artillery, and their force bristled with air defense radars and five different types of surface-to-air missile systems.

By then, the tripartite peace talks had begun in London. But Castro's extravagant public diplomacy spoke mainly the language of war and military intimidation. The Cuban media trumpeted a tale of how Cuban and FAPLA forces had delivered a crushing defeat to the SADF at Cuito Cuanavale and would now force it to withdraw by an overwhelming flanking thrust in the southwest. Military medals were struck for the "heroes of Cuito Cuanavale." Castro personally briefed African and non-aligned leaders, boasting that the South Africans were now at the negotiating table because Cuban actions had completely changed the "correlation of forces." Writing his own history, Castro publicly dared the South African leadership to run the risk of a "serious defeat" if they tangled with him, and claimed that he had refused to give Pretoria a guarantee that he would not cross into Namibian territory. Cuban propaganda organs made much of Cuba's "air superiority" over the South African Air Force's older inventory. Military maps were published with bold arrows graphically displaying the Cuban thrust toward Namibia. Cuban officials publicly warned that challenging Cuban's southern front would mean that "many white South Africans will die in battle."

At the time, it was not an easy matter to interpret Cuban intentions. Was Cuban machismo out of control? Or was this bravura performance the perfect camouflage for the decision to negotiate an honorable exit from Angola? Hard answers were scarce during the first half of 1988. It was a risky strategy—more risky, in fact, than Castro may have realized. He would be stripping some of his best units and equipment for a deployment 7,000 miles from home, adding significantly to his Angolan "commitment." His gamble would have to pay off quickly, or he could end up with the ugly choice of deescalating with nothing or becoming stuck even more deeply in the quagmire. Having tangled with the South Africans before, Castro respected them. Cuba had a technological edge in airpower and air defense technology, Soviet logistic backing, and the unity of purpose that is possible in a Leninist police state. The SADF had world-class artillery, superior knowledge of the terrain, the home-turf advantage as Cubans moved south, a large cadre of seasoned and high-spirited military leaders, and substantial manpower reserves that could be mobilized if necessary.

The isolated South Africans knew little about Soviet thinking and their expertise on the Cubans was the stuff of comic books. Castro knew dangerously little about South African politics or the baronies that made up its national security establishment. The risks of hairtrigger reactions and miscalculations were substantial. No matter what Castro's true objectives were, his bold moves risked being misperceived, triggering a major confrontation. By staking out a whole new field of operations, the Cuban leader hoped to turn the tables on Pretoria—forcing it to choose between a settlement acceptable to Cuba and the risks of military confrontation. It was a scenario fraught with dangers. A small spark—caused, for example, by a SWAPO contact in Cunene Province—could have ignited a cycle of bigger clashes engaging the honor and pride of P. W. Botha and Fidel Castro, two high-strung gentlemen.

But these things did not happen. Whatever Castro's rhetorical bombast, he could not dictate South Africa's choice, and his behavior during 1988 suggests that he realized his own limits. He could confront the South Africans with visible displays of his prowess. He could pressure them to make a choice. By moving south into Angola's war zones, the Cubans could raise the price of open-ended South African engagement. He could equalize, temporarily at least, the military scales within Angola. But it was beyond Cuba's capacity to dominate the Southern African military balance. It had been understood with the Soviets from the beginning that the Cubans would not enter Namibia; nor did Castro really have this option militarily, even with his fresh reinforcements. The strategic balance would have shifted sharply in Pretoria's favor had Castro attacked Namibia.

Castro's decision in late 1987 was to design an honorable exit from Southern Africa. But this strategy could only work if both his military and political options appeared to be credible. The Cubans would have to induce the South Africans to share their favored outcome. But Castro could not advertise his Angolan ennui or acknowledge any limits on his military options. Consequently, his risky adventure in grand strategy was dependent, in practice, on American diplomacy and South African common sense and steady nerves. To get out of Angola with Cuban honor intact, Castro would ironically seize upon the much-reviled "linkage" doctrine. If he could not become the Bolívar of Africa, spreading a wave of liberation right down to Cape Town, there was still hope. Linkage would become—as we had argued for years—the one formula by which Cubans could go home having accomplished something: the end of SADF intervention in Angola and the implementation of Resolution 435 leading to Namibian independence.

To succeed, Castro would first have to bluff a wide range of audiences (his domestic constituency, his Angolan allies, the non-aligned states, and perhaps himself) into believing that Cuba was forcing Pretoria to the table. This needed to happen by the time the face-to-face tripartite talks began in London in May so that people would not ask why *the Cubans* were at the table. Second, he would need to persuade Washington and Pretoria that while he was ready for a wider war, he preferred a balanced settlement based on linkage. None of this would work if the South Africans refused to engage at the table. Finally, he would need to persuade his MPLA allies that they were not being abandoned.

The Scorpions Maneuver in Southern Angola

Castro demonstrated his grasp of the political psychology of military action in 1988. The *real* military campaign and outcome are rather different from the picture the Cubans managed to convey. The legend of Cuito Cuanavale was gratifying for those who lusted to smash the myth of South African invincibility. The boundless arrogance of P. W. Botha met its match when the Cuban megalomaniac grabbed the mike for show-and-tell. But the South African, Angolan, and Cuban officials who accepted our mediation in 1988 knew better. They were there.

The engagements around Cuito Cuanavale began in November 1987, when the SADF and UNITA drove FAPLA back to the Cuito River just east of the town. A series of engagements punctuated the next four months, as SADF armor and artillery units, special forces, and UNITA infantry confronted FAPLA and Cuban counterparts in extraordinarily dense and difficult terrain. The South African force never exceeded a brigade in size. In April, Geldenhuys reduced it to a smaller combat group of perhaps 1,500 men, supplemented by several UNITA, SWATF, and special forces units. South Africans remained deployed in the area until the end of August 1988, when they withdrew from Angola under the Geneva Protocol agreed at the negotiating table earlier in the month.

South Africa's conduct during this strange campaign provided the raw material for Castro's victory speeches. While Castro was waging a political contest, the SADF leadership concentrated on battlefield logic. Once FAPLA's offensive had been broken, the SADF and UNITA sought to capitalize on Angolan disarray by clearing out the large region between the Cuatir and Chambinga rivers before they join the Cuito. The goal was to forestall any resumption of FAPLA offensive activity eastward through this corridor during the coming campaign season. The arrival of Cuban forces at FAPLA's side heightened the South Africans' determination to prevent any reversal of their 1987 victory. Taking the town itself, according to SADF commanders and UNITA leaders, was not the goal: UNITA could not hold it by itself; the SADF had no interest in holding a permanent position hundreds of kilometers into the deepest Angolan bush. Only if the town fell without a fight would it be temporarily occupied.

The SADF / UNITA operations from January through March 1988 were designed to drive FAPLA from its remaining toeholds on the east bank of the river. When FAPLA / Cuban defenses stiffened in February and March, Pretoria decided that a political "win" at Cuito was not worth the material and, especially, human cost of white regulars that might be required. Instead, the existing line would be held and minefields constructed against any attempts by FAPLA and the Cubans to break out and move east again toward the Lomba River and Mavinga, the strategic key to Jamba.

Pretoria emerged from its long night of diplomatic hibernation in March and April of 1988 to find that these artful military tactics were not good enough. A battle of perceptions was under way. It was too late to prevent Castro from sullying in May the SADF's image at Cuito. As the peace talks got into high gear in June through August, Geldenhuys converted the SADF position at Cuito into a bargaining chip. It still served to protect UNITA, but it also helped to deflate the Cuban balloon. Staying at Cuito would avoid the perverse imagery of an SADF withdrawal occurring after Castro's verbal taunts about his new front in the southwest. Geldenhuys was determined that there would be no withdrawal until concrete, reciprocal military agreements (including Cuban restraint) were reached. In other words, Cuban bravado helped keep the SADF engaged at Cuito. By July 1988, South African troops were receiving orders which precisely matched the diplomatic choreography at the negotiating table: simulate a larger presence, demonstrate staying power, but avoid provocation, and under no circumstances take casualties. It had become a political war. Throughout the nearly nine months of SADF presence around Cuito, there were no decisive battles; casualties among the Cubans and South Africans were modest, though FAPLA and UNITA forces paid a steeper price.

The legend of Cuito Cuanavale is that the SADF was pushed around, defeated, surrounded by hostile forces, and barely able to extricate itself. The reality is that two forces of moderate size tested and checked each other for nine months. The Cubans forestalled the further destruction of FAPLA. The SADF and UNITA consolidated their victory and pushed hard to clear the east bank of the Cuito River, but they pulled back when they realized that the price would be too high. The two forces endured a nasty and prolonged engagement in horrible conditions.

How, then, did the fighting at Cuito become a heroic Cuban legend? By proclaiming to a credulous world that the town of Cuito Cuanavale—a town under MPLA control since 1976—was the "prize" over which the entire campaign was fought, and then by crowing when you have managed not to lose it. Defining the adversary's agenda and the stakes of the battle was a Cuban art form. The South Africans were no match for Castro in the battle of perceptions. While Castro was copyrighting the legend, the South Africans had reasons of their own for not drawing excessive attention to their continuing intervention deep within Angola. Above all, they wished this to be seen as UNITA's war. That desire meshed perfectly with Castro's need to assert that he was negotiating from strength. In a subsequent speech, he offered a more candid picture: he had introduced more troops to Angola to protect FAPLA, to defend the Cubans already there, and to be "strong enough to avoid defeat."

A similar comment can be made about the Cuban thrust toward the Namibian border in the southwest. Presented as a thrust to compel the SADF's withdrawal from Angola, the potent Cuban force was primarily a political demonstration in keeping with Castro's "strutting cock" school of grand strategy. There was minimal risk in "occupying" a largely empty place. Both the Cubans and the SADF / SWATF skillfully avoided contact, apart from a few minor incidents involving SWAPO during April and May. Had Castro wished to provoke a serious encounter, it could have been arranged. Had the SADF leadership wanted to challenge the Cuban buildup, there were opportunities.

The activity in the southwest from March through June seemed both ominous and ambiguous. Like scorpions in a bottle, the rival forces avoided each other's sting. Could it be that Pretoria would permit the Cuban buildup to proceed unchallenged (sensing that it was for show)? Could it be that the Cuban leader was quietly hoping that the SADF would concentrate on defending Namibia (where he had no intention of going)? It was a difficult time for reading intentions. The rhythm of our negotiations had not yet been firmly established; in the interval between negotiating rounds, there was no standing mechanism for direct communication between the parties.

The Cubans worried that Pretoria would launch a surprise attack on their forces as they crept south from Cahama, Xangongo, and Techipa toward the large Calueque-Ruacana hydropower and water project just north of the border. Castro claimed later that he had authorized retaliatory moves (including strikes at Namibian air bases) if this happened. The South Africans were also uncertain: was this pattern of Cuban deployments designed to taunt or provoke the SADF, or was its purpose to gain the psychological edge at the bargaining table? Pretoria had only minimal, lightly armed forces in the immediate vicinity of the western Cunene / Ovamboland border. It could not be assumed that Castro's intentions were benign. Perhaps he needed an event that could be described as a final "victory"—especially after his early June warning that the SADF could suffer a "serious defeat" if it tried to thwart Cuba's plans.

By late May, the SADF began to move some heavier units into place in northern Namibia, and on June 8 Geldenhuys confirmed the call-up of the 140,000-man Citizen Force, the backbone of the SADF's conventional forces. Light contacts between advance elements had by now occurred, and Cuban planes had penetrated Namibian airspace. It appeared likely that the Cuban–FAPLA–SWAPO force centered on Techipa and Xangongo intended to continue south toward the border. The scorpions were having trouble getting out of the bottle. South African armor and artillery units engaged Cuban-FAPLA columns near Techipa on June 26. In several hours of heavy exchanges on June 27, the South Africans shot up elements of one column, claiming to have killed two to three hundred of the enemy (the Cubans conceded the loss of ten men). In a measured retaliation, Cuban Air Force MiGs bombed the dam and bridge at Calueque just north of the border. Eleven SADF men were killed in the attack, which damaged the major pumping station and water facilities serving northern Namibia. SADF armor and artillery units pulled back across the border.

Rarely since 1975 had South African and Cuban forces had a direct and bloody encounter of this sort. But having stung each other, the scorpions took a deep breath and never touched one another again. The events of June 26–27, 1988, marked a psychological watershed. It was the last significant action by the SADF and SWATF in Angola prior to their official withdrawal in late August. Geldenhuys and his men focused on converting the northern Namibian border zone into a "killing field" for would-be aggressors. This was the ideal move: it made good sense militarily and allowed the negotiations to proceed by avoiding the effects of a major engagement. For their part, the Cubans avoided actions that might risk another incident. This was a war no one wanted. To their mutual relief, Castro and P. W. Botha had failed to provoke each other. They could now concentrate on defining the principles of peace.

16

Getting the Parties to the Table, 1988

By late June 1988, the cycle of South African and Cuban military moves in 1987–88 was nearly complete. The Techipa-Calueque clashes in southwestern Angola confirmed a precarious military stalemate. That stalemate was both the reflection and the cause of underlying political decisions. In early May, my colleagues and I convened representatives of Angola, Cuba, and South Africa in London for face-to-face, tripartite talks. The political decisions leading to the London meeting formed a distinct sequence, paralleling military events on the ground, like planets moving one by one into a certain alignment.

As we have seen, the Cubans moved first, taking the MPLA down the garden path toward a settlement. In mid-December 1987, Mbinda had written me that the climate was not conducive for our next meeting. On January 7, he wrote me again proposing firm dates at the end of the month. This time, Mbinda wrote, the Cubans would have to take part. He guaranteed that they would not interject extraneous issues onto the agenda (one of our conditions), and pledged that Havana's participation would contribute to a "rapid and concrete" advance in the discussions.

Upon my arrival in Angola in late January 1988, Mbinda and I shadow-boxed awkwardly for nearly two days as I squeezed him for a concrete picture of what would happen when we met the Cuban team, headed by Jorge Risquet Valdes, Castro's principal lieutenant on African policy. I could not give Castro what he so eagerly wanted unless we got something solid in return. Mbinda had now linked the Cuban troop withdrawal ideas we had discussed in Brussels to his own five-point agenda that began with U.S. and South African aid to UNITA.

A lengthy and tiresome debate ensued, but eventually Mbinda hinted that Angola was now willing to discuss *total* Cuban withdrawal in the presence of the Cubans. To avoid a shellgame, Hank Cohen and I agreed that Cubans could join his delegation for the specific purpose of discussing Cuban withdrawal. Mbinda and General Ndalu adjourned the meeting to fetch Risquet. It was January 29, 1988. The negotiation was about to change for good. .

Risquet's presence changed the ambiance in our modest conference room at Futungo do Belas. We could hardly believe the man's body language as he strutted in my direction, eyes twinkling, and proudly introduced his colleagues to us. The white polyester safari suit, wispy beard, and corpulent frame of Castro's adviser seemed to have been borrowed from a 1950s movie. For years, Risquet had shadowed us on our Luanda visits. Now, he seemed more focused on having been admitted to the talks than on the price of admission. He lit up a long, aromatic Cohiba. Suddenly, the table seemed small as four Cubans squeezed alongside the Angolans. To Mbinda's evident distaste, the entire Angolan-Cuban delegation was soon haloed in Risquet's cigar smoke. We waited for them to compose themselves and deliver the quid pro quo that would convert our marathon into a sprint.

At this point, Ndalu spoke. The Angolans and Cubans were prepared to split the difference on the southern Cuban contingent, which would depart between twelve and twenty-four months. Now, the northern contingent could be negotiated as well; we were at last talking about *total* Cuban withdrawal. Perhaps a calendar not far from my suggestion at Brussels (three years) might work. Specific timetables would be proposed *if* progress was made on the first four items on the Angolan-defined agenda, including the issue of aid to UNITA. Risquet piped up to show how this position differed from our earlier suggestions, and said we should think in terms of "three years plus X." They did not wish to table a specific proposal, still hoping that we would engage in U.S.-Angolan horse-trading in order to obtain one.

I terminated the meeting abruptly. We had come to participate in serious negotiations, and had prepared draft documents to serve as a basis for discussion. All we had received from the Angolans and Cubans was "principles and blanks." We had nothing to take to the South Africans. We would report back to Washington that Luanda and Havana now accepted the principle of total withdrawal, but that the inclusion of the Cubans had not produced a "concrete" advance. There was nothing we could do as mediator until they had done their homework. Mbinda and Risquet pressed us to stay. They wished to go over our documents. They wanted to work out a joint press statement to register the occasion. We rejected all these ideas.

These tactics had me worried. Their attempt to link progress to a cessation of UNITA aid was a complete non-starter. We had not dealt ourselves this card in order simply to obtain yet another withdrawal proposal. As time passed, we realized that American aid to UNITA was the perfect bargaining chip for a "separate" negotiation on Angolan reconciliation—*not* for the Cuban withdrawal–Namibia negotiation. Having aligned ourselves officially with UNITA in the internal conflict, we would not simply abandon UNITA after a regional settlement.

But the January agreement in principle to total Cuban withdrawal—coming months before the action peaked at Cuito Cuanavale and Techipa-Calueque—signaled that the Angolans and Cubans now accepted the essential parameters of a linkage-based settlement.

We flew from Luanda to meet with Savimbi in Zaire the next day, January 30. It was the most constructive meeting in years. He was ecstatic about the news of total Cuban withdrawal ("a major breakthrough" and an "irreversible" step). Savimbi favored having Cubans at the table; their role in Angola was clearly decisive. He disclaimed any interest in occupying Cuito Cuanavale. He also expressed genuine anger at South African attempts to take the lion's share of captured Soviet hardware, and to posture (at U.S. expense) as a *cavalier seul* in regional affairs.

Just before the Luanda meeting, the South African government had commented that American talks with the MPLA were of no interest. When we briefed the press on our return, Pik Botha criticized U.S. officials for speaking to the press rather than talking to his government. On February 2, I called South African Ambassador Piet Koornhof to my office to lay out the position. Acceptance of the principle of total withdrawal was of fundamental importance to both our countries, but his foreign minister's remarks reflected badly on his government's seriousness. We had had enough of these periodic outbursts of Yankee bashing. It was time to clear the air. We invited Pik Botha to meet me in Europe. We also put Koornhof on notice that we might soon propose "proximity talks" if the MPLA came up with a concrete proposal. This was our first move to reengage Pretoria.

On February 8, Gorbachev announced a much-improved schedule for Soviet troop withdrawal from Afghanistan. The Soviet decision to deal with the "bleeding wound" next door, he said, could lead to an early Afghanistan accord that would have "the most profound impact on other regional conflicts." He posed the intriguing question: "Which conflict will be settled next? It is certain that more is to follow." (The Afghan Accord was eventually signed in mid-April, and a nine-month Soviet withdrawal plan began a month later.) Shultz and Armacost held further exchanges on the various regional conflicts with Shevardnadze and Vorontsov later in February. Saluting Gorbachev's speech, Shultz urged his counterpart to help persuade the Angolans to move on both Cuban withdrawal and political reconciliation with UNITA. This would put the most effective pressure on Pretoria to disengage from the Namibia-Angola conflicts. Shevardnadze expressed pleasure that the Cubans were now at the table, but grumbled that Pretoria listened to no one. He sounded a note of concern when Shultz reiterated our intention to continue support of UNITA.

Basic differences still existed between Washington and Moscow on Southern Africa. They knew by now that the Angolan conflict was a quagmire, but they faced no pressures or pain comparable to their palpable trauma in Afghanistan. They had taken no decisions about the basic shape of the deal or their role in it. They stressed that the superpowers could not act as "lawgivers" to the regional powers, and under no circumstances did Moscow wish to be perceived as muscling its clients ("legitimate governments") into a deal. The complexities of the Afghanistan endgame—and, specifically, the issues of superpower guarantees, national reconciliation, and our respective assistance to incumbent regimes and freedom fighters—acted as a brake on Soviet decisions. Unlike Afghanistan, Moscow could not act unilaterally in Southern Africa. Castro was out front; as usual, he had strong views and could be a headache for the Soviets. Moscow preferred to coast in Castro's wake during the February–April period until things clarified.

Apart from a brief flurry of face-to-face encounters back in 1984 at the time of the Lusaka Accord, the American-led negotiation had used an indirect, shuttle procedure. By early 1988, we needed a fresh dynamic and a more efficient procedure to produce political decisions. We needed to reengage Pretoria and move the parties toward proximity talks or direct negotiation. The problem was, how to do these things. As General Ndalu, the MPLA chief of staff, liked to tell us, "The water must boil before you can cook the food." We believed that a credible Angolan-Cuban proposal incorporating the principle of total Cuban withdrawal was the only way to get to the table.

The Cubans, Angolans, and Soviets had misgivings about our shuttle procedure, viewing it as a device by which we retained control of the process, filtering the parties' views and sharing them selectively as it suited us. They fretted that we misrepresented the parties' positions. They wanted to know Pretoria's "real" views. So did we. But the only way to find out was by having a serious proposal against which to test the South African commitment to linkage.

The Final Shuttle

Pik Botha agreed to meet me in Geneva on March 14. With this nailed down, we organized a March 9–11 exchange in Luanda with the MPLA and the Cubans. We would present draft documents on various aspects of an overall package agreement, leaving the crucial timetable specifics to be filled in with a new Angolan-Cuban position. We would present this material to Botha in Geneva, and then return to Luanda with South African reactions. I asked Larry Napper, my deputy director of Southern African affairs, and Angola desk officer Mike McKinley to undertake the first Luanda leg, keeping the rest of my traveling team for the Geneva session.

It would be my first encounter with Botha in two full years. We would need to cover the entire gamut of delicate bilateral and regional issues. The goal was to help Botha persuade his truculent leadership to come back into the process. We would propose proximity talks on the basis of our working documents, knowing already that Luanda and Havana favored this approach. At the end of this sequence, Robert Cabelly would see Savimbi in Africa and I would meet again with Adamishin, my Soviet counterpart, in Washington. This, at any rate, was the plan.

Napper and McKinley arrived in Luanda and promptly found themselves immersed in a ministerial-level test of wills. Justice Minister Franca Van Dunem, a Dutch-trained lawyer and yet another member of the Van Dunem clan, led the combined Angolan-Cuban team, which pushed a slew of their own documents our way. The American team tried to focus the discussion on our three working documents, each of which was prepared in English, Spanish, and Portuguese. For three straight days, two middle-ranking Foreign Service Officers went at it with two Angolan ministers, Dr. Rudolfo Puente-Ferro, Havana's foremost Angolan specialist, and José Arbesu Fraga, the head of the North American policy department of the Cuban Communist Party.

Napper's goal was to get Cuban numbers and dates that could be fitted into our detailed withdrawal schedules and verification plans. Our documents were drafted as South African–Angolan accords, which the Cubans would "witness" as interested observers. Franca's goal was to extract from us a U.S.-Angolan undertaking on the end of aid to UNITA and the establishment of diplomatic relations. This was, to Franca, the "absolute sine qua non" for providing us the detailed terms of a Cuban schedule to be contained within *their* draft "global" accord, which would be signed by Angola, Cuba, South Africa, and SWAPO.

Before even seeing their timetable, we were miles apart on both procedure and substance. Napper reminded them that the United States did not consider itself a party. Bilateral relations could not be considered until—at the earliest—the start of implementation. As for aid to UNITA, Washington would not consider this question until, at the earliest, all Cubans had left Angola. The Angolans should focus on getting South Africa out of Angola and Namibia, which would transform the SADF-UNITA relationship. Using a saying from his native Texas, the soft-spoken Napper pointed out that the Angolans were "selling the same horse twice"—giving Cuban troop withdrawal to Pretoria for Resolution 435 and offering it to Washington for the termination of UNITA aid.

Franca and da Moura accused Napper of welching on the "understanding." The United States made endless demands, but offered nothing. The U.S. delegation had no authority, and was backtracking. The U.S. government "hated" Angolans and added to their suffering. For three days, Franca and Arbesu insisted that we would get "no numbers and dates" unless we signed a formal, binding accord ending aid to UNITA effective immediately. A self-disciplined professional, with broad African and Soviet experience, Napper replied in factual tones that the MPLA and the Cubans were creating an impasse. It was essential to fill in the "blanks" in their draft accord somehow—with conditions if necessary, in pencil, with invisible ink, or whatever.

Eventually Franca blinked, giving us the new proposal as an "act of goodwill," while still demanding answers form us on the bilateral issues. The Angolan-Cuban proposal was frightful, thus validating the wisdom of our stand. All Cubans would redeploy north of the 13th parallel (approximately Angola's midsection) during the first 17 months from the start of implementation; 20,000 Cubans would be withdrawn from Angola during the second year; the remainder would be withdrawn between month thirty and month forty-eight of a *four-year* plan! The Communist allies had dropped their past distinction between the southern and northern contingents, thus simplifying matters. But the duration of the plan was outlandish. It was also something of a shellgame: Castro was in the process of increasing Cuban deployments into Angola by an amount almost equal to all those he proposed to withdraw during the first two years!

But there was a brighter side. Napper brought to Geneva the first-ever proposal for total Cuban withdrawal. We now had what we needed in procedural terms to restart the bidding process. The Luanda meeting also made headway on other, less dramatic problems. The Angolans and

Cubans appeared to grasp our point that Pretoria would not consider elevating SWAPO (one of many Namibian parties) to co-equal status with three governments. To insist on a SWAPO signature of the accords would open the way for Pretoria to demand UNITA's participation as a party. Besides, SWAPO's legitimate interests were fully reflected in the existing agreements. On our side, we listened carefully to Cuban arguments that they should sign the accords as a full party. It might produce reflexive heartburn in Washington and Pretoria, but the Cubans' interest in "face" and "role" should be accommodated if it led to substantive movement.

The Angolans and Cubans blinked in early March 1988 (before the events which Castro would trumpet as Botha's Waterloo) because they had multiple goals and were forced to choose between them. Castro's top priority was to use our settlement framework to get the South Africans to the table. That is why we got the four-year proposal while essentially ignoring the MPLA's "bilateral" condition. However outlandish its terms, we recognized it as the opening bid which the Cubans wanted to take into the endgame.

Cuban officials displayed an intensity and a sense of mission which made very clear that someone important was watching every move back home. At this stage, we still viewed Gorbachev rather than Castro as the potential ripening agent. But it gradually became clear that Castro was driving the Communist train in Angola. Castro wanted to get to the table fast. He could not fool around for months while the MPLA engaged the Americans in a futile quest to force us to abandon UNITA. He had to be sure that the South Africans would be visibly negotiating by the time that his carefully scripted military moves reached their mediagenic climax in May–June.

As we prepared to meet Pik Botha in Geneva, we faced the challenge of how to reengage an estranged pariah state. I had not spoken to him for two years, and we anticipated one of his classic *son et lumière* shows. Botha remained on the defensive within his own structure. He had sold this meeting to his colleagues by arguing that South Africa should be visibly "in the loop" when regional diplomatic contacts occurred. His Geneva delegation was composed exclusively of diplomats; defense and intelligence officials were busily spreading the word that the U.S. exercise was irrelevant.

Defense Minister Malan had gone public on March 6 with a call for direct South Africa–*Soviet* talks to resolve the Angolan conflict. There was no mention of Namibia or the U.S. settlement framework we had defined with the South Africans in 1981. Officials in Pretoria were pushing the line that perhaps it would be better if everyone just forgot about Namibia for a while and concentrated on Angola. Things had changed since 1984–85, they said. Today, it would be very difficult to persuade anyone at the top to contemplate leaving Namibia.

To say that the South Africans were behind the curve in March 1988 would be an understatement. Even after Soviet spokesmen threw Malan's bouquet back in their faces, academics, journalists, and policy types were abuzz about the Soviet factor. In the wishful thinking that often passed for policy analysis, South Africans dreamed of a new Pretoria-Moscow axis sitting astride world markets for gold, diamonds, and strategic minerals. What better way to pay back the meddlesome and sanctimonious Yanks while emasculating domestic and regional enemies? The January visit to South Africa of Franz Josef Strauss, the Bavarian conservative leader (now dead), captured the official imagination. Few men had his credibility in Pretoria. When Strauss, who had just been to Moscow, told the South Africans that Gorbachev was reappraising the value of his African empire, some read this to mean that Moscow was on the run. The more thoughtful people in various agencies realized that South Africa, too, had choices to make. But there were no grand strategists in Pretoria in March 1988 and no political consensus on Botha's team.

The issue of South Africa's role in the Angolan fighting concerned elements of white opinion. The loss of some fifty to sixty whites since September 1987 was hardly a crisis, but neither was it a negligible matter for a conscript- and reservist-based defense force, especially when the stakes were not clear. It was one thing for the SADF to defend against SWAPO in Namibia, but it was much harder to explain why white boys should die to defend Savimbi. This was why senior officials always spoke of bigger stakes, such as "stopping Soviet aggression in Angola."

In Afrikaner churches and Afrikaans-language theatres and night clubs, one could detect popular misgivings about Angola. Such mainstream white sentiment did not constitute a full-blown anti-war movement. But it unquestionably weighed on decisionmakers who had no desire to see one develop. A premium was placed on avoiding white casualties and maximizing the use of black ground troops.

These harbingers of Angolan ennui did not signal a shift to the left in white attitudes. On the contrary, Botha's National Party was crushed in two early March by-elections by the right-wing Conservative Party. While the Nats still held a comfortable 133 out of 178 parliamentary seats, a white backlash seemed to have set in against Botha's limited reform program. The unrest and militant resistance in black urban areas— and the West's failure to support Botha—fueled the white reaction. Blamed for change and violence, whites now blamed him for sanctions and isolation. This domestic climate helped explain the latest series of crackdowns: in late February 1988, the government banned virtually all activities of seventeen leading black organizations, including the United Democratic Front, plus all political activity by COSATU, the largest labor federation.

As we met with Pik Botha in Geneva in March, there was little evidence of creative thinking within his government on much of anything. Domestically, the state had smashed much of the organizational infrastructure of the black resistance and brought the level of violent unrest down. Predictably, Botha was winning the purely physical test of strength, reminding the black opposition forces once again of the limits to their ultimate bargaining power. Botha could rule, but he could no longer govern. The opposition could not overthrow him or the system he led; but it had severely undercut his legitimacy at home and overseas, and it could discredit him at every turn. Nor did it appear that he *had* an internal political strategy—beyond the crackdown—that he would like to implement. A domestic stalemate was setting in.

The South Africans were master tacticians, but they confused military power with national strategy. At around this time, a former academic colleague confirmed my impression. After spending ten days with Pretoria's military, diplomatic, and intelligence establishment, he reported to me that he had seldom seen a government so utterly confused and at cross-purposes over basic questions of policy. Given the absence of strategic guidance from top political levels, it was remarkable that SADF chief of staff Jannie Geldenhuys and his military colleagues avoided disaster in Angola during the first half of 1988. The South Africans were no longer the only serious team in the regional bush league.

Reengaging the South Africans

As we sat down in the conference room of the South African mission in Geneva on March 14, 1988, I handed Pik Botha a bluntly worded four-page letter from Shultz. Botha frowned and looked at his watch. He wished me to understand that he had not anticipated in-depth meetings and would need to leave Geneva for other European business that same afternoon. But the Shultz letter made clear that we did not view this meeting as a photo opportunity. Shultz expressed his dismay at the renewed internal repression, urging Botha to avoid a gratuitous confrontation with Western governments and public opinion. This was the time to begin rebuilding a cooperative relationship. It was essential to grasp a historic opportunity to resolve the Angola and Namibia conflicts. Agreements that would protect our respective interests were possible; the cost of failure could be high for South Africa, perhaps dangerously so.

It would have been hard for Botha to miss the purposeful tone. I sharpened the point with some very direct oral jabs. We Americans were appalled to see the cycle of bad decisions. It was almost as if Pretoria had a death wish, giving its foreign friends no ground to stand on, its white electorate no reason not to vote Conservative, and its black population no reason to believe in moderation. At times, it seemed to us that South Africans were "creating a wasteland rather than building their future."

On Angola and Namibia, I offered Botha a complete briefing and our best assessment of where the other side stood. But, first, I rebutted the innuendos planted by people in his government who disliked U.S. policy for one reason or another. If South Africans thought they could solve their problems in splendid isolation, "go ahead and try." If they thought that the SADF was on the verge of breaking the Soviets and Cubans and forcing them out of Angola, "go ahead and try."

The time had come to translate South African power into real influence by putting serious choices before the Angolans and Cubans. Moscow and Havana had large investments in Angola. In the absence of a settlement, they would hang on and keep the MPLA from collapsing. Gorbachev and Castro were not "desperate" for a deal, but they did appear open to discussing a deal. We would be seeing the Soviets again in one week to further test their position. I described our latest contacts in Luanda and the precise parameters of their new bid. Proximity talks would seem to be the logical next step.

Botha was taken aback, but he shared with us the dilemmas of a reformer amidst the grinding polarization around him. Pretoria had not turned away from the path of reform, but it was determined to restore security, he said. The Conservatives were exploiting "white fears of being overwhelmed"—a task made easier by the West's refusal to recognize the reforms already made. His government was not telling the West "to go to Hell"; it was simply "giving more attention to Africa." Good ties with the United States and Europe would be a "bonus."

Botha saw the Soviets as the key, and volunteered that the United States would necessarily play the decisive role in testing them. If Gorbachev was serious about seeking political solutions, then maybe something could be worked out. But could the MPLA afford to let the Cubans go without dealing with UNITA? Could Gorbachev really do deals in both Angola and Afghanistan? Had the Soviets really agreed that Angola was a legitimate topic the regional talks? Had they changed their position on Angola? I remarked that it was a time of flux and testing on all sides. The Soviets were no longer directly thwarting U.S. diplomacy, but nor were they helping us. On the question of Cuban intentions, I avoided sweeping theories, but pointed to what had happened since the Cubans joined the talks and assumed the lead role militarily. (Only a portion of the 15,000-man augmentation of Cuban forces had arrived at this point, but the trend was clear.)

Botha listened carefully. He had always understood our logic: Cuban withdrawal was a means gracefully to extricate the SADF from an open-ended quagmire that damaged South Africa's international standing. His president and many of his defense force colleagues felt emotionally committed to the Angola war. The real question confronting him was whether a credible settlement based on total Cuban withdrawal could be achieved. He would return home for a cabinet meeting in two days, and would need strong arguments. He was especially eager to get quick feedback on our upcoming Soviet talks in Washington.

We had told the Angolans and Cubans that I might accompany Larry Napper back to Luanda after Geneva, but this made little sense. Botha had to report home and could not tell us anything official which we could pass on. Besides, the "four-year plan" with all its conditions was hardly an act of statesmanship that we wished to reward. I instructed Napper to say that Washington had ordered me home to participate in preparations for our Soviet meetings.

I sent Cabelly along with Napper to play bad cop if necessary, and to share some sensitive impressions of the state of play within the South African government. They would say that we were working hard to engage Pretoria, and had placed a big decision in South Africa's court. But they would also emphasize that the South Africans had reacted very negatively to the four-year plan (this was an understatement; they had laughed). Coming fresh from Geneva, they could usefully coach the Angolans and Cubans on South Africa's problems with the Angolan offer: its extreme "backloading" with no Cubans leaving during the first year (by which time Namibia would be independent and Pretoria would have no leverage on the ground); and its imprecision on total numbers of Cubans and the phasing of withdrawals. In practice, we would need a more realistic proposal in order to influence Pretoria to make decisions.

Cabelly coached them on how they should rebid (again) to get Pretoria's attention. Franca listened but said he had "a bitter taste" in his mouth. The South Africans were not changing their position from 1985, except that now they had 8,000 men in Angola. (Geldenhuys's combat tactic of simulating much larger forces appears to have worked, judging by the excessive claims made by Angolan, Cuban, and SWAPO officials). Here Franca threw his hands in the air. Luanda made concessions and the United States and South Africa gave nothing. How could the United States describe itself as a mediator when it kept asking one side for more?

He had no authority to review his position. The United States should pressure South Africa to respond to the Angolan-Cuban proposal. In the meantime, Angola, with Cuban help, would continue defending itself "heroically" at Cuito.

Franca knew all the arguments and marshaled them like a trial lawyer. He was technically quite correct about the state of play: it *was* now up to Pretoria to respond to the four-year plan. But Cabelly wanted Franca to get a grip on reality. Pretoria was not under serious pressure to leave Angola and settle. Its costs and casualties were manageable in the eyes of P. W. Botha, the one man who would make the ultimate decisions. If they wished, the Angolans and Cubans could spark a real debate among the South African leadership, but their proposals had not done so.

Rather than respond directly, the Cubans spelled out in detail their logistic and technical rationale for a proposal that combined staged, northward redeployments and westward withdrawals. Their forces would have to redeploy in the midst of civil war, moving men and equipment through specified transit points to Angola's ports and airfields. This would be an organized and orderly military operation—not the flight of a defeated rabble. It was an argument we were to hear many times in the months ahead. The interesting thing, apart from the proud, demonstrative manner of the presentation, was the Cubans' calm assertion that they had already begun to prepare the plans for their withdrawal from Angola. This was on March 18, 1988, *before* Cuban reinforcements had all arrived, *before* the fighting peaked, and *before* Castro proclaimed to the world that he had altered the correlation of forces.

Another Round with Adamishin

While the rest of my team reassembled in Washington, Cabelly went to Abidjan to brief Savimbi and Félix Houphouet-Boigny, the octogenarian Ivorian leader who was among UNITA's firmest friends. Savimbi laughed at the MPLA version of the fighting: "Just because they have not lost Cuito Cuanavale, they think they have turned the war around!" But he was taken aback by Luanda's four-year plan. Cabelly reassured him that we had no intention of forcing decisions on such a lopsided basis. It was remarkable how readily the UNITA leader doubted the motives of the very people who had transformed his situation for the better! Savimbi's biggest worry was the 1988 U.S. elections and the risk that we in the State Department—also looking at the clock—would support a settlement at his expense.

Pretoria was another worry for the UNITA leader. Angered by the closer U.S. links with UNITA, Botha retaliated by downgrading communication with UNITA. Savimbi had to get along with a handful of manipulative SADF military intelligence officers who advertised their anti-American sentiments and "blackmailed" UNITA to do things for South Africa. Savimbi fretted that the South Africans were in a foul, self-destructive mood. Their anti-U.S. sentiments might end up costing him his best chance for any sort of a deal: Pretoria, he reasoned, would block our settlement drive because it needed the Cubans to remain in Angola for domestic and Namibian reasons.

The contrast between the conflicts in Afghanistan and Southern Africa was becoming increasingly clear. In our case, South Africa and Cuba had emerged as the key players. The Cubans seemed to have a coherent game plan. The South Africans clearly did not. But what about the Soviets themselves? When we met in the State Department for three hours on March 21, Anatoliy Adamishin fell short of our expectations. The Soviet deputy foreign minister offered no specific ideas for advancing the process and no concrete support for our efforts. He noted that momentum seemed to be developing toward a solution. But Moscow could only support an "honest, fair settlement"—not a onesided deal. Drawing clever distinctions, Adamishin said the Soviets supported the current momentum ("we are not holding anyone back") as well as the U.S. mediating role ("we do not tell the Angolans and Cubans you will deceive them, even though of course you will!").

We discussed the continuing SADF presence in Angola, the question of U.S. and South African aid to UNITA, and the timing and conditions for Angolan internal reconciliation. Adamishin declined to discuss the Cuban withdrawal timetable, claiming that this was not a Soviet issue. I told Adamishin that Moscow was not living up to its professed intention of supporting political solutions to regional conflicts. It was leaving Washington to do all the work, while it stayed on the sidelines, ratifying the Angolan-Cuban line. Adamishin objected: Moscow was not on the sidelines, it was supporting friends with whom it had treaty relations. The Soviets would not dictate to Luanda that it should talk to UNITA. Nor would it push its Angolan and Cuban allies toward a more forthcoming position on the Cuban timetable, as we were asking. I made clear that we had no intention of ending support for UNITA. Both superpowers were engaged in Angola. Was Moscow prepared to cut off its own military support of Luanda, I asked. These external roles were the reflection of an internal problem. Why not solve it instead of putting forward absurd, four-year proposals for Cuban withdrawal?

Adamishin and I also tangled on the subject of Castro's military moves in southern Angola. Surely Moscow did not believe that Pretoria could be bullied out of Angola by Castro? This was a "dangerous game" that would, in fact, give Pretoria's hardliners exactly what they wanted. Adamishin retorted that we Americans should be pleased with Castro's actions—could *we* get the SADF out of Angola? Not without a political context, I replied, and neither can Castro or the Soviet Union.

Adamishin summarized by saying that we agreed on the desirability of a Namibia-Angola settlement, but not on the terms of such a settlement. Moscow was less involved formally than Washington, but he did not rule out helping where this would be consistent with Soviet positions. The Soviets, he added, would not seek "ideological purity"—what was good for the parties was fine for the Soviet Union. Perhaps we were beginning to "have the feel of a common road." Earlier, Adamishin had revealed his intention to visit Havana and Luanda. He now spoke of the need for us to maintain "regular" contact. Why not write me a letter at the end of your trip, I suggested. Adamishin seemed pleased with this modest step toward practical coordination. It may have been the most important business we transacted that afternoon.

How best to interpret Adamishin's opaque performance in March 1988? Were they free-riding on our diplomacy while maintaining their image with suspicious clients? Were they using the image of U.S.-Soviet dialogue as a cover for continued behind-the-scenes obstructionism? Or, were they coaching their Marxist allies to behave constructively? Perhaps the real story revolved around Shevardnadze's gradual assertion of authority over additional arenas of Soviet policy: Adamishin had remarked that Afghanistan would soon be resolved, and that would help.

The South Africans Come to Washington

By the end of March 1988, there were still grounds for doubt about the motives of all of these characters. Things were moving, but where and why? Since we did not know, we had to play all parties off against each other. We would coach everyone to test everyone else by laying out choices. Flux would be our invisible ally. All these tools were required with the South Africans, who arrived in Washington for three days of consultations on March 28.

Neil van Heerden and Derek Auret, his top official for Namibia and Angola, expressed appreciation to be in Washington right after the Soviets left. Here was an arena where we had unique and undisputed analytical primacy, and Pretoria craved our input. At a second level, Pik Botha's ablest officials came to Washington to acquire ammunition for use back home. They made no secret of this objective as they foraged behind every statement for pertinent arguments and information. We did not hesitate to collude in this noble business.

They, like Savimbi, had some doubts. Did we have our eyes open as we worked with Gorbachev? We expanded upon the "decisive moment" line from Shultz's March 12 letter—making clear what Pretoria ought to do, but not pleading for anything. We wanted them to return home with winning arguments for moving to the table and responding to Luanda's four-year plan. But we also wanted them to return personally persuaded that it made sense to engage with us again.

Neil van Heerden knew us well, having served under then Ambassador to Washington Pik Botha in the 1970s. We knew him as one of the strongest two or three players to serve on Botha's team since he became foreign minister in 1977. It was a major blow to our cause when he left the Southern Africa desk in 1980 for five years as ambassador to Bonn (taking Auret with him for part of that time). The period from 1985 (when former Director-General and Ambassador to Washington Brand Fourie retired) to 1987 (when van Heerden became director-general at the young age of forty-eight) saw all-time lows in our relations and in the bureaucratic clout of Pik Botha's department.

Trained in political science and law at South African universities, van Heerden has the presence and the dressed-for-success look of a British merchant banker. His cool reserve and seeming nonchalance made him the perfect foil to his mercurial and intense minister. At times, van Heerden seemed aloof, as if other people's single-mindedness was actually rather boring and he would prefer to go shopping or get tickets to the theater. Understated mannerisms set him off from the more typical personae of Afrikaner bureaucrats in Pretoria.

The van Heerden mission to Washington in March 1988 became a turning point in South African foreign policy. We started by discussing Soviet motives and reviewing the prospects for U.S.-Soviet cooperation to push things along. Did we think the time had arrived when Moscow would simply "deliver" Havana and Luanda and Washington would "deliver" Pretoria? No way, we replied, but there were some emerging areas of agreement. We both believed that there was a *de facto* connection between Namibia and Angola: they would consider supporting Cuban withdrawal only in the context of Resolution 435. When did Moscow and Havana become linkage advocates, van Heerden wanted to know. We pointed out how, from the perspective of the Cubans and Soviets, getting Resolution 435 implemented by Pretoria could be presented as their "accomplishment."

And we both backed the unconditional implementation of UNSC Resolution 602 calling for immediate SADF withdrawal from Angola.

Van Heerden took this in with an icy expression. He did not yet appreciate our extremely nuanced position: we could not officially defend the SADF presence in Angola, but we had no intention of actually pressuring them to leave except as part of a series of mutually reinforcing steps.

Van Heerden declared airily that he was "frankly astounded" that we really believed Moscow was pleased to see momentum building behind our initiative. How did this jibe with the Soviets' lavish rearmament of the MPLA and the well-armed Cuban forces moving south in Angola? Why would Moscow need to go along with our settlement at all, especially after having worked so hard to block it all these years? I turned to Chas Freeman, who loved assignments like this. Moscow will not sell out the MPLA, and would prefer that it survive. But it also has come to grasp the reality of South Africa's staying power and to see through the fiction of the "armed struggle," Freeman explained. There was little pressure on Moscow, but there are growing incentives. The Soviets were on a treadmill with their tarnished African empire. A settlement would ease the financial burden, and especially the political burden on East-West relations. Gorbachev wanted deals with Reagan—the most conservative U.S. leader in decades—as insurance with any future administration. The question, Napper added, was whether Namibia and Angola would make it onto the crowded agenda of U.S.-Soviet ministerial and summit meetings. It depends on you, I added with a smile. Seldom at a loss, van Heerden noted that "we South Africans always try to be helpful."

There were hawks at home who would ask if the Americans had completely lost their skeptical faculties, van Heerden continued. How does one reply to charges that the talk of peace is an elaborate trap? We noted that there are all kinds of traps. Being portrayed as the obstacle, the party unwilling to talk, is also a trap from which it can be costly to recover. And there is the risk of a military trap. We had bluntly warned the Soviets about Castro's actions. But it was possible that the Soviets and Cubans were hoping the South Africans would get caught with their fingers in the Angolan honeypot. The way to deal with traps was to set up your own.

Van Heerden termed the four-year plan "too dreadful to contemplate," and stressed that his country's soldiers would want their gains reflected in any talks; nor could their losses (he spoke of thirty-five SADF dead) be ignored. UNITA's survival would be central in Pretoria's (especially P. W. Botha's) thinking. We pointed out how important Cuban withdrawal was to UNITA: the Cubans were vital to FAPLA air cover, air defense, logistics, maintenance, training, and the security of major urban centers. UNITA would not be restricted in any way by a Resolution 435 /

Cuban withdrawal agreement since there would be no internal cease-fire. That would only come when the MPLA and UNITA made peace with each other. We urged our visitors to think of an agreement as a win-win situation for the SADF; Cuban withdrawal would come as the direct result of South African policies since 1975. Pretoria would be "decolonizing" Angola and ridding the region of its only serious conventional adversary.

Tactically, it was South Africa's turn to make a move. We saw no prospect of eliciting a better offer from Luanda until South Africa replied to this one. However, the reply was not a precondition to holding proximity or direct talks, and could be communicated once the parties got to the table. We confirmed that Cubans would participate as one of the parties, and that our role would be as mediator (van Heerden preferred the less imposing term "facilitator"). He expressed a strong preference for delegations of subcabinet rank to lower the profile and the temperature of an initial encounter. Ndalu and Geldenhuys, who were precise counterparts, had worked well together on the military side back in 1984. The agenda would focus on exchanging and discussing proposals (the Angolan-Cuban plan, the U.S. documents, and any new proposal South Africa might make) and narrowing gaps related to a Namibia-Angola settlement.

The issue of Cubans being present at the table would trouble some of his colleagues, van Heerden noted, suggesting that the use of military force buys a seat at the table—not a popular view in the National Party. The Cubans, it would be argued, had no right being there in the first place, and South Africans should not offer concessions to get them out. We countered that we had offered a procedural concession to get a substantive result. So far, it seemed to be working. We did not attempt to coach the South Africans on Cuban motives and psychology at this stage since we remained uncertain ourselves. Further, it was easier to rely on a shared fascination with Gorbachev's innovations—a far more credible "explanation" for what was going on, both in Pretoria and Washington.

Van Heerden volunteered that this opening had come sooner than they had envisaged, catching his government somewhat unprepared. (That was an understatement.) Mike Armacost, van Heerden's counterpart, sought firm assurances that the South Africans were, indeed, thinking in terms of a Resolution 435-based settlement that would include Namibian independence. The United States would not press the Soviets to cooperate if Pretoria was playing another game. Van Heerden was categorical: South Africa did not need an endless military adventure far from its borders. The Angolan war had become something of a political issue. Moreover, the outlook was enhanced by UNITA's current strength and the SADF's high degree of self-confidence. If the Cubans forced their hand, the SADF would engage them to protect its interests.

Armacost pointed to the timing created by our election-year calendar. Sanctions could be stoked up again as an electoral gambit, but this would be less likely if a serious negotiation were under way. As for the election itself, a political change in Washington could disrupt the entire negotiating framework. Van Heerden appeared more interested in knowing whether we would soon be lame-ducked, and was impressed to hear that Reagan and Shultz were committed to going forward full tilt with the Soviet dialogue on multiple fronts. Before van Heerden's return to South Africa, I summarized the arguments for an early South African "yes." The "window" was now, before the Angolans and Cubans began wondering whether to wait for our election, before the risk of a U.S. policy change became palpable, before some military incident triggered a cycle of escalation, before the peak of our election season with all of its temptations to exploit the South African issue, and before the May summit so as to capitalize on possible Soviet interest in new areas of cooperation.

We had done what we could to bring Pretoria back. Would it be enough? Within their structure, van Heerden and Auret would not have an easy time. Our reasoning was too abstract and our perspective too "balanced" to be directly useful in their councils. But the tactical picture simplified the choice facing them. Everyone, including "those bloody Americans," had placed the ball in their court. Why not meet and reply to Luanda's latest move? The risk of meeting was less than that of refusing. South Africa would play the American game, answer the Angolan-Cuban mail, keep options open, and perhaps learn something useful in the process. It could be described as a purely incremental step; it signified almost nothing about South Africa's still-to-be-determined bottom line.

We learned of the South African decision to meet the Cubans and Angolans in mid-April. There would be no need for the intermediate step of proximity talks: this would be a face-to-face meeting. A quick check told us that it might take months to negotiate agreement on an African venue since the parties had mutually exclusive lists. We scrambled to line up some options in Britain. Despite their strong preference for an African venue, the Bothas could hardly reject Thatcher's capital. The Angolans were usually up for Western European travel. And the Cubans seldom got invited anywhere—certainly not to London. We quickly nailed down a bilateral meeting with Adamishin and Vasev in London, timed for the eve of the first round of tripartite talks between Angola, Cuba, and South Africa. Adamishin greeted me at his embassy with the words, "I want to congratulate you—you have already scored a major achievement!" The Soviets seemed about to get aboard the moving train. Now the South Africans were thinking about it, too.

17

Reflections on the Endgame, 1988

When we convened the London round of negotiations on May 2, 1988, there was no way of knowing that this was the start of a road-show that would run non-stop for the next eight months. London was the first of twelve Angolan–Cuban–South African meetings under U.S. mediation, leading to signature of the New York Accords on December 22. The people who gathered for this first dramatic, but tentative, encounter had little idea that they would do little else for the next thirty-two weeks. By midsummer, we had already busted our annual travel budget.

The Road to New York

Initially, we labored to locate venues for our trilateral meetings. It was like being the leader of a flock of ill-behaved migratory birds who argued about everything and messed up every neighborhood they visited. Durrants Hotel, a quiet, West End establishment four blocks north of London's Oxford Street, hosted us for Round One in early May. A family-run hotel catering to "discerning guests," Durrants coped as best it could when some eighty American, Angolan, Cuban, and South African delegates showed up for the first plenary in a cramped basement meeting room. Hotel staff and regulars looked stunned as our flock of ministers, generals, intelligence officers, party bureaucrats, muscular security agents, and official media elbowed their way through sedate Georgian public rooms for a place at the table, or the bar. A swarm of journalists descended on the beleaguered little hotel on George Street to stake out the historic event. In search of some privacy, the Cuban and South African chiefs of defense staff retired to a second-floor bedroom suite for some man-to-man signal sending. Neither we nor the Durrants management had quite anticipated the practical implications of the event. We were never invited back.

Despite a relatively successful opening round of exploratory talks in London, a mini-test of wills quickly developed on the question of where the next meeting should be held. The Botha government saw the peace talks as a means to obtain African entry visas and official receptions that would otherwise be denied them. There were deeper motives behind the tactical gamesmanship: Pretoria's diplomats had sold the whole process to P. W. Botha ("the old crocodile") by claiming that, whatever their results, the talks would open African doors and enhance South Africa's acceptability as a legitimate regional hegemon. The Cubans and Angolans had a contrary motive, suspecting that they were being used to help facilitate diplomatic tourism by the isolated South Africans. Moreover, their list of acceptable African sites differed sharply from Pretoria's. Later, the Cubans tried to play the same game, wangling invitations from Brazil and Mexico in hopes of adding luster to their own diplomatic standing in South America.

These and other shenanigans bogged us down immediately after the London meeting. We were not amused when the South Africans persuaded the Angolans to meet with them, separately and alone, in Brazzaville in mid-May. The meeting accomplished nothing. But it made the Cubans irate to be excluded from this cozy rendezvous. The Soviets claimed to believe that we were behind it. I rushed out to Zaire to brief its leader Mobutu, and Savimbi of UNITA, and to ask Sassou-Nguesso, the Congolese leader, what he thought he was doing by facilitating Pretoria's diversionary maneuvers. On May 18–19, I met Adamishin in Lisbon to review the logjam. African diplomacy, I remarked, was like a resort hotel with many rooms and no locks on the doors. The South Africans had rented the bridal suite and invited the MPLA to join them. Luanda could have said "no"! Far from a U.S. plot, Pretoria's tryst with Luanda was a defiant assertion of South African autonomy from both superpowers. Grinning, Adamishin declared that the Soviets and Cubans would never go astray in an African hotel, but Angolan conduct was less predictable.

It took several more weeks to untangle the snarl over venues. Finally, in mid-June, the Egyptians rescued us by offering to host our flock for Round Two. They offered us a large hotel near the Cairo airport, and proceeded to place it and all four delegations under the omnipresent gaze of well-armed Egyptian security. We felt safe and secure, though it was difficult to organize a private conversation. The Mubarak government set a high standard of constructive common sense for other African governments. The Cairo meeting came amidst the peak of military tensions in southwestern Angola—on the eve of the final clashes in the war no one in Havana or Pretoria wanted. The parties seemed jumpy at the table, engaging in provocative verbal fireworks on the opening-day plenary. But they carefully pulled back from the brink of rupture with their manhood intact and several proposals on the table for future review.

To avoid any recurrence of the tangle over venues, we decided to offer up a suitable facility in New York for Round Three in mid-July. (We eventually settled on the Coast Guard Officers' Club at Governor's Island in New York Harbor.) The main result of three days at Governor's Island was the New York Principles—the first agreed and publicly visible document of the negotiation (see Appendix 1). Soon, we would be deluged with African and non-African offers to host us. The Cairo and New York meetings effectively ended the squabbling over venues. Cape Verde hosted the next meeting in late July, a tense and inconclusive exchange between soldiers and military experts on the terms for a military disengagement. One week later, in early August, we led our flock to Geneva for Round Five, the decisive turning point where we negotiated the ending of the war and defined a procedural blueprint (a "roadmap") for building the peace. The Geneva Protocol (see Appendix 2), unpublished until much later, captured these agreements.

Brazzaville, a place of complex significance for each of the parties, was our site for Round Six (late August). When we fell short of our goal of obtaining agreement on a Cuban withdrawal schedule in this first attempt, we resumed our work in Brazzaville for Rounds Seven (early September) and Eight (late September). But consensus still eluded us. By now, the delegations had missed their first set of target dates, and nerves had begun to fray in the arduous bargaining. We returned to New York and Geneva, respectively, for Rounds Nine (October) and Ten (November). New York was a bust this time around—the Angolans and Cubans seemed to have opted for a waiting game on the eve of the presidential elections. We reassembled in Geneva in mid-November, shortly after George Bush's overwhelming victory. After nearly four days of non-stop shuttling from floor to floor of the Inter-Continental Hotel, we finally reached agreement on a twenty-seven-month Cuban withdrawal timetable. We had cracked the toughest nut.

But all delegations felt obliged to return to Brazzaville to wrap up the remaining pieces of the package. Sassou deserved this prize after sponsoring the Southern African peace process repeatedly since April

1987. Round Eleven (early December) fell apart when the South African delegation had to rush home to put out a minor political fire. We left Brazzaville frustrated once more, but returned a few days later for Round Twelve, and signed the Brazzaville Protocol on December 13. This defined the dates for signature (December 22) and implementation of the accords as April 1, 1989; confirmed a deadline for talks on verification; and created a joint commission among the parties to oversee the entire process.

On December 21, our flock descended upon New York for the signing of the bilateral and tripartite Angolan-Cuban Accords (see Appendices 4 and 5) on the following day. Last-minute maneuvers by the Angolans and Cubans converted this into a mini-Round Thirteen: we had no choice but to insert ourselves into the drafting of their own bilateral accord containing the Cuban timetable. I had returned to Washington late on the 21st in order to be able to escort Secretary Shultz up to the signing festivities the next morning, leaving Chas Freeman and my negotiating team in place to nail things down. They worked until the early hours of December 22, hammering out final details on the top of a piano in the lobby of the U.N. Plaza Hotel. This was the very day of our carefully planned signing ceremony in U.N. Headquarters! That morning the parties were jumpy, and proceded to attack each other (and us) during the actual ceremony. But they signed the interlinked trilateral and bilateral agreements. The deed was finally done, less than a month before the end of the Reagan era.

The Tripartite Process: Form and Substance

Observers often described our 1988 marathon as the "quadripartite" talks. This was odd. Technically, there were three "parties" in our flock, though it often made more sense to think of "two sides" since the Cubans were officially part of the Angolan delegation. The shape of our table confirmed the point: it was a horseshoe, with the United States at the head, the South Africans on one side, and Angolans-Cubans sitting jointly opposite them.

In reality, we were the brokers between two sides (containing three governments); we were not a party. In July, we underscored the point once again by informing the parties that the United States would not be signing the New York Principles. We stuck to that position throughout, signing no documents or side agreements with anyone. This stance offered many advantages. It protected the negotiations from the American political process, sidestepping the possible requirement for Senate ratification of an agreement to which the United States is a party. This cost us a theoretical "veto" over the terms of agreement, but we knew that the logic of our settlement framework would assure satisfactory terms. Angola and Cuba were unlikely to "sell out" on Resolution 435 and the South Africans were unlikely to "sell out" on the Cuban withdrawal schedule, placing Savimbi in jeopardy.

Our stance also protected the talks from potential Soviet pressure. We had little desire to jointly "guarantee" the behavior of the parties—and the Congress would have had even less. We also wished to avoid possible Soviet pressure to embrace high-sounding principles which would, in reality, have required us to cut off UNITA. Our unhappy experience with these issues in the Afghanistan talks during the spring of 1988 led Shultz to give me firm guidance against falling into such traps.

The formal proceedings were conducted in English, Portuguese, and Spanish. The U.S. and Cuban teams each provided simultaneous Spanish-English and English-Spanish coverage. Our interpreter also handled Portuguese in both directions. The South Africans and Angolans were content to rely on us for simultaneous interpretation. When they met bilaterally, however, we worried about their ability to hear each other. Precision and nuance of language can be of such decisive importance in a process that depends so heavily on accurate transmission and reception of signals, hints, jokes, and explanations. In our bilateral working sessions, consecutive (rather than simultaneous) translation was the norm. It permits greater precision, and gives the listener who has any facility for languages two shots at the message. It was here that we probed for every nuance in a party's sense of priorities, and coached it on the interests and fears of the "other side." We were many times blessed to have Alex Schiavo on our team. A world-class professional interpreter affiliated with the Inter-American Defense College, Schiavo was our secret weapon, often doubling as master of ceremonies and chief of protocol.

Formal exchanges at the conference table are where proposals are set forth and defended. This is the place for writing history and building a record for the domestic audience. It may also be the place for dramatic signal sending or the offering of gestures. But there were real limits to what could be done in formal plenaries. During the long road from London to New York, we spent less and less time at the plenary table. As the process matured in Cairo and New York, we conducted side meetings with individual delegations before, during, and after the formal sessions. And we encouraged the parties to hold such sessions with each other. Host government officials and media observers sometimes wondered—after two days without a formal meeting—if our ship had run aground. But they missed the point. This very looseness of structure enabled us (and others) to conduct direct diplomacy with each of the parties, opening up a vast field of possibilities.

Such working sessions in New York during the July 10–13 meetings gave us the input we required to broker an agreement on the New York Principles. To achieve closure, we listened to Angolan and South African suggestions that we convene an executive session for the heads of delegation plus one. There would be no speeches and no notetakers. When we emerged from our tiny meeting room, cheers broke out among the other delegates. The one-page text of "Principles for a Peaceful Settlement in Southwestern Africa" contained in summary form our vision of a regional security framework. The Namibia-Angola link was contained in the magic words ". . . each of these principles is indispensable to a comprehensive settlement."

By the time of Rounds Six through Eight in Brazzaville, less than 5 percent of our work was done at the horseshoe table. Our role was to play upon the dynamics between and within "the sides." Often, this could best be done by splitting off the heads of delegations to meet in a restricted, informal ambiance. This had the advantage of freeing up the working-level experts (who called themselves "juniors" or "grass") to meet more or less spontaneously. I encouraged this decentralized procedure: the creative and uninstructed exchanges of the "grass" could be highly informative. If necessary, the "elephants" could always trample on "incorrect" ideas from the "grass." At times, our mission was to intervene in the internal balances within a delegation (e.g., providing ammunition to doves or taking on burdens ourselves at the request of the hawks). Sometimes we played the Angolans and Cubans separately, coaching them on ways to influence each other as well as the South Africans. Sometimes we reached out to mobilize an intervention by U.N. Secretariat officials, the British, the Soviets, or the Congolese.

It was amusing to read accounts of the "1988 negotiations on Southern Africa," as if the peace process emerged full-blown in May of that year, the progeny of some quickie superpower liaison. In reality, the basic terms and concepts enshrined in the New York Principles, the Geneva Protocol, the Brazzaville Protocol, and the New York Accords were remarkably similar to earlier proposals from our exchanges with the parties going back to the early 1980s. But the pace and intensity of our May through December experience in 1988 was unlike anything we (or the other delegations) had previously encountered. Momentum helped keep our flock headed in the right direction. By July and August, we had established our rhythm, and the composition of delegations had stabilized. There were fewer opportunities for side games and unhelpful maneuvers. We were engaged in nearly round-the-clock improvisation, bending with the moves and signals that flowed from an endless stream of meetings and conversations.

Mediation entails collusion with everyone against everyone, bearing in mind that all parties are on the other side of the table from the mediator. We relied upon our information and a sense of humor as we sought to deploy candid assessments and unexpected confidences that shatter stereotypes. But the mediator must also learn when to shut up and hold fire, when to defer to the parties' own ideas, which may be "better" than his own overtly settlement-oriented instincts. Nothing is more valuable than the self-respect and strength of the parties. We learned to bolster their self-confidence, while pushing them to the edge of their imaginations about each other. And we battled to keep our own parochialism under control.

The continuity and intensity of the work—and the proximity of delegations working and living in the same buildings for days on end—contributed to a new chemistry. Imperceptibly, each delegation evolved from an abstraction into concrete people whose style of delivery, way of thinking, and body language became familiar. The words of specific individuals "on the other side" would be remembered and cited favorably, as a gesture of respect and a symbolic affirmation of common ground.

The sharing of confidences can be a powerful bargaining tool. Chafing under the burdens of coalition diplomacy with the "less efficient" Angolans, the Cubans also hungered for direct dealings with Washington. By now, my delegation was more deeply engaged in the conduct of U.S.-Cuban relations than any other part of our government. The Cubans relished the proper treatment we accorded them as important players. But the less attention drawn to this situation, the better. On one occasion I had to warn them that any expression of Cuban enthusiasm for our role could kill it. They got the point.

It was essential to help overcome the gulfs of culture, ignorance, pride, and fear between the parties. From May through August, we worked to nurture a dialogue between General Geldenhuys and his Cuban counterpart, General Ulises Rosales del Toro. We introduced them and facilitated their first private encounter in London in May. In New York in mid-July—after the tit-for-tat military clashes at Techipa and Calueque—we brokered some six hours of military exchanges. My Defense Department counterpart, Jim Woods, applied his deep regional expertise and disarmingly candid manner to get them to think creatively. The New York Principles needed urgent support at the military level.

But getting these men to communicate openly was a struggle. Rosales had all the political subtlety of a career soldier living in mortal fear of his micro-managing president. He tended to mix professions of peaceful intent with a thinly veiled note of intimidation. Geldenhuys spoke in crisp, soft-spoken tones, sticking to facts and avoiding flourishes. But he found it necessary gently to remind Rosales of the Boer War, when his people held the British Empire at bay for three years at the zenith of its power. In New York, Rosales told him gravely that the perilous situation in southern Angola could only be ended by a unilateral SADF withdrawal. Cuba was acting with restraint. It did not seek incidents. Why did Pretoria continue a policy of intervention within Angolan territory that "can no longer be sustained with your current strength"?

Having been dealt this card by Castro and his generals, Geldenhuys had every incentive to demand some reciprocal measures of restraint. And Castro's grandiose rhetoric about Cuban military successes only compounded the difficulty: how could Geldenhuys sell a final pull-out at home if it were being described by the other side as some sort of retreat at gunpoint?

At the edge of his mandate, Geldenhuys suggested a range of ideas that could represent a "reasonable package" for all concerned. But the Cubans and Angolans offered nothing specific—only a generalized pledge that South African withdrawal would have "positive consequences" on the ground. Rosales and Ndalu apparently had no idea what it would be like trying to sell *that* horse in Pretoria! Woods stated flatly that there would be no settlement unless the parties found common ground on how to stabilize the dangerously fluid military stand-off and to establish a channel of communication between sector commanders on the ground.

Our therapy of openness worked much more quickly with Carlos Aldana Escalante, the new head of the Cuban delegation (who replaced Jorge Risquet Valdes in Round Three in New York), and the Communist Party secretary for ideology. A rising star in the Party, Aldana had little formal diplomatic experience before 1988. A man of medium build with dark eyes and a bushy mustache, Aldana looked unprepossessing at first glance. In another life and time, he might have run a car dealership or coached a soccer team.

At first, we assumed he was a Party hack. But Aldana quickly rose in our estimation. He had a feel for reading people and situations; and he was a born craftsman of positive-sum negotiation. The contrast with Risquet was striking. In Cairo, when I probed Cuba's military intentions at the Namibian border, Risquet smiled menacingly and remarked that he could offer me "no Tylenol." Aldana looked unhappy. Afterward, we reached out to one of his associates to say bluntly what we thought of Risquet's contributions to the peace process. (We also told the Soviets and Angolans that we were less than enchanted with Risquet. They listened, while noting that Pik Botha, Pretoria's top man in Cairo, was also an acquired taste.)

In New York just a little over two weeks later, Aldana showed up as the Cuban head of delegation. (Each delegation was lowered simultaneously to the subministerial rank. This had the immediately favorable impact of reducing polemics, curtailing the intrusion of domestic politics, and limiting traveling media.) In one conversation over lunch, Aldana offered me an eloquent description of how much Cuba would gain from an honorable end to the conflicts in Southern Africa. The contrast could not have been clearer. Neil van Heerden, Jannie Geldenhuys, and Niel Barnard are the guys who need to hear your message, I responded. Tell *them* that Cuba wants a settlement. Aldana and I developed the habit of listening to each other. On this occasion, he went to the table and made a presentation which South African officials were still talking about three years later. Seizing upon van Heerden's own phraseology, Aldana called for a document of principles that would reflect "the legitimate interests of all." It should point the way to a "peace without losers," where all parties would be seen as contributing to the birth of the new state of Namibia. The "sovereign actions" of each party would be stated in positive terms. Implementing Resolution 435 would be Pretoria's primary contribution, enhancing its reputation as a "responsible party."

As for the Angolans and Cubans, they could now leave aside their "rhetoric" and "recognize that there is a linkage" between Namibia and Angola. The question was how to reflect it "so that no one is a loser." Aldana appealed for terminology stressing the free and sovereign nature of each side's contribution. Each side had its home audience. "No one could think of imposing Resolution 435 on South Africa." As for Cuba, nothing could be more honorable than Cuban troop withdrawal from Angola "of our own free will and in the context of Resolution 435 so that a new nation is born." Total Cuban withdrawal under U.N. verification *will* take place, Aldana continued, repeating for good measure that "linkage exists and its existence is accepted."

It was July 11, 1988. The room fell silent and the air was electric as van Heerden took the floor to thank the "distinguished and honorable" leader of the Cuban team for his observations. He saluted Aldana's prose and the spirit behind it. Our coaching and van Heerden's earlier gesture—putting aside the South African draft and agreeing to work on the basis of an Angolan-Cuban draft—had paid off handsomely. From then on, every intervention was larded with references to "sovereign acts."

Delegations I Have Known

The U.S. delegation in 1988 accurately reflected the recently restored interagency peace back in Washington. The keys to this happy state of affairs were three-fold. First, I enjoyed the confidence of the Secretary of State, who ensured that I had support in Washington. Second, we included my NSC and Defense Department counterparts (Hank Cohen and Jim Woods, respectively) as ranking members of our delegation. They helped present a solid front, and provided me with their leadership and counsel. Their participation reinforced the regular channel Shultz maintained with his NSC and Defense colleagues. Finally, we enjoyed constant communication with our team in Washington, headed by Chas Freeman and supported by Southern African Affairs director Gib Lanpher. Their task was to brief the top levels on every significant development and to channel feedback and guidance to us. Freeman served as my alter ego, keeping all fronts—interagency, congressional, and the media—under control back home. It was essential to have superlative backstopping by officers who could trade places with us and not miss a beat. We had it.

Cohen and Woods provided the seniority and wide experience to round out my subministerial team, thus enabling us to schedule simultaneous meetings on political-diplomatic or military matters at any level necessary. Ed Perkins, our ambassador in Pretoria, linked his mission to the negotiation and brought his "on the ground" credibility to bear with other delegates. Robert Cabelly, my special assistant, remained at my side as intelligence and policy adviser and troubleshooter. Larry Napper and John Ordway provided overall policy input and leadership on all written work, while also managing its practical and logistical aspects. They received working-level support from their Office of Southern African Affairs colleague, Mike McKinley (Angola desk), who was joined by Earl Irving (Namibia desk) at midpoint. My legal adviser, John Byerly, became an invaluable member of the team as adviser-negotiator, just as had his predecessor Nancy Ely-Raphel in the 1981–85 period. Lieutenant Colonel Charlie Snyder, my military adviser (on long-term secondment from the Army) provided essential support on the many political-military equations we confronted.

Each of these officers had unique skills. Snyder was the sort of fellow you would want in command of the police detail in a neighborhood troubled by gang wars. Southern Africa in the 1980s probably reminded him of his native Upper West Side in New York. He knew how to read the hard men of military intelligence and internal security, and he had an uncanny knack for loosening the tongues of opinionated Cubans,

Angolans, and South Africans. Byerly sported an open, hopeful manner and tried to find something constructive to say about even the most hopeless cases. One might mistake him for a guest-host on "Mr. Rogers' Neighborhood." We needed those qualities, too. His rigorous sense of "balance" and "respect" for the parties won their abiding confidence; each, in its own way, was unaccustomed to respectful treatment, least of all by Americans.

The regulars on my delegation collectively represented over 150 years of professional experience in African affairs. More important, we also represented a wide range of personal styles, political convictions, educational attainments, non-African experience, and people skills. We often argued heatedly over how to handle a specific problem. But there were no differences on achieving the settlement we had defined in 1981. This was a committed team.

The other delegations were not so fortunate. The Angolans and Cubans faced the constant challenge of coalition diplomacy. This particular alliance was subject to the specific strains of unequal power, divergent decisionmaking systems, and distinctly different interests. The Marxist brothers had little in common. Big brother was a highly militarized regional power capable of projecting its might 7,000 miles away. Little brother had become an emblem of Afro-Marxist failure, a country under rival foreign occupations. One regime featured the strategic "coherence" of Attila the Hun; the other featured an indecisive collegial leadership under a man still unable to impose himself.

Castro had the clearest strategy of any of the parties. He was transfixed by the negotiations, setting aside other business for much of the year. Our Cuban counterparts made clear just how closely "the Beard" was following each move—at the table and on the ground. We learned, for example, that the annoying presence of Cuban technicians with camcorders was partly inspired by Castro's insatiable appetite for viewing the proceedings on video cassette. Invisible but omnipresent, he kept his delegation on a short but well-defined leash. Aldana and his team knew that Castro wanted a deal and they knew what kind of deal he wanted.

General Ndalu, Franca Van Dunem, and other members of the MPLA delegation did not have such clear marching orders. The collegial structure in Luanda meant that an especially heavy burden was placed on Ndalu's shoulders to hold his delegation together and to support his president's control over it. By 1988, no one was better qualified to carry this burden than Ndalu, a man for all seasons who threatened no one in Luanda. To his portfolio as vice defense minister and FAPLA chief of staff, Ndalu had recently added the post of commander of the southwest Angolan military region. Now, as of July, he became Angola's chief diplomat in its most important negotiation. His statesmanlike instincts and graceful personal manner equipped him for the task. He knew us and the South Africans well from years of involvement in the talks. He had always been close to the Cubans, having lived there for years and married a Cuban. This would minimize the frictions that might arise in coalition diplomacy with a far stronger partner.

Like his Cuban counterpart, Ndalu had a delegation comprising diplomats, soldiers, party worthies, and omnipresent security and intelligence people. In Justice Minister Franca Van Dunem, his lead drafter and documentary negotiator, Ndalu had an internationally experienced and legally trained colleague. But he also had a man of pedantic bent who could quickly bog the discussions down in a welter of technicality. In Colonel Antonio Jose Maria, President dos Santos's security adviser, Ndalu had a mercurial and often emotional individual with lots of charm and a knack for offending people. Jose Maria, who had studied for the priesthood in his youth, enjoyed showing off his familiarity with Latin excerpts from Caesar's *Gallic Wars*.

Unlike the Cubans, we detected little evidence of an Angolan negotiating strategy, especially during the early going. The MPLA was delighted with the new situation brought about by the Cuban military reinforcements. As Ndalu and Jose Maria told us in Cairo on June 24, they enjoyed the fact that the SADF no longer held all the military cards in southern Angola, and they had relished lobbing verbal shells on the South Africans during the day's plenary. It felt good. They conceded that there were risks in the still unsettled military situation. But Ndalu seemed more impressed by the fact that Geldenhuys, his SADF opposite number, could no longer practice his doctrine of "striking SWAPO guerrillas in their lairs."

In fact, the new military stalemate in Angola felt so good to the MPLA that it just wanted it to last for a while. Cuban withdrawal—just when Cuban reinforcements were peaking—was not Luanda's top priority. And the notion of a rigorous, front-loaded withdrawal timetable (as distinguished from the Angolan-Cuban four-year plan) posed the risk of a new and sudden deterioration in their internal situation. Aldana fully grasped the emerging conflict of interest between the Cuban and Angolan governments. After the highly successful Geneva round in early August, he wanted us to know that his Angolan allies were belatedly coming to grips with the reality that the Cubans would soon be leaving. They would want maximum assurances and the longest possible timetable.

This, Aldana pointed out, was a direct constraint on Cuban freedom of maneuver in the talks. Referring to the four-year withdrawal proposal, Aldana declared that we did not need to persuade Havana to be more flexible (within reasonable limits); his government was prepared to move to a far shorter schedule. It was the Angolans whom we had to persuade. Aldana wanted to shift the onus to Washington for squaring this circle. Cuba had no blueprint to suggest, but Washington should get creative in exporing the question of Angolan reconciliation. We did not exclude the possibility that Ndalu and Aldana were colluding in this routine in hopes of forcing us to play our UNITA aid card—if not now, then later when we came to a crunch. But it was also clear that Angolan fear was a delicate issue for Havana.

We raised the question of political reconciliation at every opportunity: MPLA fear of UNITA could cause the entire negotiation to collapse over the Cuban withdrawal timetable. In the end, however, the Angolans stuck to the position that they would not deal with UNITA until "later." (The Angolans make frequent use of the Portuguese word *amanha;* a colleague once explained that this is like the Spanish *mañana,* except that it does not convey the same sense of urgency!) The Cubans remained torn between their ally and their desire to settle. It took five more months— until November 15, 1988—before the Cuban timetable was resolved. The result was a timetable that would build inexorable pressures on Luanda to deal with Savimbi. (A peace treaty between the Angolan parties was finally signed on May 31, 1991, at the very moment when the final Cuban combat troops departed from Angola, some weeks ahead of schedule.)

Aldana and Ndalu were not the only delegation with problems. The government in Pretoria had long excelled at tactics while failing at strategy. In the past, the apparent absence of strategy was often a deliberate ruse: evasive ambiguities helped to advance a "strategy" of playing for time. But Pretoria's tentative approach at the outset of the 1988 endgame was different. There was no strategic consensus. The national security establishment was best understood as a collection of egos and tendencies operating behind the scenes, while a tough, "do-your-damnedest" exterior was presented to the broader world. P. W. Botha's militarized regional policy was not unanimously supported within the broader cabinet and National Party leadership.

However, splits within the elite on Namibia and Angola remained largely out of sight. The cabinet lived in fear of its irascible leader. The problem was to find a legitimate opening to challenge Botha's natural instincts and the status quo interests of those military bureaucrats who nurtured them. Pik Botha and Neil van Heerden seized upon a series of factors—the Cuban-Angolan acceptance of the total withdrawal principle; Franz Josef Strauss's (and Margaret Thatcher's) readings of Gorbachev's thinking; the array of ammunition we provided; plus the uncertainties in the military situation—to persuade their leadership to explore the negotiating track. From the standpoint of the South African delegation, the tripartite talks might offer the chance to put incremental decisions before Botha.

South Africa's decision to come to the London meeting in May 1988 did not signify that a basic national choice had been made in favor of a settlement. Negative currents swirled around the delegation. In the early going, it had to "prove" itself at the negotiating table—holding out the hand of possible cooperation, but demonstrating requisite toughness and avoiding any hint of being pushed by anyone, especially us. Better to maintain a cool distance from the heavy-breathing American mediators, and even—in mid-May—to run off to meet the Angolans without us.

It was difficult for the South African team to explore the possibilities for a settlement in this atmosphere of political anxiety. Yet nothing could be accomplished unless it became convinced of the seriousness of both the Angolans and the Cubans. The July meeting in New York was the first occasion when the Angolans and Cubans acquired a degree of credibility in South African eyes. But the senior leadership in Pretoria still had taken no basic decisions, and still viewed the tripartite talks as, at best, an exploratory process that had produced no real results. The time had come to get beyond mere talk and polemics. Yet the recent military events at the border after Cairo had created a foul atmosphere and short tempers. The delegation, not surprisingly, walked on eggshells.

This explained its ardent (but unsuccessful) quest to achieve a military understanding to parallel the New York Principles. After Aldana's virtuoso performance, delegation members toyed with the idea of inviting Aldana and Ndalu to South Africa. Perhaps *they* could persuade the two Bothas and Malan that the Cubans were serious about a settlement. "No one will believe *us*," the South African delegates fretted to themselves. They spent long hours on the phone to Pretoria arguing their case for taking the process seriously. But Pretoria was in no rush, and remained unconvinced of the chances for a favorable deal.

Van Heerden and his colleagues faced the classic dilemma of negotiating teams which are fielded for essentially tactical or defensive purposes: How to bridge the gap between political reality at home and progress at the negotiating table. It would be impossible to produce results if they had only a listening brief. Yet it was vital to maintain the confidence of superiors and remove the dangers of poisonous strife within the ranks.

To handle this dilemma the key members made a pact to stick together and to report home *as a team.* This apparently simple principle ran against the grain of recent South African experience. For years, Pretoria's embassies and its traveling missions had contained warring fiefdoms, each with its own policy axes to grind, its own reporting networks and communications channels. Neil van Heerden (Foreign Affairs), Niel Barnard (National Intelligence Service), and Jannie Geldenhuys (SADF chief of staff) knew very well the history, and put an end to it. This time game playing within individual ministries and services would be held in check.

Van Heerden led the team and served as its principal spokesman in exchanges with other delegations. It fell to him to articulate his government's case and persuade the others of his toughness and readiness for bold decisions. He and his deputy, Derek Auret, took the lead in developing the strategems that would attract P. W. Botha's support for the process and the ultimate settlement terms. This included orchestrating official receptions for his wary president in Mozambique and Zaire in September 1988 while the Brazzaville meetings were in full swing. He also helped to launch our host, Sassou-Nguesso, and other Central African presidents on a series of meetings aimed at developing credible African sponsorship of an Angolan reconciliation process. Such events, centered on the ideal of South Africa as an African regional power, significantly helped the foreign ministry to prove itself and shape the decisionmaking process.

As South Africa's leading career diplomat at the time of maximum pariahdom, van Heerden understood the stakes. He believed that the tripartite talks represented an ideal avenue through which to regain the initiative and to reverse the negative dynamics which had gathered force against Pretoria since 1984. Our negotiation and the presence in his capital of Robin Renwick, Margaret Thatcher's extraordinarily gifted and activist ambassador, represented opportunities not to be frittered away. Van Heerden would use both to persuade his leadership that there could never be a better time to settle.

Geldenhuys took the lead in military-to-military exchanges and in the analysis of negotiating options as they affected SADF concerns in both Namibia and Angola. His ranking aide, Major General Cornelius Jacobus van Tonder, bore the title of chief director of military intelligence for the SADF. In practice, he had considerable institutional autonomy as the key figure in his own fiefdom—the SADF's clandestine operations bureaucracy. Van Tonder was a leading proponent of a "forward strategy" in Angola and Mozambique. One of Geldenhuys's many tasks was to keep tabs on van Tonder's ideological enthusiasm and to channel him toward useful activities. These included travels across Africa (jointly with Auret) to promote the UNITA cause and the need for Angolan reconciliation. Van Tonder viewed our whole enterprise with suspicion.

Even in quieter times, Geldenhuys had his work cut out for him. It was not an easy task to lead an officer corps of widely varying viewpoints and hold it together during the SADF's protracted stand-off with the advancing Cubans. His imaginative tactics—at Cuito Cuanavale and, especially, in designing a "killing field" in northern Namibia—marked him as a pro in the diplomacy of war. He helped van Heerden ride herd over the van Tonders of the SADF, who controlled Pretoria's communication channel to UNITA. Geldenhuys also had gently to steer P. W. Botha and his faithful sidekick Magnus Malan away from positions that would have killed the negotiations. Back in May and June, for example, the delegation had instructions to get Savimbi a place at the table and broaden the agenda to include a resolution of the civil war. However laudable this objective, it was a non-starter in 1988, and Geldenhuys knew it.

Niel Barnard, head of civilian intelligence, brought a key constituency onto the team. While National Intelligence did not possess the clout of the SADF's military intelligence directorate on regional military issues, it offered a distinct viewpoint on both regional and global issues (such as Soviet and Cuban intentions). In addition, its domestic intelligence function gave Barnard a major say on anything related to the African National Congress. It fell to this professor-turned-intelligence chief to offer the senior leadership a strategic assessment of the domestic consequences of a regional settlement.

Barnard also took on the assignment of getting something of tangible value in exchange for South Africa's *de facto* commitment, under the New York Principles, to cease its direct, physical support of UNITA. Barnard took the lead on van Heerden's team for negotiating a parallel commitment from the MPLA to expel the ANC from its guerrilla bases in Angola. This was another way to soften the heart of P. W. Botha (and many others). The Cubans and Angolans saw Barnard as a sort of Afrikaner Dr. Strangelove, and asked us to explain the thirty-nine-year-old intelligence chief's meteoric career trajectory. We told them to treat Barnard seriously. Once you peeled away a tough hide, he represented the emotions, fears, and hopes of Pretoria's establishment.

During negotiating rounds, the South Africans conducted themselves very carefully with other delegations, often keeping to themselves and avoiding the sort of mixing that can facilitate "walks in the woods." To outsiders, the delegation seemed cold and a little reluctant to engage. On several occasions, the South Africans abruptly struck their tents and flew home before a round of talks had run its full course. On one such occasion, the rush to the airport came at 2:00 A.M., leaving us to explain to the other side and to our Congolese hosts why the South Africans did not have the time for a more courteous departure. Sometimes, they would arrive announcing their intention to depart as soon as possible. One member of my team was so struck by this recurrent "avoidance complex" that he asked, "Chet, how do Afrikaners reproduce?"

But there was an explanation for van Heerden's conduct. He and his colleagues had begun walking down a hazardous trail. They were beginning to perceive a great prize for Pretoria at the end of that trail. As a matter of patriotic duty and personal conviction, van Heerden, Geldenhuys, and Barnard wished to blaze that trail, and then to escort their political leadership down it. But hazardous trails must be covered in small steps, one at a time. The delegation moved deliberately and stuck close to its mandate. Van Heerden's instincts were reinforced by Geldenhuys, who had studied Communist negotiating tactics. He labored to turn their game on its head by letting deadlines slip and pressures build. Geldenhuys did not believe in hanging around the negotiating site. As likely as not, this would result in further pressure to offer up concessions. It was better to make one's points, then leave the scene and let the situation "cook."

These were the delegations with which we had to deal. At one level, they were sharply asymmetrical. Castro had a clear strategy and could simply give orders to execute it. This decisiveness pulled Ndalu, his delegation, and the Angolan leadership along in his wake. We might still be at the table today were it not for the Cuban factor. The South African team had no such strategic clarity or simple, hierarchical structure. Their whole approach to the process appeared to be tentative, incremental, and even unsure. As late as Round Eleven in early December 1988, a distraught Pik Botha felt obliged to walk out and rush home to deal with yet another bout of high-level tantrums occasioned by unhelpful press stories sourced to his own traveling party.

This asymmetry presented a problem for the American mediators. Cuban-Angolan decisionmaking was faster than the South Africans', and their joint delegation often arrived with apparently clearer instructions and a more specific mandate. It was van Heerden and his colleagues who insisted that agreed documents remain *ad referendum* to cabinet meetings that might not occur for another week. The Angolan and Cuban delegation chose to view this pattern as evidence of an uncertain commitment to the process, and sought to take psychological advantage of it.

But, as we will see, the parties shared similar apprehensions about the political implications of their moves, particularly on the Cuban withdrawal timetable. There was an overall equilibrium at the table, as on the ground. The delegations finally came into roughly synchronous orbit in mid-November in Geneva, where they decided that eleven weeks and five rounds of negotiation were long enough to spend closing the deal on the Cuban timetable.

The Soviet Role

For years, Moscow's dislike for our settlement strategy had been based on the belief that they were engaged in a global, zero-sum contest. Since we had authored the settlement, it must be bad; such reflexive obstructionism was an axiom of Soviet policy. They also had procedural objections to our lead role. Successful U.S. diplomatic leadership in a key Third World hotspot risked creating a dangerous precedent for excluding the USSR from participation in similar situations elsewhere. Quite apart from the specific terms of the deal, Moscow's long-standing insecurity about its superpower status *required* Soviet officials to counter our effort. As Adamishin had remarked to me in mid-1987, "You are playing too many roles."

Moscow's gradual reappraisal of its African policies occurred as one part of an overall reassessment of Soviet global interests, power, and strategy. The first visible signs of that broader process under Gorbachev can be traced back to early 1986. It accelerated in 1987 due to a variety of factors, including the cycle of war in Afghanistan and the priorities of U.S.-Soviet ministerial and summit diplomacy during Reagan's final eighteen months. The takeover of the Moscow foreign policy machinery by Shevardnadze and his "new thinkers" did not all happen in one day. The military and intelligence bureaucracies, and above all the Communist Party had long played a dominant role in shaping African policy.

In his February 8, 1988, speech, Gorbachev took another major step, signaling explicitly that an Afghan settlement could open the way to a more constructive approach in other regional conflicts. But there would be nothing automatic about Soviet "cooperation" in Africa. They faced no inexorable pressure, as in Afghanistan. Nor was there any high-level decision by U.S. and Soviet leaders to make Africa the next candidate for cooperation. The Angolans, Cubans, and South Africans did not begin the endgame in May 1988 because of some signal they had received from Moscow and Washington. In fact, had the final settlement depended upon U.S.-Soviet political will and consensus, it would not have happened. The modern international system does not operate in that manner: regional powers such as South Africa and Cuba do not hang around awaiting superpower instructions to execute.

Instead, two distinct patterns coincided: first, the gradual transformation of superpower relations, including an agreement in principle to explore the resolution of other "regional conflicts"—e.g., conflicts beyond Europe where both the United States and the USSR had acquired a stake; and second, the ripening of the African regional peace process itself in 1987–88. These two processes occurred in separate orbits. Our job was to see if we could somehow synchronize them. We wanted to exploit Moscow's increasing openness—or, at a minimum, to neutralize Soviet conduct that could inhibit the tripartite process.

By May 1988 when the endgame began, U.S. and Soviet priorities were no longer mutually incompatible. The U.S. administration wanted to wrap up the Namibia-Angola settlement before its time ran out. Without giving up anything of substance, we were prepared to work with those who could help us get it—starting with Castro, but including Gorbachev as well. By implication, this would mean including each of them in the process in some appropriate manner and acknowledging their right to a "role." Our goal was substantive, and we were prepared to pay some procedural price to achieve it.

Soviet priorities were shifting the other way. The African empire accumulated by Brezhnev was a loser. By late 1987 and early 1988, Soviet diplomatic, academic, and media elites were increasingly frank in distancing themselves from policy commitments driven by the Party and the armed forces. Soviet realists came to see that Angola was an unmitigated military disaster: no amount of hardware and advisers could bring victory to the MPLA. Gradually, the "new thinkers" accommodated themselves intellectually to some elements of our settlement. And, gradually, they gained greater control over the foreign policy machinery affecting African issues. (It cannot have been pure coincidence that we never encountered a Soviet military or Party official during, or before, the endgame.)

If a way could be found to portray the settlement as a U.N.-based, "Soviet-supported" deal to which the Cubans and Angolans were willing parties, it might make sense to consider changing sides and joining the American peacemakers. On Gorbachev and Shevardnadze's scale of priorities, improved U.S.-Soviet relations came first. This goal depended in part on removing the major tensions provoked by ideological confrontation and military rivalry in the Third World. The trick, from the Soviet standpoint, was to convert one strategy into another without any loss of superpower status. A strategy based on unilateral ideological goals and military means would need to be replaced by one stressing universal goals and political-diplomatic means. The role of a responsible U.N. Security Council permanent member and worldwide peacemaker with Washington represented a more "modern" and "acceptable" form of superpowerdom. Moscow would exchange a weak hand as an imperial military dinosaur for one more consistent with its real resources and its domestic imperatives.

Just as we were prepared to pay a procedural price for a substantive goal, the Soviets were (by May) prepared at least to consider paying a substantive price in order to achieve procedural and status goals. Our priorities were beginning to complement rather than contradict each other. Shultz, who believed in delegating broad authority to his lieutenants, gave me a mandate to explore ways to advance our dialogue with Moscow. Eventually, Shevardnadze would take a page from Shultz's book and empower his diplomats with a similarly broad mandate. But that did not happen right away. Not until the Geneva round in August 1988 did they shed their ambivalence and begin to help move things along.

The Soviets continued to define themselves as the "ally" of Cuba and Angola, and would have been uncomfortable with a role that obliged them to behave in a visibly even-handed manner. They accepted our mediation of the tripartite process, and seemed to grasp the fundamental distinction between their "fraternal" links to Luanda and Havana and our far more complicated relations with all parties: we had sanctions in force against each of them!

The Soviets Feel Their Way

We approached the Soviets to propose a bilateral exchange immediately before the first tripartite round in London in May. We hoped to associate them with the tripartite process and give them a stake in it. We would also send a signal to the parties themselves that Washington and Moscow were "working together" to support a settlement. The Soviets accepted our initiative. For the first time in the long history of these bilateral exchanges, Soviet officials had a mandate to associate themselves with the process. Adamishin made a point of issuing press guidance from his London embassy implying that Moscow was in some way responsible for the good news. After our April 29 meeting, his Africa deputy, Vladillen Vasev, remained in London to track the trilateral talks and liaise with the Cubans and Angolans. From these modest beginnings, we launched ourselves on a case study of superpower improvisation during the final stages of the Cold War. Over the next eight months, an unusual Soviet "observer" role emerged on the fringes of the tripartite talks.

These bilateral talks were by no means harmonious, however. Adamishin fended off our efforts to talk turkey by saying that it was "not useful" to discuss specifics on the eve of the tripartite meeting. We persisted, pressing for a credible explanation of Castro's continuing military buildup in southwestern Angola. Adamishin parroted Castro's line that his moves were helping get Pretoria to negotiate. He sarcastically observed that we were, after all, discussing events taking place on Angolan territory. Cabelly, Napper, and I pointed out the extreme dangers to the peace process of such provocative behavior just north of the Namibian border. It could strengthen SADF hardliners, who would like nothing better than to have some Cuban trophies to hang over their fireplaces. The Soviets replied that the Cubans also had trophy hunters; the top soldiers could sort this out at the upcoming meeting. I asked how we should interpret this attitude to our superiors. Should we say that Moscow had assured us that Castro and dos Santos were only "trying to create opportunities for a political settlement"? If the USSR was indeed becoming a responsible superpower, it should act like one.

Adamishin protested that I was pressing him "to participate" in this negotiation. The Americans wanted everything: we wanted Moscow to remain on the sidelines, but also to hand over all the information at its disposal, he objected. The Soviets were not "real participants." If there were problems, we could talk afterwards. But, then, Adamishin flashed me a card: the Cubans would say that their military actions strengthened their hand at the table, and it would be wrong for the Americans to say that the Soviets had offerred another explanation for Cuban behavior. Smiling, I said that we would not dream of misquoting our Soviet colleague. Pleased to have gotten his point across, Adamishin joked that he would not give me any temptations.

The Soviets did not yet know how to "participate" as a non-participant. But Adamishin told me categorically that Moscow did not, in fact, want to join the formal process at the table. During the next eight months, the Soviets were never physically present in tripartite meetings or in bilateral exchanges amongst the delegations. But either Adamishin or Vasev generally traveled to the city where the talks were held, established contact with us, and camped out in the wings. We urged them to come and promptly informed them of planning details for the meetings.

What accounted for the Soviets' initially tepid and inconsequential performance during the endgame? Partly, it was inexperience: Soviet diplomats knew the arena of U.N. debate, and they were masters of legal and ideological strife. They also were expert in the hard school of East-West negotiation on European security or arms control. But they had little direct knowledge of how a great power can use its influence to make peace among regional players, herding them toward an objective even while maintaining intact its existing relations with the parties. Peacemaking was not their stock-in-trade. Their fear of appearing "disloyal" to Socialist allies seemed to be a stronger instinct.

They also had a lack of information, apart from that provided by their allies, and may have been unsure of what they should actually do as "observers." We decided that it made sense to plan regular bilateral sessions with them during a negotiating round. We began this practice in Cairo, reaching out to Vasev twice in the middle of the proceedings. This gave us the chance to provide him with a direct reading on the atmospherics, the "moves" and reactions of the parties, and the key problems we were encountering. The more candid we were, the more potentially helpful he could be. (We assumed, of course, that this was his objective. It was a calculated risk.) If we sought advice and showed some of our hand, the message might pass that we really did welcome Soviet input.

Around midnight after the first day in Cairo, we told Vasev how we had coached Pik Botha and his colleagues for the next day's meetings, suggesting that he might advise his Cuban and Angolan friends to reciprocate any gestures made in their direction. After the Cairo round, South African "spin controllers" put out the word that Vasev had taken the Angolans and Cubans to the woodshed after the stormy first day, producing a transformation in their second-day conduct. The Soviets may have quietly appreciated this backhanded compliment. But the Cubans did not, especially since they knew that it was basically a cover story aimed at explaining South Africa's own mellowness the next morning!

There may have been some initial uncertainty in Moscow as to whether the tripartite process would come to fruition on Reagan's watch. This may have accounted in part for the Soviets' absence from New York in July, when we negotiated the framework of political principles and began to pull together the political and military tracks. In hindsight, they probably wished they had taken up our invitation. No one invited them to the Cape Verde military talks.

But the basic reason for the lackluster Soviet role in the early months was that we did not yet have a consensus on the shape of the settlement. Adamishin and I spent two days in Lisbon (May 18–19) and parts of three days in Moscow (May 29–31, during the Reagan-Gorbachev summit) wrangling over this problem. The Soviets spoke airily about possible superpower "guarantees" of a settlement. But Adamishin dodged when asked to describe what this might mean in practice: he had no authority to discuss specifics because his government did not yet know what it would be asked to guarantee. (My instructions were to be exceedingly careful in discussing guarantees. They could be a Trojan Horse for another Afghan-type accord requiring that we suspend our aid to rebel forces.)

Guarantees—the Soviet minister declared to me in Lisbon—looked different depending on whether or not the United States agreed to cease supporting UNITA. The real problem was that Soviet officials continued to perceive our Resolution 435 / Cuban withdrawal package to be "ambiguous." Adamishin claimed that our governments were working for "two different settlements." The United States was not content with obtaining an independent Namibia and Cuban withdrawal; we wanted to change the Angolan government and were seeking Soviet help "to get rid of the MPLA."

I rejected the charge that we were tacitly seeking a UNITA military victory. Neither side could win a military victory. A political process was required: this was our goal, and UNITA fully shared it. Washington was not prepared, however, to help Moscow and Luanda destroy UNITA. As we pursued the matter, the Soviets claimed to smell a trap. At some stage, Washington would surface a "second linkage," demanding that an internal settlement in Angola was the precondition for a regional settlement.

It was true that Shultz, Armacost, and I had repeatedly called upon our Soviet counterparts to address the reconciliation issue. The Soviets were also aware of the bi-partisan, pro-UNITA sentiments in both the administration and Congress. Surely, they reasoned, we had a disguised agenda going well beyond our stated settlement framework. If not, why did we keep raising the subject, pressing Moscow to use its influence in Luanda to act on it now?

The Soviet minister was playing dumb, but it was true that we were advancing a complex message. We invested hours in Lisbon and Moscow trying to sort them out on Angolan reconciliation. We fully agreed, I began, that a regional settlement would create conditions for eventual reconciliation. This had long been my personal conviction, though skeptics abounded in Washington. The problem was that the absence of some parallel movement toward reconciliation now would hamper progress toward the regional settlement. Why, Adamishin insisted, unless you Americans link the two together? There were three problems with waiting, I replied. First, it would leave us superpowers engaged on opposite sides of the civil war, thus inevitably obstructing our "cooperation" on the regional track. Second, Angola's agony would continue after the regional settlement, inviting continuing involvement from across its borders. Most important, the haggling on a Cuban withdrawal timetable would, in reality, become a contest to shape the future Angolan military balance: a slow, back-loaded schedule would help the MPLA, whereas a short, front-loaded one would help UNITA. This would make it far more difficult to achieve agreement on a timetable.

Adamishin replied that Moscow supported an *internal* Angolan settlement achieved by peaceful means. But it should come after the regional settlement. If we would only drop UNITA and stop scaring the hell out of the MPLA, we would make it easier for the Cubans to leave quickly and we would induce the MPLA to take earlier steps toward reconciliation.

When the Moscow summit got under way, Adamishin and I were under instructions to see if we could come up with something for the leaders or senior ministers to endorse. But as I went over my agenda, the list of disagreements only got longer. Parallel messages to African leaders on Angolan reconciliation were a non-starter. A joint public appeal for a regional settlement *and* peace in Angola met the same fate. We argued bitterly about Moscow's refusal to urge military restraint in southern Angola. This was the Soviets' last, determined run at the issue of aid to UNITA. At one point on May 30, Adamishin declared that Moscow "could not agree to" the U.S. formula of trading Resolution 435 for Cuban withdrawal since it ignored the "third element" in the Angolan-Cuban position—namely, an end to "external aggression and interference" in Angola. An acerbic Adamishin proclaimed that if we insisted on our model, there would be no settlement.

Shultz and I decided that it was time for a basic test. In London, Jorge Risquet had suggested that September 29, 1988—the tenth anniversary of the passage of Resolution 435—become our deadline for reaching agreement. We proposed that the superpowers should jointly and publicly endorse the Cuban idea from Moscow. It would help us to measure the Soviet (and Cuban-Angolan) sense of urgency about settling. It was a graceful gesture to Castro which Gorbachev would, presumably, find hard to reject. Taken aback, Adamishin quickly said, why not? After all, it was the United States that was holding things up! But when Shultz put the matter to Shevardnadze, the Soviet minister waffled, grumbling that it would be hard to set dates for others. Since there was no joint communiqué language on specific regional conflicts, we agreed that each of us would use his own words to support the Cuban date.

The Soviets Start to Help

I did not see Adamishin again until August in Geneva. By then, the Soviets and their allies had stopped trying to link the regional settlement to our UNITA aid. The issue of guarantees had also been finessed. The New York Principles referred to the Security Council permanent members as "guarantors for the implementation of agreements that may be established." However, we informed the Soviets, Chinese, French, and British of our intention to view this principle as a political and moral appeal creating no legal obligations. They quickly agreed. And, in any event, we were not signatories of the Principles.

Adamishin arrived in Geneva with Vasev in tow prior to the formal opening of Round Five on August 2. Instead of debating the basic deal, we operated on the tacit understanding that U.S. aid to UNITA was a bilateral issue between the United States and Angola; and that national reconciliation in Angola was a separate matter, not directly linked to the package. The question of superpower guarantees was dropped for good. I made another elaborate run at interesting the Soviet team in the advantages (for Moscow) of getting the reconciliation process started on a parallel track (but unlinked). Once again, they rejoined that we should drop our UNITA aid.

Taking a Swiss franc from my pocket, I spun it on the conference table, remarking that UNITA aid and Angolan reconciliation were two sides of the same coin. Vasev quickly grasped the implications, but held his tongue. Adamishin, however, alluded delicately to "the Cuban idea" of a six-month moratorium on U.S. aid as an inducement to Luanda to open a channel of dialogue with Savimbi. I acknowledged that Aldana had, indeed, raised the idea of a moratorium for some unspecified period. But what would Moscow contribute? Would it match our restraint in its supply relationship with the MPLA? Alluding to the difficult Afghan experience, Adamishin remarked that we already knew Soviet views on "symmetry, whether positive or negative." With a twinkle in his eye, he asked, "Can't you Americans ever do anything by yourselves, without the USSR?"

Having gotten this out of our systems, Adamishin asked for advice on how we could best cooperate in Geneva. We seized the occasion to surprise the Soviets with an unexpected gesture: Larry Napper would go over with Vasev our most operational document—a "roadmap" defining the remaining stages of work along the road to a final settlement— and leave him a copy. The document was an integrated workplan, and it showed clearly how we conceptualized the sequence of agenda items before us.

Of these various tasks, achieving a military understanding was the top priority for Geneva. Without it, nothing else could happen. We urged the Soviets to use their influence with their allies to give van Heerden and Geldenhuys what they needed to sell the final withdrawal of South African forces from Angola. For the first time, we also urged the Soviets to meet with the South Africans directly. You have important cards you could play with Pretoria, we stressed. If you are serious, tell the South Africans about your more constructive regional goals, your declining interest in "armed struggle," your view of SWAPO's likely conduct in an independent Namibia, your assessment of Castro's real intentions—even your vision of South Africa itself. We wanted Geneva to be an irreversible turning point in the talks. Everyone should leave Geneva with something.

Before departing from Geneva, Adamishin gave a press conference declaring Moscow's support for an early settlement and identifying Vasev by name as the Soviet "observer" who would maintain contact with the U.S. delegation during Round Five. His comments marked a Soviet decision publicly to institutionalize their role. A few days earlier, the Soviets had publicly endorsed the New York Principles. It seemed to us that they were deciding to get visibly aboard a moving train. Whatever the real reasons for their support, Adamishin and Vasev were deeply impressed by our gesture in sharing our key negotiating document with them even before it was given to the other delegations. Our "roadmap" answered scores of factual questions and shed light on U.S. tactical thinking. This saved the Soviets from having to pester us (or others) for basic information, and it created the basis for a more dignified Soviet role. We had signaled our wish to engage them operationally in the effort. Now, it would no longer look as if they had traveled in cheap seats to crash our party.

For the veteran Vasev, the Geneva meeting must have been a high point in his career. With a loosely defined mandate from Adamishin and Shevardnadze, he was able to freelance and go with the flow. But Geneva was also a baptism of fire. My colleagues and I got three to four hours of sleep a night during those frantic days. But it seemed to us that Vasev got little more. Like a sailor in a liberty port, he thrived on the chance to implement his own rendition of "new thinking."

At Geneva, the parties negotiated a protocol containing a sweepingly ambitious set of target dates and commitments drawn from (a) our "roadmap," and (b) a dramatic, new South African proposal setting a November 1, 1988, date for the implementation of Resolution 435. The protocol contained a complex formula for SADF withdrawal from Angola (by September 1) and reciprocal military restraint by the Cubans and SWAPO. It set up a joint military commission to assure sector-level communication on the ground and reduce the risk of incidents (see Appendix 2). We also completed work on the U.S. draft tripartite treaty, which was now ready for ministerial-level review.

Vasev, as we had hoped, held the first of what became a regular series of Soviet–South African encounters; his lucid, straight-talking manner impressed the men from Pretoria. It was the beginning of a long and productive flirtation. But Vasev wanted our input to help him interpret South African tactical behavior (e.g., publicizing their proposal the moment they tabled it). He worried that Pretoria had locked its delegation in concrete on the terms for Cuban withdrawal. It was hard, Vasev reported, to persuade Luanda and Havana that this new South African seven-month plan for total withdrawal was a positive step. Vasev himself described the proposal as "linkage minus," since it called for withdrawals to begin before Resolution 435 started and to be completed by the time of the Namibian election, before independence was achieved. I told Vasev that the South Africans could probably be as flexible as the other side. Each now had an opening bid on the table and we did not take either one very seriously.

He talked openly about the problems his allies were having with certain South African demands. We asked Vasev to weigh in on several problem areas in the protocol, including the geographic definition of a highly sensitive "no-go" area for Cubans in UNITA's southeastern Angolan heartland. This was practical stuff. The action moved too fast for us to be able to isolate exactly who influenced what, but it was clear that communication with the Soviets had begun to have meaning.

At the end, Vasev showed up in my hotel suite, beaming and congratulating us on a "tremendous job." We fretted at the highly ambitious targets the parties had set themselves. We agreed that it would be vital now to prevent any incidents so that the SADF withdrawal could be completed on schedule by the end of August. Vasev later told me that the Angolans and Cubans had listened to American and Soviet advice on ways to strengthen the South African negotiating team so that it could carry the day at home. The protocol reflected such moves.

I reported to Vasev that the Angolans had shown little interest in the Cuban-Soviet notion of a moratorium on assistance to UNITA as a means of getting the reconciliation process started. Vasev predicted unofficially that if U.S. aid to UNITA stopped, Soviet military assistance to Luanda would almost automatically stop as well. Realizing that he was thinking out loud, I asked him if Moscow had an official position on a joint moratorium. There were many uncertainties about the effect of a joint moratorium, but it was a possible start toward creative thinking on how to end the civil war. If Vasev could get approval to propose it, I could raise the matter in Washington. He promised me an answer, but we never got one.

Vasev handled the next five rounds of negotiation for Moscow, and we settled into an informal but respectful relationship. I enjoyed working with this wily pro whom we had previously regarded (correctly) as the enemy of all we were trying to accomplish. Intelligent and clear-headed, he spoke with homespun authority on many subjects. Despite our age difference—Vasev was refitting the guns on Lend-Lease tanks in World War II while I was learning to walk—he showed no paternalism toward my team and me. (Vasev's interactions with his own staff were another matter.) He valued the opportunity to work with us on a serious diplomatic enterprise, applying experience and regional expertise acquired over the course of a career.

The Soviet observer respected our intensity and non-stop improvisation. He was particularly supportive of our approach to developing roadmaps and "chairman's reports" as the basis for final texts of negotiating documents. (The Geneva Protocol derived from our first such "chairman's report," and we used the technique again in Brazzaville.) On our side, we found Vasev's judgments and forecasts to be instructive. His batting average was high.

At Round Six (in Brazzaville, August 23–26), for example, we urged him to help us keep the parties from behaving like Middle East rug merchants over the Cuban withdrawal timetable. Given the gap to be bridged between Pretoria's seven-month proposal and the four-year plan of Havana and Luanda, we could spend months slicing the salami. Vasev expressed his personal preference for a short withdrawal schedule ("within reason"). But he also observed that "lots of rugs get sold in the Middle East." And, in any case, if the Angolan-Cuban delegation had instructions to move forward deliberately, those instructions would have to be carried out. Sure enough, we soon received a new Angolan-Cuban forty-two-month withdrawal timetable (down from forty-eight months!) that provoked snickers on the South African side of the table. I complained to Vasev, but he was clearly anxious to protect bargaining room for Havana and Luanda.

In the weeks to come, Vasev and I discussed in exhaustive detail every aspect of the intricate bargaining over timetables. Vasev admired our method of letting the tension build until the parties were nearly pleading with the mediator to table a possible "tie-breaker." But he feigned to be less impressed when he saw what we put forward during Round Seven in early September: a two-year schedule with a number of benchmarks and provisions drawn from our many exchanges with both sides. Supporting the negative reactions of his allies, Vasev claimed that transport factors alone ruled it out.

But it was a lame performance, and he seemed more interested to coach us on avoiding textual complexity in devising schedules and verification ideas. We should adopt the KISS principle ("Keep it simple, stupid"). Avoid recourse to elaborate and difficult treaties with annexes of fine print, he advised; agreements like that are designed to break down and to create employment for our excess lawyers. We should bear in mind that the Cubans, South Africans, and Angolans all came out of a European—not an American—legal tradition. I told Vasev that some of my best friends were lawyers; more important, small-town lawyers abounded in the South African establishment. Nonetheless, he reinforced our basic instincts. The final agreements (see Appendices 4 and 5) were remarkably concise.

Another point that caught Vasev's eye was our proposal that the parties establish a joint commission to help oversee the implementation of the entire package of accords. I described it to him as a political forum in which the parties could surface their concerns and resolve problems that arose. It would not duplicate the role of UNTAG or the U.N. Security Council, but would serve as a mechanism for ongoing contact and communication among the signatory parties. "And the U.S. would also participate as an observer, I notice," Vasev added drily. He promised to make note of our interest, and report it to his superiors.

Good, I thought to myself. He was sniffing the bait. If the Soviets developed an appetite to become an "observer" in our future commission, we would have them more firmly hooked on our entire regional approach. It was important to have Moscow with us during the implementation phase. Commission membership would ratify their nominal equality with us as regional peacemakers. This was exactly the sort of image transformation and role enhancement favored by Gorbachev and Shevardnadze. If the USSR was going to abandon the lost cause of violent revolution in Africa, why not go out in style?

The South Africans began panting almost as soon as they saw where we were headed on the joint commission: it would provide a forum of first resort and keep everyone on notice of their commitments, while limiting their recourse to the United Nations where South Africa was alone. It was not every day that Pretoria had the chance to become a founder member of a new regional entity. I argued (and believed) that this vehicle would keep the United States engaged throughout the process of implementation, reducing the risk that we would lose interest as soon as the ink dried on our treaties.

Over the next few weeks, we carefully orchestrated our sales pitch to both the Cubans and the South Africans. (The Cubans were not invited to join many clubs, either, especially by Americans.) It was hard to tell which of them was more ardent about the joint commission. We also had little doubt that Pretoria was eager for the Soviets to join—if only to keep an eye on them and keep us Americans from having a totally free ride. We would see later which of them would ask us to invite the

Soviets to join our new club as "observers." When the Cubans and Angolans finally approached us in October, we graciously acceded to their request. After a barely decent interval, the Soviets said yes. As the December 13 Brazzaville Protocol would duly record, the parties "invited" both superpowers to participate in their commission as observers. For good measure, the future government of an independent Namibia would be asked to join as a full member.

We believed it was essential—given the complexity of the diplomacy and the risk of a reversion to polarized politics—to tie the signatories and the superpowers to the settlement *during its implementation*. Too many things could go wrong. Too much time might slip by after an incident before effective action could be launched from key capitals. The global politics surrounding Southern African questions made it extremely unwise to rely on the United Nations itself to save the day.

In addition, a standing joint commission could serve as a forum for informal discussion of related regional issues and a building block for future regional cooperation. Our goal had always been to help create a framework of regional security between the Front Line States and South Africa. Having superpower support and participation in a regional mechanism would help get it launched. Finally, we wanted not only to strengthen our settlement but also to tie ourselves to its complete application and tie the Soviets to us in this endeavor. This was the way to legitimize our own legacy and to link it to the broader fabric of U.S.-Soviet relations. After all, our work as Americans in Southern Africa would not end in January 1989 when Reagan's term came to an end.

A Joint Commission Saves the Day

My final official mission to Africa came in the midst of a crisis caused by SWAPO's attempted incursion into Namibia on March 31, 1989, the eve of implementation day. I had been planning to confirm my imminent resignation from the Department of State when the news of SWAPO's attempted coup arrived in Washington. Instead, we quickly assembled a team and rushed to Luanda to begin fire-fighting under the aegis of the new joint commission. We were mystified as to how the attempted infiltration of some 2,000 men could have happened under the noses of the Angolans and Cubans unless they wittingly chose to look the other way. We were astounded that SWAPO's leaders—assuming the move had been endorsed at the top—thought that they would be allowed to get away with it. It was a miscalculation that cost SWAPO the loss of hundreds of its best fighters who died in action against South African forces in northern Namibia.

But it could have wrecked the settlement as well, had it not been for two things. First was the fortuitous presence in Namibia of Margaret Thatcher. She helped keep the South Africans from tearing up the Brazzaville and New York Accords. She also provided strong backing to Martti Ahtisaari, the U.N. Special Representative and leader of the newly arrived UNTAG mission, who had authorized the South Africans to use force to halt the SWAPO incursion. The other reason was that our joint commission was there to place the settlement back on track. Without it, the April Fools' Day fiasco could have descended into an orgy of polarized name-calling at the United Nations, reopening delicate understandings dating back to 1982 and 1978.

Castro sent Aldana and the rest of his starting line-up to Angola and on to Namibia for the emergency meeting of the commission. Their instructions were to put things back together with the South Africans. The Cubans reported to us that Castro was fit to be tied when informed of the SWAPO fiasco. No one, not even the fraternal comrades of SWAPO, was going to jeopardize *his* settlement, so painstakingly shaped over so many months. Equally striking was the Soviet response. Adamishin got to Luanda before I did. As I arrived at his embassy, he greeted me breezily: "Don't worry, Chet, I've got everything under control." Ever the wise guy, Adamishin had little idea how to proceed and seemed mainly concerned with saving his clients' face. But this was his way of telling us that Moscow had joined the ranks of the peacemakers. From Luanda, we traveled on to Mt. Etjo, a Namibian game ranch north of Windhoek where South African, U.S., Soviet, Angolan, and Cuban officials met in emergency session, accompanied by U.N. civilian and military leaders from UNTAG.

The understandings hammered out in the next forty-eight hours put the settlement back on track. The commission had a therapeutic impact on the rattled South Africans. Pik Botha summed up his feelings as we prepared to leave the game lodge: looking doe-eyed at Carlos Aldana Escalante, he remarked, "You know, Señor Aldana, I think I'm going to miss the Cubans when they actually leave Southern Africa." This episode captures the value of the joint commission. It also says something about the special importance of the chemistry established between the signatory parties themselves during the endgame. The 1988 Southern African settlement was built by Angolans, Cubans, and South Africans. They built it using an American conceptual design and American mediation. And they saved it in early April 1989 using the mechanism we had proposed to underpin the agreements.

It is difficult to pinpoint the precise Soviet contribution during the endgame. In one sense, they were free riders on our own diplomacy.

Moscow made no changes in the settlement framework. It was not Soviet pressure which got the parties to the table. We saw no evidence of Soviet arm-twisting; the Soviet practice of distancing themselves from Castro and ratcheting down their aid to Cuba did not begin until long after our settlement had been negotiated. In general, Moscow deferred to its allies and, on occasion, hid behind their ample skirts. By respecting the MPLA's sensitivities on the civil war and political reconciliation, the Soviets may actually have helped to prolong the agony.

At another level, however, their contribution to the 1988 settlement was, first, to stop opposing it, and then to associate themselves with it. This strengthened our hand with each of the parties and raised the price for bailing out. A related Soviet contribution was to urge their allies to take steps which would strengthen the South African negotiating team. Each party had home constituencies to worry about. But, as we have seen, there was a basic asymmetry between the sides. Soviet officials, deferring to U.S. expertise on South African decisionmaking, agreed that it was important to take van Heerden, Geldenhuys, and Barnard seriously. The Soviets engaged in their own version of constructive engagement with South African delegates, answering skeptical questions and demolishing stereotypes in order to make a settlement more credible in Pretoria.

Another Soviet contribution was to help clear up occasional static in U.S. communications with the Angolans and Cubans. Aldana and I achieved an excellent working relationship. But the scar tissue of hostility ran deep, making it hard at times to persuade "the Beard" in Havana that we were not engaged in some sinister ploy. Ndalu and I also developed an easygoing and cordial working link. But the U.S.-Angolan channels were by definition strained by our involvement on UNITA's side and our non-recognition policy. On occasion, the Marxist brothers became highly agitated by what they perceived to be an "identity" of U.S. and South African interests in the Cuban withdrawal issue. Vasev was able to calm them down by interpreting and explaining basic differences of motive, something he could do only because of our frequent and frank consultation. Once the Soviet "observers" became operational, each of the three parties had the benefit of regular input from two superpowers. This provided the parties with a reality check, reducing the likelihood of irrational responses and miscalculations.

From our perspective, the agreement to cooperate built up expectations, reminding the Soviets of the role they *should* be playing. As we worked to cope with the round-the-clock antics of each of the parties, it was nice to know there was someone else with whom to share burdens. We were generally lucky in our choice of Soviet counterparts. They were quick learners; their tactical acumen helped us to manage the process. On the really tough calls, they often preferred to duck rather than to lead, but at least they could laugh about it.

At the December 1988 signing ceremonies in New York and Brazzaville, George Shultz and I made generous public remarks about the Soviet contribution. This was not only the gracious thing to do; it was tactically important to salute Adamishin, Vasev, and their colleagues who had worked with us during the endgame. We had created a powerful precedent.

18

The Road to Victory

In the early months of the actual peacemaking process, I sometimes wondered if there were natural laws that governed the rhythm, tempo, and sequence in this business. It was not an instruction manual we needed, but the code or logic that would explain the final stages of peacemaking. Is it inherently best to start with concrete issues or with overarching matters of principle, with the easy questions or the hard ones? Can you get them to make peace while they are still at war, or do you, first, have to end the war? We had been preparing for seven years for the moment when everyone would come together at the same time and place. By May 1988, the parties had apparently exhausted their alternatives to our conceptual design. We had the "right" people at the table. Now what?

As mediators, we had a particular responsibility to define the agenda at each round of talks. In the early rounds, we aimed high, putting many issues forward for discussion in order to test the water. If we could get the talk rolling on one subject, the natural law of negotiation would presumably reveal itself and suggest how to proceed. In retrospect, the endgame moved through four phases:

1. Defining and reconfirming the settlement framework and obtaining reciprocal commitments in principle, May–July.
2. Ending the cross-border war and obtaining a cessation of hostilities between the SADF, SWAPO, FAPLA, and the Cubans, July–August.
3. Negotiating a compromise withdrawal timetable and an associated trilateral agreement, August–November.

4. Completing the package with an understanding on verification, setting up the Joint Commission, and agreeing upon dates for signature and implementation, November–December.

During the first phase, the sides sought commitments in principle from each other. The settlement framework had to be mutually agreeable, both in terms of what was and what was not included. Before moving to treaty language, they wanted categorical assurances on these principles. For each side, this would be the basic test of whether the other was serious. The Angolans, Cubans, and South Africans also wanted assurances that an "honorable" settlement could be achieved. No one had won on the ground. Therefore, everyone would have to win at the table. This fact would have to be fully reflected in the language, symbols, and political imagery of the deal.

From London to New York (May–July)

We started off in London on a somewhat promising note. We informed van Heerden of the ardent Angolan-Cuban desire to hear his government's response to their four-year plan. Van Heerden obliged them with a detailed, non-polemical commentary on the many problems Pretoria had with their proposal. They found this so interesting that they wanted it on paper. The South Africans obliged again. Risquet and Ndalu found the South African position on the U.N. role and Resolution 435 to be ambiguous. Full implementation of the "letter and the spirit" of the U.N. Plan was the key to the entire conflict. In response to these pointed probes, van Heerden offered a dramatic commitment. Brandishing a copy of Resolution 435 and the annexed U.N. documents describing the plan, he declared that South Africa had accepted and stood by the Namibia transition plan "precisely as it is described in these documents." And, he would recommend to his government that fresh proposals be presented at the next meeting.

Mbinda, the Angolan foreign minister, managed to get off some graceful commentary about the "very constructive" performance of van Heerden, and he stressed his government's desire for peace. Risquet observed that it would be a "joyous and proud day" in Havana when the boys came home having accomplished their historic mission. He also came up with the idea of setting Resolution 435's tenth anniversary (September 29) as a deadline for reaching agreement—an initiative that could be read as either menacing or reassuring in the context of the unsettled military situation.

We thought this was not a bad start, and we told them that the time had come to focus on hammering out a framework of principles for an agreement (they had received our draft treaty containing such principles). We also told them that it was essential to begin looking at the military situation and the question of withdrawal schedules and verification. But we were getting ahead of ourselves. It was vital to get an agreed political framework before we could stop the war and build the peace.

There were two reasons why this took time. First, Castro was locked into his own high-risk game plan as the means to an honorable exit through negotiations. He did not want to fight the SADF. He wanted a categorical South African commitment to a Resolution 435-based settlement *plus* a complete SADF withdrawal from Angola, so that he could stop his campaign of psychological intimidation without appearing to back down militarily himself. Castro's strategy placed an exceedingly heavy burden on his diplomats, and it assumed that their counterparts across the table would be able to translate his message effectively at home. Geldenhuys thought he understood this game and how to respond to it. His conversation with Rosales in London convinced him that an equitable deal could be achieved if escalatory military incidents could be avoided and if the political leadership in Havana and Pretoria wanted one. But he knew that it would not be easy to persuade his own leadership.

After all, Castro's "real" motives were not self-evident. It was possible to take from London an impression that the Cuban game was different—more elaborate and ambitious—than the Angolans'. In reality, the reverse was true, but the misperception explains, in part, why Pik Botha and Magnus Malan took the MPLA off to Brazzaville by themselves two weeks later to whisper in the Angolans' ears about reaching "alternative" arrangements without the Cubans or the superpowers. They apparently imagined that the MPLA could be split off from the Cubans in some partial deal that would stop short of full implementation of Resolution 435. This was a bad misreading of the "other side."

There was a marked lack of candor and realism at the top of the South African leadership about what it could obtain at the bargaining table. In May 1988, none of his top advisers was prepared to tell P. W. Botha that UNITA would not be joining the talks and that the settlement agenda would not include Angolan reconciliation. Whereas van Heerden and Geldenhuys were in touch with reality, at home they often faced the "wish-list" approach to foreign policymaking.

The mood was tense even before the opening exchange on June 24 in Cairo. The Angolans and Cubans had just received a South African counterproposal featuring such items as: a call for Angolan reconciliation to start in the first six weeks of the settlement; no reference whatsoever to the Cubans as parties to the negotiation; language calling for "uniformity" and "synchronization" of South African and Cuban withdrawal schedules from *both* Angola and Namibia; and a demand for all sorts of specific data on Cuban troops, including the number who had become naturalized Angolans and would be remaining behind with their Angolan wives. To top this off, Pik Botha opened up with his classic "Africa is dying" speech. The region was doomed unless "African brothers" cooperated to provide their people with jobs and clean water, to combat AIDS and overpopulation, and to find peace. It was a performance calculated to provoke a Cuban walk-out.

Mbinda attacked everything in Pretoria's proposal, starting with its title. Its terms on the timetable were as unacceptable as its interference in Angolan internal affairs. He demanded $12 billion in war reparations. Risquet slammed South African "arrogance" and dismissed the proposal as "a tasteless joke." South Africa would not achieve at the table what it had failed to achieve on the battlefield: the "myth of South African invincibility" had been forever destroyed. He noted that Havana and Luanda, in their proposal, had not interfered in South African's internal affairs, even though apartheid was a "crime against humanity." Not to be outdone, Botha went on for another forty-five minutes without notes. Could a Cuban citizen take his government to court? In South Africa, white doctors had successfully separated black Siamese twins. On a per capita basis, more South African blacks owned cars than ordinary Soviet citizens. As for reparations, he would submit damage claims for Angolan-sponsored ANC and SWAPO terrorism, and these would be higher than Angolan claims since "our property is more valuable than yours."

Did Botha want to provoke a walk-out? If so, Risquet and Mbinda disappointed him by presenting more documents, including a ten-point set of political principles. Risquet stated pointedly that Cuba would not cause a breakdown. Botha likewise refused to be provoked by "your provocations." He promised to study the document and not respond "abusively as you have done." That evening, the South Africans prepared, with our help, a counterdraft statement of political principles for a settlement. It contained no reference to Angolan internal affairs.

The next morning, Botha introduced his draft, describing it as based on "some important elements" in the Angolan-Cuban draft, which he termed "a first step toward an agreement." Before long, the sides were flattering each other's constructive ideas and evoking the "spirit of London." They quickly agreed that "experts" (i.e., the subministerial teams) should meet in two weeks in New York to prepare a single document of political principles drawing on all proposals tabled in Cairo.

Neither the fireworks at Cairo nor the military clashes at Techipa and Calueque two days after Cairo derailed the talks. Agreement on the shape and framework of the deal was now within reach, provided that mutually acceptable language could be hammered out. That was our top agenda item in New York; three days of work produced the New York Principles of July 13, 1988—our first agreed document.

Having gotten this far, what should logically come next? We proposed that the parties discuss measures of military restraint in one working group, while other delegates should focus on the end product, a package of interlocking treaties containing reciprocal commitments. The Angolans and Cubans had arrived in New York with a complex document which they called an "action plan." It sought to lay out a sequence of steps that would lead to the settlement. It took us hours of reading and discussion to grasp their basic point, which was buried in onesided argumentation about who should move first.

As Ndalu explained it, Pik Botha had been correct in Cairo to say that the negotiation must move step by step. The Angolans and Cubans would be in a position to control SWAPO forces once the SADF left Angola and Pretoria had agreed to a target date for Resolution 435 to start. Similarly, the Angolans could not take very seriously the language of a tripartite treaty which it could not sign because the SADF was still over 250 kilometers inside Angolan territory. If the SADF would just withdraw unilaterally ("with honor"!), then it would be possible to make headway on other issues.

Leaving aside the onesidedness of Ndalu's argument, it made sense to link together sequentially the parties' actions and decisions with their diplomatic work at the negotiating table. But we talked Ndalu and Aldana out of tabling their self-serving draft; the chances for agreement were much better if the mediator drafted and tabled it. They quickly pocketed the compliment, and we took over the Angolan-Cuban idea. This was the genesis of the series of "roadmaps" that served us so well in Geneva and Brazzaville. They helped us to depoliticize the agenda; and they helped the parties to develop confidence about where the exercise was headed.

From New York to Geneva (July–August)

Once the settlement framework was defined in the New York Principles, we could move on. But neither side was prepared to move to the next set of documents unless military forces could be disentangled on the ground and a physical confrontation averted. If only Rosales and Geldenhuys could have made parallel progress in their military exchanges, New York could have been an even more decisive turning point in the endgame. But, as we have seen, they fell short. Rosales blew a fine opportunity by refusing to offer Geldenhuys any tangible quid for completing SADF withdrawal from Angola—despite the latter's open hints that he was prepared to return home and argue for an immediate pullout. The root of the problem was that Rosales lacked the authority to deal at Geldenhuys's level in the New York exchange. Though nominally of the same rank, Rosales was not one of the three or four people in Havana who could answer Geldenhuys.

The risk of incidents remained high. On July 18–19, local SADF commanders unleashed their dreaded long-range artillery (G-6s) at Cuito Cuanavale after sensing that they were jeopardized by the other side's movements near a strategic bridge. Standing orders for restraint from senior commanders were being overtaken by local events that could escalate. On July 20, I passed Geldenhuys the message that the other side had agreed to an immediate meeting in Cape Verde. The Angolan, Cuban, and South African military teams assembled at Ilha do Sal (Cape Verde) with Jim Woods in the chair on July 22, a mere eight days after leaving New York. Their goal was to work out a formula covering a *de facto* cease-fire, SADF withdrawal from Angola, and reciprocal gestures of Angolan-Cuban restraint.

Ndalu opened with the statement that he had come to achieve an understanding based on total withdrawal of the SADF's remaining 3,000 men (the actual number was perhaps half of this) from Angola. He would offer guarantees for the security of the force as it withdrew over the next thirty to sixty days. Hostile actions and incidents would cease immediately. It was a thin opening bid, but at least it was specific. This time, however, the South Africans blew it. Instead of drawing the other side out further, they arrived with an elaborate and mechanistic proposal of their own. To reduce the risk of dangerous incidents, they proposed the creation of a physical break between opposing forces so that combat reaction times would be much longer—days instead of hours. As presented by van Tonder, Geldenhuys's intelligence chief, the three-phased approach would include the separation of forces, the creation of buffer zones and monitoring teams, and the completion of SADF withdrawal by around mid-September. By this time, Cuban and SWAPO forces should be some 360 kilometers north of the border!

In other words, the South Africans were now proposing to complete their long-delayed military disengagement (first announced by Geldenhuys in December 1987) if the other side would reverse the southward redeployments of Cuban, Angolan, and SWAPO forces that had taken place over the past seven months. The South Africans knew that their withdrawal represented a strong card for which it should be possible to get something in return. But this scheme bore no relationship to the new military balance on the ground near the border in the southwest.

Cuban military intelligence Brigadier General Jesus Bermudez gently replied that the Cubans would soon be going 12,000 kilometers away from the Namibian border—but not yet. His side could just as well ask the SADF to move hundreds of kilometers south of the Namibian border to achieve a separation. Bermudez suggested a ninety-day cessation of hostilities (to be extended if a date was set for Resolution 435), and offered that Cubans would not proceed south of a line from Chitado to Ngiva in the southwest sector, paralleling the border. The Angolans would guarantee the supply of water and power from Calueque to Namibia. Furthermore, they would arrange with SWAPO that it observe the *de facto* cease-fire and stay north of the 17th parallel once the Resolution 435 date was agreed.

While Geldenhuys saw merit in some of these points, he had no mandate to discuss dates for Resolution 435. Besides, SWAPO activity should cease now; and it was not enough for the Cubans just to stop moving south when they were already near the border. Woods attempted to draw up a package of reciprocal military steps, but the chemistry at Cape Verde was not conducive to cutting a straightforward deal. For one thing, the Cubans engaged in a bit of guerrilla theater by having General Arnaldo Ochoa, the commander of Cuba's Angolan forces, enter the room dressed in combat fatigues with a pistol on his hip "fresh" from the front. Ochoa's charismatic swagger did not enhance the South Africans' concentration on the work at hand. Geldenhuys was concerned over any daylight emerging between the military and diplomatic tracks, and he left before the exchanges ran their course.

Fortunately, the delegations did agree to schedule a military experts' meeting at Ruacana on the Namibia-Angola border in a few days' time. In three days of talks in the bush in late July, senior military people (with civilian "minders") worked out the institutional concepts for a joint military monitoring commission to oversee a cease-fire and separation of forces and establish military-to-military communication on the ground. My military adviser, Colonel Charlie Snyder, led our team of experts in this encounter with top Angolan, Cuban, and South African officers. It would now be up to the political leadership to decide whether and how to effect a cease-fire and SADF withdrawal.

Breakthrough at Geneva

The South Africans arrived in Geneva in early August 1988 without precise instructions. Van Heerden was unimpressed with the offers made to Geldenhuys at Cape Verde; it was essential to obtain a balanced package of military measures to set the stage for a settlement. He and Geldenhuys insisted that the military and political strands of discussion must be pulled together in an opening plenary. Ndalu and Aldana were equally preoccupied with the Cape Verde military agenda. They urged the U.S. delegation to prepare a document that would register South Africa's commitment to withdraw from Angola without implying that they had "negotiated" about it. They spoke jauntily of being prepared for "decisive" steps, but questioned the authority of the Pretoria team. We made a point of informing van Heerden that his mandate was in doubt.

On the even of the opening plenary, the South Africans cobbled together a far-reaching proposal and obtained approval for it from home. The goal was to create leverage. The key ingredient was a bold sense of timing. Earlier, we had estimated that it would take the United Nations about three months of preparation to implement Resolution 435. At Cape Verde, the Angolan-Cuban team had proposed a cease-fire for an initial period of three months. Three months would provide an appropriate window to conclude the negotiations.

On August 2, van Heerden told the plenary that his government had completed a "comprehensive review" of the talks and was now in a position to propose that November 1, 1988, be established as "D-Day," the start of Resolution 435. Under the U.N. Plan, Namibian elections would be held seven months later, around June 1, 1989. All SADF units would have to be out of Namibia by this point. Pretoria now proposed that Cuban withdrawal from Angola should be completed at the same time, thus equating the two timetables. At last, Pretoria had replied to the Angolan-Cuban four-year plan by proposing a seven-month plan (or a ten-month plan, if the Cubans took up the invitation to begin withdrawing *before* the start of Resolution 435). On the immediate military front, South Africa proposed that a *de facto* cease-fire should go into effect in eight days (August 10), at which time the SADF would begin its final withdrawal from Angola. Cuban "redeployments" and restrictions on SWAPO activity would start at the same time. The SADF would complete its withdrawal from Angola by September 1, 1988. The joint monitoring mechanism devised at Ruacana should go into effect immediately.

To top this off, van Heerden cited the New York Principles (specifically Principle "G") as requiring the MPLA government to cease offering military facilities to the African National Congress. After identifying a range of such camps, he declared that the ANC's use of Angolan territory to launch violent attacks was "unacceptable" and must cease. Van Heerden had linked all elements of the negotiation into one proposal, creating a continuum of steps that equated Pretoria's commitments with a variety of Angolan-Cuban obligations.

Ndalu and Aldana were unprepared for Pretoria's lurch to grab the initiative. Still less did they anticipate that the proposal would be published simultaneously in Pretoria and flashed around the world, upstaging them and placing them on the defensive. The Angolans and Cubans did not wish to dignify van Heerden's seven-month bid by tabling the reduction (from forty-eight to forty-two months) which they had brought with them to Geneva. By tacit agreement, the Cuban withdrawal issue was set aside for the next phase of the talks. But van Heerden's offer of specific dates for SADF withdrawal (September 1) and for the settlement itself (November 1) went to the heart of stated Angolan-Cuban interests.

U.S. mediators worked for nearly three days to produce the Geneva Protocol. In a final session, the heads of delegation could be seen pouring over military maps to define the meridians and parallels of a large quadrant in southeastern Angola where the Cubans would "not take part in offensive operations" (i.e., against UNITA). The protocol declared that a cessation of hostilities was already in effect in both Namibia and Angola. Once the SADF completed its withdrawal, Angola and Cuba would use their "good offices" to move SWAPO forces north of the 16th parallel, well away from the border. The New York Principles were reaffirmed in terms that drew attention to Pretoria's obligation not to interfere in Angolan affairs and Luanda's pledge not to allow its territory to be used for acts of violence against other states.

This was a victory for both sides. So sensitive were the reciprocal military undertakings that the protocol was classified "confidential" at Angolan-Cuban insistence. This was not surprising: the South Africans got a lot by giving a lot at Geneva. (Later, after the settlement was agreed, Pretoria published the protocol.) These military steps unlocked the way to broader progress. Now that we had effectively ended the war, the parties agreed to focus attention on the tripartite accord, working from our draft. This document converted the New York Principles into treaty language and format, and would incorporate by reference the still-to-be defined Angolan-Cuban bilateral treaty, including its Cuban withdrawal timetable. We completed work on the trilateral agreement before leaving Geneva. Now, we could turn to the Cuban timetable itself.

From the Adirondack Park to Brazzaville
(August–September)

Geneva was the crucial turning point. I found Neils van Tonder and Derek Auret keyed up about the chances for a settlement when they flew in to meet me on August 15 at the Sagamore Lodge on Lake George, New York, near my Adirondack vacation home. They described themselves as "stunned" by Vasev's candor about Cuban enthusiasm to leave Angola. Van Tonder had been "shocked" by comments from Cubans in the corridors. But they could hardly believe it. Surely, it was the MPLA which needed peace, not Castro? Not necessarily, I replied. The Cubans have all the cards; they have mounted an extraordinary military effort, but that effort makes sense only as the prelude to a dignified and early departure. They, not the MPLA, are the ones shaping the negotiation and driving it forward.

We exchanged best and worst-case analyses, factoring in the upcoming U.S. elections. For eight years, the South Africans had been telling us of their concern that their leverage would rapidly decline as soon as the UNTAG troops arrived in Namibia. By the time of the election (D-Day plus seven months) that leverage would be sharply reduced, and would decline further thereafter. This placed a premium on obtaining an early point of "irreversibility" in the withdrawal process. We discussed Cuban withdrawal schedules for four hours that day, and I urged them to get ready for the next round of bidding by analyzing their own priorities.

These South Africans knew the negotiating history in detail. They asserted that Pretoria had not officially changed or reviewed its position from 1985, but the number of Cubans had gone up over 66 percent. This made it imperative to reverse the recent augmentations in order to reestablish the status quo ante—for starters. Instead of haggling, I emphasized that we, too, wanted a credible Cuban timetable.

For the next three months, we worked non-stop to get one. My colleagues and I had no idea just how arcane and yet political a troop withdrawal schedule could become. Nor did we fully grasp until now the range of variables in a timetable: the starting point, the total duration, the degree of front- or backloading (if any), the pace of withdrawals (how many troops per month), the question of key benchmarks and links with the already established Namibia transition schedule (how many troops should leave by the time of the Namibian election), the question of defining what was to be withdrawn (men, units, equipment), the matter of stages of interim redeployment to certain geographic lines, and the question of organizing a verification regime.

A further complication was that we did not have a blank slate. Pretoria had once accepted in principle our 1985 two–year (80–20 percent) schedule, and we believed that the Cubans could live with something close to this. We knew that the MPLA was divided; those in favor of settling nonetheless based their approach on outlasting UNITA by means of the longest possible timetable. Now, however, the sides were carefully entrenched in extreme positions; each knew that the other had "backtracked" to get there. As Vasev had predicted, the parties would opt to close the vast timetable gap in small steps, keeping the maximum number of cards and forcing the other side to move first and make choices. On the other hand, the November 1 deadline created a sense of extreme pressure.

For the mediator, these problems were further complicated because we had our own interests, and the parties knew it. We had invented linkage. We cared about the settlement's impact on UNITA. Our analysis suggested that UNITA would fare well provided that the withdrawal schedule was not overly drawn out and that large numbers of Cubans would leave during the first year. This situation placed a special burden on us to prove our mediatory prowess and, within reason, our objectivity, while also advancing our own cause. The Cubans and Angolans pressed us to offer up a mediator's tie-breaker; this would either split us from Pretoria or "prove" that we were in collusion.

After several days of warm-up exercises, the real action began on August 25–26 in Brazzaville. Van Heerden politely coached Ndalu and Aldana as to what kind of proposal would enable him to move beyond Pretoria's seven-month bid from Geneva. Describing Cuban withdrawal as a "sovereign issue" for Havana and Luanda, he suggested that a pre-November 1 "gesture" was important to help offset the arrival of 15,000 fresh Cuban troops in the past six months. An "uninterrupted" flow of departures should continue thereafter. Van Heerden's tactful opener was followed by two modest but important moves by the Angolans and Cubans within twenty-four hours. After proposing a 42-month schedule and then holding overnight consultations next door in Luanda, they returned to table a 36-month plan. It contained *no* upfront "gesture" or "down payment" of Cuban departures before the start of Resolution 435. A total of 15,000 Cuban troops would leave Angola during the first year, at the end of which the remainder would be deployed north of the 13th parallel.

Though obviously an improvement, van Heerden made clear that this would not do the trick. The sides agreed on a short break. Aldana told me he needed a South African reply to his moves and a clearer sense of this new demand for a gesture. I reminded the Cuban that he was generously offering to withdraw in the first year the troops he had introduced since the spring of 1988!

Round Seven (September 6–10) began under a cloud of orchestrated press hype in both the United States and South Africa suggesting that the Cubans were preparing another offensive against UNITA (in direct violation of their Geneva commitment) and sending further reinforcements to Southern Africa. It was a false alarm; before leaving Washington, we issued press guidance stating that we could not confirm the reports. But they soured the negotiating climate and wasted the time of Rosales and Geldenhuys, who concluded that the American media were to blame! They wondered who had been briefing the media. So did we.

To compound the problem, Jonas Savimbi had refused my proposal to meet in Kinshasa right after Round Six, sending a representative instead. The UNITA leader gave a press conference to a large and sympathetic media audience at his capital of Jamba on September 3. He blasted the negotiations, attacking me personally for departing from established U.S. policy and claiming (inaccurately) that I was pressing Pretoria and UNITA to accept a 36-month timetable. His outburst came in the wake of a visit to Pretoria by the UNITA leader, a nasty letter from P. W. Botha to Reagan complaining about me, and the visit of several congressional staff members to Savimbi's bush headquarters. By mid-September, we began receiving congressional letters quoting from UNITA's bogus allegations.

But the tactic did not work in the autumn of 1988: Freeman told Shultz exactly what was going on. Our top team held together, a circumstance which probably kept the South African team from falling apart. When we got to Brazzaville, however, Aldana warned me that the Angolans were upset by Savimbi's outburst. A strong government would have viewed it as evidence of trouble in the enemy camp; but the MPLA nonetheless felt itself to be squeezed between Pretoria's seven-month demand and Savimbi's "rejection" of its 36-month bid. Now, any new move might also be "rejected" by UNITA.

The storms passed. Rosales and Geldenhuys worked out joint press guidance rebutting the scare stories. Van Heerden and I exchanged candid words about the signals which elements in our respective capitals might be passing to UNITA. It was a good sign that he had a mandate to put forward another proposal, even if it represented only a modest advance: a 12-month timetable featuring the departure of 15,000 Cubans prior to November 1; 35,000 by February 1, 1989; 45,000 by June 1; and 55,000 by November 1989. The rate of departures would be 7,000 per month in the early months. In addition, Geldenhuys wanted an artillery-range DMZ established along the border. At this rate, we would soon run out of time for any pre-November 1 "gestures."

On the second day of Round Seven we faced mounting pressure to play a more active mediatory role. This was tricky. We had not put forward a new U.S. position on Cuban troop withdrawal since 1985; Hank Cohen, Jim Woods, and I had no interest in advancing a U.S. proposal as such. But we had anticipated that such a situation might arise. We could hardly walk away, leaving the parties impatient with us and without a mandate of their own to move forward. Late in the evening of September 8 we tabled a "chairman's summary" containing (a) an anodyne review of existing positions; (b) an ambitious set of reciprocal commitments the parties were asked to consider for the pre-November 1 period; and (c) a new Cuban timetable for their review. We described the paper as an attempt to define the "zone of negotiability."

We had tried to walk a line. The paper finessed with a blank space the South African demand for pre-implementation withdrawals, suggesting instead a variety of "interim" military steps, such as the reciprocal pullback of Cuban and South African airpower, artillery tubes, and armored units from the border once the agreement was signed, but prior to D-Day. We suggested a rate of Cuban departures 50 percent below the rate called for by Pretoria and two to three times the rate contained in the Angolan-Cuban three-year plan. We called for a two-year timetable, with some 75 percent of the Cubans to leave in the first year.

Van Heerden and his team pocketed the paper and packed their bags, eager to avoid a plenary exchange with the other side. The South Africans were pleased with some aspects of the document, unhappy with others, and adamant that they had no mandate at all to react to it. Ndalu and Aldana put on a stellar performance, accusing us of multiple sins of commission, omission, and bias. But we talked it through, pointing out that we had, in fact, defined the approximate middle point and listened carefully to their substantive arguments. They objected to the form and language of our report as much as the hard numbers and dates; we took careful note for the next iteration. Vasev for his part manfully supported the Cuban-Angolan arguments.

We returned to the familiar M'Bamou Palace Hotel in Brazzaville on September 26 for Round Eight. By this time, my teammates had tried every item on the menu, with mixed results. I stayed with the reliable *bar grillé* or an occasional ham omelette containing a week's load of cholesterol. The Cubans liked to hang around the patio bar, taking in the excellent local beer and alternating their gaze between the French bathers at poolside and the imposing presence of Kinshasa, the Zairean capital, directly across the massive Congo River. Whiskey (Scotch) and room-temperature tap water (from the river) was Geldenhuys's beverage of choice; he claimed they neutralized each other. By now, our traveling troupe regularly included the United Nation's Martti Ahtisaari and his colleague, Hisham Omayad. This was invaluable in laying a groundwork of familiarity and respect between them and the South Africans with whom he would share effective power during Namibia's transition in 1989–90. Several representatives of the internal Namibian parties and swapo as well as the Soviets were also present in the wings. Our negotiations accounted for a significant share of Brazzaville's restaurant turnover during the second half of 1988.

Our meetings also became the principal order of business for President Sassou Nguesso's Foreign Ministry and protocol and security services. Sassou realized that we and the South Africans wanted to see some visible African activity on the national reconciliation front. He took the lead in organizing meetings with the leaders of neighboring countries (Zaire and Gabon) and more distant African friends of unita (Morocco and Côte d'Ivoire). But he also argued that Africans could only become credible on this matter once our regional settlement was nailed down. It was clear that he was not prepared to put his mpla relationship at risk any more than Vasev and Adamishin were. Sassou laid some useful groundwork in the fall of 1988, legitimizing the concept of "an African solution" in Angola. After Houphouet-Boigny, the Ivorian leader, hosted my rapprochement with Savimbi in Abidjan in late September, we also sought to jump-start the sending of signals between the mpla and unita (and unita and the Cubans). We handed the Congolese, the mpla, unita, and Cubans a paper on the basic principles of national reconciliation to get the ball rolling. These efforts were the genesis of subsequent initiatives on reconciliation led by Sassou, Mobutu of Zaire, and later, the Portuguese, Soviets, and Americans.

When we arrived in Brazzaville for Round Eight, we knew that this was effectively our last chance to make the November 1 deadline to start implementating the settlement. This date was central: if we failed to meet it, there was a risk that the parties' reciprocal commitment to the process could come unglued. We also knew that we had taken a major risk by tabling our chairman's summary at the end of Round Seven. Its effectiveness in forcing the pace would depend on a convergence of tactical instincts among the parties.

Unhappily, they reached opposite conclusions after studing our proposal carefully. The South Africans said they were anxious to move to closure on a protocol that would include an agreed Cuban timetable. To support this posture, they came armed with a fully developed eighteen-month plan under which 90 percent of the Cubans would depart in the first year—12,000 of them before November 1! Aldana and Ndalu arrived with a verbose commentary on our own document—but no counterbid. They told us they had a mandate to deal, but declined to do so until we had shared van Heerden's position in detail (which van Heerden no doubt expected us to do). The Marxist brothers pressed us to reveal whether or not Pretoria accepted a twenty-four-month timetable as "a basis of discussion"; if so, they could be flexible about their thirty-six-month plan.

We decided to reject the Angolan-Cuban ploy. I reminded them that I was a New Yorker, and my nose told me that they were slicing the salami. Aldana waxed eloquent: "This great goal of yours and Reagan's is at your fingertips; don't blow it over a lousy six months. You'll be a hero, and UNITA will gain a share of power." Cabelly and Napper could not contain themselves: "If van Heerden can do twenty-four months, can you?" Aldana confessed that he would prefer something a little longer. We shook our heads and said this was out of the question *unless* the schedule were much more heavily front-loaded.

The Angolans and Cubans no doubt listened carefully to this purposeful indiscretion, but the tactical morass got away from us. To force the pace, van Heerden soon bid again—this time proposing a twenty-four-month schedule with 8,000 Cubans to leave Angola before November 1. Only at this point did the other side bid, offering a thirty-month plan with a token pull-out before November 1 and 50 percent withdrawal by the end of the first year (versus the South Africans' 90 percent). (There were numerous other details such as benchmarks, pull-back lines, and monthly withdrawal rates.) Now, the South Africans had bid twice without seeing the Angolan-Cuban position and the other side had bid without knowing Pretoria's full position.

The parties' tactics had thwarted us and we had outsmarted ourselves. Aldana and Ndalu now praised the latest U.S. twenty-four-month plan as "logical" (if a bit too short) and accused van Heerden of "making foreign policy with a pocket calculator." Neither side had any further cards to play. Round Eight broke up with the parties in a testy frame of mind. It was nearly October, and we would miss our November 1 deadline. President Sassou was mournful. The mild-mannered General Ndalu summed up our feelings with an Angolan obscenity that Alex Schiavo smoothly interpreted as "it's a bitch."

From New York Back to Geneva, October–November

We got nowhere during tense consultations held at a midtown New York hotel on October 7–8. We decided to face reality by suggesting a January 1, 1989, implementation date. We also put forward a minor variation in our tie-breaker proposal to test the "seesaw" aspect of front- and backloading. One positive development was a green light from Ndalu and the Cubans for our joint commission proposal, along with the request that we ask Moscow to join.

But the parties offered no new bids. They were only six months apart on the timetable's total duration, but this only confirmed that its duration was not of equal importance to them. They remained miles apart on other details: (a) the pre-implementation "gesture" (8,000 versus 2,000); (b) the total to be withdrawn by the end of seven months (34,500 versus 18,000); (c) the point at which all Cubans would be north of the 13th parallel (four months versus twelve months); (d) the percentage of departures to be completed after one year (90 percent versus 50 percent); and (e) the residual during the final year (5,000 versus 12,000). In a final plenary, I reminded the parties that *they* were the losers if we failed. The average American, if queried about our talks, would probably guess that Namibia was a communicable disease and Angola an imported fabric. This smart-ass remark did not endear me to anybody, and we broke up growling at each other. The go-slow lasted until after Bush's election victory on November 8.

Apparently, neither Castro nor P. W. Botha was enthusiastic to become Republican Party exhibits during the climax of our election campaign. (In a U.N. address in late September, Reagan had trumpeted our eagerness to see Cuba leave Africa. Bush commented on our negotiations in glowing terms on several occasions.) It made sense, in all three capitals, to see who would win before consummating the deal. A Dukakis victory could have signified a wholesale shift of American policy.

We resumed in Geneva on November 11. Bush's massive victory implied broad continuity of global policy, but it did not necessarily signify a continued dedication to this particular diplomatic marathon. We spread the word that new administrations almost invariably bring with them basic policy reviews and personnel changes. The settlement process had come unhinged from any internal deadline, and the date for implementation had now become a topic of negotiation. January 20, 1989—inauguration day in Washington—would become the new deadline, just when we needed one.

We worked at the Cuban timetable for three straight days. Like a Rubix Cube, the number of permutations for a deal seemed almost infinite. The greatest gap was over the withdrawals to be accomplished in the first twelve months: Ndalu and Aldana wanted five times as many Cubans to remain in Angola after one year as van Heerden did! Jim Woods reduced the entire problem to a series of charts and graphs depicting five key variables; the trick was to transform apparently substantive issues into arithmetical ones and show that the delegates were no longer really arguing about basic principles. Eventually, we persuaded the parties to trade additional frontloading in the first seven months (which the South Africans now ranked first) for a merely token gesture of pre-implementation withdrawals (3,000) and heavy backloading of the final residual (which the Cubans and Angolans insisted on). With this compromise in hand, they agreed to split the difference on total duration at twenty-seven months (see Appendix 4). At the four-month benchmark, all Cubans would be redeployed north of the 15th parallel; at the seven-month benchmark, 50 percent of the Cuban troops would be withdrawn and all remaining troops would be north of parallel 13. The rate would slacken off after seven months, leading to a 66 percent withdrawal in the first year. Only 5,000 men would depart in the next six months, leaving 12,000 behind for the final nine months. *Eureka!*

It was November 15, and we had broken the back of the settlement. This was the deal that would end Africa's Thirty Years' War. This was the deal that would cap an eight-year odyssey and validate a concept that had been the object of abuse and ridicule. I thought of my superb associates who had stayed with this stock when others were selling it short. Yes, it would be okay to lift a glass with them, and with Aldana, Ndalu, and van Heerden. A few hours later, I received a cable of congratulations from Shultz which began with the prescient admonition that it might be "too soon to uncork the champagne."

The Final Lap

The remaining pieces still had to fall into place. One vital piece was an understanding on the cessation of South African support for UNITA and Angolan support for the African National Congress, respectively. Barnard and Ndalu had discussed an arrangement back in Brazzaville under which each side undertook to terminate its material and logistic assistance. Bases would be closed and personnel relocated—a point that really only affected the ANC since UNITA lived within Angola. Financial and political support were not covered: each party could remain true to its "principles."

Apparently, the needs of P. W. Botha and Jose Eduardo dos Santos were best served by a free-standing agreement bearing no formal relationship to other parts of the package. This was fine with us: we had enough problems to handle. We were also relaxed when the South Africans signaled that we were too "pro-ANC"—and the MPLA that we were too "pro-UNITA"—to qualify as a mediator on these questions. The real motive for preferring private exchanges, we sensed, was their collective embarrassment at performing these unnatural political acts in our presence. Our main interest was that they should somehow satisfy each other. It was probably best if we never found out exactly how they did it. These were governments of men, not laws or documents. Both would probably cheat, and both knew it. But Barnard and Ndalu—two men trained in the arts of coercion—had a common interest in a regional peace process if it could somehow incorporate measures to weaken their internal adversaries.

Initially, the literal-minded South Africans tabled draft language on Angola's obligations to cut off the African National Congress. But they recoiled in horror when presented with an Angolan document spelling out in black and white their obligation to cut off UNITA. A piece a paper like that could cause trouble at home. The idea of a written accord was dropped in favor of a gentleman's agreement. There was a hitch at the last minute on the eve of the main signing ceremony. We braced ourselves for trouble, but they worked it out themselves. In early January 1989, the ANC leadership in Lusaka announced its decision to "facilitate" the New York Accords— "an advance of great significance for our region"—by closing its Angolan guerrilla bases.

This side agreement contained potent symbolism, and it would set new standards of regional conduct. UNITA would lose its regional military ally at the moment when the MPLA was losing the Cubans. The ANC would lose its last remaining sanctuary within reach of South Africa just when SWAPO would become free to return home and seek power through democratic elections. The South Africans, rapidly losing credible enemies, would put Namibia on the path to independence and begin shedding their interventionist military role in neighboring countries.

Resolving the final issues was something of an anticlimax when compared with our breakthrough on the Cuban timetable. We wrestled for over two weeks (November 25 through December 13) to define the precise scenario for closure: when and where the interlocking treaties would be signed, who would sign them on behalf of the parties, and when implementation of the settlement would begin. In late November, the South Africans began to talk of pushing the signing back until after the New Year, which would push implementation back until April 1989. This unhelpful gamesmanship seemed to be related to suggestions that we should host P. W. Botha for a meeting with Reagan at the moment of signature.

Shultz managed to turn Pik Botha around in a November 27 phone call. Botha complained about U.S. pressure to rush to closure: verification still had to be worked out, and his government would not be stampeded without adequate guarantees. He had to agree, however, with Shultz's argument that delay could damage Savimbi. It was important to make a real dent in the Cuban presence before the next season for MPLA offensives rolled around in September–October.

When told that other heads of state would not attend and that a Reagan–P. W. Botha meeting could not be arranged, Pik Botha became emotional. The issue should never have been raised. Let the negotiators sign it, Botha snapped. We are disenchanted with this whole damn thing. Since we get no credit for taking the most fundamental decisions, let us get this over with now, without fanfare. Botha was caught between the emotions and hopes of his president and intense pressure from Washington and London to do the deed.

I often thought back to this exchange. It was hard for his subordinates to explain to P. W. Botha that the Americans could find no time on Reagan's calendar for a handshake at a signing ceremony that would change the course of African history. Reagan, after all, had found the time to meet Desmond Tutu, Gatsha Buthelezi, Jonas Savimbi, Joachim Chissano, Samora Machel, Robert Mugabe, Kenneth Kaunda, Quett Masire, Mobutu Sese Seko, Daniel Arap Moi, and many other African leaders. A generation of regional wars was ending, along with Cuban expansionism and South African rule over Namibia. But in the Washington world of bumper stickers and photo opportunities, shaking hands with P. W. Botha, Fidel Castro, and Jose Eduardo dos Santos is one of those special treats reserved for assistant secretaries of state.

When we arrived in Brazzaville for Round Eleven (November 30–December 3), Pik Botha and his team were still smarting from these events. So much so, in fact, that they rushed home a few days later just as we were putting the largely procedural Brazzaville Protocol to bed. Somehow, the roles of P. W. and Pik Botha in the whole process had become the topic of press commentary likely to fuel tantrums at home. Conveniently for the South Africans, we were now deeply engaged in working out understandings on U.N. verification of Cuban withdrawal. This enabled them to cover their unseemly departure with a press line citing problems with Havana on verification!

Strictly speaking, verification was between the United Nations and the Angolans and Cubans. The political reality was that we could never have obtained Pretoria's signature of the New York Accords unless we could satisfy the South Africans (and ourselves) that the program would have teeth. As a result, we had to "pre-negotiate" the plan with the parties concerned. This cleared a path for U.N. Secretariat officials who would convert our work into a U.N. agreement with Havana and Luanda. In the end, U.S. negotiators cajoled the Angolans and Cubans into accepting most of what we needed and then pressed nervous U.N. officials to back us up—all the while trying to keep the South Africans quiet. We knew all along that our own national technical means of verification (using U.S. intelligence assets) would be our principal means of checking compliance.

The U.N. verification body—to be known as the United Nations Angola Verification Mission (UNAVEM)—would be dependent in large measure on information and cooperation from the Angolans and Cubans themselves. We battled to obtain U.N. language that would include Cuban equipment as well as troops. It was important to get the criteria and definitions right. Another key goal was to obtain independent challenge inspections at the initiative of the UNAVEM commander or a member of the Security Council. This was essential as a means of bringing third-party information to bear. A lightly manned UNAVEM (a staff of about seventy was planned for) would not, by itself, generate high confidence. Resolution 435, by contrast, provided for extensive and highly intrusive monitoring and inspection of every aspect of the South African presence in Namibia during the transition. UNTAG would include up to 10,000 people.

The plan proposed to the Security Council by Perez de Cuellar on December 17, and adopted on December 20 (two days before signature day), was essentially made in Brazzaville. Separately, Pretoria sought and received an assurance of our own strong interest in Cuba's compliance with all its commitments. Pretoria could not force these issues at the United Nations by itself. On December 5, a few days after Botha had rushed home, van Heerden phoned me in Washington to say that recent storms had passed. The basic decision had been taken to proceed. The draft Brazzaville Protocol could now be signed once we had agreed on dates for the New York ceremony where the tripartite and the Angolan-Cuban Accords would be signed. He offered December 22 or 27, and I grabbed the earlier date. But we still did not have an agreed date for implementation of the settlement. The Angolans and Cubans wanted a March 1 date; we also preferred a March launch. A flurry of cables was required to sort this out. Eventually, we settled on April 1.

On December 13, the Brazzaville Protocol was signed in three languages under the gaze of Denis Sassou-Nguesso, his government and politburo, his national assembly, and the diplomatic corps. As television lights poured down on us, we began a sweaty consummation that featured consecutive translation into French (for our hosts) of speeches delivered in English, Spanish, Portuguese, and Russian. I made brief remarks (see Appendix 1) lauding everyone involved and describing the U.S. role in the process. Then came the turn of the parties. The Angolan and Cuban speakers each offered remarks targeted primarily at home constituencies and in-house historians. Pik Botha delivered a rambling, after-dinner-style stemwinder about the common interests of "African brothers" facing exploitation by "industrialized countries which set low prices for our commodities and high prices for their cars and refridgerators." For good measure, he reminded us that "if you shoot a zebra in the white stripe, the black stripe dies as well."

Anatoliy Adamishin, who had never witnessed anything quite like this before, watched Botha with his mouth open. Then he decided to grab the mike for a few choruses of new political thinking. Next, Martti Ahtisaari rose to speak. No one in the room had waited longer than he for this occasion; no one in the world was better qualified than he to take ball from here as the U.N. Special Representative for Namibia. Ahtisaari was mercifully brief and refreshingly forward-looking. I handed a bound copy of the protocol to Sassou, our patient host and facilitator, at the end of the ninety-minute ceremony. Then, like wilted flowers, we headed outdoors for a midday *coup de champagne* and barbecue.

The bilateral Angolan-Cuban treaty containing the timetable was the occasion of some last-minute arm-wrestling during the night of December 21–22. The Marxist brothers had lathered up their draft with unacceptable escape clauses and vague wordings. Chas Freeman pulled out all the stops—an imaginary phone call from Shultz calling Freeman out of a meeting with the Angolan-Cuban team, a heavy pitch to the Soviets, and an extended Freeman-Byerly disquisition on international legal practice. McKinley and Snyder nailed down the fix on a piano top in the lobby of the U.N. Plaza Hotel. Around 4:00 A.M. on the 22nd, our New York team went to bed. The signing ceremony itself began about six hours later.

"That's Some Bunch of Characters"

A large crowd of dignitaries assembled in U.N. Headquarters to view the carefully scripted ceremony co-chaired by George Shultz and Javier Perez de Cuellar. After the tripartite accord was signed, Shultz termed the event "a momentous turning point in the history of Southern Africa," one that would open up prospects for the peaceful solution of internal problems there. But his upbeat salute to peacemakers, diplomacy, the United Nations, and U.S.-Soviet dialogue did not exactly catch on when he asked the signatories to speak. Mbinda indirectly questioned U.S. good faith and demanded an end to "foreign meddling" in Angolan affairs, even while saluting me by name and pleading openly for diplomatic relations with Washington.

The Cuban foreign minister, Isidora Malmierca, had a more one-dimensional message. He had instructions to retaliate for some recent anti-Castro rhetoric by Ronald Reagan. The result was an offensive performance, attacking U.S. policy toward Angola and referring to our "contradictory and paradoxical mediating efforts." Malmierca also blasted the South Africans on human rights and other grounds, using the violent prose of a student rally. Pik Botha recounted the long history of U.N. and International Court of Justice involvement in the Namibia issue. He saluted the peaceful settlement which now existed "at least on paper." Confusingly, Botha said the settlement reflected the principle of "African solutions to African problems" and then thanked half the states in Africa for their contributions before getting around to mention the United Kingdom, Switzerland, the USSR, and the United States. But the high point was Botha's offer to give Malmierca a list of all those African leaders who wished Cuba to leave Africa. Botha then challenged Malmierca to step outside for a debate on human rights which could "carry on till late tonight—there is nothing we'd like to do more."

Malmierca wanted a right of reply. Shultz cut him off and recognized Adamishin for brief remarks which gave a large share of the credit for the settlement to "new political thinking." After listening to nearly an hour of speeches, Shultz glumly noted that it was clear "how difficult it has been, perhaps it's miraculous, that this agreement has been reached." De Cuellar invited Mbinda and Malmierca to sign their bilateral accord, made mercifully brief remarks, and the deed was done. As we left the hall, Shultz observed, "That's some bunch of characters you've been working with!"

PART V

19

Why U.S. Policy Succeeded

American diplomats faced a wide range of hurdles as we worked to bring peace to Southern Africa in the 1980s. One of these was self-imposed. The sheer ambition and complexity of our enterprise presented all the ingredients of an obstacle course. We had undertaken to resolve two distinct conflicts each of which was closely linked to a third (the UNITA-MPLA struggle) that was not formally on the agenda. Each had its own timing, balance, and rhythm. Facing several wars, we would need several perceived stalemates in order to bring the parties to abandon their unilateral options. This negotiating structure required us to shift our weight depending on the immediate issues while retaining an overall "balance" that was profoundly unsatisfying—both to the parties in Africa and to the more partisan and ideological minds within our own political system. It also set us up to look foolish when we fell short of our sweeping objectives, as we frequently did.

Only an infinitesimal percentage of our domestic audiences ever grasped the logic of our core concept: the interrelatedness of violence and change in the region as a whole. This logic and the basic moderation of U.S. policy got lost in a tangle of foreign and domestic agendas. Among those who understood what we were doing, some rejected its very balance.

Activists on the left had no real interest in our regional strategy, which was largely dismissed as a Cold War fixation with the Soviet-Cuban presence and a gift to the South Africans. They rejected the notion that the U.S. and South African governments could have any legitimate

449

common interest. By viewing South Africa as an isolated evil rather than the dominant power in a deeply troubled region, they missed the basic point. For us, the key was to define the relationship and sequence between U.S. goals and to understand the means available to achieve them. For them, the primary goal was to send the loudest possible signals on "where we stand."

Conservatives were viscerally suspicious of any State Department strategy that appeared to rely on the arts of persuasion, seduction, conversion, cooption, and other unnatural acts such as "weaning Marxists." In their view, our failure to adopt simplistic, polarized definitions of good and bad Africans meant that we flunked the strategic exam. They had their own politics of righteousness: they were transfixed by a one-dimensional imagery of African Marxism, just as the liberal left was transfixed by a stereotype of racist South Africa. Grand strategy, for hard-right conservatives, entailed the discovery of enemies. Then, we could proceed (holding our noses as necessary), relying on an off-the-shelf collection of so-called "policies": arms supplies, covert action, backing proxies, private support networks, lobbying and media blitzes, and (just like the left) congressionally mandated sanctions.

We lost domestic support because we did not meet the standards of the ideological poles in American politics. U.S. diplomacy was directly undermined by the adoption of punitive measures such as sanctions whose timing, content, and conditionality we had not chosen and could not control. This situation created endless distractions, loading our lines of communication with static and distrust. During 1985–87, South Africans, Angolans, the ANC, the Front Line States, and the Namibians all became objects of one sort of congressionally inspired sanction or another. We would joke among ourselves that someone must have dumped in various congressional offices the unsold stocks of a new computer game called "Sanctimony: How to Sock it to Racists and Marxists."

But it was not only the peculiarities of American politics that created a hurdle to effective diplomacy; it was also the peculiar character of the parties themselves and of our relations with them. The governments of Angola, Cuba, and South Africa were not simply the parties to yet another regional conflict. They were exotic political specimens, the sole exemplars of a strange history and a unique or rare political tradition. These parties were in every sense of the word "foreign" to Americans. We "understood" them by means of epithets. We "coped" with them by sewing scarlet letters in their apparel. The U.S. Department of State was one of the few institutions in our society with any incentive to engage with this odd assortment of characters instead of simply shunning them.

But we did not have a free hand to conduct this engagement under laboratory conditions. We inherited a substantial legacy of policies and precedents that could not be set aside even had we wanted to do so. That legacy included limited trading and investment ties and severe political constraints in our relationship with South Africa; the absence of recognition or diplomatic relations with Angola; the absence of diplomatic relations with Cuba; a variety of embargoes and barriers to normal economic or cultural intercourse with all of them; and, the complete absence of U.S. official presence in the Angolan capital.

Ironically, the sanctions reflex only underscored another hurdle we faced during the 1980s—the absence of coercive influence. We controlled neither carrots nor sticks in the sense of being able credibly to reward or punish the parties to the conflicts of Southern Africa. For the most part, these countries did not depend on decisions of the U.S. government as such. African nations (including South Africa) tend to be producers and exporters of primary commodities like coffee, sugar, oil, and gold. Their markets are generic and their products are fungible. With rare exceptions, U.S.-African trade relationships tend not to be unique or irreplaceable to any of the nations involved. U.S. arms supplies and economic or technical assistance programs tend to be of marginal rather than central importance in Southern Africa. U.S. investment represents but a small share of total foreign investment in the region. Those investments and the local markets they serve were so small as to barely show up in the books of major American firms.

Our primary economic "influence" in the region has been unofficial: the impact of marketplace decisions, often transmitted through and magnified by third parties in Europe. The parties cared less about the direct, physical leverage the U.S. government could bring to bear than about the intangible, symbolic influence we might wield: our ability to discredit, ostracize, legitimize, and encourage. Our coercive influence had always been limited, and it declined with the growing domestic disagreement on how, when, and whether to use it. Threats and promises which we might have found useful were undercut by our inability to guarantee delivery.

Among the many things we did not control was the variable of time. Mediators dream about controlling the pace of negotiation and possessing enforceable deadlines. But Southern Africa's wars were deeply rooted, dating back to the 1960s. The ebb and flow of events was primarily regional in origin. Since none of the parties depended on Washington for anything essential (except the chance for reduced ostracism and isolation), we did not have the means to enforce deadlines. Our most potent threat, one we found difficult to use effectively, was the threat to wash our hands and go home.

Our lack of control over timing and deadlines was partly caused by the complex negotiating structure I referred to earlier: we had to deal with multiple conflicts and "tracks." The process would only ripen when the parties could perceive the shape of an acceptable outcome on all tracks. In the case of the MPLA-UNITA track, this imposed an extraordinary burden on American negotiators. As a mediator, we worked for an outcome in the interests of both the Angolan-Cuban and the South African sides. But as an interested party and a directly involved superpower, we had to make sure that, at a minimum, Savimbi did not lose anything in the deal.

This complex negotiating structure eluded observers who preferred to blame delays and obstacles on their favored scapegoat. It complicated the art of applying time pressure on the parties. When we tried it in 1982 and again in 1984, we temporarily drove the parties toward direct side talks where they explored ways to escape from our agenda! Our use of the time factor worked fairly well in December 1983 when we piggybacked on the convenient pressure contained within the military conflict. But when we tried to force the pace and leapfrog over a procedural impasse in March 1985, our "basis for negotiation" proposal drove both sides away.

In the summer of 1985, we used the threat of mounting anti-apartheid fervor and the growth of pro-"freedom fighter" sentiment in the United States to create time pressures on both Pretoria and Luanda. Some months after we adopted limited sanctions using a presidential executive order, Pretoria delivered a useful reply to our "basis" proposal. But the South Africans probably judged it to be a safe move since the MPLA was unlikely to reciprocate. Our threat to rejoin the Angolan civil war did not work, so we went ahead and rejoined it. That worked better. Our message—that we were fed up with Luanda's delaying tactics and its pursuit of military solutions—eventually got through. But the immediate effect of our action was the opposite of a deadline: Luanda suspended the negotiations.

Toward the end of 1988, the impending change of administration provided one of the few real deadlines we ever enjoyed. One week after George Bush's victory, the tiresome logjam on the Cuban withdrawal timetable was finally broken in Geneva. But this deadline only worked because by now the parties really wanted to settle.

The combination of all these hurdles probably added years to our task. My colleagues and I did not have the "normal" range of tools to work with. Divisions within the administration and within the overall political process undercut our influence. We could not promise to terminate some sanction in return for a South African or Cuban action we wanted because other actors within the American system would have blocked us. Nor could we pick up the phone to persuade Kito or Ndalu to propose something to Pretoria—there were too many barriers to confidential communication. There was no way for me to invite a senior Cuban for a walk in the woods to test the significance of Castro's signals in 1984; it would have required a major struggle to get a license for such a discussion, a struggle that might have cost me dearly.

The Sources of U.S. Diplomatic Credibility

No single factor can explain the eventual success of U.S. diplomacy in Southern Africa. In the absence of a decisive incentive, our influence would depend partly on the parties' perception of U.S. *credibility:* as a great power, as a reliable and consistent partner in a complex process, as a uniquely placed "switchboard" for direct communication with all parties, as a competent and determined player with staying power, and as a legitimizer of preferred outcomes. We sought to maximize our credibility, and used various techniques to do it.

It was essential that we demonstrate a balanced commitment to both our Namibian and Angolan agendas. We had to communicate clearly the existence of certain shared interests with each of the relevant parties—and to do so without driving any party away.

A crucial ingredient of credibility was our ability to demonstrate mastery of the brief. After all, our strategy required us to lead allies who had invested years of effort on Southern Africa and who—in the case of Britain—knew it at least as well as we did. As for the key African parties, this negotiation was perhaps their most important foreign policy arena. Credibility required that we assemble the human talent, motivation, and knowledge base to acquire a unique advantage and make ourselves indispensable.

I wanted people around me who shared my ambitious, activist vision. I also wanted the best people I could find, colleagues to whom I could delegate and from whom I could learn. This negotiating task force or "team," as we called it, became itself a source of credibility. Organized collegially rather than hierarchically, the team had a more or less continuous, seven-days-a-week assignment to brainstorm, collect information, and implement our diplomacy.

I kept in place many of the officers inherited from my Carter administration predecessors. Their expertise, institutional memory, and personal credibility would be indispensable. The rhetoric and style of the new administration suggested a violent swing of the foreign policy pendulum. But it was my goal to build upon—not scrap—the legacy of

American policy going back to the 1970s. Gradually, my deputies and I mobilized and deployed a team with a wide-ranging expertise on numerous fronts: legal issues and the negotiating history, U.N. politics and procedures, regional military balances and security policy, peacekeeping, leadership attitudes and decisionmaking systems in a dozen allied and African governments plus the Soviet and Cuban systems, continuous and multi-sourced intelligence assessment, and the tradecraft of negotiation. The team was composed overwhelmingly of career officials.

We would also need enough talent to go around. With experience, we found it useful to sustain a fully staffed negotiating mission in the field, senior-level expertise in all missions where the negotiation was an ongoing process (e.g., New York, Lusaka, Pretoria, Maputo, London), fully literate officers in the many posts where meetings might suddenly occur, and a solid team in Washington to backstop them on multiple fronts (within the State Department, in the interagency setting, and in congressional and public affairs). There were typically up to fifteen officials in the most sensitive policy loops in Washington and perhaps another twenty to twenty-five officers deployed in our embassies in Europe and Africa and our U.N. mission in New York who were expected to be fully up to speed. (Another forty to fifty officers would acquire a general knowledge of the negotiation in the normal course of their assignments.)

Credibility comes in many forms. We achieved it, in part, by assembling and maintaining over a prolonged period the equivalent of a standing diplomatic task force. No other country operating in Africa even came close to the depth and breadth of the African team assembled under State Department leadership during the 1980s. These people came to their assignments from many educational and professional backgrounds, but their titles and ranks mattered less than their individual capacity to serve the cause. One (and sometimes more) of my deputies served as an alter ego in my absence. Team members left their posts to join or conduct diplomatic missions in capitals where they were not accredited. Middle-ranking advisers conducted delicate missions to persuade foreign heads of state and senior ministers or to lobby the leaders of guerrilla movements. Lawyers, administrative officers, security assistance experts, history PhDs, regional experts, intelligence officers, uniformed military officers, and veteran Foreign Service "generalists" all rubbed shoulders. The talented and motivated volunteers who served on this team were one of the most potent instruments of our diplomacy.

The decision in 1981 to operate within a U.N. framework and to retain Resolution 435 as the basis and pivot for a settlement provided indispensable credibility. Namibia's unique status as *de jure* U.N. terri-tory under *de facto* South African control made this approach wise and probably necessary. It enabled us to engage our allies and the African Front Line States. It shielded us from allegations that we were not seri-ous about Namibian decolonization. Without such credibility, it would have been far more difficult to resolve the outstanding issues from the pre-1981 diplomacy, to obtain improvements in the Namibia plan (such as the 1982 constitutional principles), and to force the issue of Cuban troop withdrawal onto the agenda. By building on the U.N. Plan, we also sharply reduced Pretoria's room for maneuver on Namibia.

In shaping our diplomacy in terms of U.N. frameworks and imple-menting mechanisms, we borrowed the perceived legitimacy of the world organization. Initially, we overcame South African skepticism by per-suading Pretoria's diplomats that a U.N.-based settlement could have advantages for them, neutralizing their detractors. Ironically, almost any U.N. action acknowledging the existence of the controversial Cuban withdrawal issue would help to give it international standing alongside the quasi-scriptural status of Resolution 435. At every step along the road to settlement, we considered ways to place our diplomacy under a U.N. umbrella. By the time we got to the endgame, all parties shared our determination to place the United Nations and its top officials in the scenario for signature of the final package of agreements.

At an earlier period, American negotiators gained credibility in Soviet, Cuban, and Angolan eyes by proposing that the package of agreements flowing from our diplomacy should be endorsed by the Security Council. This was, from their perspective, "correct" in light of Namibia's unique status. It was also an implicit gesture to the Soviets as a permanent mem-ber of the Security Council. Our approach rubbed off on the parties. By proposing U.N. verification of Cuban withdrawal, the Angolans and Cubans dramatized the "voluntary" and "sovereign" nature of their decision and avoided having to react to "demands." But they also con-sciously aimed at persuading the South Africans of their seriousness. It was not the United Nation's capacity to conduct verification that impressed Pretoria. Rather, the proposal further legitimized Cuban withdrawal as an integral part of the settlement. The creation of the U.N. Verification Mission in Angola (UNAVEM) thus served multiple purposes, not least to strengthen the mediator's hand with Pretoria.

The sustained U.S. commitment to a settlement became, in itself, a source of credibility. To be sure, there were some who saw us as over-ambitious, stubborn, and too coldly logical as we navigated through minefields of fear and anger. But whether they liked our approach or not, the parties generally accepted that we were seeking concrete results. Ours was a strategy for changing things. It was not a convenient posture for domestic political advantage. We did not view the peace process merely as damage-limiting "cover." Nor did we confuse power or brute force with strategy. The application of power was designed to serve a clearly defined purpose. It was not an end in itself.

Maintaining our credibility through the regional turbulence of the 1980s was a severe test. We had to walk a fine line, sustaining the idea of regional peace process in the minds of all parties while simultaneously avoiding the suggestion that Washington had more at stake than they did. We could not force the parties to implement our settlement. But we could endlessly remind them of its benefits, while working actively to discredit—if not veto—alternatives we did not like. Once we established the settlement formula and engaged the parties in negotiating within it, they became irrevocably trapped. Only we could spring the traps—by disengaging ourselves—that bound Pretoria to the Cuban issue and bound the MPLA to Resolution 435.

Credibility derived from our unwavering insistence on the linkage, which made it virtually impossible for the parties to abandon their own stake in these two constructs. When the settlement finally happened, a common reaction was that our persistence had paid off ("it worked because you never gave up"). This stubborn commitment to goals and policies which we believed to be right undoubtedly played a part in our ultimate success. But sheer doggedness and political will would not have been enough by themselves. We had a solid mandate from Reagan and, especially, Shultz, which gave us the ability to wait for the logic of events to play out. By staying with a sometimes beleaguered policy (and its practitioners), they made success possible.

The Meaning of "Leverage" in U.S. Diplomacy

To be effective, diplomacy must be backed by relevant forms of power and influence. Leverage on the behavior of other parties is essential. American leverage resulted both from the underlying diplomatic and military situation and from our decisions on how to exploit it. To give just one example: we needed the support of our allies to launch our new strategy in 1981. But they needed U.S. leadership in order to sustain any diplomatic process on Namibia and to make it credible in Pretoria. Each side gained. Our willingness to redefine the agenda enabled us to obtain a categorical commitment from the South Africans—without which nothing else would happen. As the primary recognized obstacle to a settlement, their endorsement was the logical first step. Our readiness to start with the primary obstacle—and our allies' need for U.S. leadership—gave us the freedom to use the sort of ammunition with Pretoria that might actually work. The link of Cuban troop withdrawal was like flypaper. The tactic worked. Yet, as the sole source of the linkage concept and only power prepared to back it publicly, the South Africans needed us. This gave us the leverage to insist that any changes to Resolution 435 be held within reasonable limits: in practice, we would control South African fantasizing by relying on others to veto excessive or unnecessary changes. In other words, we used linkage to complete the Namibia negotiation; and we then used the completion of the Namibia negotiation to accomplish the linkage.

We held no illusion that the parties were smitten with admiration for American policy. But we knew that closer ties with Washington were high priorities for virtually every state in the region, and especially for pariah South Africa and insecure Angola. This gave them an incentive to cooperate, or at least to go through the motions. We did nothing to dissuade people from believing that a settlement could transform the climate for bilateral relations.

In the case of the Angolans, this led to fairly specific discussion in 1984 of steps toward the full normalization of relations if they came to terms. These ideas were resuscitated halfheartedly by the Angolans from time to time during 1987–88. But the Angolans were too proud or too confused to make a direct run at the question, and they concentrated foolishly on the UNITA aid issue. For us, the notion of aiding UNITA while establishing relations with the MPLA regime was the sort of Gallic conception that was hard to sell in Washington. In the end, Luanda turned its nose up at the incremental approach to normalization that we offered in the final weeks of the Reagan era, after the December 22, 1988, signing. This left the whole question for the next administration, which promptly linked it to a settlement of the Angolan civil war.

As for the South Africans, we often discussed settlement scenarios as the context for improved relations and high-level visits. But once the focus of U.S. public and congressional attention turned to the internal situation within South Africa, our leverage quickly plummeted. The 1986 sanctions bill eliminated the strictly bilateral cards we could play to push Pretoria forward—by seizing the issue out of the hands of the executive, by enshrining sanctions terms in a static, legislative framework, and (especially) by defining U.S.-South African relations almost exclusively in terms of South Africa's domestic policies. We lost the ability to say to South Africans that a regional settlement could lead to improved relations.

Although our linkage strategy added massively to the complexity of the negotiation we inherited in 1981, it also expanded the array of trade-offs and the number of relevant parties. It was linkage, after all, which eventually prompted Castro to play his cards. This increased the long-term odds of a win-win deal. For one thing, it offered each of the key parties fresh openings to shape *both* tracks. They acquired new ways to maneuver for the high ground and to discredit or wrong-foot the other side. This explained Angola's readiness to enter into bilateral talks with Washington in early 1982 in full knowledge of our Cuban agenda, an agenda which the MPLA categorically rejected at the time. Another example of the pay-off came when the MPLA leadership agreed with their South African counterparts to cease supporting the ANC and UNITA, respectively. This side deal, worked out quietly in 1988, demonstrated that the American formula *did* address the underlying interests of the parties.

By expanding the agenda and the range of participants, our strategy permanently altered the negotiating structure. To build support for the initiative, American officials ranged far beyond the Contact Group and the Front Line States to cultivate the involvement of Cape Verde, Egypt, Congo, Zaire, Kenya, Guinea-Bissau, Senegal, Côte d'Ivoire, Nigeria, Portugal, Switzerland, Brazil, Italy, Japan, China, and Belgium. The enlarged agenda broadened the base of our influence; by increasing the stakes and the interest of third parties, this new agenda enabled us to "borrow" their influence and to mount indirect pressures on Moscow and Havana as well as on Pretoria.

At various points during the 1980s, these partners served as lobby-ists, advisers, hosts, facilitators, patrons, special channels, and co-spon-sors. Some third parties played bit parts, others major roles. We found that by engaging the ego and pride of others and saluting them profusely for their efforts, it was possible to assemble a large cast of actors to perform onstage. By the end of the decade that cast comprised much of the international community, including, of course, the Cubans and Soviets.

During the first half of the 1980s, the Mozambicans played an indis-pensable role in bringing U.S. officials together with the Angolans who had a mandate to explore a deal. Time and again, our dialogue with Luanda was renewed or restored at critical junctures through signals first passed to us in Maputo. Though further removed from the zone of conflict, Cape Verde played a parallel role, often sending along signals and offering an ideal, discreet meeting site. As interpreters of Angolan political reality, the Cape Verdean leadership was hard to beat. They were matchless champions of our strategy for achieving regional stabil-ity and internal change in Southern Africa. The Zambians advanced their own agenda by supporting ours when they sponsored the Lusaka meetings of 1984, and helped bring us to the point where Kito delivered to us the first authoritative MPLA bid on Cuban withdrawal. Zambia's Kenneth Kaunda proved to be a fair-weather friend of our strategy, but he was the closest thing to constructive leadership we could come up with among the English-speaking Front Line States.

We tapped into a very different sort of African leverage through the good offices and facilities of Zaire, Morocco, and Côte d'Ivoire to maintain frequent contact with UNITA's leadership. As leading patrons of UNITA—and, in the case of Zaire, as UNITA's primary ally in black Africa—these governments significantly broadened our strategic base by supporting UNITA and by helping us to do so. These governments, by having the vision and courage to speak out for national reconciliation in Angola while the subject was still largely taboo, helped convince the South Africans that other Africans would not ignore their responsibility to achieve peace in Angola. They also helped persuade Luanda to acknowledge that reconciliation was becoming both essential and legitimate in African eyes.

For reasons of its own, the Congo government in Brazzaville repeatedly championed our negotiations. President Sassou-Nguesso used his credibility to help reactivate the U.S.-Angolan talks in April 1987. He became our primary host-facilitator in 1988. By volunteering for this role before it became a fashionable exercise, Sassou acquired an interest in pressing the parties to achieve a settlement. The Congolese became eloquent advocates of the position that a regional settlement would lead inexorably to Angolan internal peace. They, like us, had the sequence right, even though their alliance with Luanda (and their Marxist ties to Moscow and Havana) made their logic somewhat suspect in the eyes of UNITA and its supporters.

America's allies strengthened our leverage in many ways. The Contact Group functioned as a reasonably close-knit team during 1981–82, enabling us to mount a form of man-to-man coverage on the various African parties and South Africa. U.S. diplomats gained valuable independent assessments of how to orchestrate the diplomacy of linkage. Allied officials reinforced our message by offering their African interlocutors an unvarnished analysis of American political reality. They also helped to occupy Washington's "empty chair" in Luanda, carrying our mail (as well as their own), and enabling us to interpret the twisted entrails of Angolan politics.

We needed allies who were prepared to become full partners. The number of such allies was less important than their quality. For nearly seven years, the British mobilized a powerful and effective diplomacy in Africa, Europe, New York, and the USSR in direct support of the peace process. I made it among my highest priorities to develop close working relationships with our Foreign Office counterparts. Cooperation and consultation expanded in London, Washington, New York, and African capitals, and we developed a regular exchange of information on all aspects of regional dynamics.

For nearly seven years, the British served as our principal channel of communication to the Angolans—handling and becoming thoroughly conversant with an extensive two-way flow of messages. No foreign power, and few people in Washington, knew more of the intimate details of our diplomacy. In the process, senior British officials also became knowledgeable about the politics of African policy in Washington. They became valued partners in a joint strategy of regional peacemaking. The British policy establishment—up to the level of 10 Downing Street—bolstered the Shultz-Crocker position on Southern Africa. There were times when Margaret Thatcher's diplomatic intervention in Washington did as much for us as her support in Luanda or Maputo. Thatcher, Foreign Secretary Geoffrey Howe, and their colleagues literally sustained our strategy.

Unique among our allies, the British had significant credibility in both Luanda and Pretoria. When relations with the Angolans in 1985–86, and with the South Africans in 1985–88 deteriorated, our British colleagues kept their channels warm and their powder dry. Thatcher's tough stance against indiscriminate punishment of South Africa brought special influence to bear in Pretoria when our own clout with the South Africans plummeted after the 1986 fiasco over sanctions.

Of all the diplomatic factors that strengthened leverage, our partnership with the United Kingdom was perhaps the most important. The British supported our successful campaign to reengage the South African leadership in early 1988. Once the tripartite talks began (in London) in May, British Ambassador Robin Renwick worked hard in Pretoria to smooth the way for South African negotiators as they returned home from each meeting to seek a fresh mandate. It was, therefore, a superbly appropriate coincidence that Margaret Thatcher was on hand in Namibia in April 1989 when large-scale SWAPO violations risked blowing up the settlement just as implementation was beginning. The British prime minister fired off tough warning messages to Pik Botha, Perez de Cuellar, and SWAPO's "allies" in Luanda and Havana to keep the settlement from going off the tracks. In that brief moment, the world got a glance at one of our secret weapons.

Diplomatic leverage of a very different kind became available to us when Fidel Castro decided in July 1987 to bid officially for a place at the bargaining table. Our leverage flowed directly from Cuban interest in exploring an honorable exit from its Angolan morass and Cuban eagerness to be seen playing a dignified role in world affairs. We managed to extract a significant price for agreeing to Cuban participation: the Angolan-Cuban commitment in January 1988 to the principle of total Cuban troop withdrawal. For the first time, we could aggressively explore all three dimensions of the Angolan–Cuban–Soviet triangle.

Once the Cubans joined the negotiation, we acquired a competent and professional party to sit across the table from the South Africans. At last, we had an antidote to the classic MPLA proclivity to fool around. And we could now make use of that special credibility which only the Cubans could provide by offering commitments and assurances that would strengthen our hand with Pretoria and UNITA. Only the Cubans could be credible in professing with apparent candor their enthusiasm to depart from Angola and their solemn commitment not to undertake offensive actions against UNITA.

Military Sources of Leverage

Just as we exploited the political and diplomatic angles available to us, so we sought to exploit the region's military equations as a source of leverage. We did not control—and had little influence over—these equations. Instead, we endeavored to understand them and share our analyses in a purposeful manner with all the parties involved. They often accused us of being self-interested and naive. The first charge was accurate; but we had no monopoly on naivete. In the end, we convinced them that our formula offered the best outcome available.

The United States had no intention of becoming directly involved on the side of either the MPLA government (with whom we had no relations) or the South Africans (the target of a long-standing U.S. and international arms embargo). We did provide limited hardware and training credits to other neighboring African governments such as Zaire and Botswana during the 1980s. But we generally deferred to a British lead in the security assistance field among South Africa's neighbors—a role London played skillfully in such places as Zimbabwe, Mozambique, Botswana, and Malawi.

Only minuscule U.S. budgetary resources were available to support African military aid programs, and they declined during the 1980s owing to worldwide budget pressures. Moreover, as the Mozambique case demonstrated, an activist role in this sector quickly ran into heavy seas in Congress. Despite a climate of mounting anti-apartheid fervor, there was essentially no domestic constituency for, or comprehension of, U.S. military aid to African states. And, in any case, we did not hunger for ambitious military programs. Our motives for supporting military assistance were political: to convey our support for the sovereignty and territorial integrity of countries that often faced overt or clandestine South African military pressure.

But it was just not realistic to imagine that we could make much difference merely by shipping arms. The regional military balance had less to do with hardware itself than with logistics and maintenance, doctrine and morale, training and skills, and reliable communications. This point was graphically demonstrated in Mozambique, where a huge Soviet bloc military assistance effort (including thousands of advisers) greatly exceeded in value the entire U.S. program throughout sub-Saharan Africa. Yet the Soviets did not "strengthen" Mozambique. That is why Machel and Chissano opted for the Nkomati process (with all its problems) as far preferable to the illusion of a military response to South African destabilization. Given these realities, we had no lust for military primacy in Southern Africa. Let the Soviets discover for themselves the military burdens of empire. Besides, as the peacemakers, we could live with this massive contrast in the roles of the two superpowers.

One military equation we could influence was the MPLA-UNITA balance inside Angola. The House of Representatives blocked our attempt to repeal the Clark Amendment in late 1981, and then reversed itself in July 1985. By then, Soviet and Cuban support to Luanda had grown dramatically, a major MPLA offensive against UNITA loomed, and it appeared that Luanda was dithering in the negotiations. The Reagan administration tried to use its new authority to press Luanda into constructive action. When this failed, we quickly exercised the option to help UNITA—to bolster its morale, and to show Moscow and Havana that we could exploit their vulnerability as the patrons of a beleaguered client.

The U.S. decision in 1985–86 to back its diplomacy with direct military involvement has been much debated. It was not a change of strategy but an adaptation to changing conditions on the ground. It proved to be a good investment. The resumed U.S. covert intervention did not by itself turn the tide of battle. But it raised the price of battle for Angolan and Cuban pilots, and it enhanced UNITA's battle effectiveness as well as its international standing. Some observers claimed that the U.S. intervention destroyed our credibility. Luanda, Havana, and Moscow all saw our move, more accurately, as pushing them deeper into the bog in which they were already mired. We also gained a potent card which could be played when the time was right to support political reconciliation between the Angolan parties. That card came into play when the Angolan reconciliation process finally ripened in 1990–91.

There is an irony in the U.S. decision to reenter the Angolan civil war. After all, the drive for aid to UNITA was led in part by political forces hostile to us. But instead of overturning U.S. policy, as they had hoped, this decision reinforced it. After all, we had long supported UNITA's goal of political reconciliation, and we knew that Cuban withdrawal would force the reconciliation issue. With our 1985 decision we supported this goal more directly by providing covert military assistance to UNITA. But this action would also bolster our diplomatic strategy. Tacitly, the parties had long calculated their every negotiating move in terms of trends in Angola's civil war. By reinforcing the internal stalemate, we could help destroy Angolan, Cuban, or Soviet illusions of a military victory over UNITA. This would hasten the regional settlement.

Throughout the eight-year marathon, we operated on the premise that outright victory was beyond anyone's reach. If that assumption had been wrong, we would have lacked the leverage necessary to become effective peacemakers: our settlement depended on the existence of a rough and relatively stable balance of military power in the region. But the reality of an ultimate stalemate was not enough: that stalemate had to be reinforced, accelerated—above all, clearly perceived by the various parties. We had to persuade each of them that its position (or that of its Angolan ally) was strong enough to run the risk of settlement but could not become strong enough to impose terms on the other side.

Our assessment of the underlying power realities of Southern Africa annoyed all the cheerleaders on the field. But it was correct. The Namibian and Angolan conflicts imposed real financial burdens on all the regional parties concerned: the Cubans and Soviets also began to pay when Angola's oil revenues declined in the mid-1980s. If the parties persisted in pursuing coercive options, their burdens would mount. The conflict would grow in geographic scope and technological sophistication. But none of the interlinked wars would be "won" by anyone. (The same was true of the catastrophic carnage in Mozambique.)

In a monograph published in 1981,* I elaborated on these judgments, and the events of the 1980s bore them out. Angolan factions expanded the conflict against each other without getting closer to "victory." SWAPO had no hope of forcing the SADF out of Namibia. The SADF, in turn, could push deep into Angolan territory and Namibianize the war by expanding local, territorial forces. But it could not eliminate SWAPO. The Cubans and South Africans each had escalatory options, but those options—if pressed to their logical conclusion—posed mount-

---

* *South Africa's Defense Posture: Coping with Vulnerability,* Washington Papers, Vol. 9, no. 84 (London and Beverly Hills: Sage Publications, 1981), pp. 84–91.

ing dangers and would suck the sides deeper into the Angolan bog. Each new wrinkle in military strategy by one side seemed to produce a balancing response by the other: the SADF's salient in Angola triggered the setting up of hardened firebases and air defense lines; expanded UNITA operations triggered heightened Soviet arms flows and major FAPLA counteroffensives which, in turn, led to effective SADF-UNITA reaction as FAPLA units got further and further away from their logistical support bases.

All in all, the Namibia and Angola campaigns of the 1980s were a showcase of what Edward Luttwak has termed the "paradoxical logic" of strategy:

> Within the sphere of strategy . . . where human relations are conditioned by armed conflict actual or possible, another and quite different logic is at work. It often violates ordinary linear logic *by inducing the coming together and even the reversal of opposites,* and it therefore, incidentally, tends to reward paradoxical conduct while confounding straightforwardly logical action, by yielding results ironical if not lethally self-damaging.*

The ultimate success of American strategy owes much to the leverage we derived from this coming together and reversal of opposites. The warring parties mobilized ever greater resources on their climb up the ladder of geographic and technological escalation. Yet they seemed to achieve less and less. The passage of time undermined every course of action and each advantage, inducing what Luttwak terms a "self-negating evolution," whereby success fails and defeat slides into victory. In 1987–88, the season of the peacemakers arrived during the apogee of escalatory folly. The moment of maximum risk became converted into a magic moment of opportunity. American leverage reached its peak when soldiers and politicians alike finally grasped this powerful logic of strategy. At last, the planets came into alignment.

*Edward N. Luttwak, *Strategy: The Logic of War and Peace* (Cambridge, Mass.: Harvard University Press, 1987), p. 5 (emphasis in the original).

20

The Grand Strategy of Peacemaking: Thoughts from the Front Lines

Despite the stream of commentary about "a new world order," we are still debating the likely scope and direction of change in the post-Cold War international system. The transition has only just begun. But it is already clear that there is nothing inevitable or automatic about the emergence of a decent, stable order. We are not there yet, and getting there will require more than a leap of faith. We will need strategies and leadership on multiple fronts. Peacemaking skills will be necessary because there will be lots of conflict in this transitional age. Our military power must also be available—as in "Operation Desert Storm"—to ward off the law of the jungle. We should continue to play a lead role in strengthening the institutions of regional and global security. But we must also help assure that the developing world becomes more effectively linked to the global system. Its health and security are essential if we are ever to see a worldwide system of civil societies.

The Imperative of Global Leadership

The transition to a decent world order will fail if we narrow our focus of concern to the most successful and westernized parts of the world. Too often, our debates on the post-Cold War order suggest that we should treat Africa, Latin America, the Middle East, and South and Southeast Asia as strategic backwaters unworthy of serious attention. To be sure, these regions contain the world's "bad neighborhoods," where political unrest, endemic conflict, and massive human tragedies are concentrated. But moving to the suburbs is not a viable response to the seething slums beyond our borders.

Back during the Cold War's heyday, those of us who believed that the developing nations mattered in the global scheme of things were accused of "globalism." Our sin was to believe that such places carried inherent weight in the world balance of forces and to argue that, as a consequence, Soviet behavior there was a legitimate subject of concern. This, we were told, was "Cold War reasoning." Instead of viewing the governments and societies of the South as an integral element of a global system, we were supposed to buffer them from geopolitics and support "regional solutions," averting our gaze in mute disgust if our global adversary (or some regional thug) played by other rules and took advantage of our restraint. Today, after the former Soviet leaders have disengaged from their ramshackle empires, we are again urged to retrench from much of the globe as if we, too, had somehow failed. This fallacy of equivalence leads to the dubious notion that past Soviet involvement in the developing states was the only valid rationale for our own. We must do better than this. Strategic and ethical considerations alike call for a different standard of stewardship.

Most developing societies will have to face within a generation or two the great challenges of modernization that we faced over the course of centuries. These are societies where state building, nation building, economic development, and the building of legitimate polities are all on the agenda at the same time. The old colonial-imperial structures that once contained these pressures have passed from the scene. Now, the bipolar structure has vanished as well. To be sure, the Cold War often brought with it superficial ideological alignments and "imported" rivalries, which aggravated the challenges facing the developing world. But it also brought a structure of restraints, which often channeled and even moderated the violence of these regions. Now that this era has passed, are we in the West trying to persuade ourselves that issues of war and peace, development and democratization, should only interest us when they arise in the good neighborhoods we are blessed to inhabit?

The developing world is the locus of the overwhelming majority of the world's armed conflicts, both civil and regional. This is where it will be most difficult—and also most important—to establish the rules of the game for a new world order. This is where most human beings live. Primordial questions of power, survival, identity, and legitimacy remain unanswered in many parts of this "backwater." It is no solace to know that we did not create these problems or to realize that they will not go away if we do. In today's world of demographic mobility, instant communications, and ecological interdependence, we will quickly become the victims of failure in the societies of the South. Besides, a moment's reflection would remind us that we ourselves were once a strife-torn, developing country. If we are humble enough to see our own image in their agonies of modernization—and wise enough to care—we will not abandon the bad neighborhoods, contenting ourselves with preaching at them or punishing them for their failures. Our participation must go beyond watching live television interviews of traumatized civilian victims; that is mere voyeurism. Our response should go beyond holding rock concerts to raise funds for humanitarian relief.

But what, in practical terms, *should* we be doing to build a congenial world order? A good place to start is by recognizing the sources of our past success. The West's Cold War triumph was a victory of ideas, of alliance diplomacy, and of superior military technology. Beyond the European arena, our leadership rested partly on our military muscle and economic clout. We used alliances, arms supplies, and economic support to maintain local balances and counter subversion. When appropriate, we used ground and naval force deployments and covert action to thwart aggression and raise the price of expansionism.

But it is a caricature to imagine that our policy successes rested exclusively or even primarily on such "instruments of policy." Effectiveness in foreign policy comes when power is harnessed to a strategic framework and translated into action by creative diplomacy. Such diplomacy has been indispensable to the sustained American involvement in Middle Eastern peacemaking since the 1960s. The same can be said for efforts to achieve a tolerable stability in South Asia and the Korean Peninsula. Peacemaking has been an integral component of American global strategy, not some bizarre aberration from the norm.

The sustained American drive to terminate a generation of strife in Southern Africa is another case in point. The African case may have especially lasting relevance for our transitional era since we relied less on the application of raw power than on a determined statecraft deriving its leverage from others, from the regional balance of power itself, and from the logic of the concepts to which we were committed. In the current period, there will be more cases where peacemakers must obtain some of their credibility and leverage by "borrowing" it.

The day may come when the habits of collective security through the United Nations are sufficiently developed that one could expect action from its New York headquarters without any individual great power(s) taking the lead. We may one day see regional organizations such as the Arab League or the Organization of American States playing a meaningful role as peacemakers in regional conflicts and crises. But we are far from that point today. Moreover, the African cases of the 1980s and early 1990s suggest that effective regional security mechanisms can sometimes best be improvised to suit an individual case. The 1988 settlement stayed on track in large measure because of the existence of the joint commission created at Brazzaville; a parallel joint commission had the task of putting the May 1991 Angola peace accords into effect.

There are many things we can do to encourage a decent world order. Carefully targeted support for democratization is a good investment that can, over time, help to tame the dragons of armed conflict in the bad neighborhoods. It also makes sense to establish regimes to control the spread of conventional weapons technologies. We should continue working aggressively to curb the proliferation of chemical, biological, and nuclear technologies. Innovative thinking is needed on how to build our global political and security institutions so that we *include* the parts of the world most in need of external support.

But responsible leadership requires us to go beyond these generalized goals in which we seek to improve the general environment of international life. We need to address the sources—and not just the symptoms—of conflict. This will require us to join with the leaders of the developing regions to find ways of resolving specific regional and civil conflicts. There is no substitute for becoming engaged in real problems and learning to master the strategy of peacemaking at first hand.

Peacemaking as a Strategy

There is a misconception that peacemaking is simply a rather grandiose term for what we did in Southern Africa during the final eight months of 1988. This mistakes the endgame for the hard, drawn-out struggle that preceded it. As the distinguished American diplomat Hal Saunders has pointed out, the real challenge lies in getting a conflict to the point where formal negotiation becomes possible. Viewed in this light, the pursuit of a peaceful settlement can become a long-term strategic commitment.* It may become the essential core of one's strategy

---

* See Harold H. Saunders, "The Pre-Negotiations Phase," in Diane B. Bendahmane and John W. McDonald, Jr., eds., *International Negotiation* (Washington, D.C.: Foreign Service Institute, 1984), pp. 47–56. The reader may also wish to consult I. William Zartman, "Prenegotiation: Phases and Functions," in Janice Gross Stein, ed., *Getting to the Table* (Baltimore: Johns Hopkins University Press, 1989), pp. 1–17.

toward an entire region. Such strategies tend to be incapable of surviving a test of results every six to twelve months.

Critics of American diplomacy too often apply the wrong criteria, imagining that two or three diplomatic missions without tangible and visible progress represent a failure. They mistake the chairing of meetings for peacemaking. What such criticism fails to see is that simply keeping a peace initiative alive during bad times—despite the efforts of all and sundry to kill it—represents victory. Partial accomplishments such as getting an opening bid or obtaining consensus on a basic principle can mean vital progress. The decades-long Middle East peace process is a prime example of peacemaking as grand strategy. The African peace process described in this book got its start in 1976, and it still has a ways to run.

What the peacemaker requires is a strategy for the "pre-negotiation" phase which includes everything that must occur *before* a formal negotiation can begin. In Saunders's terms, the tasks of pre-negotiation include (a) achieving a common definition of the problem; (b) producing a shared commitment to a negotiated settlement; and (c) arranging agreed procedures, formats, and terms of reference for the formal negotiations themselves. The second of these occurs only after the parties are convinced that the status quo is unacceptable. They must also see that a fair deal is available. And, the balance of forces must "permit" a settlement—i.e., a stalemate and broad equilibrium is necessary for both sides to be capable of negotiating.

Others have drawn attention to the necessary ingredients for a violent conflict to "ripen." William Zartman describes the elements of "ripening" as including: the collapse of an existing status quo; the elimination of the parties' "unilateral" options; a shift toward greater balance in the power equation; and the identification of a resolving "formula" for the deal. Zartman emphasizes that "ripe moments" come when there is a "mutually hurting stalemate" and the recent or prospective experience of an escalation in costs. Strong parties with solid negotiating mandates are also, ironically, essential.* Richard Haass's concept of "ripeness" begins with a shared perception that any agreement is better than no agreement. There must be an acceptable mechanism and an available formula that both sides can defend as honorable. Haass believes that warring parties must either be strong enough to make compromises and

---

* William Zartman, "Ripening Conflict, Ripe Moments, Formula and Mediation," in Diane B. Bendahmane and John W. McDonald, Jr., eds., *Perspectives on Negotiation* (Washington, D.C.: Foreign Service Institute, 1986), pp. 205–27.

cut a deal or too weak to avoid it: if a party is just strong enough to hang on, it will block agreement.*

The requirements of successful pre-negotiation are not a mystery. But what would a strategy of peacemaking look like, and where does one begin? Every conflict contains unique properties. It is the peacemaker's first obligation to **study the particular factors of history, culture, and power** that are found in all conflicts. The peacemaker is doomed to fail—no matter how powerful or credible or "legitimate"—unless he can place himself (like a good historian) inside the minds of the parties while remaining coldly realistic about them.

This does not mean that peacemakers must be neutral or unbiased. In fact, peacemakers typically intervene in conflicts precisely because their interests are affected, and they tend to act in support of a settlement compatible with those interests. By the same token, parties are more likely to respond to a peacemaker whose clout and prestige demand that he be taken seriously—even if that response is largely tactical or defensive. Bias (in the sense of having an interest in the issues and a preference about the outcome) is not an obstacle to success.

But ignorance or prejudice will guarantee failure. The peacemaker who tries to operate without acquiring a mastery of the problem at hand will lose a precious source of potential leverage. Equally essential is a willingness to comprehend the interests, hopes, and fears that lie behind the positions of each party. It will not be possible to design a "fair" (win-win) formula without a feel for each party's way of thinking and priorities. This is why the peacemaker must, first, invest in knowledge; no one should know the brief better than he. Procedural even-handedness and fair play are important because they signal a readiness to listen, to learn, and to protect the parties' soft parts. They also protect the peacemaker from his own parochialism. There is little room for "liking" or naively "trusting." If the various parties were not in some sense opposed to what he is doing, there would be no need for peacemaking!

The would-be peacemaker who cannot treat the parties and their concerns with respect should find another line of work. I am speaking about more than protocol and bedside manner. The list of desirable attributes for success in this field starts with **a rigorous commitment to accomplishing something and shaping events,** not posturing or finding ways to feel good. This strong orientation takes precedence over all other priorities, including domestic sentiment in the peacemaker's own country.

---

* Richard N. Haass, *Conflicts Unending: The United States and Regional Disputes* (New Haven: Yale University Press, 1990), pp. 6–29.

Obviously, peacemaking is most fruitful when a conflict is becoming ripe for resolution. But we will not come closer to a decent world order by waiting around for conflicts to end and then making our move—like the ambulance-chasing lawyer in search of a fee. **The absence of "ripeness" does not tell us to walk away and do nothing.** Rather, it helps us to identify obstacles and suggests ways of handling them and managing the problem until resolution becomes possible.

Each conflict situation will contain its own ebbs and flows, and each peacemaker will have his own rhythm. To ripen a conflict that appears to be deadlocked, it may be desirable **to shake the parties up by giving them something fresh to mull over.** Though it may be premature to table proposals, one can float basic ideas, principles, and concepts—laying them out publicly or confidentially as seems most appropriate. If the basic principles are sound, the parties will find them hard to ignore and yet difficult to respond to with a simple "yes" or "no."

Typically, in a highly polarized conflict situation, an argument will promptly break out over the conditions for accepting (or not rejecting) the new ideas. This is the game of preconditions: side A says to the mediator, only when B has done these six things on our wish list will we consider (as a sign of our political maturity and a gesture of good faith) this difficult and dangerous thing you are asking us to do. The peacemaker will also face definitional minuets over the "meaning" of the new principles. The important thing at this stage is **to block all efforts to define them in a precise, operational form.** Had we caved in to ardent South African attempts to establish a concrete definition of "total Cuban troop withdrawal," we could not have engaged the Angolans.

The peacemaker's goal at this "unripe" stage is to **establish the basic principles that could form the building blocks of a settlement.** Until such time as they are fully agreed, the imperative is to keep them alive and to gain increased legitimacy for them. This was one reason that we chose to anchor our settlement framework in the inherited, U.N.-based diplomacy.

When a peacemaker moves to lay down the conceptual framework for a settlement, this action tends to rule out and discredit the obvious alternatives. Ripening cannot take place until a consensus develops—not only about the need for a negotiated deal, but also for a specific kind of deal. If a number of approaches remain in play and appear to be equally viable and attractive, the conflict remains unripe. The peacemaker's move may prompt the parties to collude tacitly against him, escaping behind the cover of each other's non-cooperation. If this keeps happening, he can prepare his moves with one side first, and claw his way toward agreement like a skipper tacking toward the wind. There may be times when a proposed framework of principles drives the parties toward another approach which has merit. The original initiative will still have served a useful purpose by shaking things up and injecting some movement into the picture.

But the most important reason for taking the initiative is **to block the parties' unilateral options and discredit their wishful thinking.** By stating a viewpoint on the basic shape of a deal, one is stating, first, that an equitable, negotiated settlement is possible. One is also taking the position that an imposed, military solution is neither possible nor desirable. The mediator is discrediting and, hopefully, demolishing the pipe dreams and fanciful scenarios that parties tend to erect. A conflict also ripens when the mediator, as Saadia Touval and William Zartman put it, can devise and facilitate outcomes superior to any which the parties can obtain unilaterally.* This is a source of his leverage; for example, Castro could not get out of Africa "honorably" without American help.

A second dimension of ripening a conflict focuses on the procedural aspects of getting to settlement. Warring parties cannot communicate and explore doing business without having a mechanism and an appropriate forum in which to do these things. The peacemaker seeks to **become the indispensable channel** by asserting political will, demonstrating technical competence and unrivaled grasp of the brief, consistently possessing state-of-the-art information, and performing reliably (from the parties' standpoint). He illustrates how the bidding might proceed and what the structure of an agreement might look like. Will there be a shuttle or proximity talks? Would an international conference make sense? Who should participate, and who are the parties to the ultimate agreement? The origins of the 1988 New York Principles and Geneva Protocol can be found in our 1982 conversations about a "pre-implementation cease-fire" and a "procedural framework" with the MPLA and the South Africans. Over time the idea of a package of interlocking accords took shape. Before taking the plunge, the parties will want to know that **an acceptable mechanism for negotiation and an appropriate format for registering agreement** are available.

But there are no general rules governing the "correct" mechanism and procedures for peacemaking. A comparison of the so-called "Reagan Doctrine" conflicts (that is, those regional conflicts where Washington decided in the 1980s to challenge the Brezhnev Doctrine) illustrates the procedural as well as substantive uniqueness of each case. In Namibia-Angola, the United States came to play the dominant role, with support

---

* Saadia Touval and I. William Zartman, eds., *International Mediation in Theory and Practice* (Boulder, Colo.: Westview Press, 1985), pp. 260–61.

from the United Kingdom, the Contact Group, the Front Line States, other African states, the U.N. Secretariat, and (at the end) the Soviets. In the subsequent UNITA-MPLA negotiations of 1990–91, the Portuguese assumed the lead (after a Zairean-led African effort collapsed), and received strong support from the two superpowers (especially Washington).

In each of the other cases—Afghanistan, Cambodia, and Nicaragua—the actual negotiating structure has varied widely, despite the common ingredient of direct superpower interest. That is all the more true in conflicts where they are not engaged, ranging from Kashmir and Sri Lanka to Peru's Sendero Luminoso or the problems of East Timor, Cyprus, Bosnia, and Nagorno-Karabakh. The temptation to imagine that we might derive some general principles for superpower cooperation in conflict resolution is to be strenuously avoided. We tried once, back in the early 1970s, to contain superpower competition within a broad, abstract framework (the Basic Principles of Agreement), but detente broke down in the very regional conflicts we are discussing.

A case can be made for reaching out to the ex-Soviets, offering them procedural dignity in exchange for their substantive support—an approach that has proven itself in a number of cases. Arguably, a gracious, inclusive diplomacy will increase our own leverage and reward moderation. But this notion must not become a ball-and-chain on Western diplomats, especially when the ex-Soviet Union has ceased to be a recognizable global actor and has itself become a place of conflict.

For all these reasons, Western statesmen should adhere rigorously to an ad hoc approach, looking at each conflict on its merits. The peacemaker must be a tailor, not a haberdasher. When considering joint peacemaking endeavors, with the ex-Soviets or anyone else, we should apply commonsense criteria: What clout do they have with the protagonists? How "relevant" are they to the conflict at hand, and how will their participation (or non-participation) be perceived? What do we get in return for accepting or creating a role for them, and what must we pay for it? What is the cost of excluding them?

The Varieties and Sources of Leverage

The peacemaker's task is to put a leash on the dogs of war, and become an agent of purposeful change. But it is a fallacy to imagine that a peacemaker—even a powerful one—is freezing the status quo. Typically, the peacemaker is, in fact, facilitating peaceful (or less bloody) change. Sometimes, the peacemakers have promoted fundamental, even "revolutionary," change far more effectively than the revolutionaries themselves! That is why they are feared and hated by those who live off a status quo of violent polarization.

Similarly, there is a fallacy in arguing that powerful peacemakers run around the globe imposing settlements on reluctant parties. At times, the great powers may intervene to stop violence and demand cease-fires. But their action must not stop there: they have created a window for diplomacy and must use it. It would be a rare situation, indeed, where a mediator had the coercive capability to impose terms upon the parties to a conflict. Negotiation would not be necessary if the third party had such overwhelming clout. But it is equally fanciful to argue that violent international conflicts can be resolved through a bloodless, apolitical mechanism in which impotent facilitators offer T-group therapy to willing volunteers. We are not yet at the point where peace is made by immaculate conception.

For all these reasons, the peacemaker needs power and leverage to be effective. Where does this come from? Sometimes, we fall into the trap of imagining that leverage in peacemaking is like leverage in a bilateral trade or arms control negotiation. But the structure of peacemaking is fundamentally different because it is triangular. **The mediator's direct, bilateral leverage with each of the parties is most unlikely to be the decisive factor.** To be sure, there is a time and place for shifting weight from one side to another in order to strengthen or restore a stalemate. The threat of pain or the promise of reward may tip the balance among decisionmakers within a government at a particular moment.

However, the manipulation of bilateral threats and rewards is much overdone in the analysis of dispute resolution. For one thing, the peacemaker is at the center of a strange triangular logic. His gestures toward one side may drive the other into stupid behavior. Threats or sanctions toward a misbehaving party are likely to let the other side off the hook. A test of wills can develop between a reluctant party and an ardent mediator. The peacemaker who operates by doling out rewards rapidly becomes an object of manipulation. Threats and punishment can produce their own perverse effects: the mediator's objective is, presumably, to obtain forward movement *by both sides* on the settlement track, not to weaken or punish the parties.

The richest source of leverage for the peacemaker may already be built into the existing situation. How badly are the parties hurting, and how can they be persuaded that a settlement is their best option? What is it that one or the other side really wants but cannot get on its own? Is one or more of the parties isolated and eager to gain external support for its positions? Can their standing and legitimacy be put in question if they fail to cooperate? What pressures are built into the military situation, and what can be done to strengthen or accelerate the necessary stalemate?

Any successful diplomacy is based upon some form of power. In a mediatory triangle, effective leverage will more often than not be "borrowed". We borrowed leverage from all those other third parties whom we persuaded to participate in our African initiative in the 1980s, ranging from the British to the tiny nation of Cape Verde. A peacemaker also exploits the leverage within the military situation itself.

The peacemaker examines the "environment" of the conflict and the interests of other external players. Are there other third parties who crave an acknowledged role in resolving it? Great: make 'em pay. Being included and recognized is an important motivating factor for governments that are insecure about their role and status. Is there a club somewhere which one or more of the parties is eager to join? Fine: link it to performance and co-opt the admissions committee. If the current facts are not good enough, create some new ones. Build leverage through investments in your own credibility.

Then, there is the "flypaper principle." Find a way to frame a question to which it is almost impossible to say no. There is likely to be *some* hypothetical bargain that would attract even the most recalcitrant party. The flypaper principle is used with the party whose current position is perceived by everyone else to be the "main obstacle" to negotiations. The South Africans were perceived as the prime obstacle on Namibian independence in 1981. Hence, we had to take them on, and tempt them with our flypaper. The Cuban linkage was our flypaper.

When times are slow and the mediator has nothing much to work with, one can devise less ambitious forms of flypaper by posing hypothetical questions. The peacemaker's role is to place a steady, unending flow of choices before the parties. When a negotiation is becalmed, look for ways to blast the parties out of their entrenched positions—by creating and exploiting facts and posing choices.

It is generally believed that leverage comes from the ability to change the pain / reward ratio facing a party. We are accustomed by our exposure to war games to viewing such pressures and incentives as decisive. But, it is all too easy to exaggerate the degree to which peace is blocked by (a) insufficient pain, or (b) inadequate rewards in the deal. The primary obstacle confronting the peacemaker may be the parties' fears and the absence of offsetting reassurances that would give confidence. Making peace with a violent adversary is an act of faith. Increased pain (or its opposite, the removal of pain) does not address the fear–confidence equation. In fact, the two equations may not intersect.

For the peacemaker, the fear quotient in a conflict situation offers as

many types of leverage as there are varieties of fear. There is fear of the unknown (Kito Rodrigues's "wolf on every mountain"). What happens if the other side breaks its word? What if the other side's leadership is replaced by one less inclined to respect its commitments? There is the fear that political rivals at home will exploit one's readiness to consider compromises. Warring parties face the classic fear of appearing to negotiate from a position of weakness; one more concession may lead to an escalation of demands and ultimate capitulation. There is the fear of losing face in the eyes of domestic or foreign opinion; one prefers not to be seen making decisions under pressure from foreigners. What would the history books say? It is not a simple matter to answer these fears. But the peacemaker who ignores them is flying blind and missing a major source of potential leverage.

The Art of Creating Formulas

The peacemaker, by definition, is trying to convert a winner-take-all scenario into a win-win outcome. Each side must give something in order to get what it needs most. But where do we start in order to create such a formula? The odds are high that we cannot start "from scratch." Most conflicts have their own natural history etched in the memory and positions of the sides and reflected in previous phases of peacemaking. The place to start is **by deciding what to do with this inherited diplomatic legacy.** One also needs at an early stage **to decide which problems to solve now and which ones to leave for later.** My veteran Soviet counterpart Vladilen Vasev once admitted that linkage is a sound principle in international politics. But it should not be overdone, he added, because "every problem in the world, ultimately, is linked to everything else." The scope of the negotiating agenda requires careful attention.

We expanded the agenda in Southern Africa in 1981 by linking Namibia to Angola and speaking of the need for reciprocity in regional security arrangements. But the list of issues we chose *not* to address is striking. On the Angolan side, we stoutly resisted attempts (from whatever quarter) to impose internal political reconciliation as an officially linked condition of the settlement. The issue would have overloaded the negotiating circuit, preventing movement on any front.

On the Namibia side of the ledger, our predecessors had wisely omitted any resolution of the thorny problem of Walvis Bay, the territory's main port. It was one of those "killer" issues that would have ruled out any chance for consensus back in 1978. We agreed, and avoided it like the plague, sensing instinctively that the status of Walvis Bay was best left for the South Africans and Namibians to work out after independence. The original U.N. Plan also left aside the question of how a new Namibian army would be constituted, who would do it, and when. This issue was simply too hot to handle during 1981–88, and none of the parties seemed to want it raised. But the terms for forming the army were smoothly handled in 1989–90, after the election.

There may be a tide in peacemaking: at the ebb, it may take months just to arrange a meeting site; but at the flood, even the most politicized matters can fall quietly into place. The decision on what to include in a settlement formula is not simply one of avoiding the rough places. The decision must rest on a judgment about timing and whether any useful purpose is served by forcing an issue now. The original plan said nothing about the eventual Namibian constitution. We decided to negotiate a set of constitutional principles in 1981–82 because (a) democracy was less fashionable back then and we wished to see a democratic Namibia; and (b) it would help us nail Pretoria down to our new formula. That decision took nine months to implement, but it served Namibians well in 1989–90 when the constituent assembly began drafting.

Creating a formula is an analytical art. One needs to know something about a region's history and balance of power. The formula must be logically consistent with the underlying power relationships in the conflict; otherwise, one or another side will simply refuse to take it seriously—"they will never get at the peace table what they cannot achieve on the ground." The problem, of course, is that the peacemaker's analysis will likely differ from that of one or both parties. Still, it is no bad thing for a peacemaker to inform the various audiences of his considered judgment as to the basic shape of the deal. By doing so, he indicates what sort of outcome he is prepared to facilitate and why. **He defines the agenda.**

The peacemaker must analyze each of the key parties and attempt to understand their real interests and priorities. For clues, one examines (briefly) their stated positions. But other evidence tends to be more useful—decisionmaking systems, the role of key constituencies, domestic political culture and national values, and national preoccupations aside from the conflict at hand. What role does the conflict play in the party's domestic and external policies? These are analytical thickets. Warring parties seldom talk openly about their priorities. When they do, it is often in a code which foreigners are supposed to misunderstand. Few individuals in most governments are really in a position to talk about the subject authoritatively.

The mediator looks for evidence of shared interests. Warring parties may have things in common they would rather not advertise: internal problems, for example. In our 1988 endgame, a classic illustration came about when the Botha and dos Santos governments traded support for their respective allies (UNITA and the ANC) in order to weaken their respective adversaries (the ANC and UNITA). The mediator needs to keep an eye out for interests that neither coincide nor conflict. We achieved closure on a Cuban timetable which precisely reflected the parties' asymmetrical priorities about the pace, duration, and benchmarks for withdrawal. At a certain point, the schedule's overall length ceased to be an issue.

When the peacemaker faces directly incompatible interests, it may sometimes be possible to split the difference or to arrange a procedural "fix" such as an election. More often, it is necessary to find a formula that marries the parties' interests together or restructures the issues in dispute. The choice will depend upon the facts of the case and the ambition and interests of the peacemaker. Early in the 1980s, we developed the habit of saying that we had "restructured" the regional peace process. The term was apt. *Procedurally,* we reorganized the 1970s negotiating framework, placing ourselves at the center of a two-tracked exercise. *Substantively,* we changed the structure of the issues to be resolved, expanding the agenda into a regional package deal. Our decision gave us the greatest scope for strategic creativity, but it also entailed greater risks and increased our workload.

The core of any such settlement, if it is to endure, must be a sound and realistic formula that contains the raw material for numerous trade-offs between the sides. (In the African case, that formula was to offer each side the chance to improve—from its perspective—the prevailing security conditions.) By opening things up, a range of interests are brought into play, and the parties are obliged to reflect on their priorities. Like a puzzle, the conflict may have only one solution. Using trial and error, the peacemaker keeps on experimenting with new variants until the sides first come to perceive that a win-win outcome is, indeed, possible, and second, agree to select among their priorities and put aside their wish lists. Evidently, such an approach cannot work unless the formula, in its most basic sense, is equitable—and can be implemented by each side in a dignified and honorable manner.

Reflections on the Tradecraft of Mediation

During our 1988 marathon, I often wondered if the endgame required a different set of skills from those needed during pre-negotiation. Is the mediator who chairs a formal negotiation playing a different role from the foreign policy strategist who uses leverage to get warring parties to the table in the first place? What should be done differently? How does the strategy of the peacemaker relate to the tradecraft of the mediator during the endgame?

It is all part of a continuum of actions—just as the angler is fishing from the time he baits the hook, to his choice of the best means to present the lure, the strike that sets the hook, his technique for playing the fish on the line and finally bringing that fish into the angler's net. Each step is crucial to success, and each requires its own skill. The fishing analogy is instructive. It conveys the typically antagonistic relationship between the peacemaker (whose primary goal is to get the fish on the line and keep it there) and the party (which seeks to get away or, at a minimum, to have that option).

The endgame in peacemaking is akin to playing the fish from the moment when the hook is set to the joyous instant when it can be netted: the angler keeps a taut line, never permitting slack unless the fish momentarily leaps into the air in an effort to break the line or rip free of the hook. If a fish wants to dive or to surface and jump, you let it do so. You may lose the fish by trying to thwart it. And, in any case, a fish cannot be netted until it has exhausted itself (and its available options). Anyone who has ever "lost" a fish knows how many things can go wrong *after* its initial taking of the bait.

The problem with the fishing analogy is that the mediator must get *two* fish into the net to get a settlement! It is like that rare "double" known to the fly fisherman who ties two flies to his leader. The odds of getting two fish to strike at once are rather low. But it happens at times of "ripeness"—feeding frenzies. Once on the line, their actions may offset each other, inadvertently helping the fisherman to bring them in together. There is no foolproof manual that can guarantee you against losing your fish. Like military conflicts, each species of fish and each body of water are different. But the endgame of the mediator, like that of the angler, can be understood according to some general notions of tradecraft.

We have already discussed the importance of **getting the sequence right**. The parties are unlikely to "take the bait" unless they have come to accept the basic parameters of the deal being proposed. One starts with the broad principles and moves on from there. Warring parties are unlikely to take possibly irreversible steps toward military disengagement until they have come to terms with the basic deal. Nor are they likely to hammer out the specifics of essential trade-offs on the key issues until (a) the basic parameters of the deal are agreed, and (b) a climate of greater confidence exists and no side feels that it is negotiating at gunpoint. Efforts to negotiate treaty language relating to verification or guarantees make the most sense once it is reasonably clear what is to be verified or guaranteed. Institutionalized mechanisms for implementation and follow-up come at the end, when the sides have acquired a substantial stake in the success of their own efforts.

The mediator, like the fisherman, needs somehow **to keep control of the action.** This includes the action going on at home (or in the boat). If three other people are grabbing for the fishing rod or shouting conflicting advice to the angler playing the fish, the odds of a mishap grow. The mediator requires committed, full-time support at home. He must be able to rely on a mandate reflecting uncontested authority. He needs the support of colleagues at home who are as committed to success as he is.

The peacemaker requires secure reporting channels that protect him as well as the parties. Foreign parties are less likely to divulge their thinking on life-and-death security issues if the details of sensitive trades are going to appear in legislative hearings or media reports. In a democracy, there is a natural urge for openness, including full disclosure of other people's business. While respecting that urge, the mediator soon learns that the "right" to information is most often asserted by those with the strongest motivation to scuttle the negotiation. Choices must be made. One way to cope is by stoutly resisting the many pressures to sign separate understandings or side deals with the parties. A mediator whose own interests are clearly engaged in the settlement is likely to stand behind it, regardless of whether there are separate "understandings" to this effect.

As with the angler's craft, **certain things are best left to nature.** If the parties wish to meet directly and privately, any effort by the mediator to impede them will be self-defeating. Let the fish run and tire itself. There will be times when the best course is actively to facilitate such contacts. Direct, bilateral exchanges are natural acts. They permit parties to say things which are not intended for the ears of third parties, and they provide another kind of reading of each other's thought processes. If they use the occasion to whisper collusively at the expense of the peacemaker, he is in trouble anyway.

The mediator can make a difference by the ambiance and chemistry that flows from his efforts. One hopes to break down the rigid imagery of negotiating "sides" at the table by fostering a degree of informality and spontaneity. It is in the relatively unstructured give and take of informal exchanges that interesting probes and trial balloons will occur. This is where one party illustrates to the mediator or to another party the political logic of its position, including the domestic political imperatives at work. This is where the mediator engages in coaching, using his wile to elicit "gestures" and to offer reassurances about the "other side." Delicate confidences will be shared away from the plenary table.

Such message sending is not suitable for formal exchanges with lots of participants and notetakers.

The creation of **a climate where informality can thrive** is a special art. It cannot be forced. An artificial, American-style recourse to first names with total strangers is not a winning formula. Parties will become more "open" when treated respectfully, not when they are thrust into unanticipated "surprises" or corny "events." A mediator creates a sense of flow based on a step-by-step progression toward the hardest issues. This give confidence and generates momentum, making it harder to disrupt the proceedings.

Ambiance is affected by many factors: the physical setting, contrasting rhetorical styles and domestic political constraints, the ranks of delegations, language barriers and interpretation facilities, and the mediator's sense of timing and use of the clock. Only some of these are under the mediator's direct control. High-ranking delegations may bring greater authority and clearer mandates, but they also tend to bring less familiarity with the intricate detail, greater pressure from personal calendars, bigger egos and the consequent risk of tests of will, and their own traveling press contingents and domestic political concerns. For the mediator, the only situation even worse than being torn between self-important heavyweights is to be stuck with people who have no authority to take decisions.

Impatient anglers lose fish by trying to muscle them in before they are "ready" to be netted. The mediator's sense of timing will suggest when to apply pressure and when to back off and give the sides time to obtain what they need from their home bases. **The "correct" timing is a matter of feel and instinct.** A mediator will want to establish early in the process the right to take initiatives such as tabling agenda documents or blending official position papers from the parties. The presentation of single-text treaty documents with blank spaces can also be useful as an illustration of what the deal might look like on paper. Tabling of specific, compromise proposals on the core trade-offs is a more delicate issue. Once played, this card is difficult to replay and tends to lose its value. Since this move reveals where the mediator is coming from, the timing will depend on (a) how close the parties are to each other; (b) how "realistic" they are about each other; (c) the extent to which they are "stuck" in their existing positions; and (d) the degree of symmetry in the mediator's relationships with them. In the African case, we acted prematurely in 1985, assuming the risk of driving the sides away from the table. In 1988, we waited until the parties began whispering that they hoped we would move soon.

A fine touch is called for during a negotiating endgame. **The mediator's influence derives from cross-cultural insights and an ability to read other decisionmaking systems.** The arts of communication (and interpretation) become essential tools. A sense of humor can help establish common ground and trigger interesting reactions. It is sometimes important to know the things that people can laugh about. Metaphors help people put forward ideas they cannot yet articulate clearly. Distinguishing between literal meanings and rhetorical flourishes is an essential prerequisite to success. Parties do not necessarily mean what they say in remarks for the record—and may mean something very different from what they say. Literal-mindedness is to be avoided on the part of the mediator, who will need large quantities of indirection and imagination.

The legal and diplomatic traditions of various nations differ. A mediator representing our own litigious society is acculturated to think that parties will try to get away with anything not expressly prohibited by the terms of an agreement. This mentality produces lengthy documents and much fine print. It is, perhaps, more appropriate to an environment where legal actions and remedies are readily available. All countries have lawyers in their diplomatic establishments, but their traditions may differ. The mediator (from wherever) should endeavor to respect the parties' needs in this regard.

In the African case, the documents were anchored in basic principles, and the parties' commitments were stated in broad and clear terms. A hundred legal battles could have been waged over their precise operational meaning. We opted to leave those problems for the implementors. Besides, a key component of that settlement (the U.N. Plan for Namibia) had been negotiated ten years earlier. The last thing we wanted was to reopen this dossier. During implementation of the 1988 settlement, the incidents of cheating were fairly evenly balanced on all sides, and the joint commission provided a rough-and-ready court of appeal. In other cases, a more elaborate documentation may be appropriate, especially when new institutions are being created. **Let the parties shape their styles and formats.** Remember, after all, that it is **their** settlement.

Epilogue

April 22, 1989, was my final day in the Department of State. Along with other presidential appointees, I had submitted my resignation to President-elect George Bush back in December. This is standard procedure after every presidential election, assuring the victor unfettered scope to form a fresh team. I had worked for Bush in 1980 and had kept in regular touch with him during the Reagan years; he had been consistently supportive of our African efforts—making two trips to Africa during the 1980s, and hosting scores of African visitors in Washington. The incoming Secretary of State, Jim Baker, had also been an ally at the White House during the first Reagan term and during his tenure at Treasury. But Bush and Baker would want their own team of senior advisers.

For my part, I wanted a real break from government service in any event. I had no desire to remain in the Africa job. Eight-plus years were enough: soon there would be jokes about the "Assistant Secretary for Life." Yet I also recognized that I had held one of the best jobs in government, offering me an uncommon degree of responsibility and scope. Few senior officials in our fragmented, cross-wired, and congressionally micro-managed foreign policy machinery had the autonomy I had enjoyed as Shultz's African lieutenant. Consequently, it was not especially attractive to move to some other position where I would have to read three newspapers and make four phone calls each morning to learn what our "policy" would be for the day.

My immediate concern was to make certain that nothing went wrong between December 22, 1988, and April 1, 1989—the start of implementation, when the U.N. Transition Assistance Group would arrive in Namibia and the clock would start ticking on the timetables for political transition and troop withdrawals. Once the settlement began to be implemented, the move toward Namibian independence and regional peace would become irreversible. What better moment to step aside? I had been extremely fortunate to be able to bring the Southern African peace process to this happy conclusion. I could become a free man again, and my successor would have a strong legacy on which to build.

My transition back to private life began immediately after the new Joint Commission—bolstered by superb leadership from British Prime Minister Margaret Thatcher and U.N. Special Representative Martti Ahtisaari—had dealt with the crisis caused by SWAPO's aborted incursion into Namibia on April 1. The upshot of SWAPO's ploy to gain U.N.-recognized "bases" inside the territory was hundreds of SWAPO dead and a six-week delay of the settlement clock. Ironically, this mini-crisis served as a baptism of fire for our settlement, driving the signatories closer together.

After this unhappy episode, Namibia's transition to independence under U.N. supervision went off without major breakdowns. The SADF departed from its elaborate Namibian infrastructure more or less on schedule. To be sure, there was some utterly predictable wrangling between South African and U.N. authorities over security issues and electoral and voter registration procedures. But these problems were overcome. Over 40,000 refugees returned home from neighboring lands to participate in the emerging political process. The 8,000-person UNTAG operation performed effectively under the strong leadership of Ahtisaari and his deputy, Joe Legwaila of Botswana. In November, over 95 percent of Namibia's eligible voters took part in elections for the constituent assembly. To the surprise of no qualified observer, SWAPO won an absolute majority (57 percent of the votes and 41 seats in the 72-person assembly). But it fell short of the two-thirds majority that would have enabled it to dictate terms to the minority parties.

SWAPO redeemed itself by its conduct during the months that followed. It seized the high ground by proposing the adoption of our 1982 constitutional principles as the assembly's frame of reference. A strikingly democratic constitution emerged in February 1990, a few short weeks before Namibia became independent on March 21, 1990.

A flood of emotions ran through my mind as a I sat in the Windhoek stadium to witness speeches by Perez de Cuellar; Namibia's new president, Sam Nujoma; and South Africa's new president, F. W. de Klerk.

The South African flag was lowered for the last time on Namibian territory, some 105 years after the start of German colonial rule and 75 years since Pretoria took over from Berlin. Jim Baker and my successor Hank Cohen had included me in the U.S. delegation to help celebrate this sparkling diplomatic victory. Africa's last colony was free. Representatives of seventy countries attended the event, perhaps the most celebrated independence ceremony ever witnessed in Africa.

The presence amongst them of Secretary Baker and Soviet Foreign Minister Eduard Shevardnadze symbolized a new era. So, too, did the presence in Windhoek of Nelson Mandela, whom de Klerk had just freed from twenty-seven years of imprisonment back on February 11. Dramatic events were cascading across Southern Africa, just as they were rolling across Europe.

Why had the transition in Namibia gone so smoothly? Why were the Cubans leaving Angola on (or ahead of) schedule? How best to explain the sudden dramatic turn in South African politics under de Klerk since he took over from P. W. Botha in August 1989—releasing Mandela, unbanning the African National Congress and other movements driven underground thirty years ago, and committing to a vision of negotiated, democratic change? After all, neither SWAPO nor its opponents enjoyed illustrious reputations for tolerance and adherence to democratic norms. Had they wished to cheat, the Cubans might have found ready cohorts in Luanda and Moscow. (Happily, the Cubans did minimal cheating.) As for de Klerk, there were few visible markings of a historic figure in his previous career as National Party province chief and cabinet minister. What was the link between the various factors that were transforming Southern Africa? Were they simply a local reflection of some global pattern, or were they unique to the region?

As I reflected on these questions during those days in Windhoek, I shuddered. This was the historical watershed that many Southern Africans had been praying for ever since the die was cast for war and racial confrontation decades earlier. I had been dreaming about it myself for twenty-five years. What a glorious reward for years of hard slogging!

Some commentators quickly referred to Gorbachev's "new thinking" and the collapse of communism in Eastern Europe as somehow explaining the dramatic currents of change in Southern Africa. By late 1989 and early 1990, Pretoria's rulers could see that external Marxist enemies—and scapegoats—were on their knees, and the Marxist enterprise around the world had become thoroughly discredited. Losing an external enemy meant that the nationalist Afrikaners were losing their historic excuse for not facing up to imperative of sharing power with the majority of their fellow South Africans. It also made it safer and less

frightening to face up to the agenda of political negotiations with the
ANC leadership and other opposition figures. By the same token, the myth
of armed struggle was now threadbare. The ANC had lost all of its sanctuaries among the Front Line States. For Soviet-aligned regimes like
Angola's MPLA and movements like SWAPO and the ANC, their global ally
appeared to be turning away from revolutionary engagements. Violence
as a credible tool of political action was becoming suspect. Thus, the
diminished Soviet role as the enemy of one side and the ally of the other
was a factor in the new equation of early 1990.

But it was not the most important factor. After all, it was not the
Soviets who had served as the impetus in the peace process during the
crucial points of 1987–88. As we have seen, it was the regional powers,
starting with the Cubans, who finally recognized the stalemate into which
their own past actions had led them, and who began exploring the path
toward peace which we had defined. The Soviets had joined the Southern African peace train a little late in the day to be credited with having
been its engine all along! Nor could it be argued that they had coerced
Castro into disengaging: not until 1990–91 did we begin to see tangible
evidence of a dramatic decline in Soviet support for Castro's Cuba.

In fact, during the Namibian independence festivities, a principal
preoccupation of American officials was how to build upon the December 1988 settlement by energizing the internal Angolan peace process
between the MPLA government and UNITA. Our hopes for effective African leadership of this complex process had been disappointed. There
had been an initial flurry of optimism when dos Santos and Savimbi met
face to face during a June 1989 summit hosted by Zaire's President
Mobutu Sese Seko. But this initiative soon collapsed in recriminations;
Mobutu had gotten the sides together by telling each one what it wished
to hear. He lacked both the diplomatic resources and a real incentive to
end the protracted Angolan civil conflict which constituted a key element in his relationship with Washington.

Apparently, the Soviets and Angolans continued to dream that the
1988 settlement would offer them another chance to prevail over UNITA.
When Namibia achieved independence, they were not yet reconciled to
the idea of negotiating a genuine peace with UNITA. In December 1989,
they had mounted an elaborate offensive aimed at smashing UNITA militarily. A surge of U.S. supplies (and some low-key South African help)
enabled UNITA to hang on in a seesaw battle at Mavinga, and by March–
April 1990 the bloody stalemate had been reestablished. The MPLA had
once again overstretched its logistic capability, while UNITA had had
another close call. Perhaps the Angolan struggle was finally "ripening."

Baker and Cohen used their time in Windhoek to press Angolan

President dos Santos to make peace with UNITA and to probe Soviet readiness to stop fueling the Angolan war. Happily, the Portuguese had begun to discover their long-lost sense of responsibility for matters Angolan. Back in January 1990 they had signaled their interest in playing a constructive role and had invited Savimbi to Portugal in an essential (and long-overdue) act of political balancing. By April, just after the Windhoek celebrations, both Angolan parties and both superpowers had endorsed the Portuguese initiative. A first round of direct talks was held later that month in the Portuguese town of Evora, under the mediation of Secretary of State for Foreign Affairs José Durão Barroso.

I was delighted at this turn of events. Barroso had impressed me as a politically engaged and skillful diplomat. When I saw him again in Windhoek, he really seemed to have the bit between his teeth, and I told him what he already knew: no country was better placed or had a stronger incentive than Portugal to put an end to the thirty-year agony of Angola. Barroso did not need to be reminded that Lisbon would probably need the quiet support of the United States and the Soviet Union to move the parties forward.

It required some thirteen months of intense and complex negotiation to capitalize on the new opening. The pace seemed to pick up in late 1990 after Washington and Moscow began to play more actively their "observer" role in the wings. By December, Baker and Shevardnadze and their top officials had moved forcefully to assert leadership and leverage over the distrustful parties. A meeting between Soviet, American, Portuguese, MPLA, and UNITA representatives in Washington produced consensus on a series of concepts that would form the basis for agreement. This Portuguese-led, five-party negotiating framework gave Hank Cohen precisely the opportunity he required to exert leadership. He played his hand with consummate skill, pushing the Soviets forward and injecting U.S. ideas at the key points, without tredding on Portuguese toes.

Another four months were spent in developing complex transition mechanisms (election monitoring, cease-fire verification, disengagement of forces and their concentration in assembly areas, and the formation of a merged and much-reduced national army). By April 1991, the issues came down to achieving agreement on a cease-fire and defining the time-frame from the cease-fire to the national elections. By now, the MPLA's military position was under severe UNITA pressure, while both UNITA and the MPLA faced growing political pressure to come to terms on the timing. With perfect finesse, Cohen made another well-balanced intervention; he and Barroso pushed the Angolan parties to agreement on May 1, 1991. A *de facto* cease-fire took hold two weeks later, accompanied by the cessation of all external military assistance to either side in the conflict. Elections would be held on a date to be determined between September 1 and November 30, 1992. As in Namibia, U.N. monitors and observers would play a central role in carrying out the accords; as in Namibia, several joint commissions would help provide an institutional framework in which to carry out the agreements and keep the outside parties engaged. The Cubans completed their pull-out from Angola in late May, about five weeks ahead of the 1988 schedule.

Dos Santos and Savimbi signed the sixty-page package of agreements in Lisbon on May 31 in the presence of Portuguese Prime Minister Anibal Cavaco Silva. Church bells rang out across the Portuguese capital that evening, celebrating the end of a sixteen-year civil war which had wrecked Angola and cost the lives of an estimated 350,000 Angolans. As I listened to the speeches that evening and watched MPLA and UNITA leaders mingling, I knew that we were celebrating the end of an era. Angolans could now begin to shape their own destiny after centuries of foreign domination, living with foreign legacies and foreign conflicts. It was also the time for a fresh start for Portugal in Africa; peace would open up a vast, constructive potential between these peoples tied by language, blood, and culture. Certainly, it was the end of the Cold War in Africa, as Baker and his new Soviet counterpart, Aleksandr Bessmertnykh, forcefully declared at the signing ceremony. Just ten days earlier, by chance, Colonel Mengistu Haile Mariam—a leading African client of Moscow during most of his seventeen years in power—had fled Ethiopia's capital city for exile in Zimbabwe, an event that quickly led to the capture of Addis Ababa by rebel forces.

Durão Barroso and I discussed all this during Portuguese President Mario Soares's dinner in the Queluz Palace that evening. But we quickly agreed that Africa had its own rhythms as well. In several of the smaller Portuguese-speaking states, new forces of democratization had appeared, replacing single-party regimes with democratic ones. Across the continent, incumbents were under mounting pressure to open up the political process and promise free elections. This process reflected deep-seated African aspirations, as well as the fresh opportunity created by the growing reluctance of outside powers to continue support for dubious incumbents. Africa's dictators and autocrats had lost their freedom of maneuver.

In Southern Africa, a unique dynamic of peacemaking continued to spread across the subcontinent. A tentative, Italian-led process of talks had begun between the Chissano government of Mozambique and the RENAMO rebel leadership. This has proven to be one of the most intractable and complex of conflicts to terminate. In order to make peace in

Mozambique, it would be necessary to identify the political objectives of a movement which up to now had demonstrated a primarily military identity. It would also be necessary to mobilize all of Mozambique's neighbors as well as interested parties in the West to press RENAMO to come to terms with Maputo. Chissano would need to recognize that despite his many political moves—including scrapping the one-party, Marxist constitution—he would need to go further and find ways to meet RENAMO's political requirement for a measure of standing. Nonetheless, by early 1992, it appeared that the time for peace was finally coming; several protocols had been agreed in the Rome talks, and the sides were starting to look at electoral issues. A cease-fire and election date could not be too far behind.

If the civil conflict came to an end in 1992, it would be none too soon. Mozambique suffered the worst from Southern Africa's wars. By early 1992, a wrecked economy and paralyzed administrative structure stood in mute testimony to the agony of millions of refugees, displaced persons, and slaughtered innocents. The destruction inflicted on the Mozambicans had become an intolerable burden for their neighbors in Malawi, Zimbabwe, Swaziland, and South Africa itself. Defying electrified fences and the carnivores of the eastern Transvaal game parks, destitute Mozambicans had migrated into South Africa by the thousands— often carrying with them their sole possession of value, an AK-47 assault rifle, for resale within South Africa. Many African townships now had a Mozambican refugee population. And South Africa's own political violence was now being nurtured by the very weapons which South Africans had captured in Angola and inserted into Mozambique. This was the boomerang effect created by P. W. Botha's "ratcatcher," General Pieter van der Westhuizen, and the men of military intelligence.

In November 1989, six months after leaving office, I paid a private visit to Southern Africa. It was the moment of the Namibian election and a mere two months after F. W. de Klerk had received a fresh electoral mandate as P. W. Botha's successor. De Klerk had barely begun to raise the curtain on what would become the most dramatic transformation in modern South African politics. But it was clear that something was going on in Pretoria. Already, the cabinet had been restored to its proper position as the top policy council, and the military-staffed State Security Council and military-led administrative organs were being abolished. Everything was "under review," and the top tier of government was working late into the night and engaging in weekend retreats to brainstorm options.

When I met de Klerk for a quiet conversation, I found him very open, asking questions and seeking answers. What a wonderful contrast! I urged him to make use of a golden opportunity to shape history by creating political facts—not to fret about what Western nations such as ours would do to support him. A determined strategy would pull everyone else along. De Klerk had long impressed me as one of his party's most articulate and intelligent men. Now I came to realize what a good listener he was. I heard no attempt to blame Washington or make the standard excuse that basic change would produce a white backlash. On the contrary, he expressed guarded optimism that his constituency would follow decisive leadership.

After that November 1989 conversation, I left South Africa feeling more hopeful than on any previous visit. The era when South Africa's white politicians would expect their soldiers and policemen to "solve" their problems was coming to an end. Before leaving, I gave an address to a Johannesburg audience in which I expressed the belief that South Africa, too, would find peace, justice, and reconciliation. The era of negotiation was at hand.

There were many reasons for hope. Not only was the Berlin Wall coming down and the Marxist enemy starting to break up before Pretoria's eyes. Not only was the African National Congress now effectively shut off from its Front Line sanctuaries and without a serious global patron. Now, the Cubans were going home. When the last of them left in May 1991, there would be no foreign forces in Southern Africa for the first time since the Napoleonic Wars. The balance of conventional military power in Africa was shifting and the South African Defence Force no longer faced any credible threat. By the time of Namibia's independence in March 1990, SADF troops were back within South Africa's borders—ending a generation of cross-border wars.

And yet, this was no time for complacency. It was a time of rare opportunity. The 1988 Namibia settlement showed Pretoria how to defang its adversary: now, both the image and the reality of SWAPO was utterly different from the Marxist-terrorist bogeymen of yesterday. South Africa's rulers could look at their strategic and political position as strengthened, despite the "loss" of Namibia. But that would only be true if they were wise enough also to recognize that conventional military power had become less relevant to their situation. It would do little good to sit back and gloat about Cuban troop withdrawal and the relative weakness of the ANC and the neighboring states, including soon-to-be-free Namibia. *Within* South Africa, the organized black resistance was politically potent: it would be essential to deal with it politically by seizing the initiative and placing choices before it. All parties should compete in the political world of ideas.

On the external front, there was now an opportunity for major peace dividends in a country that was spending billions on defense, nuclear development, arms self-sufficiency, and strategic industries and stockpiles. Constructive diplomacy could open doors to fresh trade, investment, and political ties in Africa and beyond. The 1988 settlement also demonstrated the basic point that political strategies can produce results: it offered categorical evidence that South African interests (as defined by its government) could be successfully advanced at the negotiating table. Negotiation offered a means of creating fresh openings and acquiring new leverage. This logic would work equally well for all participants—once they became engaged in it.

On the other hand, the *failure* to adopt creative political strategies would carry a growing price, especially at home. For the reality was that the white government and its opposition had check-mated each other. Neither could move unilaterally: the black resistance had no hope of forcing the government to capitulate; but the government could no longer hope to regain the legitimacy it lost in the 1980s, except by adopting a wholly new strategy of change. Pretoria could continue a repressive form of white rule, but it could no longer govern unilaterally.

This crude balance came into being during the 1980s. But the roots of realism went back to the 1970s, when Afrikaner nationalists of de Klerk's generation first came to the tacit realization that apartheid had become a nightmare. They had watched their predecessors waste every opportunity by waiting, manipulating, evading. They understood that the ideology of racial separation and domination had been systematically subverted by socioeconomic reality, creating an ever more integrated and interdependent society. For over fifteen years, apartheid laws had become increasingly impossible to enforce. Throughout this period, the classic apartheid system was crumbling before the growing impact of black consumer power, black labor unions, and the unregulated informal sector; the unstoppable migration to the cities and towns; and the erosion of educational, residential, and job-market apartheid. The system sputtered along—an ossified and inefficient monster of state corporations, some 145 ministries reporting to separate parliaments for each ethnic group, and hundreds of thousands of bureaucrats who tried to "apply" the laws and regulations of the state. But inexorable change was occurring despite the government, which worked harder and harder to control less and less.

Not surprisingly, real GNP growth had been minimal since the late

1970s. The political violence of the 1980s reinforced a long-standing economic gloom, converting sporadic capital flight into a prolonged outflow to service debt. The Western private sector expressed its own "no confidence" vote by pulling out and refusing to extend new credit; official Western sanctions added yet another "apartheid tax" to the huge burdens already imposed on the economy by the political system.

In other words, the pressures had been growing for years, and those pressures were overwhelmingly internal. To pretend that Western sanctions themselves did the job is a myopic self-indulgence on our part, which happens also to coincide with the ANC's political interest in clinging as long as possible to a perceived "Western card" during the negotiating process. In reality, the pretense denigrates the sacrifices made in the struggle against racism and authoritarianism by millions of black and white South Africans over generations. Our sanctions were among the many apartheid taxes draining the economy (by one estimate, South Africa's GNP declined by 17 percent during 1987–91). Other pressures included the strain on white cohesion and morale of compulsory military service in the context of township strife and border wars; and the loss among thinking and self-aware Afrikaners of their sense of rectitude and their confidence in the future. The 1980s showed that the ramshackle system could no longer be defended at an acceptable price. Nor could power be seized at an acceptable price. South Africans on all sides had looked down into the abyss of civil violence—and recoiled in sober shock.

But such pressures were not the only factor that brought the Afrikaner leadership to its senses. There was also the recognition of fresh opportunity and the reinterpretation of an old threat. For at least five years before his release from prison on February 11, 1990, Nelson Mandela and members of the National Party leadership had been in sporadic communication. Elements of the Pretoria establishment found ways and means to communicate with the exiled ANC leaders, as well as with virtually every element of the black trade union, Church, and political opposition based inside the country long before the dam broke in February 1990. There is no doubt that the inclusive, healing vision conveyed by Mandela and many others made a crucial difference in opening the door to an irreversible process of negotiation. The power of their logic and their remarkable skill in addressing white fears even while remaining victims of brutal repression helps explain the apparently sudden change in Pretoria. So, too, did the consistent demand by Western leaders that the process of change lead to democracy. George Shultz's September 1987 speech insisting that we look beyond apartheid to the question of a future, post-apartheid system triggered a rolling series of draft constitutional proposals from a wide range of political groups, including the African National Congress and the National Party. However undemocratic their past, the main players were soon outdoing each other in their professions of democratic faith. Democracy came to be viewed as a form of reassurance rather than a threat to core values.

South Africa is a land cursed by divisions and by many kinds of violence. Politically motivated killings have been running above 3,000 a year since de Klerk took over, higher than some of the worst "unrest" years of the 1980s. It has taken time for the ANC to find its feet and organize itself to operate as a legal party responsible for the words and positions of its leaders—not simply a protest and resistance movement for which words are but another weapon of struggle. Weaving together the various strands of external and internal ANC-affiliated groups, and then selecting new leadership structures has been an onerous task. So, too, has been the process of getting the ANC and the Zulu-based Inkatha Party of Chief Gatsha Buthelezi to accept that each would have to make room for the other. Neither exhibited a spirit of tolerance, and both engaged in coercion and intimidation. At times, the South African government has aggravated the situation by maneuvers and actions clearly favoring Inkatha's drive for power and recognition. Key government leaders have found it difficult to accept the full implications of their strategic choice, continuing to operate as if they could still govern alone.

But the striking fact to me is how far South Africa has come in a few years, as the political arena finally caught up with the underlying realities of power and socioeconomic transformation. We have witnessed the ending of the armed struggle and the repressive state of emergency; the legalizing of the opposition, bringing the exiles and refugees home and releasing political prisoners; the establishing both of a negotiating forum and of a set of shared principles among the main political groups; the scrapping of the laws of apartheid, and setting up a variety of mechanisms to deal with the violence; and the revising of South African external policies, including sharply reduced defense spending and adherence to the Non-Proliferation Treaty and acceptance of nuclear safeguards.

South Africa is a complex place, blessed with vast natural resources, world-class entrepreneurial talent, and a rich array of institutions in all spheres of life that offer the hope that a true civil society can emerge there. Great men and women have built political movements, giant corporations, labor unions, churches, newspapers, legal institutions, a distinguished tradition of arts, music, and literature, and marvels of engineering. But until 1989–90 there was always something missing: its official political leaders had not been up to the standard set by the opposition and by leaders in these other spheres.

Until now, none of South Africa's politicians has been wholly free. Some were literally behind bars; others were imprisoned by the dogmas and institutions of racial nationalism. Often, they looked overseas for support, approval, and scapegoats. Today, those bad old habits are fading away. South Africans increasingly seem to accept Mandela's basic point that they are "doomed to co-exist." They are becoming a nation of negotiators, using their own mediators and forums to hammer out their own future.

Appendices*

1. Resolution 435, 1978

Adopted by the Security Council at its 2087th meeting on 29 September 1978

The Security Council,

Recalling its resolutions 385 (1976) and 431 (1978), and 432 (1978),

Having considered the report submitted by the Secretary-General pursuant to paragraph 2 of resolution 431 (1978) (S/12827) and his explanatory statement made in the Security Council on 29 September 1978 (S/12869),

Taking note of the relevant communications from the Government of South Africa addressed to the Secretary-General,

Taking note also of the letter dated 8 September 1978 from the President of the South West Africa People's Organization (SWAPO) addressed to the Secretary-General (S/12841),

Reaffirming the legal responsibility of the United Nations over Namibia:

* All six appendices are reprinted from United States Department of State Bureau of Public Affairs, Washington, D.C., December 1988.

ANNEX

	Timing	SAG	SWAPO	UN	Other action
(1)	At date unspecified:			UNSC passes resolution authorizing SYG to appoint UNSR and requesting him to submit plan for UN involvement. SYG appoints UNSR and dispatches UN contingency planning group to Namibia. SYG begins consultations with potential participants in UNTAG.	
(2)	As soon as possible, preferably within one week of Security Council action:			SYG reports back to UNSC. UNSC passes further resolution adopting plan for UN involvement. Provision is made for financing.	
(3)	Transitional period formally begins on date of UNSC passage of resolution adopting SYG's plan:	General cessation of hostile acts comes under UN supervision. Restriction to base of all South African forces including ethnic forces.	General cessation of hostile acts comes under UN supervision. Restriction to base	As soon as possible: UNSR and staff (UNTAG) arrive in Namibia to assume duties. UN military personnel commence monitoring of cessation of hostile acts and commence monitoring of both South African and SWAPO troop restrictions. Begin infiltration prevention and border surveillance. Begin monitoring of police forces. Begin monitoring of citizen forces, ethnic forces, and military personnel performing civilian functions. UNSR makes necessary arrangements for co-ordination with neighbouring countries concerning the provisions of the transitional arrangements.	Release of political prisoners / detainees wherever held begins and is to be completed as soon as possible.

(4)	Within six weeks:	Restriction to base continues. Force levels reduced to 12 000 men.	Restriction to base continues.	Appropriate action by UN High Commissioner for Refugees outside Namibia to assist in return of exiles. All UN activity continues.	Establishment in Namibia of provisions to facilitate return of exiles. Establishment and publication of general rules for elections. Completion of repeal of discriminatory laws and restrictive legislation. Dismantlement of command structures of citizen forces, commandos and ethnic forces, including the withdrawal of all South African soldiers attached to these units. All arms, military equipment, and ammunition of citizen forces and commandos confined to drill halls under UN supervision. AG to ensure that none of these forces will drill or constitute an organized force during the transitional period except under order of the AG with the concurrence of UNSR. AG with concurrence of UNSR determines whether and under what circumstances those military personnel performing civilian functions will continue those functions.
(5)	Within nine weeks:	Restriction to base continues. Force levels reduced to 8 000 men.	Restriction to base continues. Peaceful repatriation under UN supervision starts for return through designated entry points.	All UN activity continues.	Completion of release of political prisoners/detainees wherever held.

ANNEX

	Timing	SAG	SWAPO	UN	Other action
(6)	Within 12 weeks:	Force levels reduced to 1 500 men, restricted to Grootfontein or Oshivello or both. All military installations along northern border would by now either be deactivated or put under civilian control under UN supervision. Facilities which depend on them (e.g. hospital, power stations) would be protected where necessary by the UN.	Restrictiion to base continues.	All UN activity continues. Military Section of UNTAG at maximum deployment.	
(7)	Start of thirteenth week:				Official start of election campaign of about four months' duration.
(8)	On date established by AG to satisfaction of UNSR:				Election to Constituent Assembly.
(9)	One week after date of certification of election:	Completion of withdrawal.	Closure of all bases.		Convening of Constituent Assembly.
(10)	At date unspecified:				Conclusion of Constituent Assembly and whatever additional steps may be necessary prior to installation of new government.
(11)	By 31 December 1978 at latest:				Independence.

AG = Administrator-General; SAG = South African Government; SWAPO = South West Africa People's Organization; SYG = Secretary-General of the United Nations; UN = United Nations; UNSR = United Nations Special Representative; UNSC = United Nations Security Council; UNTAG = United Nations Transition Assistance Group

1. *Approves* the report of the Secretary-General (S/12827) for the implementation of the proposal for a settlement of the Namibian situation (S/12636) and his explanatory statement (S/12869);
2. *Reiterates* that its objective is the withdrawal of South Africa's illegal administration of Namibia and the transfer of power to the people of Namibia with the assistance of the United Nations in accordance with resolution 385 (1976);
3. *Decides* to establish under its authority a United Nations Transition Assistance Group (UNTAG) in accordance with the above-mentioned report of the Secretary-General for a period of up to 12 months in order to assist his Special Representative to carry out the mandate conferred upon him by paragraph 1 of Security Council resolution 431 (1978), namely, to ensure the early independence of Namibia through free and fair elections under the supervision and control of the United Nations;
4. *Welcomes* SWAPO's preparedness to co-operate in the implementation of the Secretary-General's report, including its expressed readiness to sign and observe the cease-fire provisions as manifested in the letter from the President of SWAPO dated 8 September 1978 (S/12841);
5. *Calls on* South Africa forthwith to co-operate with the Secretary-General in the implementation of this resolution;
6. v*Declares* that all unilateral measures taken by the illegal administration in Namibia in relation to the electoral process, including unilateral registration of voters, or transfer of power, in contravention of Security Council resolutions 385 (1976), 431 (1978) and this resolution are null and void;
7. *Requests* the Secretary-General to report to the Security Council no later than 23 October 1978 on the implementation of this resolution.

2. New York Principles, July 1988

PRINCIPLES FOR A PEACEFUL SETTLEMENT IN SOUTHWESTERN AFRICA, JULY 20, 1988

Following is the text of the agreement initialed by delegations from Angola / Cuba and South Africa in New York City on July 13, 1988. This statement was approved by their respective governments and released publicly by mutual agreement on July 20, 1988.

The Governments of the People's Republic of Angola, the Republic of Cuba, and the Republic of South Africa have reached agreement on a set of essential principles to establish the basis for peace in the southwestern region of Africa. They recognize that each of these principles is indispensable to a comprehensive settlement.

A. Implementation of Resolution 435 / 78 of the Security Council of the United Nations. The parties shall agree upon and recommend to the Secretary-General of the United Nations a date for the commencement of implementation of UNSCR 435 / 78.

B. The Governments of the People's Republic of Angola and of the Republic of South Africa shall, in conformity with the dispositions of Resolution 435 / 78 of the Security Council of the United Nations, cooperate with the Secretary-General with a view toward ensuring the independence of Namibia through free and fair elections, abstaining from any action that could prevent the execution of said Resolution.

C. Redeployment toward the North and the staged and total withdrawal of Cuban troops from the territory of the People's Republic of Angola on the basis of an agreement between the People's Republic of Angola and the Republic of Cuba and the decision of both states to solicit the on-site verification of that withdrawal by the Security Council of the United Nations.

D. Respect for the sovereignty, sovereign equality, and independence of states and for territorial integrity and inviolability of borders.

E. Non-interference in the internal affairs of states.

F. Abstention from the threat and utilization of force against the territorial integrity and independence of states.

G. The acceptance of the responsibility of states not to allow their territory to be used for acts of war, aggression, or violence against other states.

H. Reaffirmation of the right of the peoples of the southwestern region of Africa to self-determination, independence, and equality of rights.

I. Verification and monitoring of compliance with the obligations resulting from the agreements that may be established.

J. Commitment to comply in good faith with the obligations undertaken in the agreements that may be established and to resolve the differences via negotiations.

K. Recognition of the role of the Permanent Members of the Security

Council of the United Nations as guarantors for the implementation of agreements that may be established.

L. The right of each state to peace, development, and social progress.

M. African and international cooperation for the settlement of the problems of the development of the southwestern region of Africa.

N. Recognition of the mediating role of the Government of the United States of America.

3. The Geneva Protocol, 5 August 1988

Delegations representing the Governments of the People's Republic of Angola / Republic of Cuba, and the Republic of South Africa, meeting in Geneva, Switzerland, 2–5 August 1988, with the mediation of Dr. Chester A Crocker, Assistant Secretary of State for African Affairs, United States of America, have agreed as follows:

1. Each side agrees to recommend to the Secretary-General of the United Nations that 1 November 1988 be established as the date for implementation of UNSCR 435 / 78.

2. Each side agrees to the establishment of a target date for signature of the tripartite agreement among Angola, South Africa, and Cuba not later than 10 September 1988.

3. Each side agrees that a schedule acceptable to all parties for the redeployment toward the North and the staged and total withdrawal of Cuban troops from Angola must be established by Angola and Cuba, who will request on-site verification by the Security Council of the United Nations. The parties accept 1 September 1988 as the target date for reaching agreement on that schedule and all related matters.

4. The complete withdrawal of South African forces from Angola shall begin not later than 10 August 1988 and be completed not later than 1 September 1988.

5. The parties undertake to adopt the necessary measures of restraint in order to maintain the existing *de facto* cessation of hostilities. South Africa stated its willingness to convey this commitment in writing to the Secretary-General of the United Nations. Angola and Cuba shall urge SWAPO to proceed likewise as a step prior to the ceasefire contemplated in resolution 435 / 78 which will be established prior to 1 November 1988. Angola and Cuba shall use their

good offices so that, once the total withdrawal of South African troops from Angola is completed, and within the context also of the cessation of hostilities in Namibia, SWAPO's forces will be deployed to the north of the 16th parallel. The parties deemed it appropriate that, during the period before 1 November 1988, a representative of the United Nations Secretary-General be present in Luanda to take cognizance of any disputes relative to the cessation of hostilities and agreed that the combined military committee contemplated in paragraph 9 can be an appropriate venue for reviewing complaints of this nature that may arise.

6. As of 10 August 1988, no Cuban troops will deploy or be south of the line Chitado–Ruacana–Calueque–Naulila–Cuamato–N'Giva. Cuba furthermore stated that upon completion of the withdrawal of the South African troops from Angola not later than 1 September 1988 and the restoration by the People's Republic of Angola of its sovereignty over its international boundaries, the Cuban troops will not take part in offensive operations in the territory that lies east of meridian 17 and south of parallel 15 degrees, 30 minutes, provided that they are not subject to harrassment.

7. Following the complete withdrawal of South African forces from Angola, the Government of Angola shall guarantee measures for the provision of water and power supply to Namibia.

8. With a view toward minimizing the risk of battlefield incidents and facilitating exchange of technical information related to implementation of the agreements reached, direct communications shall be established not later than 20 August 1988 between the respective military commanders at appropriate headquarters along the Angola / Namibia border.

9. Each side recognizes that the period from 1 September 1988, by which time South African forces will have completed their withdrawal from Angola, and the date established for implementation of UNSCR 435, is a period of particular sensitivity, for which specific guidelines for military activities are presently lacking. In the interest of maintaining the ceasefire and maximizing the conditions for the orderly introduction of UNTAG, the sides agree to establish a combined military committee to develop additional practical measures to build confidence and reduce the risk of unintended incidents. They invite United States membership on the committee.

10. Each side will act in accordance with the Governors Island principles, including paragraph E (non-interference in the internal affairs of states) and paragraph G (the acceptance of the responsibility of

states not to allow their territory to be used for acts of war, aggression, or violence against other states).

FOR THE GOVERN-
MENT OF THE PEO-
PLE'S REPUBLIC OF
ANGOLA:

FOR THE GOVERN-
MENT OF THE REPUB-
LIC OF CUBA:

FOR THE GOVERN-
MENT OF THE REPUB-
LIC OF SOUTH AFRICA:

Geneva, 5 August 1988

4. The Brazzaville Protocol, 13 December 1988

Delegations representing the Governments of the People's Republic of Angola, the Republic of Cuba, and the Republic of South Africa,

Meeting in Brazzaville with the mediation of the Government of the United States of America,

Expressing their deep appreciation to the President of the People's Republic of the Congo, Colonel Denis Sassou-Nguesso, for his indispensable contribution to the cause of peace in southwestern Africa and for the hospitality extended to the delegations by the Government of the People's Republic of the Congo,

Confirming their commitment to act in accordance with the Principles for a peaceful settlement in southwestern Africa, initialled at New York on 13 July 1988 and approved by their respective Governments on 20 July 1988, each of which is indispensable to a comprehensive settlement; with the understandings reached at Geneva on 5 August 1988 that are not superseded by this document; and with the agreement reached at Geneva on 15 November 1988 for the redeployment to the North and the staged and total withdrawal of Cuban troops from Angola,

Urging the international community to provide economic and financial support for the implementation of all aspects of this settlement,

Agree as follows:

1. The parties agree to recommend to the Secretary-General of the United Nations that 1 April 1989 be established as the date for implementation of UNSCR 435 / 78.

2. The parties agree to meet on 22 December 1988 in New York for signature of the tripartite agreement and for signature by Angola and Cuba of their bilateral agreement. By the date of signature, Angola

and Cuba shall have reached agreement with the Secretary-General of the United Nations on verification arrangements to be approved by the Security Council.

3. The parties agree to exchange the prisoners of war upon signature of the tripartite agreement.

4. The parties agree to establish a Joint Commission in accordance with the annex attached to this protocol.

FOR THE GOVERN-MENT OF THE PEO-PLE'S REPUBLIC OF ANGOLA:	FOR THE GOVERN-MENT OF THE REPUB-LIC OF CUBA:	FOR THE GOVERN-MENT OF THE REPUB-LIC OF SOUTH AFRICA:

Brazzaville, 13 December 1988

REMARKS BY ASSISTANT SECRETARY CROCKER, DECEMBER 13, 1988

Following are remarks of Chester A. Crocker, Assistant Secretary for African Affairs, at the signing of the Brazzaville Protocol in Brazzaville, Congo, on December 13, 1988, by delegations from Angola, Cuba, and South Africa.

Today's ceremony—the signing of the Brazzaville Protocol by Angola, Cuba, and South Africa—is the culmination of many months of hard work by distinguished representatives of three sovereign governments which, faced by a stark choice of peace or war, chose to work for peace. With the signature of this protocol, the path is now clear for early signature of a tripartite agreement that will bring an end to the international conflict in southwestern Africa. This event signifies the end of a sad chapter in Africa's modern history and the beginning of a new chapter. Speaking for my government, we have high hopes that this will be a chapter that witnesses reduced internal and international strife, greater opportunity for the building of just and prosperous societies, and strengthened prospects for international cooperation in support of African development and stability.

On behalf of the delegation of the United States, which has had the honor to serve as mediator in these negotiations, and on behalf of the delegations of the three governments here present today, I would like to express our deepest gratitude to you, Mr. President [Denis Sassou-Nguesso]. As the leader of the People's Republic of the Congo, we salute your own contributions to this historic peace process in southern Africa. I recall that in April 1987 it was your invitation, while chairman of the Organization of African Unity, to meet in Brazzaville that served as a catalyst to restore and reinvigorate contact and dialogue between my government and the Government of the People's Republic of Angola. Today is the fifth occasion since that meeting nearly 2 years ago that we have assembled in Brazzaville in our joint search for peace in the region. Your hospitality, Mr. President, and the cooperation and assistance of the Government of the People's Republic of the Congo have been a vital part of this process. You have encouraged us and supported us, and we are most grateful.

It is also appropriate today to salute the determination and professionalism of the delegations from Angola, Cuba, and South Africa that over the past 8 months have met in London, Cairo, Geneva, New York, and here in Brazzaville. The process has been long, painstaking, and often frustrating for everyone concerned. Without the extraordinary dedication and skill of the principal negotiators, we would not have been able to achieve this settlement. I would also like to pay tribute to two parties who have not been present officially at the negotiating table but whose cooperation and assistance have been crucial throughout the course of these negotiations.

As mediator, we have developed a pattern of close, practical, and effective cooperation with our Soviet counterparts. Despite some differences in perspective and different roles in the negotiating process, the United States and the U.S.S.R. have been able to work cooperatively to move the process forward. It has been a case study of superpower effort to support the resolution of regional conflicts. So, I would like to salute the hard work and professional dedication of the Soviet officials who have been involved in this intensive effort over the past months.

The United Nations has the responsibility to implement UN Security Council Resolution 435 / 78 and to oversee the transition to Namibian independence, as well as to verify the withdrawal of Cuban troops from Angola. These are complex undertakings and are essential for the successful implementation of the agreements the parties are entering into. We have been fortunate to have had the benefit of the advice, support, and counsel of a real statesman, UN Secretary-General Javier Perez de Cuellar, and of another distinguished international civil servant, Under Secretary General Martti Ahtisaari, and his colleagues from the United Nations, through the negotiations.

In conclusion, I would like to say a word about my own country and its role in the search for a peaceful solution in Africa. As this protracted negotiation nears a successful conclusion, it is worth noting the ingredients that have made success possible. First, our role has been welcomed by our partners in Africa and by our friends and allies around the world. My country does not have blueprints for the solution of every problem or a mandate to play such a role. But we are prepared to involve ourselves in the search for constructive solutions when such a role is welcomed and appropriate. Second, we have been realists. We have recognized that lasting solutions can only be based on the concrete historical realities of a given situation. Just as man cannot eat slogans, neither can statesmen solve problems with rhetorical cliches and abstract formulas. Third, we have tried to chart a clear course and stick with it. This is an approach that may sometimes fall short of shifting fashions and popular hopes for instant results. But over time this is the approach that gives confidence and predictability to key decisionmakers. It is the approach that works.

5. Bilateral Agreement, 22 December 1988

Following is the unofficial U.S. translation of the original Portuguese and Spanish texts of the agreement, with annex.

AGREEMENT BETWEEN THE GOVERNMENTS OF THE PEOPLE'S REPUBLIC OF ANGOLA AND THE REPUBLIC OF CUBA FOR THE TERMINATION OF THE INTERNATIONALIST MISSION OF THE CUBAN MILITARY CONTINGENT

The Government of the People's Republic of Angola and the Republic of Cuba, hereinafter designated as the Parties,

Considering,

That the implementation of Resolution 435 of the Security Council of the United Nations for the independence of Namibia shall commence on the 1st of April,

That the question of the independence of Namibia and the safeguarding of the sovereignty, independence and territorial integrity of the People's Republic of Angola are closely interrelated with each other and with peace and security in the region of southwestern Africa,

That on the date of signature of this agreement a tripartite agreement among the Governments of the People's Republic of Angola, the Republic of Cuba and the Republic of South Africa shall be signed, containing the essential elements for the achievement of peace in the region of southwestern Africa,

That acceptance of and strict compliance with the foregoing will bring to an end the reasons which compelled the Government of the People's Republic of Angola to request, in the legitimate exercise of its rights under Article 51 of the United Nations Charter, the deployment to Angolan territory of a Cuban internationalist military contingent to guarantee, in cooperation with the FAPLA [the Angolan Government army], its territorial integrity and sovereignty in view of the invasion and occupation of part of its territory,

Noting,

The agreements signed by the Governments of the People's Republic of Angola and the Republic of Cuba on 4 February 1982 and 19 March 1984, the platform of the Government of the People's Republic of Angola approved in November 1984, and the Protocol of Brazzaville signed by the Governments of the People's Republic of Angola, the Republic of Cuba and the Republic of South Africa on December 13, 1988,

Taking into account,

That conditions now exist which make possible the repatriation of the Cuban military contingent currently in Angolan territory and the successful accomplishment of their internationalist mission,

The parties agree as follows:

Article 1

To commence the redeployment by stages to the 15th and 13th parallels and the total withdrawal to Cuba of the 50,000 men who constitute the Cuban troops contingent stationed in the People's Republic of Angola, in accordance with the pace and timeframe established in the attached calendar, which is an integral part of this agreement. The total withdrawal shall be completed by the 1st of July, 1991.

Article 2

The Governments of the People's Republic of Angola and the Republic of Cuba reserve the right to modify or alter their obligations deriving from Article 1 of this Agreement in the event that flagrant violations of the Tripartite Agreement are verified.

Article 3

The Parties, through the Secretary General of the United Nations Organization, hereby request that the Security Council verify the redeployment and phased and total withdrawal of Cuban troops from the territory of the People's Republic of Angola, and to this end shall agree on a matching protocol.

Article 4

This agreement shall enter into force upon signature of the tripartite agreement among the People's Republic of Angola, the Republic of Cuba, and the Republic of South Africa.

Signed on 22 December 1988, at the Headquarters of the United Nations Organization, in two copies, in the Portuguese and Spanish languages, each being equally authentic.

FOR THE PEOPLE'S REPUBLIC OF ANGOLA

FOR THE REPUBLIC OF CUBA

AFONSO VAN DUNEM

ISIDORO OCTAVIO MALMIERCA

Annex on Troop Withdrawal Schedule

Calendar

In compliance with Article 1 of the agreement between the Government of the Republic of Cuba and the Government of the People's Republic of Angola for the termination of the mission of the Cuban internationalist military contingent stationed in Angolan territory, the parties establish the following calendar for the withdrawal:

Time Frames

Prior to the first of April, 1989
   (date of the beginning of implementation of
   Resolution 435)   3,000 men

Total duration of the calendar
   Starting from the 1st of April, 1989   27 months

Redeployment to the north:
   to the 15th parallel   by 1 August 1989
   to the 13th parallel   by 31 Oct. 1989

Total men to be withdrawn:

by 1 November 1989	25,000 men (50%)
by 1 April 1990	33,000 (66%)
by 1 October 1990	38,000 (76%); 12,000 men remaining
by July 1991	50,000 (100%)

Taking as its base a Cuban force of 50,000 men.

6. Tripartite Agreement, 22 December 1988

AGREEMENT AMONG THE PEOPLE'S REPUBLIC OF ANGOLA, THE REPUBLIC OF CUBA, AND THE REPUBLIC OF SOUTH AFRICA

The governments of the People's Republic of Angola, the Republic of Cuba, and the Republic of South Africa, hereinafter designated as "the Parties,"

Taking into account the "Principles for a Peaceful Settlement in Southwestern Africa," approved by the Parties on 20 July 1988, and the subsequent negotiations with respect to the implementation of these Principles, each of which is indispensable to a comprehensive settlement,

Considering the acceptance by the Parties of the implementation of United Nations Security Council Resolution 435 (1978), adopted on 29 September 1978, hereinafter designated as "UNSCR 435 / 78,"

Considering the conclusion of the bilateral agreement between the People's Republic of Angola and the Republic of Cuba providing for the redeployment toward the North and the staged and total withdrawal of Cuban troops from the territory of the People's Republic of Angola,

Recognizing the role of the United Nations Security Council in implementing UNSCR 435 / 78 and in supporting the implementation of the present agreement,

Affirming the sovereignty, sovereign equality, and independence of all states of southwestern Africa,

Affirming the principle of noninterference in the internal affairs of states,

Affirming the principle of abstention from the threat or use of force against the territorial integrity or political independence of states,

Reaffirming the right of the peoples of the southwestern region of Africa to self-determination, independence, and equality of rights, and of the states of southwestern Africa to peace, development, and social progress,

Urging African and international cooperation for the settlement of the problems of the development of the southwestern region of Africa,

Expressing their appreciation for the mediating role of the Government of the United States of America,

Desiring to contribute to the establishment of peace and security in southwestern Africa,

Agree to the provisions set forth below.

(1) The Parties shall immediately request the Secretary-General of the United Nations to seek authority from the Security Council to commence implementation of UNSCR 435 / 78 on 1 April 1989.

(2) All military forces of the Republic of South Africa shall depart Namibia in accordance with UNSCR 435 / 78.

(3) Consistent with the provisions of UNSCR 435 / 78, the Republic of South Africa and People's Republic of Angola shall cooperate with the Secretary-General to ensure the independence of Namibia through free and fair elections and shall abstain from any action that could prevent the execution of UNSCR 435 / 78. The Parties shall respect the territorial integrity and inviolability of borders of Namibia and shall ensure that their territories are not used by any state, organization, or person in connection with acts of war, aggression, or violence against the territorial integrity or inviolability of borders of Namibia or any other action which could prevent the execution of UNSCR 435 / 78.

(4) The People's Republic of Angola and the Republic of Cuba shall implement the bilateral agreement, signed on the date of signature of this agreement, providing for the redeployment toward the North and the staged and total withdrawal of Cuban troops from the territory of the People's Republic of Angola, and the arrangements made with the Security Council of the United Nations for the on-site verification of that withdrawal.

(5) Consistent with their obligations under the Charter of the United Nations, the Parties shall refrain from the threat or use of force, and shall ensure that their respective territories are not used by any state, organization, or person in connection with any acts of war, aggression, or violence, against the territorial integrity, inviolability of borders, or independence of any state of southwestern Africa.

(6) The Parties shall respect the principle of non-interference in the internal affairs of the states of southwestern Africa.

(7) The Parties shall comply in good faith with all obligations undertaken in this agreement and shall resolve through negotiation and in a spirit of cooperation any disputes with respect to the interpretation or implementation thereof.

(8) This agreement shall enter into force upon signature.

Signed at New York in triplicate in the Portuguese, Spanish and English languages, each language being equally authentic, this 22nd day of December 1988.

FOR THE PEOPLE'S REPUBLIC OF ANGOLA	FOR THE REPUBLIC OF CUBA	FOR THE REPUBLIC OF SOUTH AFRICA
AFONSO VAN DUNEM	ISIDORO OCTAVIO MALMIERCA	ROELOF F. BOTHA

Further Reading

Afigbo, A. E., E. A. Ayandele, R. J. Gavin, J. D. Omer-Cooper, and R. Palmer. *The Making of Modern Africa.* Vol. 2. Harlow, Essex: Longman, 1986.

Albright, David E., ed. *Communism in Africa.* Bloomington, Ind.: Indiana University Press, 1980.

Barber, James, and John Barratt. *South Africa's Foreign Policy: The Search for Status and Security, 1945–1988.* Cambridge, Eng.: Cambridge University Press, 1990.

Bender, Gerald J., James S. Coleman, and Richard L. Sklar, eds. *African Crisis Areas and U.S. Foreign Policy.* Berkeley: University of California Press, 1985.

Berger, Peter L., and Bobby Godsell, eds. *A Future South Africa: Visions, Strategies and Realities.* Boulder, Colo.: Westview Press, 1988.

Bissell, Richard E., and Michael S. Radu, eds. *Africa in the Post-Decolonization Era.* New Brunswick, N.J., and London: Transaction Books, 1984.

Blainey, Geoffrey. *The Causes of War.* New York: Macmillan, 1988.

Bridgland, Fred. *The War for Africa: Twelve Months That Transformed a Continent.* Gibraltar: Ashanti Publishers, 1990.

Brown, Sheryl, and Kimber M. Schraub, eds. *Conflict Resolution in the Post-Cold War Third World.* Washington, D.C.: United States Institute of Peace, 1992.

Bull, Hedley. *The Anarchical Society: A Study of Order in World Politics.* New York: Columbia University Press, 1977.

Campbell, Kurt M. *Southern Africa in Soviet Foreign Policy.* London: International Institute of Strategic Studies, Adelphi Papers #227 (Winter 1987–88).

Deng, Francis M., and I. William Zartman. *Conflict Resolution in Africa.* Washington, D.C.: Brookings Institution, 1991.

Duignan, Peter, and L. H. Gann. *The United States and Africa: A History.* Cambridge, Engl.: Cambridge University Press, 1984.

Finnegan, William. *Complicated War: The Harrowing of Mozambique.* Berkeley: University of California Press, 1992.

George, Alexander L. *Forceful Persuasion: Coercive Diplomacy as an Alternative to War.* Washington, D.C.: United States Institute of Peace, 1992.

Giliomee, Hermann, and Lawrence Schlemmer. *From Apartheid to Nation Building.* New York: Oxford University Press, 1989.

Haass, Richard N. *Conflicts Unending: The United States and Regional Disputes.* New Haven and London: Yale University Press, 1990.

Harbeson, John W., and Donald Rothchild, eds. *Africa in World Politics.* Boulder, Colo: Westview Press, 1991.

Hargreaves, J. D. *Decolonization in Africa.* Harlow, Essex: Longman, 1988.

Horowitz, Donald L. *A Democratic South Africa? Constitutional Engineering in a Divided Society.* Berkeley: University of California Press, 1991.

Ikle, Fred C. *How Nations Negotiate.* New York: Harper & Row, 1964.

Isaacman, Allen and Barbara. *Mozambique: From Colonialism to Revolution, 1900–1982.* Boulder, Colo.: Westview Press, 1983.

Jabri, Vivienne. *Mediating Conflict: Decision-Making and Western Intervention in Namibia.* New York: St. Martin's Press, 1990.

Jackson, Henry F. *From the Congo to Soweto: U.S. Foreign Policy Toward Africa Since 1960.* New York: William Morrow, 1982.

James, Alan. *Peace-Keeping in International Politics.* New York: St. Martin's Press, 1991.

Jaster, Robert S., Moeletsi Mbeki, Morley Nkosi, and Michael Clough. *Changing Fortunes: War, Diplomacy, and Economics in Southern Africa.* New York: Ford Foundation and Foreign Policy Association, 1992.

Kahn, Owen Ellison, ed. *Disengagement from Southwest Africa: The Prospects for Peace in Angola and Namibia.* New Brunswick, N.J.: Transaction Publishers, 1991.

Katz, Mark N., ed. *Soviet-American Conflict Resolution in the Third World.* Washington, D.C.: United States Institute of Peace, 1991.

Kitchen, Helen, ed. *Angola, Mozambique, and the West.* New York: Praeger Publishers (The Washington Papers #130), 1987.

Lewis, Stephen R. *The Economics of Apartheid.* New York: Council on Foreign Relations Press, 1990.

Luttwak, Edward N. *Strategy: The Logic of War and Peace.* Cambridge, Mass.: Harvard University Press, 1987.

Marcum, John A. *The Angolan Revolution—The Anatomy of an Explosion, 1950–1962.* Cambridge, Mass.: MIT Press, 1969.

———. *Exile Politics and Guerrilla Warfare.* Cambridge, Mass.: MIT Press, 1978.

Mayall, James, and Anthony Payne, eds. *Fallacies of Hope: The Post-Colonial*

Record of the Commonwealth Third World. Manchester: Manchester University Press, 1991.

Mazrui, Ali A. *Africa's International Relations: The Diplomacy of Dependency and Change.* London and New York: William Heinemann, 1977.

McCormick, Shawn. *The Angolan Economy: Prospects for Growth in a Post-War Environment.* Washington, D.C.: Center for Strategic and International Studies, 1992.

Morris-Jones, W. H., and Georges Fischer, eds. *Decolonisation and After: The British and French Experience.* London: Frank Cass, 1980.

National Democratic Institute for International Affairs. *The United Nations and Namibia,* Washington, D.C., 1990.

Neuhaus, Richard John. *Dispensations: The Future of South Africa as South Africans See It.* Grand Rapids, Mich.: Wiliam B. Eerdmans Publishing Co., 1986.

Obasanjo, Olusegun. *Africa in Perspective: Myths and Realities.* New York: Council on Foreign Relations Press, 1987.

Oberdorfer, Don. *The Turn: The United States and the Soviet Union, 1983–1990.* New York: Poseidon Press, 1991.

Pakenham, Thomas. *The Scramble for Africa.* New York: Random House, 1991.

Pruitt, Dean G., and Jeffrey Z. Rubin. *Social Conflict: Escalation, Stalemate and Settlement.* New York: Random House, 1986.

Somerville, Keith. *Angola: Politics, Economic and Society.* Boulder, Colo.: Francis Pinter-Lynne Rienner, 1986.

Sparks, Donald L., and December Green. *Namibia: The Nation After Independence.* New York: Westview Press, 1992.

Thompson, W. Scott, and Kenneth M. Jensen, eds. *Approaches to Peace: An Intellectual Map.* Washington, D.C.: United States Institute of Peace, 1991.

Urquhart, Brian. *A Life in Peace and War.* New York: W. W. Norton, 1991.

Valenta, Jiri, and Frank Cibulka, eds. *Gorbachev's New Thinking and Third World Conflicts.* New Brunswick, N.J.: Transaction Books, 1990.

Vines, Alex. *RENAMO: Terrorism in Mozambique.* Bloomington, Ind.: Indiana University Press, 1991.

Wolfers, Arnold. *Discord and Collaboration: Essays on International Politics.* Baltimore: Johns Hopkins University Press, 1962.

Zartman, I. William, and Maureen R. Berman. *The Practical Negotiator.* New Haven and London: Yale University Press, 1982.

Zartman, I. William, and Saadia Touval. *International Mediation in Theory and Practice.* New York: Westview Press, 1985.

Index